D1139350

Ford
Escort
Owners
Workshop
Manual

Peter G Strasman

Models covered
All Ford Escort front wheel drive models
Hatchback, Cabriolet, Estate and Van, including XR3 & XR3i
1117 cc, 1296 cc & 1597 cc

Does not cover Diesel engine, RS 1600i or Turbo models

ISBN 1 85010 171 X

Printed in England *(686–9L5)*

ABC

THE
BOOK

Haynes Publishing Group
Sparkford Nr Yeovil
Somerset BA22 7JJ England

Haynes Publications, Inc
861 Lawrence Drive
Newbury Park
California 91320 USA

British Library Cataloguing in Publication Data

Strasman, Peter G.
    Ford Escort (front-wheel-drive) owners workshop
manual.–(Owners Workshop Manual/Haynes)
    1. Escort automobile
I. Title   II. Series
629.28'722   TL215.E78
ISBN 1-85010-171-X

Acknowledgements

Special thanks are due to the Ford Motor Company for the supply of technical information and certain illustrations. Castrol Limited provided lubrication data, and the Champion Sparking Plug Company supplied the illustrations showing the various spark plug conditions.

Thank you, also, to Sykes-Pickavant for providing some of the workshop tools, and to all the staff at Sparkford who assisted in the production of this manual.

About this manual

Its aim

The aim of this manual is to help you get the best from your car. It can do so in several ways. It can help you decide what work must be done (even should you choose to get it done by a garage), provide information on routine maintenance and servicing, and give a logical course of action and diagnosis when random faults occur. However, it is hoped that you will use the manual by tackling the work yourself. On simpler jobs it may even be quicker than booking the car into a garage and going there twice to leave and collect it. Perhaps most important, a lot of money can be saved by avoiding the costs the garage must charge to cover its labour and overheads.

The manual has drawings and descriptions to show the function of the various components so that their layout can be understood. Then the tasks are described and photographed in a step-by-step sequence so that even a novice can do the work.

Its arrangement

The manual is divided into thirteen Chapters, each covering a logical sub-division of the vehicle. The Chapters are each divided into Sections, numbered with single figures, eg 5; and the Sections into paragraphs (or sub-sections), with decimal numbers following on from the Section they are in, eg 5.1. 5.2 etc.

It is freely illustrated, especially in those parts where there is a detailed sequence of operations to be carried out. There are two forms of illustration: figures and photographs. The figures are numbered in sequence with decimal numbers, according to their position in the Chapter – Fig. 6.4 is the fourth drawing/illustration in Chapter 6. Photographs carry the same number (either individually or in related groups) as the Section or sub-section to which they relate.

There is an alphabetical index at the back of the manual as well as a contents list at the front. Each Chapter is also preceded by its own individual contents list.

References to the 'left' or 'right' of the vehicle are in the sense of a person in the driver's seat facing forwards.

Unless otherwise stated, nuts and bolts are removed by turning anti-clockwise, and tightened by turning clockwise.

Vehicle manufacturers continually make changes to specifications and recommendations, and these, when notified, are incorporated into our manuals at the earliest opportunity.

Whilst every care is taken to ensure that the information in this manual is correct, no liability can be accepted by the authors or publishers for loss, damage or injury caused by any errors in, or omissions, from the information given.

Introduction to the Ford Escort

The 'new' Escort breaks tradition with the previous Escort by having transverse engine and front wheel drive. Other than this, its construction is simple and conventional, which should make for easy servicing and maintenance.

As is the normal Ford custom, Base models are produced for the Hatchback, Estate and Van, with an extensive range of upmarket versions and options.

With the wide availability of genuine and pattern spares, these vehicles are ideal for the home mechanic who wishes to keep running costs to a minimum.

Contents

Ford Escort L model. This is the car that was dismantled in our workshop

Ford Escort GL model

Ford Escort Van

Ford Escort XR3

General dimensions, weights and capacities

Dimensions
Overall length:
Hatchback and Cabriolet .... 4059 mm (159.8 in)
Estate .... 4123 mm (162.3 in)
Van .... 4219 mm (166.1 in)
Overall width:
All models .... 1640 mm (64.6 in)
Overall height:
Hatchback (except XR3i) and Cabriolet .... 1400 mm (55.1 in)
XR3i .... 1389 mm (54.7 in)
Van .... 1568 mm (61.7 in)
Track:
Front:
Hatchback, Cabriolet and Estate .... 1400 mm (55.1 in)
Van .... 1390 mm (54.7 in)
Rear:
Hatchback, Cabriolet and Estate .... 1423 mm (56.0 in)
Van .... 1384 mm (54.5 in)

Weights
Gross vehicle weights:
1.1 Hatchback .... 1300 kg (2867 lb)
1.1 Estate .... 1375 kg (3032 lb)
1.1 Van .... 1325 kg (2922 lb)
1.3 and 1.6l Hatchback, Cabriolet and Estate .... 1375 kg (3032 lb)
1.3 and 1.6l Vans .... 1575 kg (3473 lb)
Kerb weights:
1.1 Hatchback .... 810 kg (1786 lb)
1.3 and 1.6l Hatchback and Cabriolet .... 920 kg (2029 lb)
1.6i Cabriolet .... 970 kg (2139 lb)
All Estates .... 915 kg (2018 lb)
Maximum trailer weight:
1.1 .... 300 kg (662 lb)
1.3 and 1.6l .... 900 kg (1985 lb)
Van payload:
35 models .... 491 kg (1083 lb)
55 models .... 722 kg (1592 lb)
Roof rack load .... 75 kg (165 lb) maximum, evenly distributed

Capacities
Engine oil (drain and refill):
ohv with filter change .... 3.25 litres (5.7 pints)
ohv without filter change .... 2.75 litres (4.8 pints)
ohc (except XR3i) with filter change .... 3.50 litres (6.2 pints)
ohc (except XR3i) without filter change .... 3.25 litres (5.7 pints)
ohc (XR3i) with filter change .... 3.60 litres (6.3 pints)
ohc (XR3i) without filter change .... 3.25 litres (5.7 pints)
Fuel tank:
All models (except XR3i and Van) pre May 1983 .... 40 litres (8.8 gallons)
All other models (except Van) .... 48 litres (10.5 gallons)
Van models .... 50 litres (11.0 gallons)
Cooling system:
1.1 ohv .... 5.3 litres (9.3 pints)
1.1 ohc – small radiator .... 6.2 litres (10.9 pints)
1.1 ohc – large radiator .... 7.2 litres (12.7 pints)
1.3 ohc .... 7.1 litres (12.5 pints)
1.6 ohc (except XR3i) .... 6.9 litres (12.1 pints)
1.6 ohc (XR3i) .... 7.8 litres (13.7 pints)
Transmission:
4-speed manual .... 2.8 litres (4.9 pints)
5-speed manual .... 3.1 litres (5.5 pints)
Automatic transmission .... 7.9 litres (14.0 pints)
Steering rack .... 95 cc (0.17 pint)
CV joints .... 40 g (1.5 oz) per joint

Buying spare parts and vehicle identification numbers

Buying spare parts

Spare parts are available from many sources, for example Ford garages, other garages and accessory shops, and motor factors. Our advice regarding spare part sources is as follows:

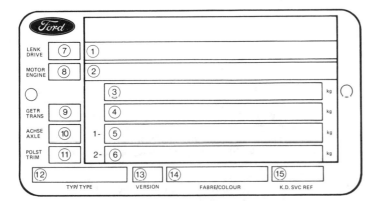

Vehicle identification (VIN) plate

1 Type Approval Number
2 Vehicle Identification Number
3 Gross vehicle weight
4 Gross train weight
5 Permitted front axle loading
6 Permitted rear axle loading
7 Steering (LHD/RHD)
8 Engine
9 Transmission
10 Axle (final drive ratio)
11 Trim (interior)
12 Body type
13 Special territory version
14 Body colour
15 KD reference (usually blank)

Officially appointed Ford garages – This is the best source of parts which are peculiar to your vehicle and are otherwise not generally available (eg; complete cylinder heads, internal gearbox components, badges, interior trim etc). It is also the only place at which you should buy parts if your vehicle is still under warranty: non-Ford components may invalidate the warranty. To be sure of obtaining the correct parts it will always be necessary to give the storeman your vehicle's engine and chassis number, and if possible, to take the 'old' part along for positive identification. Remember that many parts are available on a factory exchange scheme – any parts returned should always be clean! It obviously makes good sense to go straight to the specialists on your vehicle for this type of part for they are best equipped to supply you.

Other garages and accessory shops – These are often very good places to buy materials and components needed for the maintenance of your vehicle (eg spark plugs, bulbs, drivebelts, oils and greases, touch-up paint, filler paste, etc). They also sell general accessories, usually have convenient opening hours, charge lower prices and can often be found not far from home.

Motor factors – Good factors will stock all of the more important components which wear out relatively quickly (eg brake cylinders/pipes/hoses/seals/shoes and pads etc). Motor factors will often provide new or reconditioned components on a part exchange basis – this can save a considerable amount of money.

Vehicle identification numbers

The *Vehicle Identification Number* is located on the plate found under the bonnet above the radiator. The plate also carries information concerning paint colour, final drive ratio etc.

The *engine number* is located in one of the following places, according to engine type (photo):

Front right-hand side of engine block
Front face of cylinder block
Front left-hand side of engine block
Cylinder block above clutch bellhousing

A *tuning decal* will also be found under the bonnet (photo). This illustrates graphically the basic tuning functions, typically plug gap, ignition timing, idle speed and CO level, and (where applicable) valve clearances, points gap and dwell angle.

Typical engine number

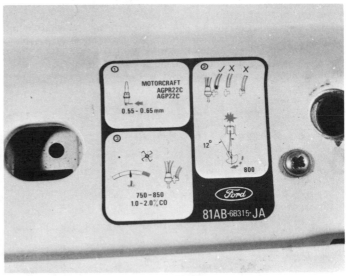

Tuning decal

Tools and working facilities

Introduction

A selection of good tools is a fundamental requirement for anyone contemplating the maintenance and repair of a motor vehicle. For the owner who does not possess any, their purchase will prove a considerable expense, offsetting some of the savings made by doing-it-yourself. However, provided that the tools purchased are of good quality, they will last for many years and prove an extremely worthwhile investment.

To help the average owner to decide which tools are needed to carry out the various tasks detailed in this manual, we have compiled three lists of tools under the following headings: *Maintenance and minor repair, Repair and overhaul*, and *Special*. The newcomer to practical mechanics should start off with the *Maintenance and minor repair* tool kit and confine himself to the simpler jobs around the vehicle. Then, as his confidence and experience grows, he can undertake more difficult tasks, buying extra tools as, and when, they are needed. In this way, a *Maintenance and minor repair* tool kit can be built-up into a *Repair and overhaul* tool kit over a considerable period of time without any major cash outlays. The experienced do-it-yourselfer will have a tool kit good enough for most repair and overhaul procedures and will add tools from the *Special* category when he feels the expense is justified by the amount of use these tools will be put to.

It is obviously not possible to cover the subject of tools fully here. For those who wish to learn more about tools and their use there is a book entitled *How to Choose and Use Car Tools* available from the publishers of this manual.

Maintenance and minor repair tool kit

The tools given in this list should be considered as a minimum requirement if routine maintenance, servicing and minor repair operations are to be undertaken. We recommend the purchase of combination spanners (ring one end, open-ended the other); although more expensive than open-ended ones, they do give the advantages of both types of spanner.

Combination spanners - 10, 11, 12, 13, 14 & 17 mm
Adjustable spanner - 9 inch
Spark plug spanner (with rubber insert)
Spark plug gap adjustment tool
Set of feeler gauges
Brake bleed nipple spanner
Screwdriver - 4 in long x $\frac{1}{4}$ in dia (flat blade)
Screwdriver - 4 in long x $\frac{1}{4}$ in dia (cross blade)
Combination pliers - 6 inch
Hacksaw (junior)
Tyre pump
Tyre pressure gauge
Oil can
Fine emery cloth (1 sheet)
Wire brush (small)
Funnel (medium size)

Repair and overhaul tool kit

These tools are virtually essential for anyone undertaking any major repairs to a motor vehicle, and are additional to those given in the *Maintenance and minor repair* list. Included in this list is a comprehensive set of sockets. Although these are expensive they will be found invaluable as they are so versatile - particularly if various drives are included in the set. We recommend the $\frac{1}{2}$ in square-drive type, as this can be used with most proprietary torque spanners. If you cannot afford a socket set, even bought piecemeal, then inexpensive tubular box wrenches are a useful alternative.

The tools in this list will occasionally need to be supplemented by tools from the *Special* list.

Sockets (or box spanners) to cover range in previous list
Reversible ratchet drive (for use with sockets)
Extension piece, 10 inch (for use with sockets)
Universal joint (for use with sockets)
Torque wrench (for use with sockets)
Mole wrench - 8 inch
Ball pein hammer
Soft-faced hammer, plastic or rubber
Screwdriver - 6 in long x $\frac{5}{16}$ in dia (flat blade)
Screwdriver - 2 in long x $\frac{5}{16}$ in square (flat blade)
Screwdriver - $1\frac{1}{2}$ in long x $\frac{1}{4}$ in dia (cross blade)
Screwdriver - 3 in long x $\frac{1}{8}$ in dia (electricians)
Pliers - electricians side cutters
Pliers - needle nosed
Pliers - circlip (internal and external)
Cold chisel - $\frac{1}{2}$ inch
Scriber
Scraper
Centre punch
Pin punch
Hacksaw
Valve grinding tool
Steel rule/straight-edge
Allen keys
Selection of files
Wire brush (large)
Axle-stands
Jack (strong scissor or hydraulic type)

Special tools

The tools in this list are those which are not used regularly, are expensive to buy, or which need to be used in accordance with their manufacturers' instructions. Unless relatively difficult mechanical jobs are undertaken frequently, it will not be economic to buy many of these tools. Where this is the case, you could consider clubbing together with friends (or joining a motorists' club) to make a joint purchase, or borrowing the tools against a deposit from a local garage or tool hire specialist.

The following list contains only those tools and instruments freely available to the public, and not those special tools produced by the vehicle manufacturer specifically for its dealer network. You will find occasional references to these manufacturers' special tools in the text of this manual. Generally, an alternative method of doing the job without the vehicle manufacturers' special tool is given. However, sometimes, there is no alternative to using them. Where this is the case and the relevant tool cannot be bought or borrowed you will have to entrust the work to a franchised garage.

Valve spring compressor
Piston ring compressor
Balljoint separator
Universal hub/bearing puller
Impact screwdriver
Micrometer and/or vernier gauge
Dial gauge
Stroboscopic timing light
Dwell angle meter/tachometer (1.1 only)
Universal electrical multi-meter
Cylinder compression gauge
Lifting tackle
Trolley jack
Light with extension lead

Buying tools

For practically all tools, a tool dealer is the best source since he will have a very comprehensive range compared with the average garage or accessory shop. Having said that, accessory shops often offer excellent quality tools at discount prices, so it pays to shop around.

Remember, you don't have to buy the most expensive items on the shelf, but it is always advisable to steer clear of the very cheap tools. There are plenty of good tools around at reasonable prices, so ask the proprietor or manager of the shop for advice before making a purchase.

Care and maintenance of tools

Having purchased a reasonable tool kit, it is necessary to keep the tools in a clean serviceable condition. After use, always wipe off any dirt, grease and metal particles using a clean, dry cloth, before putting the tools away. Never leave them lying around after they have been used. A simple tool rack on the garage or workshop wall, for items such as screwdrivers and pliers is a good idea. Store all normal spanners and sockets in a metal box. Any measuring instruments, gauges, meters, etc, must be carefully stored where they cannot be damaged or become rusty.

Take a little care when tools are used. Hammer heads inevitably become marked and screwdrivers lose the keen edge on their blades from time to time. A little timely attention with emery cloth or a file will soon restore items like this to a good serviceable finish.

Working facilities

Not to be forgotten when discussing tools, is the workshop itself. If anything more than routine maintenance is to be carried out, some form of suitable working area becomes essential.

It is appreciated that many an owner mechanic is forced by circumstances to remove an engine or similar item, without the benefit of a garage or workshop. Having done this, any repairs should always be done under the cover of a roof.

Wherever possible, any dismantling should be done on a clean flat workbench or table at a suitable working height.

Any workbench needs a vice: one with a jaw opening of 4 in (100 mm) is suitable for most jobs. As mentioned previously, some clean dry storage space is also required for tools, as well as the lubricants, cleaning fluids, touch-up paints and so on which become necessary.

Another item which may be required, and which has a much more general usage, is an electric drill with a chuck capacity of at least $\frac{5}{16}$ in (8 mm). This, together with a good range of twist drills, is virtually essential for fitting accessories such as wing mirrors and reversing lights.

Last, but not least, always keep a supply of old newspapers and clean, lint-free rags available, and try to keep any working area as clean as possible.

Standard jaw gap comparison table

Jaw gap (in)	Spanner size
0.250	$\frac{1}{4}$ in AF
0.276	7 mm
0.313	$\frac{5}{16}$ in AF
0.315	8 mm
0.344	$\frac{11}{32}$ in AF; $\frac{1}{8}$ in Whitworth
0.354	9 mm
0.375	$\frac{3}{8}$ in AF
0.394	10 mm
0.433	11 mm
0.438	$\frac{7}{16}$ in AF
0.445	$\frac{3}{16}$ in Whitworth; $\frac{1}{4}$ in BSF
0.472	12 mm
0.500	$\frac{1}{2}$ in AF
0.512	13 mm
0.525	$\frac{1}{4}$ in Whitworth; $\frac{5}{16}$ in BSF
0.551	14 mm
0.563	$\frac{9}{16}$ in AF
0.591	15 mm
0.600	$\frac{5}{16}$ in Whitworth; $\frac{3}{8}$ in BSF
0.625	$\frac{5}{8}$ in AF
0.630	16 mm
0.669	17 mm
0.686	$\frac{11}{16}$ in AF
0.709	18 mm
0.710	$\frac{3}{8}$ in Whitworth, $\frac{7}{16}$ in BSF
0.748	19 mm
0.750	$\frac{3}{4}$ in AF
0.813	$\frac{13}{16}$ in AF
0.820	$\frac{7}{16}$ in Whitworth; $\frac{1}{2}$ in BSF
0.866	22 mm
0.875	$\frac{7}{8}$ in AF
0.920	$\frac{1}{2}$ in Whitworth; $\frac{9}{16}$ in BSF
0.938	$\frac{15}{16}$ in AF
0.945	24 mm
1.000	1 in AF
1.010	$\frac{9}{16}$ in Whitworth; $\frac{5}{8}$ in BSF
1.024	26 mm
1.063	$1\frac{1}{16}$ in AF; 27 mm
1.100	$\frac{5}{8}$ in Whitworth; $\frac{11}{16}$ in BSF
1.125	$1\frac{1}{8}$ in AF
1.181	30 mm
1.200	$\frac{11}{16}$ in Whitworth; $\frac{3}{4}$ in BSF
1.250	$1\frac{1}{4}$ in AF
1.260	32 mm
1.300	$\frac{3}{4}$ in Whitworth; $\frac{7}{8}$ in BSF
1.313	$1\frac{5}{16}$ in AF
1.390	$\frac{13}{16}$ in Whitworth; $\frac{15}{16}$ in BSF
1.417	36 mm
1.438	$1\frac{7}{16}$ in AF
1.480	$\frac{7}{8}$ in Whitworth; 1 in BSF
1.500	$1\frac{1}{2}$ in AF
1.575	40 mm; $\frac{15}{16}$ in Whitworth
1.614	41 mm
1.625	$1\frac{5}{8}$ in AF
1.670	1 in Whitworth; $1\frac{1}{8}$ in BSF
1.688	$1\frac{11}{16}$ in AF
1.811	46 mm
1.813	$1\frac{13}{16}$ in AF
1.860	$1\frac{1}{8}$ in Whitworth; $1\frac{1}{4}$ in BSF
1.875	$1\frac{7}{8}$ in AF
1.969	50 mm
2.000	2 in AF
2.050	$1\frac{1}{4}$ in Whitworth; $1\frac{3}{8}$ in BSF
2.165	55 mm
2.362	60 mm

Jacking and towing

Jacking

The jack supplied in the vehicle tool kit should only be used for emergency roadside wheel changing, unless it is supplemented with axle stands.

The jack supplied with Hatchback and Estate versions is of half scissors type, while the jack supplied with the van is of full scissors type (photos).

Use the jack at the mounting points on either side of the vehicle just below the sill.

When using a trolley or other type of workshop jack, it can be placed under the front lower crossmember (provided a shaped block of wood is used as an insulator) to raise the front of the vehicle.

To raise the rear of a Hatchback (except XR3i variant) or Estate, place the jack under the right-hand suspension lower arm mounting bracket using a rubber pad as an insulator.

To raise the rear of a Van, place the jack under the centre of the axle tube, taking care not to contact the brake pressure regulating valve or the hydraulic lines.

Axle stands should only be located under the double-skinned sections of the side members at the front of the vehicle, or under the sill jacking points. At the rear of the vehicle (Hatchback or Estate), place the stands under the member to which the trailing arm is attached. On Vans, place the stands under the left spring front attachment body bracket.

Provided only one wheel at the rear of the vehicle is to be raised, Hatchback and Estate may be jacked up under the rear spring seat, or the Van under the leaf spring-to-axle tube mounting plate.

Towing

Towing eyes are fitted to the front and the rear of the vehicle for attachment of a tow rope (photos).

Always unlock the steering column if being towed by another vehicle. If servo-assisted brakes are fitted, remember that the servo is inoperative if the engine is not running.

Jack stowage (passenger vehicles)

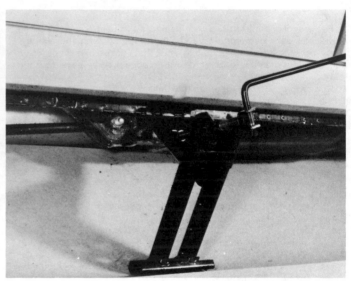

Sill jacking location (passenger vehicles)

Front towing eye

Rear towing eye

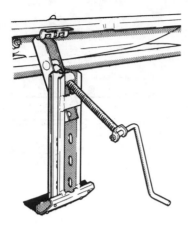

Tool kit jack (Hatchback and Estate)

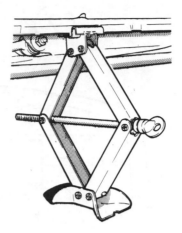

Tool kit jack (Van)

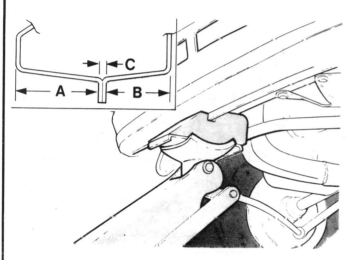

Trolley jack position at front of vehicle. Note shaped block of wood between jack head and crossmember

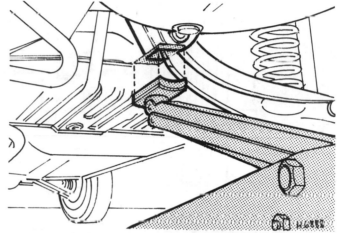

Trolley jack position at rear of vehicle (Hatchback and Estate – not XR3i). Note insulator between jack head and mounting point

A   Non load-bearing metal   C   Flange
B   Structural crossmember

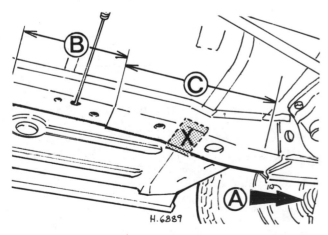

Front side members

A   To front of vehicle   C   Double-skinned area
B   Single-skinned area   X   Jacking point

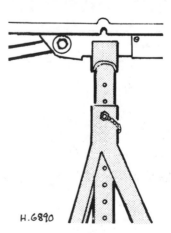

Axle stand rear mounting position (Hatchback and Estate)

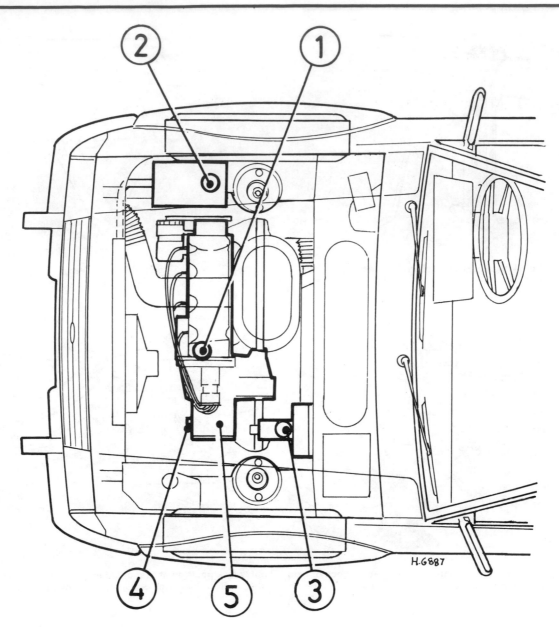

H.G887

Recommended lubricants and fluids

Component or system	Lubricant type or specification
1 Engine oil	Multigrade engine oil SAE 10W/30
2 Cooling system	Antifreeze mixture to Ford spec SSM-97B-9103-A
3 Brake hydraulic fluid	Hydraulic fluid to Ford spec SAM-6C, 9103-A
4 Manual transmission	Hypoid gear oil SAE 80EP
5 Automatic transmission	ATF to Ford spec SQM-2C9010-A
Hub bearings	Multi-purpose grease
CV joints	Molybdenum grease
Steering rack	Semi-fluid grease to Ford spec SAMIC-9106A

Safety first!

Professional motor mechanics are trained in safe working procedures. However enthusiastic you may be about getting on with the job in hand, do take the time to ensure that your safety is not put at risk. A moment's lack of attention can result in an accident, as can failure to observe certain elementary precautions.

There will always be new ways of having accidents, and the following points do not pretend to be a comprehensive list of all dangers; they are intended rather to make you aware of the risks and to encourage a safety-conscious approach to all work you carry out on your vehicle.

Essential DOs and DON'Ts

DON'T rely on a single jack when working underneath the vehicle. Always use reliable additional means of support, such as axle stands, securely placed under a part of the vehicle that you know will not give way.

DON'T attempt to loosen or tighten high-torque nuts (e.g. wheel hub nuts) while the vehicle is on a jack; it may be pulled off.

DON'T start the engine without first ascertaining that the transmission is in neutral (or 'Park' where applicable) and the parking brake applied.

DON'T suddenly remove the filler cap from a hot cooling system – cover it with a cloth and release the pressure gradually first, or you may get scalded by escaping coolant.

DON'T attempt to drain oil until you are sure it has cooled sufficiently to avoid scalding you.

DON'T grasp any part of the engine, exhaust or catalytic converter without first ascertaining that it is sufficiently cool to avoid burning you.

DON'T allow brake fluid or antifreeze to contact vehicle paintwork.

DON'T syphon toxic liquids such as fuel, brake fluid or antifreeze by mouth, or allow them to remain on your skin.

DON'T inhale dust – it may be injurious to health (see *Asbestos* below).

DON'T allow any spilt oil or grease to remain on the floor – wipe it up straight away, before someone slips on it.

DON'T use ill-fitting spanners or other tools which may slip and cause injury.

DON'T attempt to lift a heavy component which may be beyond your capability – get assistance.

DON'T rush to finish a job, or take unverified short cuts.

DON'T allow children or animals in or around an unattended vehicle.

DO wear eye protection when using power tools such as drill, sander, bench grinder etc, and when working under the vehicle.

DO use a barrier cream on your hands prior to undertaking dirty jobs – it will protect your skin from infection as well as making the dirt easier to remove afterwards; but make sure your hands aren't left slippery.

DO keep loose clothing (cuffs, tie etc) and long hair well out of the way of moving mechanical parts.

DO remove rings, wristwatch etc, before working on the vehicle – especially the electrical system.

DO ensure that any lifting tackle used has a safe working load rating adequate for the job.

DO keep your work area tidy – it is only too easy to fall over articles left lying around.

DO get someone to check periodically that all is well, when working alone on the vehicle.

DO carry out work in a logical sequence and check that everything is correctly assembled and tightened afterwards.

DO remember that your vehicle's safety affects that of yourself and others. If in doubt on any point, get specialist advice.

IF, in spite of following these precautions, you are unfortunate enough to injure yourself, seek medical attention as soon as possible.

Asbestos

Certain friction, insulating, sealing, and other products – such as brake linings, brake bands, clutch linings, torque converters, gaskets, etc – contain asbestos. *Extreme care must be taken to avoid inhalation of dust from such products since it is hazardous to health.* If in doubt, assume that they *do* contain asbestos.

Fire

Remember at all times that petrol (gasoline) is highly flammable. Never smoke, or have any kind of naked flame around, when working on the vehicle. But the risk does not end there – a spark caused by an electrical short-circuit, by two metal surfaces contacting each other, by careless use of tools, or even by static electricity built up in your body under certain conditions, can ignite petrol vapour, which in a confined space is highly explosive.

Always disconnect the battery earth (ground) terminal before working on any part of the fuel or electrical system, and never risk spilling fuel on to a hot engine or exhaust.

It is recommended that a fire extinguisher of a type suitable for fuel and electrical fires is kept handy in the garage or workplace at all times. Never try to extinguish a fuel or electrical fire with water.

Fumes

Certain fumes are highly toxic and can quickly cause unconsciousness and even death if inhaled to any extent. Petrol (gasoline) vapour comes into this category, as do the vapours from certain solvents such as trichloroethylene. Any draining or pouring of such volatile fluids should be done in a well ventilated area.

When using cleaning fluids and solvents, read the instructions carefully. Never use materials from unmarked containers – they may give off poisonous vapours.

Never run the engine of a motor vehicle in an enclosed space such as a garage. Exhaust fumes contain carbon monoxide which is extremely poisonous; if you need to run the engine, always do so in the open air or at least have the rear of the vehicle outside the workplace.

If you are fortunate enough to have the use of an inspection pit, never drain or pour petrol, and never run the engine, while the vehicle is standing over it; the fumes, being heavier than air, will concentrate in the pit with possibly lethal results.

The battery

Never cause a spark, or allow a naked light, near the vehicle's battery. It will normally be giving off a certain amount of hydrogen gas, which is highly explosive.

Always disconnect the battery earth (ground) terminal before working on the fuel or electrical systems.

If possible, loosen the filler plugs or cover when charging the battery from an external source. Do not charge at an excessive rate or the battery may burst.

Take care when topping up and when carrying the battery. The acid electrolyte, even when diluted, is very corrosive and should not be allowed to contact the eyes or skin.

If you ever need to prepare electrolyte yourself, always add the acid slowly to the water, and never the other way round. Protect against splashes by wearing rubber gloves and goggles.

When jump starting a car using a booster battery, for negative earth (ground) vehicles, connect the jump leads in the following sequence: First connect one jump lead between the positive (+) terminals of the two batteries. Then connect the other jump lead first to the negative (–) terminal of the booster battery, and then to a good earthing (ground) point on the vehicle to be started, at least 18 in (45 cm) from the battery if possible. Ensure that hands and jump leads are clear of any moving parts, and that the two vehicles do not touch. Disconnect the leads in the reverse order.

Mains electricity

When using an electric power tool, inspection light etc, which works from the mains, always ensure that the appliance is correctly connected to its plug and that, where necessary, it is properly earthed (grounded). Do not use such appliances in damp conditions and, again, beware of creating a spark or applying excessive heat in the vicinity of fuel or fuel vapour.

Ignition HT voltage

A severe electric shock can result from touching certain parts of the ignition system, such as the HT leads, when the engine is running or being cranked, particularly if components are damp or the insulation is defective. Where an electronic ignition system is fitted, the HT voltage is much higher and could prove fatal.

Routine maintenance

For modifications, and information applicable to later models, see Supplement at end of manual

Maintenance is essential for ensuring safety and desirable for the purpose of getting the best in terms of performance and economy from the vehicle. Over the years the need for periodic lubrication – oiling, greasing and so on – has been drastically reduced if not totally eliminated. This has unfortunately tended to lead some owners to think that because no such action is required the items either no longer exist or will last for ever. This is a serious delusion. It follows therefore that the largest initial element of maintenance is visual examination. This may lead to repairs or renewals.

Weekly or every 400 km (250 miles)

Check the engine oil level and top up if necessary (photo)
Check the coolant level in the expansion tank and top up if necessary (photo)
Check the battery electrolyte level and top up if necessary (photo)
Top up the fluid level in the washer reservoirs (photo)
Check brake fluid level, investigate any sudden fall in level
Check the operation of all lights
Check the operation of the horn
Check the operation of washers and wipers
Check tyre pressures, including the spare (photos)

At the first 2500 km (1500 miles) – new vehicles

Check the drivebelt tension
Check torque of inlet and exhaust manifold bolts (cold)
Check valve clearances (ohv)
Check brake hydraulic system connectors for leaks

Check idle speed, CO% (mixture) and automatic choke adjustment
Check EGR system (Sweden only)

Every 10 000 km (6000 miles)

Clean and regap spark plugs (ohv only)
Clean oil filler cap breather (ohv only)
Adjust dwell angle (mechanical ignition system)
Check ignition timing (mechanical ignition system)
Renew engine oil and filter (photo)
Check wear in disc pads
Check wear in brake shoe linings
Check steering joints for wear and gaiters for deterioration
Check tightness of roadwheel bolts
Clean fuel pump
Check and adjust drivebelt tension (ohv only)
Clean HT leads, distributor cap and coil tower (ohv only)
Lubricate distributor (ohv only)
Adjust idle speed

Every 20 000 km (12 000 miles)

Check headlamp beam alignment
Renew spark plugs
Renew contact points (1.1 only)
Lubricate distributor (1.1 only)
Clean distributor cap and HT leads
Check transmission oil level and top up if necessary (photo)

Under-bonnet view of Escort with 1.3 ohc (CVH) engine

Topping up the engine oil

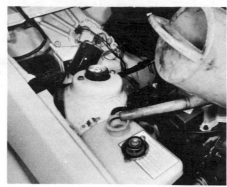

Topping up coolant expansion tank

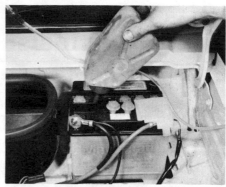

Topping up the battery

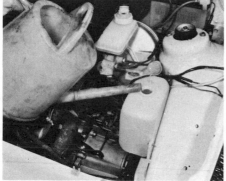

Topping up the washer fluid reservoir

Checking a tyre pressure

Spare wheel and anchor bolt

Sump drain plug

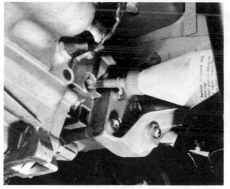

Topping up the transmission

Check driveshaft gaiters for deterioration
Check tyres for wear or damage
Check exhaust system for corrosion
Lubricate controls
Check rear hub bearing adjustment

Every 40 000 km (24 000 miles)

Renew crankcase emission filter (ohc)
Renew air cleaner element
Clean or renew emission control orifice in engine oil filler cap (ohv)

Sweden only: Check air cleaner temperature control, vacuum delay/sustain valve, ported vacuum switches and EGR system connections generally

Every 2 years

Renew antifreeze coolant mixture

Every 3 years

Renew brake hydraulic fluid by bleeding

Fault diagnosis

Introduction

The car owner who does his or her own maintenance according to the recommended schedules should not have to use this section of the manual very often. Modern component reliability is such that, provided those items subject to wear or deterioration are inspected or renewed at the specified intervals, sudden failure is comparatively rare. Faults do not usually just happen as a result of sudden failure, but develop over a period of time. Major mechanical failures in particular are usually preceded by characteristic symptoms over hundreds or even thousands of miles. Those components which do occasionally fail without warning are often small and easily carried in the car.

With any fault finding, the first step is to decide where to begin investigations. Sometimes this is obvious, but on other occasions a little detective work will be necessary. The owner who makes half a dozed haphazard adjustments or replacements may be successful in curing a fault (or its symptoms), but he will be none the wiser if the fault recurs and he may well have spend more time and money than was necessary. A calm and logical approach will be found to be more satisfactory in the long run. Always take into account any warning signs or abnormalities that may have been noticed in the period preceding the fault — power loss, high or low gauge readings, unusual noises or smells, etc — and remember that failure of components such as fuses or spark plugs may only be pointers to some underlying fault.

The pages which follow here are intended to help in cases of failure to start or breakdown on the road. There is also a Fault Diagnosis Section at the end of each Chapter which should be consulted if the preliminary checks prove unfruitful. Whatever the fault, certain basic principles apply. These are as follows:

Verify the fault. This is simply a matter of being sure that you know what the symptoms are before starting work. This is particularly important if you are investigating a fault for someone else who may not have described it very accurately.

Don't overlook the obvious: For example, if the car won't start, is there petrol in the tank? (Don't take anyone else's word on this particular point, and don't trust the fuel gauge either!). If an electrical fault is indicated, look for loose or broken wires before digging out the test gear.

Cure the disease, not the symptom. Substituting a flat battery with a fully charged one will get you off the hard shoulder, but if the underlying cause is not attended to, the new battery will go the same way. Similarly, changing oil-fouled spark plugs for a new set will get you moving again, but remember that the reason for the fouling (if it wasn't simply an incorrect grade of plug) will have to be established and corrected.

Don't take anything for granted. Particularly, don't forget that a 'new' component may itself be defective (especially if it's been rattling round in the boot for months), and don't leave components out of a fault diagnosis sequence just because they are new or recently fitted. When you do finally diagnose a difficult fault, you'll probably realise that all the evidence was there from the start.

Electrical faults

Electrical faults can be more puzzling than straightforward mechanical failures, but they are no less susceptible to logical analysis if the basic principles of operation are understood. Car electrical wiring exists in extremely unfavourable conditions — heat, vibration and chemical attack — and the first things to look for are loose or corroded connections and broken or chafed wires, especially where the wires pass through holes in the bodywork or are subject to vibration.

All metal-bodied cars in current production have one pole of the battery 'earthed', ie connected to the car bodywork, and in nearly all modern cars it is the negative (–) terminal. The various electrical components — motors, bulb holders etc — are also connected to earth, either by means of a lead or directly by their mountings. Electric current flows through the component and then back to the battery via the car bodywork. If the component mounting is loose or corroded, or if a good path back to the battery is not available, the circuit will be incomplete and malfunction will result. The engine and/or gearbox are also earthed by means of flexible metal straps to the body or subframe; if these straps are loose or missing, starter motor, generator and ignition trouble may result.

Assuming the earth return to be satisfactory, electrical faults will be due either to component malfunction or to defects in the current supply. Individual components are dealt with in Chapter 11. If supply wires are broken or cracked internally this results in an open-circuit, and the easiest way to check for this is to bypass the suspect wire temporarily with a length of wire having a crocodile clip or suitable connector at each end. Alternatively, a 12V test lamp can be used to verify the presence of supply voltage at various points along the wire and the break can be thus isolated.

If a bare portion of a live wire touches the car bodywork or other earthed metal part the electricity will take the low-resistance patch thus formed back to the battery: this is known as a short-circuit. Hopefully a short-circuit will blow a fuse, but otherwise it may cause burning of the insulation (and possible further short-circuits) or even a fire. This is why it is inadvisable to bypass persistently blowing fuses with silver foil or wire.

Spares and tool kit

Most cars are only supplied with sufficient tools for wheel changing; the *Maintenance and minor repair* tool kit detailed in *Tools and working facilities,* with the addition of a hammer, is probably sufficient for those repairs that most motorists would consider attempting at the roadside. In addition a few items which can be fitted without too much trouble in the event of a breakdown should be carried. Experience and available space will modify the list below, but the following may save having to call on professional assistance:

Spark plugs, clean and correctly gapped
HT lead and plug cap — long enough to reach the plug furthest from the distributor
Distributor rotor, condenser and contact breaker points (1.1l engines only)
Drivebelt — emergency type may suffice
Spare fuses
Set of principal light bulbs
Tin of radiator sealer and hose bandage
Exhaust bandage
Roll of insulating tape
Length of soft iron wire
Length of electrical flex
Torch or inspection lamp (can double as test lamp)
Battery jump leads
Tow-rope
Tyre valve core
Ignition waterproofing aerosol
Litre of engine oil
Sealed can of hydraulic fluid
Emergency windscreen

If spare fuel is carried, a can designed for the purpose should be used to minimise the risks of leakage and collision damage. A first aid kit and a warning triangle, whilst not at present compulsory in the UK, are obviously sensible items to carry in addition to the above.

When touring abroad it may be advisable to carry additional spares which, even if you cannot fit them yourself, could save having to wait while parts are obtained. The items below may be worth considering:

Clutch and throttle cables
Cylinder head gasket
Alternator brushes
Spare fuel pump

One of the motoring organisations will be able to advise on availability of fuel etc in foreign countries.

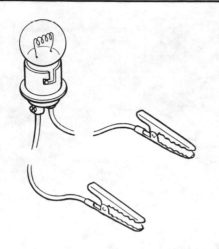

A simple test lamp is useful for tracing electrical faults

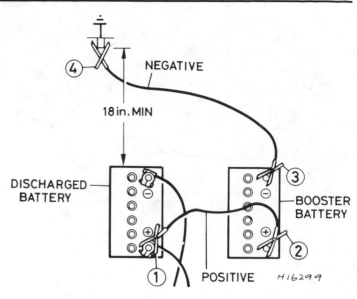

Jump start lead connections for negative earth vehicles – connect leads in order shown

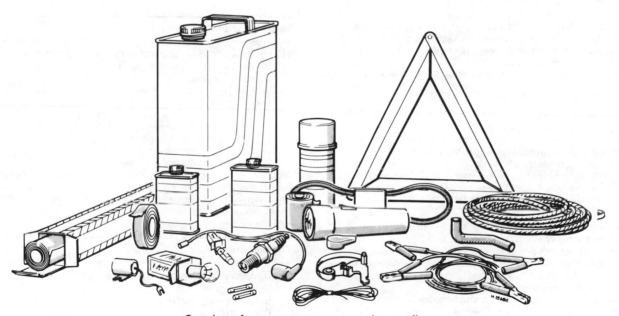

Carrying a few spares can save you a long walk

Engine will not start

Engine fails to turn when starter operated
    Flat battery (recharge, use jump leads, or push start)
    Battery terminals loose or corroded
    Battery earth to body defective
    Engine earth strap loose or broken
    Starter motor (or solenoid) wiring loose or broken
    Ignition/starter switch faulty
    Major mechanical failure (seizure) or long disuse (piston rings rusted to bores)
    Starter or solenoid internal fault (see Chapter 11)

Starter motor turns engine slowly
    Partially discharged battery (recharge, use jump leads, or push start)
    Battery terminals loose or corroded
    Battery earth to body defective
    Engine earth strap loose
    Starter motor (or solenoid) wiring loose

    Starter motor internal fault (see Chapter 11)

Starter motor spins without turning engine
    Flat battery
    Starter motor pinion sticking on sleeve
    Flywheel gear teeth damaged or worn
    Starter motor mounting bolts loose

Engine turns normally but fails to start
    Damp or dirty HT leads and distributor cap (crank engine and check for spark)
    Dirty or incorrectly gapped contact breaker points (1.1 only)
    No fuel in tank (check for delivery) (photo)
    Excessive choke (hot engine) or insufficient choke (cold engine)
    Fouled or incorrectly gapped spark plugs (remove, clean and regap)
    Other ignition system fault (see Chapter 4)
    Other fuel system fault (See Chapter 3)
    Poor compression (see Chapter 1)
    Major mechanical failure (eg camshaft drive)

Insert a nail or similar item into plug cap, crank engine with ignition on and check for spark. Note use of insulated tool. End of nail must be within 5 mm (1/5 in) of block

Checking for fuel delivery at carburettor (for fuel injection refer to Chapter 13). Remove pipe (arrowed) and crank engine (with ignition disabled)

Engine fires but will not run
 Insufficient choke (cold engine) – check adjustment
 Air leaks at carburettor or inlet manifold
 Fuel starvation (see Chapter 3)
 Ballast resistor defective (1.1l) or other ignition fault (see Chapter 4)

Engine cuts out and will not restart

Engine cuts out suddenly – ignition fault
 Loose or disconnected LT wires
 Wet HT leads or distributor cap (after traversing water splash)
 Coil or condenser failure (check for spark)
 Other ignition fault (see Chapter 4)

Engine misfires before cutting out – fuel fault
 Fuel tank empty
 Fuel pump defective or filter blocked (check for delivery)
 Fuel tank filler vent blocked (suction will be evident on releasing cap)
 Carburettor needle valve sticking
 Carburettor jets blocked (fuel contamination)
 Other fuel system fault (see Chapter 3)

Engine cuts out – other causes
 Serious overheating
 Major mechanical failure (eg camshaft drive)

Engine overheats

Ignition (no-charge) warning light illuminated
 Slack or broken drivebelt – retension or renew (Chapter 2)

Ignition warning light not illuminated
 Coolant loss due to internal or external leakage (see Chapter 2)
 Thermostat defective
 Low oil level
 Brakes binding
 Radiator clogged externally or internally
 Electric cooling fan not operating correctly
 Engine waterways clogged
 Ignition timing incorrect or automatic advance malfunctioning
 Mixture too weak
Note: *Do not add cold water to an overheated engine or damage may result*

Low engine oil pressure

Warning light illuminated with engine running
 Oil level low or incorrect grade
 Defective sender unit
 Wire to sender unit earthed
 Engine overheating
 Oil filter clogged or bypass valve defective
 Oil pressure relief valve defective
 Oil pick-up strainer clogged
 Oil pump worn or mountings loose
 Worn main or big-end bearings
Note: *Low oil pressure in a high-mileage engine at tickover is not necessarily a cause for concern. Sudden pressure loss at speed is far more significant. In any event, check the warning light sender before condemning the engine.*

Engine noises

Pre-ignition (pinking) on acceleration
 Incorrect grade of fuel
 Ignition timing incorrect
 Distributor faulty or worn
 Worn or maladjusted carburettor
 Excessive carbon build-up in engine

Whistling or wheezing noises
 Leaking vacuum hose
 Leaking carburettor or manifold gasket
 Blowing head gasket

Tapping or rattling
 Incorrect valve clearance (ohv)
 Worn valve gear
 Worn timing chain or belt
 Broken piston ring (ticking noise)

Knocking or thumping
 Unintentional mechanical contact (eg fan blades)
 Worn fanbelt
 Peripheral component fault (generator, water pump etc)
 Worn big-end bearings (regular heavy knocking, perhaps less under load)
 Worn main bearings (rumbling and knocking, perhaps worsening under load)
 Piston slap (most noticeable when cold)

Chapter 1 Engine

For modifications, and information applicable to later models, see Supplement at end of manual

Contents

Specifications

Part A : OHV engine
General

Engine type	4 cylinder in-line, overhead valve, mounted transversely with transmission at front of vehicle
Code	GLB
Capacity	1117 cc
Bore	73.96 mm (2.91 in)
Stroke	64.98 mm (2.56 in)
Compression ratio	9.15 : 1
Output	55 bhp (40 kW) at 5700 rpm
Torque	60 lbf ft (82 Nm) at 4000 rpm
Firing order	1 – 2 – 4 – 3 (No 1 at timing cover end of engine)

Cylinder block

Material	Cast iron
Number of main bearings	3
Cylinder bore (diameter):	
Standard (1)	73.940 to 73.950 mm (2.9110 to 2.9114 in)
Standard (2)	73.950 to 73.960 mm (2.9114 to 2.9118 in)
Standard (3)	73.960 to 73.970 mm (2.9118 to 2.9122 in)
Standard (4)	73.970 to 73.980 mm (2.9122 to 2.9126 in)
Oversize 0.5 mm	74.500 to 74.010 mm (2.9331 to 2.9335 in)
Oversize 1.0 mm	75.000 to 75.010 mm (2.9528 to 2.9531 in)
Main bearing shell inner diameter:	
Standard	57.009 to 57.036 mm (2.2444 to 2.2455 in)
0.254 mm undersize	56.755 to 56.782 mm (2.2344 to 2.2355 in)
0.508 mm undersize	56.501 to 56.528 mm (2.2244 to 2.2255 in)
0.762 mm undersize	56.247 to 56.274 mm (2.2144 to 2.2155 in)
Camshaft bearing inner diameter	39.662 to 39.682 mm (1.5615 to 1.5623 in)

Crankshaft
Main bearing journal diameter:
- Standard .... 56.990 to 57.000 mm (2.2437 to 2.441 in)
- Standard with yellow dot .... 56.980 to 56.990 mm (2.2433 to 2.2437 in)
- 0.254 mm undersize .... 56.726 to 56.746 mm (2.3330 to 2.2341 in)
- 0.508 mm undersize .... 56.472 to 56.492 mm (2.2233 to 2.2241 in)
- 0.762 mm undersize .... 56.218 to 56.238 mm (2.2133 to 2.2141 in)

Main bearing running clearance .... 0.009 to 0.046 mm (0.0004 to 0.0018 in)
Main bearing running clearance wear limit .... 0.056 mm (0.0022 in)
Crankpin (big-end) diameter:
- Standard .... 42.99 to 43.01 mm (1.6925 to 1.6933 in)
- 0.254 mm undersize .... 42.74 to 42.76 mm (1.6827 to 1.6835 in)
- 0.508 mm undersize .... 42.49 to 42.51 mm (1.6728 to 1.6736 in)
- 0.762 mm undersize .... 42.24 to 42.26 mm (1.6630 to 1.6638 in)

Thrust washer thickness:
- Standard .... 2.80 to 2.85 mm (0.1102 to 0.1122 in)
- Oversize .... 2.99 to 3.04 mm (0.1177 to 0.1197 in)

Crankshaft endfloat .... 0.079 to 0.279 mm (0.0031 to 0.0110 in)
Journal and crankpin out-of-round or taper – maximum permissible ... 0.0254 mm (0.001 in)

Camshaft
Number of bearings 3
Drive .... Chain (single)
Thrust plate thickness .... 4.457 to 4.508 mm (0.175 to 0.177 in)
Cam lift (inlet) .... 5.985 mm (0.236 in)
Cam lift (exhaust) .... 5.894 mm (0.232 in)
Cam length (inlet) .... 33.198 to 33.274 mm (1.307 to 1.310 in)
Cam length (exhaust) .... 33.442 to 33.518 mm (1.317 to 1.320 in)
Camshaft bearing diameter .... 39.662 to 39.682 mm (1.561 to 1.562 in)
Camshaft bearing internal diameter .... 39.662 to 39.682 mm (1.561 to 1.562 in)
Camshaft endfloat .... 0.062 to 0.193 mm (0.002 to 0.008 in)

Timing chain
Number of links 46
Length .... 438.15 mm (17.25 in)

Pistons and piston rings
Diameter:
- Standard (1) .... 73.910 to 73.920 mm (2.9098 to 2.9102 in)
- Standard (2) .... 73.920 to 73.930 mm (2.9102 to 2.9106 in)
- Standard (3) .... 73.930 to 73.940 mm (2.9106 to 2.9110 in)
- Standard (4) .... 73.940 to 73.950 mm (2.9110 to 2.9114 in)
- 0.5 mm oversize .... 74.460 to 74.485 mm (2.9315 to 2.9325 in)
- 1.0 mm oversize .... 74.960 to 74.985 mm (2.9152 to 2.9522 in)

Piston-to-bore clearance .... 0.015 to 0.050 mm (0.0006 to 0.0020 in)
Piston ring end gap:
- Compression .... 0.25 to 0.45 mm (0.010 to 0.018 in)
- Oil control .... 0.20 to 0.40 mm (0.008 to 0.016 in)

Gudgeon pin
Pin length .... 63.0 to 63.8 mm (2.48 to 2.51 in)
Pin diameter:
- White .... 20.622 to 20.625 mm (0.8118 to 0.8120 in)
- Red .... 20.625 to 20.628 mm (0.8120 to 0.8121 in)
- Blue .... 20.628 to 20.631 mm (0.8121 to 0.8122 in)
- Yellow .... 20.631 to 20.634 mm (0.8122 to 0.8124 in)

Interference fit in piston at 21°C (69.8°F) .... 0.013 to 0.045 mm (0.0005 to 0.0018 in)

Connecting rod
Big-end bore diameter .... 46.685 to 46.705 mm (1.8379 to 1.8388 in)
Small-end bore diameter .... 20.589 to 20.609 mm (0.8106 to 0.8114 in)
Bearing shell inside diameter:
- Standard .... 43.016 to 43.050 mm (1.6935 to 1.6948 in)
- 0.254 mm undersize .... 42.766 to 42.800 mm (1.6837 to 1.6850 in)
- 0.508 mm undersize .... 42.516 to 42.550 mm (1.6739 to 1.6752 in)
- 0.762 mm undersize .... 42.266 to 42.300 mm (1.6640 to 1.6654 in)
- 1.016 mm undersize .... 42.016 to 42.050 mm (1.6542 to 1.6555 in)

Big-end bearing running clearance .... 0.006 to 0.060 mm (0.0002 to 0.0024 in)

Cylinder head
Material .... Cast iron
Valve seat angle .... 45°
Valve seat width:
- Inlet .... 1.20 to 1.75 mm (0.047 to 0.068 in)
- Exhaust .... 1.20 to 1.70 mm (0.047 to 0.067 in)

Seat cutter:
- Upper correction angle .... 30°

Lower correction angle .... 75°
Valve guide bore (standard) .... 7.907 to 7.938 mm (0.3112 to 0.3125 in)

Valves – general
Operation .... Cam followers and pushrods
Inlet valve opens .... 21° BTDC
Inlet valve closes .... 55° ABDC
Exhaust valve opens .... 70° BBDC
Exhaust valve closes .... 22° ATDC
Valve clearance (cold):
    Inlet .... 0.22 mm (0.009 in)
    Exhaust .... 0.59 mm (0.023 in)
Cam follower diameter .... 13.081 to 13.094 mm (0.5149 to 0.5155 in)
Cam follower clearance in bore .... 0.016 to 0.062 mm (0.0006 to 0.0024 in)
Valve spring type .... Single
Number of coils 6
Valve spring free length .... 42.0 mm (1.654 in)

Inlet valve
Length .... 105.45 to 106.45 mm (4.1516 to 4.1909 in)
Head diameter .... 38.02 to 38.28 mm (1.4968 to 1.5071 in)
Stem diameter:
    Standard .... 7.866 to 7.868 mm (0.3097 to 0.3098 in)
    0.076 mm oversize .... 7.944 to 7.962 mm (0.3128 to 0.3135 in)
    0.38 mm oversize .... 8.249 to 8.267 mm (0.3248 to 0.3255 in)
Valve stem clearance in guide .... 0.021 to 0.070 mm (0.0008 to 0.00276 in)
Valve lift .... 9.448 mm (0.3720 in)

Exhaust valve
Length .... 105.15 to 106.15 mm (4.1398 to 4.1791 in)
Head diameter .... 29.01 to 29.27 mm (1.1421 to 1.1524 in)
Stem diameter:
    Standard .... 7.846 to 7.864 mm (0.3089 to 0.3096 in)
    0.076 mm oversize .... 7.922 to 7.940 mm (0.3119 to 0.3126 in)
    0.38 mm oversize .... 8.227 to 8.245 mm (0.3239 to 0.3246 in)
Valve stem clearance in guide .... 0.043 to 0.092 mm (0.0017 to 0.0036 in)
Valve lift .... 9.306 mm (0.3664 in)

Lubrication
Oil pump type .... Rotor, external driven by gear on camshaft
Minimum oil pressure at 80°C (175°F):
    Engine speed 750 rpm .... 0.6 kgf/cm^2 (8.5 lbf/in^2)
    Engine speed 2000 rpm .... 1.5 kgf/cm^2 (21.3 lbf/in^2)
Oil pressure warning lamp operates .... 0.32 to 0.53 kgf/cm^2 (4.5 to 7.5 lbf/in^2)
Relief valve opens .... 2.41 to 2.75 kgf/cm^2 (34.3 to 39.1 lbf/in^2)
Oil pump clearances:
    Outer rotor-to-body .... 0.14 to 0.26 mm (0.0055 to 0.0102 in)
    Inner-to-outer rotor .... 0.051 to 0.127 mm (0.0020 to 0.0050 in)
    Rotor endfloat .... 0.025 to 0.06 mm (0.0010 to 0.0024 in)
Engine oil capacity:
    Without filter change .... 2.75 litres (4.8 Imp pints)
    With filter change .... 3.25 litres (5.7 Imp pints)

Torque wrench settings

	Nm	lbf ft
Main bearing cap bolts	95	70
Connecting rod nuts	31	23
Rear oil seal retainer bolts	18	13
Flywheel bolts	68	50
Clutch pressure plate bolts	10	7
Chain tensioner bolts	8	6
Camshaft thrust plate bolts	4	3
Camshaft sprocket bolts	19	14
Timing cover bolts	10	7
Coolant pump bolts	10	7
Crankshaft pulley bolt	54	40
Coolant pump pulley bolts	10	7
Starter motor bolts	41	30
Fuel pump bolts	18	13
Oil pump bolts	19	14
Sump drain plug	25	18
Sump fixing bolts:		
Stage 1	8	6
Stage 2	11	8
Stage 3	11	8
Oil pressure sender	15	11

Coolant temperature sender	15	11
Rocker shaft pedestal bolts	38	28
Cylinder head bolts:		
Stage 1	15	11
Stage 2	48	35
Stage 3	88	65
Stage 4 (After 15 minutes delay)	109	80
Rocker cover screws	4	3
Exhaust manifold nuts and bolts	16	12
Intake manifold nuts and bolts	19	14
Carburettor flange nuts	19	14
Thermostat housing cover bolts	19	14
Engine-to-transmission bolts	41	30
Transmission oil filler plug	25	18

Part B: OHC engine
General

Engine type	4-cylinder, in-line, overhead camshaft, mounted transversely with transmission at front of vehicle
Code:	
1.1 LC	GMA
1.1 HC	GPA
1.3 HC	JPA
1.6 HC	LPA
1.6 HC/2V (Weber carburettor)	LUA
Cubic capacity:	
1.1 litre nominal	1117 cc
1.3 litre nominal	1296 cc
1.6 litre nominal	1597 cc
Bore:	
1.1	73.96 mm (2.91 in)
1.3 and 1.6	79.96 mm (3.15 in)
Stroke:	
1.1	64.98 mm (2.56 in)
1.3	64.52 mm (2.54 in)
1.6	79.52 mm (3.13 in)
Compression ratio	9.5 : 1 (except 1.1 LC 8.5 : 1)
Power output:	
1.1 LC	55 bhp (40 kW) at 6000 rpm
1.1 HC	59 bhp (43 kW) at 6000 rpm
1.3 HC	69 bhp (51 kW) at 6000 rpm
1.6 HC	79 bhp (58 kW) at 5800 rpm
1.6 HC/2V	96 bhp (71 kW) at 6000 rpm
Maximum torque:	
1.1 LC	59 lbf ft (80 Nm) at 4000 rpm
1.1 HC	62 lbf ft (84 Nm) at 4000 rpm
1.3 HC	74 lbf ft (100 Nm) at 3500 rpm
1.6 HC	92 lbf ft (125 Nm) at 3000 rpm
1.6 HC/2V	98 lbf ft (132.5 Nm) at 4000 rpm

Cylinder block

Material	Cast iron
Number of main bearings	5
Cylinder bore (diameter):	
1.1 engines:	
Standard (1)	73.94 to 73.95 mm (2.9110 to 2.9114 in)
Standard (2)	73.95 to 73.96 mm (2.9114 to 2.9118 in)
Standard (3)	73.96 to 73.97 mm (2.9118 to 2.9122 in)
Standard (4)	73.97 to 73.98 mm (2.9122 to 2.9126 in)
Oversize (A)	74.23 to 74.24 mm (2.9224 to 2.9228 in)
Oversize (B)	74.24 to 74.25 mm (2.9228 to 2.9232 in)
Oversize (C)	74.25 to 74.26 mm (2.9232 to 2.9236 in)
1.3 and 1.6 engines:	
Standard (1)	79.94 to 79.95 mm (3.1472 to 3.1476 in)
Standard (2)	79.95 to 79.96 mm (3.1476 to 3.1480 in)
Standard (3)	79.96 to 79.97 mm (3.1480 to 3.1484 in)
Standard (4)	79.97 to 79.98 mm (3.1484 to 3.1488 in)
Oversize (A)	80.23 to 80.24 mm (3.1587 to 3.1590 in)
Oversize (B)	80.24 to 80.25 mm (3.1590 to 3.1594 in)
Oversize (C)	80.25 to 80.26 mm (3.1594 to 3.1598 in)

Main bearing shell inner diameter:
Standard	58.011 to 58.038 mm (2.2839 to 2.2850 in)
Undersize 0.25 mm	57.761 to 57.788 mm (2.2740 to 2.2751 in)
Undersize 0.50 mm	57.511 to 57.538 mm ((2.2642 to 2.2653 in)
Undersize 0.75 mm	57.261 to 57.288 mm (2.2544 to 2.2554 in)

Crankshaft

Main bearing journal diameter:
Standard	57.98 to 58.00 mm (2.2827 to 2.2835 in)
Undersize 0.25 mm	57.73 to 57.75 mm (2.2728 to 2.2736 in)
Undersize 0.50 mm	57.48 to 57.50 mm (2.630 to 2.2638 in)
Undersize 0.75 mm	57.23 to 57.25 mm (2.2531 to 2.2539 in)
Main bearing running clearance	0.011 to 0.058 mm (0.0004 to 0.0023 in)

Thrust washer thickness:
Standard	2.301 to 2.351 mm (0.0906 to 0.0926 in)
Oversize	2.491 to 2.541 mm (0.0981 to 0.1000 in)
Crankshaft endfloat	0.09 to 0.30 mm (0.0035 to 0.0118 in)

Crankpin (big-end) diameter:

1.1 engines:
Standard	42.99 to 43.01 mm (1.6925 to 1.6933 in)
Undersize 0.25 mm	42.74 to 42.76 mm (1.6827 to 1.6835 in)
Undersize 0.50 mm	42.49 to 42.51 mm (1.6728 to 1.6736 in)
Undersize 0.75 mm	42.24 to 42.26 mm (1.6630 to 1.6638 in)
Undersize 1.00 mm	41.99 to 42.01 mm (1.6532 to 1.6539 in)

1.3 and 1.6 engines:
Standard	47.89 to 47.91 mm (1.8854 to 1.8862 in)
Undersize 0.25 mm	47.64 to 47.66 mm (1.8756 to 1.8764 in)
Undersize 0.50 mm	47.39 to 47.41 mm (1.8657 to 1.8665 in)
Undersize 0.75 mm	47.14 to 47.16 mm (1.8559 to 1.8567 in)
Undersize 1.00 mm	46.89 to 46.91 mm (1.8461 to 1.8468 in)
Big-end bearing running clearance	0.006 to 0.060 mm (0.0002 to 0.0024 in)

Camshaft

Number of bearings	5
Drive	Toothed belt
Camshaft thrust plate thickness	4.99 to 5.01 mm (0.1965 to 0.1972 in)

Camlift:
All except 1.6 HC/2V	5.79 mm (0.2280 in)
1.6 HC/2V	6.09 mm (0.2398 in)

Cam length – inlet:
All except 1.6 HC/2V	38.305 mm (1.5081 in)
1.6 HC/2V	38.606 mm (1.5200 in)

Cam length – exhaust:
All except 1.6 HC/2V	37.289 mm (1.4681 in)
1.6 HC/2V	37.590 mm (1.4799 in)

Camshaft bearing diameter:
1	44.75 mm (1.7618 in)
2	45.00 mm (1.7717 in)
3	45.25 mm (1.7815 in)
4	45.50 mm (1.7913 in)
5	45.75 mm (1.8012 in)
Camshaft endfloat	0.05 to 0.15 mm (0.0020 to 0.0059 in)

Pistons and piston rings

Diameter – 1.1 engines:
Standard 1	73.910 to 73.920 mm (2.9098 to 2.9102 in)
Standard 2	73.920 to 73.930 mm (2.9102 to 2.9106 in)
Standard 3	73.930 to 73.940 mm (2.9106 to 2.9110 in)
Standard 4	73.940 to 73.950 mm (2.9110 to 2.9114 in)
Standard service	73.930 to 73.955 mm (2.9106 to 2.9116 in)
Oversize 0.29 mm	74.210 to 74.235 mm (2.9217 to 2.9226 in)
Oversize 0.50 mm	74.460 to 74.485 mm (2.9315 to 2.9325 in)

Diameter – 1.3 and 1.6 engines:
Standard 1	79.910 to 79.920 mm (3.1461 to 3.1465 in)
Standard 2	79.920 to 79.930 mm (3.1465 to 3.1468 in)
Standard 3	79.930 to 79.940 mm (3.1468 to 3.1472 in)
Standard 4	79.940 to 79.950 mm (3.1472 to 3.1476 in)
Standard service	79.930 to 79.955 mm (3.1468 to 3.1478 in)
Oversize 0.29 mm	80.210 to 80.235 mm (3.1579 to 3.1589 in)
Oversize 0.50 mm	80.430 to 80.455 mm (3.1665 to 3.1675 in)

Piston-to-bore clearance:
Production	0.020 to 0.040 mm (0.00079 to 0.0016 in)
Service	0.010 to 0.045 mm (0.00039 to 0.0018 in)

Piston ring gap – 1.1 engines:
    Compression rings .... 0.25 to 0.45 mm (0.0098 to 0.0177 in)
    Oil control ring .... 0.20 to 0.40 mm (0.0079 to 0.0158 in)
Piston ring gap – 1.3 and 1.6 engines:
    Compression .... 0.30 to 0.50 mm (0.0118 to 0.0197 in)
    Oil control .... 0.4 to 1.4 mm (0.0158 to 0.0552)

Gudgeon pin

Pin length:
    1.1 engines .... 63.00 to 63.80 mm (2.480 to 2.512 in)
    1.3 and 1.6 engines .... 66.20 to 67.00 mm (2.606 to 2.638 in)
Pin diameter:
    White .... 20.622 to 20.625 mm (0.8119 to 0.8120 in)
    Red .... 20.625 to 20.628 mm (0.8120 to 0.8121 in)
    Blue .... 20.628 to 20.631 mm (0.8121 to 0.8122 in)
    Yellow .... 20.631 to 20.634 mm (0.8122 to 0.8124 in)
Play in piston .... 0.005 to 0.011 mm (0.0002 to 0.0004 in)
Interference fit in piston .... 0.013 to 0.045 mm (0.0005 to 0.0018 in)

Connecting rod

Big-end bore diameter:
    1.1 engines .... 46.685 to 46.705 mm (1.8380 to 1.8388 in)
    1.3 and 1.6 engines .... 50.890 to 50.910 mm (2.0035 to 2.0043 in)
Small-end bore diameter .... 20.589 to 20.609 mm (0.8106 to 0.8114 in)
Big-end bearing shell inside diameter:
    1.1 engines:
        Standard .... 43.016 to 43.050 mm (1.6935 to 1.6949 in)
        Undersize 0.25 mm .... 42.766 to 42.800 mm (1.6837 to 1.6850 in)
        Undersize 0.50 mm .... 42.516 to 42.550 mm (1.6739 to 1.6752 in)
        Undersize 0.75 mm .... 42.266 to 42.300 mm (1.6640 to 1.6654 in)
        Undersize 1.00 mm .... 42.016 to 42.050 mm (1.6542 to 1.6555 in)
    1.3 and 1.6 engines:
        Standard .... 47.916 to 47.950 mm (1.8865 to 1.8878 in)
        Undersize 0.25 mm .... 47.666 to 47.700 mm (1.8766 to 1.8779 in)
        Undersize 0.50 mm .... 47.416 to 47.450 mm (1.8668 to 1.8681 in)
        Undersize 0.75 mm .... 47.166 to 47.200 mm (1.8569 to 1.858 in)
        Undersize 1.00 mm .... 46.916 to 46.950 mm (1.8471 to 1.8484 in)
Big-end bearing running clearance .... 0.006 to 0.060 mm (0.0002 to 0.0024 in)

Cylinder head

Material .... Light alloy
Valve seat angle .... 45°
Valve seat width .... 1.75 to 2.32 mm (0.0689 to 0.0913 in)
    Seat cutter:
    Upper correction angle .... 18°
    Service cutter:
        1.1 engines .... 80°/70°
        1.3 and 1.6 engines .... 77°/70°
Valve guide bore:
    Standard .... 8.063 to 8.094 mm (0.3174 to 0.3187 in)
    Oversize 0.2 mm .... 8.263 to 8.294 mm (0.3253 to 0.3265 in)
    Oversize 0.4 mm .... 8.463 to 8.494 mm (0.3332 to 0.3340 in)
Camshaft bearing bore in head:
    1 .... 44.783 to 44.808 mm (1.7631 to 1.7639 in)
    2 .... 45.033 to 45.058 mm (1.7729 to 1.7739 in)
    3 .... 45.283 to 45.308 mm (1.7828 to 1.7838 in)
    4 .... 45.533 to 45.558 mm (1.7926 to 1.7936 in)
    5 .... 45.783 to 45.808 mm (1.8025 to 1.8034 in)
Valve lifter bore in head .... 22.235 to 22.265 mm (0.8754 to 0.8766 in)

Valves – general

	1.3/1.6 HC	**1.6 HC/2C**
Inlet valve opens	13° ATDC	8° ATDC
Inlet valve closes	28° ABDC	36° ABDC
Exhaust valve opens	30° BBDC	34° BBDC
Exhaust valve closes	15° BTDC	6° BTDC
Valve lift:		
Inlet	9.56 mm (0.3764 in)	10.09 mm (0.3972 in)
Exhaust	9.52 mm (0.3748 in)	10.06 mm (0.3961 in)
Valve spring free length	47.2 mm (1.8583 in)	

Inlet valve

Length:
    1.1 engines .... 135.74 to 136.20 mm (5.3441 to 5.3622 in)
    1.3 and 1.6 engines .... 134.54 to 135.00 mm (5.2969 to 5.3150 in)

Head diameter:
    1.1 engines .... 37.9 to 38.1 mm (1.4921 to 1.5000 in)
    1.3 and 1.6 engines .... 41.9 to 42.1 mm (1.6496 to 1.6575 in)
Stem diameter:
    Standard .... 8.025 to 8.043 mm (0.3159 to 0.3167 in)
    Oversize 0.2 mm .... 8.225 to 8.243 mm (0.3238 to 0.3245 in)
    Oversize 0.4 mm .... 8.425 to 8.443 mm (0.3317 to 0.3324 in)
Valve stem-to-guide clearance .... 0.020 to 0.063 mm (0.0008 to 0.0025 in)

Exhaust valve

Length:
    1.1 engine .... 132.62 to 133.08 mm (5.2213 to 5.2394 in)
    1.3 engines .... 131.17 to 131.63 mm (5.1642 to 5.1823 in)
    1.6 engines .... 131.57 to 132.03 mm (5.1800 to 5.1980 in)
Head diameter:
    1.1 engines .... 32.1 to 32.3 mm (1.2638 to 1.2717 in)
    1.3 engines .... 33.9 to 34.1 mm (1.3346 to 1.3425 in)
    1.6 engines .... 36.9 to 37.1 mm (1.4528 to 1.4606 in)
Valve stem diameter:
    Standard .... 7.999 to 8.017 mm (0.3149 to 0.3156 in)
    Oversize 0.2 mm .... 8.199 to 8.217 mm (0.3228 to 0.3235 in)
    Oversize 0.4 mm .... 8.399 to 8.417 mm (0.3307 to 0.3314 in)
Valve stem-to-guide clearance .... 0.046 to 0.089 mm (0.0018 to 0.0035 in)

Lubrication

Oil pump type .... Gear, driven by crankshaft
Minimum oil pressure at 80°C (176°F):
    At 750 rpm .... 1.0 Kgf/cm^2 (14 lbf/in^2)
    At 2000 rpm .... 2.8 Kgf/cm^2 (41 lbf/in^2)
Engine oil capacity:
    Without filter change .... 3.50 l (6.2 Imp pints)
    With filter change .... 3.75 l (6.6 Imp pints)

Torque wrench settings

	Nm	lbf ft
Main bearing cap bolts	95	70
Big-end bearing cap bolts	30	22
Oil pump mounting bolts	10	7
Oil pump pick-up tube bolt-to-block	20	15
Oil pump pick-up-to-pump	12	9
Rear oil seal carrier bolts	10	7
Sump bolts	10	7
Flywheel	85	63
Crankshaft pulley bolt	110	81
Cylinder head bolts:		
Stage 1	25	18
Stage 2	55	40
Stage 3	$\frac{1}{4}$ turn from stage 2	
Stage 4	$\frac{1}{4}$ turn from stage 3	
Camshaft thrust plate bolts	12	9
Camshaft sprocket bolt	55	40
Belt tensioner bolts	18	13
Coolant pump bolts	8	6
Rocker arm studs in head	12	9
Rocker arm nuts	24	18
Rocker cover screws	8	6
Timing cover screws	8	6
Exhaust manifold bolts	16	12
Intake manifold bolts	18	13
Carburettor mounting bolts	20	15
Thermostat housing bolts	8	6
Clutch pressure plate bolts	10	7
Engine-to-transmission bolts	41	30
Transmission oil filler plug	25	18
Fuel pump nuts	14 to 18	10 to 13
Oil pressure switch	15	11

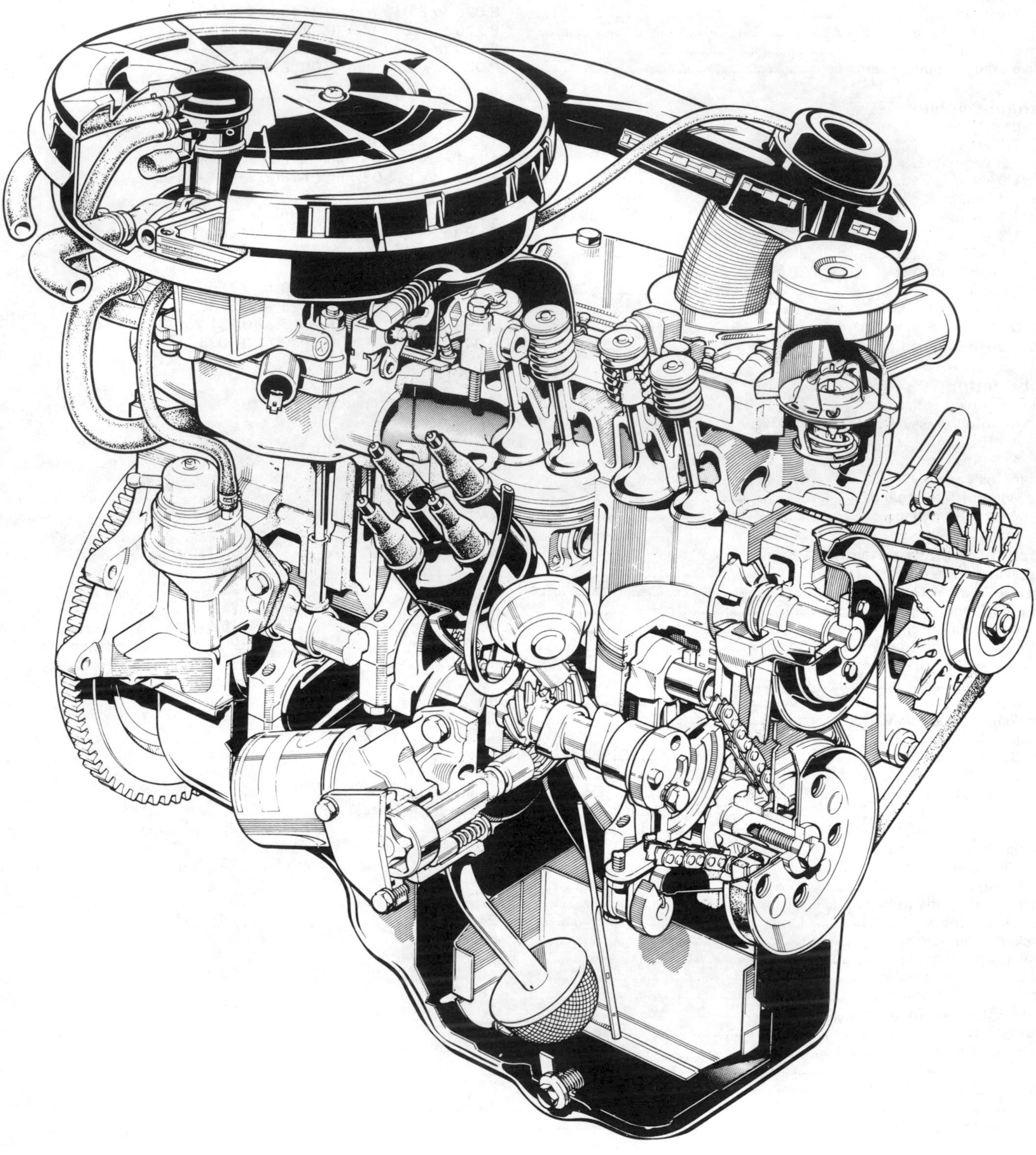

Fig. 1.1 Cutaway view of ohv engine (Sec 1)

PART A: OHV ENGINE

1 Description

The engine is of overhead valve type, based upon the 'Kent' design used in many earlier Ford models including the Fiesta.

The engine is mounted transversely at the front of the vehicle together with the transmission to form a combined power train.

The engine is of water-cooled, four-cylinder in-line type, having overhead valves operated by tappets, pushrods and rocker arms.

The camshaft is located within the cylinder block and chain-driven from the crankshaft. A gear on the camshaft drives the oil pump and the distributor, while an eccentric operates the fuel pump lever.

The cylinder head is of crossflow type, having the exhaust manifold mounted on the side opposite to the intake manifold.

The crankshaft runs in three main bearings, with endfloat controlled by semi-circular thrust washers located on either side of the centre main bearing.

The oil pump is mounted externally on the cylinder block just below the distributor, and the full-flow type oil filter is screwed directly into the oil pump.

2 Operations possible without removing engine from vehicle

The following work can be carried out without having to remove the engine:

(a) Cylinder head – removal and refitting
(b) Valve clearances – adjustment
(c) Sump – removal and refitting
(d) Rocker gear – overhaul
(e) Crankshaft front oil seal – renewal
(f) Pistons/connecting rods – removal and refitting
(g) Engine mountings – renewal
(h) Oil filter – removal and refitting
(i) Oil pump – removal and refitting

3 Operations only possible with engine removed from vehicle

1 The following work should be carried out only after the engine has been removed from the vehicle.

(a) *Crankshaft main bearings – renewal
(b) Crankshaft – removal and refitting
(c) **Flywheel – removal and refitting
(d) **Crankshaft rear oil seal – renewal
(e) Camshaft – removal and refitting
(f) Timing gears and chain – removal and refitting

2 Although it is possible to undertake the job marked * without removing the engine, and those marked ** by removing the transmission (see Chapter 6), such work is not recommended and is unlikely to save much time over that required to withdraw the complete engine/transmission.

4 Cylinder head – removal and refitting

1 If the engine is in the vehicle, carry out the preliminary operations described in paragraphs 2 to 15.
2 Open the bonnet and fit protective covers to the front wing upper surfaces.
3 Disconnect the battery earth strap. It is as well to remove the battery, so that no metal objects are placed across its terminals.
4 Remove the air cleaner. To do this, unscrew the two larger cover screws, disconnect the breather hose from the engine oil filler cap, and disconnect the vacuum pipe from the intake manifold.
5 Drain the cooling system by releasing the pressure cap on the thermostat housing and disconnecting the radiator bottom hose. Drain the coolant into a clean container if it is to be used again. Take care

against scalding if the engine is hot.
6 Disconnect the hoses from the thermostat housing.
7 Disconnect the heater hose from the upper connection on the automatic choke housing.
8 Release the throttle cable from the carburettor operating lever by moving the spring clip and removing tthe bracket fixing bolt.
9 Disconnect the fuel and vacuum pipes from the carburettor.
10 Disconnect the breather hose from the intake manifold.
11 On vehicles with servo-assisted brakes, disconnect the vacuum hose from the intake manifold.
12 Disconnect the HT leads from the spark plugs.
13 Disconnect the electrical leads from the temperature sender unit, the anti-run-on solenoid valve at the carburettor, and the radiator fan thermal switch.
14 Unbolt and remove the heated air box from the exhaust manifold.
15 Disconnect the exhaust downpipe from the manifold by unbolting the connecting flanges. Support the exhaust system at the front end.
16 Unscrew and remove the oil filler cap with breather hose.
17 Extract the four screws and remove the rocker cover.
18 Unscrew and remove the four fixing bolts and lift away the rocker shaft assembly from the cylinder head.
19 Withdraw the pushrods, keeping them in their originally fitted sequence. A simple way to do this is to punch holes in a piece of card and number them 1 to 8 from the thermostat housing end of the cylinder head.
20 Remove the spark plugs.
21 Unscrew the cylinder head bolts progressivly in the reverse order to that given for tightening (see Fig. 1.9). Remove the cylinder head.
22 To dismantle the cylinder head, refer to Section 17.
23 Before refitting the cylinder head, remove every particle of carbon, old gasket and dirt from the mating surfaces of the cylinder head and block. Do not let the removed material drop into the cylinder bores or waterways, if it does, remove it. Normally, when a cylinder head is removed, the head is decarbonised and the valves ground in as described in Section 18 to remove all trace of carbon. Clean the threads of the cylinder head bolts and mop out oil from the bolt holes in the cylinder block. In extreme cases, screwing a bolt into an oil-filled hole can cause the block to fracture due to hydraulic pressure.
24 If there is any doubt about the condition of the intake or exhaust gaskets, unbolt the manifolds and fit new ones to perfectly clean mating surfaces.
25 Locate a new cylinder head gasket on the cylinder block, making quite sure that the bolt holes, coolant passages and lubrication holes are correctly aligned.
26 Lower the cylinder head carefully into position on the block.
27 Screw in all the bolts finger tight and then tighten them in four stages and in the sequence shown in Fig. 1.9 to the specified torque.
28 Refit the pushrods in their original order.
29 Lower the rocker shaft assembly into position, making sure that the rocker adjusting screws engage in the sockets at the ends of the pushrods.
30 Screw in the rocker pedestal bolts finger tight. At this stage, some of the rocker arms will be applying pressure to the ends of the valve stems and some of the rocker pedestals will not be in contact with the cylinder head. The pedestals will be pulled down however when the bolts are tightened to the specified torque, which should now be done.
31 Adjust the valve clearances as described in the next Section.
32 Refit the rocker cover. If the gasket is in anything but perfect condition, renew it.
33 Fit the oil filler cap and breather hose and the spark plugs. Tighten these to the specified torque. They are of tapered seat type, no sealing washers being used.
34 Connect the exhaust downpipe and fit the heated air box.
35 Reconnect all electrical leads, vacuum and coolant hoses.
36 Reconnect the throttle cable. Refit the battery (if removed) and reconnect the battery terminals.
37 Fit the air cleaner.
38 Refill the cooling system as described in Chapter 2.

5 Valve clearances – adjustment

1 This operation should be carried out with the engine cold and the air cleaner and rocker cover removed.
2 Using a ring spanner or socket on the crankshaft pulley bolt, turn the crankshaft in a clockwise direction until No 1 piston is at tdc on its

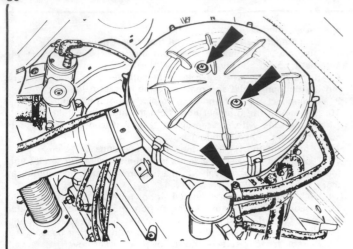

Fig. 1.2 Air cleaner detachment points (arrowed) (Sec 4)

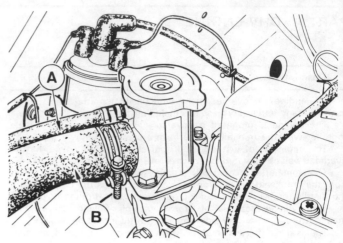

Fig. 1.3 Coolant hoses at thermostat housing (Sec 4)

A   Overflow pipe   B   Radiator top hose

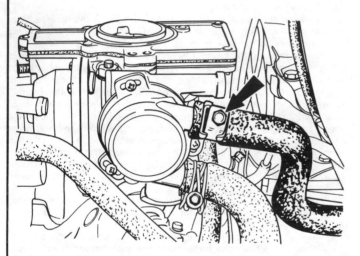

Fig. 1.4 Heater hose (arrowed) at automatic choke (Sec 4)

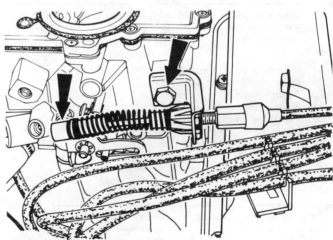

Fig. 1.5 Throttle cable connections (arrowed) at carburettor (Sec 4)

Fig. 1.6 Heated air box on exhaust manifold (Sec 4)

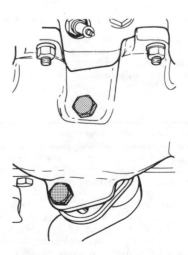

Fig. 1.7 Exhaust downpipe flange bolts (Sec 4)

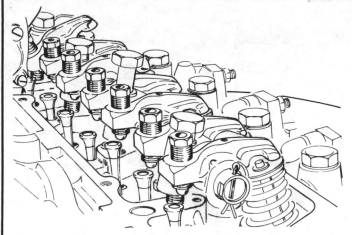

Fig. 1.8 Removing rocker gear bolts (Sec 4)

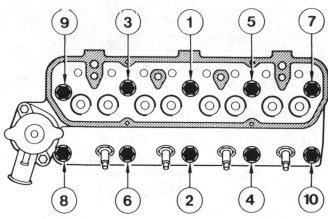

Fig. 1.9 Cylinder head bolt tightening diagram (Sec 4)

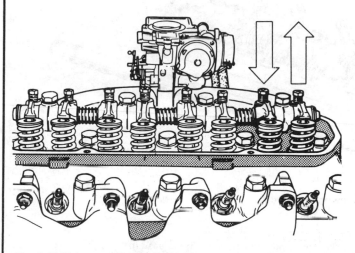

Fig. 1.10 Valves rocking indicated by movement of rocker arms (arrowed) (Sec 5)

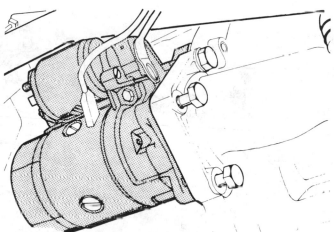

Fig. 1.11 Removing the starter motor (Sec 6)

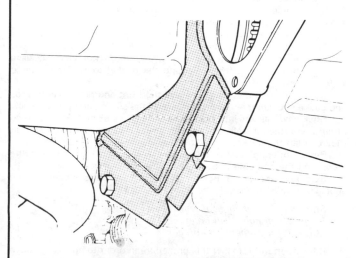

Fig. 1.12 Clutch cover plate (Sec 6)

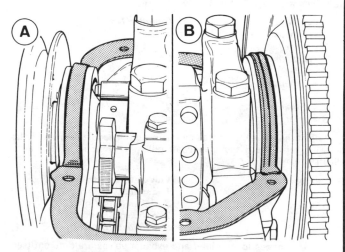

Fig. 1.13 Sump gaskets and sealing strips (Sec 6)

A   Timing cover end   B   Flywheel end

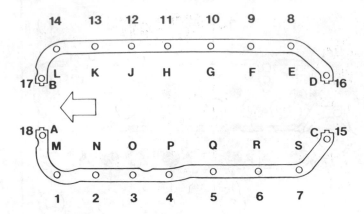

Fig. 1.14 Sump bolt tightening diagram. Arrow shows front of engine (Sec 6)

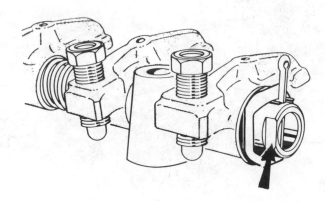

Fig. 1.15 Flat on rocker shaft (arrowed) and retaining pin (Sec 7)

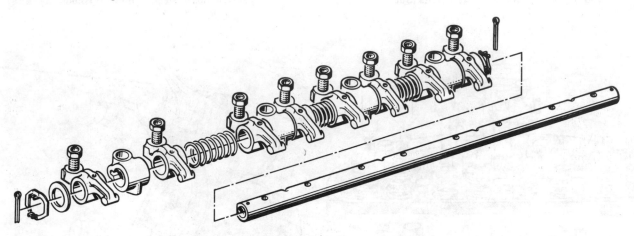

Fig. 1.16 Rocker components (Sec 7)

compression stroke. This can be verified by checking that the pulley and timing cover marks are in alignment and that the valves of No 4 cylinder are rocking. When the valves are rocking, this means that the slightest rotation of the crankshaft pulley in either direction will cause one rocker arm to move up and the other to move down.

3   Numbering from the thermostat housing end of the cylinder head, the valves are identified as follows:

Valve No	Cylinder No
1 – Exhaust	1
2 – Inlet	1
3 – Exhaust	2
4 – Inlet	2
5 – Exhaust	3
6 – Inlet	3
7 – Exhaust	4
8 – Inlet	4

4   Adjust the valve clearances by following the sequence given in the following table. Turn the crankshaft pulley 180° (half a turn) after adjusting each pair:

Valves rocking	Valves to adjust
7 and 8	1 (Exhaust), 2 (Inlet)
5 and 6	3 (Exhaust), 4 (Inlet)
1 and 2	7 (Exhaust), 8 (Inlet)
3 and 4	5 (Exhaust), 6 (Inlet)

5   The clearances for the inlet and exhaust valves are different (see Specifications). Use a feeler gauge of the appropriate thickness to check each clearance between the end of the valve stem and the rocker arm. The gauge should be a stiff sliding fit. If it is not, turn the adjuster bolt with a ring spanner. These bolts are of stiff thread type and require no locking nut. Turn the bolt clockwise to reduce the

clearance and anti-clockwise to increase it.
6   Refit the air cleaner and rocker cover on completion of adjustment.

6   Sump – removal and refitting

1   Disconnect the battery earth lead and drain the engine oil.
2   Unbolt and withdraw the starter motor. Support the motor to avoid straining the electrical wiring.
3   Unbolt and remove the clutch cover plate.
4   Extract the sump securing bolts and remove the sump. If it is stuck, prise it gently with a screwdriver but do not use excessive leverage. If it is very tight, cut round the gasket joint using a sharp knife.
5   Before refitting the sump, remove the front and rear sealing strips and gaskets. Clean the mating surfaces of the sump and cylinder block.
6   Stick new gaskets into position on the block using thick grease to retain them, then install new sealing strips into their grooves so that they overlap the gaskets.
7   Before offering up the sump, check that the gap between the sump and the oil baffle is between 2.0 and 3.8 mm.
8   Screw in the sump bolts and tighten in three stages to the specified torque in accordance with Fig. 1.14:

   Stage 1 – in alphabetical order
   Stage 2 – in numerical order
   Stage 3 – in alphabetical order

9   It is important to follow this procedure in order to provide positive sealing against oil leakage.
10   Refit the clutch cover plate and the starter motor and reconnect the battery.
11   Refill the engine with the correct grade and quantity of oil.

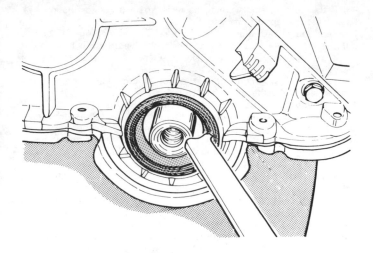

Fig. 1.17 Prising out the crankshaft front oil seal (Sec 8)

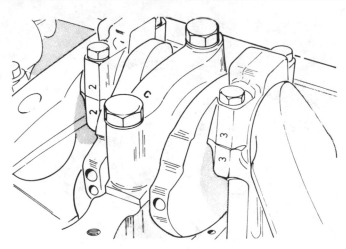

Fig. 1.18 Connecting rod big-end numbers (Sec 9)

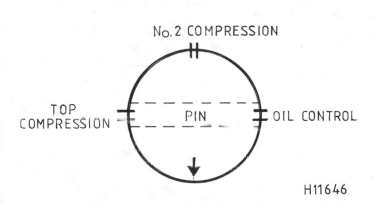

Fig. 1.19 Piston ring end gap positioning diagram (Sec 9)

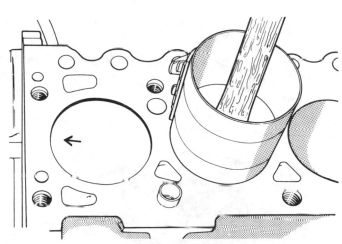

Fig. 1.20 Installing a piston/connecting rod (Sec 9)

7 Rocker gear – dismantling and reassembly

1   With the rocker assembly removed as described in Section 4, extract the split pin from one end of the rocker shaft.
2   Take off the spring and plain washers from the end of the shaft.
3   Slide off the rocker arms, support pedestals and coil springs, keeping them in their originally fitted order. Clean out the oil holes in the shaft.
4   Apply engine oil to the rocker shaft before reassembling and make sure that the flat on the end of the shaft is to the same side as the rocker arm adjuster screws. This is essential for proper lubrication of the components.

8 Crankshaft front oil seal – renewal

1   Disconnect the battery earth cable.
2   Slacken the alternator mounting and adjuster bolts and after pushing the alternator in towards the engine, slip off the drivebelt.
3   Unscrew and remove the crankshaft pulley bolt. To prevent the crankshaft turning while the bolt is being released, jam the teeth of the starter ring gear on the flywheel after removing the clutch cover plate or starter motor for access.
4   Remove the crankshaft pulley. This should come out using the hands but if it is tight, prise it carefully with two levers placed at

opposite sides under the pulley flange.
5   Using a suitable claw tool, prise out the defective seal and wipe out the seat.
6   Install the new seal using a suitable distance piece, the pulley and its bolt to draw it into position. If it is tapped into position, the seal may be distorted or the timing cover fractured.
7   When the seal is fully seated, remove the pulley and bolt, apply grease to the seal rubbing surface of the pulley, install it and tighten the securing bolt to the specified torque.
8   Refit the clutch cover or starter motor.
9   Fit and tension the drivebelt and reconnect the battery.

9 Piston/connecting rod – removal and refitting

1   Remove the cylinder head and the sump as described in Sections 4 and 6 respectively. Do not remove the oil pick-up filter or pipe, which is an interference fit.
2   Note the location numbers stamped on the connecting rod big-ends and caps, and to which side they face. No 1 assembly is nearest the timing cover and the assembly numbers are towards the camshaft side of the engine.
3   Turn the crankshaft by means of the pulley bolt until the big-end cap bolts for No 1 connecting rod are in their most accessible position. Unscrew and remove the bolts and the big-end cap complete with bearing shell. If the cap is difficult to remove, tap it off with a plastic-faced hammer.

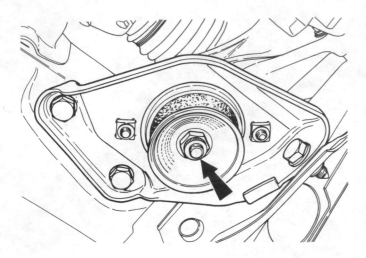

Fig. 1.21 Gearbox mounting centre bolt (arrowed) (Sec 10)

4   If the bearing shells are to be used again (refer to Section 17), keep the shell taped to its cap.

5   Feel the top of the cylinder bore for a wear ridge. If one is detected, it should be scraped off before the piston/rod is pushed out of the top of the cylinder block. Take care when doing this not to score the cylinder bore surfaces.

6   Push the piston/connecting rod out of the block, retaining the bearing shell with the rod if it is to be used again.

7   Dismantling the piston/rod is covered in Section 17.

8   Repeat the operations on the remaining piston/rod assemblies.

9   To install a piston/rod assembly, have the piston ring gaps staggered as shown in the diagram (Fig. 1.19), oil the rings and apply a piston ring compressor. Compress the piston rings.

10 Oil the cylinder bores.

11 Wipe out the bearing shell seat in the connecting rod and insert the shell.

12 Lower the piston/rod assembly into the cylinder bore until the base of the piston ring compressor stands squarely on the top of the block.

13 Check that the directional arrow on the piston crown faces towards the timing cover end of the engine and then apply the wooden handle of a hammer to the piston crown. Strike the head of the hammer sharply to drive the piston into the cylinder bore.

14 Oil the crankpin and draw the connecting rod down to engage

Fig. 1.22 Gearbox mounting insulator bolts (arrowed) (Sec 10)

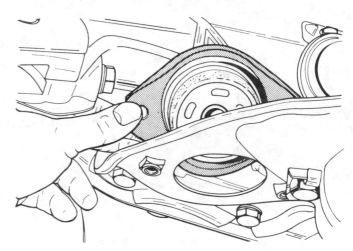

Fig. 1.23 Removing the gearbox mounting (Sec 10)

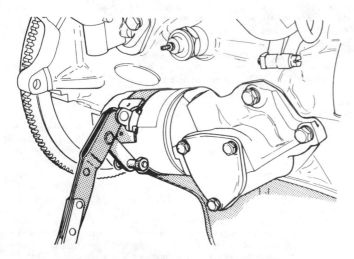

Fig. 1.24 Unscrewing the oil filter (Sec 11)

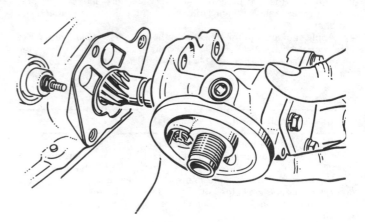

Fig. 1.25 Removing the oil pump (Sec 11)

with the crankshaft. Check that the bearing shell is still in position in the connecting rod.
15 Wipe the bearing shell seat in the big-end cap clean and insert the bearing shell.
16 Fit the cap, screw in the bolts and tighten to the specified torque.
17 Repeat the operations on the remaining pistons/connecting rods.
18 Refit the sump (Section 6) and the cylinder head (Section 4). Refill with oil and coolant.

10 Engine mountings – removal and refitting

The operations are as described in Section 32 of this Chapter.

11 Oil filter and pump – removal and refitting

1 The oil pump is externally mounted on the forward-facing side of the crankcase.
2 Using a suitable removal tool (strap wrench or similar), unscrew and remove the oil filter cartridge and discard it.
3 Unscrew the three mounting bolts and withdraw the oil pump from the engine.

4 Clean away the old gasket.
5 If a new pump is being fitted, it should be primed with engine oil before installation. Do this by turning its shaft while filling it with clean engine oil.
6 Locate a new gasket on the pump mounting flange, insert the pump shaft and bolt the pump into position.
7 Grease the rubber sealing ring of a new filter and screw it into position on the pump, using hand pressure only, not the removal tool.
8 Top up the engine oil to replenish any lost during the operations.

12 Lubrication system – description

1 Engine oil contained in the sump is drawn through a strainer and pick-up tube by an externally mounted oil pump of twin rotor design.
2 The oil is then forced through a full-flow, throw-away type oil filter which is screwed onto the oil pump.
3 Oil pressure is regulated by a relief valve integral in the oil pump.
4 The pressurised oil is directed through the various galleries and passages to all bearing surfaces. A drilling in the big-end provides lubrication for the gudgeon pins and cylinder bores. The timing chain and sprockets are lubricated by an oil ejection nozzle.

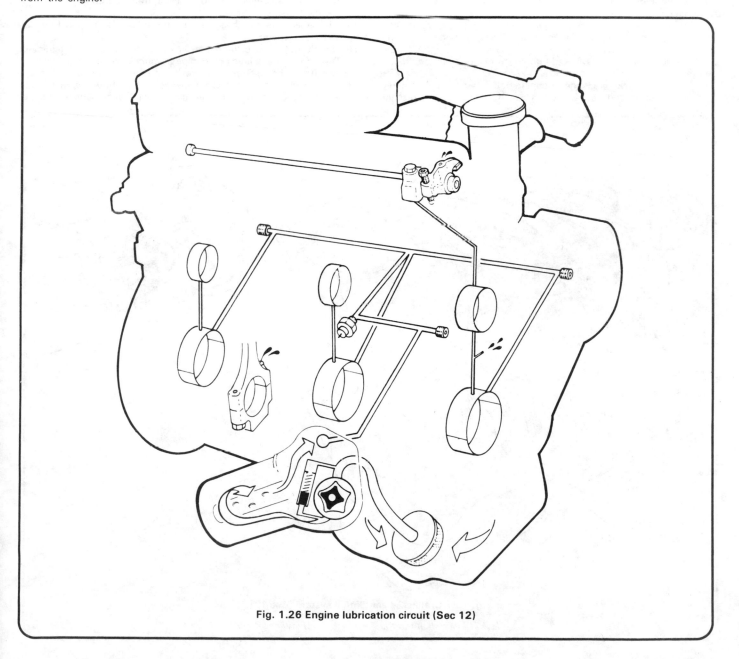

Fig. 1.26 Engine lubrication circuit (Sec 12)

13 Crankcase ventilation system – description

The system is of closed type, ensuring that blow-by gases which pass the piston rings and collect in the crankcase, also oil vapour, are drawn into the combustion chambers to be burnt.

The system consists of a vented engine oil filler cap connected by one hose to the intake manifold and by another to the air cleaner.

The gas flow is controlled by a calibrated port in the oil filler cap and by the manifold vacuum according to throttle setting.

14 Engine – method of removal

The engine should be removed from the vehicle complete with transmission (gearbox and final drive) in a downward direction.

15 Engine/transmission – removal and separation

Removal

1   Open the bonnet and remove the battery, or at least disconnect the battery earth lead. Select 4th gear to make gearchange rod reconnection easier.

2   Disconnect the windscreen washer tubing from the bonnet and then mark the position of the hinges in relation to the underside of the bonnet.

3   With the help of an assistant, unbolt the hinges from the bonnet and lift the bonnet from the vehicle.

4   Unscrew the two air cleaner retaining bolts, then lift the assembly until the breather and vacuum hoses can be identified and disconnected. Remove the air cleaner from the engine.

5   Drain the cooling system (Chapter 2), retaining the coolant if it is to be used again.

6   Disconnect the radiator top hose and the overflow tank pipe from the thermostat housing.

7   Disconnect the heater hoses from the stub on the lateral coolant pipe and from the automatic choke housing.

8   Slide the clip back and disconnect the end of the throttle cable from the carburettor throttle lever. Unbolt the cable support bracket and tie the cable assembly to one side of the engine compartment.

9   Disconnect the fuel pipe from the fuel pump and plug the pipe.

10 On vehicles equipped with power-assisted brakes, disconnect the vacuum pipe from the intake manifold.

11 Disconnect the leads from the following electrical components:

    (a) Alternator and electric fan
    (b) Oil pressure sender
    (c) Coolant temperature sender
    (d) Reversing lamp switch
    (e) Anti-run-on solenoid valve

12 Disconnect the HT and LT (distributor) wires from the coil terminals.

13 Unscrew the speedometer drive cable from the transmission and release the breather hose.

14 Disconnect the clutch cable from the release lever and from its transmission support.

15 Unbolt and remove the heater box from the exhaust manifold.

16 Disconnect the exhaust downpipe from the manifold by extracting the two flange bolts. Support the exhaust pipe to avoid straining it.

17 If the vehicle is not over an inspection pit, it should be jacked up and safety stands fitted to provide sufficient clearance beneath it to be

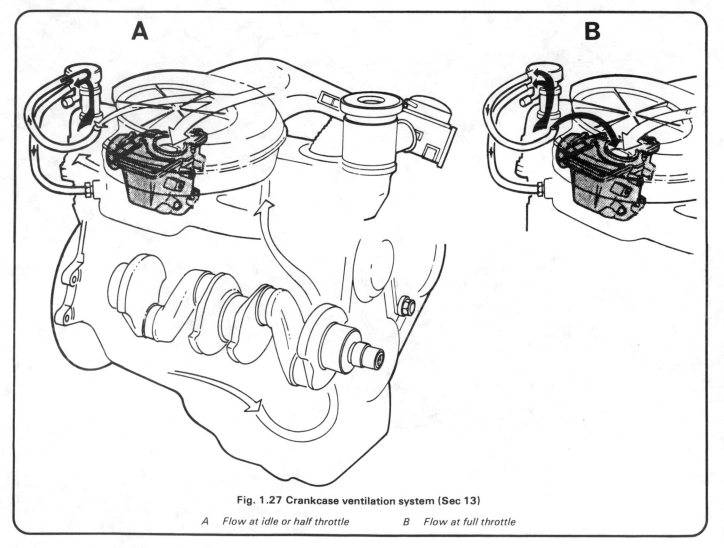

Fig. 1.27 Crankcase ventilation system (Sec 13)

A   Flow at idle or half throttle   *B   Flow at full throttle*

Fig. 1.28 Heater hose connection (arrowed) at lateral coolant pipe (Sec 15)

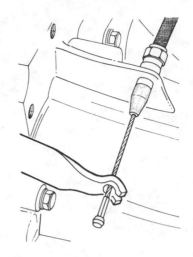

Fig. 1.29 Clutch cable connection (Sec 15)

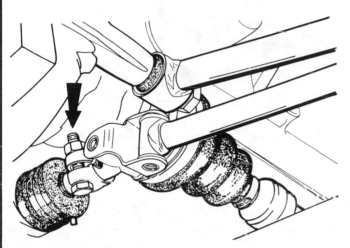

Fig. 1.30 Gearchange rod clamp bolt (arrowed) (Sec 15)

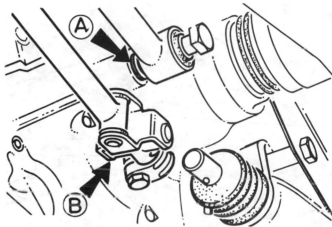

Fig. 1.31 Gearchange rod (B) and stabiliser rod (A) (Sec 15)

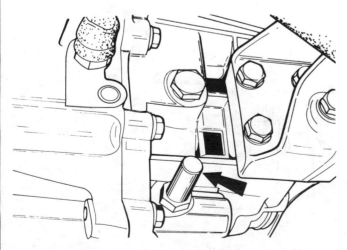

Fig. 1.32 Gearbox selector shaft cap nut (arrowed) (Sec 15)

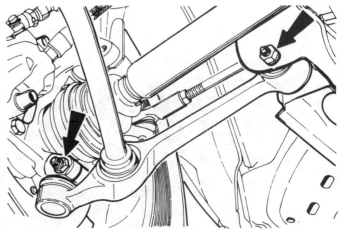

Fig. 1.33 Front suspension lower arm balljoint connection (arrowed) (Sec 15)

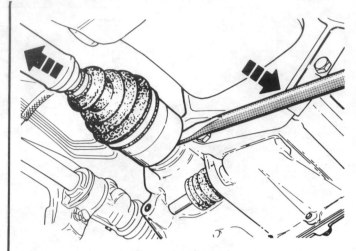

Fig. 1.34 Releasing a driveshaft (Sec 15)

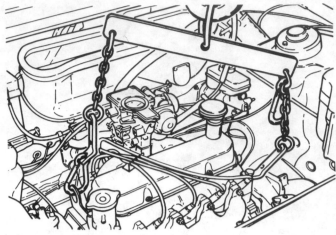

Fig. 1.35 Engine lifting points (Sec 15)

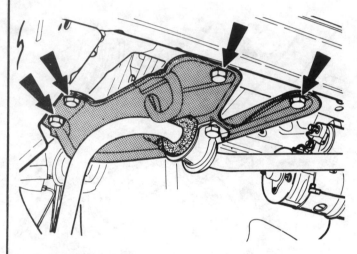

Fig. 1.36 Anti-roll bar mounting bolts (arrowed) (Sec 15)

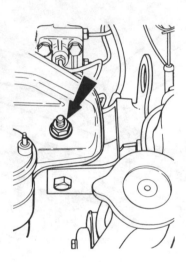

Fig. 1.37 Engine mounting to side panel (arrowed) (Sec 15)

Fig. 1.38 Engine mounting to wing apron (arrowed) (Sec 15)

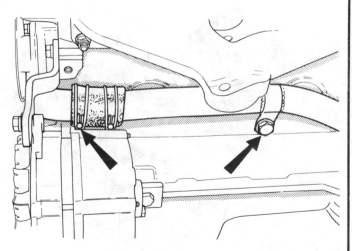

Fig. 1.39 Engine lateral coolant pipe. Hose and bracket arrowed (Sec 16)

able to remove the engine/transmission from below. A distance of 686 mm (27.0 in) is recommended between the floor and the bottom edge of the front panel.

18 Disconnect the exhaust system from its flexible mountings and remove the system complete.

19 Disconnect the starter motor leads and the engine earth strap.

20 Disconnect the gearchange rod from the gearbox selector shaft. Do this by releasing the clamp bolt and withdrawing the rod. Tie the rod to the stabiliser and then unhook the tension spring.

21 Unscrew the single bolt and disconnect the stabiliser from the gearbox. Note the washer which is located between the stabiliser trunnion and the gearbox casing.

22 Drain the gearbox. As no drain plug is fitted, this is carried out by unscrewing the cap nut on the selector shaft locking assembly. Take care not to lose the locking pin and spring.

23 Unscrew and remove the pivot bolt and nut from the inboard end of the front suspension lower arm, then remove the bolt which secures the balljoint at the outboard end of the lower arm to the stub axle carrier. An Allen key can be used to prevent the bolt turning while the nut is unscrewed.

24 The right-hand driveshaft must now be released from the transmission. Do this by inserting a lever between the inboard constant velocity (CV) joint and the transmission. With an assistant pulling the roadwheel outwards, strike the lever hard with the hand.

25 Tie the driveshaft up to the steering rack housing to prevent strain to the CV joints.

26 Restrain the differential pinion cage to prevent the cage from turning, using a plastic plug or similar. Failure to do this may make reconnection of the driveshafts difficult.

27 Release the inboard and outboard ends of the front suspension lower arm on the left-hand side of the vehicle as described for the right-hand side.

28 Disconnect the left-hand driveshaft as previously described for the right-hand one.

29 Connect a suitable hoist to the engine, preferably using a spreader bar and connecting lifting hooks at the points indicated in Fig. 1.35. Engine lifting lugs are provided.

30 Just take the weight of the engine and then remove the engine mounting through bolts.

31 Release the anti-roll (stabiliser) bar at each side of the front suspension (four bolts) and lower the bar together with the suspension lower arms.

32 Unbolt the engine mounting (complete with coolant hose support bracket) from the side member and from the wing apron panel. Place a protective board over the rear face of the radiator.

33 Carefully lower the engine/transmission and withdraw it from under the car. To ease the withdrawal operation, lower the engine/transmission onto a crawler board or a sheet of substantial chipboard placed on rollers or lengths of pipe.

Separation

34 Unscrew and remove the starter motor bolts and remove the starter.

35 Unbolt and remove the clutch cover plate from the lower part of the clutch bellhousing.

36 Unscrew and remove the bolts from the clutch bellhousing-to-engine mating flange.

37 Withdraw the transmission from the engine. Support its weight so that the clutch assembly is not distorted while the input shaft is still in engagement with the splined hub of the clutch driven plate.

16 Engine – complete dismantling

1 The need for dismantling will have been dictated by wear or noise in most cases. Although there is no reason why only partial dismantling cannot be carried out to renew such items as the timing chain or crankshaft rear oil seal, when the main bearings or big-end bearings have been knocking and especially if the vehicle has covered a high mileage, then it is recommended that a complete strip down is carried out and every engine component examined as described in Section 17.

2 Position the engine so that it is upright on a bench or other convenient working surface. If the exterior is very dirty it should be cleaned before dismantling using paraffin and a stiff brush or a water-soluble solvent.

3 Remove the coolant pipe from the side of the engine by discon-

Fig. 1.40 Alternator mounting bracket (Sec 16)

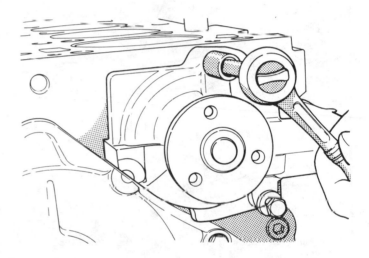

Fig. 1.41 Removing the coolant pump bolts (Sec 16)

Fig. 1.42 Removing crankshaft oil slinger (Sec 16)

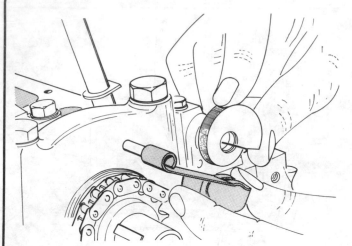

Fig. 1.43 Sliding off the chain tensioner arm (Sec 16)

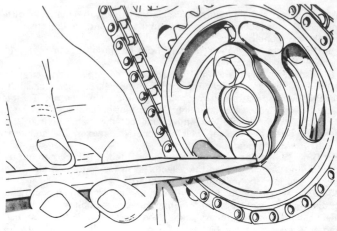

Fig. 1.44 Bending back the camshaft sprocket locktab (Sec 16)

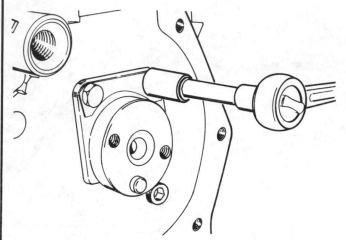

Fig. 1.45 Unbolting the camshaft thrust plate (Sec 16)

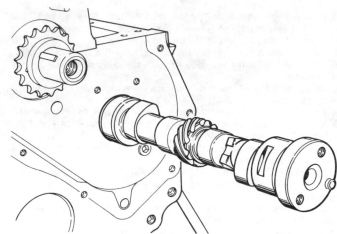

Fig. 1.46 Withdrawing the camshaft (Sec 16)

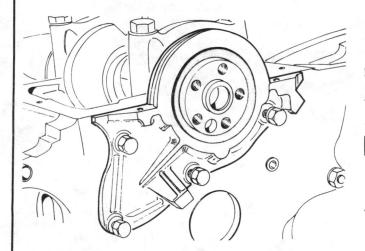

Fig. 1.47 Crankshaft rear oil seal retainer (Sec 16)

Fig. 1.48 Checking a piston ring end gap (Sec 17)

necting the hose clips and the securing bolt.

4   If not already done, drain the engine oil.

5   Remove the dipstick and unscrew and discard the oil filter.

6   Disconnect the HT leads from the spark plugs, release the distributor cap and lift it away complete with leads.

7   Unscrew and remove the spark plugs.

8   Disconnect the breather hose from the intake manifold and remove it complete with the oil filler cap.

9   Disconnect the fuel and vacuum pipes from the carburettor and unbolt and remove the carburettor.

10 Unbolt the thermostat housing cover and remove it together with the thermostat (refer to Chapter 2).

11 Remove the rocker cover.

12 Remove the rocker shaft assembly (four bolts).

13 Withdraw the pushrods, keeping them in their originally fitted order.

14 Remove the cylinder head complete with manifolds as described in Section 4.

15 Remove the bolt that holds the distributor clamp plate to the cylinder block and withdraw the distributor.

16 Unbolt and remove the fuel pump.

17 Remove the oil pump (Section 11).

18 Pinch the two runs of the coolant pump drivebelt together at the pump pulley to prevent the pulley rotating and release the pulley bolts.

19 Release the alternator mounting and adjuster link bolts, push the alternator in towards the engine and remove the drivebelt.

20 Unbolt the alternator bracket and remove the alternator.

21 Unbolt and remove the coolant pump.

22 Unscrew the crankshaft pulley bolt. To do this, the flywheel starter ring gear will have to be jammed to prevent the crankshaft from turning.

23 Remove the crankshaft pulley. If this does not pull off by hand, carefully use two levers behind it placed at opposite points.

24 Place the engine on its side and remove the sump. Do not invert the engine at this stage, or sludge and swarf may enter the oilways.

25 Unbolt and remove the timing chain cover.

26 Take off the oil slinger from the front face of the crankshaft sprocket.

27 Slide the chain tensioner arm from its pivot pin on the front main bearing cap.

28 Unbolt and remove the chain tensioner.

29 Bend back the lockplate tabs from the camshaft sprocket bolts and unscrew and remove the bolts.

30 Withdraw the sprocket complete with timing chain.

31 Unbolt and remove the camshaft thrust plate.

32 Rotate the camshaft until each cam follower (tappet) has been pushed fully into its hole by its cam lobe.

33 Withdraw the camshaft, taking care not to damage the camshaft bearings.

34 Withdraw each of the cam followers, keeping them in their originally fitted sequence by marking them with a piece of numbered tape or using a box with divisions.

35 From the front end of the crankshaft, draw off the sprocket using a two-legged extractor.

36 Check that the main bearing caps are marked F (Front), C (Centre) and R (Rear). The caps are also marked with an arrow which indicates the timing cover end of the engine, a point to remember when refitting the caps.

37 Check that the big-end caps and connecting rods have adjacent matching numbers facing towards the camshaft side of the engine. Number 1 assembly is nearest the timing chain end of the engine. If any markings are missing or indistinct, make some of your own with quick-drying paint.

38 Unbolt and remove the big-end bearing caps. If the bearing shell is to be used again, tape the shell to the cap.

39 Now check the top of the cylinder bore for a wear ring. If one can be felt, it should be removed with a scraper before the piston/rod is pushed out of the cylinder.

40 Remove the piston/rod by pushing it out of the top of the block. Tape the bearing shell to the connecting rod.

41 Remove the remaining three piston/rod assemblies in a similar way.

42 Unbolt the clutch pressure plate cover from the flywheel. Unscrew the bolts evenly and progressively until spring pressure is relieved, before removing the bolts. Be prepared to catch the clutch driven plate as the cover is withdrawn.

43 Unbolt and remove the flywheel. It is heavy, do not drop it. If necessary, the starter ring gear can be jammed to prevent the flywheel rotating. There is no need to mark the fitted position of the flywheel to its mounting flange as it can only be fitted one way. Take off the adaptor plate (engine backplate).

44 Unbolt and remove the crankshaft rear oil seal retainer.

45 Unbolt the main bearing caps. Remove the caps, tapping them off if necessary with a plastic-faced hammer. Retain the bearing shells with their respective caps if the shells are to be used again, although unless the engine is of low mileage this is not recommended (see Section 17).

46 Lift the crankshaft from the crankcase and lift out the upper bearing shells, noting the thrust washers either side of the centre bearing. Keep these shells with their respective caps, identifying them for refitting to the crankcase if they are to be used again.

47 With the engine now completely dismantled, each component should be examined as described in the following Section before reassembling.

17 Examination and renovation

1   Clean all components using paraffin and a stiff brush, except the crankshaft, which should be wiped clean and the oil passages cleaned out with a length of wire.

2   Never assume that a component is unworn simply because it looks all right. After all the effort which has gone into dismantling the engine, refitting worn components will make the overhaul a waste of time and money. Depending on the degree of wear, the overhauler's budget and the anticipated life of the vehicle, components which are only slightly worn may be refitted, but if in doubt it is always best to renew.

Crankshaft, main and big-end bearings

3   The need to renew the main bearing shells or to have the crankshaft reground will usually have been determined during the last few miles of operation when perhaps a heavy knocking has developed from within the crankcase or the oil pressure warning lamp has stayed on denoting a low oil pressure probably caused by excessive wear in the bearings.

4   Even without these symptoms, the journals and crankpins on a high mileage engine should be checked for out-of-round (ovality) and taper. For this a micrometer will be needed to check the diameter of the journals and crankpins at several different points around them. A motor factor or engineer can do this for you. If the average of the readings shows that either out-of-round or taper is outside permitted tolerance (see Specifications), then the crankshaft should be reground by your dealer or engine reconditioning company to accept the undersize main and big-end shell bearings which are available. Normally, the company doing the regrinding will supply the necessary undersize shells.

5   If the crankshaft is in good condition, it is wise to renew the bearing shells as it is almost certain that the original ones will have worn. This is often indicated by scoring of the bearing surface or by the top layer of the bearing metal having worn through to expose the metal underneath.

6   Each shell is marked on its back with the part number. Undersize shells will have the undersize stamped additionally on their backs.

7   Standard size crankshafts having main bearing journal diameters at the lower end of the tolerance range are marked with a yellow spot on the front balance weight. You will find that with this type of crankshaft, a standard shell is fitted to the seat in the crankcase but a yellow colour-coded shell to the main bearing cap.

8   If a green spot is seen on the crankshaft then this indicates that 0.25 mm (0.0098 in) undersize big-end bearings are used.

Cylinder bores, pistons, rings and connecting rods

9   Cylinder bore wear will usually have been evident from the smoke emitted from the exhaust during recent operation of the vehicle on the road, coupled with excessive oil consumption and fouling of spark plugs.

10 Engine life can be extended by fitting special oil control rings to the pistons. These are widely advertised and will give many more thousands of useful mileage without the need for a rebore, although this will be inevitable eventually. If this remedy is decided upon,

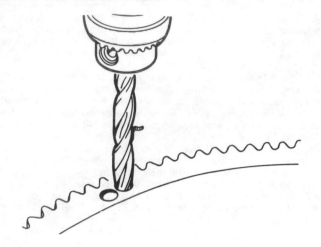

Fig. 1.49 Drilling the flywheel starter ring gear (Sec 17)

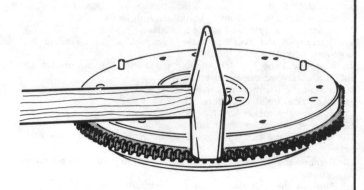

Fig. 1.50 Removing the ring gear from the flywheel (Sec 17)

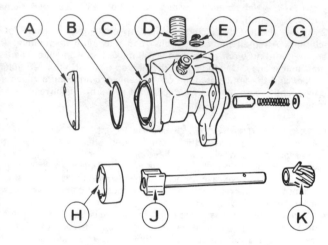

Fig. 1.51 Oil pump components (Sec 17)

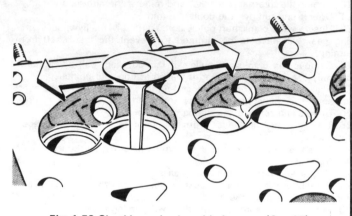

Fig. 1.52 Checking valve in guide for wear (Sec 17)

A	Cover	F	Plug
B	O-ring	G	Relief valve
C	Pump body	H	Outer rotor
D	Threaded insert	J	Inner rotor
E	Filter (relief valve)	K	Drive pinion

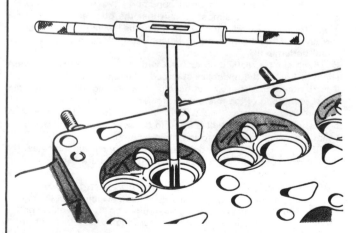

Fig. 1.53 Reaming a valve guide (Sec 17)

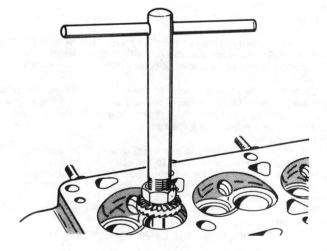

Fig. 1.54 Recutting a valve seat (Sec 17)

remove the piston/connecting rods as described in Section 9 and fit the proprietary rings in accordance with the manufacturer's instructions.

11 Where a more permanent solution is decided upon, the cylinder block can be rebored by your dealer or engineering works, or by one of the mobile workshops which now undertake such work. The cylinder bore will be measured both for out-of-round and for taper to decide how much the bores should be bored out. A set of matching pistons will be supplied in a suitable oversize to suit the new bores.

12 Due to the need for special heating and installing equipment for removal and refitting of the interference type gudgeon pin, the removal and refitting of pistons to the connecting rods is definitely a specialist job, preferably for your Ford dealer.

13 The removal and refitting of piston rings is however well within the scope of the home mechanic. Do this by sliding two or three old feeler blades round behind the top compression ring so that they are at equidistant points. The ring can now be slid up the blades and removed. Repeat the removal operations on the second compression ring and then the oil control ring. This method will not only prevent the rings dropping onto empty grooves as they are withdrawn, but it will also avoid ring breakage.

14 Even when new piston rings have been supplied to match the pistons, always check that they are not tight in their grooves and also check their end gaps by pushing them squarely down their particular cylinder bore and measuring with a feeler blade. Adjustment of the end gap can be made by careful grinding to bring it within the specified tolerance.

15 If new rings are being fitted to an old piston, always remove any carbon from the grooves beforehand. The best tool for this job is the end of a broken piston ring. Take care not to cut your fingers, piston rings are sharp. The cylinder bores should be roughened with fine glass paper to assist the bedding-in of the new rings.

Timing sprockets and chain

16 The teeth on the timing sprockets rarely wear, but check for broken or hooked teeth even so.

17 The timing chain should always be renewed at time of major engine overhaul. A worn chain is evident if when supported horizontally at both ends it takes on a deeply bowed appearance.

18 Finally check the rubber cushion on the tensioner spring leaf. If grooved or chewed up, renew it.

Flywheel

19 Inspect the starter ring gear on the flywheel for wear or broken teeth. If evident, the ring gear should be renewed in the following way. Drill the ring gear with two holes, approximately 7 or 8 mm (0.3 in) diameter and offset as shown (Fig. 1.49). Make sure that you do not drill too deeply or you will damage the flywheel.

20 Tap the ring gear downward off its register and remove it.

21 Place the flywheel in the household refrigerator for about an hour and then heat the new ring gear to between 260 and 280°C (500 and 536°F) in a domestic oven. Do not heat it above 290°C (554°F) or its hardness will be lost.

22 Slip the ring onto the flywheel and gently tap it into position against its register. Allow it to cool without quenching.

23 The clutch friction surface on the flywheel should be checked for grooving or tiny hair cracks, the latter being caused by overheating. If these conditions are evident, it may be possible to surface grind the flywheel provided its balance is not upset. Otherwise, a new flywheel will have to be fitted – consult your dealer about this.

Oil pump

24 The oil pump should be checked for wear by unbolting and removing the cover plate and checking the following tolerances:

    (a) Outer rotor to pump body gap
    (b) Inner rotor to outer rotor gap
    (c) Rotor endfloat (use a feeler blade and straight-edge across pump body)

25 Use feeler blades to check the tolerances and if they are outside the specified values, renew the pump.

Oil seals and gaskets

26 Renew the oil seals on the timing cover and the crankshaft rear retainer as a matter of routine at time of major overhaul. Oil seals are

cheap, oil is not! Use a piece of tubing as a removal and installing tool. Apply some grease to the oil seal lips and check that the small tensioner spring in the oil seal has not been displaced by the vibration caused during fitting of the seal.

27 Renew all the gaskets by purchasing the appropriate 'de-coke', short or full engine set. Oil seals may be included in the gasket sets.

Crankcase

28 Clean out the oilways with a length of wire or by using compressed air. Similarly clean the coolant passages. This is best done by flushing through with a cold water hose. Examine the crankcase and block for stripped threads in bolt holes; if evident, thread inserts can be fitted.

29 Renew any core plugs which appear to be leaking or which are excessively rusty.

30 Cracks in the casting may be rectified by specialist welding, or by one of the cold metal key interlocking processes available.

Camshaft and bearings

31 Examine the camshaft gear and lobes for damage or wear. If evident a new camshaft must be purchased, or one which has been 'built-up' such as are advertised by firms specialising in exchange components.

32 The bearing internal diameters should be checked against the Specifications if a suitable gauge is available; otherwise, check for movement between the camshaft journal and the bearing. Worn bearings should be renewed by your dealer.

33 Check the camshaft endfloat by temporarily refitting the camshaft and the thrust plate. If the endfloat exceeds the specified tolerance, renew the thrust plate.

Cam followers

34 It is seldom that the cam followers wear in their bores, but it is likely that after a high mileage, the cam lobe contact surface will show signs of a depression or grooving.

35 Where this condition is evident, renew the cam followers. Grinding out the wear marks will only reduce the thickness of the hardened metal of the cam follower and accelerate further wear.

Cylinder head and rocker gear

36 The usual reason for dismantling the cylinder head is to de-carbonise and to grind in the valves. Reference should therefore be made to the next Section, in addition to the dismantling operations described here. First remove the manifolds.

37 Using a standard valve spring compressor, compress the spring on No 1 valve (valve nearest the timing cover). Do not overcompress the spring or the valve stem may bend. If it is found that when screwing down the compressor tool, the spring retainer does not release from the collets, remove the compressor and place a piece of tubing on the retainer so that it does not impinge on the collets and strike the end of the tubing a sharp blow with a hammer. Refit the compressor and compress the spring.

38 Extract the split collets and then gently release the compressor and remove it.

39 Remove the valve spring retainer, the spring and the oil seal.

40 Withdraw the valve.

41 Repeat the removal operations on the remaining seven valves. Keep the valves in their originally fitted sequence by placing them in a piece of card which has holes punched in it and numbered 1 to 8 (from the timing cover end).

42 Place each valve in turn in its guide so that approximately one third of its length enters the guide. Rock the valve from side to side. If there is any more than an imperceptible movement, the guides will have to be reamed (working from the valve seat end) and oversize stemmed valves fitted. If you do not have the necessary reamer (tool No 21-242), leave this work to your Ford dealer.

43 Examine the valve seats. Normally, the seats do not deteriorate but the valve heads are more likely to burn away in which case, new valves can be ground in as described in the next Section. If the seats require re-cutting, use a standard cutter available from most accessory or tool stores or consult your motor engineering works.

44 Renewal of any valve seat which is cracked or beyond recutting is definitely a job for your dealer or motor engineering works.

45 If the cylinder head mating surface is suspected of being distorted due to persistent leakage of coolant at the gasket joint, then it can be checked and surface ground by your dealer or motor engineering

works. Distortion is unlikely under normal circumstances with a cast iron head.

46 Check the rocker shaft and rocker arms pads which bear on the valve stem end faces for wear or scoring, also for any broken coil springs. Renew components as necessary after dismantling as described in Section 7. If the valve springs have been in use for 50 000 miles (80 000 km) or more, they should be renewed.

47 Reassemble the cylinder head by fitting new valve stem oil seals. Install No 1 valve (lubricated) into its guide and fit the valve spring with the closer coils to the cylinder head, followed by the spring retainer. Compress the spring and engage the split collets in the cut-out in the valve stem. Hold them in position while the compressor is gently released and removed.

48 Repeat the operations on the remaining valves, making sure that each valve is returned to its original guide or if new valves have been fitted, into the seat into which it was ground.

49 On completion, support the ends of the cylinder head on two wooden blocks and strike the end of each valve stem with a plastic or copper-faced hammer, just a light blow to settle the components.

18 Cylinder head and pistons – decarbonising

1 With the cylinder head removed as described in Section 4, the carbon deposits should be removed from the combustion spaces using a scraper and a wire brush fitted into an electric drill. Take care not to damage the valve heads, otherwise no special precautions need be taken as the cylinder head is of cast iron construction.

2 Where a more thorough job is to be carried out, the cylinder head should be dismantled as described in the preceding Section so that the valves may be ground in and the ports and combustion spaces cleaned, brushed and blown out after the manifolds have been removed.

3 Before grinding in a valve, remove the carbon and deposits completely from its head and stem. With an inlet valve, this is usually quite easy, simply scraping off the soft carbon with a blunt knife and finishing with a wire brush. With an exhaust valve the deposits are very much harder and those on the head may need a rub on coarse emery cloth to remove them. An old woodworking chisel is a useful tool to remove the worst of the head deposits.

4 Make sure that the valve heads are really clean, otherwise the rubber suction cup of the grinding tool will not stick during the grinding-in operations.

5 Before starting to grind in a valve, support the cylinder head so that there is sufficient clearance under for the valve stem to project fully without being obstructed.

6 Take the first valve and apply a little coarse grinding paste to the bevelled edge of the valve head. Insert the valve into its guide and apply the suction grinding tool to its head. Rotate the tool between the palms of the hands in a back-and-forth rotary movement until the gritty action of the grinding-in process disappears. Repeat the oper-

ation with fine paste and then wipe away all traces of grinding paste and examine the seat and bevelled edge of the valve. A matt silver mating band should be observed on both components, without any sign of black spots. If some spots do remain, repeat the grinding-in process until they have disappeared. A drop or two of paraffin applied to the contact surfaces will increase the speed of grinding-in, but do not allow any paste to run down into the valve guide. On completion, wipe away every trace of grinding paste using a paraffin-moistened cloth.

7 Repeat the operations on the remaining valves, taking care not to mix up their originally fitted sequence.

8 The valves are refitted as described in Section 17.

9 An important part of the decarbonising operation is to remove the carbon deposits from the piston crowns. To do this, turn the crankshaft so that two pistons are at the top of their stroke and press some grease between these pistons and the cylinder walls. This will prevent carbon particles falling down into the piston ring grooves. Stuff rags into the other two bores.

10 Cover the oilways and coolant passages with masking tape and then using a blunt scraper remove all the carbon from the piston crowns. Take care not to score the soft alloy of the crown or the surface of the cylinder bore.

11 Rotate the crankshaft to bring the other two pistons to tdc and repeat the operations.

12 Wipe away the circle of grease and carbon from the cylinder bores.

13 Clean the top surface of the cylinder block by careful scraping.

19 Engine – reassembly

1 With everything clean, commence reassembly by oiling the bores for the cam followers and inserting them fully in their original sequence.

2 Lubricate the camshaft bearings and insert the camshaft from the timing cover end of the engine.

3 Fit the thrust plate and tighten the fixing bolts to the specified torque. The endfloat will already have been checked as described in Section 17.

4 Wipe clean the main bearing shell seats in the crankcase and fit the shells. Using a little grease, stick the semi-circular thrust washers on either side of the centre bearing so that the oil grooves are visible when the washers are installed.

5 Check that the Woodruff key is in position on the front end of the crankshaft and tap the crankshaft sprocket into place using a piece of tubing.

6 Oil the bearing shells and lower the crankshaft into the crankcase.

7 Wipe the seats in the main bearing caps and fit the bearing shells into them. Install the caps so that their markings are correctly positioned as explained at dismantling in Section 16.

8 Screw in the cap bolts and tighten evenly to the specified torque.

9 Now check the crankshaft endfloat. Ideally a dial gauge should be

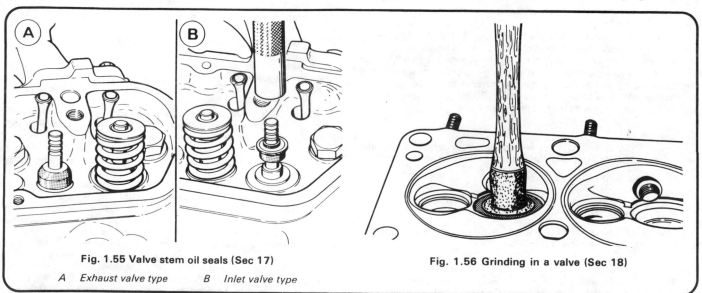

Fig. 1.55 Valve stem oil seals (Sec 17)

   A   Exhaust valve type   *B   Inlet valve type*

Fig. 1.56 Grinding in a valve (Sec 18)

used, but feeler blades are an alternative if inserted between the face of the thrust washer and the machined surface of the crankshaft balance weight after having prised the crankshaft first in one direction and then the other. Provided the thrust washers at the centre bearing have been renewed, the endfloat should be within the specified tolerance. If it is not, oversize thrust washers are available (see Specifications).

10 Rotate the crankshaft so that the timing mark on its sprocket is directly in line with the centre of the crankshaft sprocket mounting flange.

11 Engage the camshaft sprocket within the timing chain and then engage the chain around the teeth of the crankshaft sprocket. Push the camshaft sprocket onto its mounting flange. The camshaft sprocket bolt holes should now be in alignment with the tapped holes in the camshaft flange and both sprocket timing marks in alignment (Fig. 1.60). Turn the camshaft as necessary to achieve this, also withdraw the camshaft sprocket and reposition it within the loop of the chain. This is a 'trial and error' operation which must be continued until exact alignment of bolt holes and timing marks is achieved.

12 Screw in the sprocket bolts to the specified torque and bend up the tabs of a new lockplate.

13 Bolt the timing chain tensioner into position, retract the tensioner cam spring and then slide the tensioner arm onto its pivot pin. Release the cam tensioner so that it bears upon the arm.

14 Fit the oil slinger to the front of the crankshaft sprocket so that its convex side is against the sprocket.

15 Using a new gasket, fit the timing cover which will already have been fitted with a new oil seal (see Section 17). One fixing bolt should be left out at this stage as it also holds the coolant pump. Grease the oil seal lips and fit the crankshaft pulley. Tighten the pulley bolt to the specified torque.

16 Using a new gasket, bolt the crankshaft rear oil seal retainer into position. Tighten the bolts to the specified torque.

17 Locate the engine adaptor (back) plate on its dowels and then fit the flywheel.

18 Screw in and tighten the flywheel bolts to the specified torque. To prevent the flywheel turning, the starter ring gear can be jammed or a piece of wood placed between a crankshaft balance weight and the inside of the crankcase.

19 Install and centralise the clutch as described in Chapter 5.

20 The pistons/connecting rods should now be installed. Although new pistons will have been fitted to the rods by your dealer or supplier (see Section 17), it is worth checking to ensure that with the piston crown arrow pointing to the timing cover end of the engine, the oil hole in the connecting rod is on the left as shown (Fig. 1.62). Oil the cylinder bores.

21 Install the pistons/connecting rods as described in Section 9.

22 Fit the sump as described in Section 6.

23 Fit the oil pressure sender unit, if removed.

24 Turn the crankshaft until No 1 piston is at tdc (crankshaft pulley and timing cover marks aligned) and fit the oil pump complete with new gasket and a new oil filter as described in Section 11.

25 Using a new gasket, fit the fuel pump. If the insulating block became detached from the crankcase during removal, make sure that a new gasket is fitted to each side of the block.

26 Fit the coolant pump using a new gasket.

27 Fit the cylinder head as described in Section 4.

28 Refit the pushrods in their original sequence and the rocker shaft, also as described in Section 4.

29 Adjust the valve clearances (Section 5) and refit the rocker cover using a new gasket.

30 Fit the intake and exhaust manifolds using new gaskets and tightening the nuts and bolts to the specified torque.

31 Refit the carburettor using a new flange gasket and connect the fuel pipe from the pump.

32 Screw in the spark plugs and the coolant temperature switch (if removed).

33 Refit the thermostat and the thermostat housing cover.

34 Fit the pulley to the coolant pump pulley flange.

35 Fit the alternator and the drivebelt and tension the belt as described in Chapter 2.

36 Refit the distributor as described in Chapter 4.

37 Refit the distributor cap and reconnect the spark plug HT leads.

38 Bolt on and connect the coolant pipe to the side of the cylinder block.

39 Fit the breather pipe from the oil filler cap to the intake manifold and fit the cap.

40 Check the sump drain plug for tightness. A new seal should be fitted at regular intervals to prevent leakage. Refit the dipstick.

41 Refilling with oil should be left until the engine is installed in the vehicle.

20 Engine/transmission – reconnection and installation

1 This is a direct reversal of removal and separation from the transmission. Take care not to damage the radiator or front wings during installation.

Reconnection

2 Reconnection of the engine and transmission is a reversal of separation, but if the clutch has been dismantled, check that the driven plate has been centralised as described in Chapter 5.

Installation

3 First check that the engine sump drain plug is tight and that the gearbox cap nut (removed to drain the oil) is refitted together with its locking pin and spring.

4 Manoeuvre the engine/transmission under the vehicle and attach the lifting hoist. Raise the engine carefully until the engine left front mounting bolt can be located. Fit the insulator and cup to the

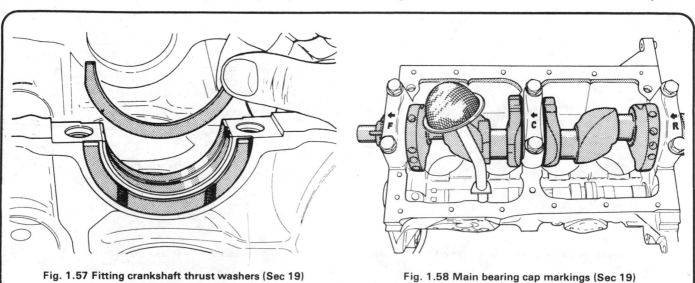

Fig. 1.57 Fitting crankshaft thrust washers (Sec 19)   **Fig. 1.58 Main bearing cap markings (Sec 19)**

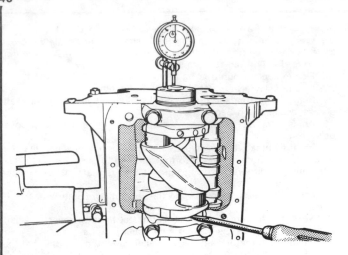

Fig. 1.59 Checking crankshaft endfloat (Sec 19)

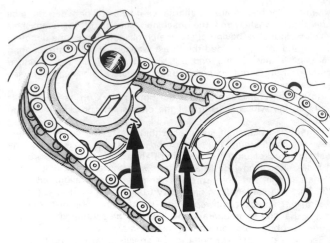

Fig. 1.60 Crankshaft and camshaft sprocket timing marks (arrowed) (Sec 19)

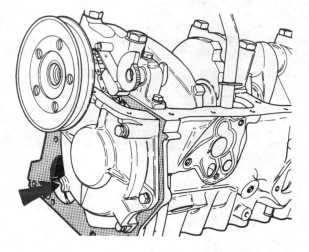

Fig. 1.61 Bolt (arrowed) which secures timing cover and coolant pump (Sec 19)

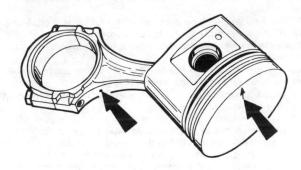

Fig. 1.62 Piston-to-connecting rod relationship. Lubrication hole and piston crown mark (arrowed) must align as shown (Sec 19)

Fig. 1.63 Fitting the fuel pump (Sec 19)

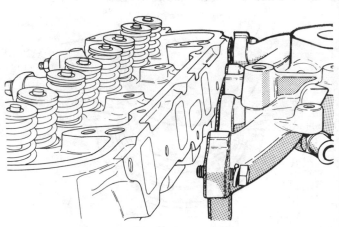

Fig. 1.64 Installing the intake manifold (Sec 19)

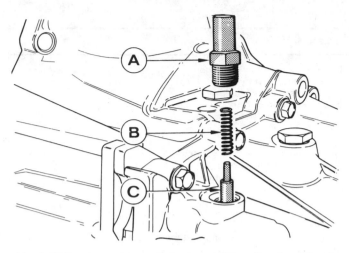

Fig. 1.65 Gearbox selector shaft cap nut (A), coil spring (B) and
locking pin (C) (Sec 20)

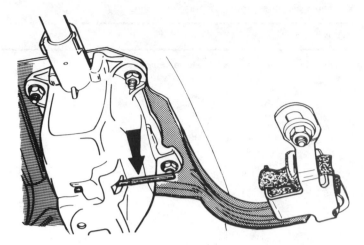

Fig. 1.66 Gearlever locked in selector housing by pin (arrowed)
(Sec 20)

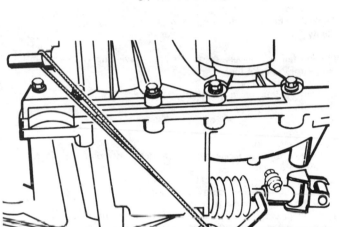

Fig. 1.67 Selector shaft retained while gearchange rod clamp
pinch-bolt is tightened (Sec 20)

underside of the mounting bracket and screw on the nut.

5   Bolt the stabiliser (anti-roll) bar mountings to the body.

6   Fit the transmission front and rear mounting through bolts and
tighten to the specified torque.

7   Release the lifting hoist and remove it.

8   If some sort of plug was used to prevent the differential pinion
cage from turning, remove the plug now. If a plug was not used, insert
a finger in the driveshaft hole and align the cage ready to receive the
driveshaft. If this is not done, the driveshaft cannot engage with the
splined pinion gear. Use a new snap-ring and reconnect the left-hand
driveshaft to the transmission by having an assistant apply pressure on
the roadwheel. Check that the snap-ring has locked in position.

9   Reconnect the left-hand lower arm of the front suspension.
Tighten the bolts to the specified torque.

10 Refit the driveshaft and suspension lower arm to the opposite side
in a similar way to that just described.

11 Reconnect the transmission stabiliser rod, making sure to insert
the washer between the rod and the transmission casing.

12 Check that the gearchange control lever is still in 4th gear position
and hook the gearchange rod tension spring to the longitudinal body
side member.

13 Pull downwards on the gearchange rod and slip it onto the end of
the selector shaft which projects from the transmission. The clamp
should be loose on the gearchange rod.

14 Using a 3.5 mm (0.14 in) diameter pin or rod, insert it as shown
(Fig. 1.66) and pull the gear lever downwards to lock it in the selector
slide. Using a pin or rod inserted into the hole in the end of the
projecting selector shaft, turn the shaft clockwise to its stop and retain
it in this position with a strong rubber band. Now tighten the clamp
pinch-bolt. Remove the temporary locking pin and connect the
gearchange rod return spring. Check the gear selection is satisfactory

15 Fit the starter motor leads to their terminals.

16 Connect the engine earth leads.

17 Refit the exhaust system and bolt the downpipe to the manifold.
Refit the heated air box which connects with the air cleaner.

18 Reconnect the clutch operating cable.

19 Reconnect the electrical leads, the fuel pipe, the brake vacuum
hose and the speedometer cable.

20 Reconnect the throttle cable and the heater hoses.

21 Reconnect the radiator coolant hoses.

22 Fill up with engine oil, transmission oil and coolant, then reconnect
the battery.

23 Refit the bonnet, bolting the hinges to their originally marked
positions. Reconnect the screen washer pipe.

24 Fit the air cleaner and reconnect the hoses and the air cleaner
intake spout.

25 Once the engine is running, check the dwell angle, timing, idle
speed and mixture adjustment (refer to Chapters 3 and 4).

26 If a number of new internal components have been installed, run
the vehicle at restricted speed for the first few hundred miles to allow
time for the new components to bed in. It is also recommended that
with a new or rebuilt engine, the engine oil and filter are changed at
the end of the running-in period.

21 Fault diagnosis (ohv engine)

Symptom	Reason(s)
Engine fails to turn over when starter operated	Discharged or defective battery Dirty or loose battery leads Defective starter solenoid or switch Engine earth strap disconnected Defective starter motor
Engine turns over but will not start	Ignition damp or wet Ignition leads to spark plugs loose Shorted or disconnected low tension leads Dirty, incorrectly set or pitted contact breaker points Faulty condenser Defective ignition switch Ignition LT leads connected wrong way round Faulty coil Contact breaker point spring earthed or broken No petrol in petrol tank Vapour lock in fuel line (in hot conditions or at high altitude) Blocked float chamber needle valve Fuel pump filter blocked Choked or blocked carburettor jets Faulty fuel pump
Engine stalls and will not start	Ignition failure – in severe rain or after traversing water splash No petrol in petrol tank Petrol tank breather choked Sudden obstruction in carburettor Water in fuel system
Engine misfires or idles unevenly	Ignition leads loose Battery leads loose on teminals Battery earth strap loose on body attachment point Engine earth lead loose Low tension lead to terminals on coil loose Low tension lead from distributor loose Dirty, or incorrectly gapped spark plugs Dirty, incorrectly set or pitted contact breaker points Tracking across distributor cap (oily or cracked cap) Ignition too retarded Faulty coil Mixture too weak Sticking engine valve Incorrect valve clearances Air leak in carburettor Air leak at inlet manifold to cylinder head, or inlet manifold to carburettor Weak or broken valve springs Worn valve guides or stems Worn pistons and piston rings
Lack of power and poor compression	Burnt out exhaust valves Sticking or leaking valves Worn valve guides and stems Weak or broken valve springs Blown cylinder head gasket (accompanied by increase in noise) Worn pistons and piston rings Worn or scored cylinder bores Ignition timing wrongly set Contact breaker points incorrectly gapped Incorrect valve clearances Incorrectly set spark plugs Mixture too rich or too weak Dirty contact breaker points Fuel filters blocked causing top end fuel starvation Distributor automatic advance weights or vacuum advance and retard mechanism not functioning correctly Faulty fuel pump giving top end fuel starvation
Excessive oil consumption	Badly worn, perished or missing valve stem oil seals Excessively worn valve stems and valve guides Worn piston rings Worn pistons and cylinder bores

Oil being lost due to leaks

Excessive piston ring gap allowing blow-by
Piston oil return holes choked

Leaking oil filter gasket
Leaking rocker cover gasket
Leaking timing case gasket
Leaking sump gasket
Loose sump plug

Unusual noises from engine

Worn valve gear (noisy tapping from top cover)
Worn big-end bearings (regular heavy knocking)
Worn main bearings (rumbling and vibration)
Worn crankshaft (knocking, rumbling and vibration)

PART B: OHC ENGINE

22 Description

This is a completely new engine, designated CVH (Compound Valve angle, Hemispherical combustion chamber) which can be described in more conventional terms as a four in-line overhead cam (ohc) engine.

The engine is mounted, together with the transmission, transversely at the front of the vehicle and transmits power through open driveshafts to the front roadwheels.

The engine is available in three capacities, 1.1, 1.3 and 1.6 litres.

The crankshaft is supported in five main bearings within a cast iron crankcase.

The cylinder head is of light alloy construction, supporting the overhead camshaft in five bearings. These bearings cannot be renewed and in the event of wear occurring, the complete cylinder head must be changed. The fuel pump is mounted on the side of the cylinder head and is driven by a pushrod from an eccentric cam on the camshaft.

The distributor is driven from the rear (flywheel) end of the camshaft.

The cam followers are of hydraulic type, which eliminates the need for valve clearance adjustment and also ensures that valve timing is always correct which is not the case if a mechanical type arrangement should be out of adjustment.

The cam followers operate in the following way. When the valve is closed, pressurised engine oil passes through a port in the body of the cam followers and four grooves in the plunger and into the cylinder feed chamber. From this chamber, oil flows through a ball type non-return valve into the pressure chamber. The tension of the coil spring causes the plunger to press the rocker arm against the valve and to eliminate any free play.

As the cam lifts the cam follower, the oil pressure in the pressure chamber increases and causes the non-return valve to close the port feed chamber. As oil cannot be compressed, it forms a rigid link between the body of the cam follower, the cylinder and the plunger which then rise as one component to open the valve.

The clearance between the body of the cam follower and the cylinder is accurately designed to meter a specific quantity of oil as it escapes from the pressure chamber. Oil will only pass along the cylinder bore when pressure is high during the moment of valve opening. Once the valve has closed, the escape of oil will produce a small amount of free play and no pressure will exist in the pressure chamber. Oil from the feed chamber can then flow through the non-return valve into the pressure chamber so that the cam follower cylinder can be raised by the pressure of the coil spring, thus eliminating any play in the arrangement until the valve is operated again.

As wear occurs between rocker arm and valve stem, the quantity of oil which flows into the pressure chamber will be slightly more than the quantity lost during the expansion cycle of the cam follower. Conversely, when the cam follower is compressed by the expansion of the valve, a slightly smaller quantity of oil will flow into the pressure chamber than was lost.

If the engine has been standing idle for a period of time, or after overhaul, when the engine is started up valve clatter may be heard. This is a normal condition and will gradually disappear within a few minutes of starting up as the cam followers are pressurised with oil.

The coolant pump is mounted on the timing belt end of the cylinder block and is driven by the toothed belt.

A gear type oil pump is mounted on the timing belt end of the cylinder block and is driven by a gear on the front end of the crankshaft.

A full-flow oil filter of throw-away type is located on the side of crankcase nearer the front of the vehicle.

23 Operations possible without removing engine from vehicle

The following work can be carried out without having to remove the engine:

(a) *Timing belt – renewal*
(b) *Camshaft oil seal – renewal*
(c) *Camshaft – removal and refitting*
(d) *Cylinder head – removal and refitting*
(e) *Crankshaft front oil seal – renewal*
(f) *Sump – removal and refitting*
(g) *Piston/connecting rod – removal and refitting*
(h) *Engine/transmission mountings – removal and refitting*

24 Operations only possible with engine removed from vehicle

1   The following work should be carried out only after the engine has been removed:

(a) *Crankshaft main bearings – renewal*
(b) *Crankshaft – removal and refitting*
(c) ** Flywheel – removal and refitting*
(d) *** Crankshaft rear oil seal – renewal*
(e) ** Oil pump – removal and refitting*

2   Although it is possible to undertake those operations marked * without removing the engine, and those marked ** by removing the transmission (see Chapter 6), such work is not recommended and is unlikely to save much time over that required to withdraw the complete engine/transmission.

25 Timing belt – removal and refitting

Note: *If fitting a new belt, refer to Chapter 13*

1   This is not a routine operation and will only normally be required after a very high mileage has been covered, or for removal of the coolant pump.

2   Disconnect the battery earth lead.

3   Release the alternator mounting and adjuster link bolts, push the alternator in towards the engine and slip the drivebelt from the pulleys.

Fig. 1.68 Cutaway view of ohc (CVH) engine (Sec 22)

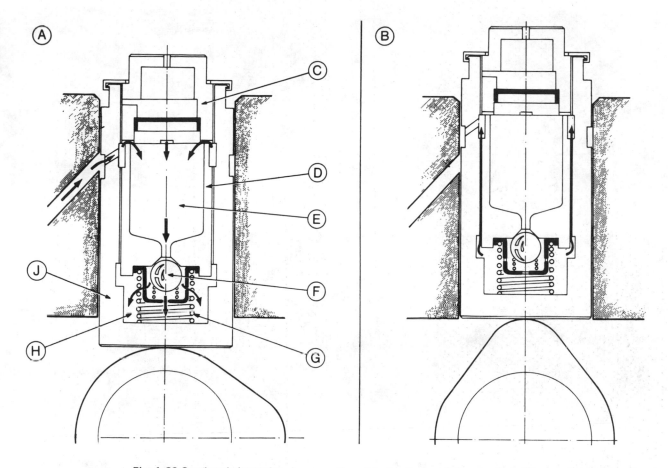

Fig. 1.69 Sectional views showing operation of hydraulic cam followers (Sec 22)

A	Valve closed	D	Cylinder	F	Non-return valve	H	Pressure chamber
B	Valve open	E	Feed chamber	G	Coil spring	J	Body
C	Plunger						

Fig. 1.70 Checking timing belt tension (Sec 25)

A   Finger pressure   X   4 to 6 mm (0.16 to 0.24 in)

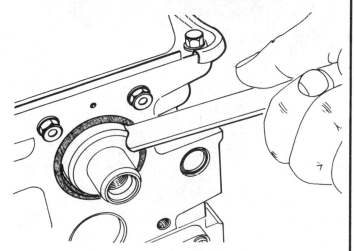

Fig. 1.71 Removing the camshaft oil seal (Sec 26)

25.4 Removing the timing belt cover

25.5A Camshaft sprocket timing mark

25.5B Crankshaft sprocket timing marks

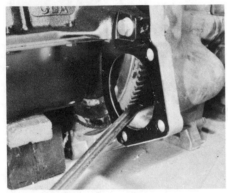
25.5C One method of jamming the flywheel ring gear

25.5D Another device for jamming the flywheel ring gear

25.8 Removing the timing belt

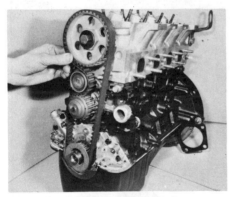
25.11 Timing belt correctly located

25.12 Crankshaft pulley and bolt

26.5 Camshaft oil seal

4   Unscrew the four bolts and remove the timing belt cover (photo).
5   Using a ring spanner on the crankshaft pulley bolt, turn the crankshaft until the timing mark on the camshaft sprocket is opposite the tdc mark on the cylinder head and the small projection on the crankshaft belt sprocket front flange is in alignment with the tdc mark on the oil pump casing. Remove the starter, jam the flywheel ring gear and unbolt and remove the crankshaft pulley (photos).
6   Slacken the bolts which secure the belt tensioner and using a large screwdriver prise the tensioner to one side to relieve spring tension on the belt. (Some tensioners do not incorporate a spring). Temporarily retighten the bolts.
7   If the original belt is to be refitted, mark it for direction of travel and also the exact tooth positions on all three sprockets.
8   Slip the timing belt from its sprockets (photo).
9   Refit by reversing the removal operations, but before engaging the belt to the camshaft and crankshaft sprockets, check that they are set to tdc as previously described. Adjust the position of the sprockets slightly if necessary, but avoid any excessive movement of the sprockets while the belt is off, as the piston crowns and valve heads may make contact with consequent damage to both components.

10   Engage the timing belt with the teeth of the crankshaft sprocket (slip the sprocket off the crankshaft if necessary to avoid kinking the belt), and then pull the belt vertically upright on its right-hand run. Keep it taut and engage it with the teeth of the camshaft sprocket. Check that the positions of the crankshaft and camshaft sprockets have not altered.
11   Wind the belt around the camshaft sprocket, around and under the tensioner idler pulley and over the coolant pump pocket (no set position for this) (photo).
12   Release the belt tensioner bolts and allow it to tension the belt under the action of its spring. If a spring is not fitted apply pressure to the tensioner so that the belt becomes taut and then tighten the right-hand tensioner bolt. Refit the crankshaft pulley and bolt (photo). Rotate the crankshaft through the two turns in a clockwise direction and align the camshaft sprocket mark with the one on the cylinder head. Now turn the crankshaft in an anti-clockwise direction through 60°. On models with a tensioner incorporating a spring, tighten the right-hand tensioner bolt.
13   Deflect the camshaft belt with the finger towards the coolant pump sprocket and check the gap between the outside diameter of the

coolant pump sprocket and the tip of the belt teeth, which should be between 4 and 6 mm (0.16 and 0.24 in).

14 If the gap is incorrect, this indicates that the belt tension is wrong. To rectify, insert a screwdriver between the tensioner pulley retainer and the engine mounting. Slacken the tensioner bolts and adjust. Tighten the bolts.

15 Always carry out belt adjustment on a cold engine.

16 Refit the belt cover, refit and adjust the vee belt and reconnect the battery. Refit the starter motor.

17 If possible, get a Ford dealer to check the timing belt tension using Special Tool 21-113.

26 Camshaft oil seal – renewal

1 Disconnect the battery earth lead.

2 Release the timing belt from the camshaft sprocket as described in the preceding Section.

3 Pass a bar through one of the holes in the camshaft sprocket to anchor the sprocket while the retaining bolt is unscrewed. Remove the sprocket.

4 Using a suitable tool, hooked at its end, prise out the oil seal.

5 Apply a little grease to the lips of the new seal and draw it into position using the sprocket bolt and a suitable distance piece (photo).

6 Refit the sprocket, tightening the bolt to the specified torque wrench setting. Thread locking compound should be applied to the threads of the bolt.

7 Refit and tension the timing belt as described in the preceding Section.

8 Reconnect the battery.

27 Camshaft – removal and refitting

1 Disconnect the battery earth lead.

2 Disconnect the crankcase ventilation hose from the intake manifold and the rocker cover.

3 Extract the two larger screws from the lid of the air cleaner, raise the air cleaner, disconnect the hoses and remove the cleaner.

4 Disconnect the pipes and remove the windscreen washer fluid reservoir from the engine compartment.

5 Disconnect the HT leads from the spark plugs, then remove the distributor cap and secure it to the left-hand side of the engine compartment.

6 Unscrew the three bolts and withdraw the distributor from the cylinder head. Note that the distributor body is marked in relation to the cylinder head.

7 Unbolt and remove the fuel pump complete with coil spring.

8 Withdraw the insulating spacer and operating pushrod.

9 Unbolt the throttle cable bracket at the carburettor and then disconnect the cable by sliding back the spring clip.

10 Remove the rocker cover.

11 Unscrew the securing nuts and remove the rocker arms and guides. Keep the components in their originally installed sequence by marking them with a piece of numbered tape or by using a suitably sub-divided box.

12 Withdraw the hydraulic cam followers, again keeping them in their originally fitted sequence.

13 Slacken the alternator mounting and adjuster link bolts, push the alternator in towards the engine and slip the drivebelt from the pulleys.

14 Unbolt and remove the timing belt cover and turn the crankshaft to align the timing mark on the camshaft sprocket with the one on the cylinder head.

15 Slacken the bolts on the timing belt tensioner, lever the tensioner against the tension of its coil spring (if fitted) and retighten the bolts. With the belt now slack, slip it from the camshaft sprocket.

16 Pass a rod or large screwdriver through one of the holes in the camshaft sprocket to lock it and unscrew the sprocket bolt. Remove the sprocket (photos).

17 Extract the two bolts and pull out the camshaft thrust plate (photos).

18 Carefully withdraw the camshaft from the distributor end of the cylinder head (photo).

19 Refitting the camshaft is a reversal of removal, but observe the following points.

20 Lubricate the camshaft bearings before inserting the camshaft into the cylinder head.

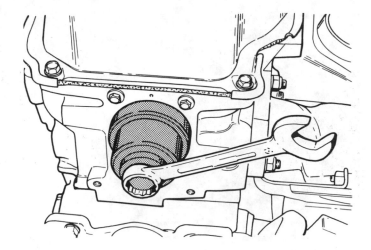

Fig. 1.72 Installing the camshaft oil seal (Sec 26)

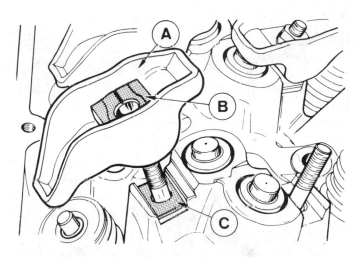

Fig. 1.73 Rocker arm components (Sec 27)

A   Rocker arm   C   Spacer plate
B   Guide

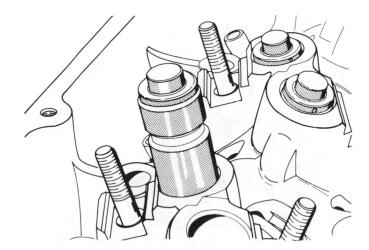

Fig. 1.74 Removing a cam follower (Sec 27)

27.16A Unscrewing the camshaft sprocket bolt

27.16B Removing the camshaft sprocket

27.17A Unscrewing the camshaft thrust plate bolts

27.17B Removing the camshaft thrust plate

27.18 Withdrawing the camshaft

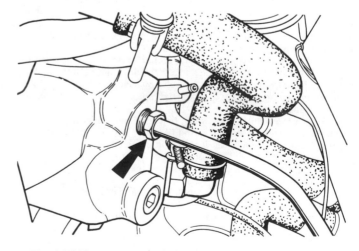

Fig. 1.75 Vacuum servo pipe-to-intake manifold connection (arrowed) (Sec 28)

21 It is recommended that a new oil seal is always fitted after the camshaft has been installed (see preceding Section). Apply thread locking compound to the sprocket bolt threads.

22 Fit and tension the timing belt as described in Section 25.

23 Oil the hydraulic cam followers with hypoid type transmission oil before inserting them into their original bores.

24 Refit the rocker arms and guides in their original sequence, use new nuts and tighten to the specified torque. It is essential that before each rocker arm is installed and its nut tightened, the respective cam follower is positioned at its lowest point (in contact with cam base circle). Turn the camshaft (by means of the crankshaft pulley bolt) as necessary to achieve this.

25 Use a new rocker cover gasket.

28 Cylinder head – removal and refitting

1 Disconnect the battery earth lead.

2 Remove the air cleaner and detach the connecting hoses.

3 Drain the cooling system (Chapter 2).

4 Disconnect the coolant hoses from the thermostat housing.

5 Disconnect the coolant hoses from the automatic choke.

6 Disconnect the throttle cable from the carburettor.

7 Disconnect the fuel pipe from the fuel pump.

8 Disconnect the vacuum servo pipe (if so equipped) from the intake manifold.

9 Disconnect the leads from the coolant temperature sender, the ignition coil, and the anti-run-on solenoid valve at the carburettor.

10 Unbolt the exhaust downpipe from the manifold by unscrewing the flange bolts. Support the exhaust pipe by tying it up with wire (photo).

11 Release the alternator mounting and adjuster link bolts, push the alternator in towards the engine and slip the drivebelt from the pulleys.

12 Unbolt and remove the timing belt cover.

13 Slacken the belt tensioner bolts, lever the tensioner to one side against the pressure of the coil spring (if fitted) and retighten the bolts.

14 With the timing belt now slack, slip it from the camshaft sprocket.

15 Disconnect the leads from the spark plugs and unscrew and remove the spark plugs.

16 Remove the rocker cover (photo).

17 Unscrew the cylinder head bolts, progressively and in the reverse sequence to that given for tightening (Fig. 1.77). Discard the bolts, as new ones must be used at reassembly

18 Remove the cylinder head complete with manifolds. Use the manifolds if necessary as levers to rock the head from the block. Do not attempt to tap the head sideways off the block as it is located on dowels, and do not attempt to lever between the head and the block or damage will result.

19 Before installing the cylinder head, make sure that the mating surfaces of head and block are perfectly clean with the head locating dowels in position. Clean the bolt holes free from oil. In extreme cases it is possible for oil left in the holes to crack the block.

20 Turn the crankshaft to position No 1 piston about 20 mm (0.8 in) before it reaches tdc.

21 Place a new gasket on the cylinder block and then locate the cylinder head on its dowels. The upper surface of the gasket is marked OBEN-TOP (photos).

22 Install and tighten the **new** cylinder head bolts, tightening them in four stages (see Specifications). After the first two stages, the bolt heads should be marked with a spot of quick-drying paint so that the paint spots all face the same direction. Now tighten the bolts (Stage 3) through 90° (quarter turn) followed by a further 90° (Stage 4). Tighten the bolts at each stage only in the sequence shown before going on to the next stage. If all the bolts have been tightened equally, the paint spots should now all be pointing in the same direction (photo).

23 Fit the timing belt as described in Section 25.

24 Refitting and reconnection of all other components is a reversal of dismantling.

25 Refill the cooling system.

29 Crankshaft front oil seal – renewal

1 Disconnect the battery earth lead.

2 Release the alternator mounting and adjuster link bolts, push the alternator in towards the engine and slip the drivebelt from the pulleys.

3 Unbolt and remove the timing belt cover and by using a spanner or socket on the crankshaft pulley bolt, turn the crankshaft until the timing mark on the camshaft sprocket is in alignment with the mark on the cylinder head.

4 Unbolt and withdraw the starter motor so that the flywheel ring gear can be jammed with a cold chisel or other suitable device and the crankshaft pulley unbolted and removed.

5 Slacken the belt tensioner bolts, lever the tensioner to one side and retighten the bolts. With the belt slack, it can now be slipped from the sprockets. Before removing the belt note its original position on the sprockets (mark the teeth with quick-drying paint), also its direction of travel.

6 Pull off the crankshaft sprocket. If it is tight, use a two-legged extractor.

7 Remove the dished washer from the crankshaft, noting that the concave side is against the oil seal.

8 Using a suitably hooked tool, prise out the oil seal from the oil pump housing.

9 Grease the lips of the new seal and press it into position using the pulley bolt and a suitable distance piece made from a piece of tubing.

10 Fit the thrust washer (concave side to oil seal), the belt sprocket and the pulley to the crankshaft.

11 Fit and tension the timing belt by the method described in Section 25.

12 Fit the timing belt cover.

13 Refit and tension the alternator drivebelt.

14 Remove the starter ring gear jamming device, refit the starter motor and reconnect the battery.

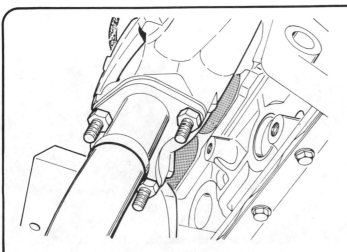

Fig. 1.76 Exhaust downpipe connection to manifold (Sec 28)

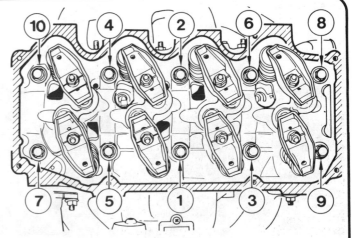

Fig. 1.77 Cylinder head bolt tightening sequence (Sec 28)

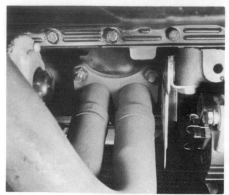

28.10 Exhaust connection to manifold

28.16 Removing the rocker cover

28.21A Fitting a cylinder head gasket

28.21B Cylinder head gasket marking

28.21C Fitting the cylinder head

28.22 Tighten cylinder head bolts to specified torque settings

30.8A Sump sealing strip

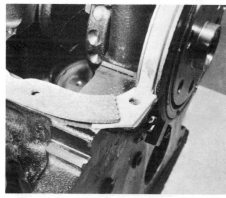

30.8B Sump gasket overlapping sealing strip

30.9A Fitting the sump

30.9B Tightening the sump bolts

30.9C Fitting the timing belt guard

30.10 Fitting the flywheel housing cover plate

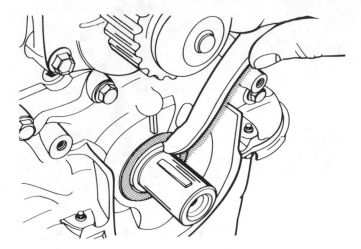

Fig. 1.78 Extracting the oil seal from the oil pump (Sec 29)

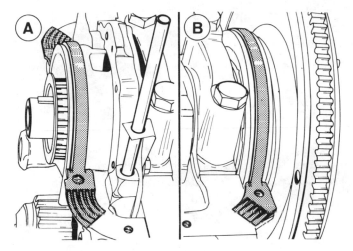

Fig. 1.79 Sump front (A) and rear (B) sealing strips (Sec 30)

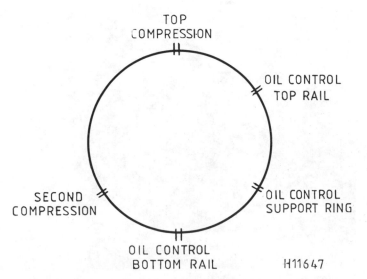

**Fig. 1.80 Piston ring gap setting diagram. Piston position is
unimportant (Sec 31)**

30 Sump – removal and refitting

1   Disconnect the battery earth lead.
2   Drain the engine oil.
3   Unbolt and remove the starter motor.
4   Unbolt and remove the cover plate from the clutch housing.
5   Unscrew the plastic timing belt guard from the front end of the engine (two bolts).
6   Unscrew the sump securing bolts progressively and remove them.
7   Remove the sump and peel away the gaskets and sealing strips.
8   Make sure that the mating surfaces of the sump and block are clean, then fit new end sealing strips into their grooves and stick new side gaskets into position using thick grease. The ends of the side gaskets should overlap the seals (photos).
9   Offer up the sump, taking care not to displace the gaskets and insert the securing bolts. Tighten the bolts in two stages to the final torque given in the Specifications. Fit the timing belt guard (photos).
10 Refit the cover plate to the flywheel housing (photo).
11 Refit the starter motor.
12 Fill the engine with oil and reconnect the battery.

31 Piston/connecting rods – removal and refitting

1   Remove the sump as described in the preceding Section and the cylinder head as described in Section 28.
2   Check that the connecting rod and cap have adjacent numbers at their big-end to indicate their position in the cylinder block (No 1 nearest timing cover end of engine) (photo).
3   Bring the first piston to the lowest point of its throw by turning the crankshaft pulley bolt and then check if there is a wear ring at the top of the bore. If there is, it should be removed using a scraper, but do not damage the cylinder bore.
4   Unscrew the big-end bolts and remove them.
5   Tap off the cap. If the bearing shell is to be used again, make sure that it is retained with the cap. Note the two cap positioning roll pins.
6   Push the piston/rod out of the top of the block, again keeping the bearing shell with the rod if the shell is to be used again.
7   Repeat the removal operations on the remaining piston/rod assemblies.
8   Dismantling a piston/connecting rod is covered in Sections 17 and 39.
9   To refit a piston/rod assembly, have the piston ring gaps staggered as shown in the diagram (Fig. 1.80). Oil the rings and apply a piston ring compressor. Compress the piston rings.
10 Oil the cylinder bores.
11 Wipe clean the bearing shell seat in the connecting rod and insert the shell (photo).
12 Insert the piston/rod assembly into the cylinder bore until the base of the piston ring compressor stands squarely on the top of the block.
13 Check that the directional arrow on the piston crown faces towards the timing cover end of the engine, then apply the wooden handle of a hammer to the piston crown. Strike the head of the hammer sharply to drive the piston into the cylinder bore and release the ring compressor (photo).
14 Oil the crankpin and draw the connecting rod down to engage with the crankshaft. Make sure the bearing shell is still in position.
15 Wipe the bearing shell seat in the big-end cap clean and insert the bearing shell (photo).
16 Fit the cap, screw in the bolts and tighten them to the specified torque (photos).
17 Repeat the operations on the remaining pistons/connecting rods.
18 Refit the sump (Section 30) and the cylinder head (Section 28). Refill the engine with oil and coolant.

32 Engine/transmission mountings – removal and refitting

The information below also applies to ohv engines
1   The engine mountings can be removed if the weight of the engine/transmission is first taken by one of the three following methods.
2   Either support the engine under the sump using a jack and a block of wood, or attach a hoist to the engine lifting lugs. A third method is

31.2 Connecting rod and cap matching numbers

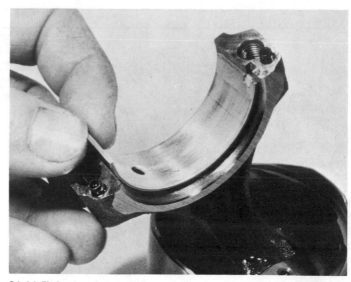
31.11 Fitting bearing shell to connecting rod

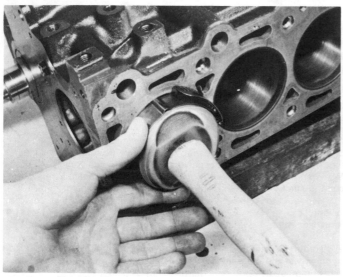
31.13 Installing a piston/connecting rod

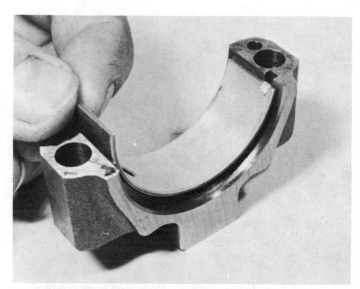
31.15 Fitting a bearing shell to a big-end cap

31.16A Fitting a big-end cap

31.16B Tightening a big-end cap bolt

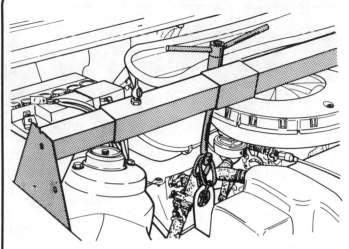

Fig. 1.81 Typical engine support bar (Sec 32)

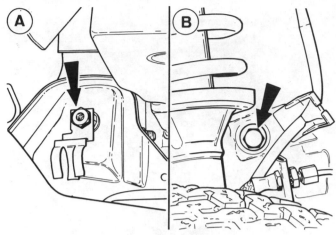

Fig. 1.82 Rear right-hand engine mounting (Sec 32)

A   Side member attachment   B   Wing inner panel
                                    attachment

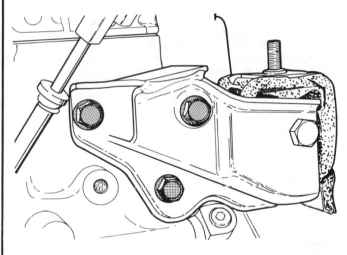

Fig. 1.83 Rear right-hand engine mounting bracket (Sec 32)

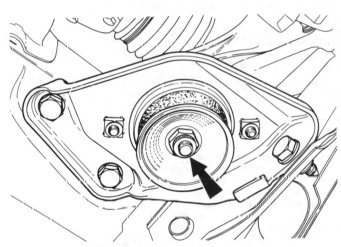

Fig. 1.84 Rear left-hand engine mounting (centre bolt arrowed)
(Sec 32)

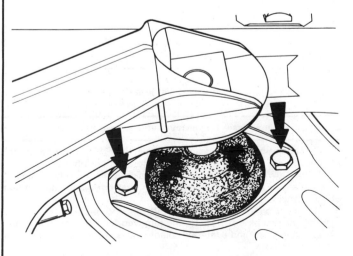

Fig. 1.85 Front left-hand flexible mounting (Sec 32)

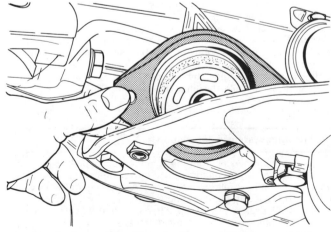

Fig. 1.86 Extracting front left-hand flexible mounting (Sec 32)

33.3 Screwing on an oil filter cartridge

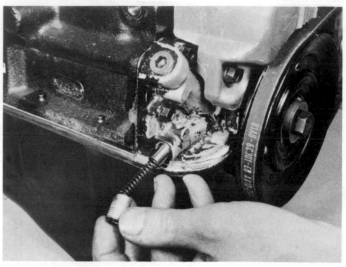

34.1 Oil pressure relief valve

to make up a bar with end pieces which will engage in the water channels at the sides of the bonnet lid aperture. Using an adjustable hook and chain connected to the engine lifting lugs, the weight of the engine can be taken off the mountings.

Rear mountings
3   Unbolt the mounting, according to type from the body member or panel, also from the engine or transmission. With the mounting withdrawn, the centre bolt can be unscrewed and the flexible component detached.

Front left-hand mounting
4   Removal of the front mounting on the transmission requires a different removal procedure. Remove the centre bolt from the mounting and then using one of the methods described, raise the transmission just enough to be able to unbolt and remove the two insulator bolts and withdraw the insulator.

All mountings
5   Refitting of all mountings is a reversal of removal. Make sure that the original sequence of assembly of washers and plates is maintained.

33 Oil filter – removal and refitting

1   The oil filter is of throw-away screw-on cartridge type, mounted on the right-hand side of the crankcase.
2   The filter should be unscrewed using a strap or chain wrench.
3   When fitting a new filter, smear the rubber sealing ring with grease and screw it on as tightly as possible using hand pressure only, not a tool (photo).
4   After starting the engine, the oil pressure warning light will stay on for a few seconds while the filter fills with oil. This is normal after fitting a new filter.

34 Lubrication system – description

1   The oil pump draws oil from the sump through a pick-up pipe and then supplies pressurised oil through an oilway on the right-hand side of the engine into a full-flow oil filter. A pressure relief valve is incorporated inside the pump casing (photo).
2   Filtered oil passes out of the filter casing through the central threaded mounting stud into the main oil gallery.
3   Oil from the main gallery lubricates the main bearings, and the big-end bearings are lubricated from oilways in the crankshaft.
4   The connecting rods have an oil hole in the big-end on the side towards the exhaust manifold. Oil is ejected from this hole onto the gudgeon pins and cylinder bores.
5   The oil pressure warning switch is located next to the oil filter and

connected by an internal passage to the main oil gallery. Oil from this passage is supplied to the centre camshaft bearing.
6   Oil is provided to the other camshaft bearings by means of a longitudinal drilling within the camshaft.
7   The hydraulic cam followers (tappets) are supplied with oil through the grooves in the camshaft bearing journals and oilways in the cylinder head.
8   The contact face of the rocker arm is lubricated from ports in the tappet guides, while the end faces of the valve stems are splash lubricated.

35 Crankcase ventilation system – description

1   The system is of closed type, in which oil and blow-by fumes are extracted from the crankcase and passed into the intake manifold, after which they are burnt during the normal combustion cycle.
2   At light throttle openings, the emissions are drawn out of the rocker cover, through a control orifice in the crankcase ventilation filter and into the intake manifold. Under full throttle conditions the gas flow routing is still as just described, but in addition the gases are drawn through a filter and pass into the air cleaner.
3   This arrangement offsets any tendency for the fuel/air ratio to be adversely affected at full throttle.
4   Models intended for operation in countries with strict emission control laws also have an exhaust gas recirculation system. This is considered in Chapter 3.

36 Engine – method of removal

The engine should be removed from the vehicle complete with transmission (gearbox and final drive) in a downward direction.

37 Engine/transmission – removal and separation

1   The operations are as described in Section 15 of this Chapter for removal of the ohv type engine, with one addition (photos).
2   Before lowering the engine/transmission from the vehicle, unbolt (two bolts) and remove the plastic belt guard from the timing belt end of the sump.
3   It should also be noted that with the ohc engine, the exhaust manifold heated air box need not be removed for disconnection of the exhaust downpipe, and a lateral coolant pipe is not fitted at the side of the cylinder block.

38 Engine – complete dismantling

1   The need for dismantling will have been dictated by wear or noise

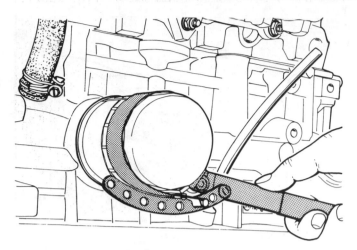

Fig. 1.87 Removing the oil filter (Sec 33)

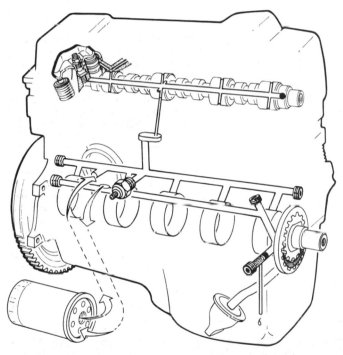

Fig. 1.88 Engine lubrication system (Sec 34)

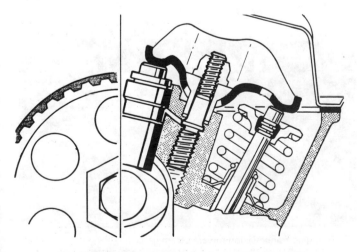

Fig. 1.89 Sectional view of valve rocker (Sec 34)

in most cases. Although there is no reason why only partial dismantling cannot be carried out to renew such items as the oil pump or crankshaft rear oil seal, when the main bearings or big-end bearings have been knocking and especially if the vehicle has covered a high mileage, then it is recommended that a complete strip-down is carried out and every engine component examined as described in Section 39.

2   Position the engine so that it is upright and safely chocked on a bench or other convenient working surface. If the exterior of the engine is very dirty it should be cleaned before dismantling, using paraffin and a stiff brush or a water-soluble solvent.

3   Remove the alternator, the mounting bracket and exhaust heat shield, and the adjuster link (photos).

4   Disconnect the heater hose from the coolant pump.

5   Drain the engine oil and remove the filter.

6   Jam the flywheel starter ring gear to prevent the crankshaft turning and unscrew the crankshaft pulley bolt. Remove the pulley.

7   Unbolt and remove the timing belt cover (4 bolts).

8   Slacken the two bolts on the timing belt tensioner, lever the tensioner against its spring pressure and tighten the bolts to lock it in position.

9   With the belt now slack, note its running direction and mark the mating belt and sprocket teeth with a spot of quick-drying paint. This is not necessary if the belt is being renewed.

10 Disconnect the spark plug leads and remove the distributor cap complete with HT leads.

11 Unscrew and remove the spark plugs.

12 Disconnect the crankcase ventilation hose from its connector on the crankcase.

13 Remove the rocker cover.

14 Unscrew the cylinder head bolts in the reverse order to tightening (Fig. 1.77) and discard them. New bolts must be used at reassembly.

15 Remove the cylinder head complete with manifolds.

16 Turn the engine on its side. Do not invert it as sludge in the sump may enter the oilways. Remove the sump bolts, withdraw the sump and peel off the gaskets and sealing strips.

17 Remove the bolts from the clutch pressure plate in a progressive manner until the pressure of the assembly is relieved and then remove the cover, taking care not to allow the driven plate (friction disc) to fall to the floor.

18 Unbolt and remove the flywheel. The bolt holes are offset so it will only fit one way.

19 Remove the engine adaptor plate.

20 Unbolt and remove the crankshaft rear oil seal retainer.

21 Unbolt and remove the timing belt tensioner and take out the coil spring. (This spring is not used on all models).

22 Unbolt and remove the coolant pump.

23 Remove the belt sprocket from the crankshaft using the hands or if tight, a two-legged puller. Take off the thrust washer.

24 Unbolt the oil pump and pick-up tube and remove them as an assembly.

25 Unscrew and remove the oil pressure switch (photo).

26 Turn the crankshaft so that all the pistons are half-way down the bores, and feel if a wear ridge exists at the top of the bores. If so, scrape the ridge away, taking care not to damage the bores.

27 Inspect the big-end and main bearing caps for markings. The main bearings should be marked 1 to 5 with a directional arrow pointing to the timing end. The big-end caps and connecting rods should have adjacent matching members towards the oil filter side of the engine. Number 1 is at the timing end of the engine. Make your own marks if necessary.

28 Unscrew the bolts from the first big-end cap and remove the cap. The cap is located on two roll pins, so if the cap requires tapping off make sure that it is not tapped in a sideways direction.

29 Retain the bearing shell with the cap if the shell is to be used again.

30 Push the piston/connecting rod out of the top of the cylinder block, again retaining the bearing shell with the rod if the shell is to be used again.

31 Remove the remaining pistons/rods in a similar way.

32 Remove the main bearing caps, keeping the shells with their respective caps if the shells are to be used again. Lift out the crankshaft.

33 Take out the bearing shells from the crankcase, noting the semi-circular thrust washers on either side of the centre bearing. Keep the shells identified as to position in the crankcase if they are to be used again.

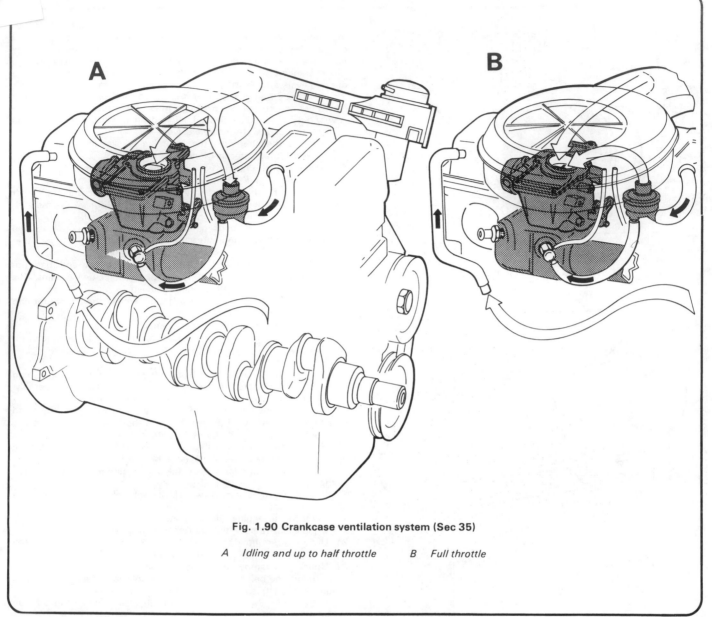

Fig. 1.90 Crankcase ventilation system (Sec 35)

A   Idling and up to half throttle   B   Full throttle

37.1A Removing engine/transmission

37.1B Engine/transmission lowered from vehicle

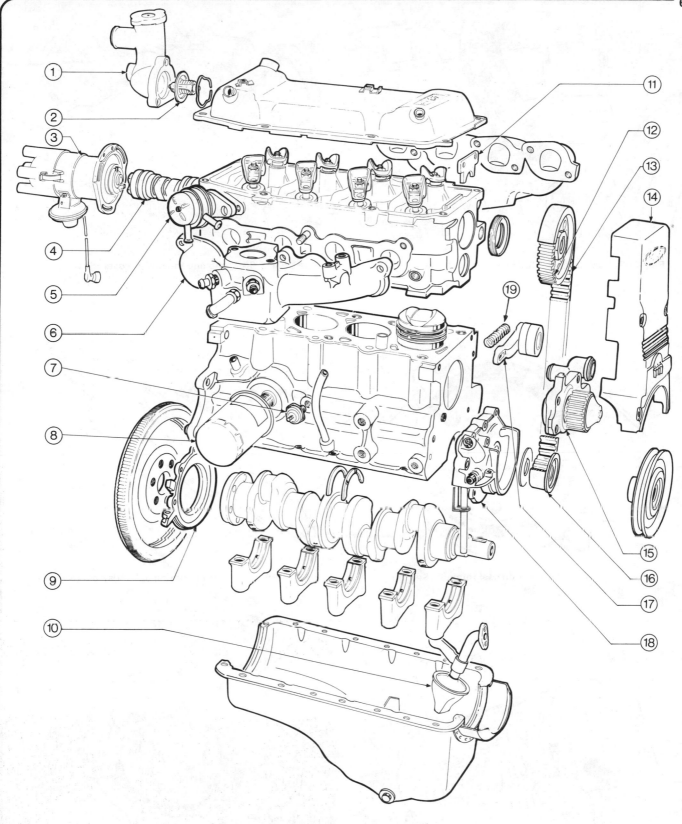

Fig. 1.91 Exploded view of engine (Sec 38)

1	Thermostat housing	7	Oil pressure switch
2	Thermostat	8	Oil filter
3	Distributor	9	Oil seal retainer
4	Camshaft	10	Oil pump intake pipe and strainer
5	Fuel pump		
6	Intake manifold		

11	Camshaft thrust plate	16	Crankshaft belt sprocket
12	Camshaft belt sprocket	17	Timing belt tensioner
13	Timing belt	18	Oil pump
14	Timing belt cover	19	Belt tensioner spring (not fitted to all models)
15	Coolant pump		

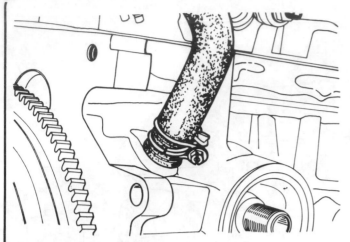

Fig. 1.92 Crankcase ventilation hose attachment (Sec 38)

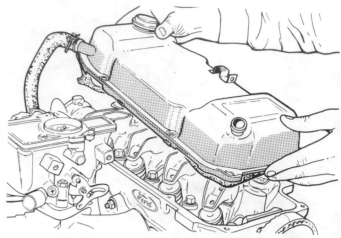

Fig. 1.93 Removing the rocker cover (Sec 38)

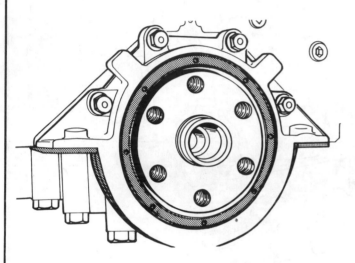

Fig. 1.94 Crankshaft rear oil seal retainer (Sec 38)

Fig. 1.95 Removing the timing belt tensioner (Sec 38)

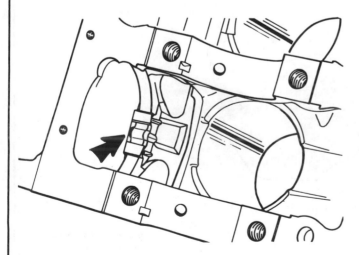

Fig. 1.96 Crankcase ventilation baffle (arrowed) (Sec 38)

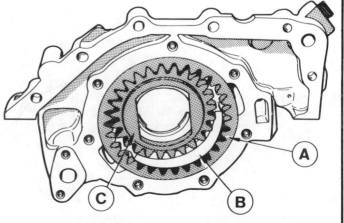

Fig. 1.97 Oil pump with cover plate removed (Sec 39)

A   Driven gear   C   Driving gear
B   Spacer

38.3A Removing alternator mounting bolt

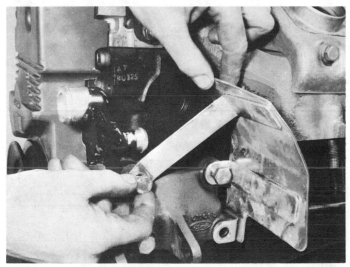

38.3B Alternator heat shield

38.25 Unscrewing the oil pressure switch

34 Prise down the spring arms of the crankcase ventilation baffle and remove it from inside the crankcase just below the ventilation hose connection.

35 The engine is now completely dismantled and each component should be examined as described in the following Section before reassembling.

39 Examination and renovation

Crankshaft, bearings, cylinder bores and pistons

1 Refer to paragraphs 1 to 15 of Section 17. The information applies equally to the ohc engine, except that standard sized crankshafts are unmarked and the following differences in the piston rings should be noted.

2 The top rings are coated with molybdenum. Avoid damaging the coating when fitting the rings to the pistons.

3 The lower (oil control) ring must be fitted so that the manufacturer's mark is towards the piston crown, or the groove towards the gudgeon pin. Take care that the rails of the oil control ring abut without overlapping.

Timing sprockets and belt

4 It is very rare for the teeth of the sprockets to wear, but attention should be given to the tensioner idler pulley. It must turn freely and smoothly, be ungrooved and without any shake in its bearing. Otherwise renew it.

5 Always renew the coil spring (if fitted) in the tensioner. If the engine has covered 80 000 km (50 000 miles) then it is recommended that a new belt is fitted, even if the original one appears in good condition.

Flywheel

6 Refer to paragraphs 19 to 23 of Section 17.

Oil pump

7 The oil pump is of gear type, incorporating a crescent shaped spacer. Although no wear limit tolerances are specified, if on inspection there is obvious wear between the gears or between the driven gear and the pump casing, the pump should be renewed. Similarly if a high mileage engine is being reconditioned, it is recommended that a new pump is fitted.

Oil seals and gaskets

8 Renew the oil seals in the oil pump and in the crankshaft rear oil seal retainer as a matter of routine at time of major overhaul. It is recommended that the new seals are drawn into these components using a nut and bolt and distance pieces, rather than tapping them into position, to avoid distortion of the light alloy castings.

9 Renew the camshaft oil seal after the camshaft has been installed.

10 Always smear the lips of a new oil seal with grease, and check that the small tensioner spring in the oil seal has not been displaced during installation.

11 Renew all gaskets by purchasing the appropriate engine set, which usually includes the necessary oil seals.

Crankcase

12 Refer to paragraphs 28 to 30 of Section 17.

Camshaft and bearings

13 Examine the camshaft gear and lobes for damage or wear. If evident, a new camshaft must be purchased, or one which has been built-up, such as are advertised by firms specialising in exchange components.

14 The bearing internal diameters in the cylinder head should be checked against the Specifications if a suitable gauge is available, otherwise check for movement between the camshaft journal and the bearing. If the bearings are proved to be worn, then a new cylinder head is the only answer as the bearings are machined directly in the cylinder head.

15 Check the camshaft endfloat by temporarily refitting the camshaft and thrust plate. If the endfloat exceeds the specified tolerance, renew the thrust plate.

39.35A Using a socket to install a valve stem oil seal

39.35B Valve stem oil seal installed

39.35C Valve components

39.36 Inserting a valve into its guide

39.37A Fitting a valve spring

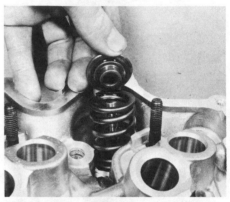

39.37B Fitting a valve spring retainer

39.38 Inserting a split collet

39.42 Installing a hydraulic cam follower

39.43A Fitting a rocker arm spacer plate

39.43B Fitting a rocker arm and guide

39.43C Tightening a rocker arm nut

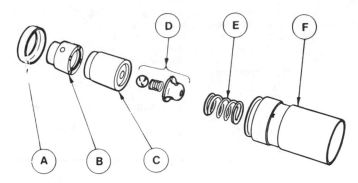

Fig. 1.98 Exploded view of hydraulic cam follower (Sec 39)

A   Crimped retainer   D   Non-return valve
B   Plunger   E   Coil spring
C   Cylinder   F   Body

Fig. 1.99 Special valve spring compressing tool (Sec 39)

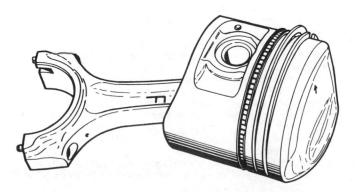

Fig. 1.100 Piston/connecting rod alignment (Sec 41)

Cam followers

16 It is seldom that the hydraulic type cam followers (tappets) wear in their cylinder head bores. If the bores are worn then a new cylinder head is called for.

17 If the cam lobe contact surface shows signs of a depression or grooving, grinding out the wear surface will not only remove the hardened surface of the follower but may also reduce its overall length to a point where the self-adjusting capability of the cam follower is exceeded and valve clearances are not taken up, with consequent noisy operation.

18 The cam follower can be dismantled for renewal of individual components after extracting the circlip, but after a high mileage it is probably better to renew the follower complete. After reassembly of a cam follower, do not attempt to fill it with oil but just smear the parts with a little oil during assembly.

Cylinder head and rocker arms

19 The usual reason for dismantling the cylinder head is to decarbonise and to grind in the valves. Reference should therefore be made to the next Section in addition to the dismantling operations described here.

20 Remove the intake and exhaust manifolds and their gaskets, also the thermostat housing (Chapter 2).

21 Unscrew the nuts from the rocker arms and discard the nuts. New ones must be fitted at reassembly.

22 Remove the rocker arms and the hydraulic cam followers, keeping them in their originally fitted sequence. Keep the rocker guide and spacer plates in order.

23 The camshaft need not be withdrawn but if it is wished to do so, first remove the thrust plate and take the camshaft out from the rear of the cylinder head.

24 The valve springs should now be compressed. A standard type of compressor will normally do the job, but a forked tool (Part No 21-097) can be purchased or made up to engage on the rocker stud using a nut and distance piece to compress it.

25 Compress the valve spring and extract the split collets. Do not overcompress the spring, or the valve stem may bend. If it is found when screwing down the compressor tool that the spring retainer does not release from the collets, remove the compressor and place a piece of tubing on the retainer so that it does not impinge on the collets and place a small block of wood under the head of the valve. With the cylinder head resting flat down on the bench, strike the end of the tubing a sharp blow with a hammer. Refit the compressor and compress the spring.

26 Extract the split collets and then gently release the compressor and remove it.

27 Remove the valve spring retainer, the spring and the valve stem oil seal. Withdraw the valve.

28 Valve removal should commence with No 1 valve (nearest timing cover end). Keep the valves and their components in their originally installed order by placing them in a piece of card which has holes punched in it and numbered 1 to 8.

29 To check for wear in the valve guides, place each valve in turn in its guide so that approximately one third of its length enters the guide. Rock the valve from side to side. If any more than the slightest movement is possible, the guides will have to be reamed (working from the valve seat end) and oversize stemmed valves fitted. If you do not have the necessary reamer (Tool No 21-071 to 21-074), leave this work to your Ford dealer.

30 Examine the valve seats. Normally the seats do not deteriorate, but the valve heads are more likely to burn away, in which case new valves can be ground in as described in the next Section. If the seats require recutting, use a standard cutter, available from most accessory or tool stores.

31 Renewal of any valve seat which is cracked or beyond recutting is definitely a job for your dealer or motor engineering works.

32 If the rocker arm studs must be removed for any reason, a special procedure is necessary. Warm the upper ends of the studs with a blow-lamp flame (**not** a welder) before unscrewing them. Clean out the cylinder head threads with an M10 tap and clean the threads of oil or grease. Discard the old studs and fit new ones, which will be coated with adhesive compound on their threaded portion. Screw in the studs without pausing, otherwise the adhesive will start to set and prevent the stud seating.

33 If the cylinder head mating surface is suspected of being distorted, it can be checked and surface ground by your dealer or motor engineering works. Distortion is possible with this type of light alloy

head if the bolt tightening method is not followed exactly, or if severe overheating has taken place.

34 Check the rocker arm contact surfaces for wear. Renew the valve springs if they have been in service for 80 000 km (50 000 miles) or more.

35 Commence reassembly of the cylinder head by fitting new valve stem oil seals (photos).

36 Oil No 1 valve stem and insert the valve into its guide (photo).

37 Fit the valve spring (closer coils to cylinder head), then the spring retainer (photos).

38 Compress the spring and engage the split collets in the cut-out in the valve stem. Hold them in position while the compressor is gently released and removed (photo).

39 Repeat the operations on the remaining valves, making sure that each valve is returned to its original guide or new valves have been fitted, into the seat into which it was ground.

40 Once all the valves have been fitted, support the ends of the cylinder head on two wooden blocks and strike the end of each valve stem with a plastic or copper-faced hammer, just a light blow to settle the components.

41 Fit the camshaft (if removed) and a new oil seal as described in Section 26.

42 Smear the hydraulic cam followers with hypoid type transmission oil and insert them into their original bores (photo).

43 Fit the rocker arms with their guides and spacer plates, use new nuts and tighten to the specified torque. It is important that each rocker arm is installed only when its particular cam follower is at its lowest point (in contact with the cam base circle) (photos).

44 Refit the exhaust and intake manifolds and the thermostat housing, using all new gaskets.

40 Cylinder head and pistons – decarbonising

1 With the cylinder head removed as described in Section 28, the carbon deposits should be removed from the combustion surfaces using a blunt scraper. Take great care as the head is of light alloy construction and avoid the use of a rotary (power-driven) wire brush.

2 Where a more thorough job is to be carried out, the cylinder head should be dismantled as described in the preceding Section so that the valves may be ground in, and the ports and combustion spaces cleaned and blown out after the manifolds have been removed.

3 Before grinding in a valve, remove the carbon and deposits completely from its head and stem. With an inlet valve this is usually quite easy, simply a case of scraping off the soft carbon with a blunt knife and finishing with a wire brush. With an exhaust valve, the deposits are very much harder and those on the valve head may need a rub on coarse emery cloth to remove them. An old woodworking chisel is a useful tool to remove the worst of the valve head deposits.

4 Make sure that the valve heads are really clean, otherwise the rubber suction cup grinding tool will not stick during the grinding-in operations.

5 Before starting to grind in a valve, support the cylinder head so that there is sufficient clearance under it for the valve stem to project fully without being obstructed, otherwise the valve will not seat properly during grinding.

6 Take the first valve and apply a little coarse grinding paste to the bevelled edge of the valve head. Insert the valve into its guide and apply the suction grinding tool to its head. Rotate the tool between the palms of the hands in a back-and-forth rotary movement until the gritty action of the grinding-in process disappears. Repeat the operation with fine paste and then wipe away all trace of grinding paste and examine the seat and bevelled edge of the valve. A matt silver mating band should be observed on both components, without any sign of black spots. If some spots do remain, repeat the grinding-in process until they have disappeared. A drop or two of paraffin is applied to the contact surfaces will speed the grinding process, but do not allow any paste to run down into the valve guide. On completion, wipe away every trace of grinding paste using a paraffin-moistened cloth.

7 Repeat the operations on the remaining valves, taking care not to mix up their originally fitted sequence.

8 An important part of the decarbonising operation is to remove the carbon deposits from the piston crowns. To do this (engine in vehicle), turn the crankshaft so that two pistons are at the top of their stroke and press some grease between the pistons and the cylinder walls.

This will prevent carbon particles falling down into the piston ring grooves. Plug the other two bores with rag.

9 Cover the oilways and coolant passages with masking tape and then using a blunt scraper, remove all the carbon from the piston crowns. Take great care not to score the soft alloy of the crown or the surface of the cylinder bore.

10 Rotate the crankshaft to bring the other two pistons to tdc and repeat the operations.

11 Wipe away the circles of grease and carbon from the cylinder bores.

12 Clean the top surface of the cylinder block by careful scraping.

41 Engine – reassembly

1 With everything clean and parts renewed where necessary, commence reassembly by inserting the ventilation baffle into the crankcase. Make sure that the spring arms engage securely (photo).

2 Insert the bearing half shells into their seats in the crankcase, making sure that the seats are perfectly clean (photo).

3 Stick the semi-circular thrust washers on either side of the centre bearing with thick grease. Make sure that the oil channels face outwards (photo).

4 Oil the bearing shells and carefully lower the crankshaft into position (photos).

5 Insert the bearing shells into the main bearing caps, making sure that their seats are perfectly clean. Oil the bearings and install the caps to their correct numbered location and with the directional arrow pointing towards the timing belt end of the engine (photos).

6 Tighten the main bearing cap bolts to the specified torque (photo).

7 Check the crankshaft endfloat. Ideally a dial gauge should be used, but feeler blades are an alternative if inserted between the face of the thrust washer and the machined surface of the crankshaft balance web, having first prised the crankshaft in one direction and then the other (photo). Provided the thrust washers at the centre bearing have been renewed, the endfloat should be within specified tolerance. If it is not, oversize thrust washers are available (see Specifications).

8 The pistons/connecting rods should now be installed. Although new pistons will have been fitted to the rods by your dealer or supplier due to the special tools needed, it is worth checking to ensure that with the piston crown arrow or cast nipple in the piston oil cut-out pointing towards the timing belt end of the engine, the F mark on the connecting rod or the oil ejection hole in the rod big-end is as shown (Fig. 1.100).

9 Oil the cylinder bores and install the pistons/connecting rods as described in Section 31.

10 Fit the oil pressure switch and tighten to the specified torque.

11 Before fitting the oil pump, action must be taken to prevent damage to the pump oil seal from the step on the front end of the crankshaft. First remove the Woodruff key and then build up the front end of the crankshaft using adhesive tape to form a smooth inclined surface to permit the pump seal to slide over the step without its lip turning back or the seal spring being displaced during installation (photo).

12 If the oil pump is new, pour some oil into it before installation in order to prime it and rotate its driving gear a few turns (photo).

13 Align the pump gear flats with those on the crankshaft and install the oil pump complete with new gasket. Tighten the bolts to the specified torque (photos).

14 Remove the adhesive tape and tap the Woodruff key into its groove (photo).

15 Bolt the oil pump pick-up tube into position (photos).

16 To the front end of the crankshaft, fit the thrust washer (belt guide) so that its concave side is towards the pump (photo).

17 Fit the crankshaft belt sprocket. If it is tight, draw it into position using the pulley bolt and a distance piece. Make sure that the belt retaining flange on the sprocket is towards the front of the crankshaft and the nose of the shaft has been smeared with a little grease before fitting (photo).

18 Install the coolant pump using a new gasket and tightening the bolts to the specified torque (photos).

19 Fit the timing belt tensioner and its coil spring (where fitted). Lever the tensioner fully against spring pressure and temporarily tighten the bolts.

20 Using a new gasket, bolt on the rear oil seal retainer, which will have been fitted with a new oil seal and the seal lips greased (photo).

41.1 Crankcase ventilation baffle

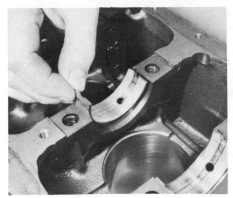

41.2 Inserting a main bearing shell into the crankcase

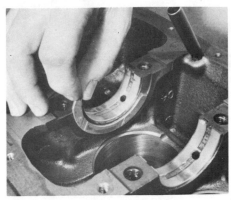

41.3 Crankshaft thrust washer

41.4A Lubricating a main bearing shell

41.4B Installing the crankshaft

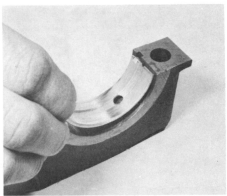

41.5A Fitting a bearing shell to a main bearing cap

41.5B Fitting a main bearing cap

41.5C Main bearing cap markings

41.6 Tightening a main bearing cap bolt

41.7 Checking crankshaft endfloat with a feeler blade

41.11 Building up front end of crankshaft with tape

41.12 Priming the oil pump

41.13A Oil pump ready for installation

41.13B Tightening the oil pump bolts

41.14 Crankshaft Woodruff key

41.15A Oil pump pick-up tube

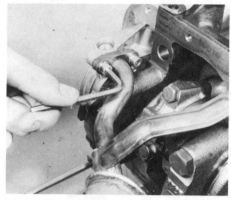
41.15B Tightening oil pick-up tube bolt

41.16 Crankshaft timing belt guide

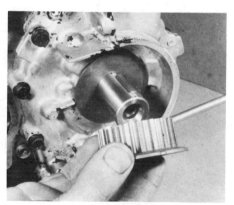
41.17 Fitting crankshaft timing belt sprocket

41.18A Fitting the coolant pump

41.18B Tightening a coolant pump bolt

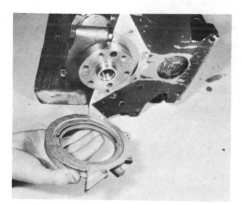
41.20 Crankshaft rear oil seal and retainer

41.21A Fitting the engine adaptor plate

41.21B Installing the flywheel

41.21C Flywheel bolt coated with thread sealant

41.21D Tightening the flywheel bolts

41.24A Fitting the intake manifold gasket

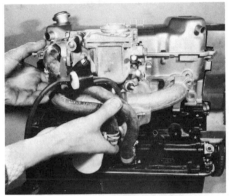

41.24B Installing the intake manifold

41.24C Fitting the exhaust manifold gasket

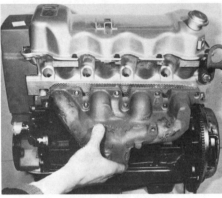

41.24D Installing the exhaust manifold

41.24E Tightening the exhaust manifold nuts

41.26 Tightening the rocker cover bolts

41.27A Connecting the crankcase ventilation rear hose

41.27B Connecting the crankcase ventilation front hose

41.32 Engine mounting (right-hand rear)

41.33 Alternator mounting bracket

42.4 Connecting the transmission to the engine

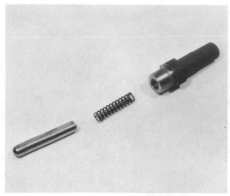
42.6A Gearbox cap nut, spring and plunger

42.6B Fitting gearbox cap nut assembly

42.8 Engine mounting (front left-hand)

42.9 Engine mounting (rear left-hand)

42.10A Engine mounting stud and nut (right-hand rear)

42.10B Engine mounting wing inner panel bolt (right-hand rear)

42.15A Suspension lower arm inner pivot bolt

42.15B Anti-roll bar ready for installation

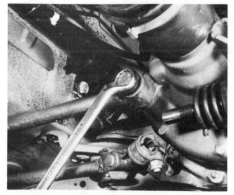
42.16 Connecting the transmission stabiliser rod

42.17 Gearchange rod tension spring

42.18 Sliding the clamp onto the transmission selector shaft

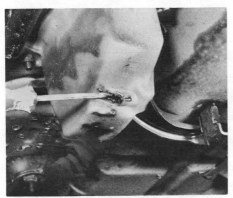

42.19 Locking the gear lever into the selector slide

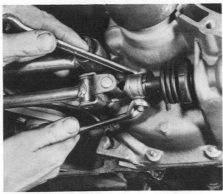

42.20 Tightening the gearchange rod clamp bolt

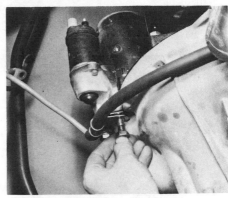

42.22A Starter motor cable clip

42.22B Transmission earthing points

42.24 Manifold heated air box

42.25 Connecting the clutch cable

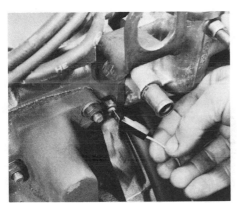

42.26A Coolant temperature sender lead

42.26B Electric fan thermal switch

42.27 Oil pressure switch and lead

42.28 Connecting the lead to the anti-run-on valve

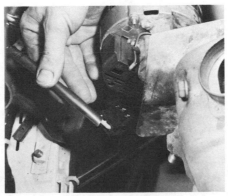

42.29 Alternator connecting plug

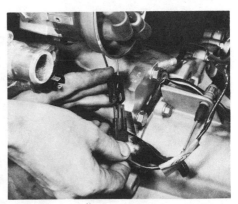

42.30A Distributor LT lead connecting plug

42.30B Ignition coil

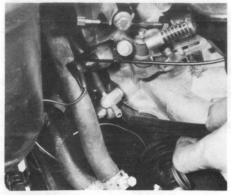

42.30C Manifold vacuum pipe take-off

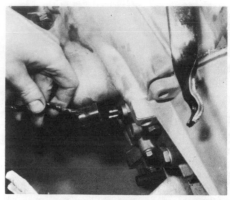

42.31 Connecting the leads to the reversing lamp switch

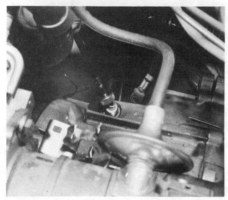

42.32 Speedometer cable connection at transmission

42.33 Connecting the fuel pipe to the fuel pump

42.34 Connecting the brake vacuum pipe to the intake manifold

42.35A Tightening a hose clip

42.35B Heater hose branch connection at rear bulkhead

42.36 Fitting the throttle cable balljoint retaining clip

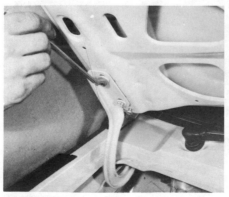

42.38A Bolting up a bonnet hinge

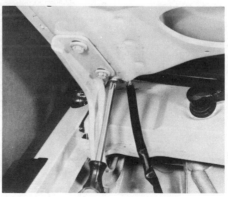

42.38B Bonnet bonding strap screw

21 Engage the engine adaptor plate on its locating dowels and then offer up the flywheel. It will only go on in one position as it has offset holes. Insert new bolts and tighten to the specified torque. The bolts are pre-coated with thread sealant (photos).

22 Fit the clutch and centralise it (refer to Chapter 5).

23 With the engine resting on its side (not inverted unless you are quite sure that the pistons are not projecting from the block), fit the sump, gaskets and sealing strips as described in Section 30.

24 Fit the cylinder head as described in Section 28, using new bolts. Refit the manifolds (photos).

25 Install and tension the timing belt as described in Section 25.

26 Using a new gasket, fit the rocker cover (photo).

27 Reconnect the crankcase ventilation hoses between the rocker cover and the crankcase (photos).

28 Screw in a new set of spark plugs, correctly gapped, and tighten to the specified torque – this is important. If the specified torque is exceeded, the plugs may be impossible to remove.

29 Fit the timing belt cover.

30 Fit the crankshaft pulley and tighten the bolt to the specified torque while the flywheel ring gear is locked to prevent it turning.

31 Smear the sealing ring of a new oil filter with a little grease, and screw it into position using hand pressure only.

32 Install the engine mounting brackets, if removed (photo).

33 Refit the ancillaries. The alternator bracket and alternator (Chapter 11), the fuel pump (Chapter 3), the thermostat housing (Chapter 2), and the distributor (Chapter 4) (photo).

34 Fit the distributor cap and reconnect the HT leads.

35 Check the tightness of the oil drain plug and insert the dipstick.

42 Engine/transmission – reconnection and installation

1 This is a direct reversal of removal and separation of the engine from the transmission. Take care not to damage the radiator or front wings during installation.

Reconnection

2 Check that the clutch driven plate has been centralised as described in Chapter 5.

3 Make sure that the engine adaptor plate is correctly located on its positioning dowels.

4 Smear the splines of the transmission input shaft with a little grease and then, supporting the weight of the transmission, connect it to the engine by passing the input shaft through the splined hub of the clutch plate until the transmission locates on the dowels (photo).

5 Screw in the flange bolts and tighten to the specified torque.

Installation

6 First check that the engine sump drain plug is tight and that the gearbox cap nut (removed to drain the oil) has been refitted with its locking pin and spring (photos).

7 Manoeuvre the engine/transmission under the vehicle and attach a lifting hoist to the engine lugs.

8 Raise the engine/transmission carefully until the engine front left mounting bolt can be located. Fit the insulator and cup to the underside of the mounting bracket and screw on the nut (photo).

9 Fit the left-hand rear mounting (photo).

10 Fit the right-hand rear mounting. Make sure that the sequence of mounting washers and plates is as originally located, and don't forget the wing inner panel bolt which secures the rear mounting, (photos).

11 Release the lifting hoist and remove it.

12 If some sort of plug was used to prevent the differential pinion cage from turning, extract it now. If a plug was not used, insert the finger into the driveshaft hole in the transmission and align the cage ready to receive the driveshaft.

13 Using a new snap-ring, reconnect the left-hand driveshaft to the transmission by applying pressure inwards on the roadwheel. Check that the snap-ring has locked securely in position. It is sometimes difficult to fully engage the driveshaft and its snap-ring in the differential unless the driveshaft is raised to a horizontal attitude. In this case, the hub assembly should be raised and it will be easier to do if the roadwheel is first removed to reduce the weight.

14 Reconnect the left-hand lower arm of the front suspension. Tighten the bolts to the specified torque. When tightening the balljoint pinch-bolt, the bolt head can be prevented from turning by inserting an Allen key into its socket head. Although this is not the correct tool, it

will serve as an alternative. Where the socket is rounded through abuse, mole grips can be used.

15 Refit the driveshaft and suspension lower arm to the opposite side in a similar way to that just described. Reconnect the anti-roll bar (photos).

16 Reconnect the transmission stabiliser rod, making sure to insert the washer between the rod and the transmission casing (photo).

17 Check that the gearchange control lever is still in 4th gear position, and hook the gearchange rod tension spring to the longitudinal body side member (photo).

18 Pull downwards on the gearchange rod and slip it onto the selector shaft which projects from the transmission. The clamp should be loose on the gearchange rod (photo).

19 Using a 3.5 mm (0.14 in) diameter rod or pin, insert it as shown and pull the gear lever downwards to lock it in the selector slide. When inserting the rod, point it upward to 'feel' the cut-out in the gear lever before prising it downwards (photo). Now turn your attention to the gearbox.

20 Using a pin or rod, inserted into the hole in the end of the projecting selector shaft, turn the shaft clockwise to its stop and retain it in this position with a strong rubber band. Now tighten the clamp pinch-bolt (photo).

21 Remove the locking pins and connect the gearchange rod return spring.

22 Reconnect the starter motor and the engine earth leads. Fit the drivebelt plastic cover to the front end of the sump (photos).

23 Refit the exhaust system and connect the exhaust downpipe to the manifold.

24 Fit the heated air box which connects with the air cleaner (photo).

25 Connect the clutch operating cable. No adjustment is required (refer to Chapter 5) (photo).

26 Reconnect the lead to the coolant temperature sender switch and the electric fan sender switch (photos).

27 Reconnect the lead to the oil pressure warning switch (photo).

28 Reconnect the lead to the anti-run-on solenoid valve on the carburettor (photo).

29 Reconnect the alternator leads (photo).

30 Reconnect the distributor LT leads and the HT lead to the ignition coil. Reconnect the distributor vacuum pipe (photos).

31 Reconnect the leads to the reversing lamp switch (photo).

32 Reconnect the speedometer drive cable to the transmission (photo).

33 Reconnect the fuel pipe to the fuel pump (photo).

34 Reconnect the brake vacuum pipe (if so equipped) to the intake manifold (photo).

35 Reconnect the coolant hoses and the heater hoses, including those to the automatic choke housing, and the overflow pipe to the expansion tank (photos).

36 Connect the throttle cable to the carburettor (photo).

37 Fill up with engine oil, transmission oil and coolant, reconnect the battery.

38 Install the bonnet, bolting the hinges to their originally marked positions. Reconnect the bonding strap (for radio interference suppression) (photos).

39 Reconnect the windscreen washer pipe.

40 Fit the air cleaner and reconnect its hoses and air intake spout.

41 Once the engine is running, check the dwell angle (if applicable), timing, idle speed and mixture adjustment (refer to Chapters 3 and 4).

42 If a number of new internal components have been installed, run the vehicle at a restricted speed for the first few hundred miles to allow time for the new components to bed in. It is also recommended that with a new or rebuilt engine, the engine oil and filter are changed at the end of the running-in period.

43 Fault diagnosis (ohc engine)

Refer to Section 21, but (except on 1.1 models) ignore all reference to mechanical type contact breaker points.

Rough engine idling or misfiring may also be caused on ohc engines by a slack or worn timing belt which has jumped a sprocket tooth.

A certain amount of 'chatter' is normal when starting an engine with hydraulic valve lifters, but the noise should disappear as the lifters fill with oil.

Chapter 2
Cooling, heating and ventilation systems

For modifications, and information applicable to later models, see Supplement at end of manual

Contents

Specifications

System type .... Radiator with expansion tank, belt-driven coolant pump and electric radiator fan. Semi-pressurised system on 1.1l engines; fully pressurised on 1.3l and 1.6l engines

Radiator type .... Crossflow, fin on tube

Thermostat
Type .... Wax
Opening temperature .... 85° to 89°C (185° to 193°F)
Fully open temperature .... 99° to 102°C (210° to 216°F)

Coolant pump
Type .... Centrifugal with vee belt drive (ohv) or driven from toothed timing belt (ohc)
Drivebelt tension (ohv) .... 12.5 mm (0.5 in) total deflection at centre of longest run

Pressure cap rating
1.1 .... 0.9 kgf/cm² (13 lbf/in²)
1.3 and 1.6 .... 0.85 kgf/cm² (12 lbf/in²)

Capacity
1.1 ohv .... 5.3 litres (9.3 pints)
1.1 ohc (small radiator) .... 6.2 litres (10.9 pints)
1.1 ohc (large radiator) .... 7.2 litres (12.7 pints)
1.3 ohc .... 7.1 litres (12.5 pints)
1.6 ohc .... 6.9 litres (12.1 pints)

Antifreeze
Recommended concentration (UK) .... 45% by volume

Torque wrench settings

	Nm	lbf ft
Coolant pump bolts	8	6
Radiator mounting bolts	8	6
Thermostat housing bolts:		
ohv	19	14
ohc	8	6
Coolant pump pulley bolts (ohv)	10	7
Fan shroud-to-radiator bolts	8	6
Fan motor-to-shroud nuts	8	6

1 Description

The cooling system on all models comprises a radiator, a coolant pump, a thermostat and an electrically-operated radiator fan. The system is pressurised and incorporates an overflow container.

The system used on the ohv engine differs from that used on the ohc engine in layout and location of components. The coolant pump on the ohv engine is driven by the alternator drivebelt, while the pump on the ohc engines is driven by the toothed timing belt.

The electric radiator fan is controlled by a thermal switch located in the thermostat cover except on early 1.1 engines where the fan operates continuously with the ignition switched on.

The cooling system operates in the following way. When the coolant is cold, the thermostat is shut and coolant flow is restricted to the cylinder block, cylinder head, intake manifold and the vehicle interior heater matrix.

As the temperature of the coolant rises the thermostat opens, allowing initially partial and then full circulation of the coolant through the radiator.

If the vehicle is in forward motion then the inrush of air cools the coolant as it passes across the radiator. If the coolant temperature rises beyond a predetermined level, due for example to ascending a gradient or being held up in a traffic jam, then the electric fan will cut in (not 1.1 with standard equipment) to supplement normal cooling.

On 1.1 engines, coolant expansion is taken care of by a pressure relief valve on the cap of the thermostat housing. This allows coolant to pass through an overflow tube into the expansion tank. As the system cools and coolant is drawn back into the system, the vacuum valve also incorporated in the cap opens to prevent a vacuum condition occurring.

On 1.3 and 1.6 engines, the expansion tank is of degas type and the necessary pressure/vacuum relief valve is incorporated in the tank cap.

2 Maintenance

1.1 engines

1   At the intervals recommended in Routine Maintenance at the beginning of this manual, visually check the coolant level in the expansion tank. If topping up is required, use antifreeze mixture of the same strength as the original coolant used for filling the system.
2   Only top up the expansion tank, *do not remove the cap from the thermostat housing.*
3   Regularly inspect all coolant hoses for security of clips and for evidence of deterioration of the hoses.
4   Frequent topping up of the system will indicate a leak, as under normal conditions the addition of coolant is a rare occurrence.
5   At specified intervals check the tension of the coolant pump drivebelt (ohv engines only) and adjust if necessary (see Section 11).

1.3 and 1.6 engines

6   The maintenance procedure is similar to that described for the 1.1 engine except that if the addition of coolant is required to the expansion tank and the engine is hot, *remove the pressure cap from the expansion tank very carefully,* having first covered it with a cloth to prevent any possibility of scalding.
7   Top up to between the marks on the tank.
8   No attention will be needed to the coolant pump drive alone as on these engines, the pump is driven by the toothed timing bolt.
9   If the electric radiator cooling fan has not been heard to operate for some time, a simple test can be carried out to check that the fan motor is serviceable. Switch on the ignition and pull the lead from the temperature sensor which is screwed into the thermostat housing. Bridge the two contacts of the lead connecting plug, when the fan should operate. Although this test does not of course prove the function of the temperature switch, the switch is unlikely to be faulty if there has been an indication of normal temperature during the preceding period of motoring.

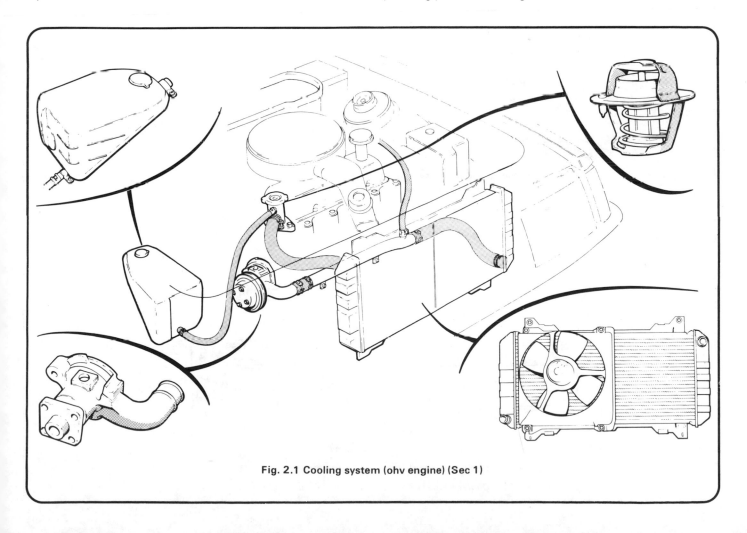

Fig. 2.1 Cooling system (ohv engine) (Sec 1)

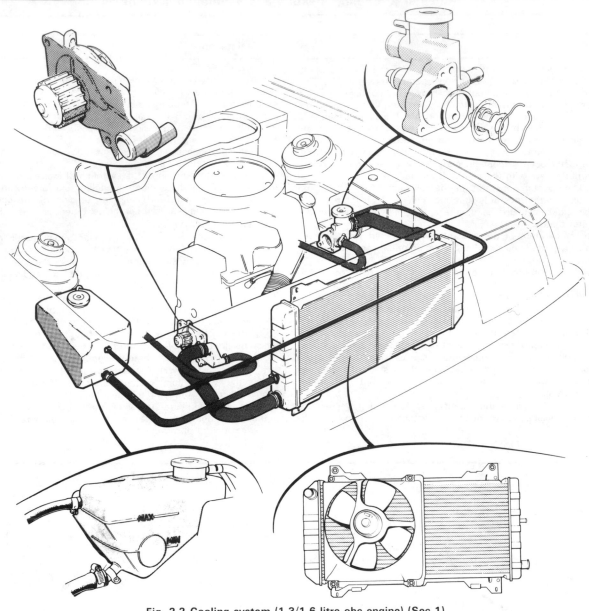

Fig. 2.2 Cooling system (1.3/1.6 litre ohc engine) (Sec 1)

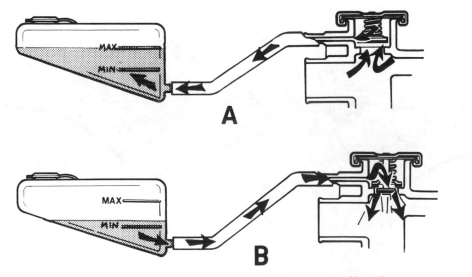

Fig. 2.3 Expansion tank/pressure cap operating modes (Sec 1)

A   Coolant expansion   B   Coolant contraction

All engines

10 Renew the coolant (antifreeze) mixture at the intervals specified in Routine Maintenance.

Safety note

11 Take particular care when working under the bonnet with the engine running, or ignition switched on, on vehicles fitted with a temperature-controlled radiator cooling fan. As the coolant temperature rises the fan may suddenly actuate so make sure that ties, clothing, hair and hands are away from the fan. Remember that the coolant temperature will continue to rise for a short time after the engine is switched off.

---

3 Cooling system – draining, flushing and refilling

1 It is preferable to drain the system when the coolant is cold. If it must be drained when hot, release the pressure cap very slowly, having first covered it with a cloth to avoid any possibility of scalding.
2 Set the heater control to maximum heat position.
3 Place a container under the radiator and release the bottom hose. Allow the system to drain.
4 Provided the coolant is of the correct antifreeze mixture then no flushing should be necessary and the system can be refilled immediately as described below.
5 Where the system has been neglected however, and rust or sludge is evident at draining, then the system should be flushed through with a cold water hose inserted into the thermostat housing (thermostat

removed – see Section 5 or 6) until the water flows clean from the disconnected bottom hose and the radiator.
6 In severe cases, the drain plug on the cylinder block can be unscrewed to assist sludge removal and flushing (photo).
7 If the radiator is suspected of being clogged, remove it and reverse flush it as described in Section 8.
8 When the coolant is being changed, it is recommended that the overflow pipe is disconnected from the expansion tank and the coolant drained from the tank. If the interior of the tank is dirty, remove it and thoroughly clean it out. Evidence of oil within the expansion tank may indicate a leaking cylinder head gasket.
9 Reconnect the radiator and expansion tank hoses, and refit the cylinder block drain plug (if removed).
10 Using the correct antifreeze mixture, fill the system through the thermostat housing filler neck slowly until the coolant is nearly overflowing. Wait a few moments for trapped air to escape and add more coolant. Repeat until the level does not drop and refit the cap.
11 Pour similar strength coolant into the expansion tank up to the level marked and fit the cap. Start the engine and run it to normal operating temperature. Once it has cooled, check and carry out any final topping up *to the expansion tank only*.

---

4 Coolant mixtures – general

1 Never operate the vehicle with plain water in the cooling system. Apart from the danger of freezing during winter conditions, an important secondary purpose of antifreeze is to inhibit the formation of

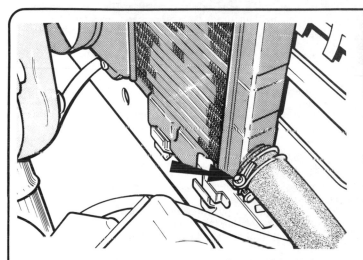

Fig. 2.4 Radiator bottom hose clip (arrowed) (Sec 3)

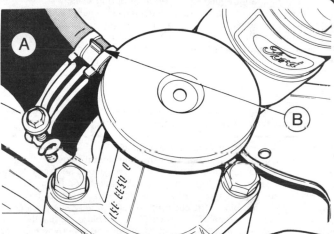

Fig. 2.5 Thermostat housing (ohv) (Sec 5)

A   Radiator top hose   B   Expansion tank hose

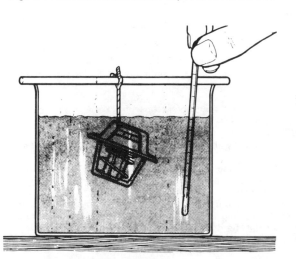

Fig. 2.6 Checking the thermostat (Sec 5)

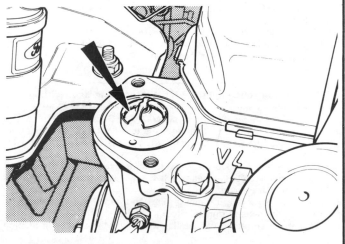

Fig. 2.7 Thermostat (ohv) arrowed (Sec 5)

3.6 Cylinder block drain plug

rust and to reduce corrosion. This is particularly important with the ohc engine which has an alloy cylinder head.

2   Use a reliable brand of antifreeze with a glycol base – never one containing methanol which will evaporate during use.

3   Renew the coolant at the specified intervals. Although the antifreeze properties of the coolant will remain indefinitely, the effectiveness of the rust and corrosion inhibitors will gradually weaken.

4   Even in climates where antifreeze is not required, never use plain water but use one of the branded corrosion inhibitors available.

5   A percentage of 45% antifreeze will protect the system adequately against all danger from frost, rust and corrosion.

5 Thermostat (ohv engine) – removal, testing and refitting

1   Drain the cooling system as described in Section 3.

2   Disconnect the two hoses from the thermostat housing.

3   Unbolt and remove the thermostat housing bolts and remove the cover. If it is stuck tight, tap it off with a plastic-faced hammer.

4   Extract the thermostat. If it is stuck tight in its seat, do not lever it out by its bridge piece but cut round it with a very sharp knife.

5   To test the thermostat, first check that in a cold condition its valve plate is closed. Suspend it in a pan of water and gradually heat the water; at or near boiling the valve plate should be fully open. A more accurate assessment of the opening and closing points of the thermostat can be made if a suitable thermometer is placed in the water and results compared with the temperatures given in the Specifications. Check that the thermostat closes again as the water cools down.

6   Refitting is a reversal of removal. Always use a new gasket and apply a little jointing compound to the threads of the thermostat housing bolts before screwing them in.

6 Thermostat (ohc engine) – removal, testing and refitting

1   Drain the cooling system as described in Section 3.

2   Disconnect the three hoses from the thermostat housing (photos).

3   Disconnect the lead from the fan thermal switch on the thermostat housing.

4   Unscrew and remove the three bolts and remove the thermostat housing from the cylinder head. If it is stuck, tap it off gently with a plastic-faced hammer (photo).

5   Extract the spring retaining ring and remove the thermostat followed by its sealing ring (photos).

6   Test the thermostat in a similar way to that described in Section 5.

7   Refitting is a reversal of removal. Always use a new sealing ring and apply jointing compound to the threads of the thermostat housing securing bolts. Never use the old joint gasket.

7 Radiator fan – removal and refitting

1   Disconnect the battery.

2   Pull the wiring connector plug from the rear of the fan motor and unclip the wiring from the fan cowl (photo).

3   Unscrew the two fan retaining bolts from the base of the cowl, followed by the two upper bolts.

4   Carefully lift the fan assembly from the engine compartment, taking care not to damage the radiator.

5   Extract the retaining circlip and take off the fan from the motor shaft.

6   Unscrew the three nuts and separate the motor from the shroud.

7   Reassembly and refitting are reversals of the removal and dismantling operations.

8 Radiator – removal, repair and refitting

1   Drain the cooling system as described in Section 3. Retain the coolant if it is fit for further service.

2   Release the retaining clips and disconnect all the hoses from the radiator (photo).

3   Disconnect the wiring plug from the rear of the radiator fan motor.

4   Unscrew and remove the two mounting bolts and carefully lift the radiator, complete with cowl and fan, from the engine compartment. The base of the radiator is held in place by lugs (photos).

5   If the purpose of removal was to thoroughly clean the radiator, first reverse flush it with a cold water hose. The normal coolant flow is from left to right (from the thermostat housing to the radiator) through the matrix and out of the opposite side.

6   If the radiator fins are clogged with flies or dirt, remove them with a soft brush or blow compressed air from the rear face of the radiator. It is recommended that the fan assembly is first removed as described in the preceding Section. In the absence of a compressed air line, a strong jet from a water hose may provide an alternative method of cleaning.

7   If the radiator is leaking, it is recommended that a reconditioned or new one is obtained from specialists. Home repairs are seldom successful. If the radiator, due to neglect, requires the application of chemical cleaners, then these are best used when the engine is hot and the radiator is in the vehicle. Follow the manufacturer's instructions precisely and appreciate that there is an element of risk in the use of most de-scaling products, especially in a system which incorporates alloy and plastic materials.

8   Refit the radiator by reversing the removal operations, but make sure that the rubber lug insulators at its base are in position.

9   Fill the system as described in Section 3.

9 Coolant pump (ohv engine) – removal and refitting

1   Drain the cooling system as described in Section 3.

2   Release the coolant pump pulley bolts now while the drivebelt is still in position. Any tendency for the pulley to turn as the bolts are unscrewed can be restrained by depressing the top run of the belt.

3   Release the alternator mounting and adjuster link bolts, push the alternator in towards the engine and slip the drivebelt from the coolant pump pulley.

4   Disconnect the coolant hose from the pump. Remove the previously slackened pulley bolts and take off the pulley.

5   Unbolt the coolant pump and remove it.

6   Peel away the old gasket from the engine block and clean the surface.

7   No provision is made for repair and if the pump is leaking or noisy, it should be renewed.

8   Refitting is a reversal of removal. Use a new gasket, smeared with jointing compound, and apply the same compound to the threads of the fixing bolts. Tighten the bolts to the specified torque.

9   Adjust the drivebelt tension as described in Section 11 and refill the cooling system.

10 Coolant pump (ohc engine) – removal and refitting

1   Drain the cooling system as described in Section 3.

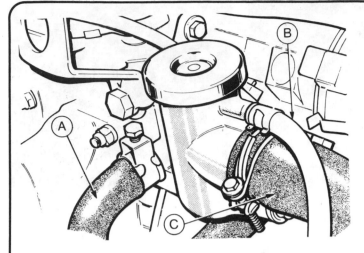

Fig. 2.8 Thermostat housing (ohc) (Sec 6)

A   Heater hose   C   Radiator hose
B   Expansion tank hose

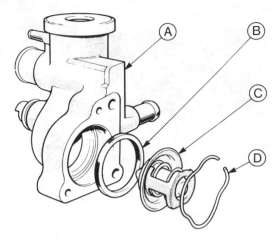

Fig. 2.9 Thermostat fitting components (ohc) (Sec 6)

A   Housing   C   Thermostat
B   Sealing ring   D   Retaining clip

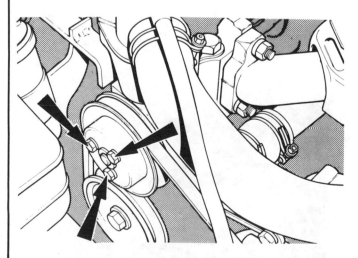

Fig. 2.10 Fan cowl and radiator mounting bolts (Sec 7)

A   Radiator bolts   B   Fan cowl bolts

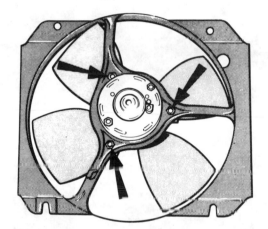

Fig. 2.11 Fan motor mounting nuts (arrowed) (Sec 7)

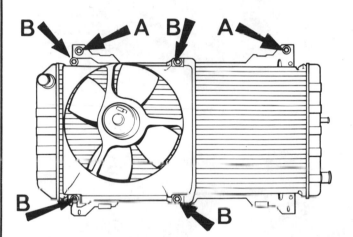

Fig. 2.12 Coolant pump pulley bolts, arrowed (ohv) (Sec 9)

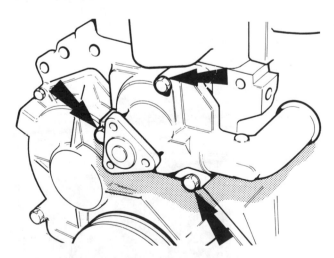

Fig. 2.13 Coolant pump mounting bolts (ohv) arrowed (Sec 9)

6.2A Disconnecting coolant hose from thermostat housing (ohc)

6.2B Disconnecting heater hose from thermostat housing (ohc)

6.2C Disconnecting radiator hose from thermostat housing (ohc)

6.4 Removing the thermostat housing (ohc)

6.5A Thermostat retaining clip (ohc)

6.5B Removing the thermostat (ohc)

6.5C Thermostat sealing ring (ohc)

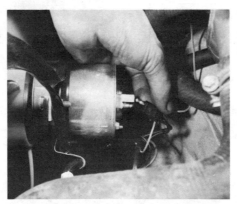

7.2 Radiator fan motor plug

8.2 Releasing radiator hose clip

8.4A Unbolting the radiator

8.4B Removing the radiator

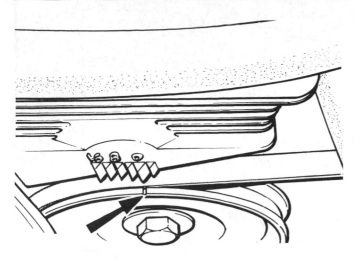

Fig. 2.14 TDC marks (ohc) (Sec 10)

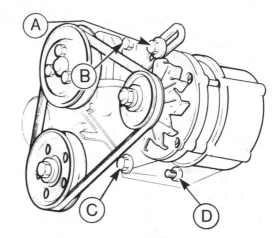

Fig. 2.15 Alternator adjuster and mounting bolts (Sec 11)

A   Adjuster link clamp bolt   C   Lower front mounting bolt
B   Adjuster link-to-block bolt   D   Lower rear mounting bolt

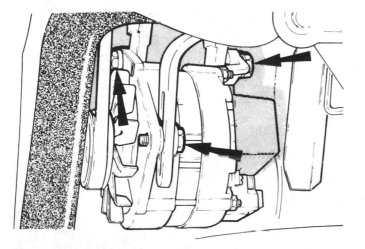

Fig. 2.16 Alternator and adjuster link bolts, arrowed (ohc) (Sec 11)

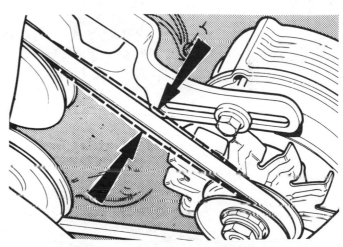

Fig. 2.17 Drivebelt tension checking points (Sec 11)

2   Release the alternator mountings and adjuster strap bolt, push the alternator in towards the engine and slip the drivebelt from the pulley.
3   Apply a spanner to the crankshaft pulley bolt and turn the crankshaft until the notch on the pulley is opposite the tdc mark on the belt cover scale.
4   Remove the timing belt cover and check that the camshaft and the crankshaft sprockets are aligned with their timing marks (see Chapter 1). This will prove that No 1 piston is at tdc, not No 4 piston. If the marks are not aligned, turn the crankshaft through another complete turn.
5   Using a spot of quick-drying paint, mark the teeth of the belt and their notches on the sprockets so that the belt can be re-engaged in its original position in relation to the sprocket teeth.
6   Slacken the belt tensioner bolts and slide the tensioner to relieve the tautness of the belt, then slip the belt from the crankshaft sprocket, tensioner pulley and the coolant pump sprocket.
7   Release the clamps and disconnect the hoses from the coolant pump.
8   Remove the timing belt tensioner.
9   Unscrew the four bolts and remove the coolant pump from the engine cylinder block.
10 Clean away the old gasket and ensure that the mating surfaces of the pump and block are perfectly clean.
11 Position a new gasket (on the cylinder block) which has been smeared both sides with jointing compound. Offer up the coolant pump, screw in the bolts and tighten to the specified torque.

12 Fit the belt tensioner, but with the mounting bolts only screwed in loosely.
13 Reconnect and tension the timing belt as described in Chapter 1, Section 25.
14 Refit the timing belt cover.
15 Fit the alternator drivebelt and tension it as described in the next Section.
16 Reconnect the coolant hoses to the pump and the bottom hose to the radiator.
17 Fill the cooling system as described in Section 3.

11 Drivebelt – removal, refitting and tensioning

1   A conventional vee drivebelt is used to drive the alternator and coolant pump pulleys on ohv engines, and the alternator pulley on ohc engines, power being transmitted from a pulley on the front end of the crankshaft.
2   To remove a belt, slacken the alternator mounting bolts and the bolts on the adjuster link, push the alternator in towards the engine and slip the belt from the pulleys.
3   Fit the belt by slipping it over the pulley rims while the alternator is still loose on its mountings. Never be tempted to remove or fit a belt by prising it over a pulley without releasing the alternator. Either the pulley will be damaged or the alternator or coolant pump will be distorted.

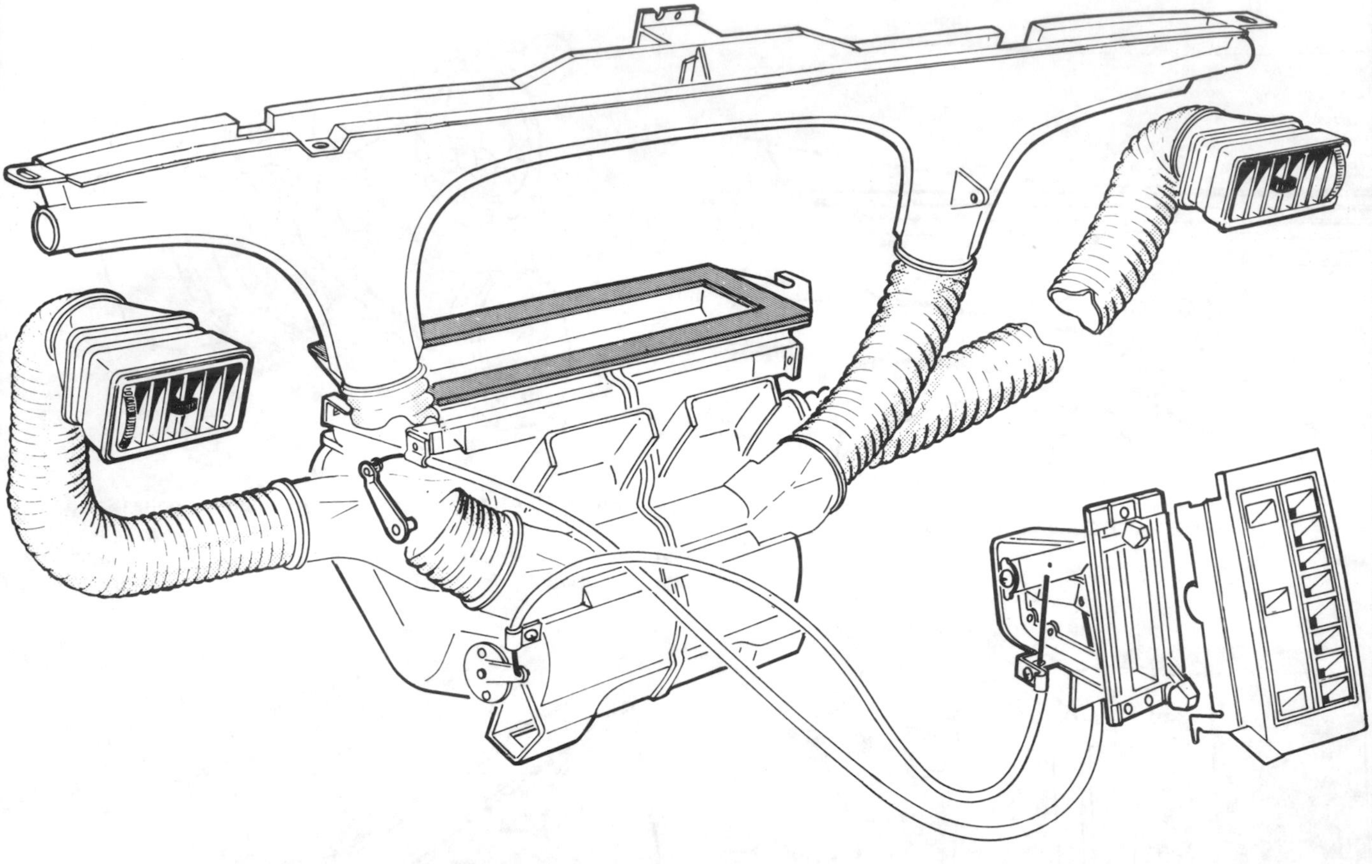

Fig. 2.18 Heater/ventilation system – Base model (Sec 12)

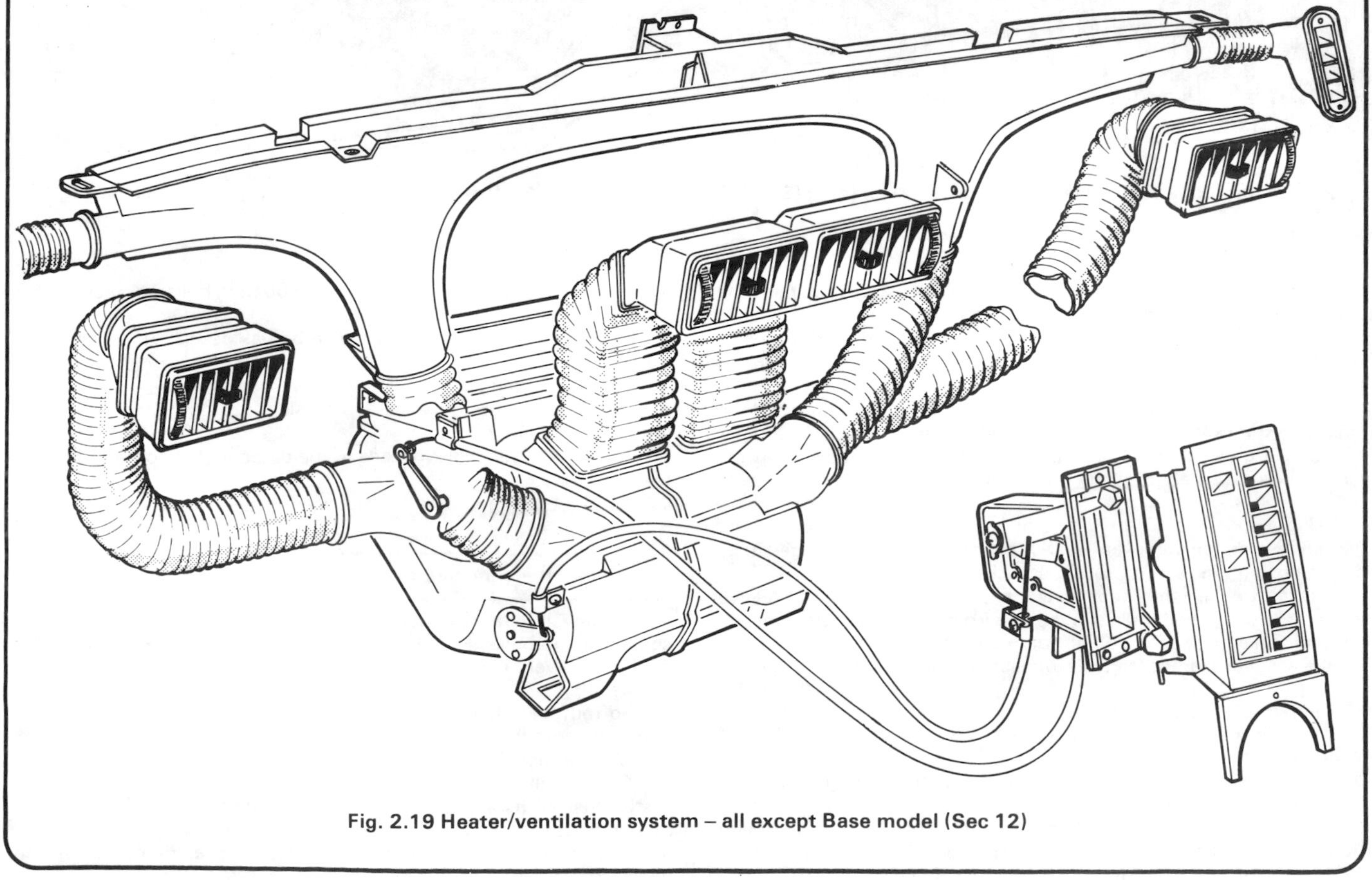

Fig. 2.19 Heater/ventilation system – all except Base model (Sec 12)

4   To retension the belt, pull the alternator away from the engine until the belt is fairly taut and nip up the adjuster strap bolt. Check that the total deflection of the belt is 12.5 mm (0.5 in) at the mid point of its longest run. A little trial and error may be required to obtain the correct tension. If the belt is too slack, it will slip and soon become glazed or burnt and the coolant pump (ohv) and alternator will not perform correctly, with consequent overheating of the engine and low battery charge. If the belt is too tight, the bearings in the alternator and/or coolant pump will soon be damaged.

5   Do not lever against the body of the alternator to tension the belt or damage may occur.

12 Heating and ventilation system – description

The heater is of the type which utilises waste heat from the engine coolant. The coolant is pumped through the matrix in the heater casing where air, force-fed by a duplex radial fan, disperses the heat into the vehicle interior.

Fresh air enters the heater or the ventilator ducts through the grille at the rear of the bonnet lid. Air is extracted from the interior of the vehicle through outlets at the rear edges of the doors.

There are differences between the heater used on Base models and other versions in the Escort range. On Base models, a two-speed fan switch is used instead of the three-position switch used on other versions. On all models except the Base version, central and side window vents are incorporated in the facia panel.

The heater/ventilator controls are of lever type, operating through cables to flap valves which deflect the air flowing through the heater both to vary the temperature and to distribute the air between the footwell and demister outlets.

13 Heater controls – adjustment

1   Incorrect airflow direction is most likely to be due to the control cables being out of adjustment. Adjust the cables as follows.
2   Set both the control levers at about 2.0 mm (0.08 in) up from their lowest setting.
3   Release the securing bolts on the cable clamps and pull the temperature control and air direction flap valve arms to the COLD and CLOSED positions respectively. Check to see that the setting of the levers on the control panel has not changed and retighten the cable clamps.

14 Heater controls – removal and refitting

1   Working inside the vehicle, remove the dash lower trim panel from the right-hand side. The panel is secured by two metal tags and two clips.
2   Detach the air ducts from the right-hand side of the heater casing and swivel them to clear the control cables.
3   Disconnect the control cables from the heater casing.
4   Giving a sharp jerk, pull the knobs from the control levers on the facia panel, then press the control indicator plate downwards and remove it.
5   Unscrew and remove the two screws which are now exposed and which hold the control lever assembly in position.
6   Carefully withdraw the control unit with the cables from the facia and disconnect the wire from the illumination lamp.
7   Refitting is a reversal of removal. On completion, adjust as described in the preceding Section.

15 Heater – removal and refitting

1   Disconnect the battery earth lead.
2   Working within the engine compartment, disconnect the coolant hoses from the heater pipe stubs at the rear bulkhead. Raise the ends of the hoses to minimise loss of coolant.
3   The heater matrix will still contain coolant and should be drained by blowing into the upper heater pipe stub and catching the coolant which will be ejected from the lower one.
4   Remove the cover plate and gasket from around the heater pipe

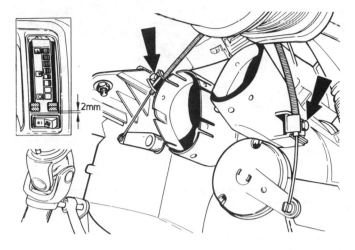

Fig. 2.20 Heater control cable connections (arrowed) (Sec 13)

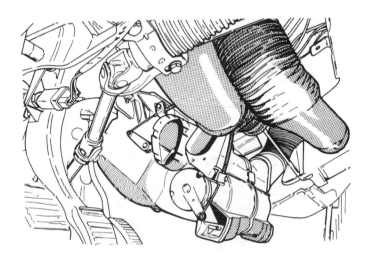

Fig. 2.21 Heater air ducts disconnected (Sec 14)

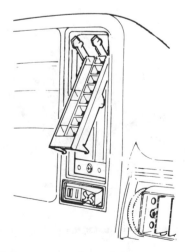

Fig. 2.22 Heater control panel plate removal (Sec 14)

stubs. This is held to the bulkhead by two self-tapping screws.

5   Working inside the vehicle, remove the dash lower trim panels from both sides. The panels are held in position by clips and tags.

6   Pull the air distribution ducts from the heater casing and swivel them as necessary to clear the control cables.

7   Disconnect the control cables from the heater casing and the flap arms.

8   Remove the two heater mounting nuts and lift the heater assembly out of the vehicle, taking care not to spill any remaining coolant on the carpet.

9   Refitting is a reversal of removal. Check that the heater casing seal to the cowl is in good order, otherwise renew it. Adjust the heater controls on completion as described in Section 13.

10 Top up the cooling system (Section 3) and reconnect the battery.

17.3 Heater motor/fan (cover removed)

16 Heater casing – dismantling and reassembly

1   With the heater removed from the vehicle as previously described, extract the two securing screws and slide the matrix out of the heater casing.

2   If further dismantling is necessary, cut the casing seal at the casing joint, prise off any securing clips and separate the two halves of the casing.

3   Remove the air flap valves. It should be noted that the lever for the air distribution valve can only be removed when the mark on the lever is in alignment with the one on the gearwheel.

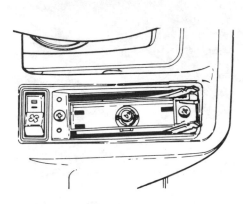

Fig. 2.23 Heater control unit securing screws (Sec 14)

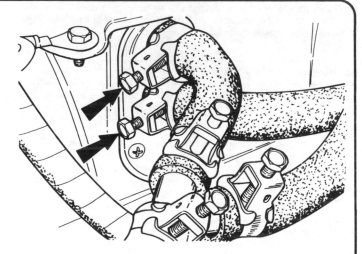

Fig. 2.24 Heater hose connections at bulkhead (arrowed) (Sec 15)

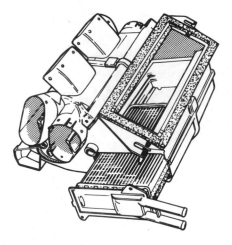

Fig. 2.25 Withdrawing heater matrix from casing (Sec 16)

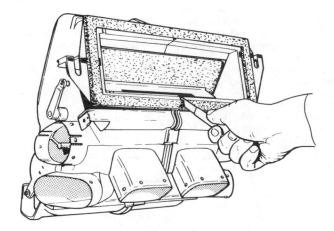

Fig. 2.26 Cutting heater casing seal (Sec 16)

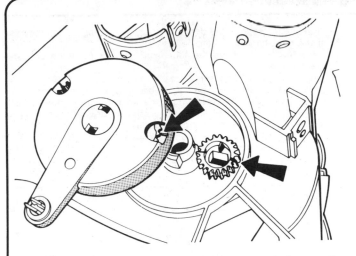

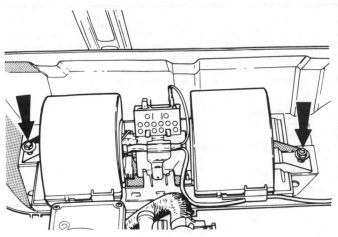

Fig. 2.27 Air distribution valve lever and gear marks (arrowed) (Sec 16)

Fig. 2.28 Heater motor/fan mounting bolts (arrowed) (Sec 17)

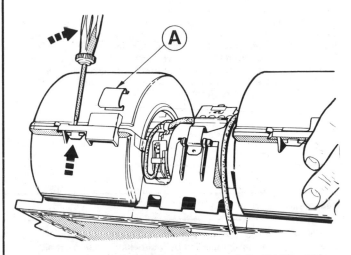

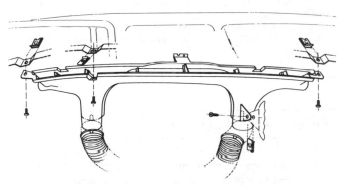

Fig. 2.29 Removing heater fan cover and clip (A) (Sec 17)

Fig. 2.30 Demister nozzle fixing screw locations (Sec 18)

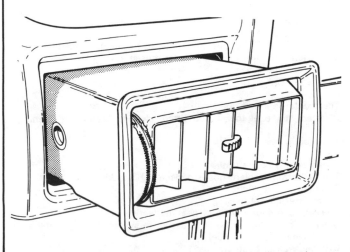

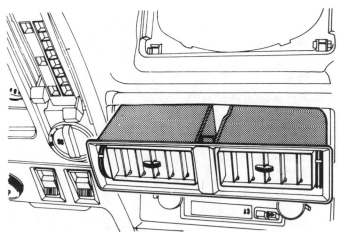

Fig. 2.31 Removing a face level vent nozzle (Sec 19)

Fig. 2.32 Removing the face level centre vent (Sec 20)

4   If the heater matrix is leaking, it is best to obtain a new or reconditioned unit. Home repairs are seldom successful. A blocked matrix can sometimes be cleared using a cold water hose and reverse flushing, but avoid the use of searching chemical cleaners.

5   Reassembly is a reversal of removal. Take care not to damage the fins or tubes of the matrix when inserting it into the casing.

17 Heater motor/fan – removal and refitting

1   Open the bonnet, disconnect the battery and pull off the rubber seal which seals the air intake duct to the bonnet lid when the lid is closed.

2   Prise off the five spring clips from the plenum chamber cover and detach the cover at the front.

3   Disconnect the wiring harness multi-plug and the earth lead at its body connection adjacent to the heater pipe stub cover plate on the engine compartment bulkhead (photo).

4   Unscrew and remove the fan housing mounting nuts and lift the housing from the engine compartment.

5   Insert the blade of a screwdriver and prise off the securing clips so that the fan covers can be removed.

6   Remove the resistor and lift out the motor/fan assembly.

7   Reassembly and refitting are reversals of dismantling and removal.

18 Demister nozzle – removal and refitting

1   Disconnect the battery earth lead.

2   Remove the dash lower trim panels.

3   Remove the shrouds from the upper part of the steering column. The upper section of the shroud is secured by one screw while the lower one is held by three screws.

4   Remove the instrument cluster cowl and the instrument cluster as described in Chapter 11.

5   Pull the hoses from the demister nozzles and then detach the hose from the right-hand side vent.

6   Unscrew and remove the four fixing screws from the demister nozzle assembly.

7   As the upper fixing screw of the crash pad also secures the demister nozzle, the crash pad must be removed by extracting four screws. One screw is located under the ashtray, one screw at each windscreen pillar and after pulling the crash pad forward the last screw may be extracted, also releasing the demister nozzle.

8   Remove the demister by drawing it downward and to the side with the front door wide open.

9   Refitting is a reversal of the removal procedure.

19 Face level vent (right or left-hand) – removal and refitting

1   Remove the dash lower trim panels.

2   Reach up behind the facia panel and pull the hose from the vent nozzle.

3   Apply pressure to the rear of the nozzle to eject it from the front of the facia.

4   Refit by reversing the removal operations.

20 Face level vent (centre) – removal and refitting

1   Prise up the loudspeaker grille and remove it from its spring clips. Extract the speaker mounting screws and withdraw the speaker (if fitted) until the leads can be disconnected and the speaker removed.

2   Pull the hoses from the centre vent assembly by inserting the hand into the aperture left by removal of the loudspeaker grille.

3   Extract the screw which secures the rear of the centre vent and push the vent out of the front of the facia panel.

4   Refitting is the reverse of the removal procedure.

21 Fault diagnosis – cooling system

Symptom	Reason(s)
Heat generated in engine not being successfully disposed of by radiator	Insufficient water in cooling system Drivebelt slipping (accompanied by a shrieking noise on rapid engine acceleration) – ohv only Radiator core blocked or radiator grille restricted Bottom coolant hose collapsed, impeding flow Thermostat not opening properly Ignition timing incorrect or automatic advance malfunctioning (accompanied by loss of power and perhaps misfiring) Carburettor incorrectly adjusted (mixture too weak) Exhaust system partially blocked Oil level in sump too low Blown cylinder head gasket (water/steam being forced down the expansion tank overflow pipe under pressure) Engine not yet run-in Brakes binding
Too much heat being dispersed by radiator	Thermostat jammed open Incorrect grade of thermostat fitted allowing premature opening of valve Thermostat missing
Leaks in system	Loose clips on water hoses Top or bottom coolant hoses perished and leaking Radiator core leaking Thermostat gasket leaking Pressure cap spring worn or seal ineffective Blown cylinder head gasket (pressure in system forcing water/steam down expansion tank pipe) Cylinder wall or head cracked
Oil in expansion tank (may be ignored if slight oil deposit present initially after major overhaul or decarbonising)	Blown cylinder head gasket Cracked head or block

22 Fault diagnosis – heating and ventilating system

Symptom	Reason(s)
Lack of heat in vehicle interior, poor air distribution or demisting/defrosting capability	Thermostat faulty or of incorrect type Heater matrix blocked Coolant pump not operating due to slipping belt (ohv) or eroded impeller Incorrectly adjusted heater controls Blower motor inoperative due to blown fuse or other fault Disconnected ducts or hoses for air distribution Overcooling in cold weather by continuously running radiator fan Deteriorated seal at bonnet lid-to-air intake.

Chapter 3 Fuel and exhaust systems

For modifications, and information applicable to later models, refer to Supplement at end of manual

Contents

Specifications

System type .... Rear mounted fuel tank, mechanically-operated fuel pump, thermostatically controlled air cleaner and Ford variable venturi (VV) or Weber dual venturi (2V) carburettor

Fuel tank
Capacity .... 40 litres (8.8 gallons)

Fuel grade
1.1 LC engine .... 91 octane
1.1, 1.3 and 1.6 HC engines .... 97 octane

Fuel pump
Type .... Non-repairable, camshaft driven

Air cleaner
Element type .... Paper, disposable
Heat sensor rating:
  With Ford VV carburettor .... 20°C (68°F) ± 2°C (3°F)
  With Weber 2V carburettor .... 28°C (82°F) ± 2°C (3°F)

Carburettors
Types:
  Ford variable venturi (VV) .... Downdraught with sonic idle circuit, coolant-heated automatic choke and anti-run-on valve
  Weber dual venturi (2V) .... Fixed jet with electrically-heated automatic choke and anti-run-on valve

Engine	Carburettor number
1.1 ohv	79BF–9510–KCB
1.1 ohc	81SF–9510–KAA
1.3 ohc	81SF–9510–KCA
1.6 ohc	81SF–9510–KFA
1.6 ohc (certain versions only)	81SF–9510–AA

Application:
  Ford VV .... 1.1 ohv / 1.1 ohc / 1.3 ohc / 1.6 ohc
  Weber 2V .... 1.6 ohc (certain versions only)

Ford carburettor tuning data
Idle speed .... 750 to 850 rpm (fan in operation)
Idle mixture setting (CO level) .... 1.0 to 2.0%
Main metering rod:
  1.1 ohv .... FCH
  1.1 ohc .... FDA
  1.3 ohc .... FDK
  1.6 ohc .... FCX

Weber carburettor tuning data
Idle speed .... 775 to 825 rpm (fan in operation)
Idle mixture setting (CO level) .... 1.0 to 1.50%
Fast idle setting (high cam) .... 2600 to 2800 rpm

Float level setting	35.0 mm (1.38 in)
Throttle barrel diameter	32/34
Venturi diameter	24/25
Main jet	112/125
Air jet	160/150
Emulsion tube	F30/F30
Idle jet	50/60

Torque wrench settings

	Nm	lbf ft
Carburettor flange nuts:		
Ford	19	14
Weber	20	15
Exhaust manifold-to-downpipe nuts:		
1.1	38	28
1.3 and 1.6	44	32
Exhaust downpipe-to-main system coupling (1.3 and 1.6 only)	44	32
Exhaust joint U-bolts	44	32
Fuel pump mounting bolts	18	13

1 Description

The fuel system on all models comprises a rear-mounted fuel tank, a mechanical fuel pump, a carburettor and an air cleaner.

The type of carburettor varies between the different engines used (see Specifications). An automatic choke is fitted to all versions.

The idle mixture screw is of tamperproof type and no adjustment of the fuel/air mixture is normally required as the carburettors are set during production to comply with current regulations governing exhaust emissions.

2 Fuel pump – cleaning

1 At the intervals specified in Routine Maintenance, the filter in the fuel pump should be cleaned.
2 To do this, place a piece of rag around the pump body to catch the fuel which will drain out when the cover is removed.
3 Unscrew and remove the single cover screw and lift off the cover.
4 Take out the rubber sealing ring and the filter screen from inside the cover.
5 Clean the screen by brushing it in clean fuel, then fit it into the cover, noting the projections on some screens which centralise it.
6 Fit the sealing ring. If it is not in good order, renew it.
7 Locate the cover on the pump body. On some pumps, the cover is correctly installed when the notch in the cover engages in the groove in the pump body.
8 Screw in the retaining screw, but do not overtighten it provided it is making a good seal.

3 Fuel pump – testing, removal and refitting

1 The fuel pump may be quite simply tested by disconnecting the fuel inlet pipe from the carburettor and placing its open end in a container.
2 Disconnect the LT lead from the negative terminal of the ignition coil to prevent the engine firing.
3 Actuate the starter motor. Regular well-defined spurts of fuel should be seen being ejected from the open end of the fuel inlet pipe.
4 Where this is not evident and yet there is fuel in the tank, the pump is in need of renewal. The pump is a sealed unit and cannot be dismantled or repaired.
5 On ohv engines, the fuel pump is mounted on the cylinder block and is actuated by a lever which is in direct contact with an eccentric cam on the camshaft.
6 On ohc engines, the pump is mounted on the cylinder head and is actuated by a push-rod from an eccentric cam on the camshaft.
7 To remove the pump, disconnect and plug the fuel inlet and outlet hoses at the pump and then unbolt it from the engine (photos).
8 Retain any insulating spacers and remove and discard the flange gaskets.
9 On ohc engines, withdraw the push-rod with coil spring (photo).

10 Refitting is a reversal of removal, but use new flange gaskets. If crimped type hose clips were used originally, these will have been destroyed when disconnecting the fuel hoses. Renew them with conventional nut and screw or plastic ratchet type clips.

4 Air cleaner – description

1 The air cleaner is of renewable paper element type, and is thermostatically controlled to provide air at the most suitable temperature for combustion with minimum emission levels.
2 This is accomplished by drawing in both cold and hot air (from the exhaust manifold box) and mixing them. The proportion of hot and cold air is varied by the position of a deflector flap which itself is controlled by a vacuum diaphragm. The vacuum pressure is monitored by a heat sensor within the air cleaner casing to ensure that according to the temperature requirements of the carburettor, the appropriate degree of intake manifold vacuum is applied to the air deflector flap to alter the volume of hot or cold air being admitted (photo).

5 Air cleaner element – renewal

1 A circular or oval type air cleaner may be fitted according to vehicle model, engine capacity and carburettor.
2 To remove the lid of the round type air cleaner, extract the three screws (photo).
3 Remove and discard the paper element and wipe out the air cleaner casing (photo).
4 Place the new element in position and refit the lid.
5 Renewal of the oval type element is similar, except that the lid is held by two bolts.

6 Air cleaner – removal and refitting

Round type
1 Unscrew and remove the two larger headed screws from the cover.
2 The air cleaner assembly can now be lifted off the carburettor sufficiently far to be able to disconnect the vacuum hose, the crankcase (flame trap) emission hose and the cold air intake duct.

Oval type
3 The procedure is similar to that just described, but there are three securing bolts which hold the air cleaner to its mounting struts.
4 The air intake is held to the radiator grille support rail by two self-tapping screws, but this does not normally require removal.

Both types
5 Refitting of both types is a reversal of removal.

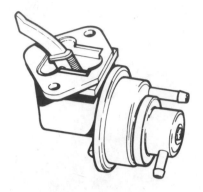

Fig. 3.1 Fuel pump (ohv engine type) (Sec 2)

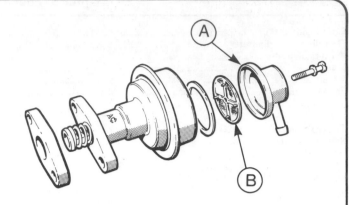

Fig. 3.2 Fuel pump (ohc engine type) (Sec 2)

A   Cover   B   Filter screen

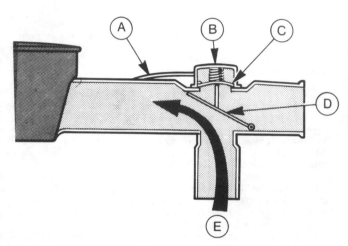

Fig. 3.3 Air cleaner flap valve under high vacuum conditions
(Sec 4)

A   Vacuum pipe to heat sensor   D   Flap valve
B   Diaphragm unit   E   Hot air flow
C   Diaphragm

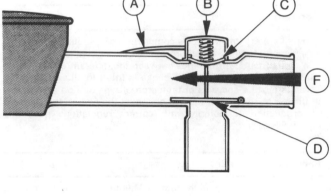

Fig. 3.4 Air cleaner flap valve under low vacuum conditions
(Sec 4)

A   Vacuum pipe to heat sensor   D   Flap valve
B   Diaphragm unit   F   Cool air flow
C   Diaphragm

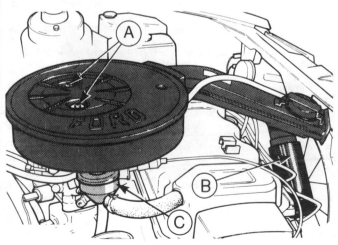

Fig. 3.5 Circular type air cleaner (Sec 5)

A   Air cleaner fixing screws   C   Crankcase ventilation flame
B   Heated air intake   trap

Fig. 3.6 Oval type air cleaner (Sec 5)

A   Fixing bolts   B   Heated air intake

3.7A Unbolting fuel pump (ohc)

3.7B Removing fuel pump (ohc)

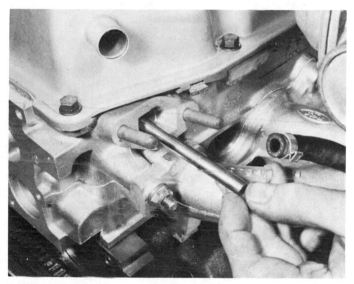

3.9 Withdrawing fuel pump operating rod (ohc)

4.2 Air cleaner intake ducts

5.2 Removing air cleaner lid screws

5.3 Air cleaner element

7 Fuel tank – removal and refitting

Passenger vehicles

1 The fuel tank will normally only need to be removed if it is severely contaminated with sediment or other substance, or requires repair.

2 As there is no drain plug incorporated in the tank, the best time to remove it is when it is nearly empty. If this is not possible, syphon as much fuel as possible from the tank into a container which can be sealed, but before doing so, observe the following precautions:

  (a) Disconnect the battery
  (b) Do not smoke or bring naked lights near
  (c) Avoid placing the vehicle over an inspection pit as the fuel vapour is heavier than air

3 With the rear of the vehicle raised and supported securely, disconnect the flexible hose connection between the sections of rigid fuel line at the front face of the tank. On some models (with Weber carburettor) dual pipelines are used, the second one being a fuel return line which returns excess fuel from the carburettor.

4 Disconnect the electrical leads from the tank sender unit.

5 Brush away all adhering dirt and disconnect the tank filler pipe and vent pipes from the tank pipe-stubs (photo).

6 Support the tank and unscrew the nuts from the supporting straps (photo).

7 Lower the tank until the fuel hoses can be detached from the sender unit and from their retaining clips.

8 If the tank is to be cleaned out, repaired or renewed, remove the sender unit. To do this, unscrew the unit in a clockwise direction using the special tool (23-014) or a suitable lever engaged behind the tabs.

9 If the tank contains sediment or water, clean it out by shaking vigorously using paraffin as a solvent. After several changes, rinse out finally with petrol.

10 If the tank is leaking, leave repair to a specialist company. Attempting to weld or solder the tank without it first having been steamed out for several hours is extremely dangerous.

11 Refit the sender unit using a new sealing ring.

12 Refit the tank into the vehicle by reversing the removal operations. Check all connections for leaks after the tank has been partly filled with fuel.

Van

13 The fuel tank on the van is located under the floor pan towards the middle of the vehicle, with the filler cap located just to the rear of the driver's door.

14 The operations just described for passenger vehicles will apply.

8 Carburettors – general description

1 The carburettor will be the Ford variable venturi (VV) type or the Weber dual venturi (2V) unit. Refer to the Specifications for application.

Ford (VV)

2 The carburettor incorporates an automatic choke, coolant-heated from the intake manifold (photo).

3 The fuel inlet is controlled by a 'Viton' tipped needle valve and a float. No adjustment is provided for. The float chamber is vented into the carburettor air intake.

4 The air control system is based upon a pivot type air valve which opens or closes the venturi in accordance with the engine air requirements (photo). The valve is actuated by a vacuum-controlled diaphragm. At idle, the valve is held in its almost closed position by the diaphragm return spring. Once the accelerator pedal is depressed, the demand for air increases as does the vacuum level in the venturi which actuates the diaphragm and air valve until the forces of return spring and vacuum are in balance.

5 The sonic idle system achieves very low emission levels. This is largely due to the method of atomisation of the fuel droplets, which utilise the speed of the airstream at the discharge tube. This airstream is at supersonic level and produces a shock wave which atomises the fuel droplets as they pass through.

6 The main fuel control system comprises a pick-up tube, main and

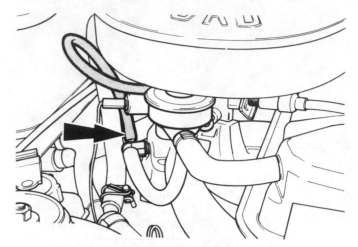

Fig. 3.7 Air cleaner vacuum connection to intake manifold (arrowed) (Sec 5)

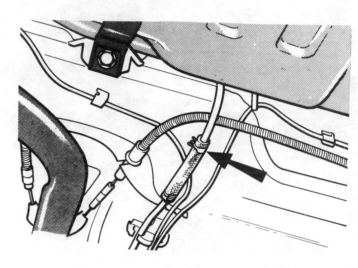

Fig. 3.8 Fuel supply pipe connection at tank (arrowed) (Sec 7)

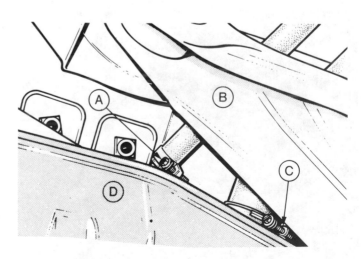

Fig. 3.9 Fuel tank connections (Sec 7)

A   Vent pipe   C   Filler pipe and clip
B   Suspension arm   D   Fuel tank

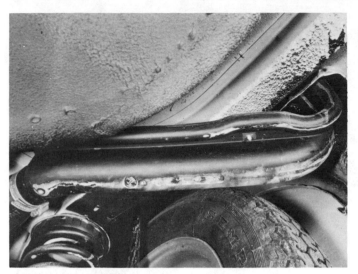

7.5 Fuel tank filler and vent pipes

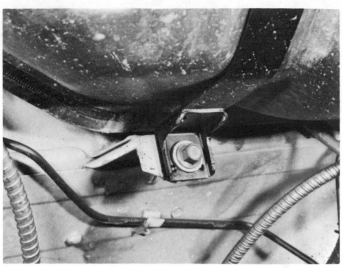

7.6 Fuel tank mounting strap nut

secondary jets and a tapered metering rod. Fuel is drawn through the system by reason of the vacuum created in the venturi.

7 The accelerator pump is vacuum-controlled to enrich the mixture in the venturi as soon as a fall in vacuum is sensed in the intake manifold. During prolonged idle, when the under-bonnet temperature rises, the fuel in the accelerator pump reservoir is liable to boil and vaporise. To offset this condition, which could cause enrichment of the idle mixture, a pump back bleed is fitted to bleed this vapour back into the float chamber. A vacuum break hole is incorporated in the system to obviate any tendency for high vacuum conditions at the fuel outlet to pull fuel through the accelerator pump circuit.

8 An anti-run-on (anti-dieseling) valve is fitted into the carburettor (photo). Its purpose is to block the idle system when the ignition is switched off to prevent any tendency for the engine to run on.

Weber (2V)

9 The carburettor incorporates an automatic choke which is electrically-heated, power being supplied from the alternator to prevent the choke element from being energised until the engine is actually running.

10 The idle system is of conventional fixed jet type, with an anti-run-on valve screwed into the idle fuel gallery. The valve is solenoid-operated and cuts off the supply of fuel as soon as the ignition is switched off.

11 The power valve system fitted to Weber carburettors provides additional fuel during high engine load conditions when the fuel from the main jets is insufficient to meet the needs of the engine. The main jets are calibrated to provide fuel up to approximately three-quarter throttle only in sufficient volume to give good consumption and to meet emission control regulations. A supplementary system is therefore required at full throttle conditions. The system comprises a spring-loaded diaphragm valve, which is controlled by vacuum, and a fuel jet.

9 Ford VV carburettor – in-car adjustments

1 The following adjustments can be carried out without having to remove the carburettor from the engine.

Idle speed

2 With the engine at normal operating temperature, connect a tachometer in accordance with the manufacturer's instructions. Do not remove the air cleaner.

3 Start the engine, run it at 3000 rpm for 30 seconds and then let it idle. Turn the idle speed adjusting screw in or out as necessary to bring the speed to that given in the Specifications (photo).

4 Switch off the engine and remove the tachometer.

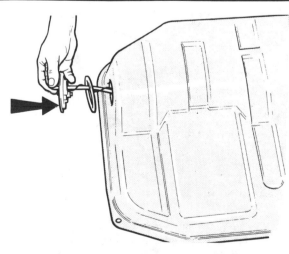

Fig. 3.10 Fuel tank sender unit (arrowed) (Sec 7)

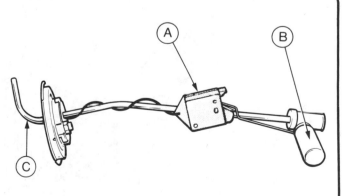

Fig. 3.11 Fuel tank sender unit details (Sec 7)

A   Rheostat   C   Fuel outlet pipe
B   Float

8.2 Ford VV carburettor, choke housing side

8.4 Ford VV carburettor, air valve arrowed

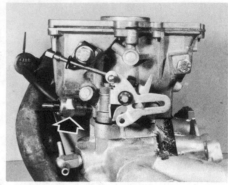

8.8 Ford VV carburettor, fuel cut-off solenoid arrowed

Idle mixture

5   This is set during production and the adjusting screw is sealed with a plug in order to conform to emission control regulations operating in certain countries.

6   The mixture may be in need of adjustment under one of the following conditions:

    (a) After carburettor overhaul
    (b) After a high mileage when engine characteristics may have changed slightly due to carbon build-up, wear or other factors

7   To adjust the mixture accurately, a CO (exhaust gas) analyser should be connected to the vehicle in accordance with the manufacturer's instructions. Also connect a tachometer.

8   Have the engine at normal operating temperature.

9   Using a thin, sharp screwdriver, prise out the tamperproof plug which covers the mixture screw.

10 Start the engine and run it at 3000 rpm for 30 seconds, then allow it to return to idle. Turn the mixture screw in (weak) or out (rich) until the CO level is within the specified range as indicated on the analysing equipment. The adjustment must be carried out within 30 seconds; otherwise, again increase the engine speed for 30 seconds before continuing with the adjustment.

11 Once the mixture is correct, adjust the idle speed as previously described, then re-check the mixture.

12 Switch off the engine and remove the tachometer and the exhaust gas analyser. Fit a new tamperproof plug to the mixture screw.

13 In the absence of a suitable exhaust gas analyser, an approximate setting of the mixture screw may be made by turning the screw inwards (engine idling) until the idle speed just begins to drop. Unscrew the screw the smallest amount necessary to achieve smooth

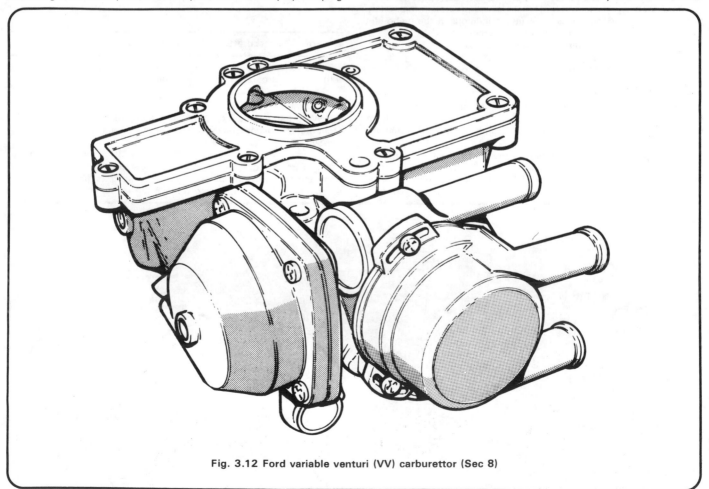

Fig. 3.12 Ford variable venturi (VV) carburettor (Sec 8)

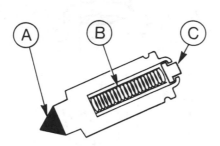

Fig. 3.13 Fuel inlet needle valve (Sec 8)

A   Viton tip   C   Plunger
B   Spring

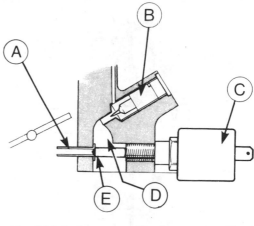

Fig. 3.14 Anti-run-on valve arrangement (Sec 8)

A   Sonic discharge tube   D   Bypass air channel
B   Mixture screw   E   Viton tip
C   Anti-run-on valve

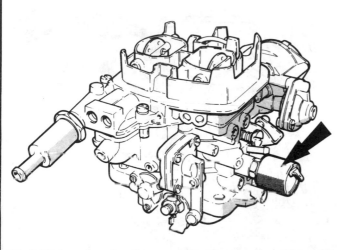

Fig. 3.15 Location of anti-run on valve (arrowed) on Weber 2V carburettor (Sec 8)

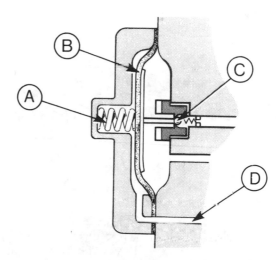

Fg. 3.16 Weber 2V power valve system during part throttle (Sec 8)

A   Diaphragm return spring   C   Power valve
B   Diaphragm   D   Manifold high vacuum

9.3 Ford VV carburettor control screws
1   Idle speed
2   Mixture (plugged)

9.15 Choke housing insulating disc

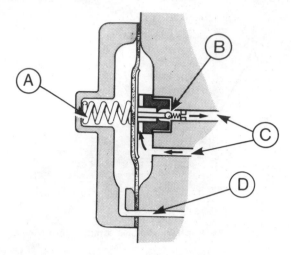

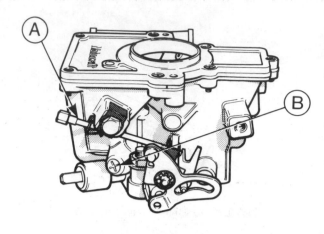

Fig. 3.17 Weber 2V power valve system during full throttle (Sec 8)

A	Diaphragm return spring	C	Fuel flow
B	Power valve	D	Manifold low vacuum

Fig. 3.18 Adjustment screws (Ford VV carburettor) (Sec 9)

A   Idle speed   B   Idle mixture

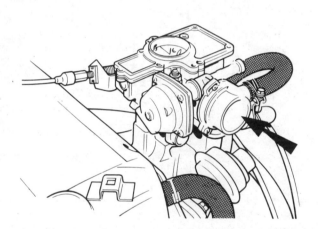

Fig. 3.19 Automatic choke housing cover (arrowed) (Ford VV carburettor) (Sec 9)

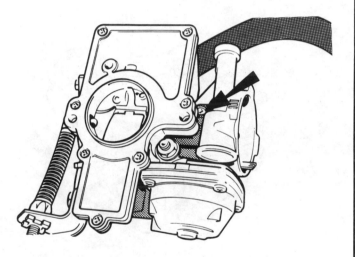

Fig. 3.20 Choke housing tamperproof plug (arrowed) (Ford VV carburettor) (Sec 9)

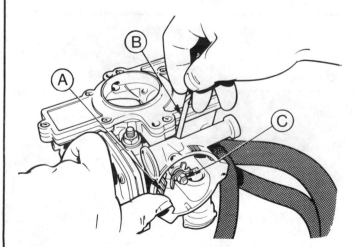

Fig. 3.21 Aligning choke central shaft (Ford VV carburettor) (Sec 9)

A	Lever held clockwise	C	Choke shaft nut
B	Twist drill as alignment rod		

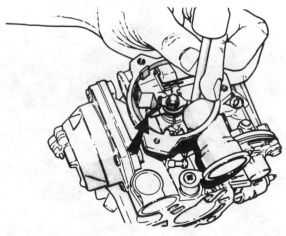

Fig. 3.22 Use a suitable tool to prevent the pull-down lever (arrowed) moving when being bent (Ford VV carburettor) (Sec 9)

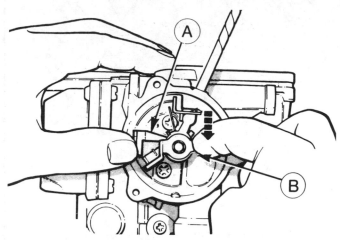

Fig. 3.23 Choke pull-down/fast idle setting (Sec 9) (Ford VV carburettor)

A Bi-metal lever held fully rotated   B Vacuum piston fully down

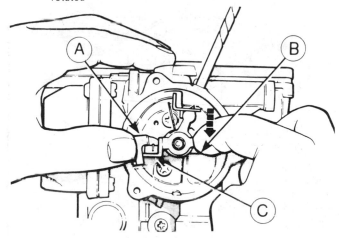

Fig. 3.24 Choke correctly adjusted (Ford VV carburettor) (Sec 9)

A Bi-metal lever fully rotated   C Pull-down lever just in contact with bi-metal lever
B Vacuum piston fully down

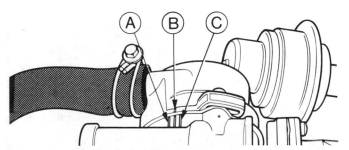

Fig. 3.25 Choke housing alignment (Ford VV carburettor) (Sec 9)

A Lean   C Rich
B Index

Note: Index mark B to be aligned with setting line C on 1.6 engine

idle. The CO level of the exhaust gas should be checked by your dealer at the earliest opportunity and further adjustment carried out as may be necessary.

Automatic choke
14 Remove the air cleaner as described in Section 6.
15 Note the relative positions of the choke housing and cover. Extract the three cross-head screws which retain the choke housing cover and

withdraw the cover, but without disconnecting the coolant hoses from it. Take out the insulating disc (photo).
16 Using a sharp thin screwdriver, prise out the tamperproof plug which is located behind the choke housing.
17 Look into the hole left by removal of the plug, at the same time turning the choke operating lever until the drilling in the choke central shaft lines up with the plug hole.
18 Insert a drill of the appropriate diameter (ohv – 3 mm/0.120 in; 1.3 ohc – 3.3 mm/0.130 in; 1.1 and 1.6 ohc – 3.4 mm/0.134 in) to retain the alignment.
19 Loosen the nut that holds the choke linkage to the choke shaft.
20 Rotate the choke lever fully clockwise to its stop and retighten the central nut. Do not overtighten the nut.
21 Withdraw the twist drill used for alignment.
22 Do not fit a new tamperproof plug until the check and adjustment described below has been carried out.

Choke pull-down/fast idle
23 Working inside the choke housing, bend back the pull-down operating lever with a pair of pliers so that movement of the vacuum piston is not restricted. To prevent the pull-down lever moving whilst it is being bent, insert a twist drill into the hole in the choke housing just above the piston bore (Fig. 3.22).
24 Align the central shaft as described in paragraph 17. Now insert a drill of the appropriate diameter (ohv – 3.3 mm/0.130 in, 1.1 ohc – 4.4 mm/0.170 in, 1.3 ohc – 3.8 mm/0.150 in, early 1.6 ohc (with A stamped on choke housing) – 3.7 mm/0.146 in, late 1.6 ohc – 4.3 mm/0.169 in) to retain the alignment.
25 Push the vacuum piston to the lowest point of its travel and then hold the choke lever fully clockwise on ohv, 1.3 ohc and late 1.6 ohc models or anti-clockwise on 1.1 ohc and early 1.6 ohc models (identified by letter A stamped on the choke housing). This simulates the choke pull-down/fast idle setting.
26 Check that a clearance exists between the pull-down lever and the bi-metal choke lever. If it does not, repeat the piston/lever bending operation (paragraph 23).
27 Now bend the pull-down lever so that it just contacts the bi-metal lever.
28 Remove the drill used for alignment and fit a new tamperproof plug.

Reassembly
29 With the automatic choke now adjusted, locate a new gasket on the housing and offer up the housing cover so that the bi-metal coil engages in the central slot of the choke lever.
30 Screw in the retaining screws only finger tight.
31 Rotate the choke housing cover so that it is aligned with the housing in the position noted during its removal, then tighten the screws.
32 Refit the air cleaner.

10 Weber 2V carburettor – in-car adjustments

Idle speed and mixture adjustment
1 These operations are as described for the Ford carburettor in Section 9. The mixture screw is fitted with a tamperproof plug.

Fast idle
2 Remove the air cleaner as described earlier in this Chapter.
3 Have the engine at normal operating temperature, with a tachometer connected in accordance with the manufacturer's instructions.
4 With the engine switched off, partially open the throttle by moving the cable at the carburettor. Close the choke plates with the fingers and hold them closed while the throttle is released. This has the effect of setting the choke mechanism in the high cam/fast idle position.
5 Release the choke valve plates and without touching the throttle pedal, start the engine by just turning the key. Record the engine speed shown on the tachometer and compare the figure with that specified.
6 Where necessary turn the fast idle screw in or out to adjust the fast idle speed.
7 Refit the air cleaner.

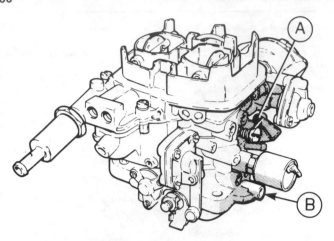

Fig. 3.26 Weber 2V carburettor adjustment screws (Sec 10)

A   Idle speed   B   Mixture (with tamperproof plug)

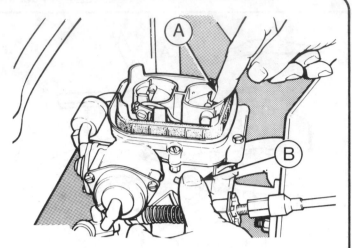

Fig. 3.27 Check fast idle (Weber 2V) (Sec 10)

A   Choke plate held closed   B   Throttle held partially open

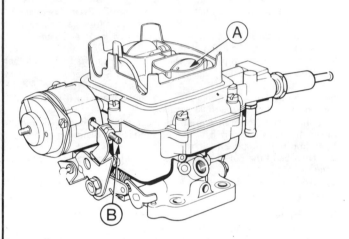

Fig. 3.28 Fast idle adjustment (Weber 2V) (Sec 10)

A   Choke plates open   B   Fast idle adjustment screw

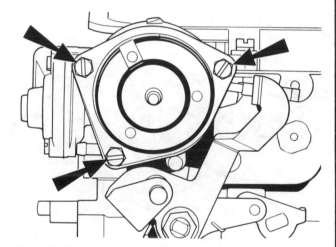

Fig. 3.29 Choke housing cover screws (arrowed) (Weber 2V carburettor) (Sec 10)

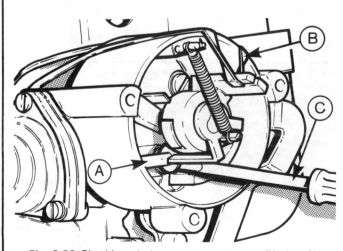

Fig. 3.30 Checking choke vacuum pull-down (Weber 2V carburettor) (Sec 10)

A   Diaphragm operating rod   C   Screwdriver
B   Rubber band

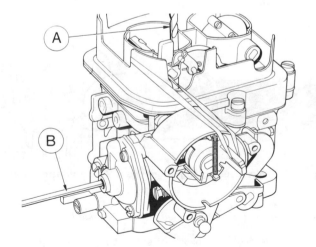

Fig. 3.31 Adjusting choke vacuum pull-down (Weber 2V carburettor) (Sec 10)

A   Twist drill as gauge rod   B   Screwdriver

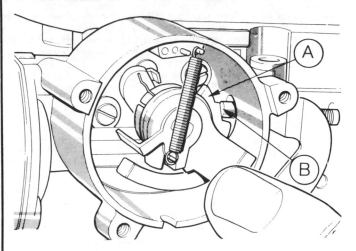

Fig. 3.32 Checking choke phasing (Weber 2V carburettor) (Sec 10)

A   Fast idle cam   B   Fast idle adjustment screw

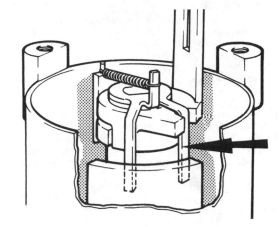

Fig. 3.33 Choke phase adjustment tag (arrowed) (Weber 2V carburettor) (Sec 10)

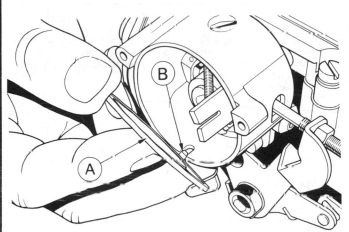

Fig. 3.34 Fitting choke heat shield (Weber 2V carburettor) (Sec 10)

A   Heat shield   B   Locating peg

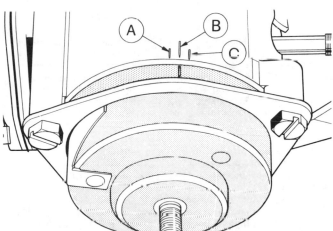

Fig. 3.35 Choke housing alignment marks (Weber 2V) (Sec 10)

A   Rich   C   Lean
B   Index

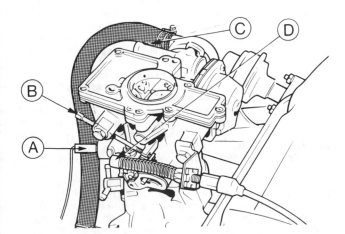

Fig. 3.36 Disconnection points (Ford VV carburettor) (Sec 11)

A   Anti-run-on valve   C   Coolant hoses
B   Idle speed screw   D   Throttle linkage

Fig. 3.37 Disconnection points (Weber 2V carburettor) (Sec 12)

A   Anti-run-on valve   C   Accelerator cable
B   Supply to electric choke

Automatic choke

8   Remove the air cleaner.

9   Disconnect the electric lead to the automatic choke.

10 Unscrew and remove the three screws which hold the automatic choke housing cover in position. Withdraw the cover and bi-metal coil, followed by the internal heat shield.

11 The choke plate pull-down should now be adjusted. To do this, fit a rubber band to the choke plate lever, open the throttle to allow the choke plates to close and then secure the band to keep the plates closed.

12 Using a screwdriver, push the diaphragm open to its stop and measure the clearance between the lower edge of the primary choke plate and the air horn using a twist drill or other gauge rod. Where the clearance is outside that specified (5.5 mm/0.22 in), remove the plug from the diaphragm housing and turn the screw, now exposed, in or out as necessary.

13 Refit the plug and remove the rubber band.

14 The choke phasing must now be checked and adjusted. Hold the throttle partially open and set the fast idle cam so that the fast idle screw is located on the centre step of the cam. Release the throttle so that the cam is held in this position.

15 Push the choke plates downward until the step on the cam jams against the fast idle screw. Now measure the clearance between the lower edge of the primary choke plate and the air horn using a twist drill or gauge rod of suitable diameter (2.0 mm/0.08 in).

16 Where necessary, bend the tag (arrowed in Fig. 3.33) to adjust the clearance.

17 Refit the heat shield, making sure that the locating peg is correctly engaged in the notch in the housing.

18 Offer up the cover and engage the bi-metal coil with the slot in the choke lever which projects through the cut-out in the heat shield.

19 Screw in the retaining screws finger tight and then rotate the cover to set the cover mark opposite the centre index line.

20 Reconnect the lead to the choke.

11 Ford VV carburettor – removal and refitting

1   Remove the air cleaner as described earlier in this Chapter.

2   If the engine is hot, depressurise the cooling system by carefully removing the pressure cap as described in Chapter 2.

3   Disconnect the coolant hoses from the automatic choke housing and tie them up as high as possible to minimise loss of coolant.

4   Pull off the electrical lead from the anti-run-on valve on the carburettor.

5   Disconnect the distributor vacuum pipe.

6   Disconnect the throttle cable by pulling the spring clip to release the end fitting from the ball-stud and then unscrewing the cable bracket fixing bolt.

7   Disconnect and plug the fuel inlet hose from the carburettor. If

13.4 Removing top cover (Ford VV carburettor)

crimped type hose clips are used, cut them off and fit screw type clips at reassembly.

8   Unscrew the two carburettor mounting flange nuts and lift the carburettor from the intake manifold. Remove the idle speed screw if necessary for access to the nut.

9   Refitting is a reversal of removal, but make sure that a new flange gasket is used on perfectly clean mating surfaces.

12 Weber 2V carburettor – removal and refitting

1   The operations are very similar to those described for the Ford carburettor in the preceding Section except for the following differences:

(a) *The choke is electrically-heated, disconnect the electrical lead instead of coolant hoses. There is no need to tie the electrical lead up as high as possible*

(b) *A fuel return hose will require disconnection from the carburettor as well as the fuel supply hose*

(c) *The carburettor is held by four nuts instead of two*

13 Ford VV carburettor – overhaul

1   Complete overhaul of the carburettor is seldom required. It will usually be found sufficient to remove the top cover and mop out fuel, dirt and water from the fuel bowl and then blow through the accessible jets with air from a tyre pump or compressed air line. Do not direct air pressure into the accelerator pump air bleed or outlet, or the air valve vent, or diaphragm damage may occur.

2   To completely dismantle a carburettor, carry out the following operations, but remember that for a unit which has been in service for a high mileage it may be more economical to purchase a new or reconditioned one rather than to renew several individual components.

3   Remove the carburettor from the engine as described in Section 11 and clean away external dirt.

4   Extract the seven screws and lift off the top cover and gasket (photo).

5   Drain the fuel from the float bowl.

6   Using a thin sharp screwdriver, prise out the metering rod tamperproof plug.

7   Unscrew and withdraw the main metering rod, making sure to keep the air valve closed during the process.

8   Extract the four cross-head screws and detach the main jet body and gasket. Take out the accelerator pump outlet one-way valve ball and weight by inverting the carburettor and allowing the components to drop out.

9   Lift out the float, the float spindle and the fuel inlet needle valve.

10 Extract the four cross-head screws and remove the air control vacuum diaphragm housing, the return spring and the spring seat. The diaphragm can be removed after the circlip is extracted.

11 Invert the carburettor, remove the three cross-head screws and detach the accelerator pump diaphragm, taking care not to lose the return spring.

12 Clean out all drillings, jets and passages in the carburettor with compressed air – never by probing with wire. Examine all components for wear or damage; renew gaskets and diaphragms as a matter of routine. Many necessary components will be supplied in repair kit form. The throttle linkage and air valve mechanism are particularly subject to wear, as are the diaphragm return springs to compression. Renew as necessary.

13 Commence reassembly by making sure that the metering rod bias spring is correctly installed to the air valve.

14 Fit the accelerator pump assembly, making sure that the gasket-faced side of the diaphragm is towards the cover.

15 Reconnect and refit the air valve control vacuum diaphragm housing, making sure that the vacuum hole in the diaphragm is in alignment with the gallery in the carburettor body and the housing.

16 Fit the fuel inlet needle valve, the float and the float pivot pin. The needle valve should be so installed that the spring-loaded plunger on the valve will be in contact with the float once fuel has entered the float bowl.

17 Insert the accelerator pump ball and weight into the pump discharge passage.

18 Use a new gasket and fit the main jet body.

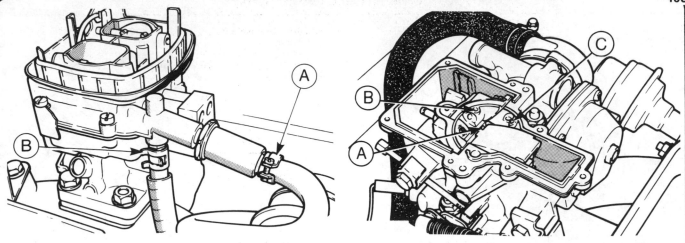

Fig. 3.38 Fuel hoses (Weber 2V carburettor) (Sec 12)

A   Fuel inlet   B   Fuel return (to tank)

Fig. 3.39 Top cover removed from Ford carburettor (Sec 13)

A   Accelerator pump discharge   B   Accelerator pump air bleed
     pipe   C   Air valve diaphragm vent

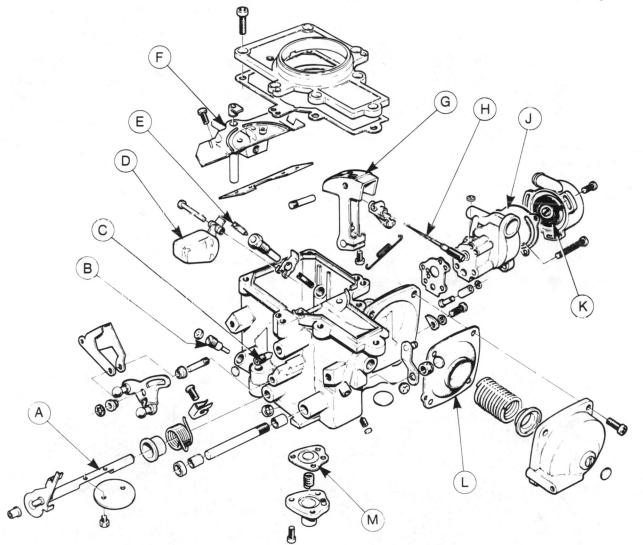

Fig. 3.40 Exploded view of Ford VV carburettor (Sec 13)

A   Throttle spindle   E   Fuel inlet needle valve   J   Choke assembly   valve control)
B   Mixture adjustment screw F   Main jet body   K   Bi-metal coil and choke   M   Accelerator pump
C   Bypass adjuster   G   Air valve   housing cover   diaphragm
D   Float   H   Metering rod   L   Vacuum diaphragm (air

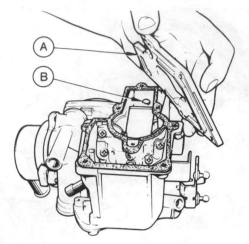

Fig. 3.41 Removing top cover from Ford carburettor (Sec 13)

A   Top cover   B   Metering rod tamperproof
plug

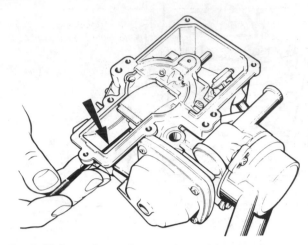

Fig. 3.42 Removing main metering rod (arrowed) from Ford carburettor (Sec 13)

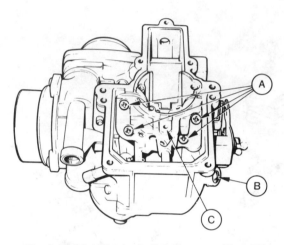

Fig. 3.43 Main jet body fixing screws (Sec 13)

A   Screws   C   Main jet body
B   Mixture screw tamperproof
plug

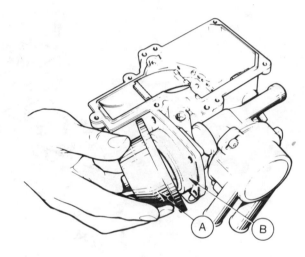

Fig. 3.44 Removing air valve control diaphragm from Ford carburettor (Sec 13)

A   Housing   B   Diaphragm

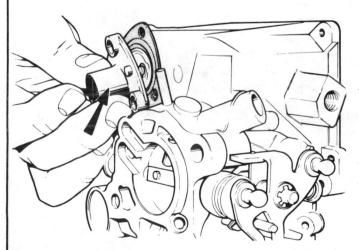

Fig. 3.45 Removing accelerator pump housing (arrowed) from Ford carburettor (Sec 13)

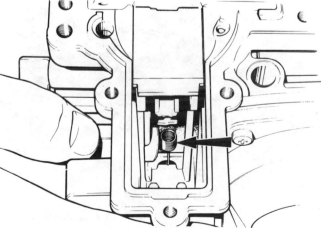

Fig. 3.46 Metering rod bias spring (arrowed) correctly located on air valve of Ford carburettor (Sec 13)

19 Very carefully slide the metering rod into position, hold the air valve closed and screw in the rod until its shoulder is aligned with the vertical face of the main jet body. If the rod binds when screwing it in, do not force it but check the reason. Do not overtighten it.
20 Fit a new tamperproof plug to the metering rod hole.
21 Fit the top cover with a new gasket.
22 Once the carburettor has been fitted to the engine, the idle speed and mixture must be checked and adjusted as described in Section 9. If by any chance the mixture screw was removed at overhaul, screw it in very gently until it seats and then unscrew it three full turns. This will provide a basic setting to get the engine started.

14 Weber 2V carburettor – overhaul

1 Complete overhaul of the carburettor is seldom required and it will usually be found sufficient to clean the carburettor and inspect it.
2 To do this, remove the air cleaner as described earlier in this Chapter and disconnect the fuel flow and return hoses.
3 Unscrew the fuel filter at the inlet union.
4 Disconnect the lead from the electrically-heated choke.
5 Remove the carburettor upper body by extracting the six securing screws and then holding the fast idle operating lever clear of the choke housing.
6 Mop out the fuel from the float chamber and extract the jets from the carburettor main body, but identify their locations before removal.

7 Clean all jets, galleries, drillings and the filter using air pressure. Never probe a jet with wire.
8 Reassembly is a reversal of dismantling.
9 To completely dismantle the carburettor, carry out the following operations, but note that with a unit which has been in service for a high mileage it may be more economical to purchase a new or reconditioned carburettor rather than to renew several individual components.
10 Remove the carburettor from the engine as described in Section 12 and clean away external dirt.
11 Remove the upper body as described in paragraph 5.
12 If the upper body must be disconnected, the fuel filter, float and fuel inlet needle valve can be removed.
13 Remove the jets and the accelerator pump supply tube from the main body, having noted their original locations.
14 Remove the accelerator pump diaphragm (4 screws).
15 Remove the power valve diaphragm (3 screws).
16 Clean the jets and drillings with compressed air – do not probe with wire.
17 Examine all components for wear or damage, renew gaskets and diaphragms as a matter of routine. Many necessary components will be supplied in repair kit form. The throttle linkage is particularly subject to wear and the diaphragm return springs to compression. Renew as necessary.
18 Commence reassembly by fitting the accelerator pump and power valve.
19 Fit the main and idle jets and the fuel filter.

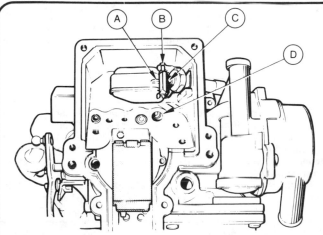

Fig. 3.47 Needle valve detail on Ford carburettor (Sec 13)

A Float
B Float pivot pin
C Fuel inlet needle valve
D Accelerator pump discharge passage

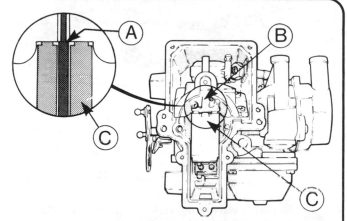

Fig. 3.48 Main metering rod adjustment on Ford carburettor (Sec 13)

A Shoulder on rod
B Main jet body
C Air valve

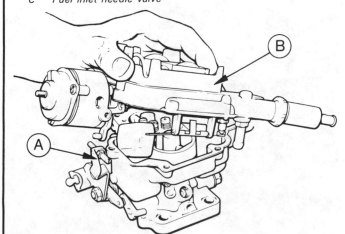

Fig. 3.49 Removing Weber carburettor upper body (Sec 14)

A Fast idle lever
B Upper body

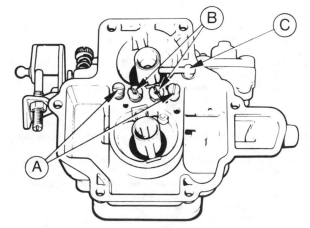

Fig. 3.50 Location of jets in Weber carburettor (Sec 14)

A Idle jets
B Combined main and air correction jets
C Accelerator pump supply tube

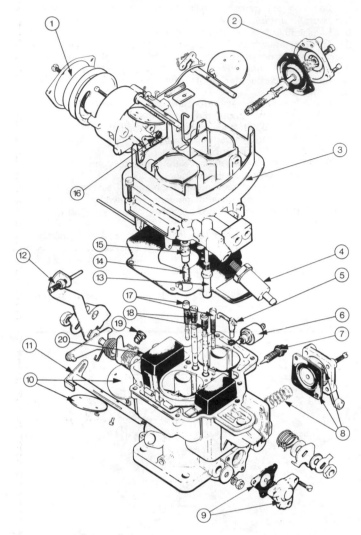

Fig. 3.51 Exploded view of the Weber 2V carburettor (Sec 14)

1   Choke housing cover
2   Choke pull-down diaphragm
3   Upper body
4   Fuel filter
5   Accelerator discharge tube
6   Anti-run-on valve
7   Mixture screw
8   Accelerator pump assembly
9   Power valve diaphragm
    assembly
10 Throttle valve plates
11 Secondary throttle spindle

12 Fast idle adjuster
13 Fuel return connection
14 Fuel inlet needle valve
15 Needle valve housing
16 Seal
17 Idle jets
18 Combined emulsion tube,
    air correction and main
    jets
19 Idle speed adjustment
    screw
20 Float

20 Locate a new body gasket in position and then fit the needle valve assembly and the float.
21 Check the float setting. To do this, hold the carburettor body vertically so that the float is hanging down and closing the needle valve. Measure the distance between the surface of the gasket and the base of the float. If adjustment is necessary to achieve the correct setting (see Specifications), bend the tag (A in Fig. 3.52).
22 Fit the upper body to the main body and secure with the six screws.
23 Once the carburettor has been fitted to the engine, the idle speed and mixture must be checked and adjusted as described in Section 10. If by any chance the mixture screw was removed at overhaul, screw it in very gently until it seats and then unscrew it three full turns. This will provide a basic setting to get the engine started.

15 Throttle linkage – adjustment

1   Remove the air cleaner from the carburettor.
2   Depress the accelerator pedal fully and hold it open using a block of wood.
3   Turn the adjusting sleeve at the cable bracket until the throttle lever at the carburettor is just in the wide open position.
4   Remove the block of wood and then with an assistant depressing the accelerator pedal, check that the throttle lever at the carburettor moves to the wide open position. Readjust as necessary.

16 Accelerator cable – renewal

1   Working within the vehicle, remove the dash lower insulation panel.
2   Disconnect the cable from the upper end of the accelerator pedal arm. Do this by sliding off the spring clip to release the cable end from the ball-stud (photo).
3   Working under the bonnet, release the cable from the bulkhead. This is probably more easily carried out if an assistant can punch the cable grommet out from inside the vehicle.
4   Remove the air cleaner.
5   The cable must now be detached from its bracket on the carburettor. Prise out the clip and then depress the four lugs on the retainer simultaneously so that the retainer can be slid out of the bracket. Take care not to damage the outer cable.
6   Disconnect the end of the cable from the ball-stud on the carburettor throttle lever by sliding back the spring retaining clip.
7   Fit the new cable by reversing the removal procedure then adjust as described in the preceding Section.

17 Accelerator pedal – removal and refitting

1   The accelerator pedal can be removed once the cable has been disconnected from it as described in the preceding Section.
2   Unbolt the pedal support bracket. On LHD models two nuts are accessible from inside the engine compartment and one from the interior of the vehicle; on RHD models the two bolts are accessible from inside the vehicle.
3   Refitting is the reverse of the removal procedure. Adjust the throttle linkage if necessary as described in Section 15.

18 Manifolds – description

Removal and refitting of the manifolds is covered in Chapter 1.

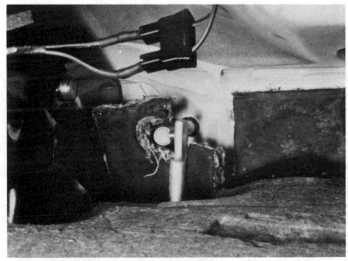

16.2 Accelerator cable connection under dash

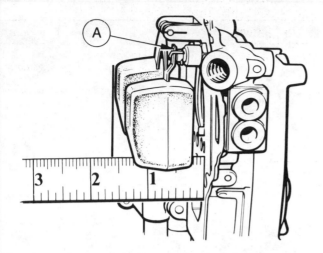

Fig. 3.52 Checking float setting on Weber carburettor (Sec 14)

A   Adjustment tag

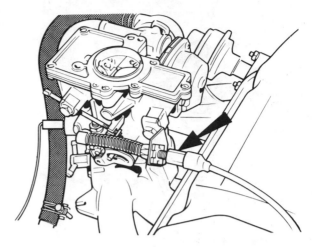

Fig. 3.53 Throttle cable adjustment sleeve (arrowed) (Sec 15)

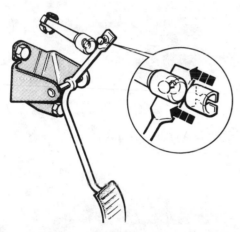

Fig. 3.54 Accelerator cable connection to pedal (Sec 16)

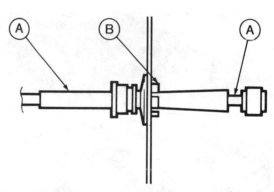

Fig. 3.55 Accelerator cable fixing at bulkhead (Sec 16)

A   Accelerator cable   B   Grommet

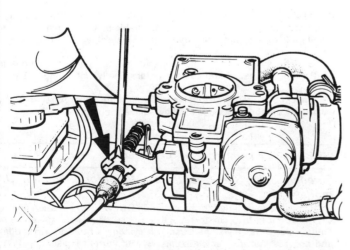

Fig. 3.56 Prising off cable retaining clip (arrowed) (Sec 16)

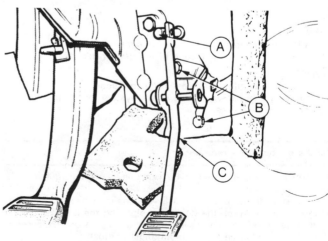

Fig. 3.57 Accelerator pedal (RHD) (Sec 17)

A   Cable   C   Pedal arm
B   Fixing bolts

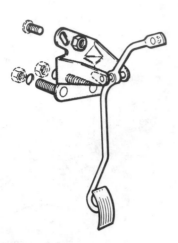

Fig. 3.58 Accelerator pedal (LHD))Sec 17

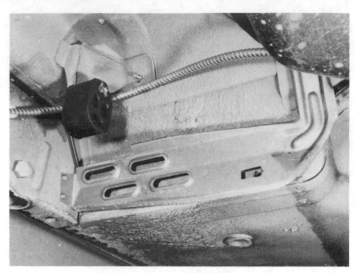

19.3A Exhaust flexible mounting and heat baffle

19.3B Silencer mounting

19.3C Expansion box mounting

Intake

1   The intake manifold is of light alloy construction and is coolant-heated to improve the atomisation of the fuel/air mixture.

Exhaust

2   The exhaust manifold is of cast iron construction and incorporates a heated air box as part of the air intake system for the thermostatically controlled air cleaner.

19 Exhaust system – renewal

1   The exhaust system fitted to 1.1 versions as original equipment is of one-piece construction.
2   The system fitted to 1.3 and 1.6 versions is of two-section type, with a coupling between the dual downpipe and the main system.
3   All systems incorporate a silencer and an expansion box, and the system is suspended on rubber mountings (photos).
4   The system can be renewed in sections as coupling sleeves are supplied so that an old section can be cut out and a new one inserted without the need to renew the entire system at the same time.
5   It is recommended when working on an exhaust system that the complete assembly be removed from under the vehicle by releasing the downpipe from the manifold and unhooking the flexible suspension hangers.

6   Assemble the complete system, but do not fully tighten the joint clips until the system is back in the vehicle. Use a new exhaust manifold/flange gasket and check that the flexible mountings are in good order.
7   Set the silencer and expansion box in their correct attitudes in relation to the rest of the system before finally tightening the joint clips.
8   Check that with reasonable deflection in either direction, the exhaust does not knock against any adjacent components.

20 Emission control system – description

Sweden only. See Chapter 13 for information on UK models.

1   On vehicles destined for operation in Sweden, an emission control system is fitted in order to reduce the level of noxious gases being emitted from the vehicle exhaust. The system is fitted to 1.6 models and ensures that the vehicle complies with current legislation.
2   The arrangement used is an Exhaust Gas Recirculation (EGR) system which redirects a small quantity of exhaust gas back into the intake manifold in order to reduce peak combustion temperatures and pressures. In turn, this has the effect of reducing the emissions of noxious gases by up to 60%.

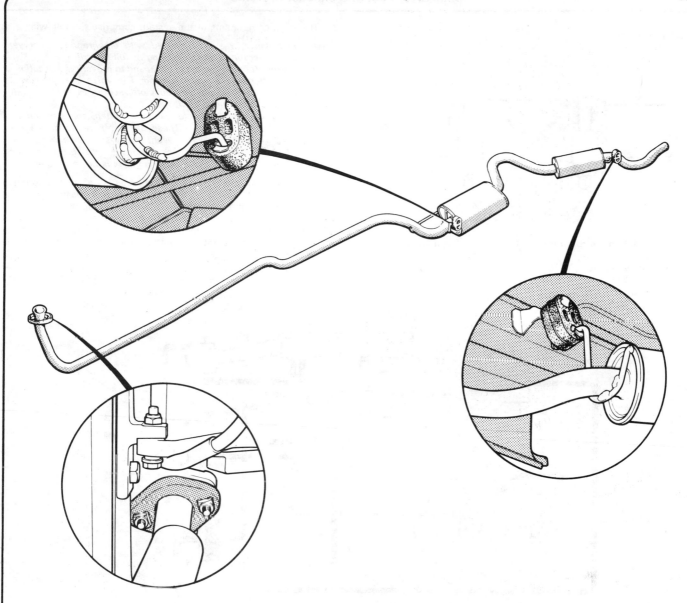

Fig. 3.59 Exhaust sustem (1.1 l engine) (Sec 19)

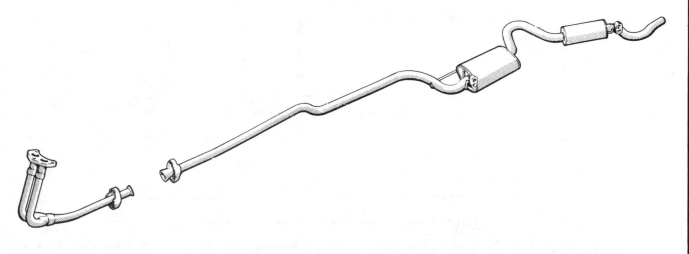

Fig. 3.60 Exhaust system (1.3 l and 1.6 l engine) (Sec 19)

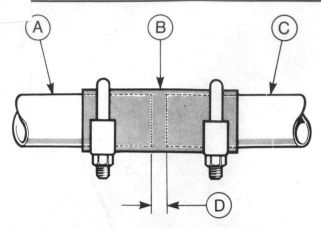

Fig. 3.61 Exhaust pipe connecting sleeve (typical) (Sec 19)

A   Exhaust pipe
B   Sleeve
C   Exhaust pipe

D   Gap between pipe ends
    (11.0 mm 0.4 in)

3   The main components of the system comprise the following:

   (a)   *EGR valve, vacuum-operated with diaphragms, to prevent EGR operating during cranking or full throttle*

   (b)   *Ported Vacuum Switch (PVS), used to prevent the injection of exhaust gases at cold starting. The valve is responsive to coolant temperature and cuts off vacuum to the EGR valve when the engine is cold*

   (c)   *Speed sensor, solenoid vacuum switch, microswitch and vacuum sustain valve. These are components of the EGR control system which prevent the system becoming operational at low engine speeds and at light throttle cruising when the formation of noxious gases is not a problem*

4   In addition to the foregoing components, a dual diaphragm distributor is fitted, also a fuel trap to prevent fuel passing down the vacuum hose and damaging the distributor diaphragm.

5   It should be realised that for optimum reduction of exhaust gas CO level, the good tune of the engine (carburettor and ignition) and the efficiency of the temperature controlled air cleaner are essential requirements.

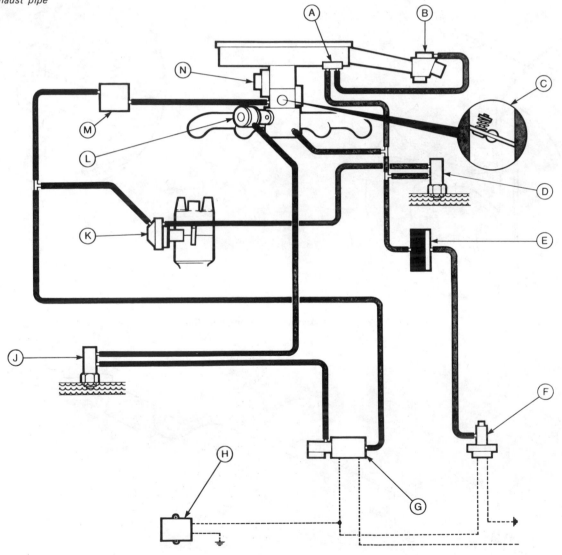

Fig. 3.62 Layout of emission control system (Sec 20)

A   Air cleaner heat sensor
B   Vacuum diaphragm unit
C   Deceleration valve (in carburettor venturi)

D   Two-port PVS (distributor retard cut-out)
E   Vacuum sustain valve
F   Vacuum-operated microswitch

G   Two-way solenoid
H   Speed sensor
J   Two-part PVS (EGR cold cut-out)

K   Dual diaphragm distributor
L   EGR valve
M   Fuel trap

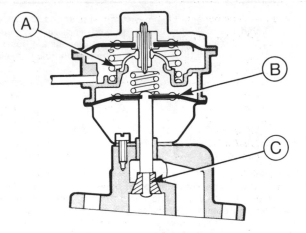

Fig. 3.63 EGR valve (low vacuum state shown) (Sec 20)

A   Upper diaphragm return   B   Lower diaphragm
    spring   C   Pintle valve

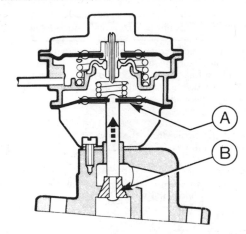

Fig. 3.64 EGR valve (high vacuum state shown) (Sec 20)

A   Lower diaphragm   B   Pintle valve

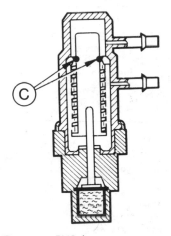

Fig. 3.65 Two-port PVS (wax sensor type) (Sec 20)

C   O-ring (valve closed)

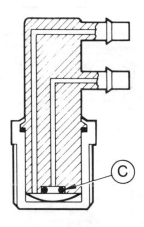

Fig. 3.66 Two-port PVS (bi-metal disc type) (Sec 20)

C   O ring (valve open)

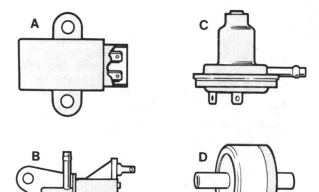

Fig. 3.67 EGR system control components (Sec 20)

A   Speed sensor   C   Vacuum-operated
B   Solenoid vacuum switch   microswitch
                             D   Vacuum sustain valve

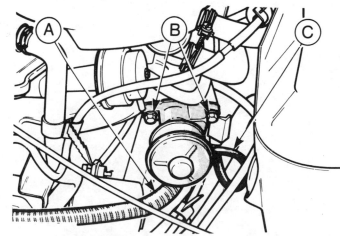

Fig. 3.68 Location of EGR valve (Sec 21)

A   Exhaust gas supply hose C   Vacuum supply hose
B   Mounting bolts

21 EGR system components – removal and refitting

1   Testing of the various components of the system is not within the scope of the home mechanic due to the need for a vacuum pump and gauge, but if a fault has been diagnosed by a service station having the necessary equipment, the renewal of a defective component can be carried out in the following way.

EGR valve
2   Disconnect the hoses from the valve. Unbolt the two mounting bolts and remove the valve.

Speed sensor
3   This is located on the left-hand side of the engine compartment rear bulkhead. Disconnect the wiring from the sensor and extract its two self-tapping mounting screws.

PVS
4   Check that the cooling system is not under pressure by removing the pressure cap (see Chapter 2). Disconnect the vacuum hoses from the switch and unscrew the switch. Plug the tapped hole in the intake manifold to prevent loss of coolant.

Solenoid valve
5   This is located adjacent to the Speed Sensor. Disconnect the vacuum hoses and the electrical lead from the switch and remove the single self-tapping mounting screw.

Microswitch
6   This too is located adjacent to the Speed Sensor. Disconnect the vacuum hose and electrical leads from the switch and then extract the two self-tapping mounting screws.

22 Fault diagnosis – fuel system

Symptom	Reason(s)
Fuel consumption excessive	Air cleaner choked giving rich mixture
	Leak from tank, pump or fuel lines
	Float chamber flooding due to incorrect level or worn needle valve
	Carburettor incorrectly adjusted
	Idle speed too high
	Incorrect valve clearances (ohv)
Lack of power, stalling or difficult starting	Faulty fuel pump
	Leak on suction side of pump or in fuel line
	Intake manifold or carburettor flange gaskets leaking
	Carburettor incorrectly adjusted
Poor or erratic idling	Weak mixture (screw tampered with)
	Leak in intake manifold
	Leak in distributor vacuum pipe
	Leak in crankcase extractor hose
	Leak in brake servo hose (if fitted)

Note: *High fuel consumption and poor performance are not necessarily due to carburettor faults. Make sure that the ignition system is properly adjusted, that the brakes are not binding and that the engine is in good mechanical condition, before tampering with the carburettor.*

Chapter 4 Ignition system

For modifications, and information applicable to later models, see Supplement at end of manual

Contents

Specifications

Part A: Mechanical system (1.1 engines)

General

System type .... Battery, coil, distributor with mechanical contact breaker
Polarity .... Negative earth
Firing order:
  OHV engines .... 1-2-4-3 (No 1 at timing cover end)
  CVH engines .... 1-3-4-2 (No 1 at timing belt end)

Ignition timing

Pre-1984 model year (ie, ohv and cvh) .... 12° btdc at 750 to 850 rpm
1984 model year onwards (ie, ohv only) .... 6° btdc at 750 to 850 rpm

Distributor

Make .... Bosch (all engines) or Lucas (CVH only)
Drive:
  OHV engines .... Gear on camshaft
  CVH engines .... Offset dogs on rear of camshaft
Rotation of rotor arm .... Anti-clockwise viewed from cap
Contact breaker points gap:
  Bosch distributor .... 0.4 to 0.5 mm (0.016 to 0.020 in)
  Lucas distributor .... 0.4 to 0.6 mm (0.016 to 0.024 in)
Dwell angle .... 48° to 52°
Condenser capacity:
  Bosch distributor:
    OHV engines .... 0.20 µF
    CVH engines .... 0.235 to 0.315 µF
  Lucas distributor .... 0.21 to 0.29 µF

Advance characteristics * at 2000 engine rpm, no load:

	Mechanical	Vacuum	Total
OHV (pre-1984)	5° to 11°	18° to 26°	23° to 37°
OHV (1984 on)	3° to 9°	13° to 21°	16° to 30°
CVH HC	5° to 11°	14° to 22°	19° to 33°
CVH LC	1.5° to 7.5°	16° to 24°	17.5° to 31.5°

Crankshaft degrees; initial advance not included

Coil

Type .... Oil-filled, low voltage with 1.5 ohm ballast resistor
Output:
  OHV engines .... 23 kV minimum
  CVH engines .... 25 kV minimum
Primary resistance .... 1.2 to 1.4 ohms
Secondary resistance .... 5000 to 9000 ohms

Spark plugs

Type:
  OHV engines .... Motorcraft AGRF 22 or equivalent
  CVH engines (HC) .... Motorcraft Super AGPR 12C, AGP 12C or equivalent

CVH engines (LC) .... Motorcraft Super AGP 22C   *AGPR 22C (?)*
Electrode gap: *'7 / .8 mm*
OHV engines .... 0.75 mm (0.030 in)
CVH engines .... 0.60 mm (0.025 in)

HT lead resistance
OHV engines .... 23 000 ohms maximum per lead
CVH engines .... 17 500 ohms maximum per lead

Torque wrench settings

	Nm	lbf ft
Spark plugs:		
OHV engines	13 to 20	10 to 15
CVH engines	25 to 38	18 to 28
Distributor clamp pinch-bolt (ohv)	4	3
Distributor clamp plate bolt (ohv)	10	7
Distributor mounting bolts (CVH)	7	5

Part B: Electronic system (1.3 and 1.6 engines)
General
System type .... Battery, coil, distributor incorporating electronic module
Polarity .... Negative earth
Firing order .... 1-3-4-2 (No 1 at timing belt end of engine)

Ignition timing .... 12° btdc at 800 rpm

Distributor
Type .... Bosch or Lucas breakerless, driven by offset dogs on rear of camshaft
Rotation direction .... Anti-clockwise viewed from cap

Advance characteristics* at 2000 engine rpm, no load:

	Mechanical	Vacuum	Total
1.3	2.4° to 8.4°	14° to 22°	16.4° to 30.4°
1.6 (Ford carburettor)	0.8° to 6.8°	18° to 26°	18.8° to 32.8°
1.6 (Weber carburettor)	6.0° to 12.0°	14° to 22°	20.0° to 34.0°

Crankshaft degrees; initial advance not included

Coil
Type .... Lucas or Bosch high output (30 kV minimum)
Primary resistance .... 0.72 to 0.88 ohms
Secondary resistance .... 4500 to 7000 ohms

Spark plugs
Type:
1.3 .... Motorcraft AGP22C
1.6 (Weber carburettor) .... Motorcraft Super AGP12C or Super AGPR12C
1.6 (Ford carburettor) .... Motorcraft Super AGPR12C
Electrode gap .... 0.75 mm (0.030 in)

HT lead resistance .... 17 500 ohms maximum per lead

Torque wrench settings

	Nm	lbf ft
Distributor mounting bolts	7	5
Distributor cap screws:		
Bosch	4	3
Lucas	2.25	1.66
Module fixing screws	1.4	1.03
Spark plugs	25 to 38	18 to 28

PART A: MECHANICAL SYSTEM (1.1 ENGINES)

1 Description

A conventional ignition system is used on the 1.1 litre engined models and comprises a coil, a distributor with mechanical contact breaker, a ballast resistor and spark plugs.

On ohv engined models, the distributor is driven from a skew gear on the camshaft. On CVH-engined models, it is driven by offset dogs on the end of the camshaft. It incorporates both centrifugal and vacuum advance capability. Lucas distributors have a secondary cam, giving the points vertical movement to reduce pitting.

The coil is mounted on the wing inner panel and is of the oil-filled type.

The ballast resistor is a grey coloured wire, built into the loom on ohv models, which runs between the ignition switch and the coil. Its purpose is to limit the battery voltage to the coil during normal running to seven volts. During starting, the ballast resistor is bypassed to give full battery voltage at the coil to facilitate quick starting of the engine.

The spark plugs are of small diameter and require a long reach 16 mm ($\frac{5}{8}$ in AF) socket to remove them instead of a conventional spark plug spanner. On ohv engines they are of the taper seat type.

The HT leads are of suppressed type, of carbon cored construction.

Always pull them from the spark plugs by gripping the terminal rubber insulator, not the cable itself. The leads are numbered, No 1 being at the spark plug nearest the timing cover end of the engine.

2 Maintenance

1   Apart from the Routine Maintenance service items described in this Chapter, periodically check the rotor arm and distributor cap for cracks and renew them if evident.
2   Wipe the HT leads free from oil and grease and check the security of all ignition system connections.
3   Make sure that all earth connections from the battery, engine and transmission are tight and that the contact is being made between the surfaces of clean metal – not rusted or corroded.
4   For removal and refitting of the ignition switch, refer to Section 19.

3 Contact breaker gap – adjustment

1   This will normally only be required after new contact breaker points have been fitted, but it is worthwhile checking the adjustment at about halfway through the service interval in case the gap has

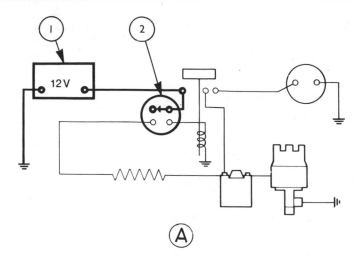

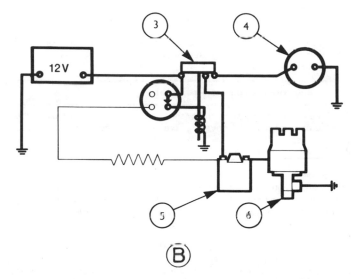

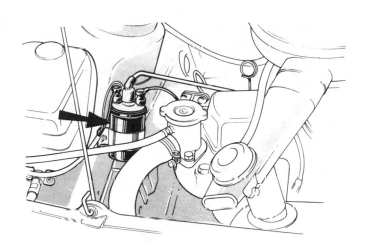

Fig. 4.1 Ignition coil (ohv engine) (Sec 1)

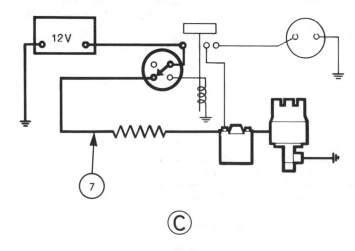

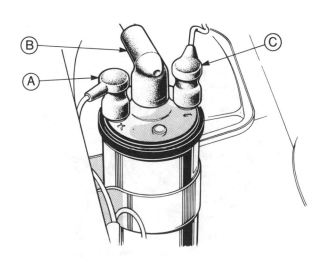

Fig. 4.2 Ignition coil terminals (Sec 1)

Fig. 4.3 Ignition circuit showing action of ballast resistor (Sec 1)

A Positive (LT to switch)	C Negative (LT to distributor)
B HT lead to distributor cap	

A	Ignition switch off (O)	2	Ignition switch
B	Ignition switch in START position (III)	3	Starter solenoid
		4	Starter motor
C	Ignition switch in normal running position (II)	5	Ignition coil
		6	Distributor
1	Battery	7	Ballast resistor

altered due to wear on the contact breaker cam follower heel.
2   Prise down the retaining clips or remove the securing screws, as appropriate, and remove the distributor cap and rotor.
3   Apply a spanner to the crankshaft pulley bolt and turn the crankshaft until the distributor points are fully open, with the heel of the cam follower on the highest point of one of the lobes of the cam.
4   Using feeler blades, check the points gap. If the blade is not a sliding fit, release the screw at the fixed contact so that the contact will move stiffly and adjust the gap. Retighten the screw, refit the rotor and cap. Take care not to contaminate the points with oil from the feeler gauges.
5   This method of adjustment should be regarded as 'second best' as on modern engines, setting the points gap is usually carried out by measuring the dwell angle.
6   The dwell angle is the number of degrees through which the distributor cam turns during the period between the instants of closure and opening of the contact breaker points. Checking the dwell angle not only gives a more accurate setting of the contact breaker gap, but this method also evens out any variations in the gap which could be caused by pitting of the points, wear in the distributor shaft or its bushes, or difference in height of any of the cam peaks.
7   The dwell angle should be checked with a dwell meter connected in accordance with the maker's instructions. Refer to the Specifications for the correct dwell angle. If the dwell angle is too large, increase the points gap. If it is too small, reduce the gap.
8   The dwell angle should always be adjusted before checking and adjusting the ignition timing (see Section 5).

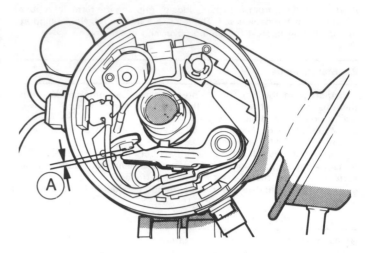

Fig. 4.4 Contact breaker points gap (A) (Sec 3)

4   Contact breaker points – renewal

1   Disconnect the leads from the spark plugs, prise down the distributor cap clips or remove the screws, and place the cap and leads to one side.
2   Remove the rotor arm.
3   Pull off the contact breaker LT lead from the points.
4   Unscrew and remove the screw from the fixed contact arm. Take great care not to drop the screw into the interior of the distributor; if necessary, cover the openings in the baseplate with rag before starting to remove the screw. If the screw is dropped, retrieve it before proceeding any further by removing the distributor (Section 7) and inverting it.
5   With the screw removed, lift out the contact breaker assembly.
6   Dressing the points on a strip of emery cloth is not recommended, and they should be renewed if they are in poor condition or they have completed their specified period of service (see Routine Maintenance).
7   Fit the new contact breaker set, but leave the securing screw loose at this stage until the gap has been set using feeler blades as described in the preceding Section.
8   On Lucas distributors, make sure that the secondary movement cam is engaged with its pin, and that both washers are refitted with the securing screw.
9   Apply a little high melting-point grease to the distributor cam. (Grease may be supplied with the new contact breaker set).
10 Refit the rotor arm and the distributor cap and reconnect the spark plug leads.
11 Check and adjust the dwell angle (Section 3) and the ignition timing (next Section).

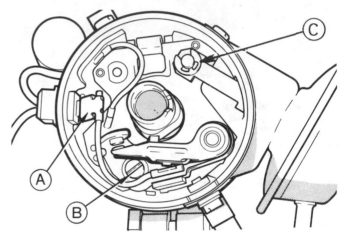

Fig. 4.5 Contact breaker points removal – Bosch, ohv (Sec 4)

A   LT lead connector   C   Vacuum advance strut
B   Securing screw   circlip

5   Ignition timing – checking and adjusting

1   This will be required whenever one of the following operations has been carried out.

  (a) Contact breaker points adjusted or renewed
  (b) Distributor removed and refitted
  (c) Change of fuel octane rating

2   Before checking the timing, check and adjust the dwell angle as described in Section 3, with the engine at normal operating temperature.
3   Increase the contrast of the notch in the crankshaft pulley and the appropriate mark on the timing index (refer to Specifications) by applying quick-drying white paint.
4   Connect a timing light (stroboscope) in accordance with the manufacturer's instructions.

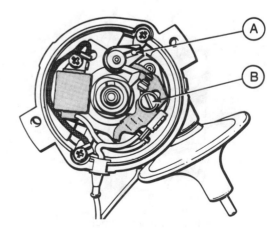

Fig. 4.6 Contact breaker points removal – Lucas, CVH (Sec 4)

A   Secondary movement cam   B   Securing screw

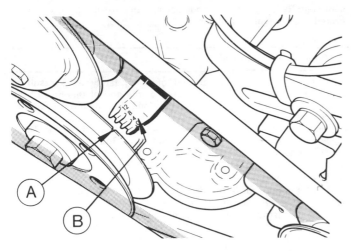

Fig. 4.7 Ignition timing marks – ohv (Sec 5)

A   *Crankshaft pulley notch*   B   *Timing cover scale*

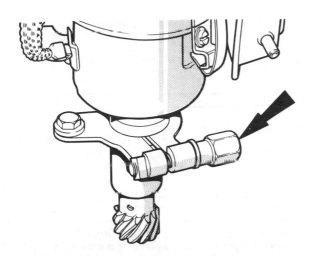

Fig. 4.8 Distributor clamp plate pinch-bolt (arrowed) – ohv (Sec 5)

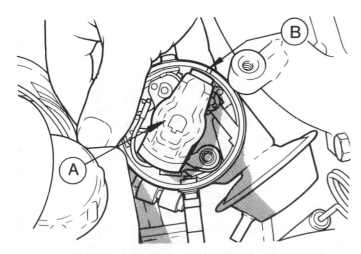

Fig. 4.9 Rotor arm (A) with rim alignment mark made after withdrawing the distributor (B) (Sec 7)

5   Start the engine and allow it to idle at the specified speed.
6   Disconnect the vacuum pipe from the distributor and plug the pipe with a piece of rod.
7   If the timing light is now directed at the engine timing marks, the pulley notch will appear to be stationery and opposite the specified mark on the scale. If the marks are not in alignment, release the distributor clamp pinch-bolt (ohv engines) or securing bolts (CVH engines) and turn the distributor in whichever direction is necessary to align the marks.
8   Retighten the pinch-bolt or securing bolts, switch off the engine, remove the timing light and reconnect the vacuum pipe.
9   It may now be necessary to check and adjust the engine idle speed if the distributor setting has to be varied to any extent.

6   Distributor advance – checking

1   A secondary use of the timing light is to check that the centrifugal and vacuum advance functions of the distributor are working.
2   The tests are not of course precise as would be the case if sophisticated equipment were used, but will at least indicate the serviceability of the unit.
3   With the engine idling, timing light connected and vacuum pipe disconnected and plugged as described in the preceding Section, increase the engine speed to 2000 rpm and note the approximate distance which the pulley mark moves out of alignment with the mark on the scale.
4   Reconnect the vacuum pipe to the distributor and repeat the test when for the same increase in engine speed, the alignment differential of the timing marks should be greater than previously observed. Refer to the Specifications for typical figures.
5   A further check of the vacuum advance can be made by removing the distributor cap after the engine has been switched off, disconnecting the distributor vacuum pipe at its suction end, and sucking the pipe. The suction should be sufficient to move the distributor baseplate slightly.
6   If these tests do not prove positive, renew the vacuum unit as described in Section 8.
7   Some models are equipped with a spark delay/sustain valve in the vacuum line from carburettor to distributor, the purpose of which is to delay vacuum advance under certain part throttle conditions. If such a valve is suspected of malfunctioning, it should be tested by substitution, or taken to a Ford dealer for specialised checking. The main effect of the valve is to reduce exhaust emission levels and it is unlikely that malfunction would have a noticeable effect on engine performance.
8   If a ported vacuum switch (PVS) is fitted in the vacuum line, its purpose is to bypass the spark sustain valve when normal engine operating temperature (as sensed by the temperature of the coolant flowing round the inlet manifold) has been reached.
9   For further information on the spark delay/sustain valve and ported vacuum switch refer to the emission control information in Chapter 13.

7   Distributor – removal and refitting

OHV engines
1   Disconnect the leads from the spark plugs, remove the distributor cap and place the cap with the leads to one side.
2   Disconnect the LT lead from the coil negative terminal and disconnect the distributor vacuum pipe.
3   Using a ring spanner or socket on the crankshaft pulley bolt, turn the crankshaft until No 1 piston is at tdc. Verify this by checking that the timing cover mark is aligned with the notch on the crankshaft pulley and that the rotor arm (contact end) is pointing to the No 1 spark plug lead contact in the distributor cap when fitted. Do not turn the crankshaft again until after the distributor has been refitted.
4   Mark the position of the rotor arm on the rim of the distributor body.
5   Mark the position of the distributor body in relation to the cylinder block.
6   Remove the bolt which holds the distributor clamp plate to the cylinder block, do not remove the distributor by releasing the clamp pinch-bolt.
7   Withdraw the distributor without turning the body, then make a further mark on the rim to indicate the new position of the rotor arm.
8   To install the original distributor, hold it over its hole in the cylinder

block so that the body mark made before removal is aligned with the one on the cylinder block (No 1 piston still at tdc).

9   When the distributor is installed, the meshing of the drive and driven gears will cause the rotor arm to rotate in an anti-clockwise direction. This must be anticipated by positioning the rotor arm in line with the mark made in paragraph 7.

10 Install the distributor and check that the rotor arm and distributor body marks are aligned with the marks made before removal. Tighten the clamp plate bolt.

11 If the distributor was removed without marking its position, or if a new distributor is being fitted, install the distributor in the following way.

12 Set No 1 piston to tdc. To do this, remove No 1 spark plug and place the finger over the plug hole. Turn the crankshaft pulley bolt until compression can be felt, which indicates that No 1 piston is rising on its firing stroke. Continue turning until the timing marks for tdc are in alignment.

13 Hold the distributor over its hole in the cylinder block so that the vacuum unit is aligned with the engine oil dipstick guide tube.

14 Set the rotor arm to anticipate its rotation as the gears mesh on installation, remembering that the arm will turn in an anti-clockwise direction and should take up a final position with its contact end opposite No 1 spark plug lead contact (as if the distributor cap is fitted).

15 Release the clamp plate pinch-bolt and install the distributor. Check that the body and rotor arm are correctly positioned, then swivel the clamp plate as necessary to be able to screw in the clamp plate bolt. Tighten the clamp plate pinch-bolt.

16 Fit the distributor cap and reconnect the HT and LT leads.

17 Check the timing as described in Section 5 and then reconnect the vacuum pipe to the distributor.

CVH engines

18 Refer to Section 14. Instead of disconnecting the multi-plug from the distributor, disconnect the LT lead from the coil.

8 Distributor vacuum unit – removal and refitting

1   This will normally only be required if a new unit is to be fitted due to a fault having been diagnosed in the old one.

2   Remove the distributor cap and the rotor arm. Disconnect the vaccum pipe from the unit.

3   Extract the circlip which holds the vacuum advance actuating rod to the pivot post (Bosch distributors only).

4   Extract the two screws which hold the unit to the distributor body, tilt the unit downwards to release the actuating rod from the pivot post and then withdraw the unit.

5   Refitting is a reversal of removal, but apply a little grease to the

pivot post. Refitting may be made easier if the distributor baseplate is rotated slightly with the fingers.

9 Condenser – renewal

1   If the condenser is suspected of being faulty as a result of reference to the Fault Diagnosis chart at the end of this part of the Chapter, it may be removed and a new one fitted without having to remove the distributor.

2   Release the HT leads from the spark plugs, take off the distributor cap and place the cap and the leads to one side. Remove the rotor arm.

3   Disconnect the LT lead from the coil negative terminal.

OHV engines

4   Mark the position of the distributor body in relation to the clamp plate and then release the clamp plate pinch-bolt.

5   Turn the distributor approximately 120° in a clockwise direction to expose the condenser and extract its securing screw. Pull off its lead connecting block and remove the condenser.

6   Refitting is a reversal of removal.

7   Check the ignition timing on completion (Section 5).

CVH engines

8   Remove the condenser retaining screw.

9   On Lucas distributors, slide the contact spring away from the plastic retainer and remove the LT connector from the spring. Remove the condenser and wire.

10 On Bosch distributors, unclip the points-to-condenser wire and remove the condenser by sliding the grommet from the distributor body.

11 On all distributors, refitting is a reversal of the removal procedure.

10 Distributor – overhaul

1   Dismantling of the distributor should not be taken beyond the renewal of components described in earlier Sections of this Chapter.

2   Internal components are not supplied as spares. In the event of severe wear having taken place, obtain a new or reconditioned unit.

11 Spark plugs, HT leads and distributor cap – general

For CVH engines, refer also to Section 17

1   The spark plugs should be removed at the intervals described in Routine Maintenance. Before unscrewing the plugs, pull off the leads

Fig. 4.10 Removing condenser from distributor – ohv (Sec 9)

A   Condenser lead   B   Condenser securing screw

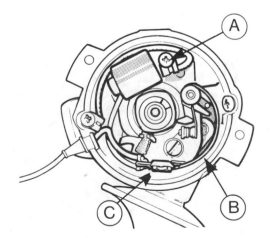

Fig. 4.11 Condenser removal – Lucas, CVH (Sec 9)

A   Securing screw   C   Wire connector
B   Contact spring

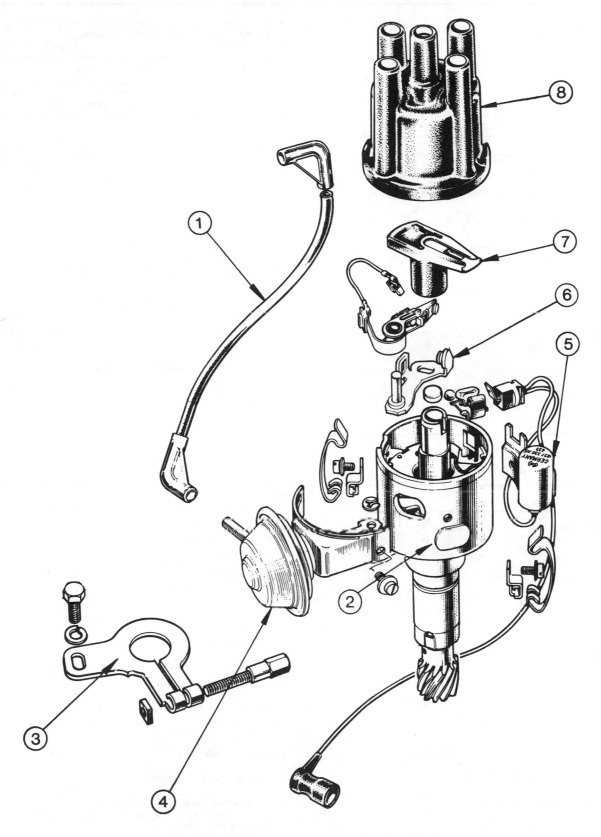

Fig. 4.12 Distributor components – ohv (Sec 10)

| 1 | Vacuum pipe | 3 | Distributor clamp plate | 5 | Condenser | 7 | Rotor arm |
| 2 | Distributor body | 4 | Vacuum unit | 6 | Contact breaker | 8 | Distributor cap |

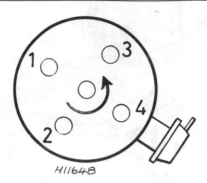

Fig. 4.13 HT lead connecting diagram – ohv (Sec 11)

and brush out any grit from the plug recesses to avoid it dropping into the cylinders as the spark plugs are unscrewed.

2   The appearance of a removed spark plug can give some indication of the condition or state of tune of the engine, but as modern engines run on a weaker fuel/air mixture in order to conform to current emission control regulations, a rather whiter appearance of the spark plug electrode area must be expected than was the case on older cars. As the mixture control is preset during production, a black appearance of the plug electrode will normally be due to oil passing worn piston rings or valve stem oil seals, unless the carburettor has been tampered with.

3   Either clean the spark plugs and re-gap them or renew them according to mileage interval. Cleaning the electrodes with a wire brush may leave conductance paths so an abrasive type cleaning device is to be preferred, but wash the plugs thoroughly in petrol to remove any abrasive powder, particularly from the threads if they were oily.

4   Always bend the outer electrode with a proper spark plug gapping tool to set the gaps to the specified clearance.

5   When installing the plugs use a long reach socket, apply a little grease to the threads of the plugs and tighten them only to the specified torque wrench setting. Overtightening may damage the plug or its seat.

6   Periodically wipe over the HT leads with a fuel-moistened cloth. Only pull the leads off by their rubber connectors.

7   The sockets on the distributor cap should be cleaned if they appear corroded when a lead is detached. A smear of petroleum jelly (not grease) applied to the ferrule on the end of the HT lead will help to prevent corrosion.

8   Never cut a carbon cored type of HT lead in order to insert a radio suppressor. Apart from it being unnecessary, the cable will be ruined.

9   Examine the inside of the distributor cap. If the contacts are corroded or are excessively burnt, or if the carbon centre contact is worn away, renew the cap. Make sure that the leads are installed in their correct firing order.

12 Fault diagnosis – mechanical ignition system

Symptom	Reason(s)
Engine fails to start	Discharged battery
	Loose battery connections
	Oil on contact points
	Disconnected ignition leads
	Faulty condenser
	Damp HT leads or distributor cap
	Faulty coil
	Mechanical fault (eg distributor drive)
	Ignition timing grossly incorrect (after overhaul)
Engine starts and runs but misfires	Faulty spark plug
	Cracked distributor cap
	Cracked rotor arm
	Worn advance mechanism
	Incorrect spark plug gap
	Incorrect contact points gap
	Faulty condenser
	Faulty coil
	Incorrect timing
	Poor earth connections
Engine fires but will not run	Ballast resistor or associated component defective
Engine overheats and lacks power	Seized advance weights in distributor
	Perforated or disconnected vacuum pipe
	Incorrect ignition timing
Engine pinks	Timing too advanced
	Advance mechanism stuck
	Broken centrifugal weight spring
	Low fuel octane rating
Contact points badly burnt	Poor earth connections at battery or engine/body earth straps
	Faulty condenser

Measuring plug gap. A feeler gauge of the correct size (see ignition system specifications) should have a slight 'drag' when slid between the electrodes. Adjust gap if necessary

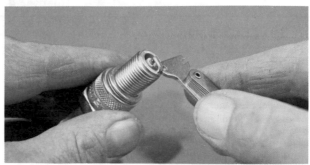

Adjusting plug gap. The plug gap is adjusted by bending the earth electrode inwards, or outwards, as necessary until the correct clearance is obtained. Note the use of the correct tool

Normal. Grey-brown deposits, lightly coated core nose. Gap increasing by around 0.001 in (0.025 mm) per 1000 miles (1600 km). Plugs ideally suited to engine, and engine in good condition

Carbon fouling. Dry, black, sooty deposits. Will cause weak spark and eventually misfire. Fault: over-rich fuel mixture. Check: carburettor mixture settings, float level and jet sizes; choke operation and cleanliness of air filter. Plugs can be re-used after cleaning

Oil fouling. Wet, oily deposits. Will cause weak spark and eventually misfire. Fault: worn bores/piston rings or valve guides; sometimes occurs (temporarily) during running-in period. Plugs can be re-used after thorough cleaning

Overheating. Electrodes have glazed appearance, core nose very white — few deposits. Fault: plug overheating. Check: plug value, ignition timing, fuel octane rating (too low) and fuel mixture (too weak). Discard plugs and cure fault immediately

Electrode damage. Electrodes burned away; core nose has burned, glazed appearance. Fault: pre-ignition. Check: as for 'Overheating' but may be more severe. Discard plugs and remedy fault before piston or valve damage occurs

Split core nose (may appear initially as a crack). Damage is self-evident, but cracks will only show after cleaning. Fault: pre-ignition or wrong gap-setting technique. Check: ignition timing, cooling system, fuel octane rating (too low) and fuel mixture (too weak). Discard plugs, rectify fault immediately

PART B: ELECTRONIC SYSTEM (1.3 & 1.6 ENGINES)

13 Description and maintenance

One of two systems may be fitted, Bosch or Lucas. Interchanging of alternative makes of component should not be done, except for the coil. Never fit a coil from a conventional mechanical breaker system.

The system includes a breakerless distributor driven from the flywheel end of the camshaft.

The electronic module, which is usually remotely sited on these systems, is integrated in the distributor on the Ford Escort.

A high output type ignition coil is located on the side of the engine compartment.

Ignition adjustments (dwell angle and timing) have been eliminated from routine service operations.

The breakerless distributor has no mechanical contact breaker or condenser, these components being replaced by a trigger wheel, a trigger plate and a pick-up coil. The rotor arm is driven at half engine speed and rotates in an anti-clockwise direction when viewed from the transmission.

The electronic amplifier module may be one of two different makes – Bosch or AC Delco (used on the Lucas distributor). The module is a sealed unit, which should be treated with care, and is connected to the distributor body by a multi-plug.

The action of the distributor is to provide a pulse to the electronic module, which in turn triggers the ignition to fire the fuel/air mixture through the spark plug electrodes. This pulse is created by a magnetic signal generating system within the distributor.

Spark advance and distribution is carried out in an identical way to that used in conventional mechanical breaker systems. A dual diaphragm type distributor is fitted to emission control models (Sweden).

Maintenance consists of keeping all electrical connections secure, the HT leads and distributor cap clean. Inspect the distributor cap and rotor arm for cracks if misfiring occurs (refer to Section 17).

Repair and overhaul operations should be limited to those described in this Chapter as the supply of spare parts is restricted to the distributor cap, the rotor arm, electronic module, drive dog and vacuum diaphragm unit.

Safety note

The voltage produced from the HT circuit on an electronic ignition system is considerably greater than that from a conventional system. In consequence, take extra precautions when handling the HT leads with the engine running. ALthough not lethal, the shock experience could be severe.

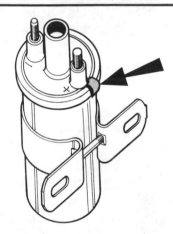

Fig. 4.14 Lucas type coil (electronic ignition). Clip is arrowed (Sec 13)

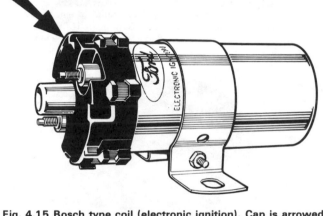

Fig. 4.15 Bosch type coil (electronic ignition). Cap is arrowed (Sec 13)

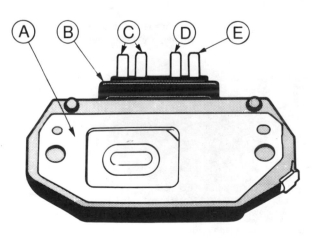

Fig. 4.16 Base of electronic amplifier module (Sec 13)

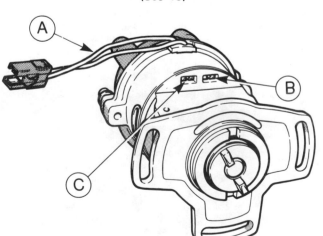

Fig. 4.17 Distributor connecting point for electronic module (Sec 13)

A	Module	D	Feed from ignition switch
B	Flexible seal	E	To coil LT terminal
C	To distributor trigger coil		

A	LT leads to coil and ignition feed	B	Module to trigger coil socket
		C	Module to coil LT lead socket

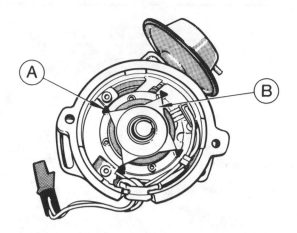

Fig. 4.18 Pulse triggering device (Bosch) (Sec 13)

A   Stator   B   Trigger wheel

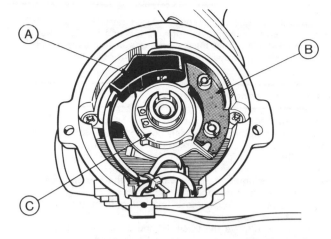

Fig. 4.19 Pulse triggering device (Lucas) (Sec 13)

A   Trigger coil   C   Trigger wheel
B   Stator

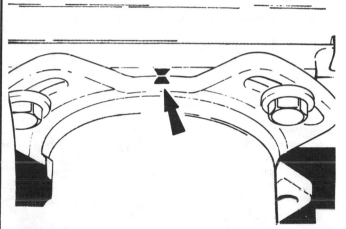

Fig. 4.20 Distributor and cylinder head alignment marks (arrowed)
(Sec 14)

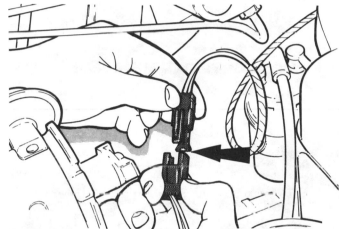

Fig. 4.21 Distributor multi-plug LT connections (arrowed) (Sec 14)

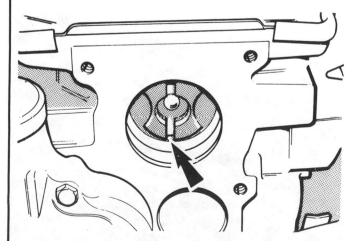

Fig. 4.22 Distributor offset drive dogs (arrowed) (Sec 14)

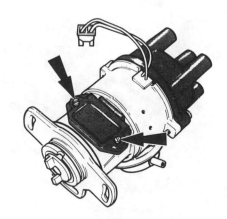

Fig. 4.23 Module securing screws (arrowed) (Sec 15)

Care should be taken not to knock the distributor when the ignition is switched on and the engine not running. It is possible for the engine to fire on one cylinder under these conditions, with resultant injury to the hands if engaged in overhaul or adjustment operations.

14 Distributor – removal and refitting

Original unit

1   The original distributor is precisely positioned for optimum ignition timing during production and marked accordingly with a punch mark on the distributor mounting flange and the cylinder head.

2   Disconnect the HT leads from the spark plugs.

3   Extract the distributor cap screws, lift off the cap and position it with the leads to one side (photo).

4   Disconnect the wiring harness multi-plug from the distributor. Disconnect the vacuum pipe.

5   Unscrew and remove the three distributor flange mounting bolts and withdraw the distributor from the cylinder head (photos).

6   Before refitting the distributor, check the condition of the oil seal and renew it if necessary (photo).

7   Hold the distributor so that the punch marks on the distributor body and the offset drive dog are in approximate alignment, then insert the distributor into its recess.

14.3 Removing a distributor cap screw

14.5A Two of the distributor mounting bolts. The third bolt is not visible

14.5B Removing the distributor

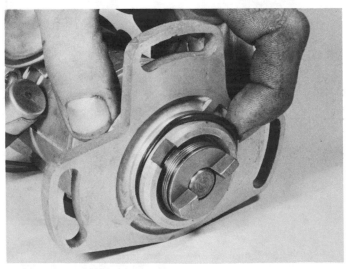

14.6 Check the condition of the oil seal

14.14 Ignition timing marks

8 Check that the drive components have engaged and then rotate the distributor until the punch marks on flange and head are in alignment. Insert the bolts and tighten to the specified torque.

9 Reconnect all the disconnected components.

New unit

10 Where a new distributor is being installed, its flange will obviously not have a punch mark and it must therefore be fitted in the following way.

11 Hold the distributor in approximately its fitted position, making sure that the vacuum unit is horizontal and towards the right-hand side when viewed from the roadwheel. Also ensure that the drive dog is in approximately the correct alignment to engage with the offset segments of the camshaft dog.

12 Locate the distributor on the cylinder head. When you are sure that the drive dogs are fully engaged, screw in the flange bolts so that they are not only positioned centrally in the flange slots, but still allow the distributor to be rotated stiffly.

13 Reconnect the distributor cap, the spark plug leads and the LT multi-plug, but not the vacuum pipe, which should be plugged.

14 Using a little quick-drying white paint, increase the contrast of the timing notch in the crankshaft pulley and the appropriate mark (see Specifications) on the timing belt cover scale (photo).

15 Connect a timing light (stroboscope) in accordance with the manufacturer's instructions.

16 Start the engine, allow it to idle and point the timing light at the timing marks. They should appear stationary and in alignment. If they are not, rotate the distributor as necessary to bring them into line and then tighten one of the distributor bolts.

17 Switch off the engine, remove the timing light and then tighten all the distributor mounting bolts to the specified torque.

18 Punch mark the distributor flange at a point exactly opposite the mark on the cylinder head. Future installation can then be carried out as described in paragraphs 1 to 9 of this Section.

19 Reconnect the vacuum pipe to the distributor.

20 If it is wished to check the advance characteristics of the distributor, refer to Section 6.

15 Ignition amplifier module – removal and refitting

1 Remove the distributor as described in the preceding Section.

2 Extract the two screws which hold the module to the distributor body and pull the module from its multi-plug.

3 Before refitting, check that the rubber grommet is in good condition. If not, renew it.

4 Coat the metal rear face of the module with special heat sink compound available from your dealer. This is to ensure good earthing contact.

5 Refit the distributor as described in Section 14.

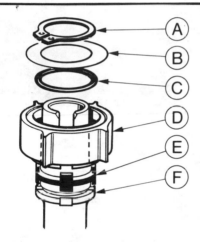

Fig. 4.24 Trigger wheel components (Lucas) (Sec 16)

A	Circlip	D	Trigger wheel
B	Washer	E	Toothed collar
C	O-ring	F	Shaft slots

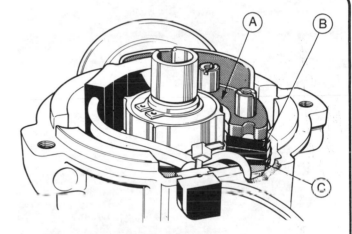

Fig. 4.25 Distributor signal operating system (Lucas) (Sec 16)

| A | Stator | C | Baseplate (upper) |
| B | Permanent magnets | | |

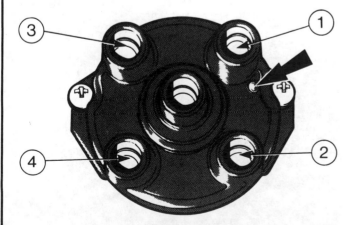

Fig. 4.26 Distributor cap HT connections. Arrowed dimple denotes No 1 plug lead (Sec 17)

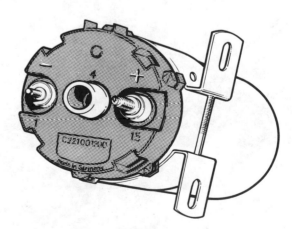

Fig. 4.27 Ignition coil terminals (Sec 18)

16 Distributor – overhaul

1   As noted in Section 13, distributor spare parts are not generally available. In the event of malfunction or mechanical wear occurring in the distributor itself, a new unit must be obtained.

2   The rotor arm is simply pulled off the shaft once the cap has been withdrawn (two screws) from the distributor (photo).

3   Access to the trigger wheel and associated components is gained by removing the plastic shield (photo).

4   The trigger wheel on both Lucas and Bosch distributors is secured to the shaft by a circlip.

5   If it is wished to remove the distributor baseplate to gain access to the vacuum unit, **do not** slacken the screws which hold the permanent magnet in position on the Lucas distributor, or the air gap will be altered. The baseplate is secured by three screws.

6   As the baseplate is lifted away, the vacuum unit operating lever can be disconnected. The vacuum unit is secured to the distributor body by two screws.

7   Do not drop or strike the distributor or its components, some of which are both mechanically and electrically fragile.

16.2 Removing the rotor arm

16.3 Removing distributor plastic shield

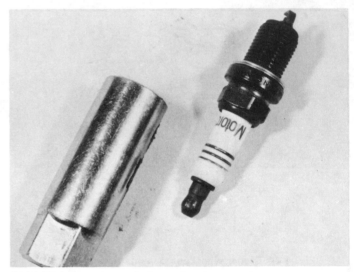

17.1A Miniature type spark plug and socket wrench

17.1B Connecting a spark plug HT lead

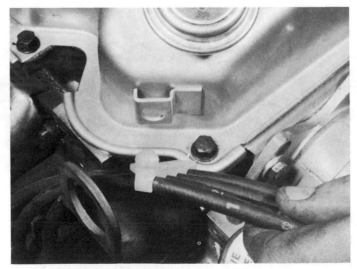

17.1C HT lead support clip and rocker cover bracket

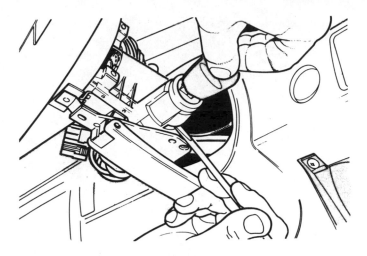

Fig. 4.28 Removing ignition lock cylinder (Sec 19)

Fig. 4.29 Ignition key positions (Sec 19)

O   Off
I   Ignition off, radio on,
     steering unlocked
II   Ignition on

III Start engine (repeat
     operation only after
     returning key to position I)

17 Spark plugs, HT leads and distributor cap – general

1   In general, the same remarks apply as were made in Section 11. Note however that a different type of plug is used, and that its electrode gap and tightening torque are different (photos).
2   Only remove plugs from the CVH engine when it is warm or cold – never when it is hot.
3   Note that the firing order on the CVH engine is different from the ohv engine.

18 Ignition coil – general

1   The LT connections to the coil used with electronic ignition cannot be confused as the terminals are of different size.
2   Never fit a coil from a conventional ignition system into an electronic ignition system otherwise the amplifier module may be damaged.

19 Ignition lock cylinder – removal and refitting

This operation also applies to cars with mechanical ignition systems.
1   Disconnect the battery earth terminal, then remove the steering column lower shroud.
2   Insert the ignition key into the lock and turn to position I.
3   Using a screwdriver, depress the cylinder retaining clip and withdraw the lock cylinder by pulling on the key.
4   Refit by simply pushing the cylinder into position with the key held in position I.
5   Refer to Chapter 9, for details of steering column lock removal.

20 Fault diagnosis – electronic ignition system

Symptom	Reason(s)
Engine fails to start	Discharged battery Loose battery connections Disconnected ignition leads Crack in distributor cap or rotor Faulty amplifier module
Engine starts and runs but misfires	Faulty spark plug Crack in distributor cap Cracked rotor arm Worn advance mechanism Faulty coil Poor earth connections
Engine overheats and lacks power	Perforated or disconnected vacuum pipe Faulty centrifugal or advance mechanism
Engine pinks	Advance mechanism stuck Low fuel octane rating

Note: *Any of the foregoing symptoms could be caused by incorrect timing, but unless the distributor mounting bolts have become slack this is unlikely as the timing is preset during production with the distributor flange and cylinder head punch marks aligned.*

Chapter 5 Clutch

Contents

Specifications

General
Type .... Single dry plate, diaphragm spring
Actuation .... Cable with automatic adjuster

Driven plate
Diameter:
    1.1 Hatchback .... 165 mm (6.5 in)
    1.1 Van and Estate and 1.3 models .... 190 mm (7.5 in)
    1.6 (all models) .... 200 mm (7.9 in)
Lining thickness .... 3.20 mm (0.126 in)
Number of torsion springs 4

Pedal stroke .... 155 mm (6.1 in)

Torque wrench settings

	Nm	lbf ft
Pressure plate cover-to-flywheel:		
165 mm diam (6.5 in)	10	7
190/200 mm diam (7.5/7.9 in)	18	13

1 Description

The clutch is of single dry plate type wih a diaphragm spring pressure plate.

Actuation is by cable and the pendant mounted pedal incorporates a self-adjusting mechanism.

The release bearing is of ball type and is kept in constant contact with the fingers of the diaphragm spring by the action of the pedal self-adjusting mechanism. In consequence, there is no pedal free movement adjustment required.

When the clutch pedal is released, the adjustment pawl is no longer engaged with the teeth on the pedal quadrant, the cable being tensioned however by the spring which is located between the pedal and the quadrant. When the pedal is depressed the pawl engages in the nearest vee between the teeth. The particular tooth engagement position will gradually change as the components move to compensate for wear in the clutch driven plate and stretch in the cable.

The size of the clutch varies according to engine capacity (see Specifications).

2 Clutch pedal – removal and refitting

1 Below the instrument panel, bend back the retaining tabs, extract the clips and remove the lower insulating panel.

2 At the transmission, prise the clutch release lever and detach the clutch cable from the fork at its end.

LHD models

3 Pull out the spring clip, take off the plain and wave washers and slide the pedal from the shaft.

4 As the pedal is withdrawn, detach the clutch cable from it.

5 The pedal can now be dismantled as necessary in order to renew the bushes, spring or adjustment mechanism.

6 To refit, first set the pawl with its spring so that the pawl is in contact with the smooth part of the quadrant.

7 Refit the clutch pedal to its shaft, which should have been greased with molybdenum disulphide grease.

8 Connect the clutch cable to the pedal.

9 At the transmission, connect the cable to the clutch release lever.

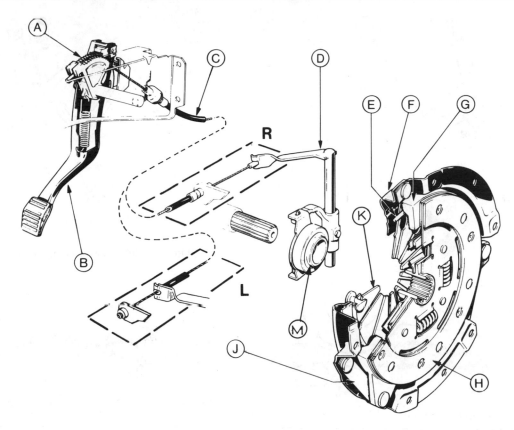

Fig. 5.1 Clutch arrangement (Sec 1)

A	Automatic adjuster	E	Fulcrum ring	H	Driven plate (friction disc)
B	Clutch pedal	F	Cover	J	Steel straps
C	Clutch cable	G	Pressure plate	K	Diaphragm spring
D	Release assembly				

L — LHD cable arrangement
M — Release bearing
R — RHD cable arrangement

10 Operate the clutch pedal two or three times and refit the dash lower insulating panel.

RHD versions

11 Extract the retaining clip securing the brake pedal to the master cylinder pushrod.
12 Detach the clutch cable from the pedal.
13 Remove the central retaining clip from the pedal cross-shaft. Note the position of the spacers and washers, then withdraw the cross-shaft towards the heater. Lift off the clutch and brake pedals.
14 The pedal can now be dismantled as necessary in order to renew the bushes, spring or adjustment mechanism.
15 To refit, first set the pawl with its spring so that the pawl is in contact with the smooth part of the quadrant.
16 Position the pedals in the support bracket and refit the cross-shaft, which should have been greased with molybdenum disulphide grease. Ensure that the washers are refitted in the same position as noted during removal then refit the central retaining clip to the cross-shaft.
17 Refit the master cylinder pushrod to brake pedal retaining clip.
18 Connect the clutch cable to the pedal and, at the transmission end, to the release lever.
19 Operate the clutch pedal two or three times and refit the dash lower insulating panel.

3 Clutch operating cable – renewal

1 The cable is released from the release lever and the pedal as described in the preceding Section.
2 On LHD vehicles, draw the cable towards the engine compartment rear bulkhead and remove the cable retainer and its bush.
3 On RHD vehicles, remove the plastic clip which secures the cable to the steering rack housing.
4 Refit the clutch by reversing the appropriate removal operations.

On RHD vehicles, align the white band on the cable with the paint spot on the steering rack housing before fitting the cable securing clip.

4 Clutch – method of access

1 The usual method of access to the clutch assembly is by removing the transmission as described in Chapter 6.
2 If the engine is also being removed for major overhaul then the engine/transmission will be removed as a combined unit and separated later.

5 Clutch – removal

1 With the flywheel exposed, unbolt the clutch pressure plate. Unscrew the retaining bolts in a diagonal sequence a turn at a time until the pressure of the diaphragm spring is relieved. Remove the bolts completely.
2 Carefully prise the pressure plate from its locating dowels and remove it. Take care not to allow the driven plate to fall, as will certainly happen as the pressure of the plate is withdrawn.

6 Clutch – inspection and renovation

1 The most likely reason for dismantling the clutch will be due to the occurence of faults described in Section 8.
2 Unless the vehicle has been used under conditions of very low traffic density and in fairly flat terrain, the clutch driven plate will certainly require renewal any time after 80 000 km (50 000 miles) have been covered.
3 Under dense traffic driving conditions, in hilly country or if the

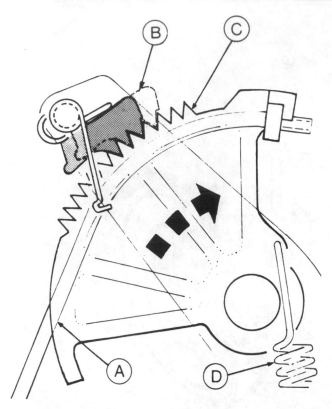

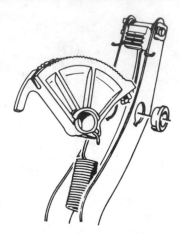

Fig. 5.4 Clutch pedal components (Sec 2)

Fig. 5.2 Clutch cable automatic adjuster (Sec 1)

A   Cable   C   Toothed quadrant
B   Pawl   D   Tension spring

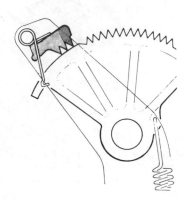

Fig. 5.5 Automatic adjuster setting ready for pedal refitting (Sec 2)

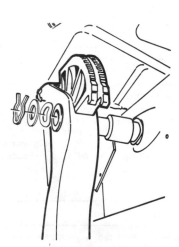

Fig. 5.3 Removing the clutch pedal (Sec 2)

ommended that all the components are renewed at the same time. If the driven plate has had a short life however, due to adverse operating conditions, then the pressure plate assembly will probably give further service until the next driven plate renewal stage is reached.

7   If the pressure plate is not renewed, examine it very closely for scoring of the pressure plate face, cracking of the diaphragm spring fingers or rust or corrosion. If any of these conditions are evident, renew the assembly.

8   Now check the contact surface of the flywheel. If it is grooved or deeply scored, the flywheel must be renewed or refinished. Refer to Chapter 1, Section 17 or 39. Hair cracks are usually a sign of overheating due to excessive clutch slip.

9   A pilot bearing is not used in the centre of the flywheel/crankshaft rear flange as the input shaft is supported independently on two bearings within the transmission housing.

10   Finally, check the condition of the clutch release bearing. If it is noisy when turned with the fingers or is obviously worn, it must be renewed. It is always best to renew it at time of clutch overhaul as it has a hard life and failure at a later date will mean removing the transmission again for this one component to be changed.

---

7   Clutch – installation and centralising

1   Check that the contact surfaces of the flywheel and pressure plate are clean and free from oil or grease.

2   Offer up the driven plate to the flywheel. Make sure that the projecting hub of the driven plate is **not** against the flywheel. The plate is usually marked FLYWHEEL SIDE (photo).

3   Hold the driven plate in position and then locate the pressure

driver is 'heavy footed' and seldom matches the speed of the engine to that of the transmission when changing gear, then clutch renewal may be required at half the mileage just mentioned or even earlier.

4   Examine the friction linings of the driven plate. If they are worn down to the rivet heads then renew the plate. Don't attempt to re-line the plate with new linings yourself, it is seldom satisfactory.

5   If the friction linings appear oil-stained, renew the driven plate and before fitting it, rectify the oil leak. This will probably mean renewal of the crankshaft rear oil seal or the transmission input shaft oil seal.

6   It is difficult to decide whether to renew the clutch pressure plate at the same time as the driven plate is renewed. If a really good mileage has been covered by the old components then it is rec-

7.2 Driven plate marking

7.3 Installing the clutch

7.7 Tightening the pressure plate cover bolts. Note driven plate centralising tool

7.10 Clutch release bearing attachment to fork (roll pin arrowed)

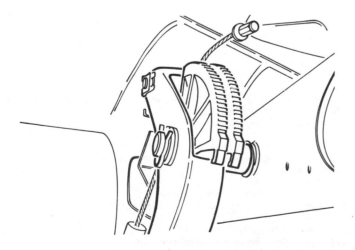

Fig. 5.6 Connecting clutch cable to pedal (Sec 3)

plate/cover assembly on its positioning dowels on the flywheel, so trapping the driven plate (photo).

4 Insert the retaining bolts, but only screw them in finger tight.

5 The clutch driven plate must now be centralised in order to facilitate mating of the transmission to the engine. To do this, a clutch alignment tool is needed. Either purchase one of the several multi-purpose types available from motor accessory stores, or the official tool (21-052), or use an old input shaft or make up something by winding tape around a rod until suitable diameters are achieved.

6 The tool should be passed through the splined hub of the driven plate and its end engaged in the centre hole in the flywheel. The action of engaging the end of the tool in the flywheel will move the driven plate so as to centralise it.

7 Without moving the driven plate or tool, tighten the pressure plate cover bolts to the specified torque in a diagonal sequence and in a progressive manner (photo).

8 Withdraw the alignment tool.

9 Smear the splines of the input shaft and the release bearing hub sliding surfaces with molybdenum disulphide grease.

10 Connect the release bearing to the fork, noting that it is only retained at its upper point by being hooked over a roll pin (photo).

11 The transmission can now be reconnected to the engine as described in Chapter 6.

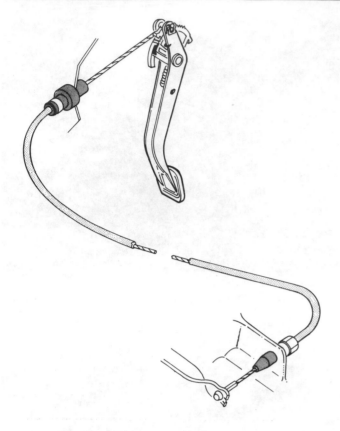

Fig. 5.7 Clutch cable routing (RHD) (Sec 3)

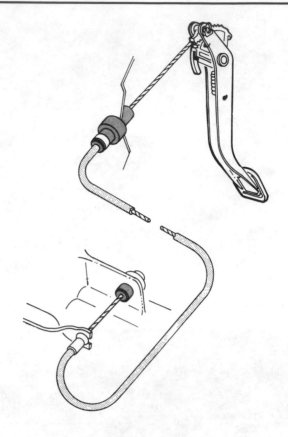

Fig. 5.8 Clutch cable routing (LHD) Sec 3

8   Fault diagnosis – clutch

Symptom	Reason(s)
Judder when taking up drive	Loose engine/transmission mountings Worn friction linings Oil saturated linings Worn splines on input shaft or clutch driven plate
Clutch spin (failure to disengage) so that gears cannot be meshed	Driven plate sticking on input shaft splines due to rust. May occur after standing idle for long periods Damaged or misaligned pressure plate assembly
Clutch slip (increase in engine speed does not result in comparable increase in road speed – particularly on gradients)	Friction surfaces worn or oil contaminated Weak clutch engagement due to fault in automatic cable adjuster or weak diaphragm spring
Noise evident on depressing clutch pedal	Dry, worn or damaged release bearing Play between driven plate and input shaft splines
Noise evident as clutch pedal released	Distorted driven plate Weak or broken driven plate torsion springs Distorted or worn input shaft Release bearing loose on mounting hub

Chapter 6 Transmission

For modifications, and information applicable to later models, refer to Supplement at end of manual

Contents

Specifications

Transmission type .... 4 forward speeds and 1 reverse, synchromesh on all forward gears

Ratios (:1)

Gear ratios:

	1.1 l and 1.3 l	1.6 l
1st	3.58	3.15
2nd	2.04	1.19
3rd	1.35	1.28
4th	0.95	0.95
Reverse	3.77	3.62

Final drive ratios:

	Car	Van
1.1l	4.06	4.29
1.3l	3.84	4.29
1.6l	3.58	4.06
XR3	3.84	-

Speedometer drive
Worm .... 21 teeth
Pinion:
    With 145 SR 13 types .... 20 teeth
    With all other types .... 19 teeth

Mainshaft and input shaft snap-ring thickness .... 1.86 to 1.89, 1.94 to 1.97 and 2.01 to 2.04 mm (0.0732 to 0.0744, 0.0764 to 0.0776 and 0.0791 to 0.0803 in)

Lubrication
Lubricant type .... SAE 80EP gear oil to Ford spec SQM-2C9008-A
Lubricant capacity .... 2.8 litres (4.9 pints)

Torque wrench settings

	Nm	lbf ft
Transmission bellhousing-to-engine bolts	41	30
Transmission housing section bolts	25	18
Cover plate bolts	12	9
Selector interlock cap nut	30	22
Crownwheel bolts	110	81
Gearchange housing-to-floor nuts	15	11
Gearchange rod clamp bolt	18	13
Oil filler plug	25	18
Stabiliser rod-to-transmission bolt	55	40

1 Description

The gearbox and differential are housed in a two section light alloy casting which is bolted to the transversely mounted engine.

Drive from the engine/transmission is transmitted to the front roadwheels through open driveshafts.

The engine torque is transmitted to the gearbox input shaft. Once a gear is selected, power is then transmitted to the main (output) shaft. The helically cut forward speed gears on the output shaft are in constant mesh with the corresponding gears on the input shaft.

Synchromesh units are used for 1st/2nd and 3rd/4th gear selection and operate as follows.

When the clutch pedal is depressed and the gearchange lever is moved to select a higher gear, the synchro baulk ring is pressed onto the gear cone. The friction generated causes the faster rotating gear on the input shaft to slow until its speed matches that of the gear on the output shaft. The gears can then be smoothly engaged.

When changing to a lower gear, the principle of operation is similar except that the speed of the slower rotating gear is increased by the action of the baulk ring on the cone.

Reverse gear is of the straight cut tooth type and is part of the 1st/2nd synchro unit. A sliding type reverse idler gear is used.

The torque from the gearbox output shaft is transmitted to the crownwheel which is bolted to the differential cage and thence through the differential gears to the driveshafts.

All adjustment to the differential and its bearings has been obviated by the inclusion of two diaphragm springs which are located in the smaller half of the transmission housing. Any tolerances which may exist are taken up by the sliding fit of the outer bearing ring in the smaller section of the housing.

Gear selection is obtained by rotary and axial movements of the main selector shaft (transmitted through a selector dog bolted to the selector shaft) and two guide levers to the guide shaft which also carries a selector dog.

Rotary movement of the main selector shaft engages a cam on the guide shaft selector dog either in the cut-out of the 1st/2nd or 3rd/4th gear selector fork or in the aperture in the reverse gear guide lever.

Axial movement of the selector shaft moves the appropriate selector fork on the guide shaft or reverse idler gear through the medium of the guide lever, so engaging the gear.

The selected gear is locked in engagement by a shift locking plate which is carried on the guide shaft selector dog and a spring-loaded interlock pin located in the smaller housing section.

2 Maintenance

1   The only maintenance required is to check and top up, if necessary, the oil level in the transmission at the intervals specified in Routine Maintenance at the beginning of this manual.

2   A combined level/filler plug is fitted and the correct oil level is established when the oil is just seen to be running out of the plug hole when the vehicle is on level ground.

3   Regular oil changing is not specified by the manufacturers, but the oil can be drained if necessary (prior to removal of the unit or after traversing a flooded road for example) by removing the selector shaft locking mechanism (Fig. 6.2).

3 Gearchange mechanism – adjustment

1   This is not a routine operation and will normally only be required after dismantling, to compensate for wear or to overcome any 'notchiness' evident during gear selection.

2   To set the linkage correctly, refer to Chapter 1, Section 20 or 42.

4 Gearchange mechanism – removal, overhaul and refitting

1   Before commencing removal operations, engage 4th gear.

2   Unscrew the gear lever knob, slide the rubber gaiter up the lever and remove it.

3   If the vehicle is not over an inspection pit, jack it up and fit axle stands.

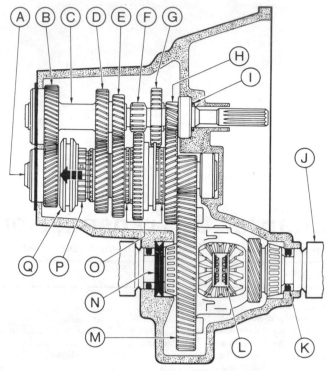

Fig. 6.1 Cutaway view of transmission (Sec 1)

A Mainshaft	K Oil seal
B 4th gear	L Driveshaft snap-ring
C Input shaft	M Crownwheel
D 3rd gear	N Diaphragm springs
E 2nd gear	O 1st/2nd synchro with
F Reverse gear	reverse gear
G Reverse idler gear	P 3rd/4th synchro
H 1st gear	Q 3rd/4th synchro sleeve
I Input shaft oil seal	(4th gear engaged)
J Driveshaft inboard	
CV joint	

4   Unhook the tension spring which runs between the gearchange rod and the side member.

5   Slacken the clamp bolt and pull the gearchange rod from the selector shaft which projects from the transmission.

6   Unbolt the end of the stabiliser from the transmission housing. Note the washer between the stabiliser trunnion and the transmission.

7   Still working under the vehicle, unbolt the gearchange housing from the floor. Withdraw the housing/stabiliser from the vehicle.

8   To dismantle, unbolt the housing from the stabiliser and detach the gearchange lever with plastic cover and the stabiliser from the slide block.

9   Detach the gearchange rod from the slide block. This is done by unclipping the upper guide shell and withdrawing the rod.

10   The gear lever can be removed by prising off the rubber spring retaining clip and withdrawing the spring, half shell and plastic cover.

11   Renew any worn components and reassemble by reversing the dismantling procedure, but observe the following points.

12   Make sure that the cut-out at the edge of the plastic cover is aligned with the curve in the gearchange lever as shown.

13   The gear lever must locate in the shift rod cut-out.

14   To install the gearchange mechanism to the vehicle, offer it up from below and loosely attach it to the floor pan.

15   Reconnect the stabiliser to the gearbox, remembering to fit the washer between the trunnion and the gearbox.

16   The mechanism should now be secured to the floor pan by tightening the nuts to the specified torque.

17   Reconnect the gearchange rod to the shaft at the gearbox as described in Chapter 1, Section 20 or 42.

18   Working inside the vehicle, refit the gaiter and the knob to the gear lever.

19   Lower the vehicle to the ground.

5 Transmission – removal and refitting

1   Engage 4th gear and disconnect the battery earth lead.
2   Support the weight of the engine either by using a jack and block of wood under the sump or by attaching a hoist (refer to Chapter 1, Section 10 or 32).
3   Disconnect the speedometer cable from the transmission after unscrewing the retaining nut.
4   Disconnect the clutch control cable from the release lever. This is simply done by levering the release lever until the cable can be slipped out of its forked end.
5   Unscrew and remove the top four bolts which hold the gearbox flange to the engine.
6   Release the gearbox breather tube from the side rail.
7   Move the heater hose which runs between the thermostat housing and the heater to one side of the engine compartment and retain it with a piece of wire. This will prevent it obstructing the transmission during removal.
8   If the vehicle is not over an inspection pit, raise its front end and fit axle stands.
9   Working under the vehicle, disconnect the leads from the starter motor and the reversing lamp switch.
10 Unbolt and remove the starter motor.
11 Unbolt and remove the cover plate from the lower face of the clutch housing.
12 Disconnect the gearchange rod from the gearbox selector shaft by releasing the clamp pinch-bolt and pulling the rod towards the rear of the vehicle. Unhook the tension spring from the gearchange rod.
13 Unbolt the stabiliser rod from the side of the transmission, noting that there is a washer between the trunnion of the rod and the transmission casing.
14 Tie the gearchange rod and the stabiliser rod to the steering rack using a piece of wire.
15 Drain the oil from the transmission into a suitable container. As a drain plug is not fitted, unscrew the selector shaft locking assembly which includes the nut, cap, spring and interlock pin.
16 Unscrew and remove the balljoint retaining bolt from the outboard end of the right-hand track control arm. The bolt is of Torx type, having a socket head, and in the absence of the correct tool, an Allen key may be used to stop the bolt turning while the nut is unscrewed. Alternatively, use a pair of mole grips on the bolt head.
17 Disconnect the right-hand driveshaft from the transmission. Do this by inserting a lever between the constant velocity joint and the transmission. With an assistant pulling the roadwheel outwards, strike the end of the lever to release the joint from the differential. In order to prevent the differential pinions from turning and obstructing the driveshaft holes, insert a plastic plug or similar.
18 Tie up the disconnected driveshaft to avoid putting any strain on the joints.
19 Disconnect the suspension arm and the driveshaft from the left-hand side in a similar manner.
20 Check that the engine/transmission is still securely supported and unbolt the front left-hand mounting from the transmission.
21 Unscrew and remove the centre bolt from the mounting flexible component.

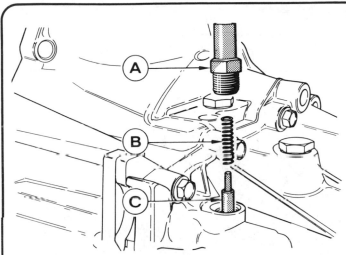

Fig. 6.2 Selector shaft cap nut (A), spring (B) and interlock pin (C) (Sec 2)

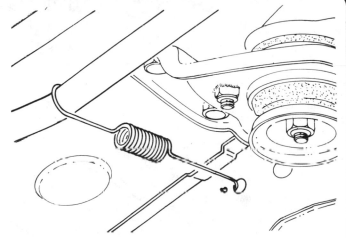

Fig. 6.3 Gearchange rod tension spring (Sec 4)

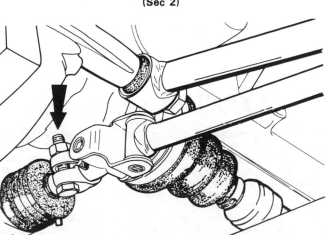

Fig. 6.4 Gearchange rod clamp bolt (arrowed) (Sec 4)

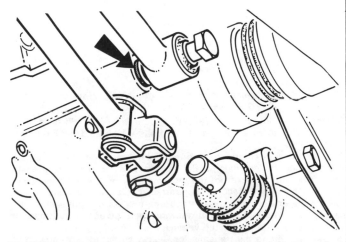

Fig. 6.5 Gearchange rod and stabiliser disconnected. Note washer (arrowed) (Sec 4)

5.31 Transmission mounting bracket

5.33 Pinion gear displaced in differential

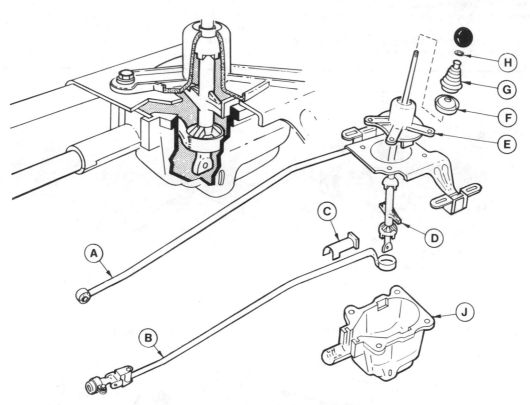

Fig. 6.6 Gearchange mechanism (Sec 4)

A	Stabiliser	D	Gear lever
B	Gearchange rod	E	Housing
C	Guide shell		

F	Spring carrier	H	Circlip
G	Rubber spring	J	Slide block

22 Unscrew and remove the centre bolt from the left-hand rear mounting and then remove the three bolts which hold the mounting bearer plate.

23 Unscrew and remove the two remaining bolts from the lower part of the clutch housing/engine flange. On 1.3 and 1.6 litre models detach the anti-roll bar from the crossmember on the left-hand side.

24 With the engine securely supported, withdraw the transmission towards the side of the engine compartment until the input shaft clears the clutch driven plate splined hub and then lower the transmission and remove it from under the vehicle.

25 Before refitting the transmission, lightly smear the splined part of the input shaft with a little grease, also the thrust bearing guide sleeve.

26 If the clutch has been dismantled, make sure that the driven plate has been centralised as described in Chapter 5.

27 Check that the engine adaptor plate is correctly located on its dowels.

28 With the transmission positioned on the floor below the vehicle, lift it up and engage the input shaft in the splined hub of the clutch driven plate. Obtain the help of an assistant for this work as the weight of the gearbox must not hang upon the input shaft while it is engaged in the driven plate.

29 Push the transmission into full engagement with the engine and check that the unit sits on its locating dowels and that the adaptor plate has not been displaced. Any reluctance for the transmission to mate with the engine may be due to the splines of the input shaft and clutch driven plate not engaging. Try swivelling the transmission slightly, or have your assistant rotate the crankshaft by applying a spanner to the crankshaft pulley bolt.

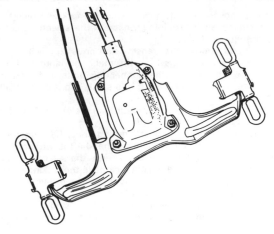

Fig. 6.7 Stabiliser rod assembly removed from floor (Sec 4)

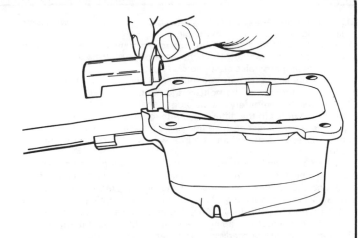

Fig. 6.8 Removing guide shell (Sec 4)

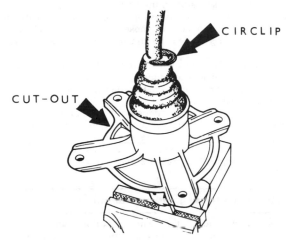

Fig. 6.9 Extracting rubber spring retaining circlip (Sec 4)

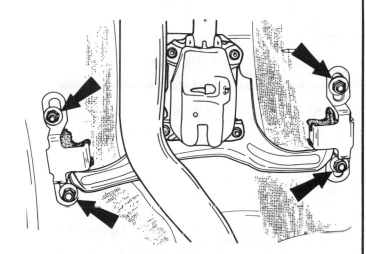

Fig. 6.10 Gearchange mechanism mounting nuts (arrowed)
(Sec 4)

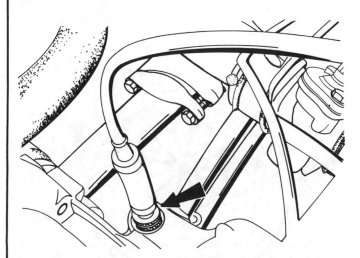

Fig. 6.11 Speedometer cable knurled retaining ring (arrowed)
(Sec 5)

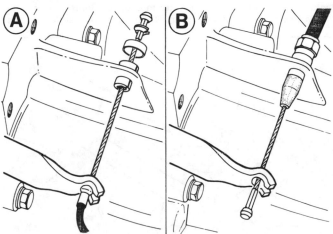

Fig. 6.12 Clutch cable attachment (Sec 5)

A   LHD   B   RHD

30 Once the transmission is fully engaged, screw in the two lower retaining bolts to hold it to the engine.
31 Refit the front and rear mountings to the transmission and to the body side member (photo). Refit the anti-roll bar left-hand mounting. Remove the engine hoist or support device.
32 Insert the selector shaft interlock pin, spring and cap bolt, having smeared the threads of the bolt with jointing compound.
33 Remove the temporary plastic plugs used to prevent displacement of the pinion gears in the differential. If plugs were not used, insert the finger into each driveshaft hole and align the pinion gear splined hole ready to accept the driveshaft. A mirror will assist in correct alignment (photo).
34 Fit a new snap-ring to the splined end of the left-hand driveshaft and insert the shaft into the transmission. Turn the shaft as necessary to engage the splines with those on the pinion gear. Once engaged, have an assistant push hard on the roadwheel until the snap-ring engages with the shaft fully home. Any reluctance to engage may be due to the driveshaft not being in a sufficiently horizontal attitude. In this event, remove the roadwheel in order to reduce the weight while the hub assembly is lifted.
35 Reconnect the suspension track control arm.
36 Repeat all the operations and refit the right-hand driveshaft.
37 Connect the stabiliser rod to the transmission making sure to insert the washer between the trunnion of the rod and the transmission casing.
38 Reconnect and adjust the gearchange rod as described in Chapter 1, Section 20 or 42.
39 Refit the gearchange rod tension spring.
40 Refit the starter motor.
41 Connect the leads to the starter motor and to the reversing lamp switch.
42 Fit the cover plate to the clutch housing.
43 Lower the vehicle to the ground.
44 Fit the upper bolts to the clutch housing/engine flange.
45 Reconnect the clutch operating cable.
46 Connect the speedometer drive cable to the transmission.
47 Fill the unit with the correct quantity and grade of oil.
48 Reconnect the battery earth lead.
49 Locate the transmission breather hose in the aperture in the longitudinal member.
50 Check the selection of all gears, and check the torque wrench settings of all nuts and bolts which were removed now that the weight of the vehicle is again on the roadwheels.

6 Transmission – removal of major assemblies

1 With the gearbox removed from the vehicle, clean away external dirt and grease using paraffin and a stiff brush or a water-soluble solvent. Take care not to allow water to enter the transmission.
2 Unscrew the lockbolt which holds the clutch release fork to the

shaft and remove the shaft, followed by the fork and release bearing.
3 If not removed for draining, unscrew the selector shaft cap nut, spring and interlock pin.
4 Unbolt and remove the transmission housing cover.
5 Remove the snap-rings from the main and input shaft bearings.
6 Unscrew and remove the connecting bolts and lift the smaller housing from the transmission. If it is stuck, tap it off carefully with a plastic-headed mallet.
7 Extract the swarf collecting magnet and clean it. Take care not to drop the magnet or it will shatter.
8 Withdraw the selector shaft, noting that the longer portion of smaller diameter is at the bottom as the shaft is withdrawn.
9 Remove the selector shaft coil spring, the selector forks and the shift locking plate. Note the roll pin located in the locking plate cut-out.
10 Withdraw the mainshaft, the input shaft and reverse gear as one assembly from the transmission housing.
11 Lift the differential assembly from the housing.
12 The transmission is now dismantled into its major assemblies.

7 Transmission – dismantling (general)

1 The need for further dismantling will depend upon the reasons for removal of the transmission in the first place.
2 A common reason for dismantling will be to renew the synchro units. Wear or malfunction in these components will have been obvious when changing gear by the noise or by the synchro, being easily 'beaten'.
3 The renewal of oil seals may be required as evident by pools of oil under the vehicle when stationary.
4 Jumping out of gear may mean renewal of the selector mechanism, forks or synchro sleeves.
5 General noise during operations on the road may be due to worn bearings, shafts or gears and when such general wear occurs, it will probably be more economical to renew the transmission complete.
6 When dismantling the geartrains, always keep the components strictly in their originally installed order.

8 Transmission housing and selector mechanism – overhaul

1 To remove the mainshaft bearing, break the plastic roller cage with a screwdriver. Extract the rollers and the cage, the oil slinger and retainers. Remove the bearing outer track.
2 When fitting the new bearing, also renew the oil slinger.
3 When renewing the input shaft oil seal, drive the old seal out by applying the drift inside the bellhousing (photos).
4 The constant velocity (CV) joint oil seals should be renewed at time of major overhaul.
5 The differential bearing tracks can be removed, using a drift inserted from the large housing section.

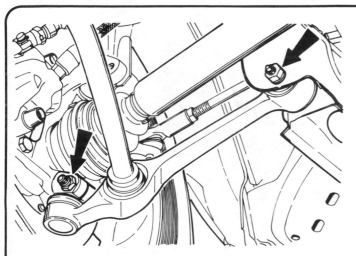

Fig. 6.13 Suspension arm disconnection points (arrowed) (Sec 5)

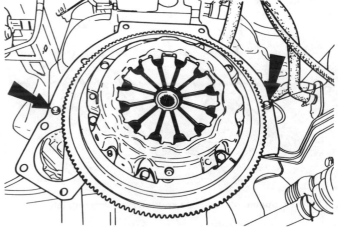

Fig. 6.14 Locating dowels for engine adaptor plate and transmission (arrowed) (Sec 5)

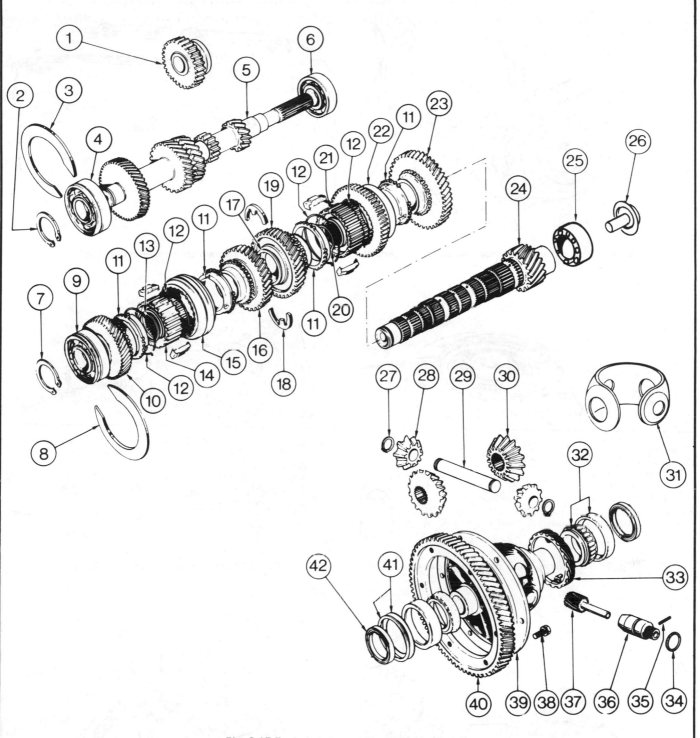

Fig. 6.15 Exploded view of transmission (Sec 6)

1 Reverse idler gear	12 Spring	22 1st/2nd synchro sleeve with reverse gear	32 Tapered roller bearing
2 Circlip	13 Circlip	23 1st speed gear	33 Speedometer drivegear
3 Snap-ring	14 3rd/4th synchro	24 Mainshaft	34 O-ring
4 Bearing	15 Synchro sleeve	25 Bearing	35 Roll pin
5 Input shaft	16 3rd speed gear	26 Oil slinger	36 Speedo drive pinion bearing
6 Bearing	17 Segment anchor ring	27 Circlip	37 Speedo drive pinion
7 Circlip	18 Semi-circular thrust segment	28 Differential pinion	38 Crownwheel bolts
8 Snap-ring	19 2nd speed gear	29 Differential shaft	39 Differential case
9 Bearing	20 Circlip	30 Pinion gear (driveshaft)	40 Crownwheel
10 4th gear	21 1st/2nd synchro hub	31 Thrust cage	41 Diaphragm springs
11 Baulk ring			42 Oil seal

139

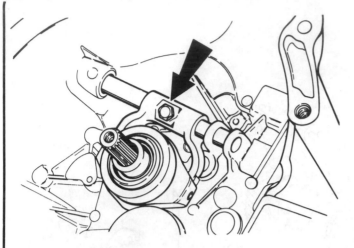

Fig. 6.16 Clutch release bearing fork lockbolt (arrowed) (Sec 6)

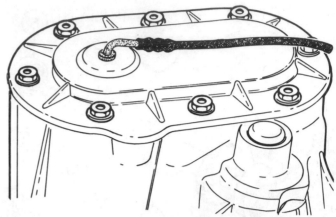

Fig. 6.17 Transmission cover plate (Sec 6)

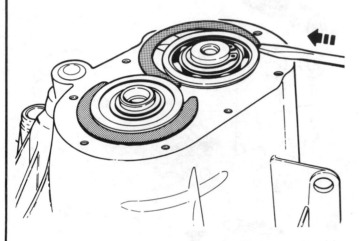

Fig. 6.18 Removing shaft snap-rings (Sec 6)

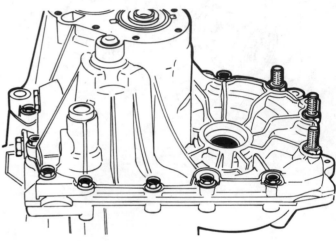

Fig. 6.19 Smaller housing section (Sec 6)

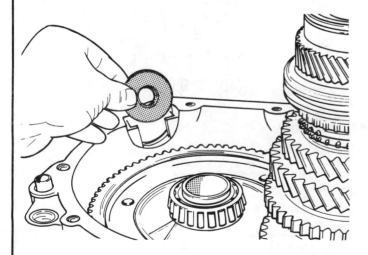

Fig. 6.20 Removing magnetic disc (Sec 6)

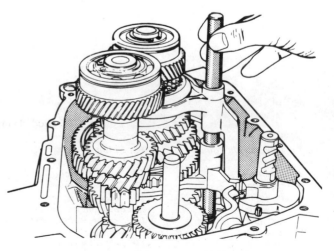

Fig. 6 21 Withdrawing selector shaft (Sec 6)

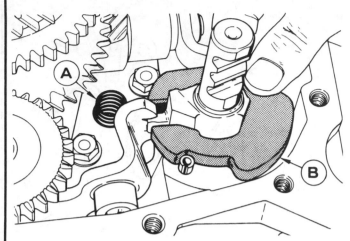

Fig. 6.22 Selector shaft coil spring (A) and shift lockplate (B) (Sec 6)

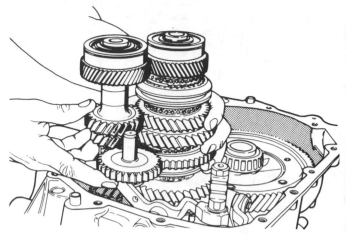

Fig. 6.23 Withdrawing the gear trains (Sec 6)

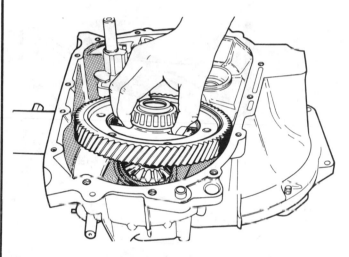

Fig. 6.24 Withdrawing the differential (Sec 6)

Fig. 6.25 Breaking the mainshaft bearing plastic cage (Sec 8)

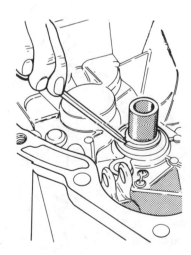

Fig. 6.26 Removing the input shaft oil seal (Sec 8)

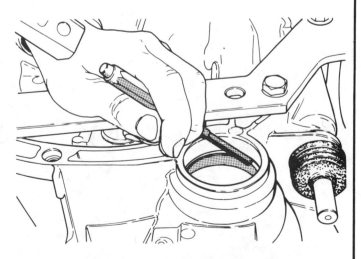

Fig. 6.27 Removing a differential bearing track (Sec 8)

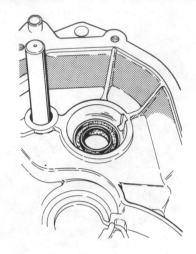

Fig. 6.28 Input shaft oil seal correctly installed (Sec 8)

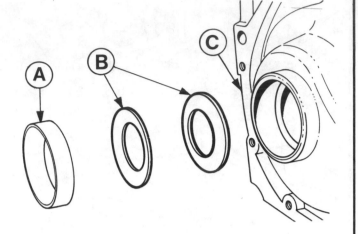

Fig. 6.29 Differential bearing preload diaphragm springs (Sec 8)

A   Bearing track   C   Small housing section
B   Diaphragm springs

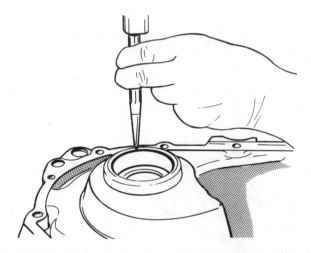

Fig. 6.30 Staking bearing track in small housing section (Sec 8)

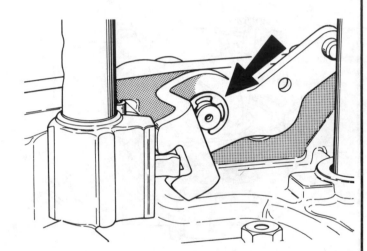

Fig. 6.32 Reverse selector lever retaining clip (arrowed) (Sec 8)

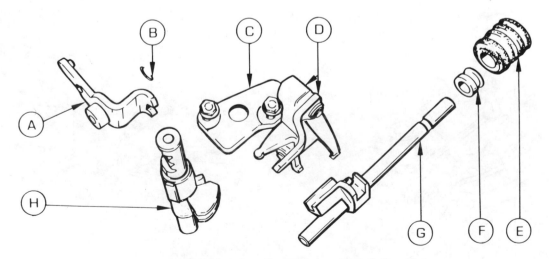

Fig. 6.31 Exploded view of selector mechanism (Sec 8)

A   Reverse selector lever   C   Guide lever retaining   D   Guide levers   F   Oil seal
B   Circlip   plate   E   Flexible gaiter   G   Selector shaft with dog
                                                                                      H   Guide shaft with dog

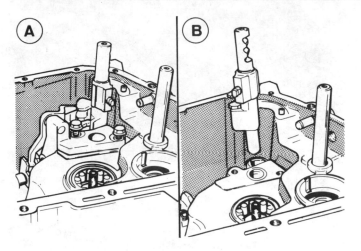

Fig. 6.33 Dismantling selector mechanism (Sec 8)

A   *Removing retaining plate*   B   *Removing guide shaft*

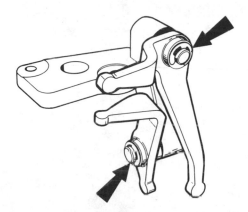

Fig. 6.34 Guide lever retaining circlips (arrowed) (Sec 8)

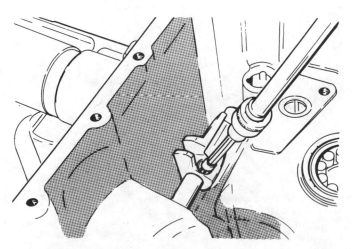

Fig. 6.35 Extracting lockscrew which secures dog to selector shaft (Sec 8)

6   The differential bearing outer track and the diaphragm adjustment springs can be driven out of the smaller housing section using a suitable drift such as a piece of tubing.

7   Refit the input shaft oil seal so that its lips are as shown (Fig. 6.28). Apply grease to all the oil seal lips and check that the lip retaining spring has not been displaced during installation of the seal.

8   When installing the differential diaphragm springs and bearing track to the smaller housing section, note that the spring convex faces are towards each other. Stake the track with a light blow from a punch. This is only to hold the track during assembly of the remainder of the transmission.

9   If the selector mechanism is worn, sloppy or damaged, dismantle it by extracting the circlip and taking off the reverse selector lever (photo).

10   Remove the guide lever retaining plate and the guide shaft. Two bolts hold these components in place.

11   Extract the two circlips and detach the guide lever from the retaining plate.

12   To remove the main selector shaft, pull the rubber gaiter up the shaft and then extract the single socket screw which secures the selector dog. Withdraw the shaft.

13   The selector shaft plastic bushes and oil seal should be renewed.

14   Reassembly is a reversal of dismantling, but when fitting the rubber gaiter make sure that its drain tube will point downward when installed in the vehicle. Use new circlips at reassembly.

9   Mainshaft – overhaul

Dismantling

1   Extract the circlip which holds the bearing to the shaft.

2   Using a puller, engaged behind 4th speed gear, draw off the gear and the bearing from the end of the mainshaft (photo).

3   Discard the bearing.

4   Extract the circlip and remove the 3rd/4th synchro with 3rd gear, using hand pressure only.

5   Remove the anchor ring and the two thrust semi/circular segments, then take 2nd gear from the mainshaft.

6   Extract the circlip and take off 1st/2nd gear synchro unit with 1st gear.

7   The mainshaft is now completely dismantled. Do not attempt to remove the drive pinion gear (photo).

Synchronisers

8   The synchro units can be dismantled and new components fitted after extracting the circular retaining springs.

9   When reassembling the hub and sleeve, align them so that the cut-outs in the components are in alignment ready to receive the sliding keys.

10   The two springs should have their hooked ends engaged in the same sliding key, but must run in opposing directions as shown in Fig. 6.38.

11   The baulk rings should be renewed if they do not 'stick' when pressed and turned onto the gear covers, or if a clearance no longer exists between the baulk ring and the gear when pressed onto its cone.

Reassembly

12   With all worn or damaged components renewed, commence reassembly by oiling the shaft and then sliding 1st gear onto the shaft so that the gear teeth are next to the pinion drivegear (photo).

13   Fit 1st/2nd synchro baulk ring (photo).

14   Fit 1st/2nd synchro so that reverse gear teeth on the unit are furthest from 1st gear (photo).

15   Fit the circlip to secure the synchro to the mainshaft (photo).

16   Slide on the synchro baulk ring (photo).

17   Slide on 2nd speed gear (photo).

18   Fit 2nd gear so that the cone is towards the baulk ring.

19   Fit the thrust semi-circular segments and their anchor ring (photos).

20   To the shaft fit 3rd gear so that its teeth are towards 2nd gear (photo).

21   Fit the baulk ring (photo).

22   Slide on 3rd/4th synchro so that its serrated edge is towards the shaft drive pinion gear (photo).

8.3A Transmission housing oil seal

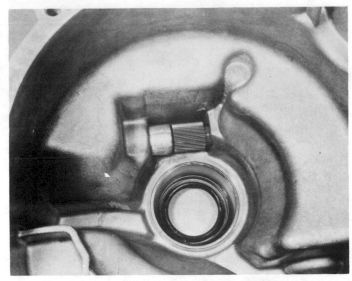

8.3B Transmission housing oil seal and speedometer driven gear

8.9 Selector mechanism

9.2 Removing 4th gear and bearing from mainshaft

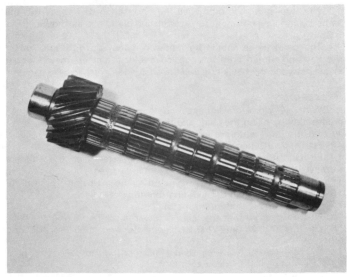

9.7 Mainshaft stripped

9.12 Fitting 1st speed gear to mainshaft

9.13 Fitting 1st/2nd baulk ring

9.14 Fitting 1st/2nd synchro with reverse gear

9.15 Fitting synchro securing circlip to mainshaft

9.16 Fitting 1st/2nd synchro baulk ring

9.17 Fitting 2nd speed gear to mainshaft

9.19A Thrust segments installed

9.19B Thrust segment anchor ring installation

9.20 Fitting 3rd speed gear to mainshaft

9.21 Fitting 3rd/4th synchro baulk ring

9.22 Fitting 3rd/4th synchro to mainshaft. Note that serrated edge is downwards

9.23 Securing 3rd/4th synchro with circlip

9.24 Fitting last (4th) synchro baulk ring to mainshaft

9.25 Fitting 4th speed gear to mainshaft

9.26A Installing mainshaft bearing

9.26B Using tubing to drive on mainshaft bearing

9.27A Fitting mainshaft bearing circlip

9.27B Mainshaft fully assembled

23 Secure the synchro to the mainshaft with the circlip (photo).
24 Fit the baulk ring (photo).
25 Fit 4th gear (photo).
26 Fit the bearing so that its circlip groove is nearer the end of the shaft. Apply pressure only to the bearing centre track, using a press or a hammer and a piece of suitable diameter tubing (photos).
27 Fit the circlip to secure the bearing to the shaft. The mainshaft is now fully assembled (photos).

10 Input shaft – overhaul

1 The only components which can be renewed are the two ball-bearing races (photo).
2 Remove the securing circlip from the larger one and extract both bearings with a two-legged extractor or a press (photos).
3 When fitting the new bearings, apply pressure to the centre track

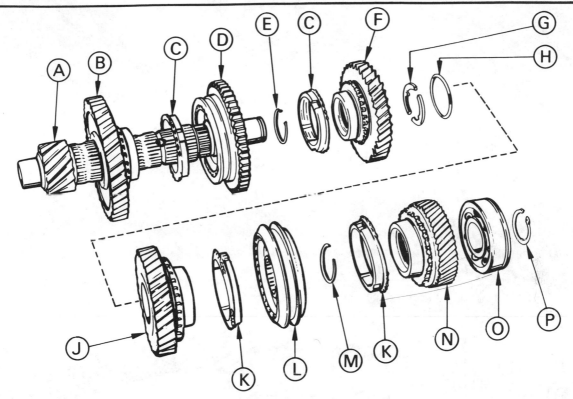

Fig. 6.36 Exploded view of mainshaft (Sec 9)

A Mainshaft/drive pinion gear
B 1st speed gear
C 1st/2nd synchro baulk ring
D 1st/2nd synchro with reverse gear
E Circlip
F 2nd speed gear
G Semi-circular thrust segments
H Anchor ring for thrust segments
J 3rd speed gear
K 3rd/4th synchro baulk ring
L 3rd/4th synchro
M Circlip
N 4th speed gear
O Bearing
P Circlip

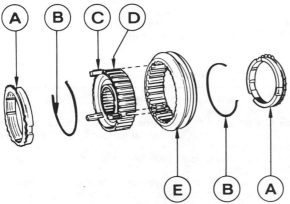

Fig. 6.37 Synchroniser dismantled (Sec 9)

A Baulk ring
B Key retaining spring
C Sliding key
D Hub
E Sleeve

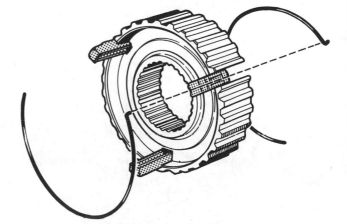

Fig. 6.38 Fitting direction of synchro springs (Sec 9)

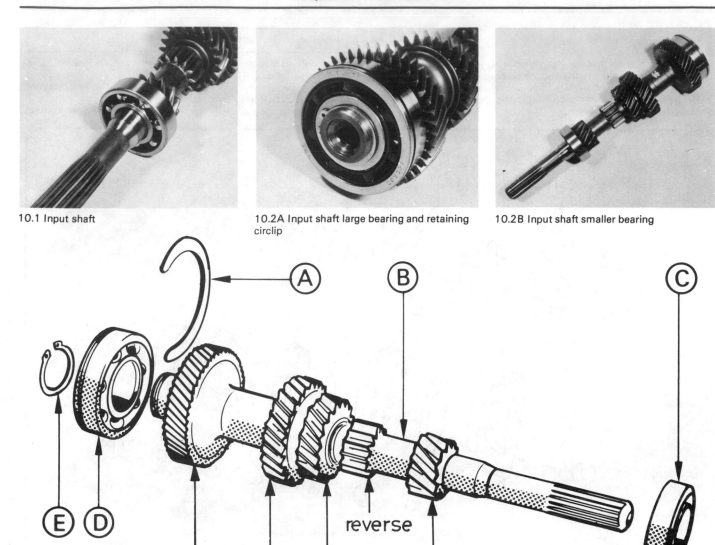

10.1 Input shaft

10.2A Input shaft large bearing and retaining circlip

10.2B Input shaft smaller bearing

Fig. 6.39 Input shaft components (Sec 10)

A Bearing snap-ring   C   Bearing   D   Bearing   E   Circlip
B Input shaft

only, using a press or a piece of suitable diameter tubing and a hammer. When installing the larger bearing, make sure that the circlip groove is nearer the end of the shaft.

11 Differential – overhaul

1   With the differential removed from the transmission housing, twist both drive pinions out of the differential case.

2   Extract one of the circlips from the end of the differential shaft, press the shaft out of the differential case and extract the pinions and the cage.

3   The differential tapered roller bearings can be drawn off using a two-legged extractor.

4   The crownwheel can be separated from the differential case after removing the six securing bolts. Tap the components apart using a plastic mallet.

5   If the crownwheel is to be renewed, then the gearbox mainshaft should be renewed at the same time, as the gear teeth are matched and renewal of only one component will give rise to an increase in noise during operation on the road.

6   Reassembly is a reversal of dismantling, but make sure that the deeply chamfered edge of the inside diameter is against the differential case. Tighten all bolts to the specified torque.

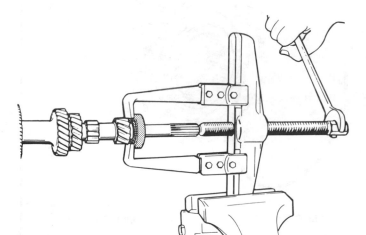

Fig. 6.40 Removing an input shaft bearing (Sec 10)

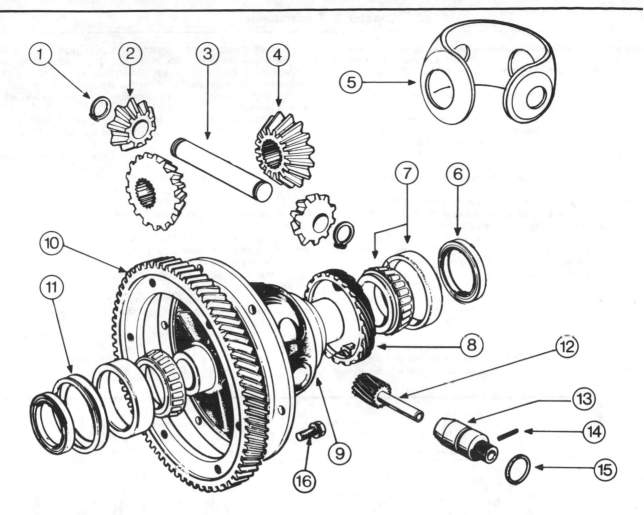

Fig. 6.41 Exploded view of the differential (Sec 11)

1	Circlip	6	Oil seal
2	Pinion gear	7	Tapered roller bearing
3	Shaft	8	Speedometer worm drivegear
4	Drive pinion gear	9	Differential case
5	Thrust cage		

10	Crownwheel	14	Roll pin
11	Diaphragm springs	15	O-ring
12	Speedometer drive pinion	16	Crownwheel retaining bolt
13	Bearing		

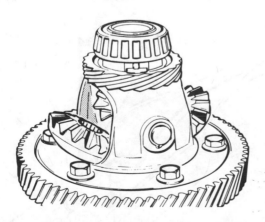

Fig. 6.42 Sliding drive pinions from differential case (Sec 11)

Fig. 6.43 Extracting differential case shaft circlip (Sec 11)

7 The pinion gears should be held in position by inserting plastic plugs or similar so that they will be in correct alignment for eventual installation of the driveshafts, refer to Section 5 of this Chapter.

12 Transmission – reassembly

1 With the larger housing section on the bench, lubricate the differential bearings with gear oil and insert the differential assembly into the housing (photos).

2 Slide reverse idler gear onto its shaft, at the same time engaging the selector lever in the groove of the gear which should be pointing downward (photo).

3 In order to make installation of the mainshaft and input shaft easier, lift the reverse idler gear so that its selector lever is held by the reversing lamp switch spring-loaded ball (photo).

4 Mesh the gears of the mainshaft and the input shaft and install both geartrains into the transmission housing simultaneously (photo).

5 Lower the reverse idler gear and its selector lever.

6 Fit the shift locking plate (photo).

7 Engage 1st/2nd selector fork with the groove in the mainshaft synchro sleeve. This fork has the shorter actuating lever (photo).

8 Engage 3rd/4th selector fork with the groove in its synchro sleeve. Make sure that the end of this fork actuating lever is engaged with the shift locking plate (photo).

9 Insert the coil spring in the selector shaft hole and pass the shaft downwards through the holes in the forks. Make sure that the longer section of the reduced diameter of the rod is pointing downward (photos).

10 Actuate the appropriate selector fork to engage 4th gear. Do this by inserting a rod in the hole in the end of the selector shaft which projects from the transmission casing and turning the shaft fully clockwise to its stop, then pushing the shaft inwards (photo).

11 Insert the magnetic swarf collector in its recess, taking care not to drop it (photo).

12 Locate a new gasket on the housing flange, install the smaller housing section and screw in and tighten the bolts to the specified torque (photos).

13 Fit the snap-rings to the ends of the main and input shafts. Cut-outs are provided in the casing so that the bearings can be levered upwards to expose the snap-ring grooves. Snap-rings are available in three thicknesses and the thickest possible ring should be used which will fit into the groove. If any difficulty is experienced in levering up the bearing on the input shaft, push the end of the shaft from within the bellhousing (photo).

14 Tap the snap-rings to rotate them so that they will locate correctly in the cut-outs in the cover gasket which should now be positioned on the end of the housing. Fit a new gasket (photo).

15 Fit the cover plate, screw in the bolts and tighten them to the specified torque (photos).

16 Fit the interlock pin, spring and cap nut for the selector shaft locking mechanism. The threads should be coated with jointing compound before installation.

17 Refit the clutch release shaft, lever and bearing into the bellhousing (photos).

18 The transmission is now ready for installation in the vehicle. Wait until it is installed before filling with oil.

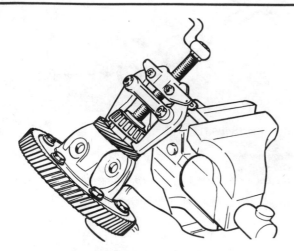

Fig. 6.44 Removing a differential bearing (Sec 11)

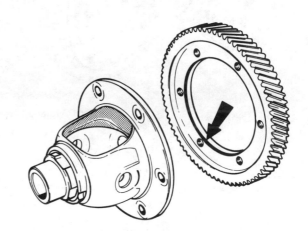

Fig. 6.45 Crownwheel chamfered edge (arrowed) (Sec 11)

Fig. 6.46 Reverse selector lever supported on reversing lamp switch plunger ball (Sec 12)

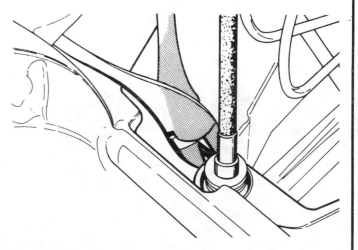

Fig. 6.47 Extracting speedometer pinion retaining roll pin (Sec 13)

12.1A Interior of transmission larger housing

12.1B Installing differential

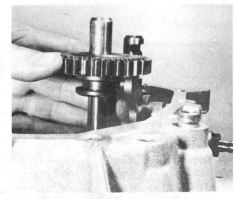

12.2 Fitting reverse idler gear

12.3 Reverse idler gear supported in raised position

12.4 Installing the geartrains

12.6 Fitting shift locking plate

12.7 Fitting 1st/2nd selector fork

12.8 Fitting 3rd/4th selector fork

12.9A Inserting selector shaft coil spring

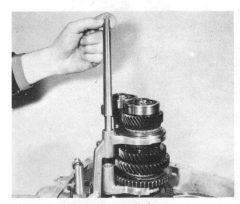

12.9B Installing selector shaft

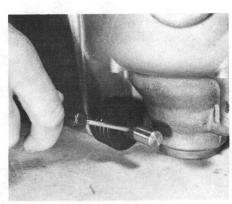

12.10 Turning selector shaft to stop

12.11 Magnetic swarf collector

12.12A Locating housing flange gasket

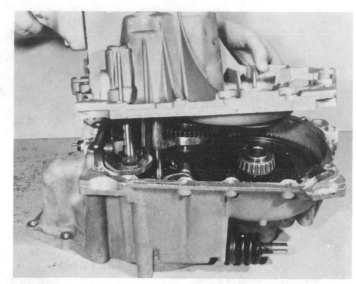
12.12B Fitting transmission smaller housing

12.12C Tightening housing section connecting bolts

12.13A Raising bearing for snap-ring installation

12.13B Fitting bearing snap-ring

12.14 Bearing snap-rings and gasket in position

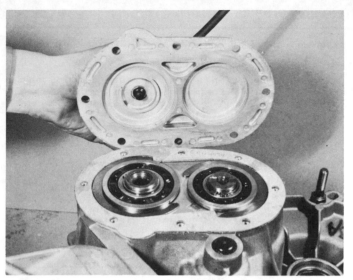

12.15A Fitting transmission cover plate and gasket

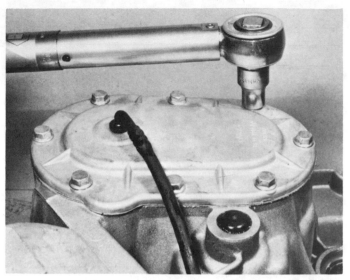

12.15B Tightening cover plate bolts. Note breather tube

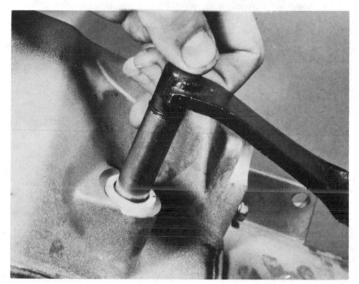

12.17A Inserting clutch release shaft

12.17B Tightening clutch release fork bolt

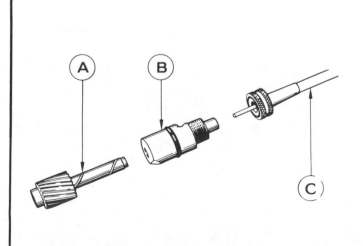

Fig. 6.48 Speedometer drive components (Sec 13)

A   Pinion gear   C   Drive cable
B   Bearing and O-ring seal

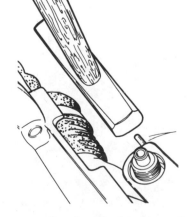

Fig. 6.49 Driving in speedometer pinion roll pin (Sec 13)

13 Speedometer driven gear – removal and refitting

1   This work may be done without having to remove the transmission from the vehicle.
2   Using a pair of side cutting pliers, lever out the roll pin which secures the speedometer drive pinion bearing in the transmission housing.
3   Withdraw the pinion bearing together with the speedometer drive cable. Separate the cable from the pinion by unscrewing the knurled ring.
4   Slide the pinion out of the bearing.
5   Always renew the O-ring on the pinion bearing before refitting.
6   Insert the pinion and bearing into the transmission housing using a back-and-forth twisting motion to mesh the pinion teeth with those of the drivegear. Secure with the roll pin.
7   Reconnect the speedometer cable.

14 Fault diagnosis – transmission

Symptom	Reason(s)
Weak or ineffective synchromesh	Synchronising cones worn, split or damaged Baulk ring synchromesh dogs worn or damaged
Jumps out of gear	Broken selector shaft interlock spring Gearbox coupling dogs badly worn Selector fork rod groove badly worn
Excessive noise	Incorrect grade of oil in gearbox or oil level too low Bush or needle roller bearings worn or damaged Gear teeth excessively worn or damaged Shaft bearing circlips allowing excessive endplay
Noise when cornering	Driveshaft or wheel bearing worn Diffential bearing worn

Chapter 7 Driveshafts

For modifications, and information applicable to later models, see Supplement at end of manual

Contents

Specifications

Type
Right hand .... Tubular, three-section with two constant velocity (CV) joints
Left-hand .... Solid, three-section with two CV joints

Driveshaft identification marks
1.1 models .... Yellow
1.3 and 1.6 models .... Blue

Lubrication
Lubricant capacity (each joint) .... 40g (1.5 oz)
Lubricant type .... Grease to S-MIC-75-A/SQM-IC-9004-A

Torque wrench settings

	Nm	lbf ft
Lower suspension arm balljoint pinch-bolt	58	43
Lower suspension arm inboard pivot bolt	60	44
Driveshaft/hub nut	230	170
Caliper mounting bolts	60	44
Roadwheel bolts	80	59
Transmission oil filler plug	25	18
Transmission cap nut	30	22

1 Description and maintenance

1 The two open driveshafts are of unequal length with the longer (hollow) one having a greater diameter than the shorter (solid) one.
2 Each driveshaft consists of three sections: the inboard end, namely a splined output shaft and constant velocity joint, the outboard end, being the splined front hub spindle and constant velocity joint, and a centre shaft with splined ends.
3 The inboard ends of the driveshaft are retained in the differential gears by the engagement of snap-rings. The outboard ends are secured to the hub by a nut which is staked after tightening.
4 The constant velocity joints are lubricated and sealed by flexible gaiters. The only maintenance required is a visual inspection, for splits in the gaiter or an oil leak from the inboard oil seal. A leakage of grease from the hub seal will indicate that the hub bearing oil seal is in need of renewal and this is described in Section 3 of Chapter 10.
5 Where a driveshaft gaiter is split, it must be renewed immediately to avoid the entry of dirt and grit (see Section 3 or 4).

2 Driveshaft inboard oil seal – renewal

1 Raise the front end of the vehicle and support on stands placed under the jacking points on the side members.
2 Drain the transmission oil by unscrewing and removing the cap nut from the selector shaft locking mechanism. Take care not to lose the spring and interlock pin which will be ejected.
3 Unscrew and remove the pinch-bolt and nut and disconnect the suspension lower track control arm from the hub carrier.
4 On 1.3 and 1.6 models, which have a front anti-roll bar, disconnect the track control arm from the body at its inboard end by removing the pivot bolt.
5 With an assistant pulling the roadwheel, insert a lever between the inboard constant velocity joint and the transmission. Strike the end of the lever, so prising the driveshaft out of the transmission. Tie the driveshaft to the steering rack housing to avoid strain on the CV joints caused by excessive deflection of the driveshaft.
6 Using a tool with a hook at its end, prise out the oil seal from the differential housing. Take care not to damage the seal housing.
7 Wipe out the oil seal seat, apply grease to the lips of a new oil seal and tap it into position using a piece of tubing or similar as a drift.
8 Using a mirror, check that the pinion gear within the differential is in correct alignment to receive the driveshaft. If not, insert the finger to align it.
9 Fit a new snap-ring to the driveshaft and then offer it up to engage it in the transmission (photos).
10 Have your assistant push inwards on the roadwheel until the snap-ring is fully engaged. If any difficulty is experienced in pushing the driveshaft fully home, remove the roadwheel to reduce weight and lift the hub assembly until the driveshaft is in a more horizontal attitude.
11 Reconnect the suspension track control arm and lower the vehicle to the ground. Tighten nuts and bolts to the specified torque when the weight of the vehicle is again on its roadwheels.

12 Fill the transmission with oil after having refitted the selector cap nut assembly.

3 Driveshaft inboard joint bellows – renewal

1 Jack up the front of the vehicle and support securely. Wipe the driveshaft free from dirt and grease.
2 Disconnect the front suspension track control arm balljoint from the hub carrier by removing the pinch-bolt and nut. The bolt is of socket headed (Torx) type and can be prevented from rotating in the absence of a special tool by using an Allen key.
3 On 1.3 and 1.6 models, which have an anti-roll bar, disconnect the track control arm from the body at its inboard end by removing the pivot bolt.
4 Disconnect both clamps from the bellows on the inboard driveshaft joint and slide the bellows off the CV joint and along the shaft.
5 Wipe enough grease from the joint to expose the circlip which secures it to the shaft. Using a pair of circlip pliers, extract the circlip.
6 Pull the driveshaft out of the joint and slide the bellows off the end of the shaft.
7 To fit the new bellows, slide them onto the shaft and then connect the driveshaft to the CV joint. The circlip should be engaged in its groove in the joint and the shaft slid through it until the circlip snaps into its groove in the shaft.

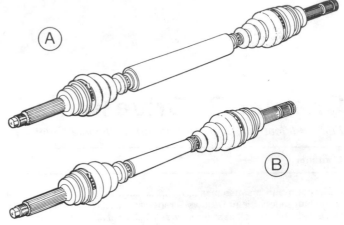

Fig. 7.1 The driveshafts (Sec 1)

A   Right-hand (tubular)   B   Left-hand (solid)

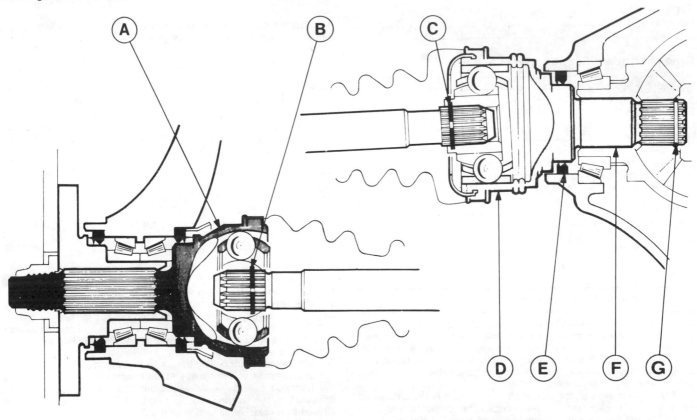

Fig. 7.2 Sectional view of driveshaft constant velocity (CV) joints (Sec 1)

A Outboard joint	C Circlip	E Oil seal	G Snap-ring
B Circlip	D Inboard joint	F Inboard driveshaft	

8 Replenish the joint with grease of the specified type and then pull the bellows over the joint.
9 Set the length of the bellows (A in Fig. 7.9) to the appropriate dimension:

1.1	127 mm (5.0 in)
1.3 and 1.6	132 mm (5.19 in)

10 Fit the bellows clamps and tighten.
11 Reconnect the track control arm, tighten all bolts and lower the

vehicle. Finally tighten all fastenings to the specified torque when the weight of the vehicle is again on its wheels.

4 Driveshaft outboard joint bellows – renewal

1 Unless the driveshaft is to be removed completely for other repair work to be carried out (refer to Section 5), the following method of bellows renewal is recommended to avoid having to disconnect the driveshaft from the hub carrier.

2.9A Connecting left-hand driveshaft to transmission

2.9B Connecting right-hand driveshaft to transmission

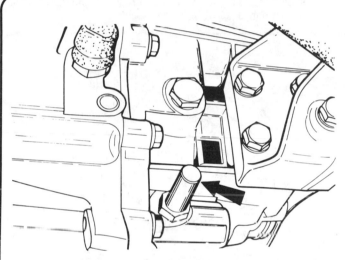

Fig. 7.3 Transmission selector mechanism cap nut (arrowed) (Sec 2)

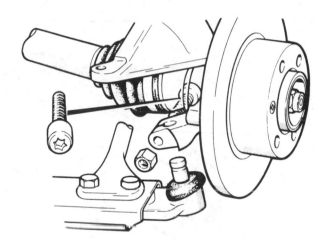

Fig. 7.4 Suspension arm balljoint disconnected (Sec 2)

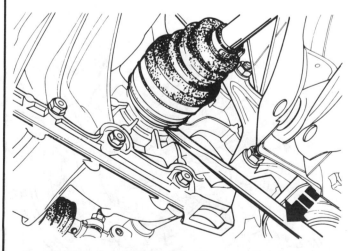

Fig. 7.5 Releasing a driveshaft from the transmission (Sec 2)

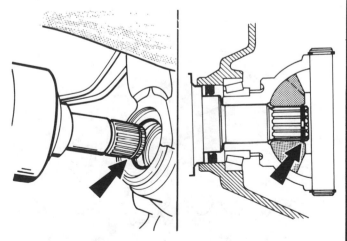

Fig. 7.6 Inserting driveshaft into transmission (left) and driveshaft snap-ring fully engages with differential pinion gear (arrowed, right) (Sec 2)

2   Remove the inboard joint bellows as described in the preceding Section.

3   Release the clamps on the outboard joint bellows and slide the bellows along the driveshaft until they can be removed from the inboard end of the shaft.

4   Thoroughly clean the driveshaft before sliding on the new bellows. Replenish the outboard joint with specified lubricant and slide the bellows over the joint, setting its overall length to the appropriate dimension:

1.1   70 mm (2.75 in)
1.3 and 1.6   82 mm (3.22 in)

5   Fit and tighten the bellows clamps but make sure that the crimped part of the clamp nearest the hub does not interfere with the hub carrier as the driveshaft is rotated.

6   Refit the inboard bellows and connect the driveshaft to the transmission as described in the preceding Section.

5 Driveshaft – removal and refitting

1   Slacken the roadwheel bolts and then raise the front of the vehicle.
2   Remove the roadwheel.
3   Refit two of the roadwheel bolts as a means of anchoring the disc

when the hub nut is unscrewed (the disc retaining screw is not strong enough to prevent the disc from rotating).

4   Have an assistant apply the footbrake and then unscrew the staked hub nut and remove it together with the plain washer.

5   Remove the temporary wheel bolts.

6   Unbolt the caliper and tie it up to the suspension strut to prevent strain on the flexible hose.

7   Disconnect the inboard end of the driveshaft as described in Section 2, paragraphs 2 to 5.

8   Support the driveshaft on a jack or by tying it up.

9   Extract the small retaining screw and withdraw the brake disc from the hub.

10   It may now be possible to pull the hub from the driveshaft. If it does not come off easily, use a two-legged puller.

11   Withdraw the driveshaft complete with CV joints. If both driveshafts are being removed at the same time then the differential pinion gears must be retained in alignment with their transmission casing holes by inserting pieces of plastic tubing or dowel rods.

12   To refit the driveshaft, first engage it in the splines of the hub carrier while supporting the shaft in a horizontal attitude to avoid strain on the CV joints.

13   Using the original nut and distance pieces of varying lengths, draw the driveshaft into the hub carrier.

14   Remove the old nut and distance pieces and fit the washer and a new nut, but only finger tight at this stage.

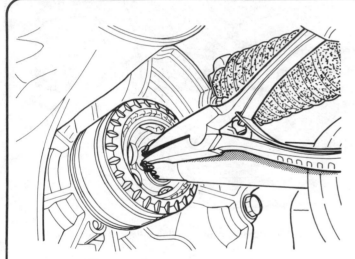

Fig. 7.7 Releasing joint circlip (Sec 3)

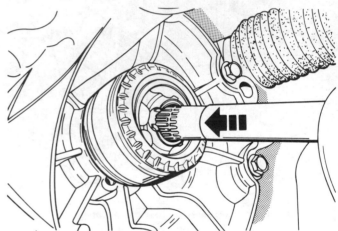

Fig. 7.8 Engaging driveshaft with CV joint (Sec 3)

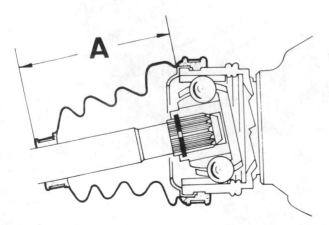

Fig. 7.9 Driveshaft inboard joint bellows setting diagram (Sec 3)

For (A) refer to text

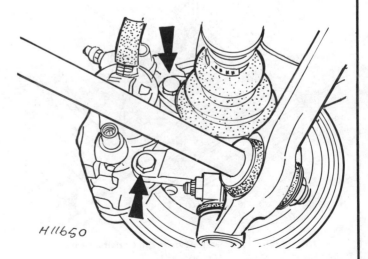

Fig. 7.10 Brake caliper mounting bolts (arrowed) (Sec 5)

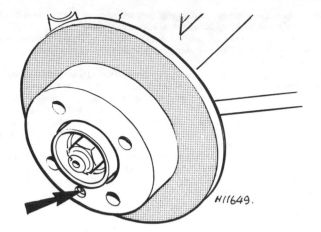

Fig. 7.11 Brake disc retaining screw (arrowed) (Sec 5)

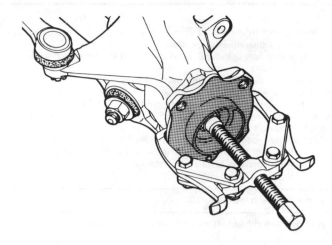

Fig. 7.12 Withdrawing hub from driveshaft (Sec 5)

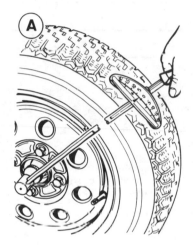

Fig. 7.13 Tightening hub nut (Sec 5)

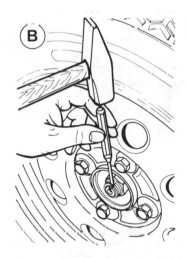

Fig. 7.14 Staking hub retaining nut (Sec 5)

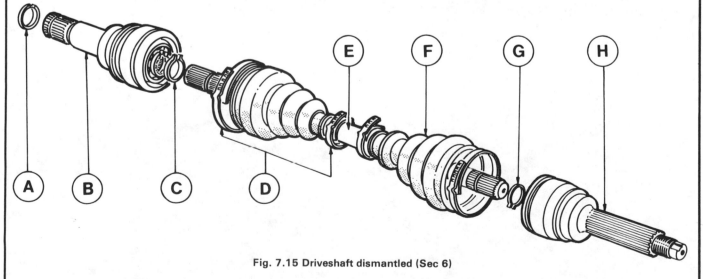

Fig. 7.15 Driveshaft dismantled (Sec 6)

A	Snap-ring	C	Circlip
B	Inboard joint	D	Bellows clamps

E	Driveshaft	G	Circlip
F	Gaiter	H	Outboard joint

15 Fit the brake disc and caliper.

16 Connect the inboard end of the driveshaft and the suspension components as described in Section 2.

17 Temporarily screw in two wheel bolts and then have an assistant apply the footbrake.

18 Tighten the hub nut to the specified torque. In the absence of a suitable torque wrench with a high enough range, full pressure on a knuckle bar or pipe extension about 457 mm (18 in) in length should give approximately the correct torque. Once tight, stake the nut into the shaft groove. Fit the roadwheel and lower the vehicle.

19 Tighten the roadwheel bolts and then check the torque wrench settings of the other front suspension attachments now that the weight of the vehicle is on the roadwheels.

6 Driveshaft – overhaul

1 Remove the driveshaft as described in the preceding Section.

2 Clean away external dirt and grease, release the bellows clamps and slide the bellows from the CV joint.

3 Wipe away enough lubricant to be able to extract the circlip and then separate the CV joint with its splined shaft section from the main member of the driveshaft.

4 Thoroughly clean the joint components and examine for wear or damage to the balls, cage, socket or splines. A repair kit may provide a solution to the problem but if the socket requires renewal, this will of course include the splined section of shaft and will prove expensive. If both joints require renewal of major components, then a new driveshaft or one which has been professionally reconditioned may prove to be more economical.

5 Reassemble the joint by reversing the dismantling operations. Use a new circlip if necessary and pack the joint with the specified quantity of lubricant. When fitting the bellows, set their length in accordance with the information given in Section 3 or 4 according to which joint (inboard or outboard) is being worked upon.

6 Refit the driveshaft as described in Section 5.

7 Fault diagnosis – driveshafts

Symptom	Reason(s)
Knock when taking up drive or on overrun	Wear in joint Wear in shaft splines Loose roadwheel bolts
Noise, especially on turns	Lack of lubrication Wear in joint Loose hub retaining nut
Leakage of lubricant	Split bellows or loose retaining clamp Faulty oil seal at differential end of shaft Faulty oil seal at roadwheel end of shaft (refer to Chapter 10)

Chapter 8 Braking system

For modifications, and information applicable to later models, refer to Supplement at end of manual

Contents

Specifications

System type	Hydraulic, dual circuit, discs front, drums rear. Servo standard or option according to model. Handbrake mechanical to rear wheels only

Disc brakes

Caliper type	Single piston, sliding type
Disc diameter	239.45 mm (9.43 in)
Disc thickness:	
1.1 and 1.3 (solid)	10.0 mm (0.39 in)
1.6 (ventilated)	24.0 mm (0.95 in)
Minimum disc thickness (after refinishing):	
1.1 and 1.3 (solid)	8.7 mm (0.34 in)
1.6 (ventilated)	22.7 mm (0.89 in)
Maximum disc run-out	0.15 mm (0.006 in)
Caliper cylinder diameter	54.0 mm (2.12 in)
Minimum pad friction material thickness	1.5 mm (0.06 in)

Drum brakes

Passenger vehicles:	
Drum diameter	180.0 mm (7.2 in)
Shoe width	30.0 mm (1.2 in)
Wheel cylinder diameter	19.05 mm (0.75 in)
Minimum shoe friction lining thickness	1.0 mm (0.04 in)
Van:	
Drum diameter	203.2 mm (8.0 in)
Shoe width	38.1 mm (1.5 in)
Wheel cylinder diameter	22.2 mm (0.875 in)
Minimum shoe friction lining thickness	1.0 mm (0.04 in)

Master cylinder

Type	Tandem
Cylinder diameter	20.64 mm (0.813 in)

Servo diameter .... 200 mm (7.87 in)

Torque wrench settings

	Nm	lbf ft
Caliper mounting bolts	60	44
Rear backplate fixing bolts	24	17
Hydraulic unions	14	10
Brake pressure valve mounting bolts (passenger vehicles)	24	17
Caliper piston housing screws	24	17
Pressure regulator valve mounting bolts (Van)	25	19

1 Description

The braking system is of four-wheel hydraulic type, with discs at the front and drums at the rear.

The hydraulic system is of dual circuit type, each circuit controls one front brake and one rear brake linked diagonally.

The calipers are of single piston, sliding piston housing type. The discs are of solid type on 1.1 and 1.3 models but of ventilated type on 1.6 versions.

The rear brakes are of leading and trailing shoe design with a self-adjusting mechanism. To compensate for the greater lining wear of the leading shoe, its friction lining is thicker than that on the trailing shoe.

The master cylinder incorporates a reservoir cap which has a fluid level switch connected to a warning lamp on the instrument panel.

A vacuum servo is standard on some models and optional on others. When fitted to RHD versions, because of the location of the servo/master cylinder on the left-hand side of the engine compartment the brake pedal is operated through a transverse rod on the engine compartment rear bulkhead.

A brake pressure regulating control valve is fitted into the hydraulic circuit to prevent rear wheel locking under conditions of heavy braking and (on vans) to compensate for load variation.

The floor-mounted handbrake control lever operates through cables to the rear wheels only.

2 Maintenance

1 At weekly intervals, check the fluid level in the translucent reservoir on the master cylinder. The fluid will drop very slowly indeed over a period of time to compensate for lining wear, but any sudden drop in level or the need for frequent topping up should be investigated immediately.

2 Always top up with hydraulic fluid which meets the specified standard and has been left in an airtight container. Hydraulic fluid is hygroscopic (absorbs moisture from the atmosphere) and must not be stored in an open container. Do not shake the tin prior to topping up. Fluids of different makes can be intermixed provided they all meet the specification.

3 Inspect the thickness of the friction linings on the disc pads and brake shoes as described in the following Sections, at the intervals specified in Routine Maintenance.

4 The rigid and flexible hydraulic pipes and hoses should be inspected for leaks or damage regularly. Although the rigid lines are plastic-coated in order to preserve them against corrosion, check for damage which may have occurred through flying stones, careless jacking or the traversing of rough ground.

5 Bend the hydraulic flexible hoses sharply with the fingers and examine the surface of the hose for signs of cracking or perishing of the rubber. Renew if evident.

6 Renew the brake fluid at the specified intervals and examine all rubber components (including master cylinder and piston seals) with a critical eye, renewing where necessary.

3 Disc pads (without wear sensors) – inspection and renewal

1 At the intervals specified in Routine Maintenance, place a mirror between the roadwheel and the caliper and check the thickness of the friction material of the disc pads. If the material has worn down to 1.5 mm (0.060 in) or less, the pads must be renewed as an axle set (four pads).

2 Slacken the roadwheel bolts, raise the front of the vehicle and remove the roadwheels.

3 Remove the retaining clip (photo).

4 Using a 7 mm Allen key, unscrew the bolts until they can be withdrawn from the caliper anchor brackets (photos).

5 Withdraw the piston housing and tie it up with a length of wire to prevent strain on the flexible hose (photo).

6 Withdraw the inboard pad from the piston housing (photo).

7 Withdraw the outboard pad from the anchor bracket (photo).

8 Clean away all residual dust or dirt, taking care not to inhale the dust as being asbestos based it is injurious to health.

9 Using a piece of flat wood, a tyre lever or similar, push the piston squarely into its bore. This is necessary in order to accommodate the new thicker pads when they are fitted.

10 Depressing the piston will cause the fluid level in the master cylinder reservoir to rise, so anticipate this by syphoning out some fluid using an old hydrometer or poultry baster. Take care not to drip hydraulic fluid onto the paintwork, it acts as an effective paint stripper!

11 Commence reassembly by fitting the inboard pad into the piston housing. Make sure that the spring on the back of the pad fits into the piston.

12 Fit the outboard pad into the anchor bracket.

13 Locate the piston housing and screw in the Allen bolts to the specified torque.

14 Fit the retaining clip (photo).

15 Repeat the operations on the opposite brake.

16 Apply the footbrake hard several times to position the pads against the disc and then check and top up the fluid in the master cylinder reservoir.

17 Fit the roadwheels and lower the vehicle.

18 Avoid heavy braking (if possible) for the first hundred miles or so when new pads have been fitted. This is to allow them to bed in and reach full efficiency.

4 Disc pads (with wear sensors) – inspection and renewal

1 The operations are very similar to those just described in the preceding Section, but once the roadwheel is removed and before the caliper is dismantled, disconnect the multi-plug for the wear sensor lead and unclip the lead from the bleed screw.

2 When reassembling, once the inboard pad is located in the piston housing, feed the wear sensor lead through the opening in the caliper and then attach it to the bleed nipple clip.

3 Where the cable has become unwound, loosely coil the surplus wire so that slack is taken out yet enough flexibility (25 mm/1 in) is still allowed for pad wear. The coiled wire must on no account be stretched.

5 Caliper – removal, overhaul and refitting

1 Slacken the roadwheel bolts, raise the front of the vehicle and remove the roadwheel.

2 Disconnect the brake flexible hose from the caliper. This can be carried out in one of two ways. Either disconnect the flexible hose from the rigid hydraulic pipeline at the support bracket by unscrewing the union, or, once the caliper is detached, hold the end fitting of the hose in an open-ended spanner and unscrew the caliper from the hose. Do not allow the hose to twist.

3 If wear sensors are fitted to the pads, disconnect the lead plug.

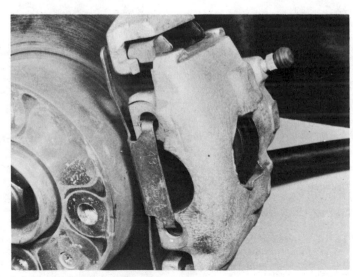

3.3 Disc pad retaining clip

3.4A Unscrewing caliper bolt

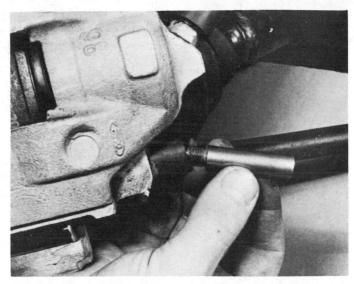

3.4B Removing bolt from caliper anchor bracket

3.5 Withdrawing caliper piston housing

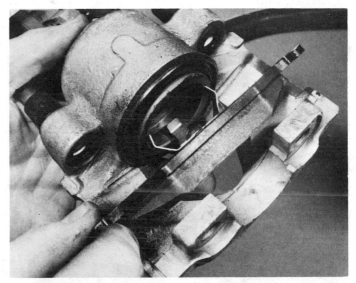

3.6 Removing inboard pad

3.7 Removing outboard pad

3.14 Fitting pad retaining clip

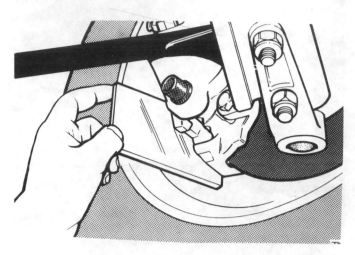

Fig. 8.1 Checking disc pad wear (Sec 3)

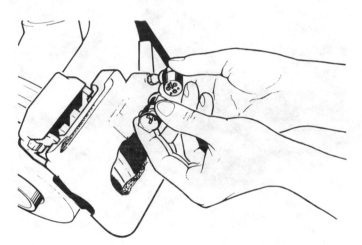

Fig. 8.2 Disconnecting disc pad wear sensor plug (Sec 4)

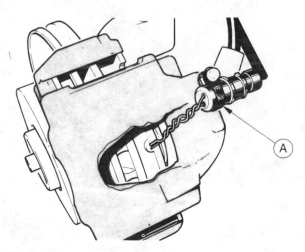

Fig. 8.3 Disc pad sensor (A) clipped to bleed screw (Sec 4)

4   Unscrew and remove the two caliper mounting bolts and remove the caliper.
5   Brush away all external dirt and pull off the piston dust-excluding cover.
6   Apply air pressure to the fluid inlet hole and eject the piston. Only low air pressure is needed for this, such as is produced by a foot-operated tyre pump.
7   Using a sharp pointed instrument, pick out the piston seal from the groove in the cylinder bore. Do not scratch the surface of the bore.
8   Examine the surfaces of the piston and the cylinder bore. If they are scored or show evidence of metal-to-metal rubbing, then a new piston housing will be required. Where the components are in good condition, discard the seal and obtain a repair kit.
9   Wash the internal components in clean brake hydraulic fluid or methylated spirit only, nothing else.
10 Using the fingers, manipulate the new seal into its groove in the cylinder bore.
11 Dip the piston in clean hydraulic fluid and insert it squarely into its bore.
12 Connect the rubber dust excluder between the piston and the piston housing and then depress the piston fully.
13 Install the caliper by reversing the removal operations. Tighten the mounting bolts to the specified torque.
14 Bleed the brake hydraulic circuit (see Section 13).

6   Brake disc – examination, removal and refitting

1   Raise the front of the vehicle and remove the roadwheel.
2   Examine the surface of the disc. If it is deeply grooved or scored or if any small cracks are evident, it must either be refinished or renewed. Any refinishing must not reduce the thickness of the disc to below a certain minimum (see Specifications). Light scoring on a brake disc is normal and should be ignored.
3   If disc distortion is suspected (refer to Fault Diagnosis, Section 20), the disc can be checked for run-out using a dial gauge or feeler blades located between its face and a fixed point as the disc is rotated.
4   Where the run-out exceeds the specified figure, renew the disc.
5   To remove a disc, unbolt the caliper, withdraw it and tie it up to the suspension strut to avoid strain on the flexible hose.
6   Extract the small disc retaining screw and pull the disc from the hub.
7   If a new disc is being installed, clean its surfaces free from preservative.
8   Refit the caliper and the roadwheel and lower the vehicle to the floor.

7   Rear brake linings – inspection and renewal

Passenger vehicles

1   Due to the fact that the rear brake drums are combined with the hubs, which makes removal of the drums more complicated than is the case with detachable drums, inspection of the shoe linings can be carried out at the specified intervals by prising out the small inspection plug from the brake backplate and observing the linings through the hole using a mirror (photo).
2   A minimum thickness of friction material must always be observed on the shoes, if it is worn down to this level, renew the shoes.
3   Do not attempt to re-line shoes yourself but always obtain factory re-lined shoes.
4   Renew the shoes in an axle set (four shoes), even if only one is worn to the minimum.
5   Slacken the roadwheel bolts, raise the rear of the vehicle and support it securely. Remove the roadwheels.
6   Release the handbrake fully.
7   Tap off the hub dust cap, remove the split pin, nut lock, nut and thrust washer (photos).
8   Pull the hub/drum towards you and then push it back enough to be able to take the outer bearing from the spindle (photo).
9   Remove the hub/drum and brush out any dust taking care not to inhale it (photo).
10 Remove the shoe hold-down spring from the leading shoe (photo). Do this by gripping the dished washer with a pair of pliers, depressing it and turning it through 90°. Remove the washer, spring and the hold-

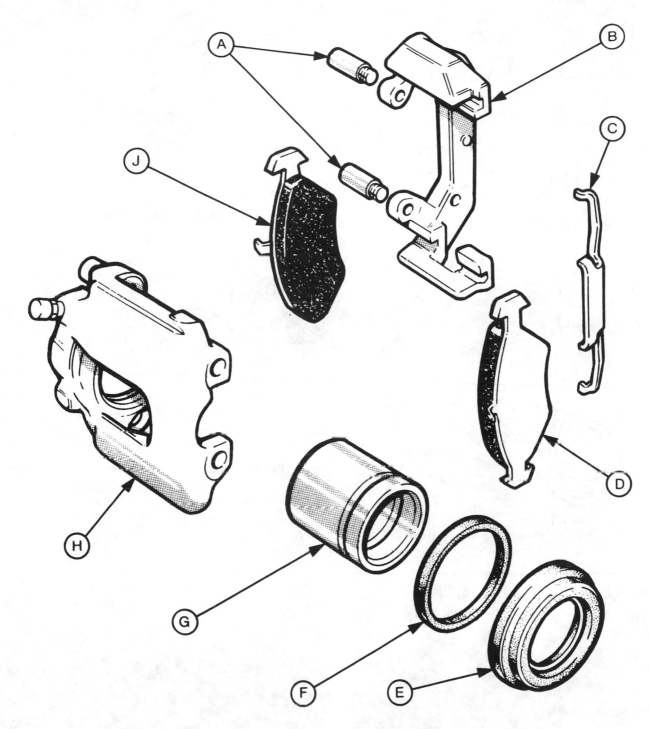

Fig. 8.4 Exploded view of disc caliper (Sec 5)

A	Anchor bolts	D	Disc pad	F	Piston seal	H	Cylinder body
B	Anchor bracket	E	Dust excluder	G	Piston	J	Disc pad
C	Retaining clip						

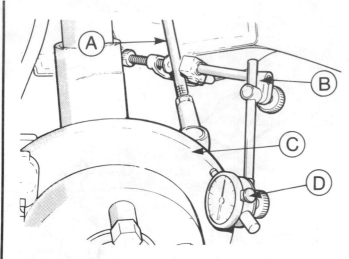

Fig. 8.5 Using a dial gauge to check disc run-out (Sec 6)

A   Track rod   C   Disc
B   Gauge support   D   Zeroing knob

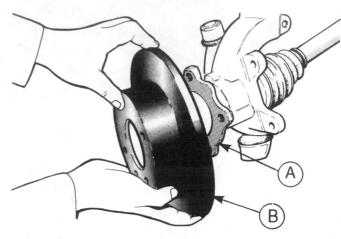

Fig. 8.6 Removing brake disc (Sec 6)

A   Hub   B   Disc

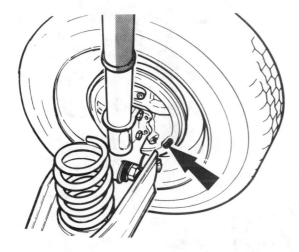

Fig. 8.7 Rear brake shoe inspection plug (arrowed) (Sec 7)

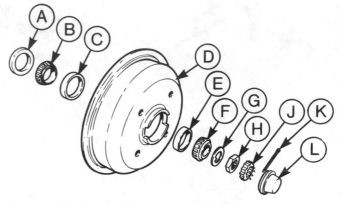

Fig. 8.8 Rear hub/drum components (passenger vehicles) (Sec 7)

A   Oil seal   F   Tapered roller bearing
B   Tapered roller bearing   (outer)
     (inner)   G   Thrust washer
C   Bearing track   H   Nut
D   Hub/drum   J   Nut lock
E   Bearing track   K   Split pin
                                L   Grease cap

7.1 Checking rear brake lining wear with a mirror

7.7A Removing rear hub dust cap

7.7B Extracting rear hub split pin

7.7C Unscrewing rear hub nut

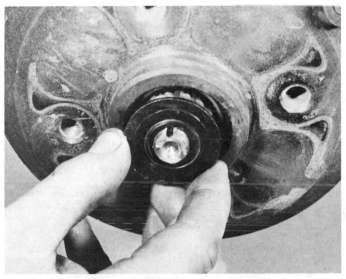

7.7D Removing rear hub thrust washer

7.8 Removing rear hub outer bearing

7.9 Rear hub/drum removed

7.10 Releasing brake shoe hold-down washer

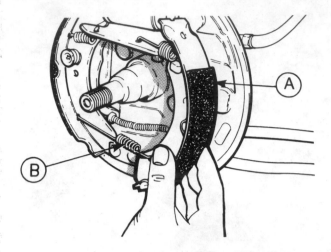

Fig. 8.9 Withdrawing leading shoe (Sec 7)

A   Shoe   B   Spring

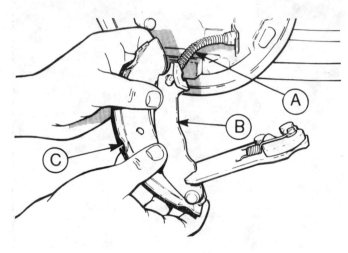

Fig. 8.10 Handbrake cable attachment to shoe (Sec 7)

A   Cable   C   Shoe
B   Lever

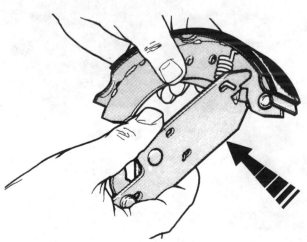

Fig. 8.11 Separating trailing shoe from spacer strut (arrowed)
(Sec 7)

down post. Note the locations of the leading and trailing shoes and the cut-back of the linings at the leading ends.

11 Pull the leading shoe outwards and upwards away from the backplate.

12 Twist the shoe to unhook it from its return springs. If you have any doubt about remembering into which holes the springs engage, mark or sketch them.

13 Remove the trailing shoe in a similar way, at the same time withdrawing the spacer strut.

14 Release the end of the handbrake cable from the lever on the shoe.

15 Disconnect the trailing shoe from the spacer strut by pulling the shoe outwards and twisting the shoe spring.

16 Commence reassembly by installing the trailing shoe. Do this by engaging the handbrake lever return spring to the shoe. Hook the spacer strut onto the spring and lever it into position.

17 Locate the webs of the trailing shoe on the wheel cylinder and the fixed abutment, making sure that the lower end of the handbrake lever is correctly located on the face of the plastic plunger and not trapped behind it.

18 Fit the trailing shoe hold-down post and spring. Hold the leading shoe in position.

19 Connect the larger shoe return spring at the lower (abutment) position between both shoes.

20 Holding the leading shoe almost at right-angles to the backplate, connect the spring between it and the strut and then engage the bottom end of the shoe behind the abutment retainer plate.

21 Swivel the shoe towards the backplate so that the cut-out in its web passes over the quadrant lever. Fit the shoe hold-down post, spring and washer.

22 Centralise the shoes within the backplate by tapping them if necessary with the hand, then fit the hub/drum and slide the outer bearing onto the spindle.

23 Fit the thrust washer and nut and whilst rotating the drum, tighten the nut to a torque of 24 Nm (17 lbf ft). Unscrew the nut one half a turn and then screw the nut up again, but this time only finger tight.

24 Without altering the position of the nut, fit the nut lock so that suitable cut-outs align with the split pin hole. Insert a new split pin and bend the ends **around** the spindle, **not** over the end of it or the pin may rub on the inside of the dust cap.

25 Depress the brake pedal hard several times to actuate the self-adjusting mechanism and to bring the shoes up close to the drum.

26 Refit the roadwheel and lower the vehicle to the floor.

Vans

27 On Van versions, the brake drum is separate from the hub and can be removed for inspection of the shoes without the need to remove the hub as well.

28 Apart from this difference, renewal of the brake shoes is as described in the preceding paragraphs for passenger cars.

8   Rear wheel cylinder – removal, overhaul and refitting

1   Remove the rear brake shoes as described in the preceding Section.

2   Disconnect the fluid pipeline from the wheel cylinder and cap the end of the pipe to prevent loss of fluid. A bleed screw rubber dust cap is useful for this.

3   Unscrew the two bolts which hold the wheel cylinder to the brake backplate and remove the cylinder with sealing gasket.

4   Clean away external dirt and then pull off the dust-excluding covers.

5   The pistons will probably shake out. If they do not, apply air pressure (from a tyre pump) at the fluid inlet hole to eject them.

6   Examine the surfaces of the pistons and the cylinder bores for scoring or metal-to-metal rubbing areas. If evident, renew the complete cylinder assembly.

7   Where the components are in good condition, discard the rubber seals and dust excluders and obtain a repair kit.

8   Any cleaning should be done using hydraulic fluid or methylated spirit – nothing else.

9   Reassemble by dipping the first piston in clean hydraulic fluid and inserting it into the cylinder. Fit a dust excluder to it.

10 From the opposite end of the cylinder body, insert a new seal, spring, a second new seal, the second piston and the remaining dust excluder. Use only the fingers to manipulate the seals into position and make quite sure that the lips of the seals are the correct way round.

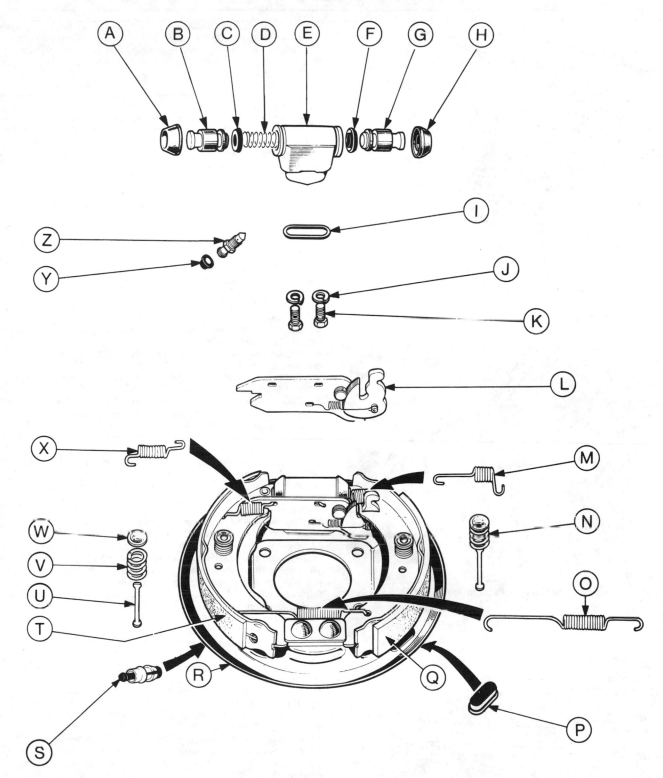

Fig. 8.12 Exploded view of rear brake assembly (Sec 7)

A	Dust excluder	H	Dust excluder	O	Return spring	U	Hold-down post
B	Piston	I	Gasket	P	Inspection hole plug	V	Spring
C	Seal	J	Spring washer	Q	Leading shoe	W	Dished washer
D	Spring	K	Mounting bolt	R	Backplate	X	Return spring
E	Cylinder body	L	Adjuster strut	S	Handbrake lever plunger	Y	Dust cover
F	Seal	M	Return spring	T	Trailing shoe	Z	Bleed screw
G	Piston	N	Hold-down spring				

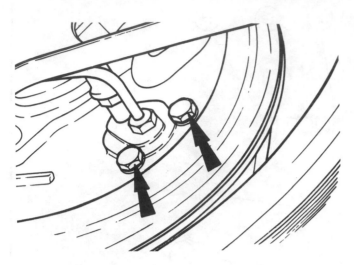

Fig. 8.13 Rear wheel cylinder retaining bolts (arrowed) (Sec 8)

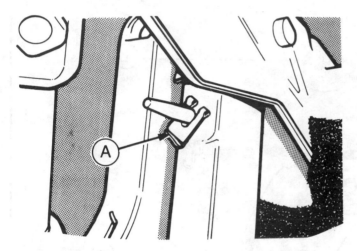

Fig. 8.14 Pushrod-to-brake pedal attachment clip (A) (Sec 10)

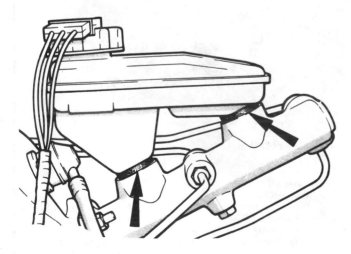

**Fig. 8.15 Master cylinder reservoir sealing rings (arrowed)
(Sec 10)**

11 Bolt the wheel cylinder to the backplate, reconnect the fluid line and refit the shoes (Section 7).
12 Refit the brake drum and roadwheel and lower the vehicle to the floor.
13 Bleed the hydraulic circuit (Section 13).

9 Brake drum – inspection and renewal

1 Whenever a brake drum is removed, brush out dust from it, taking care not to inhale it as it contains asbestos and is injurious to health.
2 Examine the internal friction surface of the drum. If deeply scored, or so worn that the drum has become pocketed to the width of the shoes, then the drums must be renewed.
3 Regrinding is not recommended as the internal diameter will no longer be compatible with the shoe lining contact diameter.

10 Master cylinder – removal, overhaul and refitting

1 Syphon out as much fluid as possible from the master cylinder reservoir using an old battery hydrometer or a poultry baster. Do not drip the fluid onto the paintwork or it will act as an effective paint stripper.
2 Disconnect the pipelines from the master cylinder by unscrewing the unions.
3 Disconnect the leads from the level warning switch in the reservoir cap. Remove the cap (photo).
4 Working inside the vehicle, remove the spring clip which retains the pushrod to the pedal arm.
5 Working within the engine compartment, unbolt the master cylinder from the bulkhead and remove it.
6 Clean away external dirt and then detach the fluid reservoir by tilting it sideways and gently pulling. Remove the two rubber seals.
7 Secure the master cylinder carefully in a vice fitted with jaw protectors.
8 Unscrew and remove the piston stop bolt.
9 Pull the dust excluder back from around the pushrod and using circlip pliers, extract the circlip which is now exposed.
10 Remove the pushrod, dust excluder and washer.
11 Withdraw the primary piston assembly, which will already have been partially ejected.
12 Tap the end of the master cylinder on a block of wood and eject the secondary piston assembly.
13 Examine the piston and cylinder bore surfaces for scoring or signs of metal-to-metal rubbing. If evident, renew the cylinder complete.
14 Where the components are in good condition, dismantle the primary piston by unscrewing the screw and removing the sleeve. Remove the spring, retainer, seal and the shim. Prise the second seal from the piston.
15 Dismantle the secondary piston in a similar way.
16 Discard all seals and obtain a repair kit.
17 Cleaning of components should be done in brake hydraulic fluid or methylated spirit only – nothing else.
18 Using the new seals from the repair kit, assemble the pistons, making sure that the seal lips are the correct way round.
19 Dip the piston assemblies in clean hydraulic fluid and enter them into the cylinder bore.
20 Fit the pushrod complete with new dust excluder and secure with a new circlip.
21 Engage the dust excluder with the master cylinder.
22 Depress the pushrod and screw in the stop bolt.
23 Locate the two rubber seals and push the fluid reservoir into position.
24 It is recommended that a small quantity of fluid is now poured into the reservoir and the pushrod operated several times to prime the unit.
25 Refit the master cylinder by reversing the removal operations.
26 Bleed the complete hydraulic system on completion of the work (see Section 13).

11 Pressure regulating valve – removal and refitting

Passenger vehicles

1 The brake pressure regulating valve is located within the engine compartment, just above the aperture in the wing inner panel through which the tie-rod passes (photo).

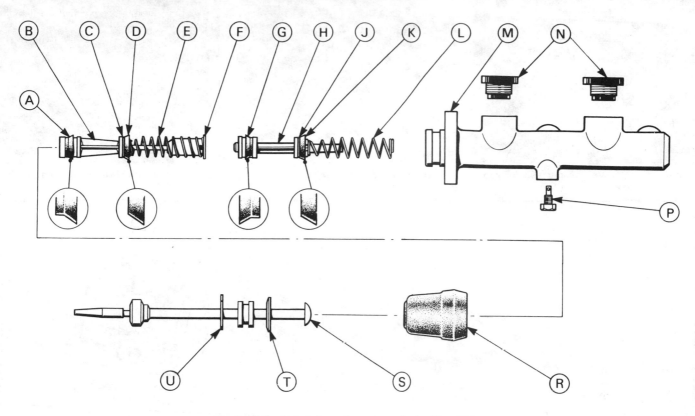

Fig. 8.16 Exploded view of master cylinder (Sec 10)

A	Seal	F	Retainer	L	Spring	R	Bolt
B	Primary piston	G	Seal	M	Cylinder body	S	Pushrod
C	Shim	H	Secondary piston	N	Reservoir seals	T	Washer
D	Seal	J	Shim	P	Piston stop bolt	U	Circlip
E	Spring	K	Seal				

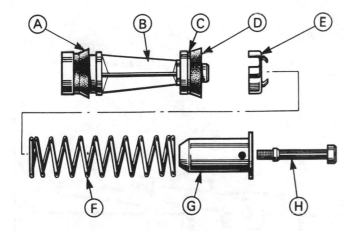

Fig. 8.17 Primary piston dismantled (Sec 10)

A	Seal	E	Retainer
B	Piston	F	Spring
C	Shim	G	Sleeve
D	Seal	H	Screw

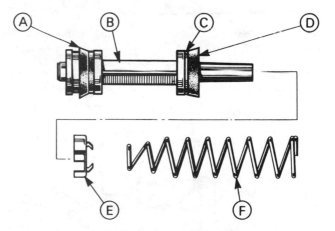

Fig. 8.18 Secondary piston dismantled (Sec 10)

A	Seal	D	Seal
B	Piston	E	Retainer
C	Shim	F	Spring

2   Unscrew the unions and disconnect the pipelines from the valve. Cap the ends of the pipes with bleed nipple dust caps to prevent loss of fluid.

3   Unscrew the valve mounting bolts and remove the valve.

4   Refitting is a reversal of removal, but bleed the complete hydraulic system when the work is finished (see Section 13).

Vans

5   The pressure regulating valve used on vans is mounted on the underside of the vehicle above the rear axle tube. It is connected to the axle by a rod.

6   The valve is of the 'light laden' type and reacts to suspension height according to vehicle load.

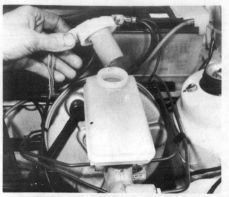
10.3 Removing master cylinder reservoir cap

11.1 Location of pressure regulating valve (passenger vehicles)

12.2 Extracting flexible hose clip from bracket

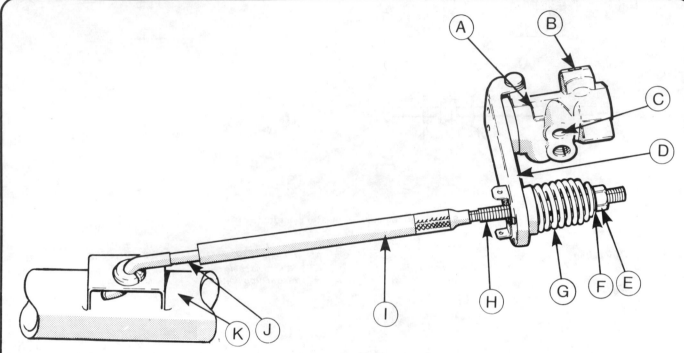

Fig. 8.19 Pressure regulating valve (Van) (Sec 11)

A	Valve body	D	Actuating lever	G	Control spring	J	Link rod
B	Fluid outlet	E	Adjuster nut	H	Adjuster rod	K	Rear axle tube
C	Fluid inlet	F	Linkage retaining clip	I	Spacer tube		

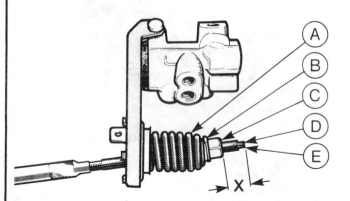

Fig. 8.20 Pressure regulating valve (Van) adjustment diagram (Sec 11)

A	Control spring	D	Threaded rod
B	Linkage retaining clip	E	Flats
C	Adjuster nut	X	10 to 12 mm (0.4 to 0.5 in)

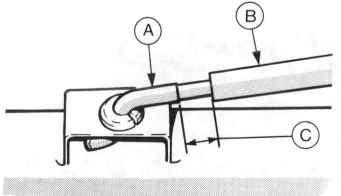

Fig. 8.21 Pressure regulating valve (Van) linkage adjustment diagram with original roadsprings (Sec 11)

A	Link rod	C	18.5 to 20.5 mm
B	Spacer tube		(0.76 to 0.84 in)

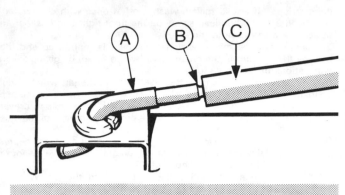

Fig. 8.22 Pressure regulating valve (Van) linkage adjustment diagram with new roadspring(s) (Sec 11)

A   Link rod   C   Spacer tube
B   Groove

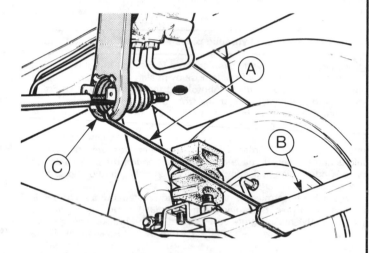

Fig. 8.23 Pressure regulating valve (passenger vehicles) fixing bolts (A) (Sec 11)

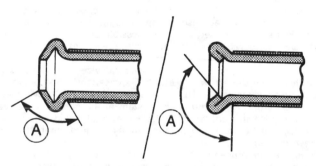

Fig. 8.24 Brake pipe flare (Sec 12)

A   Protective coating removed
    before flaring

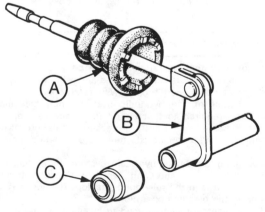

Fig. 8.25 Pressure regulating valve lever (Van) retained in open position (Sec 13)

A   Wire   C   Lever
B   Spring

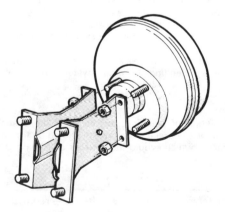

Fig. 8.26 Servo and mounting bracket (Sec 14)

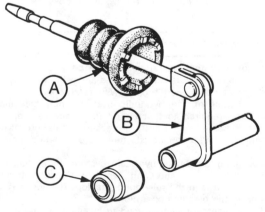

Fig. 8.27 Brake servo connecting linkage (RHD) (Sec 14)

A   Grommet   C   Bush
B   Link

7   The valve should never be dismantled but it must be adjusted whenever the valve itself, the axle tube, spring or shock absorber have been removed, refitted or renewed.

8   Follow this adjustment procedure provided the original road-springs have been refitted, but when new valve linkage has been installed. Measure the dimension X (Fig. 8.20) and if necessary adjust the position of the nut to make the dimension between 10 and 12 mm (0.4 and 0.5 in). Rotate the spacer tube so that the dimension C (Fig. 8.21) is between 18.5 and 20.5 mm (0.76 and 0.84 in). Crimp the end of the spacer tube adjacent to the knurled section of the tube to prevent the tube from rotating.

9   If the original roadsprings have been refitted and also the original valve linkage, hold the threaded adjustment rod by means of its flats and turn the adjusting nut in either direction until the correct dimensions are obtained.

10   If one or both rear roadsprings have been renewed, carry out the adjustment procedure described in paragraph 8, except that the end of the spacer tube should be aligned with the groove in the link rod (Fig. 8.22).

11   If the pressure regulating valve must be removed, first disconnect the hydraulic pipelines from the valve and cap the pipes.

12   Unbolt the valve from its mounting bracket, lower the valve and slide the spacer tube assembly off the link rod. Remove the link rod.

13   Refitting is a reversal of removal, but bleed the brakes (Section 13) and adjust the valve as described above.

12 Flexible and rigid hydraulic pipes – removal and installation

1   Inspection has already been covered in Section 2 of this Chapter.

2   Always disconnect a flexible hose by prising out the spring anchor clip from the support bracket (photo) and then using two close-fitting spanners, disconnect the rigid line from the flexible hose.

3   Once disconnected from the rigid pipe, the flexible hose may be unscrewed from the caliper or wheel cylinder.

4   When reconnecting pipeline or hose fittings, remember that all union threads are to metric sizes. No copper washers are used at unions and the seal is made at the swaged end of the pipe, so do not try to wind a union in if it is tight yet still stands proud of the surface into which it is screwed.

5   A flexible hose must never be installed twisted, but a slight 'set' is permissible to give it clearance from an adjacent component. Do this by turning the hose slightly before inserting the bracket spring clip.

6   Rigid pipelines can be made to pattern by factors supplying brake components.

7   If you are making up a brake pipe yourself, observe the following essential requirements.

8   Before flaring the ends of the pipe, trim back the protective plastic coating by a distance of 5.0 mm (0.2 in).

9   Flare the end of the pipe as shown (Fig. 8.24).

10   The minimum pipe bend radius is 12.0 mm (0.5 in), but bends of less than 20.0 mm (0.8 in) should be avoided if possible.

13 Hydraulic system – bleeding

1   This is not a routine operation but will be required after any component in the system has been removed and refitted or any part of the hydraulic system has been 'broken'. Where an operation has only affected one circuit of the hydraulic system, then bleeding will normally only be required to that circuit (front and rear diagonally opposite). If the master cylinder or the pressure regulating valve have been disconnected and reconnected, then the complete system must be bled.

2   When bleeding the brake hydraulic system on a Van, tie the pressure regulating valve actuating lever to the right-hand rear roadspring so that it is in the fully open position. This will ensure full fluid flow during the bleeding operations.

3   One of three methods can be used to bleed the system.

Bleeding – two-man method

4   Gather together a clean jar and a length of rubber or plastic bleed tubing which will fit the bleed screw tightly. The help of an assistant will be required.

5   Take care not to spill fluid onto the paintwork as it will act as a paint stripper. If any is spilled, wash it off at once with cold water.

6   Clean around the bleed screw on the front right-hand caliper and attach the bleed tube to the screw.

7   Check that the master cylinder reservoir is topped up and then destroy the vacuum in the brake servo (where fitted) by giving several applications of the brake foot pedal.

8   Immerse the open end of the bleed tube in the jar, which should contain two or three inches of hydraulic fluid. The jar should be positioned about 300 mm (12.0 in) above the bleed nipple to prevent any possibility of air entering the system down the threads of the bleed screw when it is slackened.

9   Open the bleed screw half a turn and have your assistant depress the brake pedal slowly to the floor and then quickly remove his foot to allow the pedal to return unimpeded.

10   Observe the submerged end of the tube in the jar. When air bubbles cease to appear, tighten the bleed screw when the pedal is being held fully down by your assistant.

11   Top up the fluid reservoir. It must be kept topped up throughout the bleeding operations. If the connecting holes to the master cylinder are exposed at any time due to low fluid level, then air will be drawn into the system and work will have to start all over again.

12   Repeat the operations on the left-hand rear brake, the left-hand front and the right-hand rear brake in that order (assuming that the whole system is being bled).

13   On completion, remove the bleed tube. Discard the fluid which has been bled from the system unless it is required for bleed jar purposes, never use it for filling the system.

Bleeding – with one-way valve

14   There are a number of one-man brake bleeding kits currently available from motor accessory shops. It is recommended that one of these kits should be used whenever possible as they greatly simplify the bleeding operation and also reduce the risk of expelled air or fluid being drawn back into the system.

15   Connect the outlet tube of the bleeder device to the bleed screw and then open the screw half a turn. Depress the brake pedal to the floor and slowly release it. The one-way valve in the device will prevent expelled air from returning to the system at the completion of each stroke. Repeat this operation until clean hydraulic fluid, free from air bubbles, can be seen coming through the tube. Tighten the bleed screw and remove the tube.

16   Repeat the procedure on the remaining bleed nipples in the order described in paragraph 12. Remember to keep the master cylinder reservoir full.

Bleeding – with pressure bleeding kit

17   These too are available from motor accessory shops and are usually operated by air pressure from the spare tyre.

18   By connecting a pressurised container to the master cylinder fluid reservoir, bleeding is then carried out by simply opening each bleed screw in turn and allowing the fluid to run out, rather like turning on a tap, until no air bubbles are visible in the fluid being expelled.

19   Using this system, the large reserve of fluid provides a safeguard against air being drawn into the master cylinder during the bleeding operations.

20   This method is particularly effective when bleeding 'difficult' systems or when bleeding the entire system at time of routine fluid renewal.

All systems

21   On completion of bleeding, top up the fluid level to the mark. Check the feel of the brake pedal, which should be firm and free from any 'sponginess' which would indicate air still being present in the system.

14 Vacuum servo unit and linkage (RHD) – removal and refitting

1   Working inside the vehicle, remove the spring clip which attaches the pushrod to the arm of the brake pedal.

2   Disconnect the pipelines from the master cylinder.

3   Unscrew the nuts which hold the servo to its mounting bracket, also the servo support brace to the body.

4   Disconnect the vacuum hose from the servo.

5   Detach the linkage arm spring at the rear of the servo and then

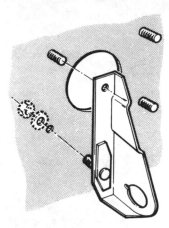

Fig. 8.28 Servo linkage driver's side support bracket (RHD) (Sec 14)

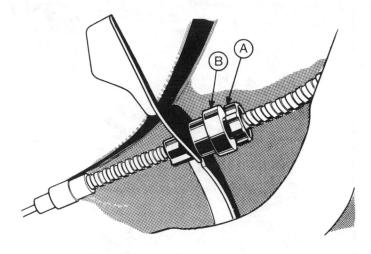

Fig. 8.29 Handbrake cable adjuster nut (A) and sleeve (B) (Sec 16)

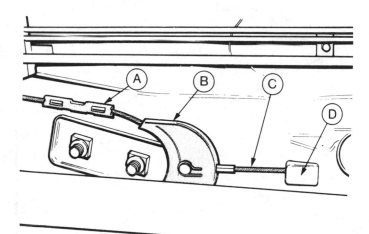

Fig. 8.30 Handbrake cable equaliser (Sec 17)

A   Cable connector   C   Primary cable
B   Equaliser   D   Cable guide

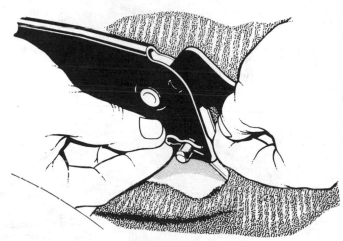

Fig. 8.31 Handbrake control lever clevis pin and clip (Sec 17)

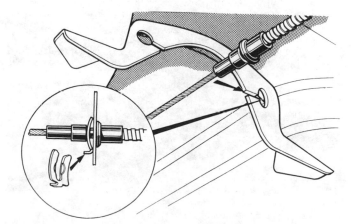

Fig. 8.32 Handbrake cable connector and body guide (Sec 17)

pull the servo forward until the servo operating rod can be unclipped from the linkage.

6   Remove the servo from the vehicle. It must be renewed if defective, no repair is possible.

7   If necessary, the rest of the servo operating linkage can be removed from under the instrument panel once the covering and cowl side trim have been removed from above the brake pedal inside the vehicle. Unbolt the connecting link bracket from the driver's side.

8   Refitting is a reversal of removal. Bleed the hydraulic system on completion.

15 Vacuum servo unit (LHD) – removal and refitting

1   Detach the spring clip which connects the pushrod to the arm of the brake pedal.

2   Disconnect and cap the pipelines from the master cylinder.

3   Unscrew the retaining nuts and remove the master cylinder from the servo unit.

4   Disconnect the servo vacuum hose.

5   Unscrew the servo mounting nuts and remove the servo from the engine compartment. It must be renewed if defective, no repair is possible.

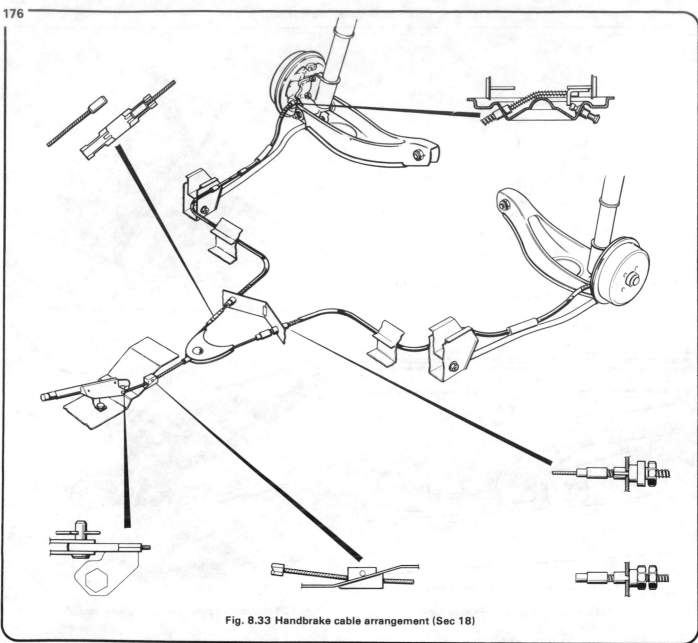

Fig. 8.33 Handbrake cable arrangement (Sec 18)

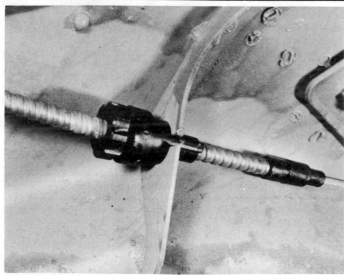

16.5 Handbrake cable adjuster nut and sleeve

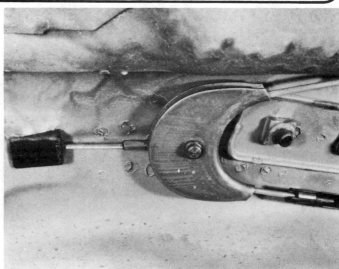

17.2 Handbrake cable equaliser

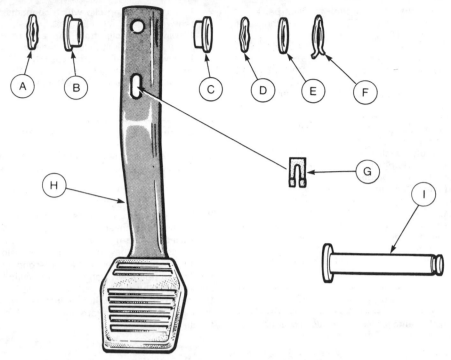

Fig. 8.34 Brake pedal components (Sec 18)

A Washer	D Washer	F Spring clip	H Pedal
B Bush	E Washer	G Pushrod clip	I Pedal pivot shaft
C Bush			

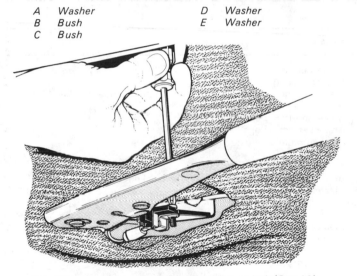

Fig. 8.35 Removing handbrake warning switch (Sec 19)

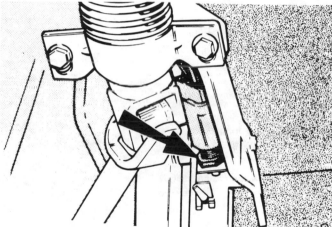

Fig. 8.36 Brake stop-lamp switch showing locknut (arrowed) (Sec 19)

6   Refitting is a reversal of removal. Bleed the hydraulic system on completion.

16 Handbrake – adjustment

Also see Chapter 13

1   Adjustment of the handbrake is normally automatic by means of the self-adjusting mechanism working on the rear brake shoes.
2   However, due to cable stretch, occasional inspection of the handbrake adjusters is recommended. Adjustment must be carried out if the movement of the control lever becomes excessive.
3   Make sure that the handbrake is fully off.
4   Grip each adjuster plunger between finger and thumb and check for in and out movement. If the total movement (both sides added together) is between 1.0 and 2.5 mm (0.04 and 0.10 in), then adjustment is satisfactory. If there is no movement or if it exceeds that specified, adjust in the following way.
5   Make sure that the keyed sleeve on the cable conduit is engaged in its bracket slot. Unlock the adjusting nut by levering between the shoulders of nut and sleeve (photo).

6   Now turn the adjuster nut to eliminate slackness from the cable so that it is just possible to rotate the adjustment plungers. Give the adjuster nut a further $\frac{1}{4}$ to $\frac{1}{2}$ turn.
7   Apply the handbrake control lever fully to seat the adjuster nut against its sleeve.
8   If adjustment of the cable does not alter the plunger movement then the handbrake cable must be binding or the brake mechanism is at fault.

17 Handbrake cables – renewal

Also see Chapter 13
Primary cable

1   Raise the vehicle on ramps or axle stands, or position it over an inspection pit.
2   Extract the spring clip and clevis pin and disconnect the primary cable from the equaliser (photo).
3   Working inside the vehicle, disconnect the cable from the hand-brake control lever, again by removal of clip and pin. Drift out the cable

guide to the rear and withdraw the cable through the floor pan.

4   Refitting is a reversal of removal. Adjust the handbrake if necessary as described in Section 16.

Secondary cable

5   Unlock the adjuster nut from its sleeve by prising their shoulders apart.

6   Slacken the handbrake cable by turning the adjuster nut.

7   Release the cable connector from its body guide by extracting the spring clip and passing the inner cable through the slit in the guide.

8   Now disconnect the cable from its body guide on the right-hand side of the vehicle.

9   Separate the cable assembly/equaliser from the primary cable by extracting the spring clip and clevis pin.

10 Release the cable from the body guides.

11 Remove the rear roadwheels and the brake drums.

12 Release the shoe hold-down spring so that the shoe can be swivelled and the handbrake lever unclipped from the relay lever.

13 Remove the cable ends through the brake backplates and withdraw the complete cable assembly from the vehicle.

14 Refitting is a reversal of removal. Grease the cable groove in the equaliser and adjust the handbrake as described in Section 16.

18 Brake pedal – removal and refitting

1   Working within the vehicle, remove the under-dash cover panel (if fitted).

2   Extract the spring clip which connects the pushrod to the arm of the brake pedal.

3   Extract the circlip from the end of the pedal pivot shaft and withdraw the shaft with clutch pedal and the flat and wave washers.

4   Renew the bushes as necessary.

5   Reassembly and refitting are reversals of removal and dismantling. Apply a little grease to the bushes when installing.

19 Brake warning lamps – description and renewal

1   As already mentioned, all models are fitted with a low fluid level warning switch in the master cylinder reservoir cap and a brake pedal stop-lamp switch.

2   Some versions have front disc pad wear sensors and a handbrake 'ON' warning switch.

3   Warning indicator lamps are mounted on the instrument panel. Their renewal is covered in Chapter 11.

4   Access to the handbrake switch is obtained after removal of the centre console, the switch cover is below it. Extract the switch retaining screw to remove it and disconnect the electrical lead from it.

5   The stop-lamp switch can be removed by disconnecting the leads and unscrewing the locknut which holds the switch to its bracket.

6   When fitting the switch, adjust its position by screwing it in or out so that it does not actuate during the first 5.0 mm (0.2 in) of pedal travel.

20 Fault diagnosis – braking system

Symptom	Reason(s)
Pedal travels almost to floorboards before brakes operate	Brake fluid level too low Caliper leaking Master cylinder leaking (bubbles in master cylinder fluid) Brake flexible hose leaking Brake line fractured Brake system unions loose Rear automatic adjusters seized
Brake pedal feels springy	New linings not yet bedded-in Brake discs or drums badly worn or cracked Master cylinder securing nuts loose
Brake pedal feels spongy and soggy	Caliper or wheel cylinder leaking Master cylinder leaking (bubbles in master cylinder reservoir) Brake pipeline or flexible hose leaking Unions in brake system loose Air in hydraulic system
Excessive effort required to brake car	Pad or shoe linings badly worn New pads or shoes recently fitted – not yet bedded-in Harder linings fitted than standard causing increase in pedal pressure Linings and brake drums contaminated with oil, grease or hydraulic fluid Servo unit inoperative or faulty
Brakes uneven and pulling to one side	Linings and discs or drums contaminated with oil, grease or hydraulic fluid Tyre pressures unequal Seized hydraulic cylinder on one side of vehicle Brake caliper loose Brake pads or shoes fitted incorrectly Different type of linings fitted at each wheel Anchorages for front suspension or rear suspension loose Brake discs or drums badly worn, cracked or distorted
Brakes tend to bind, drag or lock-on	Air in hydraulic system Wheel cylinders seized Handbrake cables too tight
Wheels lock during heavy braking	Pressure regulating valve defective

Chapter 9 Steering

For modifications, and information applicable to later models, see Supplement at end of manual

Contents

Specifications

Steering gear

Type	Rack-and-pinion with universally jointed steering shaft and deformable column
Lubricant capacity	95 cc (0.17 pint)
Pinion turning torque	0.6 to 1.3 Nm (5 to 12 lbf in)
Tie-rod inner balljoint preload (articulation effort)	2.27 kg (5.0 lb)
Rack slipper shim thickness availability	0.127 mm (0.005 in), 0.19 mm (0.007 in), 0.25 mm (0.010 in), 0.38 mm (0.015 in) and 0.50 mm (0.020 in)
Paper gasket thickness	0.14 mm (0.0055 in)
Turning circle:	
Between kerbs	10.05 m (32.9 ft)
Between walls	10.56 m (34.6 ft)

Front wheel alignment

Tolerance permitted when checking	1.5 mm (0.06 in) toe-in to 5.5 mm (0.22 in) toe-out
Adjust to	1.0 mm (0.04 in) toe-in to 3.0 mm (0.12 in) toe-out

Castor and camber angles (nominal, for reference only):

	Castor	Camber
1.1 Saloon, Base and L:		
Standard	3° 11' to 1° 17'	2° 26' to 0° 26'
Heavy duty	3° 10' to 1° 10'	2° 55' to 0° 55'
1.1 GL and Ghia:		
Standard	3° 09' to 1° 09'	2° 11' to 0° 11'
Heavy duty	3° 06' to 1° 06'	2° 38' to 0° 38'
1.3, 1.6 Base and L:		
Standard	3° 33' to 1° 33'	2° 47' to 0° 47'
Heavy duty	3° 10' to 1° 10'	2° 57' to 0° 57'
1.3, 1.6 GL and Ghia:		
Standard	3° 31' to 1° 31'	2° 30' to 0° 30'
Heavy duty	3° 09' to 1° 09'	2° 42' to 0° 42'
1.6 XR3	3° 39' to 1° 39'	2° 22' to 0° 22'
Estate (all models):		
Standard	3° 38' to 1° 38'	2° 53' to 0° 53'
Heavy duty	3° 16' to 1° 16'	2° 53' to 0° 53'
Van 35 and 55	2° 24' to 0° 24'	2° 17' to 0° 17'
Maximum side to side variation:		
Castor	1° 0'	
Camber	1° 15'	

Torque wrench settings

	Nm	lbf ft
Steering wheel nut	32	24
Steering gear mounting bolts	48	35
Tie rod balljoint taper pin nuts	28	20
Coupling pinch-bolt	54	40
Tie-rod end locknut	66	48
Pinion bearing cover bolts	22	16
Rack slipper cover bolts	9	6

1 Description

The steering is of rack-and-pinion type, with a safety steering column which incorporates a universally jointed lower shaft and a convoluted column tube.

The pinion of the steering gear is supported in a needle roller bearing at its lower end and in a ball-bearing at its upper end. Pinion bearing preload adjustment has been eliminated.

The steering tie-rods are attached to the steering rack by means of balljoints working in nylon seats. The balljoints are precisely preloaded, set and locked in position during production.

The tie-rod outer balljoints are of screw-on type with a locking nut.

Rack-to-pinion contact is maintained by a spring-loaded slipper working against a cover plate which is located on the housing using selective shims.

The tie-rods are adjustable for lengths in order to vary the front wheel alignment. Other steering angles are set in production and cannot be adjusted.

Integral lock stops are built into the steering gear and these are also non-adjustable.

The steering gear is lubricated with a semi-fluid grease but in case of difficulty in supply, use Hypoy 90 oil.

The steering wheel is located on a hexagon section shaft instead of the more conventional splined type. This arrangement makes the wheel easier to remove once the nut has been removed.

The steering column lock provides greater security through the large number of lock engagement slots in the column. It is impossible to remove the lock from the column unless the cylinder has first been unlocked.

2 Maintenance and precautions

1 Regularly check the condition of the steering gear bellows and the tie-rod balljoint dust excluders. If split, they must be renewed immediately and in the case of the steering gear, the lubricant cleared out and fresh injected (see Section 3).
2 With an assistant turning the steering wheel from side-to-side, check for lost motion at the tie-rod end balljoints. If evident, renew the balljoints (see Section 4) as no repair or lubrication is possible.
3 When the front wheels are raised, avoid turning the steering wheel rapidly from lock-to-lock. This could cause hydraulic pressure build-up, with consequent damage to the bellows.

3 Steering gear bellows – renewal

1 At the first indication of a split or grease leakage from the bellows, renew them.
2 Raise the front of the vehicle and support it securely.
3 Turn the wheels slowly to full lock to give access to the tie-rod balljoint.
4 Release the tie-rod end locknut, but only unscrew it one quarter of a turn.
5 Extract the split pin and remove the nut from the balljoint taper pin.
6 Using a suitable balljoint extractor, separate the balljoint taper pin from the eye of the steering arm (photo).
7 Unscrew the balljoint from the end of the tie-rod.
8 Release the clips from both ends of the damaged bellows and slide them from the rack and the tie-rod.
9 Turn the steering wheel gently to expel as much lubricant as possible from the rack housing. It is recommended that the bellows on the opposite side are released by detaching their inboard clip, turning the bellows back and clearing the lubricant as it is also ejected at this end of the rack housing.
10 Smear the narrow neck of the new bellows with specified grease and slide them over the tie-rod into position on the rack housing.
11 If new bellows are being fitted to the pinion end of the rack, leave both ends of the bellows unclamped at this stage.
12 If the bellows are being fitted to the rack support bush end of the rack housing, clamp only the inner end of the bellows and leave the outer end unfastened.
13 Screw on the tie-rod end until the locknut requires only $\frac{1}{4}$ turn to lock it.

Fig. 9.1 Steering mechanism (Sec 1)

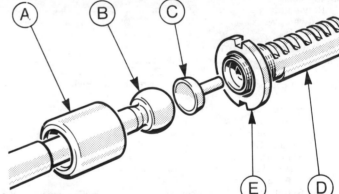

Fig. 9.2 Tie-rod inner balljoint components (Sec 1)

A Ball housing   D Rack
B Tie-rod ball   E Lockring
C Ball seat

14 Connect the tie-rod end balljoint to the steering arm, tighten the nut to the specified torque and insert a new split pin.
15 Add 95 cc (0.17 pint) of the specified lubricant to the pinion end of the rack housing. Move the steering slowly from lock-to-lock to assist the entry of the lubricant into the steering gear.
16 When all the lubricant is injected, fit the bellows clamps. Where the original bellows clamping was by means of soft iron wire, this should be discarded and proper clips used instead.
17 Lower the vehicle to the floor.
18 If the position of the tie-rod locknut was not altered from its original setting, the front wheel alignment (toe) will not have altered, but it is recommended that the alignment is checked at the earliest opportunity as described in Section 11.

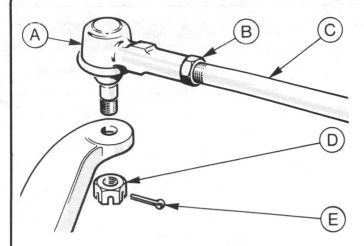

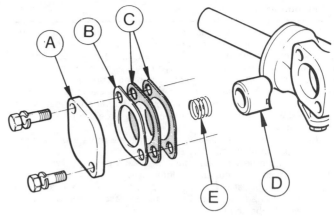

Fig. 9.3 Tie-rod outer balljoint (Sec 1)

A Balljoint D Castellated nut
B Locknut E Split pin
C Tie-rod

Fig. 9.4 Rack slipper components (Sec 1)

A Cover plate D Slipper
B Gasket E Spring
C Shims

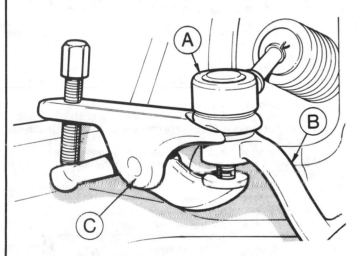

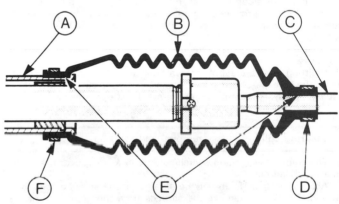

Fig. 9.5 Separating a balljoint from the steering arm (Sec 3)

A Balljoint C Tool
B Steering arm

Fig. 9.6 Rack bellows fitting diagram (Sec 3)

A Rack housing D Retaining clamp
B Bellows E Application of grease
C Tie-rod F Retaining clamp

3.6 Disconnecting a track rod end balljoint

5.1 Removing steering wheel trim

5.2 Unscrewing steering wheel retaining nut

4 Tie-rod end balljoint – renewal

1 If as the result of inspection the tie-rod end balljoints are found to be worn, remove them as described in the preceding Section.

2 When the balljoint nuts are unscrewed, it is sometimes found that the balljoint taper pin turns in the eye of the steering arm to prevent the nut from unscrewing. Should this happen, apply pressure to the top of the balljoint using a length of wood as a lever to seat the taper pin while the nut is unscrewed. When this condition is met with, a balljoint extractor is unlikely to be required to free the taper pin from the steering arm.

3 With the tie-rod end removed, wire brush the threads of the tie-rod and apply grease to them.

4 Screw on the new tie-rod end to take up a position similar to the original. Due to manufacturing differences, the fitting of a new component will almost certainly mean that the front wheel alignment will require some adjustment. Check this as described in Section 11.

5 Connect the balljoint to the steering arm as described in Section 3.

5 Steering wheel – removal and refitting

1 According to model, either pull off the steering wheel trim or prise out the insert which carries the Ford motif at the centre of the steering wheel (photo). Insert the ignition key and turn it to position I.

2 Hold the steering wheel from turning and have the front road-wheels in the straight-ahead attitude, while the steering wheel retaining nut is unscrewed using a socket with extension (photo).

3 Remove the steering wheel from the shaft. No effort should be required to remove the steering wheel as it is located on a hexagonal section shaft which does not cause the binding associated with splined shafts (photo).

4 Note the steering shaft direction indicator cam which has its peg uppermost.

5 Refitting is a reversal of removal. Check that the roadwheels are still in the straight-ahead position and locate the steering wheel so that the larger segment between the spokes is uppermost.

6 Steering column lock – removal and refitting

1 To remove the ignition switch/column lock, the shear head bolt must be drilled out.

2 Access for drilling can only be obtained if the steering column is lowered. To do this, remove the shrouds from the upper end of the column by extracting the fixing screws. Disconnect the battery earth lead.

3 Unscrew the bonnet release lever mounting screw and position the lever to one side.

4 Disconnect the steering column clamps. The lower one is of bolt and nut type, while the upper one is of stud and nut design.

5 Lower the shaft/column carefully until the steering wheel rests on the seat cushion.

6 Centre-punch the end of the shear bolt which secures the steering column lock and then drill it out. Remove the ignition switch/column lock.

7 When fitting the new lock, check for correct operation and then tighten the securing bolt until its head breaks off.

8 Raise the steering column and reconnect the clamps.

9 Refit the bonnet release lever and the column shrouds.

7 Steering column – removal, overhaul and refitting

1 Disconnect the battery.

2 Turn the ignition key and rotate the steering wheel to bring the front roadwheels to the straight-ahead position.

3 Working within the engine compartment, unscrew and remove the pinch-bolt which holds the steering shaft to the splined pinion shaft of the rack-and-pinion gear.

4 Remove the steering wheel as described in Section 5.

5 Remove the direction indicator cam from the top end of the steering shaft.

6 Extract the fixing screws and remove the upper and lower shrouds from the upper end of the steering column (photos).

7 Remove the insulation panel from the lower part of the dash panel (photo).

8 Extract the screw, remove the bonnet release lever mounting and place it to one side (photo).

9 Take out the fixing screws and remove the switches from the steering column (photo).

10 Disconnect the wiring harness multi-plug at the side of the column.

11 Unbolt the upper and lower clamps from the steering column and then withdraw the column/shaft into the vehicle. If any difficulty is experienced in separating the lower shaft from the pinion gear, prise the coupling open very slightly with a screwdriver.

12 Wear in the column bearings can be rectified by renewing them. Access to them is obtained by extracting the tolerance ring from the upper end of the column and then withdrawing the shaft from the lower end of the column. The lower bearing and spring will come with it. Make sure that the steering column lock is unlocked before withdrawing the shaft.

13 If the upper bearing is to be renewed, first remove the lock assembly by drilling out the shear head bolt. The upper bearing may now be levered out of its seat.

14 Commence reassembly by tapping the new upper bearing into its seat in the lock housing.

15 Locate the column lock on the column tube and screw in a new shear head bolt until its head breaks off.

16 Insert the conical spring into the column tube so that the larger diameter end of the spring is against the lowest convolution of the collapsible section of the column tube.

17 Slide the lower bearing onto the shaft so that its chamfered edge will mate with the corresponding one in the column lower bearing seat when the shaft is installed.

18 Insert the shaft into the lower end of the steering column. Make sure that the lock is unlocked and pass the shaft up carefully through the upper bearing.

19 Fit the bearing tolerance ring.

20 Fit the direction indicator cancelling cam to the top of the shaft, making sure that the peg will be uppermost when the column is in the in-car attitude.

21 Fit the steering wheel to the shaft, screwing on the nut sufficiently tightly to be able to pull the lower bearing into the column tube with the bearing slots correctly aligned with the pegs on the tube.

22 Refit the column, making sure to engage the coupling at its lower end with the splined pinion shaft.

23 Bolt up the column upper and lower clamps.

24 Reconnect the wiring harness multi-plug.

25 Refit the combination switches to the steering column.

26 Reconnect the bonnet release lever.

27 Fit the column shrouds.

28 Check that the steering wheel is correctly aligned (wheels in the straight-ahead position). If not, remove the steering wheel and realign it.

29 Tighten the steering wheel nut to the specified torque and then insert the motif into the centre of the steering wheel.

30 Refit the insulation panel to the lower dash.

31 Tighten the coupling pinch-bolt at the base of the steering shaft.

32 Reconnect the battery.

8 Steering gear – removal and refitting

1 Set the front roadwheels in the straight-ahead position.

2 Raise the front of the vehicle and fit safety stands.

3 Working under the bonnet, remove the pinch-bolt from the coupling at the base of the steering column shaft.

4 Extract the split pins from the tie-rod balljoint taper pin nuts, unscrew the nuts and remove them.

5 Separate the balljoints from the steering arms using a suitable tool.

6 Flatten the locktabs on the steering gear securing bolts and unscrew and remove the bolts. Withdraw the steering gear downwards to separate the coupling from the steering shaft and then take it out from under the front wing.

7 Refitting is a reversal of removal. If a new rack-and-pinion assembly is being installed, the tie-rod ends will have to be removed

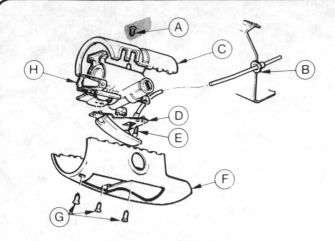

Fig. 9.7 Steering upper column attachments (Sec 6)

A	Screw	E	Screw
B	Bonnet release cable	F	Lower shroud
C	Upper shroud	G	Screws
D	Bonnet release lever	H	Lock housing

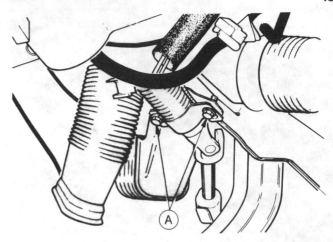

Fig. 9.8 Steering column lower clamp bolts (A) (Sec 6)

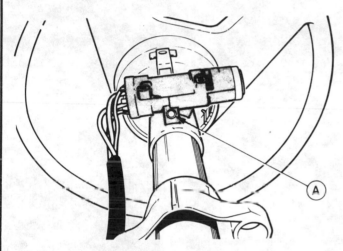

Fig. 9.9 Steering column lock (Sec 6)

A   Shear head bolt

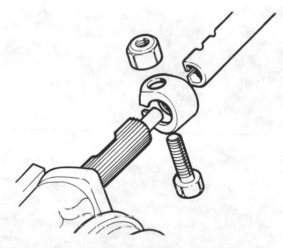

Fig. 9.10 Steering shaft coupling and pinch-bolt (Sec 7)

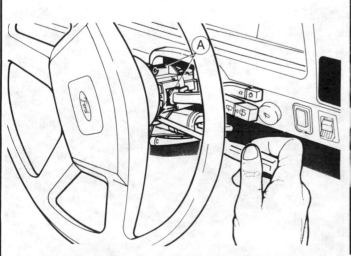

Fig. 9.11 Steering column combination switch fixing screws (A) (Sec 7)

6.3 Steering wheel removed

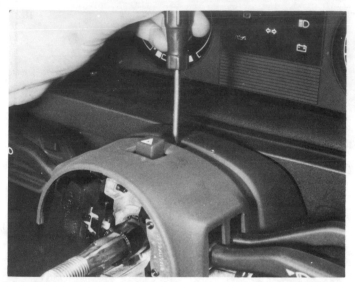

7.6A Extracting upper shroud screw

7.6B Removing lower shroud

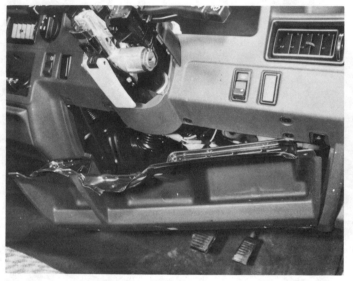

7.7 Removing dash lower panel

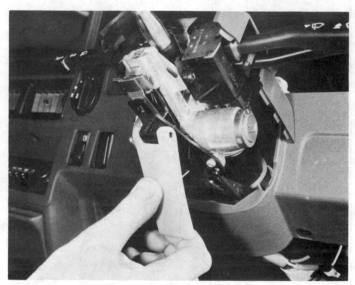

7.8 Bonnet release lever

7.9 Extracting a steering column switch screw

7.11 Steering column lower mounting

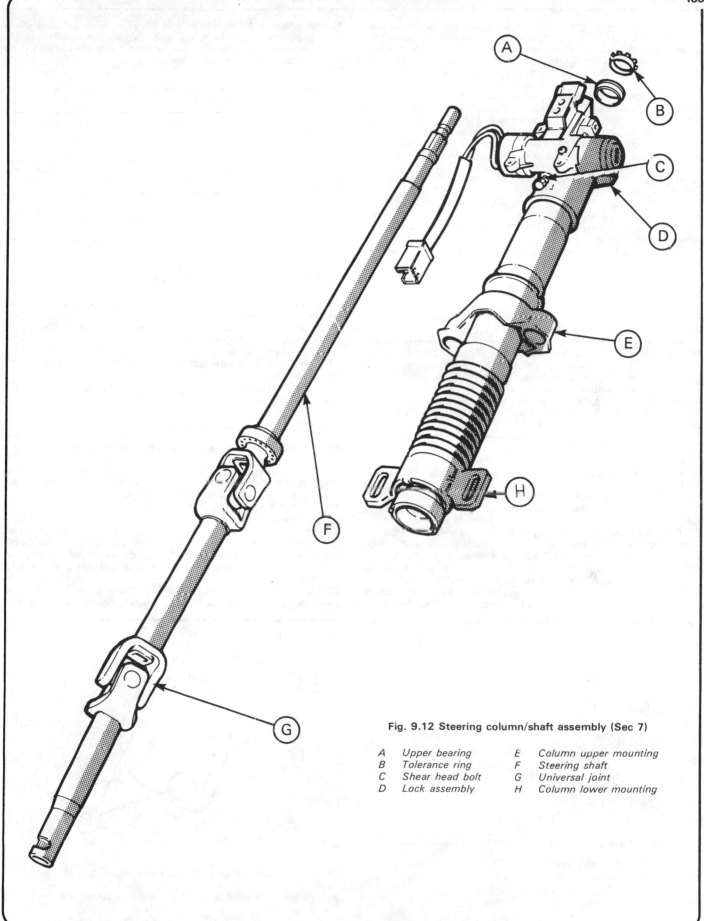

Fig. 9.12 Steering column/shaft assembly (Sec 7)

A	Upper bearing	E	Column upper mounting
B	Tolerance ring	F	Steering shaft
C	Shear head bolt	G	Universal joint
D	Lock assembly	H	Column lower mounting

from the original unit and screwed onto the new tie-rods to approximately the same setting. If a note was not made of the position of the original tie-rod ends on their rods, inspection of the threads will probably indicate their original location. In any event it is important that the new tie-rod ends are screwed on an equal amount at this stage.

8   Make sure that the steering gear is centred. Do this by turning the pinion shaft to full lock in one direction and then count the number of turns required to rotate it to the opposite lock. Now turn the splined pinion shaft through half the number of turns just counted.

9   Check that the roadwheels and the steering wheel are in the straight-ahead attitude, offer up the steering gear and connect the shaft coupling without inserting the pinch-bolt.

10 Bolt up the gear housing and lock the bolts with their lockplate tabs.

11 Reconnect the tie-rod ends to the steering arms. Use new split pins.

12 Tighten the coupling pinch-bolt to the specified torque. Lower the vehicle to the floor.

13 If the tie-rod ends were disturbed or if a new assembly was installed, check and adjust the front wheel alignment as described in Section 11.

9   Rack slipper bearing – adjustment

1   This operation may be required if a knocking or rattling noise is heard when traversing rough ground or uneven road surfaces.

2   Remove the steering gear as described in the preceding Section and mount the assembly in a vice (fitted with jaw protectors) so that the rack slipper cover plate is uppermost.

3   Unbolt and remove the cover plate, together with shim pack and gasket.

4   Ideally, a dial gauge should be used to record the rack slipper height deflection as the rack is moved from lock-to-lock by turning the pinion.

5   Using a micrometer, make up a shim pack greater in thickness by 0.015 to 0.150 mm (0.0006 to 0.006 in) than the dial gauge deflection. The shim pack thickness must include the gasket.

6   Refit the spring, shims and gasket and tighten the bolts to the specified torque.

7   Now check the turning torque of the splined pinion. The correct torque is given in the Specifications. If a suitable torque wrench with splined connector is not available, wind a length of cord round the splined pinion shaft, attach it to a spring balance and take a reading just as the balance is pulled to start the pinion turning.

8   Where a dial gauge is not available, and the reason for adjustment is steering knock, then remove one shim at a time and check the

turning torque with the cord as just described until sufficient shims have been removed to bring the torque within the specified range. With a factory-assembled rack, it is unlikely that stiff steering will be encountered, requiring the addition of shims.

10   Steering gear – overhaul

1   The following operations should only be carried out by home mechanics having a reasonable level of engineering skill and the necessary tools.

2   If the steering gear has given good service over a high mileage then it is strongly recommended that a new or factory reconditioned unit is installed, rather than overhaul the original assembly.

3   Remove the steering gear from the vehicle as described in Section 8.

4   Remove the tie-rod ends and the bellows as described in Section 3.

5   Drain the lubricant by turning the splined pinion shaft from lock-to-lock.

6   Mount the gear in a vice fitted with jaw protectors.

7   Centre-punch the pins which secure the balljoint housings at the ends of the rack.

8   Drill out the pins using a 4.9 mm ($\frac{5}{32}$ in) diameter drill. Do not drill deeper than 9.5 mm (0.4 in).

9   Using a C-spanner and an open-ended spanner, release the balljoint housings from their locknuts.

10 Withdraw the housings, tie-rods and ball seats.

11 Unbolt and remove the rack slipper cover plate, shim pack, gasket, spring and slipper.

12 Unbolt and remove the pinion bearing cover plate and remove the gasket and the pinion oil seal.

13 Withdraw the pinion/bearing assembly.

14 Withdraw the rack from the housing.

15 With the steering gear dismantled, clean and inspect all components. Renew the pinion shaft seal as a matter of routine, also the cover plate gaskets.

16 If the pinion upper bearing is worn it can only be renewed as an assembly with the pinion. The pinion lower bearing, which is of needle roller type, can be renewed independently.

17 The rack support bush is renewable.

18 Commence reassembly by inserting the rack into the housing.

19 Insert the pinion/bearing into the housing. Do this with the rack held central in the housing. Once installed, check that the flat on the end of the pinion shaft is at 90° to the centre-line of the rack and facing the correct way according to whether the vehicle is RHD or LHD (see Fig. 9.19).

20 Locate a new gasket in position and fit the pinion bearing cover plate and the oil seal. Apply some jointing compound to the bolt

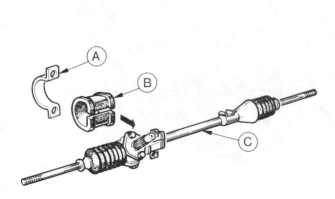

Fig. 9.13 Steering rack mounting components (Sec 8)

A   Clamping saddle   C   Rack housing
B   Rubber insulator

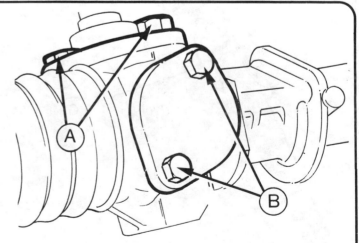

Fig. 9.14 Cover plate identification (Sec 9)

A   Pinion cover plate bolts   B   Rack slipper cover plate bolts

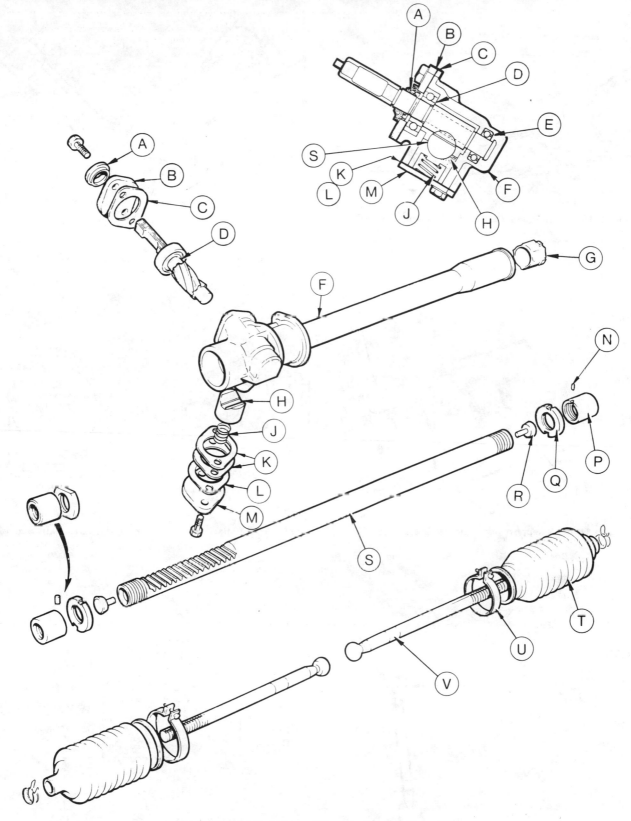

Fig. 9.15 Exploded view of the steering gear (Sec 10)

A	Pinion oil seal	F	Housing	L	Gasket	R	Ball seat
B	Cover plate	G	Rack support bush	M	Cover plate	S	Rack
C	Gasket	H	Rack slipper	N	Lockpin	T	Bellows
D	Pinion/bearing assembly	J	Spring	P	Ball housing	U	Bellows clamp
E	Bearing	K	Shims	Q	Lockring	V	Tie-rod

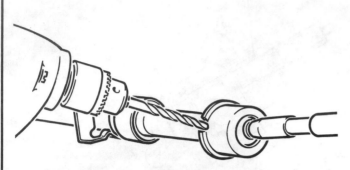

Fig. 9.16 Drilling out a ball housing lockpin (Sec 10)

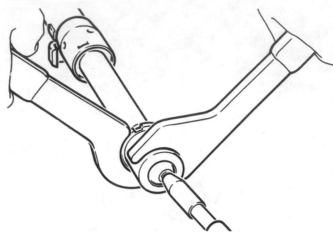

Fig. 9.17 Unscrewing ball housing and lockring (Sec 10)

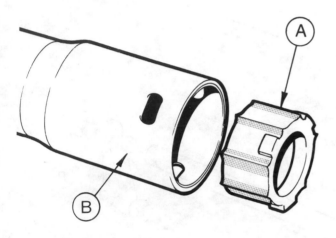

Fig. 9.18 Rack support bush and retainers (Sec 10)

A   Bush   B   Rack housing

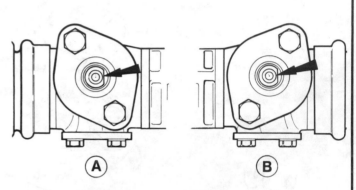

Fig. 9.19 Pinion alignment – note flat (arrowed) (Sec 10)

A   LHD   B   RHD

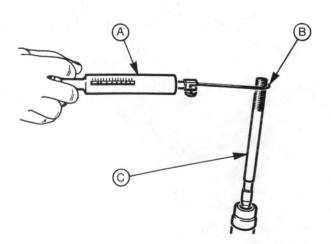

Fig. 9.20 Checking tie-rod inner balljoint preload (Sec 10)

A   Spring balance   C   Tie-rod
B   Attachment point

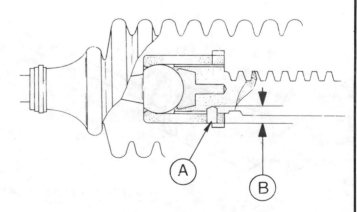

Fig. 9.21 Tie-rod inner balljoint pin locking diagram (Sec 10)

A   Hole   B   Maximum depth

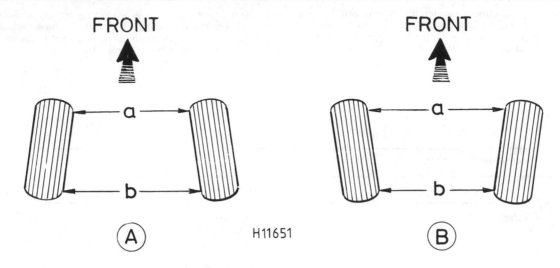

Fig. 9.22 Front wheel alignment (Sec 11)

A   Toe-in (a less than b)   B   Toe-out (a greater than b)

threads before screwing them in. Tighten the bolts to the specified torque.
21 Fit the rack slipper, the spring, the selected shim pack (refer to Section 9), the gasket and the cover plate.
22 Assemble the tie-rod balljoints to their seats at the ends of the rack. Make sure that the ball seats are lubricated with the specified grease or if not available, with SAE 90 transmission oil.
23 The preload (articulation effort) of the tie-rod balljoints must now be measured and adjusted. Do this by tightening the ball housing until the force required to move the tie-rod from the mid-point of its arc of travel is as given in the Specifications. To measure this, attach a spring balance to the threaded part of the tie-rod about 6.0 mm (0.25 in) from the end of the rod.
24 Adjust the ball housing as necessary to achieve the specified setting and then using a C-spanner, tighten the locking ring nut without moving the position of the ball housing. Recheck the setting.
25 The ball housings/locknuts must now be pinned. Do this by centre-punching the joint between the housing and the lockring and drilling carefully down the joint faces. The hole must be 4.0 mm ($\frac{5}{32}$ in) in diameter and with a maximum depth of 9.5 mm (0.4 in). These new holes must be drilled even if it was found that the original holes came into alignment when the ball preload was finally adjusted.
26 Insert new pins into the holes and retain them by peening over the edges of their holes.
27 Fit one set of bellows and secure with clamps at both ends. Make sure that the bellows are not twisted and if wire was used to secure them originally, discard it in favour of proper clips.
28 Add 95 cc (0.17 pt) of the specified lubricant. Move the rack from lock-to-lock to assist the entry of the lubricant into the steering gear.
29 Fit the second set of bellows and their clamps.
30 Re-check the pinion turning torque (see Section 9). Readjust the thickness of the shim pack if necessary.

11 Steering angles and wheel alignment

1 When reading this Section, reference should also be made to Chapter 10 in respect of front and rear suspension arrangement.
2 Accurate front wheel alignment is essential to good steering and for even tyre wear. Before considering the steering angles, check that the tyres are correctly inflated, that the roadwheels are not buckled, the hub bearings are not worn or incorrectly adjusted and that the steering linkage is in good order.
3 Wheel alignment consists of four factors,:

Camber is the angle at which the road wheels are set from the vertical when viewed from the front or rear of the vehicle. Positive camber is the angle (in degrees) that the wheels are tilted outwards at the top, from the vertical.

Castor is the angle between the steering axis and a vertical line when viewed from each side of the vehicle. Positive castor is indicated when the steering axis is inclined towards the rear of the vehicle at its upper end.

Steering axis inclination is the angle, when viewed from the front or rear of the vehicle, between the vertical and an imaginary line drawn between the upper and lower suspension swivel balljoints or upper and lower strut mountings.

Toe is the amount by which the distance between the front inside edges of the roadwheel runs differs from that between the rear inside edges. If the distance at the front is less than that at the rear, the wheels are said to toe-in. If the distance at the front inside edges is greater than that at the rear, the wheels toe-out.
4 Due to the need for precision gauges to measure the small angles of the steering and suspension settings, it is preferable to leave this work to your dealer. Camber and castor angles are set in production and are not adjustable. If these angles are ever checked and found to be outside specification then either the suspension components are damaged or distorted, or wear has occurred in the bushes at the attachment points.
5 If you wish to check front wheel alignment yourself, first make sure that the lengths of both tie-rods are equal when the steering is in the straight-ahead position. This can be measured reasonably accurately by counting the number of exposed threads on the tie-rod adjacent to the balljoint assembly.
6 Adjust if necessary by releasing the locknut from the balljoint assembly and the clamp at the small end of the bellows.
7 Obtain a tracking gauge. These are available in various forms from accessory stores, or one can be fabricated from a length of steel tubing, suitably cranked to clear the sump and bellhousing, and having a setscrew and locknut at one end.
8 With the gauge, measure the distance between the two inner rims of the roadwheels (at hub height) at the rear of the wheel. Push the vehicle forward to rotate the wheel through 180° (half a turn) and measure the distance between the wheel inner rims, again at hub height, at the front of the wheel. This last measurement should differ from the first one by the specified toe-in/toe-out (see Specifications).
9 Where the toe setting is found to be incorrect, release the tie-rod balljoint locknuts and turn the tie-rods by an equal amount. Only turn them through a quarter turn at a time before re-checking the alignment. Do not grip the threaded part of the tie-rod during adjustment and make sure that the bellows outboard clip is released otherwise the bellows will twist as the tie-rod is rotated. When each tie-rod is viewed from the rack housing, turning the rods clockwise will increase the toe-out. Always turn the tie-rods in the same direction when viewed from the centre of the vehicle, otherwise they will become unequal in length. This would cause the steering wheel spoke alignment to alter and also cause problems on turning with tyre scrubbing.

10 On completion of adjustment, tighten the tie-rod end locknuts without altering the setting of the tie-rods. Hold the balljoint assembly at the mid-point of its arc of travel (flats are provided on it for a spanner) while the locknuts are tightened.

11 Finally, tighten the bellows clamps.

12 Rear wheel alignment is set in production and is not adjustable, but when dismantling the tie bar, it is essential that all washers are refitted in their original positions as they control the wheel setting for the life of the vehicle (see Chapter 10).

12 Fault diagnosis – steering

Symptom	Reason(s)
Steering feels vague, vehicle wanders	Uneven tyre pressures Worn tie-rod end balljoints Incorrect pinion adjustment
Stiff and heavy steering	Tyres under-inflated Dry suspension strut swivels Tie-rod end balljoints dry or corroded Incorrect toe setting Other steering angles incorrect Pinion adjusted too tightly Steering column misaligned

Chapter 10 Suspension

For modifications, and information applicable to later models, see Supplement at end of manual

Contents

Specifications

Front suspension

Type .... Independent, MacPherson strut.
1.1 with tie-rod to lower arm, 1.3 and 1.6 with anti-roll bar

For steering and suspension angles refer to Specifications, Chapter 9

Rear suspension

Type:
    Passenger vehicles .... Independent with coil springs, hydraulic shock absorbers and tie-bars.
    Van .... Tubular axle located by semi-elliptic leaf springs and hydraulic shock absorbers

Toe setting .... 1.63 mm (0.06 in) toe-out to 3.87 mm (0.15 in) toe-in

Camber (passenger vehicles) at specified ride height ....

Camber	Ride height
–3°15′ to –1°15′	340 to 349 mm
–3°00′ to –1°00′	350 to 359 mm
–2°45′ to –0°45′	360 to 369 mm
–2°30′ to –0°30′	370 to 379 mm
–2°00′ to 0°00′	380 to 389 mm
–1°45′ to +0°15′	390 to 399 mm
–1°30′ to +0°30′	400 to 409 mm
–1°00′ tp +1°00′	410 to 419 mm
–0°45′ to +1°15′	420 to 429 mm

Maximum variation between sides .... 1°00′

Roadwheels and tyres

Application:
    Pressed steel (Lo series) .... 13 x 4.50, 13 x 5.00
    Pressed steel (Hi series) .... 13 x 5.00
    Cast alloy .... 14 x 5.50
Tyres:
    Passenger vehicles .... 145 SR 13, 155 SR 13, 175/70 SR 13, 175/70 HR 13 or 185/60 HR 14, depending on model
    Van .... 155 SR 13 or 165 RR 13

Tyre pressures (cold) in bar (lbf/in²)

	Front	Rear
Passenger vehicles, up to 3 occupants	1.8 (26)	1.8 (26)
Passenger vehicles, fully laden	2.0 (28)	2.3 (33)
Van, 155 SR 13 tyres:		
Up to 2 occupants	1.8 (26)	1.8 (26)
Fully laden	1.8 (26)	2.6 (37)
Van, 165 RR 13 tyres:		
Up to 2 occupants	1.8 (26)	1.8 (26)
Fully laden	1.8 (26)	3.0 (43)

Torque wrench settings

	Nm	lbf ft
Front suspension		
Hub retaining nut	230	170
Arm inboard pivot bolt	60	44
Arm balljoint pinch-bolt	58	43
Balljoint-to-lower arm bolts (1.1)	85	62
Suspension strut-to-stub axle carrier	85	62
Tie-bar-to-body bracket	50	37
Tie-bar bracket-to-body	50	37
Strut piston rod nut	50	37
Strut top mounting bolts	22	16
Anti-roll bar clamp bolts	50	37
Anti-roll bar-to-suspension arm	110	80
Rear suspension (passenger vehicles)		
Suspension arm inboard pivot bolt	85	62
Suspension arm outboard pivot bolt	65	48
Shock absorber top mounting nuts	50	37
Shock absorber bottom mounting bolts	85	62
Brake backplate bolts	50	37
Tie-bar-to-body pivot bolt	85	62
Tie-bar-to-stub axle carrier nut	85	62
Rear suspension (Van)		
Shock absorber upper mounting pivot bolt	45	33
Shock absorber lower mounting pivot bolt	45	33
Spring U-bolt nuts	40	29
Spring shackle eye bolts	80	59
Shock absorber upper mounting bracket bolts	25	18
Roadwheels		
Fixing bolts	80	59

1   Description

1   The front suspension is of independent type with MacPherson struts. On 1.1 models, the fabricated type suspension lower arm is positively located by a tie-bar; on 1.3 and 1.6 versions, the forged type suspension lower arm is located by an anti-roll bar (photo).

2   The rear suspension on passenger vehicles is independent, incorporating a lower-arm, a tie-bar and a coil spring with hydraulic shock absorber (photo).

3   On Vans, the rear suspension consists of a transverse axle tube mounted on semi-elliptic leaf springs with hydraulic shock absorbers.

2   Maintenance

This comprises a regular inspection of all suspension flexible bushes for wear, and periodically checking the torque wrench settings of all bolts and nuts with the weight of the vehicle on its roadwheels.

3   Front hub bearings – removal and refitting

1   Slacken the roadwheel bolts, raise the front of the vehicle and remove the roadwheel.

2   Refit two of the roadwheel bolts as a means of anchorage for the disc when the hub nut is unscrewed.

3   Have an assistant apply the footbrake and then unscrew the staked hub nut and remove it together with the plain washer. This nut is very tight.

4   Remove the temporary wheel bolts.

5   Unbolt the brake caliper and tie it up to the suspension strut to avoid strain on the flexible hose.

6   Withdraw the hub/disc. If it is tight, use a two-legged puller.

7   Extract the split pin and unscrew the castellated nut from the tie-rod end balljoint.

8   Using a suitable balljoint splitter, separate the balljoint from the steering arm.

9   Unscrew and remove the special Torx pinch-bolt which holds the lower arm balljoint to the stub axle carrier.

1.1 One side of the front suspension (forged type suspension arm)

1.2 One side of the rear suspension

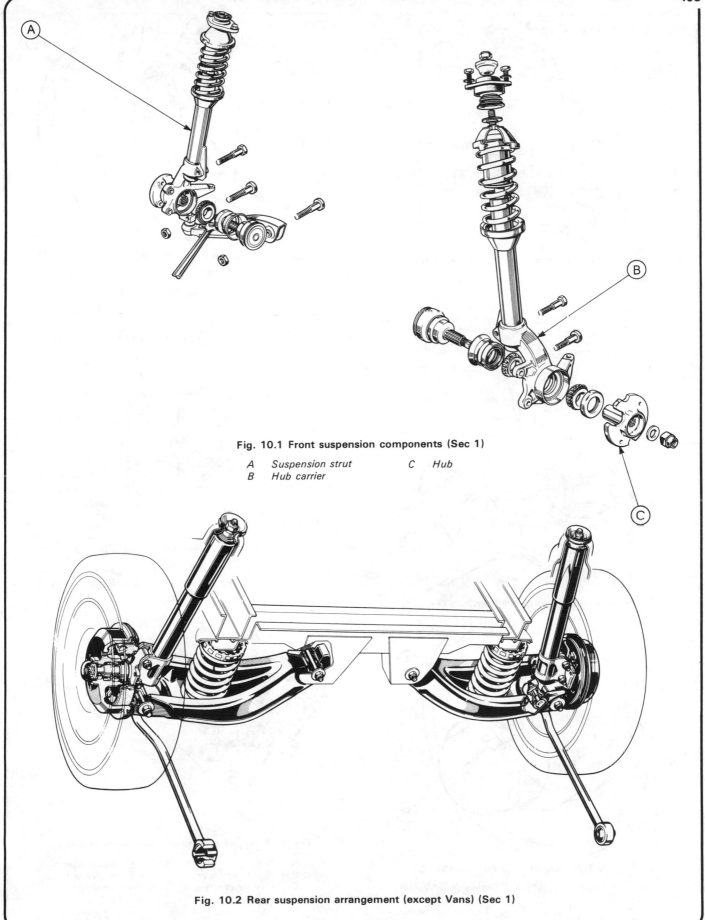

Fig. 10.1 Front suspension components (Sec 1)

A   Suspension strut   C   Hub
B   Hub carrier

Fig. 10.2 Rear suspension arrangement (except Vans) (Sec 1)

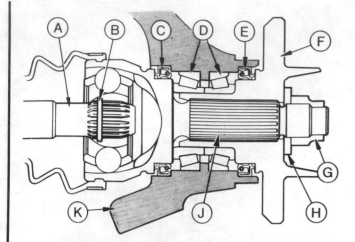

Fig. 10.3 Front hub sectional view (Sec 3)

A   Driveshaft (intermediate
    section)
B   Circlip
C   Oil seal
D   Tapered roller bearings
E   Oil seal
F   Hub
G   Retaining nut
H   Washer
J   Driveshaft (outboard
    section)
K   Hub carrier

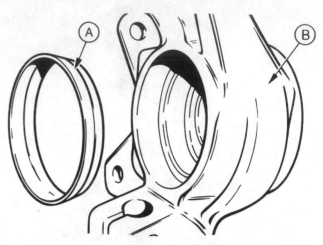

Fig. 10.4 Hub carrier (B) and dust shield (A) (Sec 3)

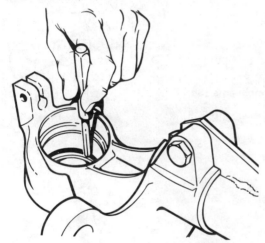

Fig. 10.5 Removing bearing tracks from hub carrier (Sec 3)

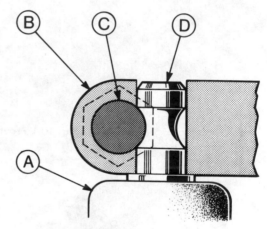

Fig. 10.6 Balljoint pinchbolt (Sec 3)

A   Balljoint
B   Hub carrier
C   Bolt
D   Balljoint stud

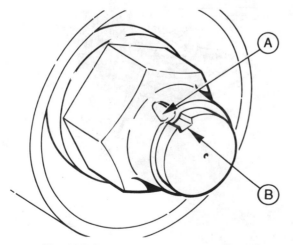

Fig. 10.7 Staking of front hub nut (Sec 3)

A   Nut collar   B   Groove in driveshaft

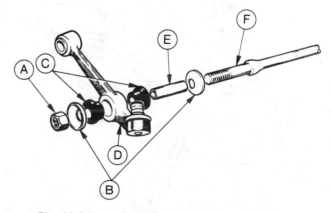

Fig. 10.8 Forged type suspension lower arm (Sec 4)

A   Nut
B   Dished washers
C   Flexible bushes
D   Suspension arm
E   Steel sleeve
F   Anti-roll bar

4.3 Front suspension lower control arm disconnected at the inboard end

4.4A Removing balljoint pinch-bolt

4.4B Torx type balljoint pinch-bolt

4.4C Disconnecting lower control arm at the outboard end

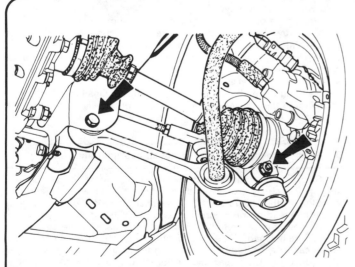

Fig. 10.9 Suspension arm pivot bolt and balljoint pinchbolt (arrowed) (Sec 4)

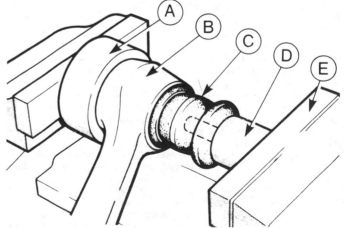

Fig. 10.10 Method of fitting suspension arm flexible bush (Sec 4)

A	Tubular spacer	D	Pilot
B	Lower arm	E	Vice jaw
C	Bush		

10 Support the driveshaft on a block of wood and remove the bolt which holds the stub axle carrier to the base of the suspension strut.
11 Using a suitable lever, separate the carrier from the strut by prising open the clamp jaws.
12 Support the driveshaft at the outboard CV joint and pull the stub axle carrier clear of the driveshaft.
13 Remove the stub axle carrier and grip it in a vice fitted with jaw protectors.
14 Using pliers, pull out the dust shield from the groove in the stub axle carrier.
15 Prise out the inner and outer oil seals.
16 Lift out the bearings.
17 With a suitable drift, drive out the bearing tracks.
18 Clean away all the old grease from the stub axle carrier.
19 Drive the new bearing tracks squarely into their seats using a piece of suitable diameter tubing.
20 Liberally pack grease into the bearings, making sure to work plenty into the spaces between the rollers.
21 Install the bearing to one side of the carrier, then fill the lips of the new oil seal with grease and tap it squarely into position.
22 Fit the bearing and its seal to the opposite side in a similar way.
23 Fit the dust shield by tapping it into position using a block of wood.
24 Smear the driveshaft splines with grease, then install the carrier over the end of the driveshaft.
25 Connect the carrier to the suspension strut and tighten the bolt to the specified torque.
26 Reconnect the suspension lower arm balljoint to the carrier and secure by passing the pinch-bolt through the groove in the balljoint stud.
27 Reconnect the tie-rod to the steering arm, tighten the castellated nut to the specified torque and secure with a new split pin.
28 Install the hub/disc and push it on to the driveshaft as far as it will go using hand pressure.
29 In the absence of the special hub installer tool (14-022), draw the hub/disc onto the driveshaft by using a two or three-legged puller with legs engaged behind the carrier. On no account try to knock the hub/disc into position using hammer blows or the CV joint will be damaged.
30 Grease the threads at the end of the driveshaft, fit the plain washer and screw on a new nut, finger tight.
31 Fit the brake caliper, tightening the mounting bolts to the specified torque.
32 Screw in two wheel bolts and have an assistant apply the footbrake.
33 Tighten the hub nut to the specified torque. This is a high torque and if a suitably calibrated torque wrench is not available, use a socket with a knuckle bar 18 in (457.2 mm) in length. Applying maximum leverage to the knuckle bar should tighten the nut to very close to its specified torque.
34 Stake the nut into the driveshaft groove.
35 Remove the temporary roadwheel bolts.
36 Fit the roadwheel and lower the vehicle to the floor. Fully tighten the roadwheel bolts.

4 Front suspension lower arm (forged type) – removal, overhaul and refitting

1 This type of suspension arm is used on 1.3 and 1.6 models.
2 Raise the front of the vehicle and support it securely.
3 Unbolt and remove the pivot bolt from the inboard end of the suspension arm (photo).
4 At the outboard end of the suspension arm, disengage the arm from the hub carrier by unscrewing and removing the pinch-bolt (photos).
5 Unscrew and remove the nut, washer and bush from the end of the anti-roll bar. Withdraw the suspension arm.
6 Renewal of the pivot bush at the inboard end of the suspension arm is possible using a nut and bolt, or a vice, and suitable distance pieces. Apply some brake hydraulic fluid to facilitate installation of the new bush. If the balljoint is worn or corroded, renew the suspension arm complete.
7 Refitting the arm is a reversal of removal. Tighten all nuts and bolts to the specified torque when the weight of the vehicle is again on the roadwheels.

5 Front suspension lower arm (fabricated type) – removal, overhaul and refitting

1 This type of suspension arm is used only on 1.1 models.
2 Unscrew and remove the pivot bolt from the inboard end of the suspension arm.
3 Unscrew and remove the two nuts which hold the suspension arm to the tie-bar. Remove the suspension arm.
4 Renewal of the pivot bush is carried out in a similar way to that described in Section 4.
5 If the balljoint is worn or corroded, renew it by unbolting it from the suspension arm.
6 Refitting the arm is a reversal of removal. Tighten all nuts and bolts to the specified torque when the weight of the vehicle is again on the roadwheels.

6 Front anti-roll bar – removal and refitting

The anti-roll bar is used in conjunction with the forged type suspension arm found on 1.3 and 1.6 models.
1 Jack up the front of the vehicle and support it securely on stands.
2 Flatten the lockplate tabs and unbolt the clamps which hold the anti-roll bar to the body.
3 Disconnect the ends of the anti-roll bar by unscrewing the nuts, and removing the washers and the bushes. Note that the nut on the right-hand side of the anti-roll bar has a left-hand thread and is unscrewed in a clockwise direction.
4 Unscrew a pivot bolt from the inboard end of one of the suspension arms.
5 Withdraw the anti-roll bar from the vehicle. To facilitate sliding the bushes from the bar, smear the bar with some brake fluid.
6 Refitting is a reversal of removal. Tighten all nuts and bolts to the specified torque after the weight of the vehicle is again on the roadwheels.
7 Lock the clamp bolts by bending up the lockplate tabs.

7 Front tie-bar – removal and refitting

The tie-bar is used in conjunction with the fabricated type suspension arm on 1.1 models.
1 Jack up the front of the vehicle and support securely on axle stands.
2 Unscrew and remove the nut which holds the tie-bar to the large pressed steel mounting bracket. Take off the dished washer and the rubber insulator.
3 Separate the balljoint from the hub carrier by removing the pinch-bolt, which is of Torx type.
4 Unbolt the opposite end of the tie-bar from the suspension arm.
5 Withdraw the tie-bar from its pressed steel bracket and take off the remaining washer, insulator and steel sleeve.
6 Where necessary the bush in the pressed steel mounting bracket can be renewed if the old bush is drawn out using a bolt, nut and suitable distance pieces.
7 Refitting the tie-bar is a reversal of removal. Finally tighten all nuts and bolts to the specified torque only when the weight of the vehicle is again on its roadwheels.

8 Front suspension strut – removal, overhaul and refitting

1 Slacken the roadwheel bolts, raise the front of the vehicle and support it securely on stands, then remove the roadwheel.
2 Support the underside of the driveshaft on blocks or by tying it up to the rack-and-pinion steering housing.
3 Remove the pinch-bolt which holds the base of the suspension strut to the hub carrier. Using a suitable tool, lever the sides of the slot in the carrier apart until it is free from the strut.
4 Working at the upper end of the strut, unbolt the top mounting from the wing inner panel (photo).
5 Withdraw the complete strut assembly from under the front wing.
6 Clean away external dirt and mud.
7 If the strut has been removed due to oil leakage or to lack of damping, then it should be renewed with a new or factory recondi-

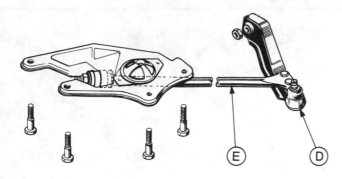

Fig. 10.11 Fabricated type suspension arm (Sec 5)

D   *Suspension arm*   E   *Tie-bar*

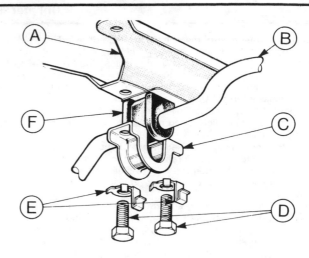

Fig. 10.12 Anti-roll bar mounting (Sec 6)

A	*Body*	D	*Bolts*
B	*Anti-roll bar*	E	*Lockplates*
C	*Clamp*	F	*Flexible bush*

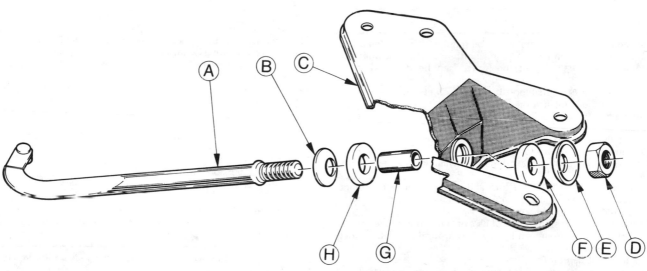

Fig. 10.13 Tie-bar and associated components (Sec 7)

| A | *Tie-bar* | C | *Mounting bracket* | E | *Dished washer* | G | *Steel sleeve* |
| B | *Dished washer* | D | *Nut* | F | *Front insulator (black)* | H | *Rear insulator (natural)* |

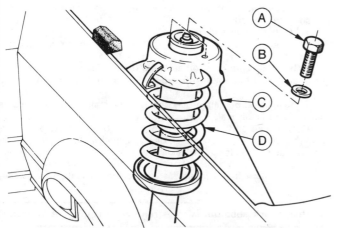

Fig. 10.14 Front strut top mounting (Sec 8)

| A | *Bolt* | C | *Wing inner panel* |
| B | *Washer* | D | *Strut* |

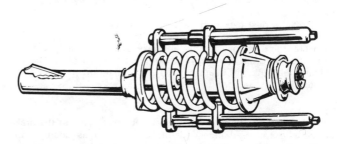

Fig. 10.15 Typical spring compressor in position (Sec 8)

tioned unit. Dismantling of the original strut is not recommended and internal components are not generally available.

8   Before the strut is exchanged, the coil spring will have to be removed. To do this, a spring compressor or compressors will be needed. These are generally available from tool hire centres or they can be purchased at most motor accessory shops.

9   Engage the compressor over three coils of the spring and compress the spring sufficiently to release spring tension from the top mounting.

10   Once the spring is compressed, unscrew and remove the nut from the end of the piston rod which retains the top mounting. As there will be a tendency for the piston rod to turn while the nut is unscrewed, provision is made at the end of the rod to insert a 6 mm Allen key to hold the rod still.

11   Remove the top mounting and lift off the spring and compressor.

12   The compressor need not be released if the spring is to be fitted immediately to a new strut. If the compressor is to be released from the spring, make sure that you do it slowly and progressively.

13   Fit the spring to the strut, making sure that the ends of the coils locate correctly in the shaped parts of the spring seats.

14   Fit the top mounting components, being very careful to maintain the correct order of assembly of the individual components.

15   Gently release and remove the spring compressor.

16   Refitting of the strut is a reversal of removal.

8.4 Front strut top mounting

9 Rear hub bearings – adjustment

1   This adjustment will normally only be required if, when the rear of the vehicle is raised and the top and bottom of the roadwheel are gripped and 'rocked', a slight movement can be detected in the bearings.

2   Raise the vehicle and support it securely on stands, then remove the roadwheel. Fully release the handbrake.

3   Using a hammer and cold chisel, tap off the dust cap from the end of the hub.

4   Extract the split pin and take off the nut retainer.

5   Tighten the hub nut to a torque of between 20 and 25 Nm (15 and 18 lbf ft), at the same time rotating the roadwheel in an anti-clockwise direction.

6   Unscrew the nut one half a turn and then tighten it only finger tight. Check that the slightest amount of endfloat can be detected. Endfloat **must not** be eliminated entirely.

7   Fit the nut retainer so that two of its slots line up with the split pin hole. Insert a new split pin, bending the end **around** the nut, **not** over the end of the stub axle.

8   Tap the dust cap into position.

9   Repeat the operations on the opposite hub, refit the roadwheels and lower the vehicle to the floor.

10 Rear hub bearings – removal and refitting

Passenger vehicles

1   Raise the rear of the vehicle and support it securely. Remove the roadwheel.

2   Tap off the dust cap from the end of the hub.

3   Extract the split pin and remove the nut retainer.

4   Unscrew and remove the nut and take off the thrust washer.

5   Pull the hub/drum towards you, then push it back slightly. This will now leave the outboard bearing ready to be taken off the stub axle.

6   Withdraw the hub/drum.

Vans

7   The operations are similar to those just described, but the brake drum can be removed independently of the hub as soon as the roadwheel has been withdrawn and the drum securing screw extracted.

All models

8   Prise the oil seal from the hub and take out the inboard taper roller bearing.

9   Using a suitable punch, drive out the bearing outer tracks, taking care not to burr the bearing seats.

10   If new bearings are being fitted to both hubs, do not mix up the bearing components but keep them in their individual packs until required.

11   Drive the new bearing tracks squarely into their hub recesses.

12   Pack both bearings with the specified grease, working plenty into the rollers. Be generous, but there is no need to fill the cavity between the inner and outer bearings.

13   Locate the inboard bearing and then grease the lips of a new oil seal and tap it into position.

14   Fit the hub onto the stub axle, taking care not to catch the oil seal lips.

15   Fit the outboard bearing and the thrust washer and screw on the nut.

16   Adjust the bearings as described in Section 9.

17   With Van versions, refit the brake drum.

18   Fit the roadwheel, lower the vehicle to the floor.

11 Rear shock absorber (passenger vehicles) – removal, testing and refitting

1   Slacken the roadwheel bolts, raise the rear of the vehicle and remove the roadwheel.

2   Support the suspension lower arm with a jack.

3   Open the tailgate and lift the parcels tray to expose the shock absorber top mounting (photo).

4   Remove the cap and then unscrew the nut from the shock absorber spindle. To prevent the spindle turning, use an Allen key in the socket provided.

5   Take off the cap and insulator.

6   Working under the wheel arch, release the brake flexible hose from the shock absorber.

7   Unbolt the shock absorber lower mounting and withdraw the shock absorber, together with cup and bump rubber, from under the rear wing.

8   To test the shock absorber, grip its lower mounting in a vice so that the unit is vertical.

9   Fully extend and retract the shock absorber ten or twelve times. Any lack of resistance in either direction will indicate the need for renewal, as will evidence of leakage of fluid.

10   Refitting is a reversal of removal, but if a new unit is being installed, prime it first in a similar way to that described for testing.

12 Rear shock absorber (Van) – removal, testing and refitting

1   Disconnect the shock absorber lower mounting by unscrewing the pivot bolt.

2   Unbolt the top mounting bracket from the body and withdraw the unit.

3   Test as described in the preceding Section and refit by reversing the removal operations.

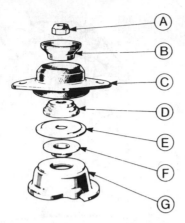

Fig. 10.16 Front strut top mounting components (Sec 8)

A   Nut   E   Thrust washer
B   Retainer   F   Thrust bearing
C   Top mounting   G   Spring upper seat
D   Spacer

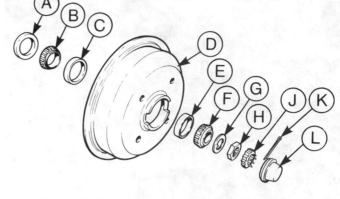

Fig. 10.17 Rear hub components (not Vans) (Sec 9)

A   Oil seal   G   Thrust washer
B   Tapered roller bearing   H   Nut
C   Bearing track   J   Nut retainer
D   Drum/hub   K   Split pin
E   Bearing track   L   Dust cap
F   Bearing

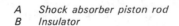

Fig. 10.18 Prising oil seal from rear hub/drum (Sec 10)

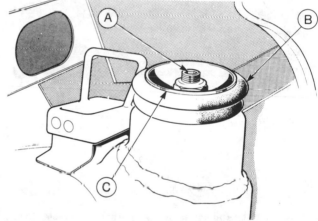

Fig. 10.19 Rear shock absorber top mounting (passenger vehicles) (Sec 11)

A   Shock absorber piston rod   C   Cup
B   Insulator

Fig. 10.20 Unscrewing shock absorber top nut (Sec 11)

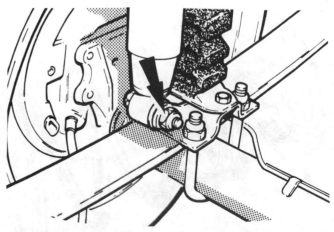

Fig. 10.21 Rear shock absorber lower mounting (arrowed) on Van (Sec 12)

11.3 Rear shock absorber top mounting

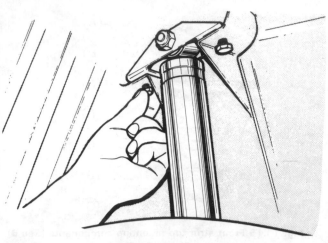

Fig. 10.22 Rear shock absorber top mounting on Van (Sec 12)

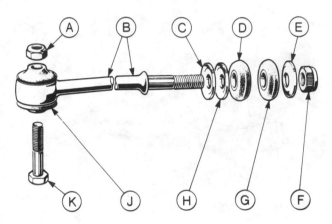

Fig. 10.23 Rear tie-rod components – passenger vehicles (Sec 13)

A	Nut	F	Nut
B	Tie-bar	G	Flexible bush
C	Washer	H	Washer
D	Flexible bush	J	Flexible bush
E	Washer	K	Pivot bolt

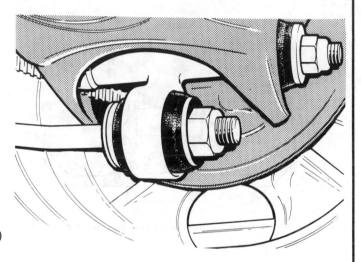

Fig. 10.24 Tie-bar attachment to rear hub carrier (Sec 13)

Fig. 10.25 Rear coil spring and insulating pad (arrowed) (Sec 14)

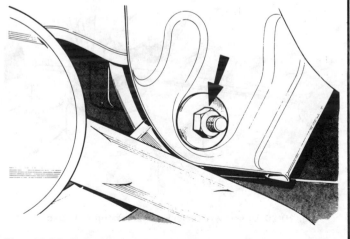

Fig. 10.26 Rear suspension lower arm attachment to body (arrowed) (Sec 15)

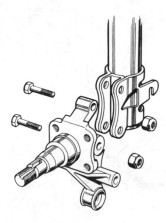

Fig. 10.27 Rear stub axle carrier (Sec 16)

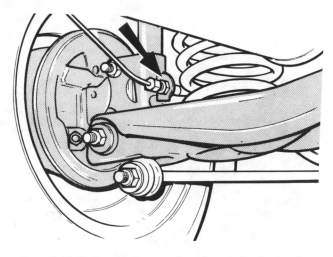

Fig. 10.28 Brake pipe connection at rear shock absorber (passenger vehicles) (Sec 17)

13 Rear tie-bar – removal and refitting

1   Before attempting to remove a tie-bar, note the location of all washers and bushes. These control the rear wheel alignment and they must be returned to their original locations.
2   Raise the rear of the vehicle and support with stands.
3   Unscrew and remove the pivot bolt from the eye at the front end of the tie-bar.
4   Unscrew the nut from the rear end of the tie-bar, take off the washers and bushes as the tie-bar is withdrawn and keep them in strict sequence for refitting.
5   Renewal of the tie-bar flexible bush is quite easily carried out using sockets or distance pieces and applying pressure in the jaws of a vice.
6   Refit the tie-bar by reversing the removal operations.

14 Rear coil spring (passenger vehicles) – removal and refitting

1   Slacken the roadwheel bolts, raise the rear of the vehicle and support it securely. Remove the roadwheel.
2   Support the suspension lower arm by placing a jack beneath it.
3   Disconnect the shock absorber upper mounting as described in Section 11.
4   Remove the pivot bolt from the outboard end of the suspension arm.
5   Lower the jack under the suspension arm slowly and lift out the coil spring and its insulating pad.
6   Refitting is a reversal of removal. On XR3 versions, the plastic sleeved end of the coil spring must be at the upper end when the spring is installed.

15 Rear suspension lower arm (passenger vehicles) – removal and refitting

1   Raise the rear of the vehicle and support it securely on stands.
2   Unscrew and remove the pivot bolt from the inboard end of the suspension arm.
3   Unscrew and remove the pivot bolt from the outboard end of the suspension arm.
4   Withdraw the arm from the vehicle.
5   Refitting is a reversal of removal.

16 Rear stub axle carrier (passenger vehicles) – removal and refitting

1   Raise the rear of the vehicle and support it on stands.
2   Remove the roadwheel.
3   Remove the hub/drum, the brake assembly and the brake backplate as described in Chapter 8.
4   Support the lower arm on a jack.

5   Unscrew and remove the pivot bolt from the outboard end of the suspension arm.
6   Unscrew the two bolts which hold the lower end of the shock absorber to the stub axle carrier.
7   Carefully note the location of washers and bushes and disconnect the tie-bar from the stub axle carrier.
8   Lift the stub axle carrier from the vehicle.
9   Refitting is a reversal of removal.

17 Rear suspension (passenger vehicles) – removal and refitting

1   Raise the rear of the vehicle and support on stands.
2   Disconnect the handbrake cable at the connection to the primary cable and from the body guides (refer to Chapter 8).
3   Disconnect the tie-rod from its body bracket.
4   Unscrew and remove the pivot bolt from the inboard end of the suspension arm.
5   Disconnect the flexible brake hose and cap the end to prevent loss of fluid.
6   Place a jack under the suspension arm.
7   Disconnect the shock absorber upper mounting as described in Section 11.
8   Lower the jack under the suspension arm and withdraw the suspension assembly from the vehicle.
9   Remove the suspension assembly from the opposite side in a similar way.
10 Refitting is a reversal of removal. Bleed the brake hydraulic system on completion and adjust the handbrake.
11 Tighten all nuts and bolts to the specified torque when the weight of the vehicle has been lowered onto the roadwheels.

18 Rear roadspring (Van) – removal and refitting

1   To remove the single leaf type rear roadspring from the van, raise the rear of the vehicle and support it securely under the body members.
2   Unscrew the spring U-bolt nuts and withdraw the bump rubber plate complete with shock absorber lower attachment.
3   Disconnect the shackle from the rear end of the roadspring and pull the spring downward.
4   Unscrew and remove the spring front eye bolt and nut.
5   Remove the spring from under the vehicle.
6   Refit by reversing the removal operations, but do not tighten the nuts to the specified torque until the weight of the vehicle has been lowered onto the roadwheels.
7   Adjust the brake regulator valve as described in Section 11 of Chapter 8.

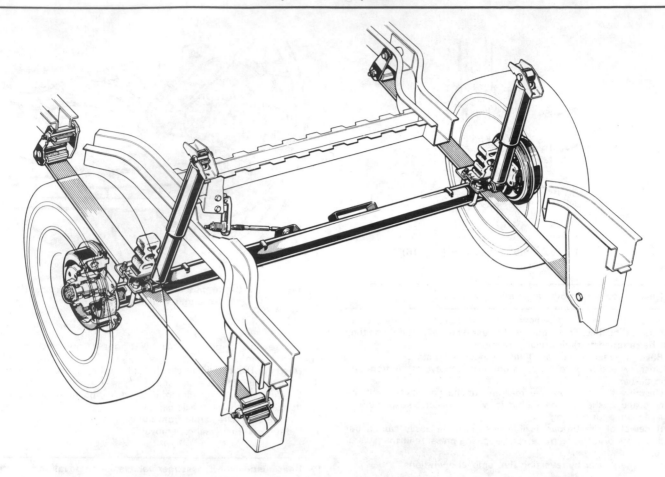

Fig. 10.29 Rear suspension (Van) (Sec 18)

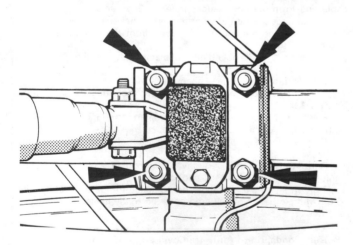

Fig. 10.30 Rear spring U-bolt nuts (Van) (Sec 18)

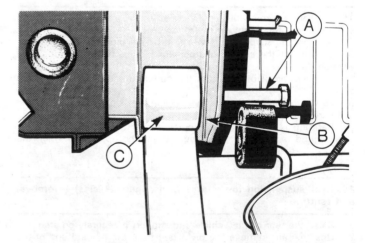

Fig. 10.31 Rear spring front eye bolt (Van) (Sec 18)

A   Pivot bolt   C   Spring eye
B   Mounting bracket

4   The bump rubber mounting plate is secured above the spring by two small bolts.
5   When fitting the new bump rubber, note the locating tag which must engage in the slot in the mounting plate.

19 Rear spring bushes and bump rubber (Van) – renewal

1   This work can be carried out once the spring has been removed as described in the preceding Section.
2   The bushes can be pressed out of the spring eyes in a vice using a socket or piece of tubing (36 mm) to locate on the metal sleeve of the bush. An alternative method is to draw the bushes out using a bolt, nut, washers and distance pieces.
3   Refit using similar methods.

20 Rear suspension (Van) – removal and refitting.

1   Raise the rear of the vehicle and support it securely under the body members.

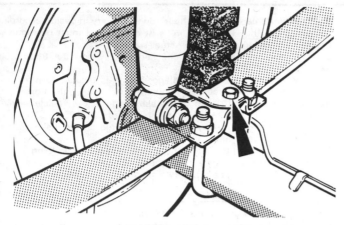

Fig. 10.32 Rear spring bump rubber fixing bolt (Van) (Sec 19)

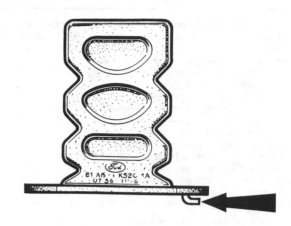

Fig. 10.33 Rear spring bump rubber locating tag (Van) (Sec 19)

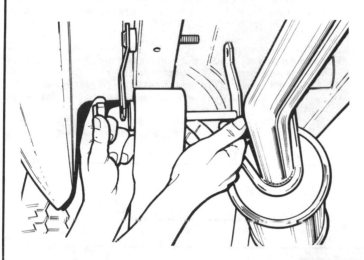

Fig. 10.34 Removing rear spring shackle plates (Van) (Sec 21)

Fig. 10.36 Rear ride height measurement diagram (Sec 22)

For A refer to Specifications

Fig. 10.35 Types of rear wheel, balance weights and bolts

A   Steel
B   Steel
C   Alloy

F   Steel wheel weight
G   Alloy wheel weight

2 Support the axle tube on a jack. preferably of trolley type.
3 Disconnect the handbrake secondary cable by withdrawing the spring clip and clevis pin from the equaliser.
4 Disconnect and plug the fuel supply pipe.
5 Unhook the exhaust system from its flexible mountings and support it to prevent strain.
6 Disconnect the brake hydraulic hoses at the rear axle support bracket. Plug or cap the pipes to prevent loss of fluid.
7 Disconnect the rear ends of the roadsprings by unbolting the shackle plates from the body members.
8 Unbolt the shock absorber upper mountings.
9 Remove the pivot bolts from the roadspring front eyes.
10 Withdraw the axle/suspension from under the vehicle, lowering it as necessary, and disconnecting the brake pressure valve link rod from its spacer tube during the process.
11 Refitting is a reversal of removal, but observe the following points:

  (a) *Clean and grease the pressure valve link rod*
  (b) *Tighten nuts and bolts to the specified torque only when the weight of the vehicle is on the roadwheels*
  (c) *Bleed the brake hydraulic system and adjust the brake pressure valve as described in Chapter 8*

21 Roadwheels and tyres – general

1 One of three types of roadwheel may be fitted, depending upon particular model and wheel size (see Specifications). Two types are of pressed steel construction while the third is of aluminium alloy.
2 The wheels are retained to the hubs by bolts, but the bolt design varies according to the type of wheel.
3 Radial tyres are fitted as original equipment to all models.

4 The centre caps used on the roadwheels vary in design according to model, but they are all of press fit design and must be removed before unscrewing the bolts on steel wheels.
5 Tyre pressures should be checked weekly and the tread wear examined.
6 Always have the wheels balanced. If it is desired to move the position of the roadwheels to minimise tyre wear, only move them front to rear or rear to front of the same side of the vehicle – never from side to side with radial tyres.
7 Periodically clean away the mud deposited on the inside rims of the roadwheels and touch up any rusty areas.
8 Avoid damaging the wheel rims through careless kerbing.
9 Whenever changing a roadwheel, always locate the jack as recommended in the introductory Section of this manual

22 Rear suspension angles – measurement

1 The rear wheel toe and camber angles are set in production and do not require adjustment.
2 If checking the angles confirms that they are outside the specified tolerance, then this is due to damage or severely worn components.

Passenger vehicles
3 When checking rear wheel camber, the rear riding height must first be measured in order to be able to read off the appropriate camber from the table given in the Specifications.
4 Measure the height between the centre of the rear wheel and the highest point of the wheel arch cut-out as shown in Fig. 10.36 (dimension A).
5 The variation in riding height is due to the different rate of settlement of individual suspension components and springs.

23 Fault diagnosis – suspension

Symptom	Reason(s)
Steering feels vague, car wanders and floats at speed	Tyre pressures uneven Shock absorbers worn Broken roadspring Suspension geometry incorrect Suspension pick-up points out of alignment
Stiff and heavy steering	Suspension geometry incorrect Dry or corroded suspension balljoints Low tyre pressures
Wheel wobble and vibration	Roadwheel bolts loose Wheels/tyres out of balance Worn hub bearings Weak front coil springs Weak front struts

Chapter 11 Electrical system

For modifications, and information applicable to later models, see Supplement at end of manual

Contents

Specifications

System type .... 12V, negative earth with belt-driven alternator and pre-engaged starter motor

Battery .... 12V Lead/acid, 35 to 50 Ah depending upon vehicle model

Alternator

	Bosch	Lucas	Motorola
Rated output (13.5V at 6000 rpm engine speed)	28A (G1-28A)	28A (A115/28)	28A (265 OD)
	35A (K1-35A)	35A (A115/36)	35A (2652 F)
	45A (K1-45A)	45A (A133/45)	45A (2627 G)
	55A (K1-55A)	55A (A133/55)	
Maximum continuous speed	15 000 rpm	15 000 rpm	15 000 rpm

Minimum brush length .... 5.0 mm (0.197 in)   5.0 mm (0.197 in)   4.0 mm (0.157 in)
Regulator voltage at 4000 rpm, 3 to 7A load .... 13.7 to 14.6V   13.7 to 14.6V   13.7 to 14.6V

Stator winding resistance (ohms/phase) ....

$0.2 \begin{array}{l} +0.02 \\ -0 \end{array}$ (G1 - 28A)

$0.13 \begin{array}{l} +0.013 \\ -0 \end{array}$ (K1 - 35A)

$0.09 \begin{array}{l} +0.009 \\ -0 \end{array}$ (K1 - 45A)

$0.07 \begin{array}{l} +0.007 \\ -0 \end{array}$ (K1 - 55A)

0.198 ± 0.005 (A115/28)
0.133 ± 0.005 (A115/36)
0.098 ± 0.01 (A133/45)
0.203 ± 0.01 (A133/55)

0.35 ± 5% (2650 D)
0.35 ± 5% (2652 F)
0.28 ± 5% (2627 G)

Rotor winding resistance (ohms at 20°C) ....

$3.4 \begin{array}{l} +0.34 \\ -0 \end{array}$ (G1 - 28A and K1-35A)

$4.0 \begin{array}{l} +0.34 \\ -0 \end{array}$ (K1 - 45A and K1 - 55A)

3.25 ± 5% (A115/28)
3.2 ± 5% (A115/36, A133/45 and A133/55)

4 ± 0.2 (all models)

Starter motor
Type .... Pre-engaged
Make:
    Lucas .... 8M 90 or 9M 90
    Bosch .... 0.8 kW, 0.85 kW or 0.9 kW
    Nippondenso .... 0.6 kW or 0.9 kW
Number of brushes .... 4, except Nippondenso 0.6 kW which has 2
Minimum brush length:
    Lucas .... 8.0 mm (0.32 in)
    Bosch .... 10.0 mm (0.39 in)
    Nippondenso 0.6 kW .... 10.0 mm (0.39 in)
    Nippondenso 0.9 kW .... 9.0 mm (0.35 in)
Minimum commutator dimension:
    Lucas .... 2.05 mm (0.08 in) thick
    Bosch .... 32.8 mm (1.29 in) diameter
    Nippondenso .... 0.6 mm (0.02 in) thick
Armature endfloat:
    Lucas .... 0.25 mm (0.010 in)
    Bosch .... 0.30 mm (0.012 in)
    Nippondenso .... 0.60 mm (0.024 in)
Number of pinion teeth (all models) 10
Number of flywheel teeth (all models) 135

Bulbs
Headlamp:
    Halogen 60/55
    Tungsten 50/45W
Front parking lamp 4W
Front indicator lamp 21W
Side repeater lamp 5W
Stop/tail lamp 21/5W
Reversing lamp 21W
Rear foglamp 21W
Rear indicator lamp 21W
Rear licence plate lamp 5W
Auxiliary lamp (Halogen) 55W
Foglamp (Halogen) 55W
Instrument cluster warning lamps 1.3W
Panel illumination 2.6W
Cigar lighter illumination 1.4W
Glove compartment lamp 2W
Luggage compartment lamp 10W
Interior lamp 10W

Torque wrench settings

	Nm	lbf ft
Electric window motor mounting bolts	5	4
Electric window regulator mounting bolts	5	4
Horn bracket bolt	35	26
Foglamp mounting bolt	9	7
Auxiliary lamp mounting bolt	45	33

1 Description

The electrical system is of 12V, negative earth type. The major components include an alternator, a pre-engaged starter and a lead/acid battery.

The electrical equipment varies according to the particular model. The system is fully fused, with circuit breakers and any necessary relays incorporated in the fuse box.

2 Battery – maintenance

1 The modern battery seldom requires topping up but nevertheless, the electrolyte level should be inspected weekly as a means of providing the first indication that the alternator is overcharging or that the battery casing has developed a leak.

2 When topping up is required, use only distilled water or melted ice from a refrigerator (frosting not ice cubes).

3 Acid should never be required if the battery has been correctly filled from new, unless spillage has occurred.

4 Inspect the battery terminals and mounting tray for corrosion. This is the white fluffy deposit which grows at these areas. If evident, clean it away and neutralise it with ammonia or baking soda. Apply petroleum jelly to the terminals and paint the battery tray with anti-corrosive paint.

5 With normal motoring, the battery should be kept in a good state of charge by the alternator and never need charging from a mains charger.

6 However, as the battery ages, it may not be able to hold its charge and some supplementary charging may be needed. Before connecting the charger, disconnect the battery terminals or better still, remove the battery from the vehicle.

7 An indication of the state of charge of a battery can be obtained by checking the electrolyte in each cell using a hydrometer. The specific gravity of the electrolyte for fully charged and fully discharged conditions at the electrolyte temperature indicated, is listed below.

Fully discharged	Electrolyte temperature	Fully charged
1.098	38°C (100°F)	1.268
1.102	32°C (90°F)	1.272
1.106	27°C (80°F)	1.276
1.110	21°C (70°F)	1.280
1.114	16°C (60°F)	1.284
1.118	10°C (50°F)	1.288
1.122	4°C (40°F)	1.292
1.126	−1.5°C (30°F)	1.296

8 There should be very little variation in the readings between the different cells, but if a difference is found in excess of 0.025 then it will probably be due to an internal fault indicating impending battery failure. This assumes that electrolyte has not been spilled at some time and the deficiency made up with water only.

9 The cells have individual filler/vent caps on the battery fitted as original equipment. The battery plates should always be covered to a depth of 6.0 mm (0.25 in) with electrolyte.

10 Keep the top surface of the battery casing dry.

3 Battery – removal and refitting

1 Open the bonnet and support it on its stay.

2 The battery is mounted at the rear of the engine compartment.

3 Disconnect the negative (earth) lead, followed by the positive lead.

4 Unbolt and remove the clamps from the nibs at the base of the battery casing.

5 Lift the battery from its location, taking care not to spill electrolyte on the paintwork.

6 Refitting is a reversal of removal.

4 Alternator – description, maintenance and precautions

1 One of three different makes of alternator may be fitted, dependent upon model and engine capacity. The maximum output of the alternator varies similarly.

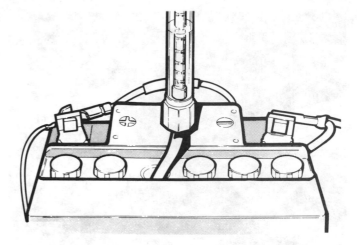

Fig. 11.1 Checking battery electrolyte specific gravity (Sec 2)

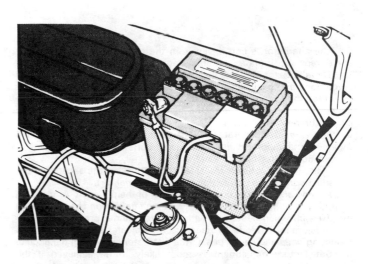

Fig. 11.2 Battery clamp bolts (arrowed) (Sec 3)

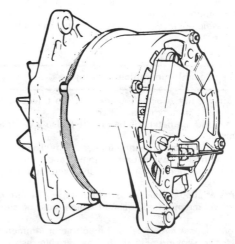

Fig. 11.3 Bosch alternator (Sec 4)

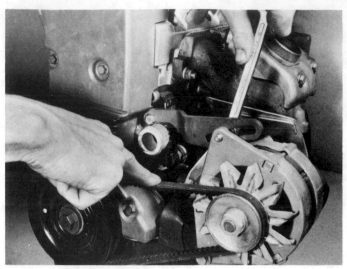

4.6 Checking drivebelt tension

2   The alternator is belt-driven from the crankshaft pulley, it is fan-cooled and incorporates a voltage regulator.
3   The alternator provides a charge to the battery at very low engine revolutions and basically consists of a stator in which a rotor rotates. The rotor shaft is supported in ball-bearings, and slip rings are used to conduct current to and from the field coils through the medium of carbon brushes.
4   The alternator generates ac (alternating current) which is rectified by an internal diode system to dc (direct current) which is the type of current needed for battery storage.
5   Maintenance consists of occasionally checking the security of the electrical connections and wiping away external dirt.
6   At regular intervals, check the tension of the drivebelt. At the mid-point of the longest run of the belt, total belt deflection should be 10.0 mm (0.4 in) when depressed with moderate finger pressure (photo).
7   Adjustment is made by releasing the adjuster strap bolt and the mounting bolts and gently prising the alternator away from the engine.
8   Satisfactory adjustment is most likely to be achieved if the alternator bolts are not fully released so that the unit pivots only stiffly.
9   To renew the drivebelt, push the alternator in towards the engine as far as it will go and slip the belt from the pulley. Never attempt to prise the belt off the pulleys without releasing the alternator mountings. Recheck the tension of a new belt after the engine has run a few miles.
10 Never connect the battery leads to the wrong terminals, or disconnect a battery lead as a means of stopping the engine, or damage to the alternator may result.
11 If electric welding is being carried out on the vehicle, always disconnect the battery.

5   Alternator (Bosch) – in-vehicle testing

1   Before carrying out this test, check that the drivebelt tension is correct and that the battery is well charged.
2   A voltmeter and ammeter will be required, also a variable resistor and a tachometer.
3   Check the charging circuit wiring for continuity. To do this, pull out the alternator multi-plug, switch on the ignition and connect a 0 - 20V voltmeter between a good earthing point and each multi-plug terminal in turn.
4   The voltmeter should indicate battery voltage. If a zero reading is observed, this will mean an open-circuit which must be checked and repaired.
5   Rig the output test circuit using the voltmeter, ammeter and the variable resistor as shown in Fig. 11.8. The variable resistor must be capable of carrying a current of 30 amps.

6   Switch on the headlamps, the heater blower motor and the heated rear window. Start the engine and run it at 3000 rpm. Vary the resistance to increase the load current. The rated output (see Specifications) should be reached without the voltage dropping below 13V.
7   Switch off the engine and accessories and dismantle the test circuit.
8   Rig the 'positive side' volt drop test circuit (Fig. 11.9) and reconnect the regulator multi-pin plug.
9   Switch on the headlamps, start the engine and check the voltage drop.
10 Run the engine at 3000 rpm. If the voltage drop is in excess of 0.5V, a high resistance is indicated on the positive side of the charging circuit. This must be located and remedied.
11 Switch off the headlamps and the engine.
12 Rig the 'negative side' voltage drop test circuit (Fig. 11.10).
13 Switch on the headlamps, start the engine and check the voltage drop. Run the engine at 3000 rpm and check the voltage reading. If the voltage drop is in excess of 0.25V then a high resistance is indicated on the negative (earth) side of the charging circuit which must be located and remedied. Check all earth terminals, earth straps etc for security.
14 Switch off the headlamps and the engine, and disconnect the test circuit.
15 Rig the control voltage test circuit (see Fig. 11.11). Start the engine and check the regulator voltage. Run the engine at 2000 rpm and observe the ammeter reading. When this falls to between 3 and 5A, check the reading on the voltmeter which should be between 13.7 and 14.5V. If the reading is outside this range, then the integral regulator is faulty.
16 Switch off the ignition and dismantle the test circuit.
17 Refit the alternator multi-plug.
18 Where a fault is discovered as a result of the foregoing tests and its cause is not visually evident, the alternator must be overhauled as described in Section 10.

6   Alternator (Lucas) – in-vehicle testing

1   Remove the multi-plug and the alternator rear cover, then check the wiring circuit for continuity as described for the Bosch alternator in Section 5.
2   Check the alternator output as described in Section 5.
3   Check the 'positive side' voltage drop as described in Section 5.
4   Check the 'negative side' voltage drop as described in Section 5.
5   Check the control voltage as described in Section 5, but run the engine at 3000 rpm and check the voltage is between 13.7 and 14.5V when the current falls below 10A.

7   Alternator (Motorola) – in-vehicle testing

1   To test this alternator, in addition to a voltmeter (0 to 20V) and an ammeter (50A), a rheostat (variable resistor) will be required, also a tachometer unless the vehicle is already equipped with one.
2   With the ignition off, check the voltage on one phase of the stator winding. Do this by connecting the voltmeter between the stator winding and a good earth and between the stator winding and the battery positive terminal.
3   If the voltmeter shows a reading in either case, it will indicate that a positive rectifier diode is shorting.
4   With the ignition switched off, check the voltage at the output terminal on the alternator and at the battery positive terminal.
5   The reading shown on the voltmeter should be the same at both test points. Otherwise, check for broken leads and for loose or corroded terminals.
6   Check the field current by rigging a test circuit as shown in Fig. 11.19, but use a rheostat (variable resistance) in series with the ammeter to protect the meter in the event of a short-circuit in the field windings.
7   Start the engine and run it at 3000 rpm. Reduce the rheostat resistance if necessary and check the field current, which should be 1 to 4 amps.
8   If the current is less than 1 amp, check the alternator brushes and slip rings. If the current is much more than 4 amps, a short-circuit is indicated.
9   To carry out a voltage comparison test, switch on the ignition,

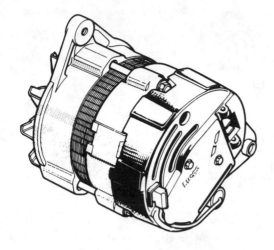

Fig. 11.4 Lucas alternator (Sec 4)

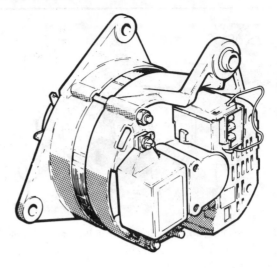

Fig. 11.5 Motorola alternator (Sec 4)

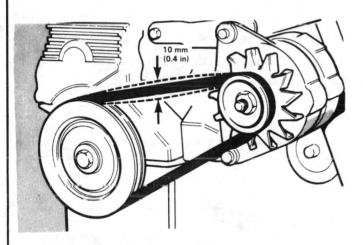

Fig. 11.6 Alternator drivebelt deflection (Sec 4)

10 mm
(0.4 in)

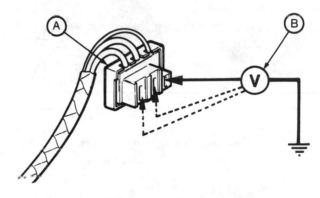

Fig. 11.7 Checking charging circuit continuity (Bosch) (Sec 5)

A   Multi-plug   B   Voltmeter

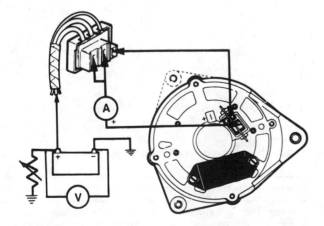

Fig. 11.8 Checking alternator output (Bosch) (Sec 5)

A   Ammeter   B   Voltmeter

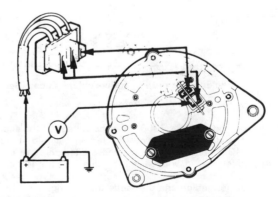

Fig. 11.9 Checking volt drop (positive side) – Bosch (Sec 5)

V   Voltmeter

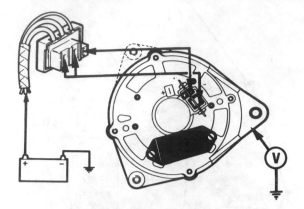

Fig. 11.10 Checking volt drop (negative side) – Bosch (Sec 5)

V   Voltmeter

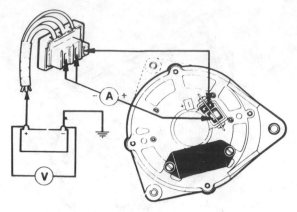

Fig. 11.11 Checking regulator control linkage (Bosch) (Sec 5)

A   Ammeter   V   Voltmeter

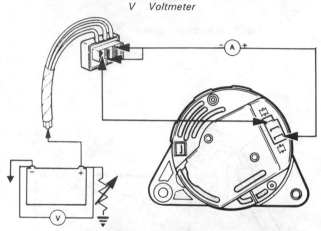

Fig. 11.12 Checking alternator output (Lucas) (Sec 6)

A   Ammeter   V   Voltmeter

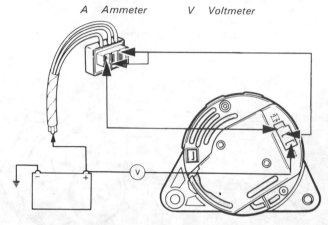

Fig. 11.13 Checking volt drop (positive side) – Lucas (Sec 6)

V   Voltmeter

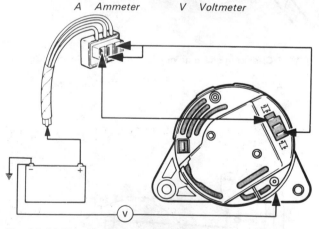

Fig. 11.14 Checking volt drop (negative side) – Lucas (Sec 6)

V   Voltmeter

Fig. 11.15 Checking regulator control voltage (Lucas) (Sec 6)

A   Ammeter   V   Voltmeter

start the engine and run it at 3000 rpm. The voltage at the alternator output terminal and at the battery positive terminal should be identical and between 13.7 and 14.7V at an ambient temperature of 25°C (77°F). Any difference in voltage will be due to corroded or loose terminals.

10 Switch off the ignition and dismantle the test rig.

11 Disconnect the regulator, short out the output terminal to the field terminal, switch on the ignition and run the engine at a fast idle. Check the voltage between the output terminal and a good earth. If the output voltage attains a level of between 14 and 16V, but failed to reach 14V when the test described in paragraph 9 was carried out, then the regulator is at fault. If the output voltage does not rise and no fault was found in the field circuit during testing (paragraph 7), then the stator or the rectifier diodes are faulty.

12 Switch off the ignition and dismantle the test rig.

8   Alternator – removal and refitting

1   The operations are similar for all makes of alternator.

2   Disconnect the battery and disconnect the multi-plug or leads from the rear of the alternator. Remove the heat shield (where fitted).

3   Release the mounting and adjuster link bolts, push the alternator in towards the engine and slip the drivebelt from the pulley.

4   Unscrew and remove the mounting bolts and adjuster link bolt and withdraw the alternator from the engine (photo).

5   Refit by reversing the removal operations, and adjust the drivebelt tension as described in Section 4.

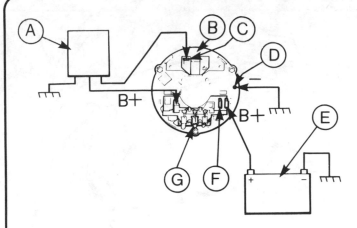

Fig. 11.16 Motorola alternator connections (Sec 7)

A Regulator   E Battery
B Alternator   F Multi-plug output
C Field   G Stator winding
D Earth

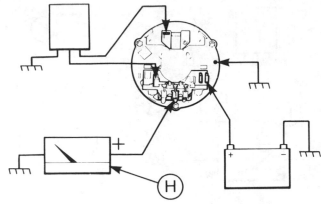

Fig. 11.17 Checking phase voltage (Motorola) (Sec 7)

H Voltmeter

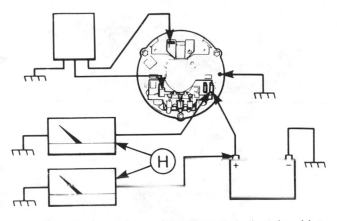

Fig. 11.18 Checking voltage at output terminals and positive terminals (Motorola) (Sec 7)

H Voltmeters

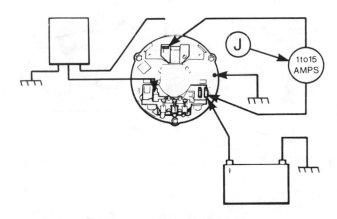

Fig. 11.19 Testing field circuits (Motorola) (Sec 7)

J Ammeter

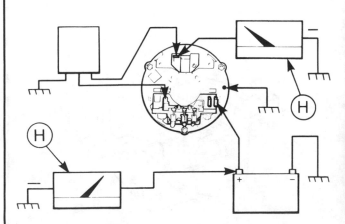

Fig. 11.20 Comparing output and battery voltage (Motorola) (Sec 7)

H Voltmeters

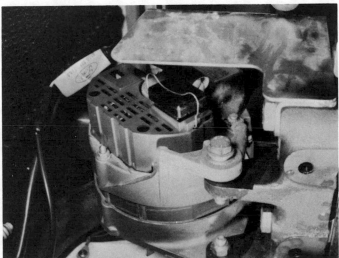

8.4 Alternator mounting bolts

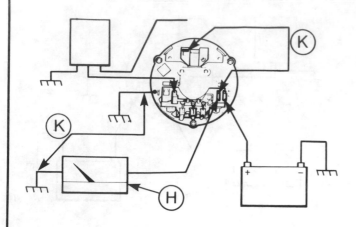

Fig. 11.21 Checking voltage between output terminal and earth (Sec 7)

H   Voltmeter   K   Connecting leads

Fig. 11.22 Regulator screws (arrowed) (Sec 9)

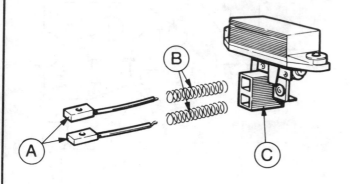

Fig. 11.23 Brush box (Bosch) (Sec 9)

A   Brushes   C   Brush box
B   Springs

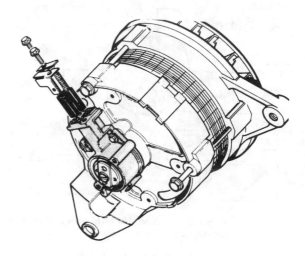

Fig. 11.24 Brush box (Lucas) (Sec 9)

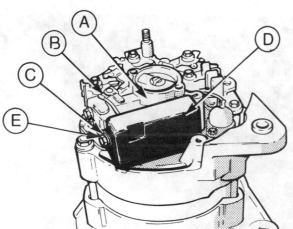

Fig. 11.25 Regulator (Lucas) (Sec 9)

A   Brush box   D   Regulator
B   Field link   E   Retaining screw
C   Plastic spacer

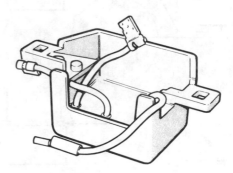

Fig. 11.26 Regulator (Motorola) (Sec 9)

9 Alternator brushes and regulator – renewal

1   With the alternator removed from the engine, clean the external surfaces free from dirt.

Bosch

2   Extract the regulator screws from the rear cover and withdraw the regulator. Check the brush length, if less than the specified minimum, renew them.

3   Unsolder the brush wiring connectors and remove the brushes and the springs.

4   Refit by reversing the removal operations.

Lucas

5   Remove the alternator rear cover.

6   Extract the brush box retaining screws and withdraw the brush assemblies from the brush box.

7   If the length of the brushes is less than the specified minimum, renew them. Refit by reversing the removal operations.

8   To remove the regulator, disconnect the wires from the unit and unscrew the retaining screw.

9   Refit by reversing the removal operations, but check that the small plastic spacer and the connecting link are correctly located.

Motorola

10 Extract the two regulator securing screws, disconnect the two

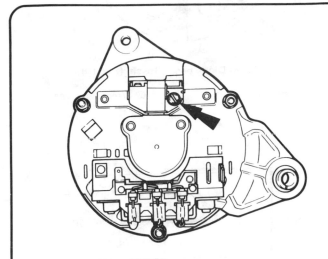

Fig. 11.27 Brush box retaining screw (arrowed) (Motorola) (Sec 9)

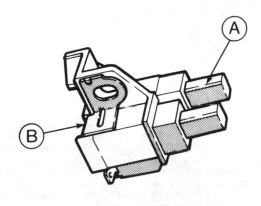

Fig. 11.28 Brush box (Motorola) (Sec 9)

A   Brush   B   Brush box

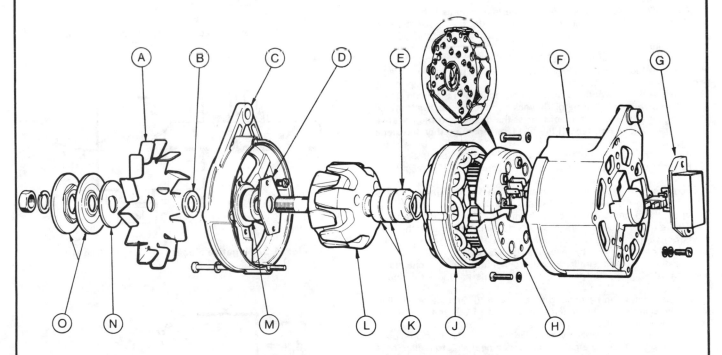

Fig. 11.29 Exploded view of Bosch alternator (Sec 10)

A	Fan	D	Drive end bearing	G	Brush box and regulator	L	Rotor
B	Spacer		retaining plate	H	Rectifier diode pack	M	Drive end bearing
C	Drive end housing	E	Slip ring end bearing	J	Stator	N	Spacer
		F	Slip ring end housing	K	Slip rings	O	Pulley

regulator leads and withdraw the unit.

11 Extract the brush box retaining screw and pull and tilt the brush box from its location, taking care not to damage the brushes during the process.

12 If necessary, unsolder the brush connections.

13 Fit the new brushes by reversing the removal operations.

10 Alternator (Bosch) – overhaul

1 With the alternator removed from the vehicle, unscrew the pulley retaining nut. To prevent the pullley rotating, place an old drivebelt in the pulley grooves and grip both runs of the belt in a vice as close to the pulley as possible.

2 Take off the washer, pulley, fan, spacer and the Woodruff key.

3 Remove the brush box.

4 Remove the tie-bolts and separate the drive end housing and rotor from the slip ring end housing.

5 Press out the rotor from the drive end housing.

6 Remove the drive end bearing and its retainer.

7 Remove the slip ring end bearing from the rotor shaft.

8 Extract the rectifier diode pack retaining screws and lift out the stator and the rectifier pack.

9 Unsolder the stator-to-diode pack connections, using a pair of pliers as a heat sink to prevent the heat spreading to the diodes.

10 With the alternator dismantled, check the positive diodes by connecting a 12V supply through a 5W test bulb wired to form a circuit through one of the diodes. Connect to the positive section of the diode pack with the negative terminal attached to the upper side of one of the diodes. Connect the positive terminal to the lower surface of the diode. The test lamp should illuminate if the diode is in good condition.

11 Repeat the operations on the remaining two positive diodes.

12 Reverse the test circuit terminals so that the positive one goes to the upper side of the diode and the negative one to the lower surface. If the test bulb lights up, the diode is defective.

13 To check the field diodes, connect the test lamp as shown in Fig. 11.32 with the negative terminal coupled to the brush box terminal and the positive one to the diode. The bulb will light up if the diode is in good condition.

14 Repeat the test on the remaining two diodes.

15 Now reverse the terminals and repeat the test. If the bulb lights up then the diode is defective.

16 Now check the negative diodes by connecting the test lamp circuit to the negative section of the diode pack so that the positive terminal is attached to the top surface of one of the diodes and the negative terminal to the under surface. If the test lamp lights up then the diode is in good condition.

17 Repeat the test operations on the remaining two diodes.

18 Reverse the test circuit terminals and repeat. If the bulb lights up then that particular diode is defective.

19 To check the rotor and stator insulation, a 110V ac power supply and test lamp will be required and as this is unlikely to be available, the testing of these items will probably have to be left to your dealer.

20 Where the suitable voltage supply is available, make the test circuit between one slip ring contact and one of the rotor poles. If the test lamp lights up then the insulation is defective.

21 Test the stator in a similar way by connecting between one stator cable and the lamination pack. If the bulb lights up, the insulation is defective.

22 An ohmmeter can be used to determine rotor and stator winding continuity. Connect as shown (Figs. 11.35 and 11.36) and refer to the Specifications for resistance values.

23 Commence reassembly by resoldering the stator-to-diode pack connections, again using a pair of pliers as a heat sink to reduce heat spread.

24 Install the stator and diode pack into the slip ring end housing.

25 Press the slip ring end housing onto the rotor shaft.

26 Refit the drive end bearing and secure with its retainer plate.

27 Fit the rotor into the drive end housing and assemble the rotor and drive end housing to the slip ring end housing.

28 Refit the brush box and the fan/pulley assembly. Make sure that the pulley spacer has its concave face against the fan as it acts as a vibration damper.

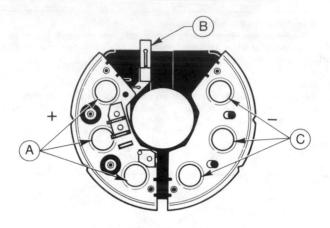

Fig. 11.30 Diode pack (Bosch) (Sec 10)

A   Positive diodes   C   Negative diodes
B   Brush box terminal

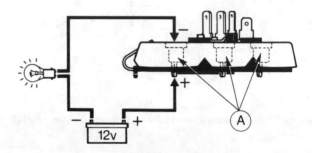

Fig. 11.31 Positive diodes (A) – Bosch (Sec 10)

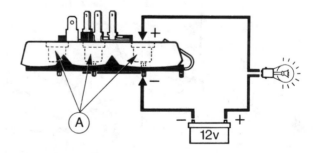

Fig. 11.32 Negative diodes (A) – Bosch (Sec 10)

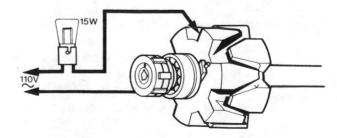

Fig. 11.33 Checking rotor winding insulation (Bosch) (Sec 10)

11 Alternator (Lucas) – overhaul

1 With the alternator removed from the vehicle and cleaned, remove the pulley and fan as described in the preceding Section, paragraph 1.
2 Remove the rear cover.
3 Remove the regulator.
4 Remove the surge protection diode and the brush box.
5 Unsolder the stator connections from the rectifier pack, using a pair of pliers as a heat sink as described in the preceding Section.
6 Extract the three bolts and remove the pack.
7 Checking the diodes should be carried out in a similar way to that described in the preceding Section, but note the different design of the diode pack.
8 Remove the tie-bolts, separate the drive end and slip ring end housing and withdraw the stator.
9 Unsolder the leads from the slip rings and remove the slip rings from the rotor shaft.
10 Press out the slip ring end bearing and the rotor assembly from the slip ring end housing. Press off the slip ring end bearing.
11 To facilitate extraction of the drive end bearing circlip, apply light pressure to the rear face of the bearing.
12 Remove the circlip, thrust washer, the drive end bearing and shim pack.
13 Check the rotor and stator for winding continuity and insulation as described in the preceding Section, paragraphs 19 to 22.
14 Commence reassembly by fitting the drive end bearing shim pack, the bearing and the thrust washer. If the original bearing is being used again, work some high melting point grease into it. Fit the retaining circlip.
15 Make sure that the rotor wires are correctly located in their grooves in the rotor shaft and install the slip ring end bearing to the shaft. If the original bearing is being used, work some high melting point grease into it. Refit the slip rings and resolder their leads.
16 Fit the rotor assembly to the slip ring end housing.
17 Locate the stator in the slip ring end housing and reconnect the slip ring and drive end housings. Pull the housings evenly together by tightening the tie-bolts.
18 Fit the rectifier diode pack and resolder the stator-to-rectifier diode pack wiring.
19 Fit the brush box and the surge protection diode.
20 Fit the regulator, the rear cover and the pulley/fan assembly.

12 Alternator (Motorola) – overhaul

1 With the alternator removed from the engine and cleaned, remove the pulley/fan assembly as described in Section 10, paragraph 1.
2 Remove the rear cover and the regulator.
3 Remove the brush box.
4 Check the rotor by connecting test probes from an ohmmeter to each slip ring. The resistance must be within the limits given in the Specifications.
5 Connect an ohmmeter between a slip ring and the alternator housing. No reading should be indicated.
6 Check the stator insulation by connecting the ohmmeter between the alternator housing and each stator phase winding in turn. No reading should be indicated.
7 Unsolder the stator-to-diode bridge connections and remove the bridge.
8 Test the diode bridge using a 5W test lamp and 12V supply. Connect the indicator lamp between each positive diode phase

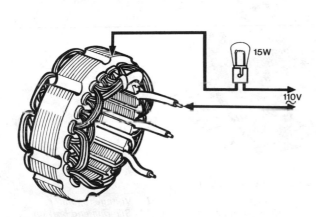

Fig. 11.34 Checking stator winding insulation (Bosch) (Sec 10)

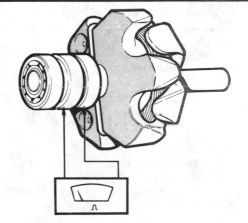

Fig. 11.35 Checking rotor winding continuity (Bosch) (Sec 10)

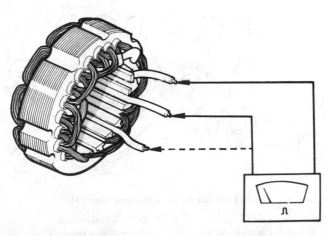

Fig. 11.36 Checking stator winding continuity (Bosch) (Sec 10)

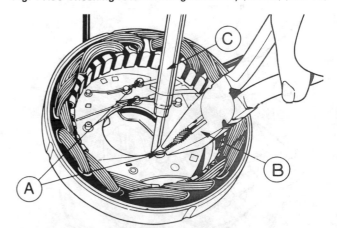

Fig. 11.37 Soldering stator-to-diode pack connections (Bosch) (Sec 10)

A   Stator pack   C   Soldering iron
B   Pliers

terminal and the B+ terminal as shown (Fig. 11.48). The lamp should light up if the diode is in good condition.

9   Reverse the test lead probes and the lamp should not light up unless the diode is faulty.

10   To check the negative diodes, connect the test lamp between each phase terminal and earth. If the diode is in good condition, the bulb should light up. Now reverse the test probes when the bulb should not light up unless the diode is faulty.

11   Remove the tie-bolts, separate the drive end and slip ring end housings and withdraw the stator.

12   Pull off the rear bearing using a two-legged extractor.

13   Unsolder the wires from the slip rings.

14   Extract the three screws which hold the bearing plate at the drive end and press out the bearing assembly.

15   Commence reassembly by installing the drive end bearing and the bearing plate and screws. If the original bearing is being used, work some high melting point grease into it.

16   Locate the inner slip ring on the rotor shaft, making sure that the lead holes are correctly aligned. Press the slip ring into position and solder the lead.

17   Install the outer slip ring in a similar way.

18   Fit the rotor and drive end bearing to the drive end housing. If the original bearing is being used, work some high melting point grease into it.

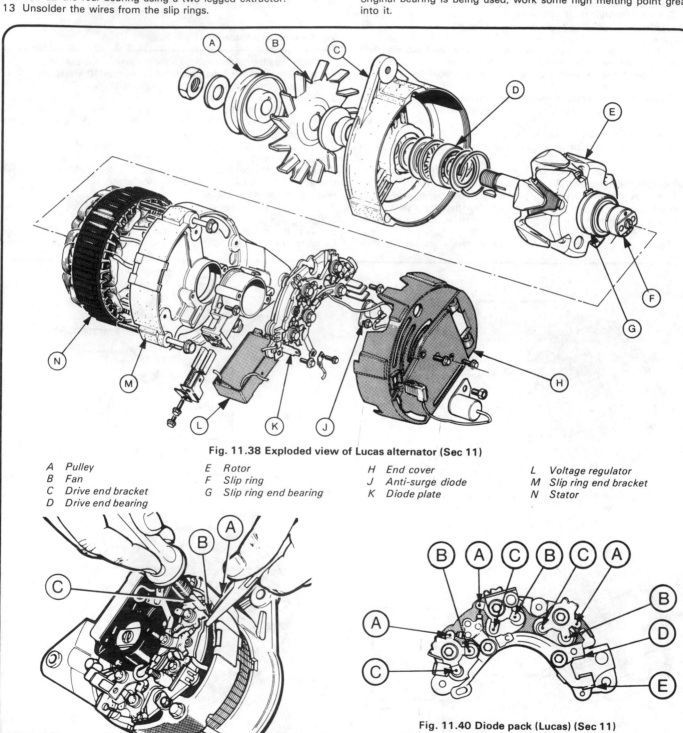

Fig. 11.38 Exploded view of Lucas alternator (Sec 11)

A	Pulley	E	Rotor	H	End cover	L	Voltage regulator
B	Fan	F	Slip ring	J	Anti-surge diode	M	Slip ring end bracket
C	Drive end bracket	G	Slip ring end bearing	K	Diode plate	N	Stator
D	Drive end bearing						

Fig. 11.39 Unsoldering stator/diode connections (Lucas) (Sec 11)

A   Rectifier pack   C   Soldering iron
B   Pliers

Fig. 11.40 Diode pack (Lucas) (Sec 11)

A   Field diodes   D   Field terminal
B   Positive diodes   E   Positive terminal
C   Negative diodes

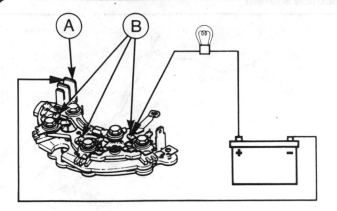

Fig. 11.41 Checking positive diodes (Lucas) (Sec 11)

A   *Positive terminals*   B   *Positive diodes*

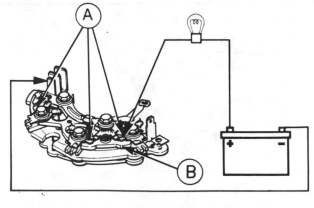

Fig. 11.42 Checking field diodes (Lucas) (Sec 11)

A   *Field diodes*   B   *Field plate*

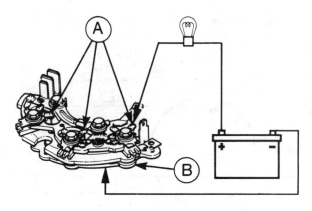

Fig. 11.43 Checking negative diodes (Lucas) (Sec 11)

A   *Negative diodes*   B   *Negative plate*

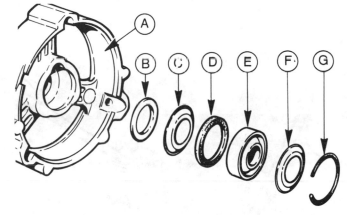

Fig. 11.44 Drive end bearing components (Lucas) (Sec 11)

A   *Drive end housing*   E   *Drive end bearing*
B   *Felt ring*   F   *Thrust washer*
C   *Thrust washer*   G   *Circlip*
D   *O-ring*

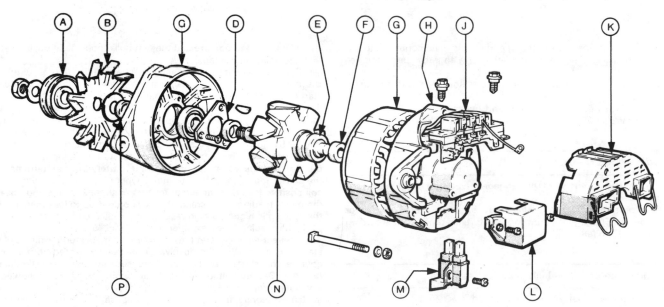

Fig. 11.45 Exploded view of Motorola alternator (Sec 12)

A   *Pulley*   D   *Drive end bearing*   G   *Stator*   L   *Regulator*
B   *Fan*   *retaining plate*   H   *Slip ring end bearing*   M   *Brush box*
C   *Drive end bearing*   E   *Slip ring*   J   *Diode bridge*   N   *Rotor*
                        F   *Slip ring end bearing*   K   *End cover*   P   *Spacer*

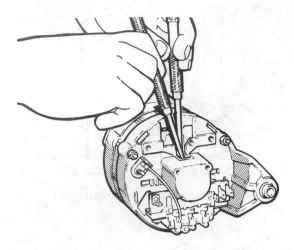

Fig. 11.46 Checking rotor resistance (Motorola) (Sec 12)

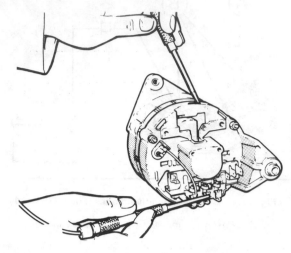

Fig. 11.47 Checking stator insulation (Motorola) (Sec 12)

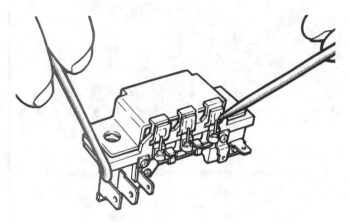

Fig. 11.48 Checking positive diodes (Motorola) (Sec 12)

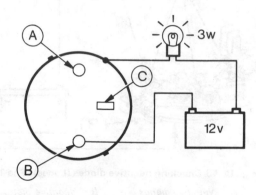

Fig. 11.49 Checking solenoid winding (Sec 14)

A   Battery terminal   C   Spade terminal
B   Feed terminal

19   Locate the stator in the slip ring end housing and connect it to the drive end housing. Pull the assemblies evenly together using the tie-bolts.
20   Fit the diode bridge and resolder the stator/diode wiring connections.
21   Fit the brush box, the regulator and the rear cover.
22   Fit the Woodruff key and the fan/pulley assembly.

13 Starter motor – description

The starter motor is of pre-engaged type and incorporates an integral solenoid.

One of three different makes may be fitted, Lucas, Bosch or Nippondenso. The power output of the starter motor varies according to make and model.

14 Starter motor – in-vehicle testing

1   Check that the battery is fully charged.
2   First test the solenoid. To do this, disconnect the battery negative lead and both leads from the solenoid. Check the continuity of the solenoid windings by connecting a test lamp (12V with 2 to 3W bulb) between the starter feed terminal and the solenoid body. The lamp should light up.
3   Now make the test circuit as shown in Fig. 11.50, using a higher wattage (18 to 21W) bulb. Energise the solenoid by applying 12V between the spade terminal and the starter feed terminal. The solenoid

should be heard to operate and the test bulb should light up, indicating that the solenoid contacts have closed.
4   Connect a voltmeter directly between the battery terminals. Disconnect the positive LT lead from the ignition coil and operate the starter. The voltmeter should indicate not less than 10.5V.
5   Now connect the voltmeter between the starter main terminal and the body of the starter motor. Operate the starter, with the coil LT lead still disconnected. The reading on the voltmeter should be no more than 0.5V lower than that indicated during the test described in paragraph 4. If it is, check the battery-to-starter motor wiring.
6   Connect the voltmeter between the battery positive terminal and the starter motor main feed terminal. Operate the starter (with the LT coil positive lead disconnected) for two or three seconds and observe the meter readings. A reading of 12V should drop to less than 1.0V. If the reading is higher, a high resistance is indicated (refer to paragraph 7). If the reading is lower, refer to paragraph 8.
7   Connect the voltmeter between the two main stud terminals of the starter solenoid. With the positive LT lead disconnected from the coil, operate the starter for two or three seconds and note the meter readings. Battery voltage (12V) should be indicated first, followed by a voltage drop to less than 0.5V. If outside this tolerance, a faulty switch or connections may be the cause, or loose or corroded terminals in the circuit.
8   Connect a voltmeter between the battery negative terminal and the starter motor main casing. With the positive LT lead disconnected from the coil, operate the starter for two or three seconds. If the earth line is satisfactory, the reading should be less than 0.5V. If it is 0.6V or more then there is a high resistance in the earth return side of the circuit. This may be due to a loose or corroded connection either at the battery or at the engine block.

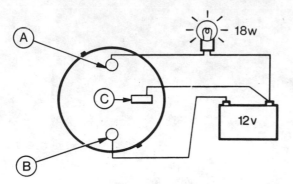

Fig. 11.50 Checking solenoid for continuity (Sec 14)

A   *Battery terminal*   C   *Spade terminal*
B   *Feed terminal*

15 Starter motor – removal and refitting

1   Disconnect the battery.
2   Working from under the vehicle, disconnect the main starter motor cable and the two wires from the starter solenoid (photo).
3   Unbolt the starter motor and withdraw it from its location (photo).
4   Refit by reversing the removal operations.

16 Starter motor (Bosch) – overhaul

1   With the starter motor removed from the vehicle and cleaned, grip the starter motor in the jaws of a vice which have been fitted with soft metal protectors.
2   Disconnect the field winding connector link from the solenoid stud.
3   Extract the solenoid fixing screws and withdraw the solenoid yoke from the drive end housing and the solenoid armature. Unhook the solenoid armature from the actuating lever.
4   Extract the two screws and remove the commutator end cap and rubber seal.
5   Wipe away any grease and withdraw the C-clip and shims.
6   Remove the tie-nuts and remove the commutator end housing.
7   Remove the brushes by prising the brush springs clear and sliding the brushes from their holders. Remove the brushplate.
8   Separate the drive end housing and armature from the yoke by tapping apart with a plastic-faced hammer.
9   Remove the tie-studs to release the drive pinion clutch stop bracket.
10 Withdraw the armature assembly and unhook the actuating arm from the drive pinion flange.
11 To remove the drive pinion from the armature shaft, drive the stop collar down the shaft with a piece of tubing to expose the clip. Remove the clip from its groove and slide the stop collar and drive pinion off the shaft.
12 Examine the components and renew as necessary.

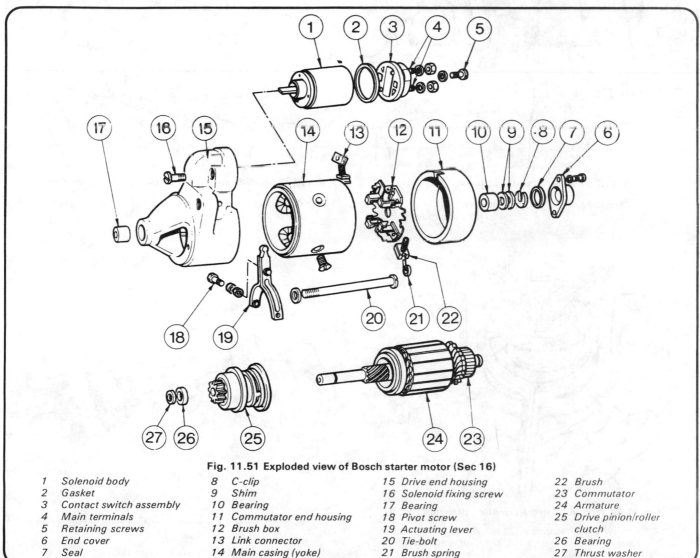

Fig. 11.51 Exploded view of Bosch starter motor (Sec 16)

1	Solenoid body	8	C-clip	15	Drive end housing
2	Gasket	9	Shim	16	Solenoid fixing screw
3	Contact switch assembly	10	Bearing	17	Bearing
4	Main terminals	11	Commutator end housing	18	Pivot screw
5	Retaining screws	12	Brush box	19	Actuating lever
6	End cover	13	Link connector	20	Tie-bolt
7	Seal	14	Main casing (yoke)	21	Brush spring

22	Brush
23	Commutator
24	Armature
25	Drive pinion/roller clutch
26	Bearing
27	Thrust washer

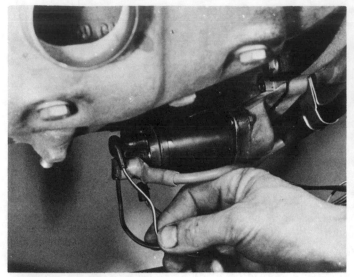

15.2 Starter solenoid connections

15.3 Removing the starter motor

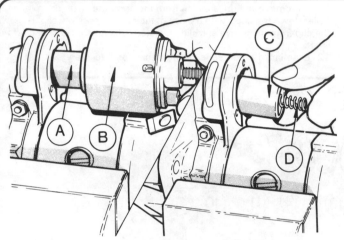

Fig. 11.52 Solenoid removal (Bosch) (Sec 16)

A   Armature   C   Armature
B   Yoke   D   Armature return spring

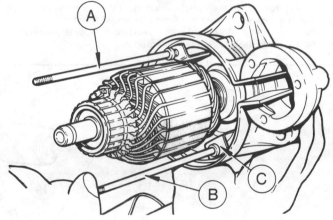

Fig. 11.53 Tie-studs and clutch stop bracket (Bosch) (Sec 16)

A   Stud   C   Clutch stop bracket
B   Stud

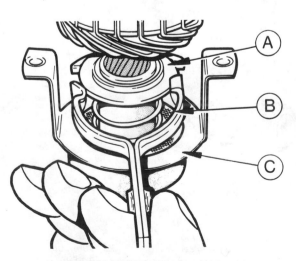

Fig. 11.54 Withdrawing the armature (Bosch) (Sec 16)

A   Actuating arm locating   B   Actuating arm
    flange   C   Clutch stop bracket

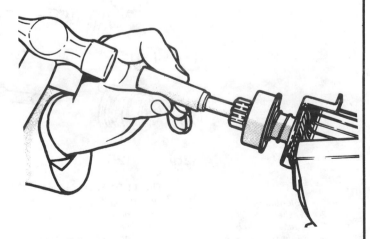

**Fig. 11.55 Driving down armature shaft stop collar (Bosch)
(Sec 16)**

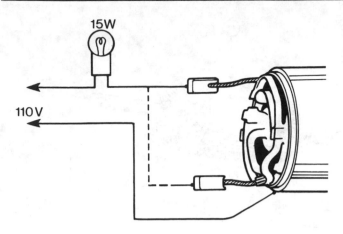

Fig. 11.56 Testing field winding for continuity (Bosch) (Sec 16)

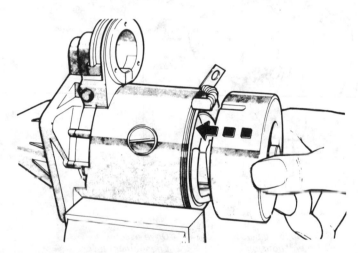

Fig. 11.57 Fitting commutator end housing and rubber insulator (Bosch) (Sec 16)

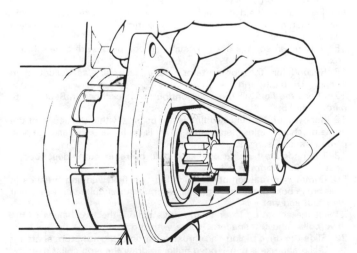

Fig. 11.58 Checking armature endfloat (Bosch) (Sec 16)

13 If the brushes have worn to less than the specified minimum, renew them as a set. To renew the brushes, cut their leads at their midpoint and make a good soldered joint when connecting the new brushes.

14 The commutator face should be clean and free from burnt spots. Where necessary burnish with fine glass paper (**not** emery) and wipe with a fuel-moistened cloth. If the commutator is in really bad shape it can be skimmed on a lathe provided its diameter is not reduced below the specified minimum.

15 The field winding can be checked for continuity only if a 110V ac power source is available, probably a job for your dealer. Where facilities are to hand, connect the test lamp between each field winding brush in turn and a clean, unpainted area of the yoke. The test lamp should not light up.

16 Renew the end housing bushes, which are of self-lubricating type and should have been soaked in clean engine oil for at least 20 minutes before installation.

17 Commence reassembly by sliding the drive pinion and stop collar onto the armature shaft. Fit the C-clip into the shaft groove and then use a two-legged puller to draw the stop collar over the clip.

18 Align the clutch retaining bracket and secure it with the two tie-studs.

19 Fit the rubber insert into the drive end housing.

20 Guide the yoke over the armature and tap home onto the drive end housing.

21 Fit the brush plate, the brushes and their springs.

22 Guide the commutator end housing into position, at the same time sliding the rubber insulator into the cut-out in the commutator housing. Secure the commutator end housing with the stud nuts and washers.

23 Slide the armature into position in its bearings so that the shaft has the maximum projection at the commutator bearing end.

24 Fit sufficient shims onto the armature shaft to eliminate endfloat when the C-clip is installed, which should now be done.

25 Fit the armature shaft bearing cap seal, apply a little lithium-based grease to the end of the shaft and refit the bearing cap with its two screws.

26 Apply some grease to the solenoid armature hook and engage the hook with the actuating arm in the drive end housing. Check that the solenoid armature return spring is correctly located and then guide the solenoid yoke over the armature. Align the yoke with the drive end housing and fit the three securing screws.

27 Connect the field wire link to the solenoid terminal stud

17 Starter motor (Lucas) – overhaul

1 With the starter removed from the vehicle and cleaned, grip it in a vice fitted with soft metal jaw protectors.

2 Remove the plastic cap from the commutator endplate.

3 Using a very small cold chisel, remove the star clip from the end of the armature shaft. Do this by distorting the prongs of the clip until it can be removed.

4 Disconnect the main feed link from the solenoid terminal.

5 Unscrew the two mounting nuts and withdraw the solenoid from the drive end housing, at the same time unhooking the solenoid armature from the actuating lever.

6 Extract the two drive end housing fixing screws. Guide the housing and the armature clear of the yoke.

7 Withdraw the armature from the drive end housing and the actuating lever assembly will come out with it, complete with plastic pivot block and rubber pad.

8 Use a piece of tubing to drive the stop collar down the armature shaft to expose the C-clip. Remove the C-clip and take off the stop collar and drive pinion.

9 To separate the actuating lever from the drive pinion, extract the C-clip and remove the spacer. Separate the two halves of the plastic drive collar and withdraw the actuating lever.

10 Remove the commutator endplate screws and tap the plate free of the yoke.

11 Lift the plate far enough to give access to the two field winding brushes. Disconnect two of the brushes from the brush box to permit complete removal of the commutator endplate.

12 The brush box and commutator endplate are only supplied as a complete assembly and should be renewed together if necessary.

13 Examine all the components for wear. If the brushes have worn to

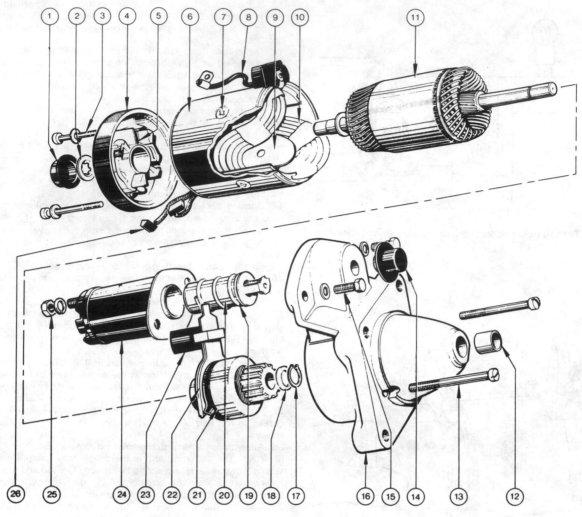

Fig. 11.59 Exploded view of Lucas starter motor (Sec 17)

1	Dust cap	8	Link connector	15	Solenoid fixing screw	21	Drive assembly
2	Star clip	9	Pole screw	16	Drive end housing	22	Engagement lever
3	Endplate bolt	10	Field coils	17	C-clip	23	Pivot
4	Endplate	11	Armature	18	Spacer	24	Solenoid body
5	Brush housing	12	Bearing	19	Return spring	25	Terminal nut and washer
6	Main casing (yoke)	13	Housing screws	20	Solenoid armature	26	Brushes
7	Pole screw	14	Dust cover				

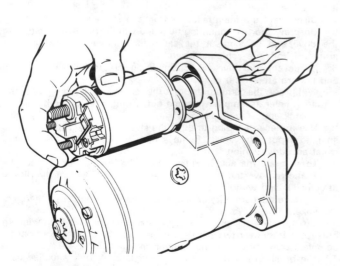

Fig. 11.60 Removing the solenoid (Lucas) (Sec 17)

less than the specified minimum length, renew them as a set.

14 Two of the brushes come complete with the commutator endplate terminal, but the field winding brushes will have to be cut and new ones soldered. Cut the original leads 6.0 mm (0.25 in) from the field winding conductor.

15 New brush springs are only supplied complete with a new brush box.

16 Recondition the commutator where necessary as described in Section 16, paragraph 14.

17 Check the field winding for continuity as described in Section 16, paragraph 15.

18 Renewal of the field winding is not usually within the scope of the home mechanic unless a pressure driver is available to release the pole piece retaining screws.

19 The endplate bearing bushes should be renewed as described in Section 16, paragraph 16.

20 Commence reassembly by locating two field winding brushes in their brush box channels. Align the commutator endplate and secure it with four screws.

21 Fit the actuating lever to the drive pinion, the two halves of the drive collar and the spacer. Secure with the C-clip.

22 Slide the drive pinion and thrust collar onto the armature shaft. Fit the C-clip and use a two-legged puller to draw the stop collar over the clip.

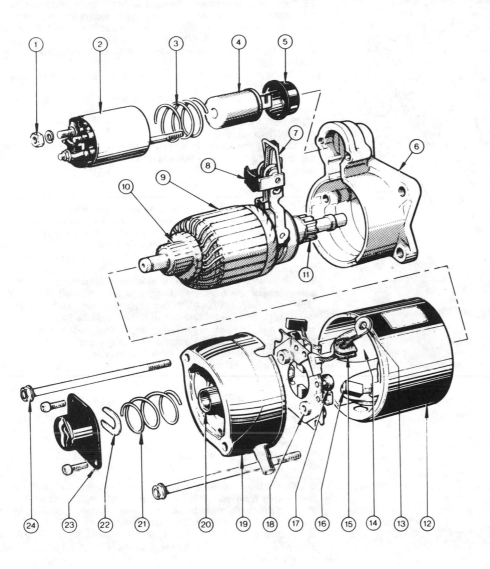

Fig. 11.61 Exploded view of Nippondenso starter motor (Sec 18)

1   Solenoid terminal nut
2   Solenoid body
3   Return spring
4   Solenoid armature
5   Seal
6   Drive end housing
7   Actuating lever
8   Pivot
9   Armature
10 Commutator
11 Drivepinion/roller
    clutch
12 Main casing
13 Link connector
14 Pole shoe
15 Seal
16 Brush
17 Brush spring
18 Brush plate
19 Commutator end housing
20 Bush
21 Spring
22 C-clip
23 End cover
24 Tie-bolt

23 Hook the plastic pivot block over the actuating arm, position the rubber pad and insert into the solenoid mounting housing.
24 Guide the armature into the drive end housing.
25 Guide the armature and drive end housing through the yoke and align the armature shaft with the endplate bush. Secure the yoke and housing with two fixing screws.
26 Fit a new star clip to the end of the armature shaft, making sure that it is firmly fixed to eliminate shaft endfloat. Fit the plastic cap.
27 Locate the solenoid armature onto the actuating arm, guide the solenoid yoke over the armature and secure with studs and nuts.
28 Refit the connecting link between the solenoid and the main feed terminal.

18 Starter motor (Nippondenso) – overhaul

1   With the starter motor removed from the engine and cleaned, secure it in a vice with jaws protected with soft metal.
2   Disconnect the field winding connector from the solenoid terminal.
3   Remove the solenoid retaining nuts.
4   Withdraw the solenoid and unhook the armature hook from the actuating lever.
5   Remove the bearing cap (two screws).

6   Slide the C-washer from its groove in the armature shaft and take off the coil spring.
7   Unbolt and remove the rear housing cover.
8   Withdraw two field brushes and remove the brush gear mounting plate.
9   Withdraw the armature and drive end housing from the main housing.
10 Withdraw the armature and the actuating lever from the drive end housing. Remove the actuating lever.
11 Use a piece of tubing to tap the stop collar down the armature shaft to expose the C-clip. Remove the clip and pull off the stop collar and drive pinion.
12 Inspect all components for wear. If the brushes have worn down to less than the specified minimum, renew them as a set. To do this, the original brush leads will have to be cut at the midpoint of their length and the new ones joined by soldering.
13 Recondition the commutator as described in Section 16, paragraph 14.
14 Check the field winding for continuity as described in Section 16, paragraph 15.
15 The endplate bearing bushes should be renewed where necessary as described in Section 16, paragraph 16.
16 Commence reassembly by sliding the drive pinion and stop collar onto the armature shaft. Fit the C-clip and using a two-legged puller, draw the stop collar over the clip.

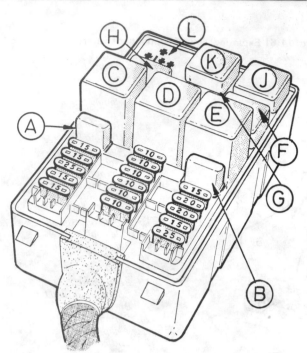

Fig. 11.62 Fuse and relay box (Sec 19)

A   Overload circuit breaker   F   Auxiliary driving lamp
    (central door locking)   relay
B   Overload circuit breaker   G   Spare
    (electric windows)   H   Ignition relay
C   Wiper delay relay   J   Tailgate heated window
D   Headlamp wash relay   relay
E   Direction indicator relay   K   Foglamp relay
                                    L   Spare

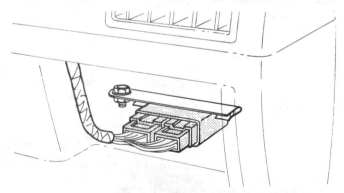

Fig. 11.63 Auxiliary relay (central door locking) (Sec 19)

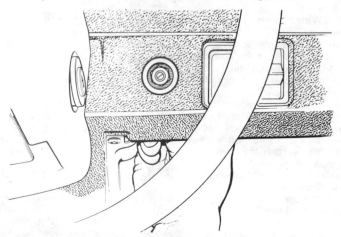

Fig. 11.64 Removing wiper delay switch (Sec 20)

17 Align the actuating lever in the drive end housing. Guide the
armature into position, at the same time locating the actuating lever
onto the drive pinion flange.
18 Tap the yoke into engagement with the drive end housing.
19 Locate the brush plate, aligning the cut-outs in the plate with the
loops in the field winding. The brush assembly will be positively
located when the fixing screws are screwed in.
20 Position the brushes in their brush box locations and retain with
their springs.
21 Guide the commutator end housing into position and secure with
the fixing nuts.
22 To the commutator end of the armature shaft, fit the coil spring
and the C-clip.
23 Smear the end of the shaft with lithium-based grease and then fit
the cap (two screws).
24 Connect the solenoid armature hook onto the actuating lever in
the drive end housing. Align the solenoid yoke and fit the two fixing
bolts.

19 Fuses, relays and circuit breakers – general

1   These are combined in one box under the bonnet (photo).
2   The fuses are numbered to identify the circuit which they protect
and the circuits are represented by symbols on the plastic cover of the
box (photo).
3   When an accessory or other electrical component or system fails,
always check the fuse first. The fuses are coloured red (10A), blue
(15A) or yellow (20/25A). Never replace a fuse with one of higher
rating or bypass it with tinfoil, and if the new fuse blows immediately,
check the reason before renewing again. The most common cause of
a fuse blowing is faulty insulation creating a short-circuit.
4   Spare fuses are carried in the fuse box lid.
5   Relays are of the plug-in type and are used for the following
circuits (as applicable):

   Auxiliary foglamp
   Heated rear window
   Auxiliary driving lamp
   Direction indicators
   Headlamp washer
   Windscreen wiper delay
   Ignition relay

6   Circuit breakers are only fitted to vehicles equipped with electrically-operated front windows or a central door locking system.
7   Vehicles with a central door locking system also have an additional relay located under the instrument panel.
8   Where a radio/cassette player is installed, an in-line 2A fuse is
located in the power line and is accessible once the dash lower trim
panel has been removed.

20 Switches – removal and refitting

Disconnect the battery before removing any switches.
1   Reference should also be made to Chapter 9 for details of steering
column switches and to Chapter 8 for braking system switches.

Wiper delay switch
2   Remove the switch knob and the bezel nut.
3   Withdraw the switch through the parcels tray and disconnect it
from the wiring harness.

Rear washer/wiper switch
4   Using a screwdriver, gently prise the switch from the facia panel.
5   Disconnect the switch multi-plug.

Load space lamp switch
6   Open the tailgate and remove the trim panel.
7   Disconnect the lead from the switch and remove the single switch
fixing screw.

Instrument cluster light switch
8   Open the small tidy tray by pulling it downwards.
9   Extract the two screws from its top edge.

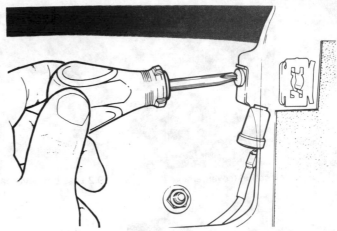

Fig. 11.65 Removing tailgate washer/wiper switch (Sec 20)

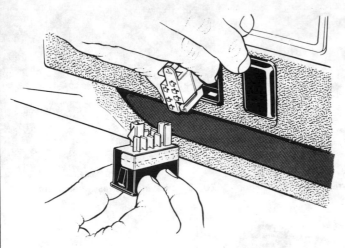

Fig. 11.66 Removing load space lamp switch (Sec 20)

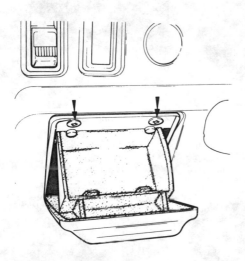

Fig. 11.67 Facia tidy tray securing screws (arrowed) (Sec 20)

Fig. 11.68 Removing heater blower motor switch (Sec 20)

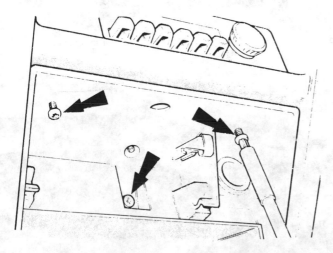

Fig. 11.69 Ashtray housing screws (arrowed) (Sec 21)

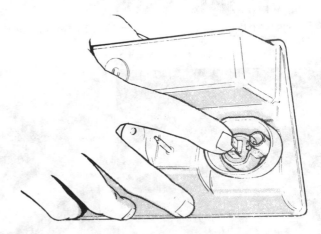

Fig. 11.70 Removing the cigar lighter (Sec 21)

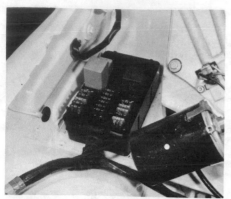

19.1 Fuse box location (cover removed)

19.2 Fuse box cover carries circuit information

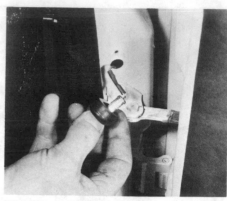

20.15 Removing courtesy lamp switch

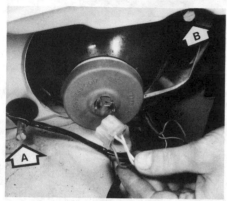

22.2 Disconnecting headlamp plug
A Vertical beam adjuster
B Horizontal beam adjuster

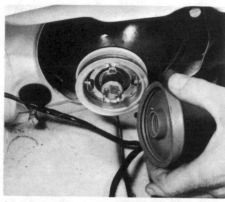

22.3 Headlamp rubber cover

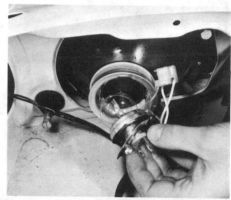

22.4 Removing headlamp bulb

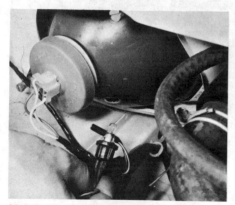

22.6 Parking lamp bulb

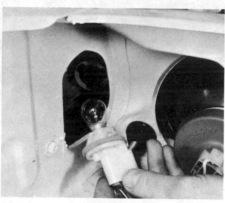

22.7 Front indicator bulb

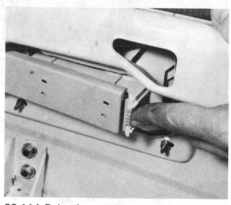

22.11A Releasing rear lamp cluster

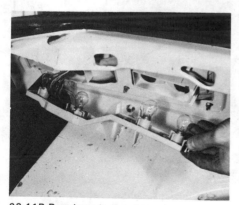

22.11B Rear lamp bulb holder

22.17A Rear number plate lamp

22.17B Rear number plate lamp bulb

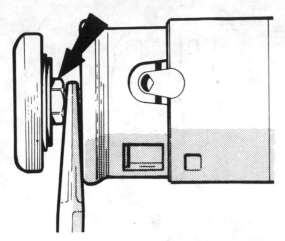

Fig. 11.71 Removing cigar lighter element coil. Release locknut (arrowed) (Sec 21)

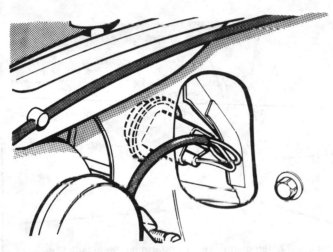

Fig. 11.72 Front direction indicator bulb holder (Sec 22)

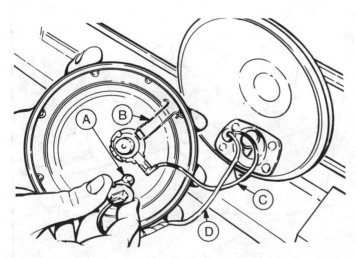

Fig. 11.73 Auxiliary lamp bulb holder (Sec 22)

A	Bulb	C	Earth wire
B	Clip	D	Feed wire

10 Pull the knob from the switch and unscrew the bezel nut.
11 Remove the switch through the tidy tray aperture and disconnect the electrical leads from it.

Heater blower motor switch
12 Pull off the switch knob.
13 Reach behind the facia panel and squeeze the switch retaining tangs. Pull the switch out of the panel and disconnect the wiring from it.

Courtesy lamp switch
14 Extract the single screw which holds the switch to the door pillar.
15 Withdraw the switch from its rubber shroud and disconnect the electrical lead. To prevent the lead falling back into the pillar, tape it to retain it (photo).
16 Smearing the switch with petroleum jelly will help to prevent corrosion which often causes failure.

All switches
17 Refitting is the reverse of the removal procedure. Reconnect the battery and check for correct operation on completion.

21 Cigar lighter   removal and refitting

1   Disconnect the battery.
2   Remove the ashtray, and after extracting the fixing screws withdraw the ashtray housing.
3   Disconnect the electrical leads and remove the bulb holder from the lighter.
4   Pull out the lighter element and then press the lighter body and the illumination ring from the ashtray.
5   Remove the illumination ring from the lighter body.
6   To remove the coil from the element, release the locknut while gripping the spindle with a pair of pliers.
7   Refitting is a reversal of removal.

22 Bulbs (exterior lamps) – renewal

Headlamp
1   Open the bonnet.
2   Working inside the engine compartment, pull the multi-plug from the rear of the headlamp (photo).
3   Remove the rubber gaiter and rotate the bulb securing clip or extract the spring clip according to type (photo).
4   Withdraw the bulb (photo).
5   Fit the bulb, avoiding handling it with the fingers. If you have touched it, wipe the bulb with a pad moistened in methylated spirit.

Front parking lamp
6   The operations are similar to those just described for the headlamp bulb. Twist the parking lamp bulb holder from the headlamp units (photo).

Front indicator lamp
7   Working inside the engine compartment, twist the bulb holder from the rear of the lamp (photo).
8   Remove the bulb from the holder.

Auxiliary lamp and foglamp
9   Remove the single lens securing screw, pull the lens/reflector forward and disconnect the lead from the spade terminal.
10 Release the bulb holder retaining clip and take out the bulb. Do not handle a bulb with the fingers, but if the glass is touched, clean it with a pad moistened in methylated spirit.

Rear lamps
Car
11 Open the tailgate, depress the catch on the bulb holder and pull it from its location (photos).
12 Remove the bulb from its holder
Estate
13 Open the tailgate and remove the rear trim panel.

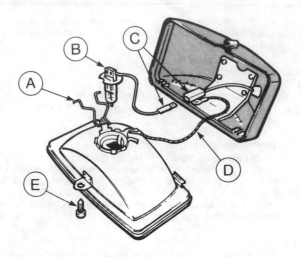

Fig. 11.74 Foglamp bulb holder (Sec 22)

A   Bulb clip   D   Earth wire
B   Bulb   E   Lens screw
C   Connector

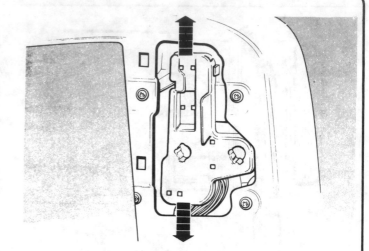

Fig. 11.75 Rear lamp bulb holder (Estate) (Sec 22)

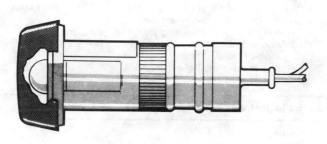

Fig. 11.76 Side repeater lamp (Sec 22)

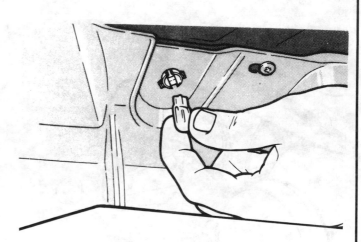

Fig. 11.77 Removing glove compartment lamp bulb (Sec 23)

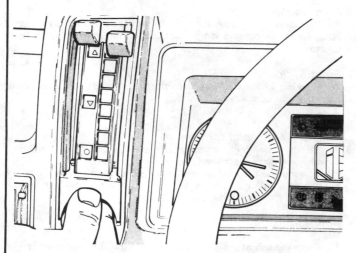

Fig. 11.78 Removing heater control panel trim (Sec 23)

Fig. 11.79 Hazard warning switch bulb and cover (Sec 23)

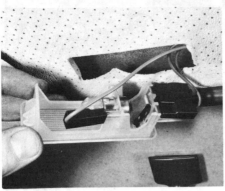

23.7 Interior roof lamp

24.4 Headlamp unit removed

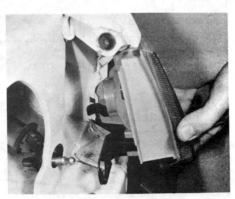

24.9 Front indicator lamp removed

14 Release the bulb holder by pressing one clip up and the other one down with the thumbs.

Van

15 Remove the rear trim panel and twist the individual bulb holders in an anti-clockwise direction.

Rear number plate lamp

Car and Estate

16 Reach under the rear bumper and disconnect the wiring multi-plug.

17 Squeeze the tangs which retain the lamp to the bumper, pull and remove. The base of the lamp contains the bulb which is removed by gently pulling (photos).

Van

18 Insert a thin screwdriver into the slot between the lamp and bumper and prise it from the bumper.

19 Withdraw the wiring through the cut-out until the multi-plug can be disconnected.

20 Separate the lens from the base by twisting the base.

Side repeater lamp

21 Release the lamp from the wing by reaching up under the wing and squeezing the lamp retaining tangs.

22 Push out the lamp and twist the bulb holder from it in an anti-clockwise direction. Pull the bulb gently from its holder.

All lamps

23 Replacement of the bulb and holder is a reversal of removal in all cases.

23 Bulbs (interior lamps) – renewal

Glove compartment lamp

1 This is simply a matter of gently pulling the bulb from its holder.

Heater control illumination lamp

2 Slide the heater control levers to the top of their travel.

3 Pull off the heater motor switch knob and then unclip the control trim panel from the facia.

4 Pull the bulb from the lamp socket.

Hazard warning switch

5 Grip the switch cover and pull it off.

6 Gently pull the bulb from its socket.

Interior front lamp

7 Carefully prise the lamp from its location and remove the bulb from its spring contact on the lamp body (photo).

Luggage compartment lamp

8 Using a thin screwdriver, prise the lamp from its location.

9 Remove the bulb from its spring contact clip.

10 Refitting the bulb is a reversal of removal.

24 Exterior lamps – removal and refitting

Headlamp

1 Remove the radiator grille as described in Chapter 12.

2 Working inside the engine compartment, disconnect the headlamp multi-plug and pull out the parking lamp bulb holder.

3 Twist the top and side clip plastic heads through 90° to release them from their retainers.

4 With the headlamp unit released, pull it sharply forward off its ball-stud (photo).

Front direction indicator lamp

5 Working inside the engine compartment, disconnect the indicator bulb holder from the lamp.

6 Remove the headlamp as described in earlier paragraphs of this Section.

7 Remove the spring clip from the ball-headed bolt and remove the bolt.

8 Remove the lower adjuster by turning the knurled collar.

9 Release the lamp from its retaining clips and tangs, the latter by prising up with a screwdriver (photo).

Rear lamp

10 Remove the bulb holder as described in Section 22.

11 Remove the lamp retaining nuts (cars, vans) or the screws (Estates) and remove the lamp assembly from the body.

All lamps

12 Refitting is a reversal of removal for all lamp assemblies. Check headlight alignment if necessary.

25 Headlamps, auxiliary lamps and foglamps – beam alignment

1 It is recommended that this work is left to your dealer who will have the necessary equipment to align the lamp beams accurately.

2 In an emergency however, an acceptable result can be obtained by carrying out the following operations.

3 Have the vehicle on level ground, parked head-on to a wall or screen, and normally laden. Check that the tyre pressures are correct and the front of the vehicle is 10 m (33 ft) from the wall.

4 Unless a darkened building is available, the work will have to be done during the hours of darkness.

5 Mark on the wall or screen two crosses in the places indicated in Fig. 13.136 in Chapter 13.

6 Switch on the lamps (headlamps on dipped beam) and adjust the lamps until the brightest spots coincide with the crosses on the wall.

26 Auxiliary warning system – description

1 This is fitted to certain models in the new Escort range and is basically a means of warning the driver through an indicator lamp that

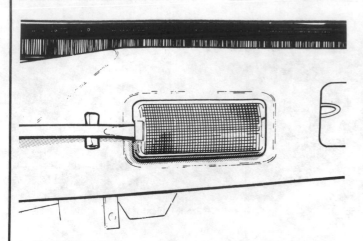

Fig. 11.80 Removing luggage compartment lamp (Sec 23)

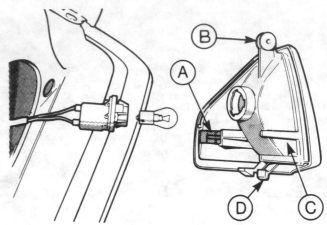

Fig. 11.81 Front direction indicator lamp removed (Sec 24)

A Spring clip   C Support bracket slide
B Tapped fixing   D Lamp base support

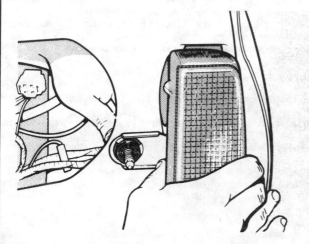

Fig. 11.82 Headlamp lower adjuster

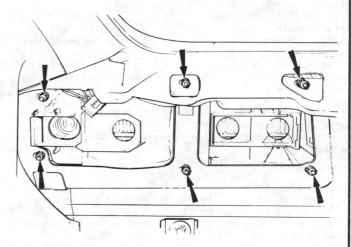

Fig. 11.83 Rear lamp fixing nuts (car) (Sec 24)

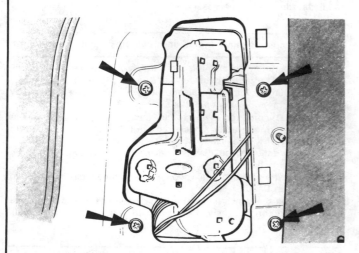

Fig. 11.84 Rear lamp fixing screws (Estate) (Sec 24)

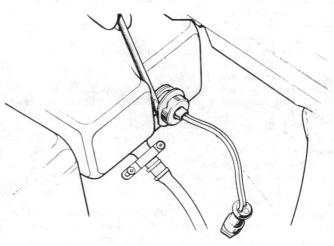

Fig. 11.85 Low coolant level switch (Sec 27)

a fluid level is low or the disc pad friction linings are worn.

2 When the ignition is first switched on, all warning lamps will illuminate as a means of verifying that all bulbs are working. This illumination period is of five seconds duration.

3 The system embraces the following components:

Fuel low level warning lamp. Activated by a sensor in the fuel level transmitter when the quantity of fuel in the tank falls below 7.0 litres (1.5 gallons).

Coolant low level warning lamp. Activated by a float-operated reed switch mounted in the expansion vessel.

Washer fluid low level warning lamp. A similar device to the coolant switch, it activates when the fluid is down to about 25% of capacity.

Engine oil low level warning lamp. Activated by a dipstick whose resistance increases when its marked lower section is not immersed in oil.

Brake pad wear indicator. The sensing of worn disc pads is carried out by an electrode built into the pad. When the friction material has worn down to about 2 mm (0.079 in) thick, the electrodes contact the brake disc and complete the warning lamp circuit.

27 Auxiliary warning system – removal and refitting of components

1 To remove the low coolant level and washer fluid switches, drain the containers and lever the switches out of their sealing grommets with a screwdriver.

2 To remove the indicator control assembly, first disconnect the battery.

3 Remove the speaker and grille as described in Section 53.

4 Disconnect the multi-plug from the warning indicator control assembly and then remove the two nylon fixing nuts which hold the assembly in position on the dash panel.

5 Take great care not to drop or knock the assembly, or its micro electronic circuit could be damaged.

6 Refitting is a reversal of removal.

28 Instrument cluster glass – removal and refitting

1 Remove the instrument cluster bezel by extracting the two retaining screws and pulling the bezel from its lower clips.

2 Extract the six glass securing screws.

3 Refitting is a reversal of removal.

29 Instrument cluster – removal and refitting

1 Disconnect the battery.

2 Extract the screws and pull the instrument panel bezel from the panel. The two clips at the base of the bezel will release by the pulling action (photos).

3 Extract the two screws which hold the cluster to the facia panel (photo).

4 Remove the dash under-trim panel, reach up and disconnect the cable from the speedometer by depressing the serrated plastic ring (photo).

5 Gently pull the cluster forwards and to one side so that the wiring multi-plug can be disconnected. Withdraw the cluster (photo).

6 Refitting is a reversal of removal.

30 Instrument cluster printed circuit – removal and refitting

1 Remove the instrument cluster as described in the preceding Section.

2 Place the cluster face downwards on a clean bench and remove all the bulb holders and multi-plug retainers (photo).

29.2A Extracting instrument cluster bezel screw

29.2B Removing instrument cluster bezel

29.3 Extracting instrument cluster screw

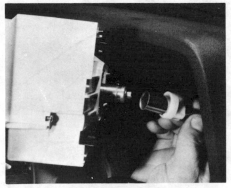
29.4 Disconnecting speedometer drive cable

29.5 Speedometer cable and multi-pin plug disconnected from instrument panel

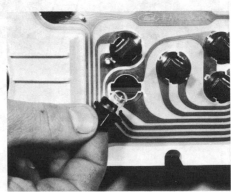
30.2 Instrument cluster bulb holder

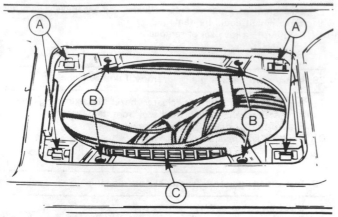

Fig. 11.86 Loudspeaker fixings (A,B) and auxiliary warning system control assembly (C) (Sec 27)

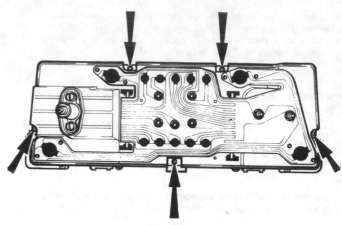

Fig. 11.87 Instrument cluster halves retaining screws (arrowed) (Sec 32)

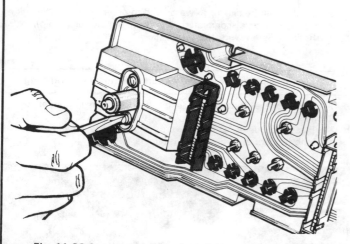

Fig. 11.88 Speedometer head retaining screws (Sec 32)

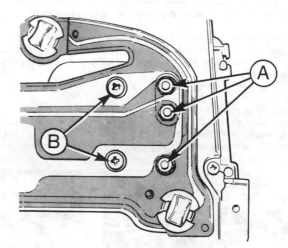

Fig. 11.89 Tachometer fixing screws (B) and terminal nuts (A) (Sec 33)

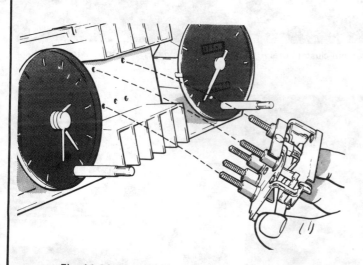

Fig. 11.90 Fuel and temperature gauge (Sec 34)

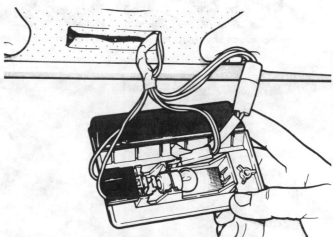

Fig. 11.91 Removing roof-mounted clock (Sec 36)

3 Remove the terminal nuts and washers.
4 Very carefully prise the printed circuit from its fixing pegs and remove it.
5 Refitting is a reversal of removal.

31 Speedometer cable – removal and refitting

1 Disconnect the battery and remove the instrument cluster as described in Section 29.
2 Disconnect the cable from the transmission and release it from its clips and grommet.
3 Withdraw the cable through the bulkhead.
4 Refitting is a reversal of removal. The inner and outer cables are supplied as a complete assembly.

32 Speedometer – removal and refitting

1 Remove the instrument cluster as described in Section 29.
2 Split the cluster by extracting the securing screws.
3 Remove the speedometer fixing screws and remove the unit.
4 Refit by reversing the removal operations.

33 Tachometer – removal and refitting

The operations are very similar to those described for the speedometer in the preceding Section.

34 Fuel and temperature gauges – removal and refitting

1 Access to these instruments is obtained in a similar way to that described for the speedometer (Section 32).
2 Remove the five fixing nuts and withdraw the fuel gauge, temperature gauge and voltage stabiliser as an assembly. The individual components cannot be obtained separately. Refit by reversing the removal operations.

35 Clock (facia-mounted) – removal and refitting

1 Disconnect the battery.
2 Remove the instrument cluster (Section 29).
3 Separate the cluster as previously described.
4 Unscrew the two fixing nuts and remove the clock.
5 Refit by reversing the removal operations.
6 The clock can be adjusted by depressing the button and turning the hands.

36 Clock (roof-mounted, digital) – removal and refitting

1 Disconnect the battery.
2 Extract the two screws which hold the clock to the header panel.
3 Disconnect the clock and courtesy lamp wiring plug.
4 Detach the lamp from the clock.
5 Refit by reversing the removal operations. Once the battery is reconnected, the time must be set in the following way.
6 Turn the ignition key to position II. The clock will indicate a random time and the colon will be flashing at one second intervals to prove that the clock is running.
7 Using a ballpoint pen or similar, gently depress the upper recessed button. For each depression of the button, the clock will advance one hour.
8 If the clock indicates am instead of pm advance the clock through a full twelve hours.
9 To regulate the minutes, depress the lower recessed button. For each depression, the clock will advance one minute.
10 The colon will now be static and the set time will not advance until the stop/start button is depressed. This is a feature of great advantage when setting the clock accurately to a radio time check. Once the clock has started, the colon will flash.
11 To set the calendar function, again turn the ignition key to position II. Depress the function control once. The clock will now indicate a random date. Continue adjustment within four seconds of having depressed the function button.
12 Using a ballpoint pen or similar, depress the upper recessed button.
13 For each successive depression of the button the clock calendar will advance one day.
14 Once the correct day is obtained move the ballpoint pen to the lower recessed button and depress to obtain the correct month.
15 The clock automatically compensates for months of varying numbers of days.

37 Horn – removal and refitting

1 Disconnect the battery.
2 Disconnect the lead from the horn.
3 Unscrew the single bolt and remove the horn and bracket.
4 Refitting is a reversal of removal.

38 Windshield/tailgate wiper blades and arms – removal and refitting

1 Pull the wiper arm away from the glass until the arm locks.
2 Depress the small clip on the blade and slide the blade out of the hooked part of the arm.

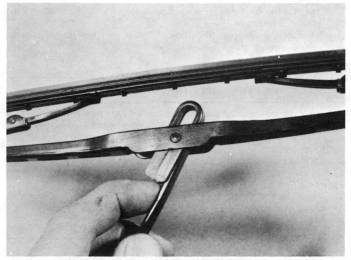
38.2 Disconnecting wiper blade from arm

38.3 Unscrewing wiper arm nut

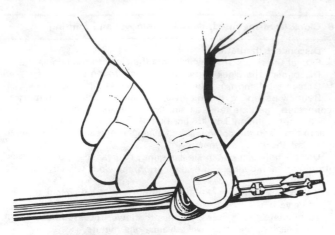

Fig. 11.92 Pushing back wiper blade rubber (Sec 39)

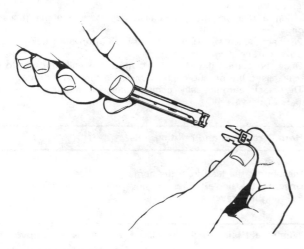

Fig. 11.93 Refitting wiper blade rubber insert clip (Sec 39)

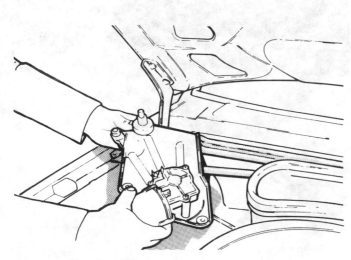

Fig. 11.94 Withdrawing windscreen wiper motor (Sec 40)

3   Before removing the wiper arms it is worthwhile marking their parked position on the glass with a strip of masking tape as an aid to refitting. Raise the plastic nut cover (photo).
4   Unscrew the nut which holds the arm to the pivot shaft and pull the arm from the shaft splines.
5   Refit by reversing the removal operations.

39 Wiper blade rubber – renewal

1   Remove the wiper blade as described in the preceding Section.
2   Using the thumb, draw back the rubber insert until the spring clip can be removed.
3   Slide the rubber insert from the blade.
4   Refit by reversing the removal operations.

40 Windscreen wiper motor and linkage – removal and refitting

1   Remove the wiper arms and blades as previously described.
2   Disconnect the battery.
3   Remove the nut covers, the fixing nuts, washers and spacers from the pivot shafts.
4   Disconnect the wiper motor wiring at the multi-pin plugs.
5   Unscrew the two fixing bolts and withdraw the motor complete with linkage from the engine compartment (photo).
6   Remove the spacers from the pivot shafts.
7   The motor can be separated from the linkage by removing the nut from the crankarm and then unbolting the motor from the mounting.
8   Refitting is a reversal of removal, but connect the motor crankarm when the link is aligned with it as shown in Fig. 11.95.

41 Tailgate wiper motor – removal and refitting

1   Disconnect the battery and remove the wiper arm/blade assembly.
2   Remove the pivot shaft nut, spacer and outer seals.
3   Open the tailgate and remove the trim panel (refer to Chapter 12).
4   Release the earth lead and unscrew the two wiper motor mounting bolts.
5   Disconnect the multi-pin plug and remove the motor from the tailgate.
6   Take off the pivot shaft seal, spacer and bracket from the motor.
7   Refit by reversing the removal operations.

42 Windscreen washer pump – removal and refitting

1   Drain the washer fluid container.
2   Disconnect the lead and washer pipe.
3   Ease the top of the washer pump away from the fluid container and remove it (photo).
4   Refitting is a reversal of removal; check that the pump sealing grommet is a good fit.

43 Windscreen washer jets – removal and refitting

1   Open the bonnet and disconnect the washer pipe from the jet.
2   If the pipe stub on the jet assembly is now pushed to one side, the jet retaining tang will be released and the jet can be removed from the bonnet grille slots.
3   Refit by reversing the removal operations. The end of the plastic washer pipe should be warmed in very hot water to make it easier to push onto the jet pipe stub and so avoid breaking it.
4   Adjustment of the jet spray pattern can be done using a pin in the jet nozzle.

44 Tailgate washer pump (car) – removal and refitting

1   Remove the load space trim panel as described in Chapter 12.
2   Disconnect the pump leads at the multi-plug.

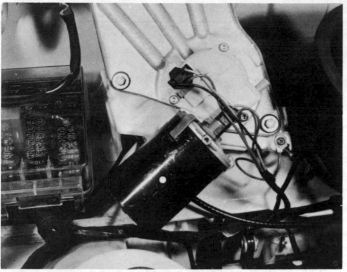

40.5 Wiper motor and gear within engine compartment

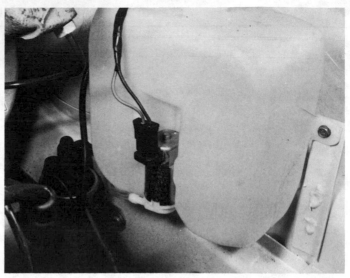

42.3 Windscreen washer fluid reservoir and pump

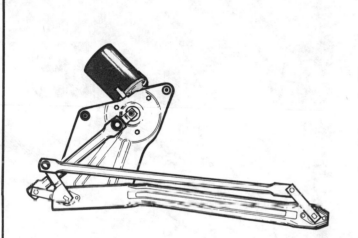

Fig. 11.95 Wiper motor crankarm alignment for refitting (Sec 40)

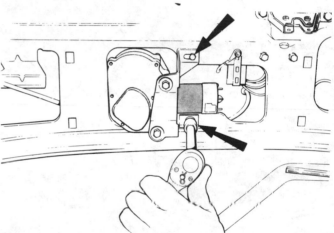

Fig. 11.96 Tailgate wiper motor mounting bolts (arrowed) (Sec 41)

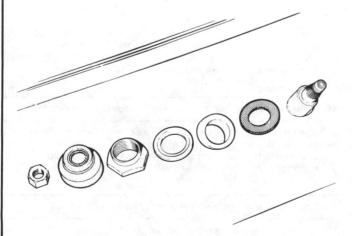

Fig. 11.97 Tailgate wiper pivot components (Sec 41)

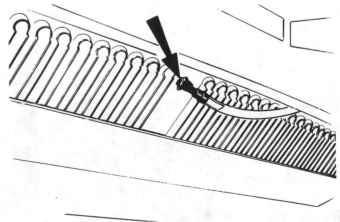

Fig. 11.98 Windscreen washer jet (arrowed) at bonnet grille (Sec 43)

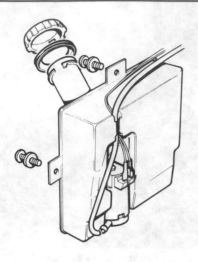

Fig. 11.99 Tailgate washer reservoir and pump (car) (Sec 44)

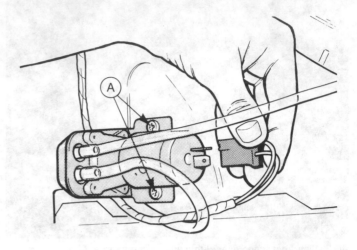

Fig. 11.100 Tailgate washer pump retaining screws (A) (Estate)
(Sec 45)

Fig. 11.101 Draining headlamp washer fluid reservoir (Sec 46)

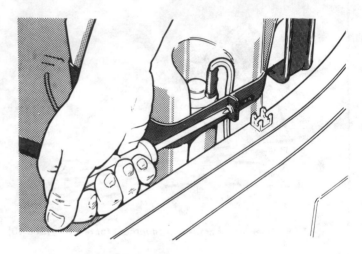

Fig. 11.102 Washer fluid reservoir clamp screw (Sec 46)

Fig. 11.103 Removing headlamp washer pump (Sec 46)

3   Unscrew the three reservoir mounting screws, and remove the reservoir until the fluid pipe can be pulled from the pump.
4   With the reservoir removed, pull the pump from its reservoir seal.
5   Refit by reversing the removal operations.

45 Tailgate washer pump (Estate) – removal and refitting

1   Open the tailgate, raise the spare wheel cover and disconnect the electrical leads and fluid pipe from the pump.
2   Extract the two securing screws and remove the pump.
3   Refitting is a reversal of removal.

46 Headlamp washer pump – removal and refitting

1   Drain the washer reservoir by syphoning, and disconnect the electrical leads from the pump.
2   Disconnect the fluid pipe from the pump.
3   Release the reservoir clamp screw.
4   Ease the top of the pump from the reservoir and remove it upwards.
5   Refitting is a reversal of removal.

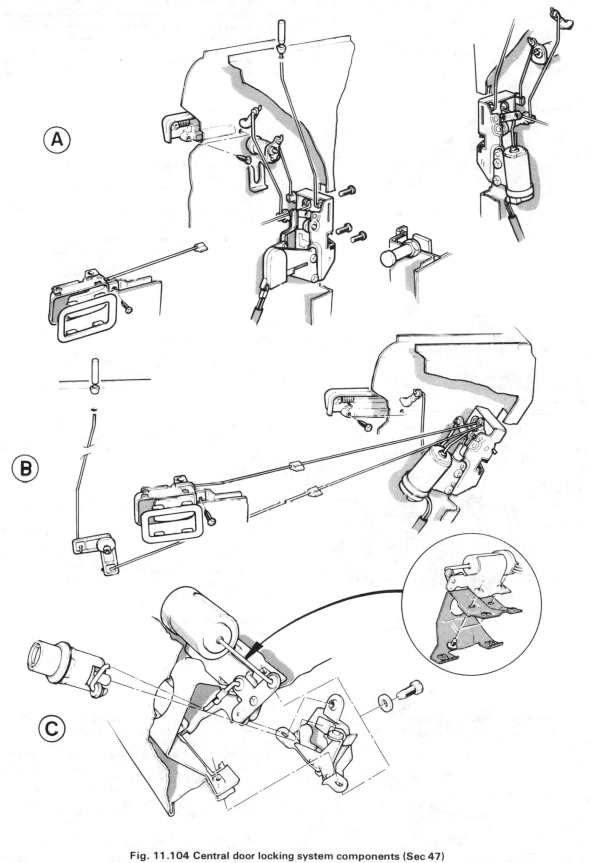

Fig. 11.104 Central door locking system components (Sec 47)

A   Front door components   C   Tailgate components
B   Rear door components

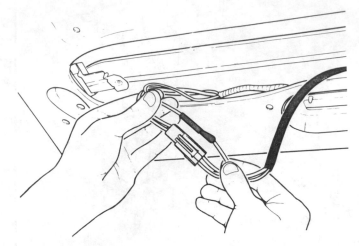

Fig. 11.105 Door lock switch connections (Sec 48)

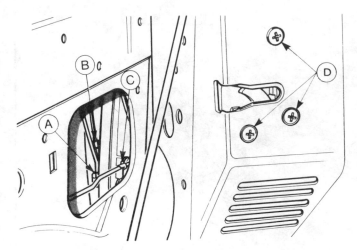

Fig. 11.106 Door locking rod attachment (Sec 48)

A   Clip   C   Clip
B   Clip   D   Lock retaining screws

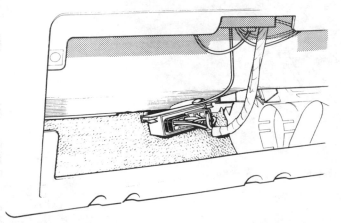

Fig. 11.107 Solenoid relay (central door locking) (Sec 48)

47 Central door locking system – description

1   This system is available as an option on certain models.
2   The system allows all door locks and the tailgate lock to be operated by the driver by turning the key or using the door lock plunger inside the vehicle.
3   The door locks, with the exception of the one on the driver's door, are actuated by solenoids.
4   An overload circuit breaker is located in the fuse box to protect the system.

48 Central door locking system components – removal and refitting

Switch
1   Raise the driver's door lock fully.
2   Disconnect the battery.
3   Remove the door trim panel (Chapter 12).
4   Disconnect the wiring plugs inside the door cavity and release the wires from their clips.
5   Release the lock control rods and remove the lock fixing screws.
6   Remove the lock from the door interior by guiding it round the glass guide channel.
7   Extract the two screws and remove the switch from the lock.

Solenoid control relay
8   Disconnect the battery.
9   Remove the under-facia trim panel from the passenger side.
10   Pull the relay from its securing clips.
11   Disconnect the multi-plug and remove the relay.

Solenoid (rear door)
12   Disconnect the battery.
13   Remove the door trim panel (Chapter 12).
14   Remove the bellcrank and operating lever by extracting the securing screws.
15   Release the operating rod rubber insulators from the door and disconnect the wiring.
16   Extract the lock securing screws, push the lock into the door cavity and then withdraw the lock with operating rods through the cut-out in the door panel.
17   Extract the screws and disconnect the solenoid from the lock.

Solenoid (front door)
18   Disconnect the battery.
19   Remove the door trim panel (Chapter 12).
20   Disconnect the lock operating rods and extract the three lock fixing screws.
21   Release the wiring from the clips, manoeuvre the lock round the door glass guide channel and remove it through the cut-out in the door panel.
22   Separate the solenoid from the lock after extracting the fixing screws.

Solenoid (tailgate)
23   Disconnect the battery.
24   Open the tailgate and remove the trim panel (Chapter 12).
25   Remove the lock rod clip and then prise out the clip which retains the lock cylinder. Remove the cylinder.
26   Slightly lower the tailgate and working through the lock cylinder hole, move the lock lever away from its spring until the lock engages.
27   Disconnect the solenoid wiring.
28   Extract the lock fixing bolts and remove the lock.
29   Insert a screwdriver through the aperture left by removal of the lock and unscrew the two solenoid fixing screws. Withdraw the solenoid.
30   Refitting of all components is a reversal of removal.

49 Electrically-operated windows – description

1   These can be installed as an option on certain models.
2   The electric motor drivegear engages directly with the window regulator mechanism.

3   When the ignition is switched on, power is supplied through a relay mounted in the fuse box.
4   When a control switch is actuated, the motor operates to lower or raise the window.
5   A circuit breaker type of overload protection is provided.

50 Electrically-operated window system – removal and refitting of components

Switch
1   Disconnect the battery.
2   Carefully lever the switch from the armrest and disconnect the multi-plug connector.
3   Refit by reversing the removal operations.

Motor
4   Lower the window fully on the door that is being dismantled.
5   Disconnect the battery.
6   Remove the door trim panel (Chapter 12).
7   Disconnect the motor wiring multi-plugs and retaining clips.
8   Remove the mounting screws from the motor and the regulator (three screws each).
9   Extract the retaining screw from the door glass channel. Detach the channel from the door and remove the door glass (see Chapter 12).
10 Grip the motor mounting plate in one hand and the regulator in the other. Raise the regulator and at the same time pull the motor towards the hinge end of the door.
11 Slowly twist the motor in a clockwise direction and at the same time fold the regulator over the top of the motor so that it comes to rest on the lock side of the door.
12 Rotate the motor mounting in an anti-clockwise direction until a corner of the mounting comes into view in the cut-out of the door.
13 Move the assembly so that this corner projects through the cut-out and then turn the whole assembly in a clockwise direction and guide it out of the cut-out.
14 Remove the two Allen screws from the regulator travel stop, and the single screw from the regulator gear guide.
15 Extract the circlip from the motor driveshaft and remove the drivegear.
16 Move the regulator to expose the motor mounting bolts. Extract the bolts and separate the motor from the regulator.
17 Reassembly and refitting are reversals of removal and dismantling.

51 In-vehicle entertainment equipment – general

1   The following Sections (52 to 55) cover radio/cassette player equipment fitted during production which is of Ford manufacture.
2   Where equipment is to be installed at a later date and is not necessarily of Ford make, refer to Section 56.

52 Radio – removal and refitting

1   Disconnect the battery.
2   Pull off the control knobs, the tuning knob spacer and the tone control lever. Remove the cover panel.
3   Extract the four fixing screws from the front of the radio.
4   Pull the radio far enough from the facia to be able to disconnect the aerial, power supply and earth leads and the speaker wires.
5   Unscrew the two nuts which hold the receiver to the mounting plate. Remove the mounting plate.
6   Take off the rear support bracket and locating plate.
7   Refitting is a reversal of removal.
8   Where a radio/cassette player is installed, the operations are identical.

53 Loudspeaker (facia-mounted) – removal and refitting

1   Carefully prise up the speaker grille using a small screwdriver. Lift it from the facia.

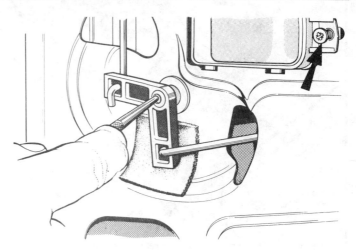

Fig. 11.108 Removing bellcrank securing screw (central door locking). Remote control handle screw is arrowed (Sec 48)

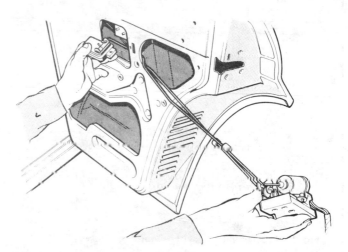

Fig. 11.109 Withdrawing door lock mechanism (central door locking) (Sec 48)

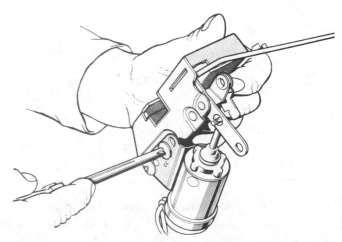

Fig. 11.110 Detaching solenoid from lock (central door locking) (Sec 48)

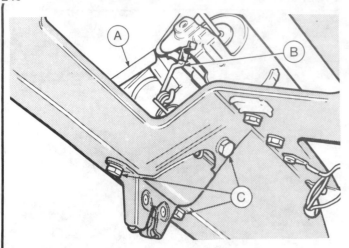

Fig. 11.111 Tailgate lock (central door locking) (Sec 48)

A   *Cylinder retaining clip*   C   *Lock retaining bolts*
B   *Lock rod clip*

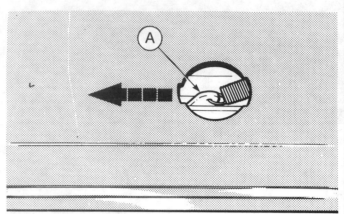

Fig. 11.112 Moving tailgate lock lever (A) to engage lock (Sec 48)

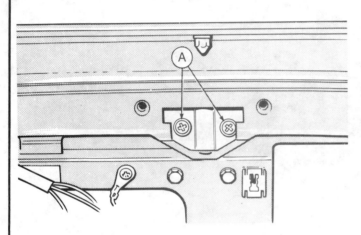

Fig. 11.113 Tailgate solenoid mounting screws (A) (Sec 48)

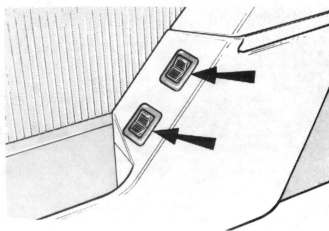

Fig. 11.114 Electric window switches (arrowed) (Sec 50)

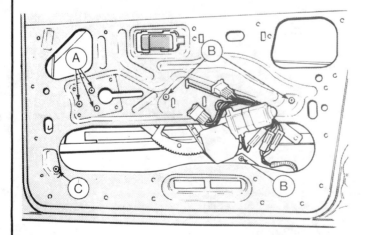

Fig. 11.115 Electric window winding mechanism (Sec 50)

A   *Regulator mounting screws*   C   *Glass channel fixing screw*
B   *Motor mounting screws*

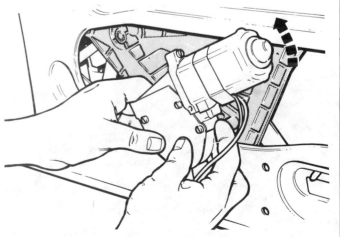

Fig. 11.116 Removing window motor/regulator (Sec 50)

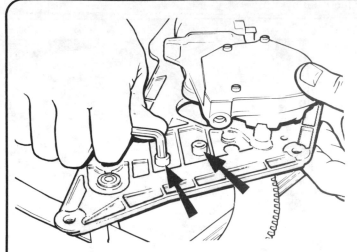

Fig. 11.117 Electric window regulator travel stop screws (arrowed) (Sec 50)

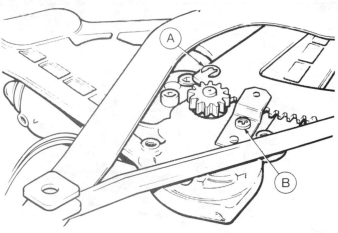

Fig. 11.118 Drivegear retaining circlip (electric window winder) (Sec 50)

A   Circlip   B   Gear guide retaining screw

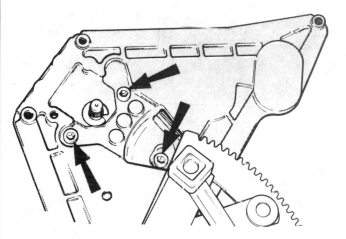

Fig. 11.119 Motor mounting bolts (arrowed) (electric window winder) (Sec 50)

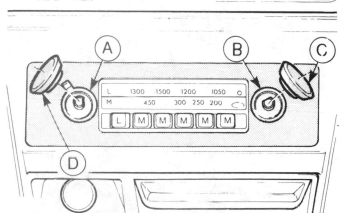

Fig. 11.120 Radio controls (Sec 52)

A   Tone lever   C   Tuning knob
B   Spacer   D   On/off knob

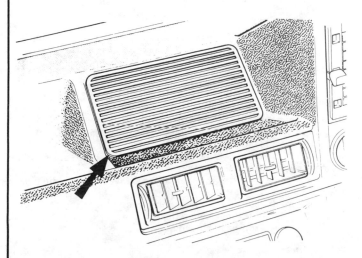

Fig. 11.121 Facia-mounted speaker grille. Prising position is arrowed (Sec 53)

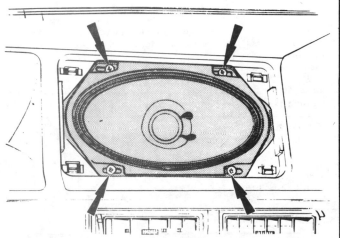

Fig. 11.122 Loudspeaker retaining screws (arrowed) (Sec 53)

Fig. 11.123 Cowl-mounted speaker grille clip (arrowed) (Sec 54)

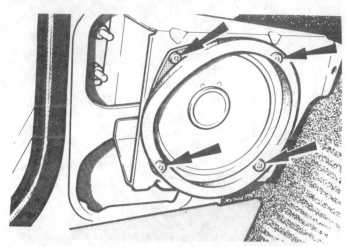

Fig. 11.124 Cowl-mounted speaker screws (arrowed) (Sec 54)

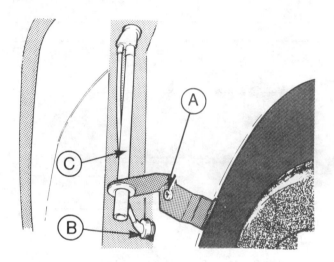

Fig. 11.125 Aerial lower mounting (Sec 55)

A   Bracket screw   C   Aerial tube
B   Grommet

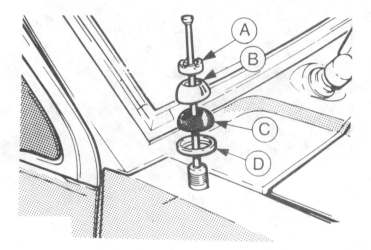

Fig. 11.126 Aerial wing mounting components (Sec 55)

A   Collar nut   C   Spacer
B   Bezel   D   Seal

2   Extract the speaker mounting screws which are now exposed.
3   Lift the speaker up until the connecting wires can be disconnected. The wires have different connecting terminals to prevent incorrect connections.
4   Refitting is a reversal of removal.

54 Loudspeaker (cowl panel mounted) – removal and refitting

1   Prise out the grille retaining clip.
2   Extract screws as necessary to be able to remove the cowl panel/grille.
3   Extract the four speaker mounting screws and withdraw the speaker until the leads can be disconnected at the rear of the speaker.
4   Refitting is a reversal of removal.

55 Aerial – removal and refitting

Manually-operated type

1   Withdraw the radio as described in Section 52 until the aerial lead can be pulled out of the receiver socket.
2   Working under the front wing, release the aerial inner wing bracket.

3   Prise out the grommet and pull the aerial lead through the hole in the inner wing.
4   Unscrew the aerial collar retaining nut.
5   Withdraw the aerial, spacers and seal.
6   Refitting is a reversal of removal.

Power-operated type

7   Carry out the operations described in paragraph 1.
8   Lower the bottom facia insulation panel and disconnect the red and white aerial feed cables.
9   Working under the front wing, extract the self-tapping screw which secures the aerial lower bracket.
10   Prise out the grommet and pull the aerial lead through the hole in the inner wing.
11   Unscrew the aerial upper retaining nut and lower the aerial from its location. Take off the seals and spacers.
12   Refitting is a reversal of removal.

All aerials

13   If a new aerial is being installed, it will have to be trimmed to the radio. To do this, tune in the receiver with maximum volume to a weak station near 1400 kHz (214 m) on the AM scale.
14   Insert a thin screwdriver into the trim screw hole provided in the receiver and turn the screw until maximum volume is obtained.

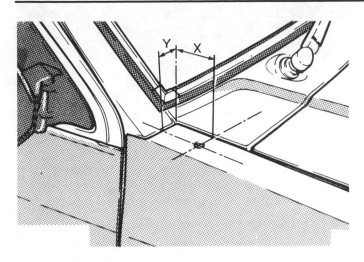

Fig. 11.127 Aerial wing mounting hole diagram (Sec 56)

X = 50 mm (1.97 in)   *Y = 18.5 mm (0.73 in)*

15 Make sure that the aerial mounting is making a good earth connection (bare metal with the body panel).

---

56 Radio equipment (non-standard) – installation

1   This Section covers briefly the installation of in-vehicle entertainment equipment purchased from non-Ford sources.

Radio/cassette player

2   It is recommended that a standard sized receiver is purchased and fitted into the location provided in the facia panel or centre console.
3   A fitting kit is normally supplied with the radio or cassette player.
4   Connections will be required as follows:

(a) Power supply, taken from the ignition switch so that the radio is only operational with the ignition key in position I or II. Always insert a 2A in-line fuse in the power lead

(b) Earth. The receiver must have a good clean earth connection to a metal part of the body

(c) Aerial lead. From an aerial which itself must be earthed. Avoid routing the cable through the engine compartment or near the ignition, wiper motor or flasher relay

(d) Loudspeaker connections, between speaker and receiver

5   Location of the aerial is a matter of choice. A roof-mounted or rear wing-mounted aerial usually provides the most interference-free reception but if a front wing position is preferred, mount the aerial as

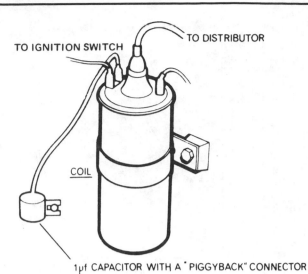

Fig. 11.128 Radio interference suppressor capacitor fitted to coil + terminal (Sec 56)

shown in Fig. 11.127. Cut the hole by drilling and filing or by means of a tank hole cutter. Paint the edges of the hole to prevent rusting.
6   If the radio is being installed for the first time, interference will almost certainly present a problem when the engine is running.
7   The ignition HT leads will have been suppressed during production, but a $1\mu F$ capacitor should be connected between the + terminal of the coil and the coil mounting bracket bolt.
8   Sometimes an in-line choke can be fitted into the power supply lead as close as possible to the radio to reduce interference.
9   The alternator often gives rise to a whine through the radio which can be eliminated by connecting a 1.0 to 3.0 μF capacitor between the large terminal (B+) on the alternator and earth.
10 Further interference suppression will be on a trial and error basis. Sometimes bonding straps should be connected between the bonnet and rear bulkhead.
11 Interference from electric motors, flasher units or front disc pads is usually not serious enough to suppress and can be tolerated.

---

57 Tailgate window element – general

1   The tailgate glass heater element is fixed to the interior surface of the glass. When cleaning the window use only water and a leather or soft cloth, and avoid scratching with rings on the fingers.
2   Avoid sticking labels over the element and packing luggage so that it can rub against the glass.
3   In the event of the element being damaged, it can be repaired using one of the special conductive paints now available.

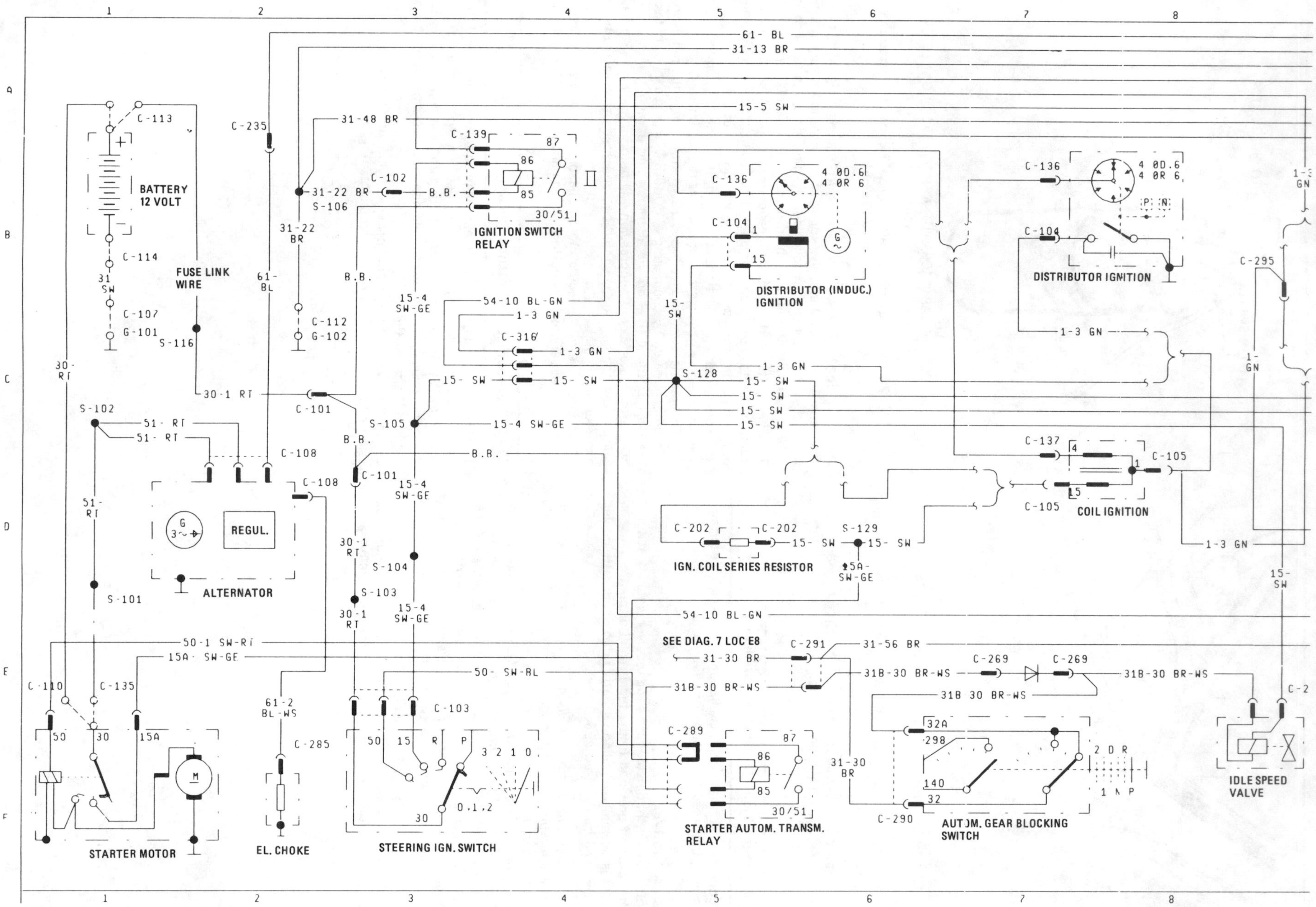

Fig. 11.129 Wiring diagram for starting and charging (diagram 1) (For key see page 259)

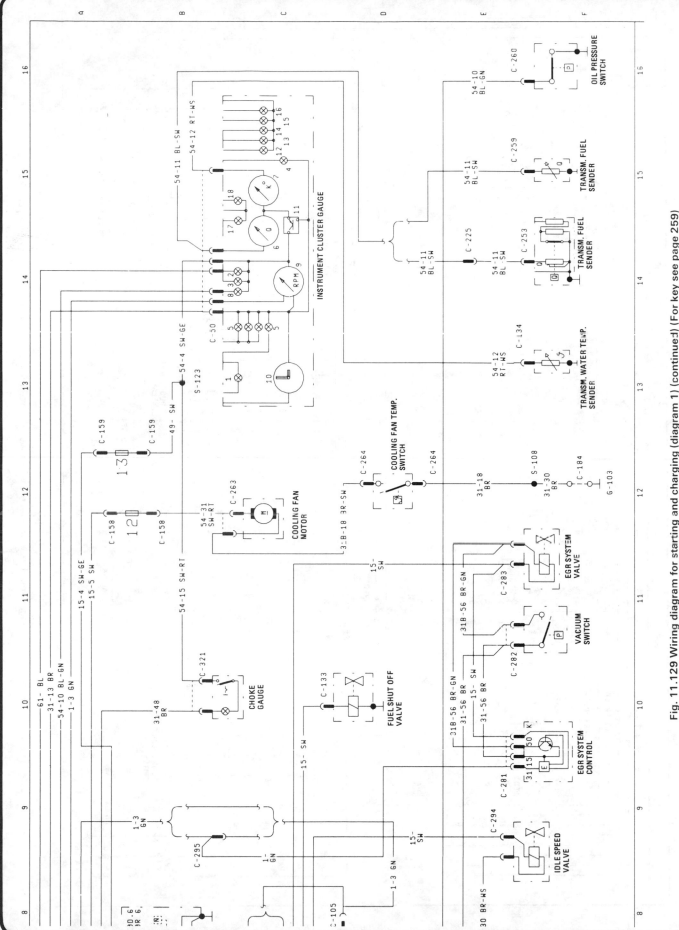

Fig. 11.129 Wiring diagram for starting and charging (diagram 1) (continued) (For key see page 259)

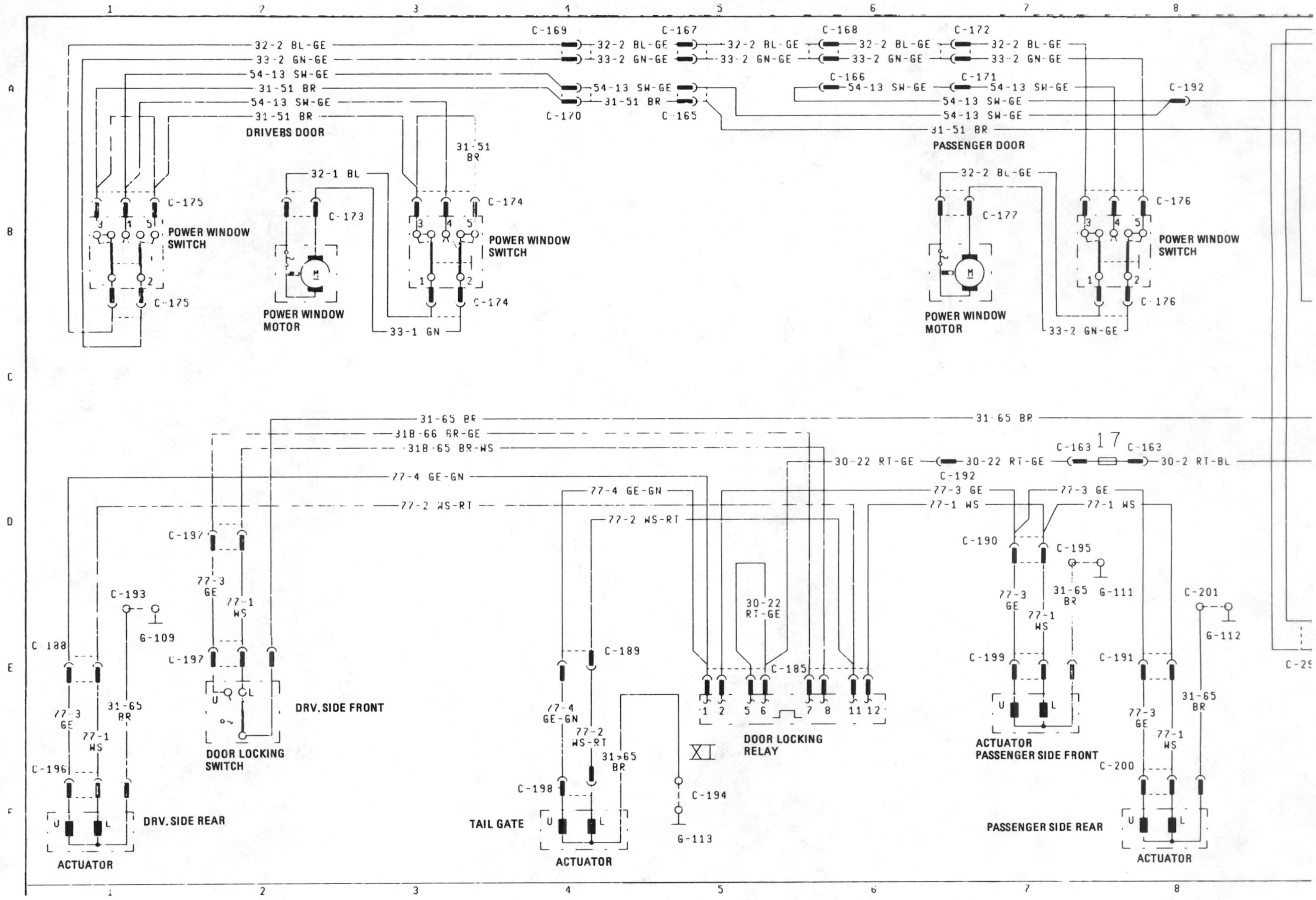

Fig. 11.130 Wiring diagram for central locking, electric windows and exterior lights (diagram 2) (For key see page 259)

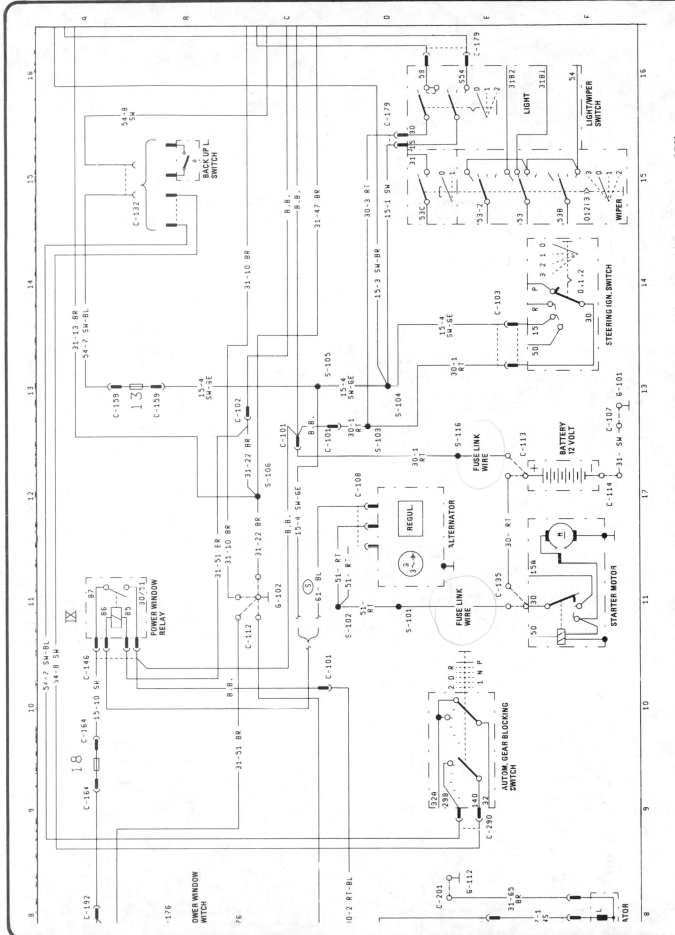

Fig. 11.130 Wiring diagram for central locking, electric windows and exterior lights (diagram 2) (continued) (For key see page 259)

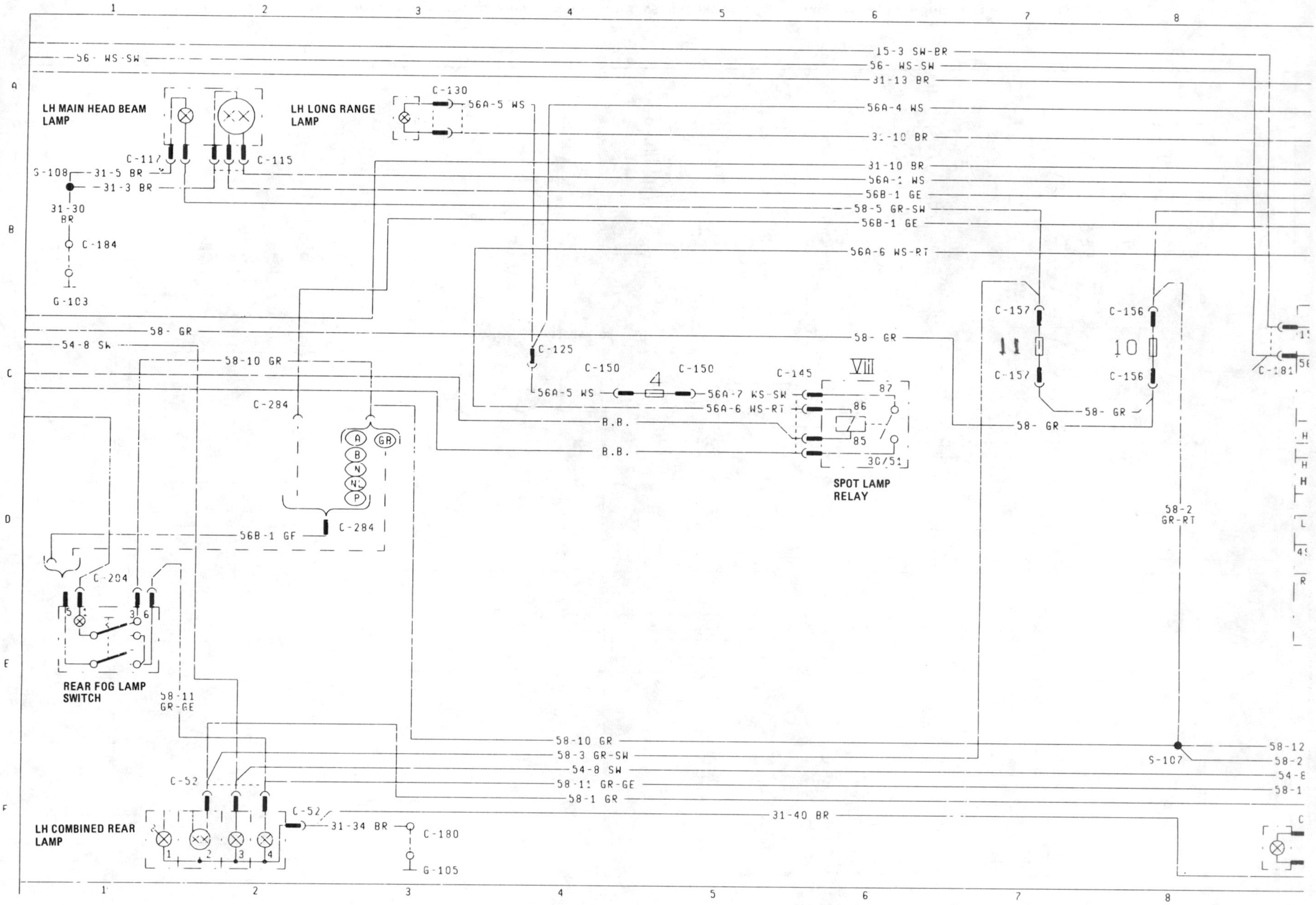

Fig. 11.131 Wiring diagram for exterior lights (diagram 3) (For key see page 259)

SPOT LAMP RELAY

LH LONG RANGE LAMP

LH MAIN HEAD BEAM LAMP

REAR FOG LAMP SWITCH

LH COMBINED REAR LAMP

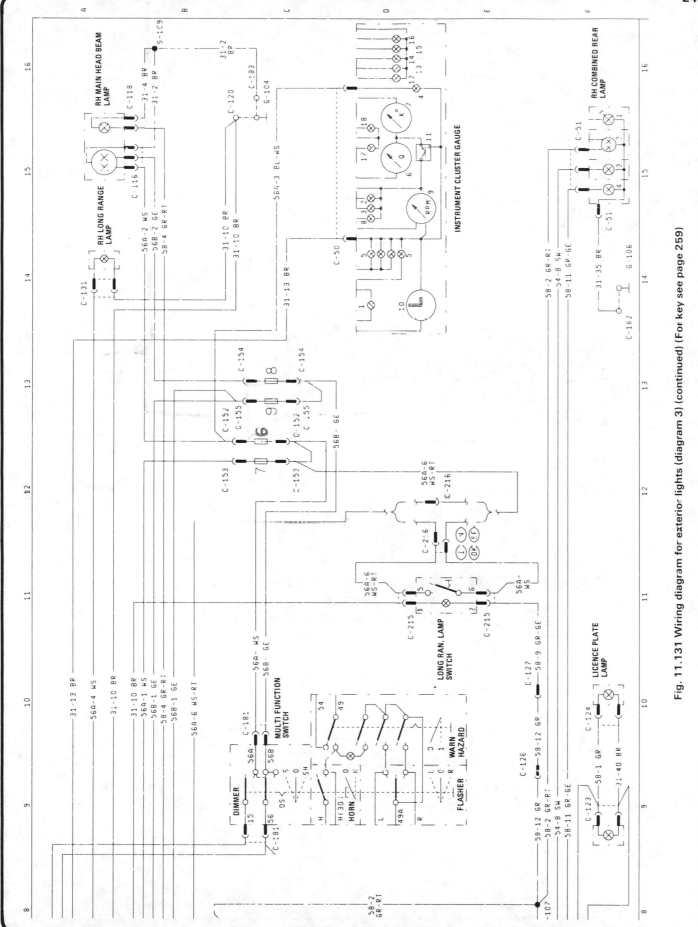

Fig. 11.131 Wiring diagram for exterior lights (diagram 3) (continued) (For key see page 259)

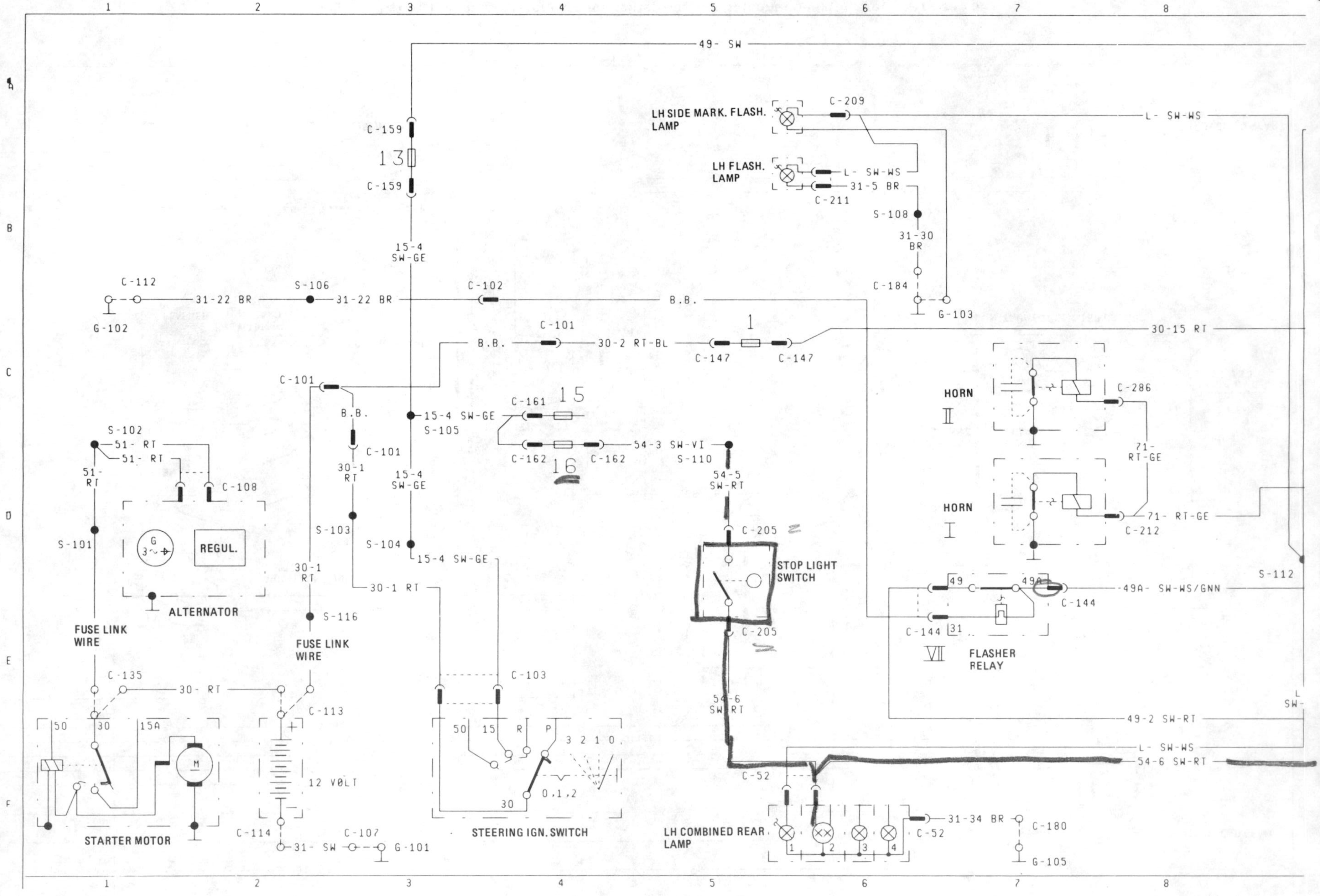

Fig. 11.132 Wiring diagram for indicating and warning systems (diagram 4) (For key see page 259)

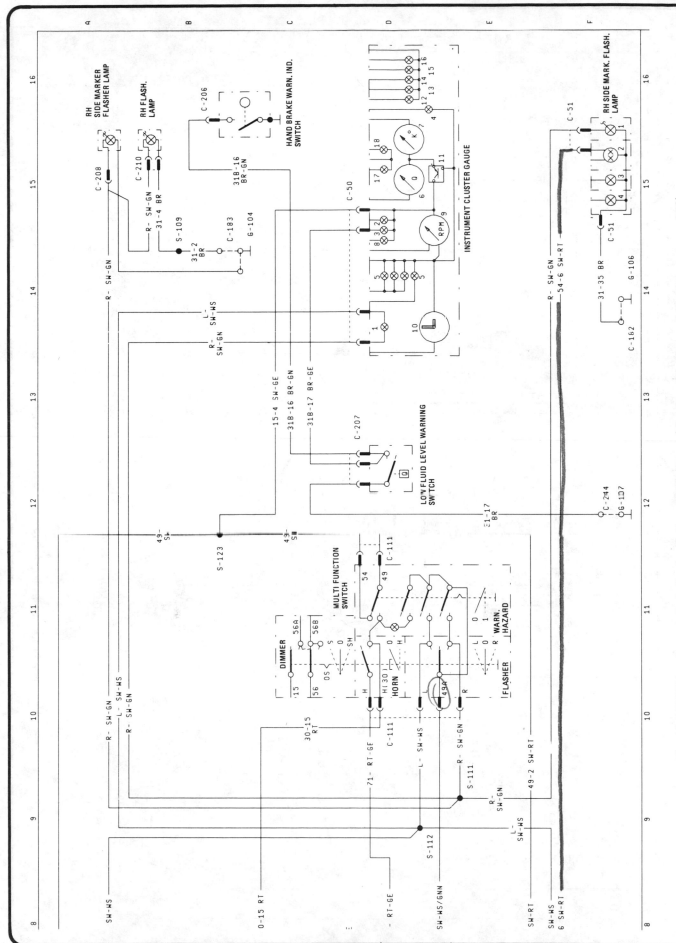

Fig. 11.132 Wiring diagram for indicating and warning systems (diagram 4) (continued) (For key see page 259)

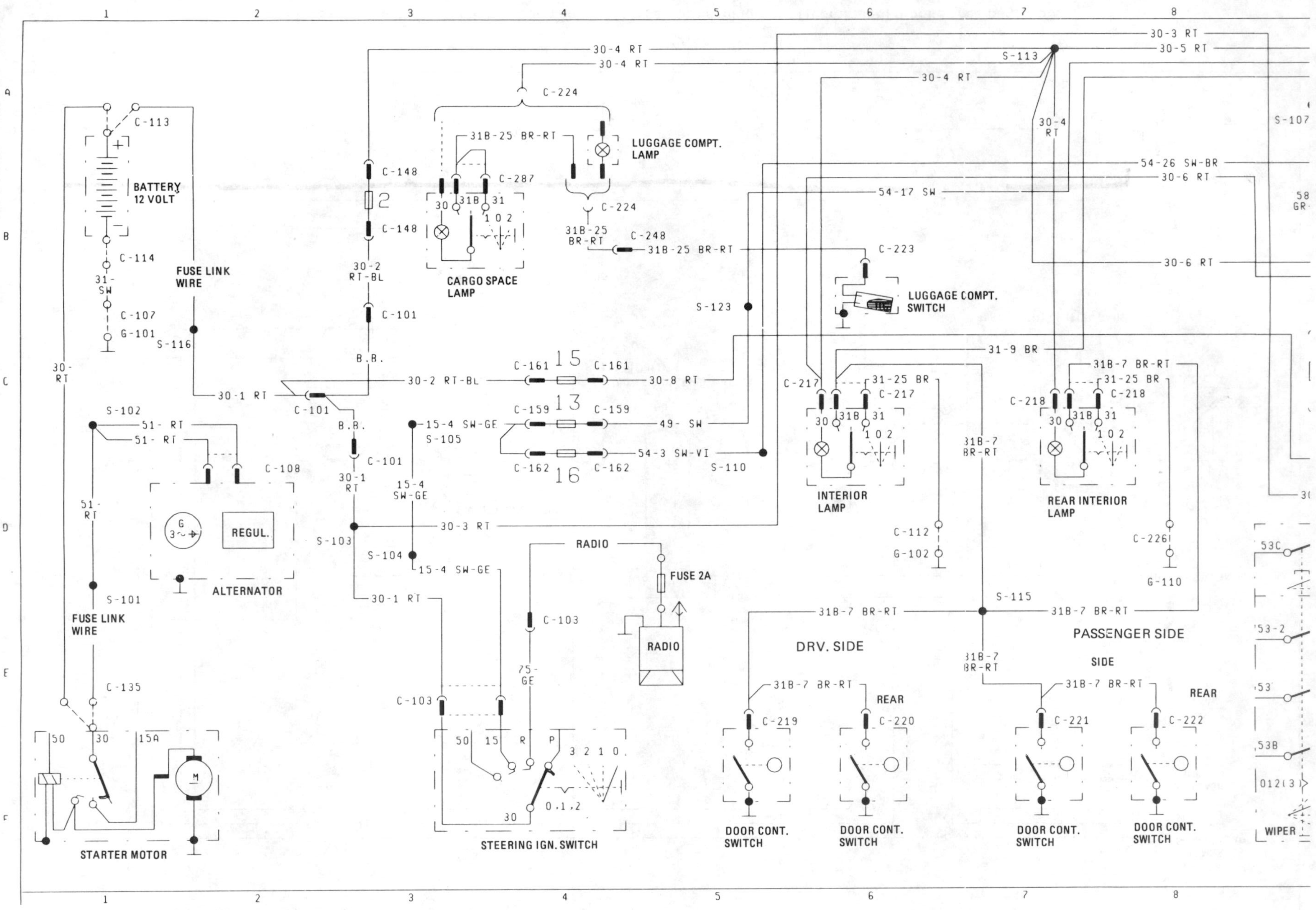

Fig. 11.133 Wiring diagram for interior lights and heated rear window (diagram 5) (For key see page 259)

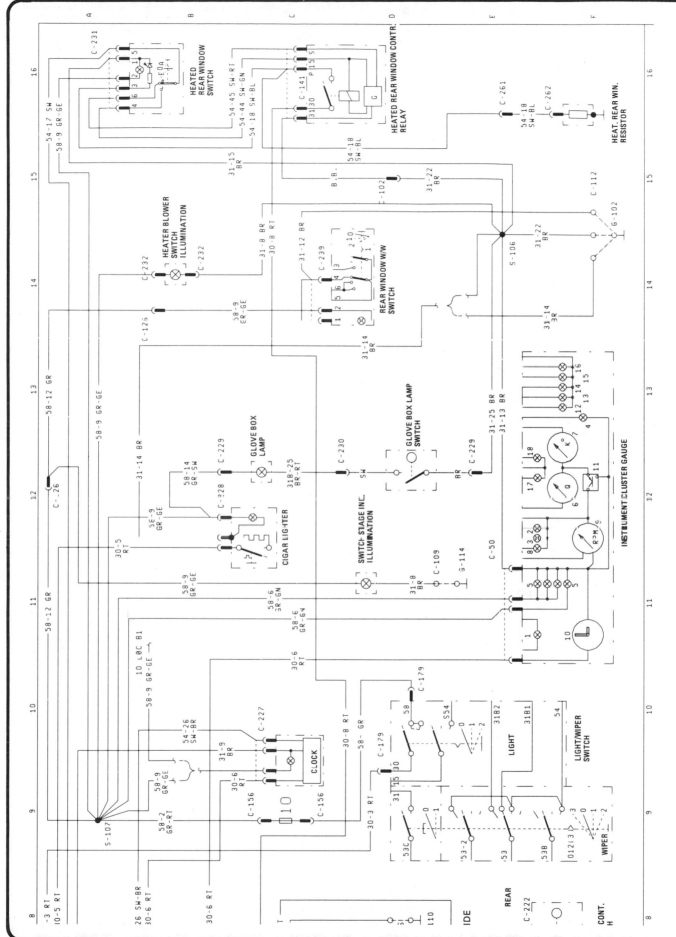

Fig. 11.133 Wiring diagram for interior lights and heated rear window (diagram 5) (cont'nued) (For key see page 259)

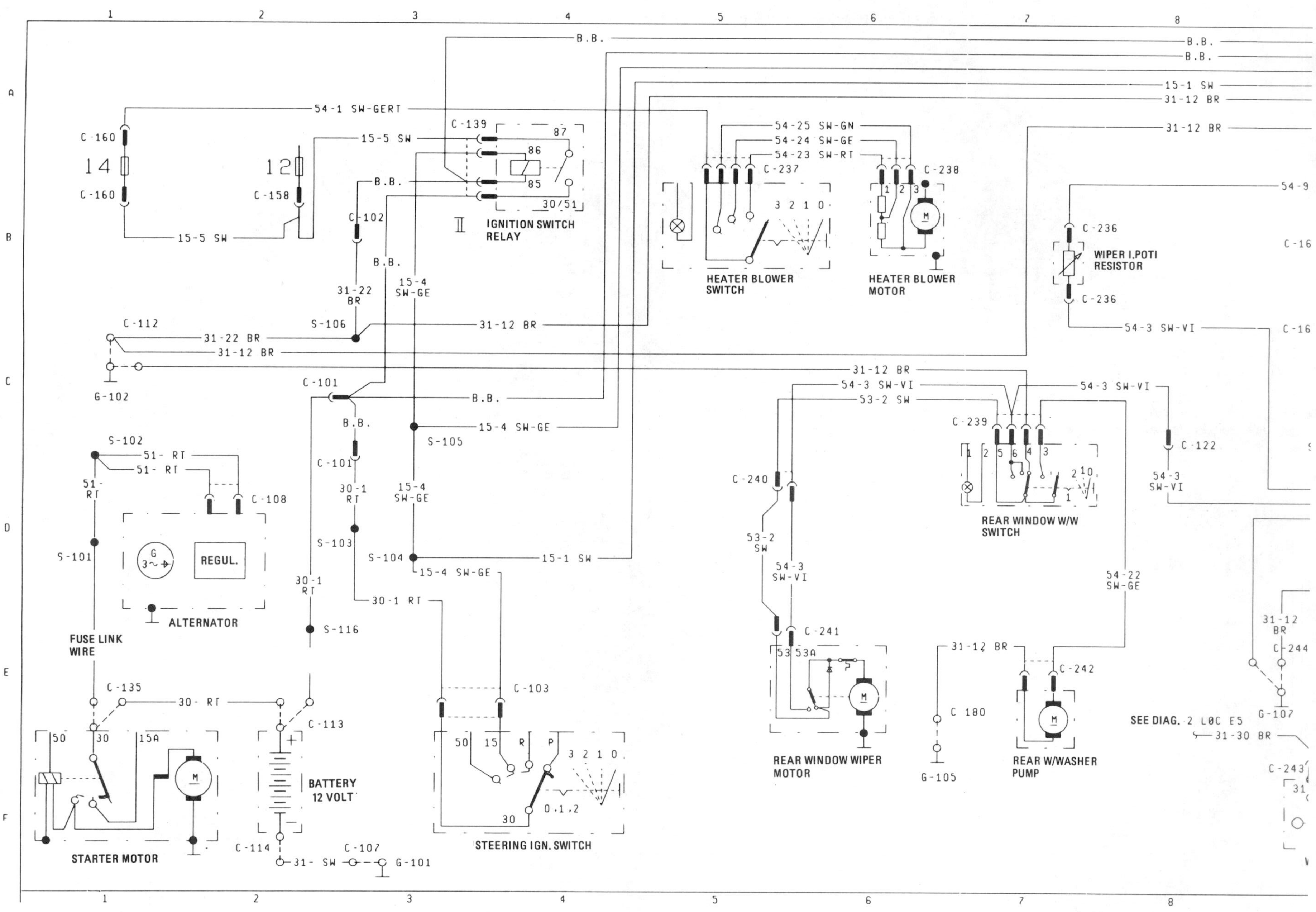

Fig. 11.134 Wiring diagram for heater fan and wash/wipe systems (diagram 6) (For key see page 259)

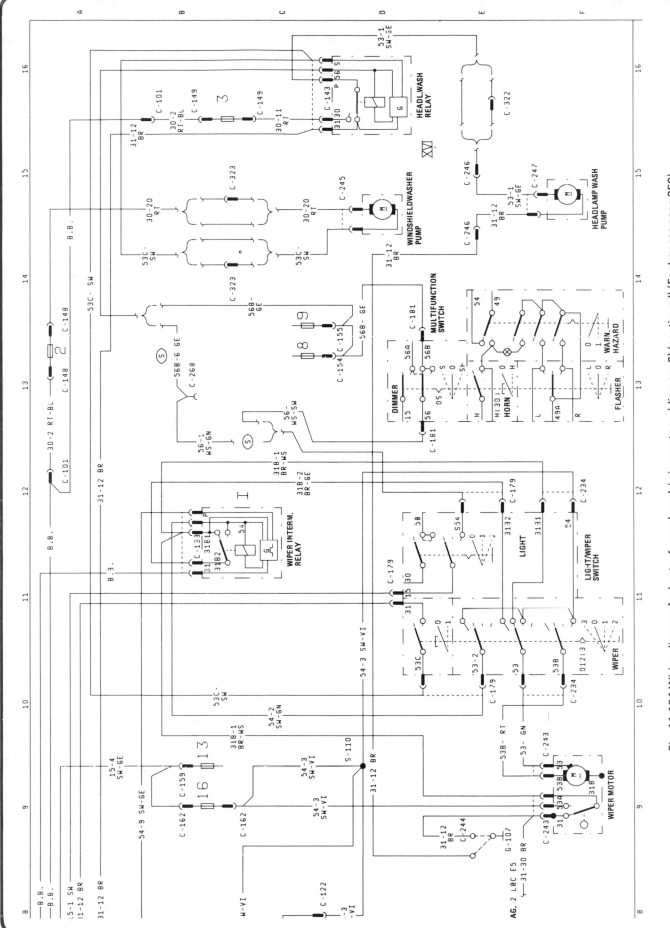

Fig. 11.134 Wiring diagram for heater fan and wash/wipe systems (diagram 6) (continued) (For key see page 259)

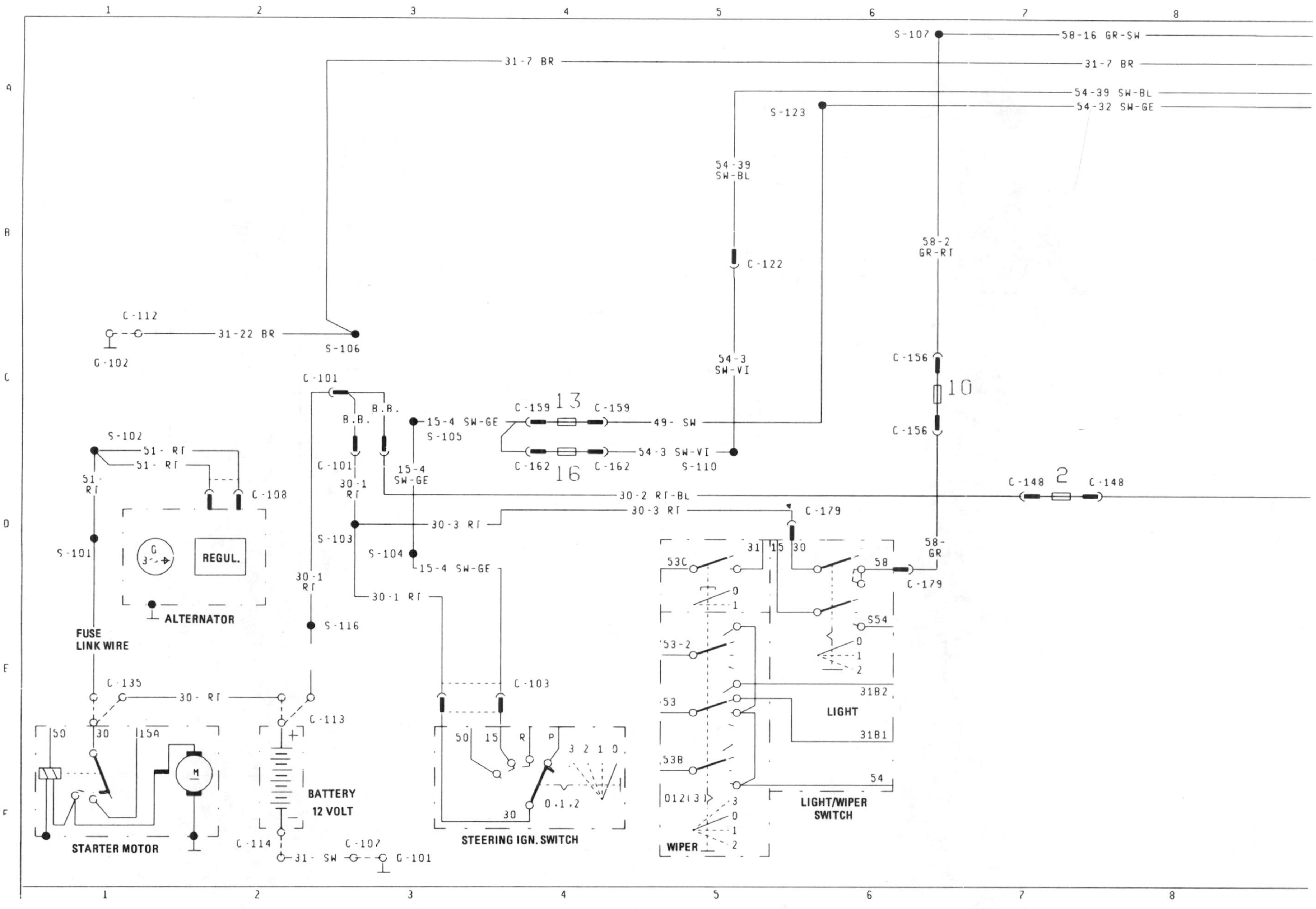

Fig. 11.135 Wiring diagram for auxiliary warning systems and Econo-lights (diagram 7) (For key see page 259)

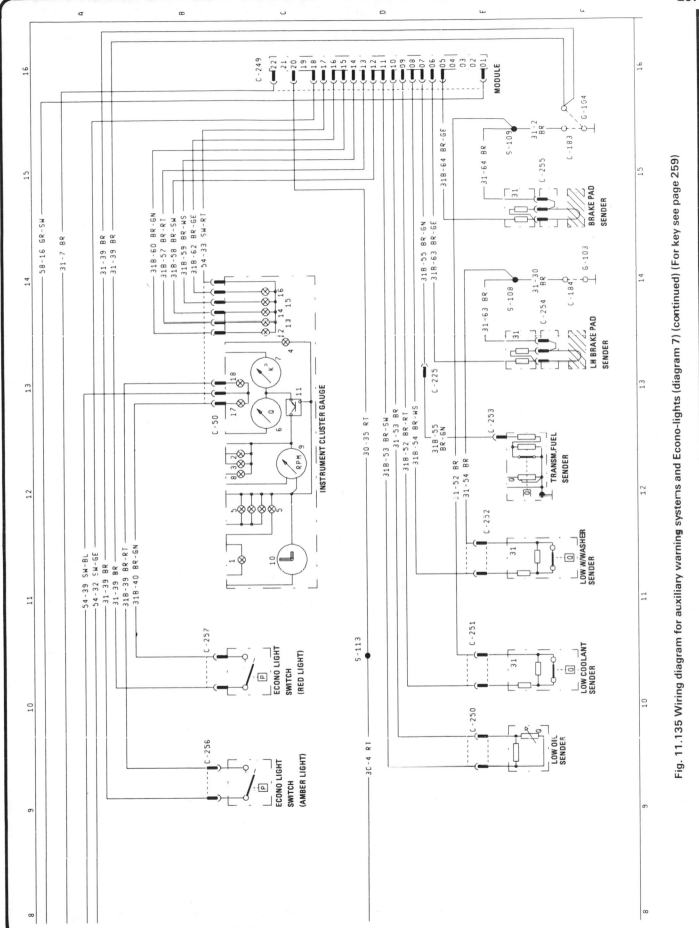

Fig. 11.135 Wiring diagram for auxiliary warning systems and Econo-lights (diagram 7) (continued) (For key see page 259)

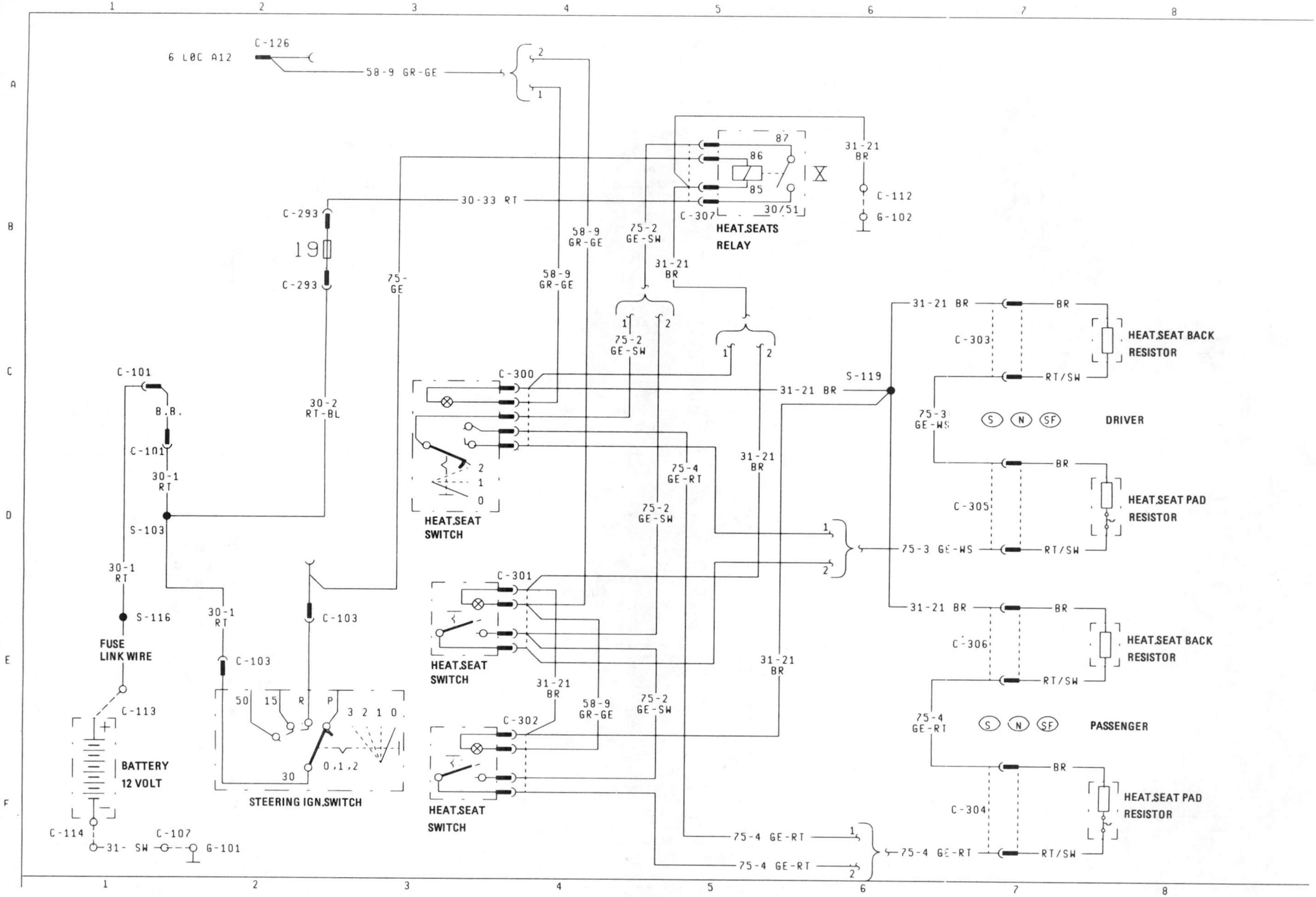

Fig. 11.136 Wiring diagram for heated rear seats (diagram 8) (For key see page 259)

Note that diagrams 9, 10 and 11 are in the Supplement

Wiring diagrams index

Note that diagrams 9, 10 and 11 are in the Supplement

Colour code

BL	Blue	GN	Green	RT	Red	VI	Violet
BR	Brown	GR	Grey	SW	Black	WS	White
GE	Yellow	RS	Pink				

58 Fault diagnosis – electrical system

Symptom	Reason(s)
Starter fails to turn engine	Battery discharged Battery defective internally Leads loose, or terminals corroded Loose connections at starter motor Engine earth strap loose, broken or missing Starter motor faulty or solenoid not functioning Starter motor brushes worn Commutator dirty or worn Starter motor armature faulty Field coils earthed
Starter turns engine very slowly	Battery in discharged condition Starter brushes badly worn, sticking or brush wires loose Loose wires in starter motor circuit
Starter spins but does not turn engine	Pinion or flywheel gear teeth broken or worn Battery discharged
Starter motor noisy or excessively rough engagement	Pinion or flywheel gear teeth broken or worn Starter motor retaining bolts loose
Battery will not hold charge for more than a few days	Battery defective internally Electrolyte level too low or electrolyte too weak due to leakage Plate separators no longer fully effective Battery plates severely sulphated Alternator drivebelt slipping Battery terminal connections loose or corroded Alternator not charging Short-circuit causing continual battery drain Integral regulator unit not working correctly
Ignition light fails to go out, battery runs flat in a few days	Alternator drivebelt loose and slipping or broken Alternator brushes worn, sticking, broken or dirty Alternator brush springs weak or broken Internal fault in alternator

Failure of individual electrical equipment to function correctly is dealt with under the headings listed below

Horn

Symptom	Reason(s)
Horn operates all the time	Horn push either earthed or stuck down Horn cable to horn push earthed
Horn fails to operate	Blown fuse Cable or cable connection loose, broken or disconnected Horn has an internal fault
Horn emits intermittent or unsatisfactory noise	Cable connections loose Horn incorrectly adjusted

Lights

Symptom	Reason(s)
Lights do not come on	If engine not running, battery discharged Wire connections loose, disconnected or broken Light switch shorting or otherwise faulty Light bulb filament burnt out or bulbs broken
Lights give very poor illumination	Lamp glasses dirty Lamps badly out of adjustment
Lights work erratically – flashing on and off, especially over bumps	Battery terminals or earth connection loose Lights not earthing properly Contacts in light switch faulty

Wipers

Symptom	Reason(s)
Wiper motor fails to work	Blown fuse Wire connections loose, disconnected or broken Brushed badly worn Armature worn or faulty Field coils faulty

Symptoms	Reason(s)
Wiper motor works very slowly and takes excessive current	Commutator dirty, greasy or burnt
	Armature bearings dirty or unaligned
	Armature badly worn or faulty
Wiper motor works slowly and takes little current	Brushes badly worn
	Commutator dirty, greasy or burnt
	Armature badly worn or faulty
Wiper motor works but wiper blades remain static	Wiper motor gearbox parts badly worn

Electrically operated windows

Glass will only move in one direction	Defective switch
Door glass slow to move	Stiff regulator or glass guide channels
Door glass will not move:	
With motor running	Binding glass guide channels
	Faulty regulator
Motor not running	Faulty relay
	Blown fuse
	Fault in motor
	Broken or disconnected wire

Central door locking system

Complete failure	Blown fuse
	Faulty master switch
	Faulty relay
	Broken or disconnected wire
Latch locks but will not unlock, or unlocks but will not lock	Faulty master switch
	Poor contact in pulse relay multi-plugs
	Faulty relay
One solenoid will not operate	Poor circuit connections
	Broken wire
	Faulty solenoid
	Binding bellcrank rod
	Binding driver's remote control lock button
	Fault in latch

Chapter 12 Bodywork

For modifications, and information applicable to later models, see Supplement at end of manual

Contents

Specifications

For details of sizes and weights, refer to the introductory sections of this manual.

Torque wrench setting

	Nm	lbf ft
All seat belt anchor bolts	35	26

1 Description

The body is of welded steel construction. The model range includes 3 and 5-door hatchbacks, a 3-door estate car and a van.

L, LG and Ghia versions are available, offering a difference in trim and equipment, and there is also an XR3 model which is the sports derivative and which has a rear spoiler, a tachometer and other items to differentiate it from other 1.6 Escorts.

The body is of monocoque construction and is of energy-absorbing design.

Rust and corrosion protection is applied to all new vehicles and includes zinc phosphate dipping and wax injection of box sections and door interiors.

All body panels are welded, including the front wings, so it is recommended that major body damage repairs are left to your dealer.

2 Bodywork – maintenance

1 Regular maintenance consists of a weekly wash with plenty of water. Apart from improving the appearance of the vehicle, washing removes abrasive dust and will prolong the life of the paintwork gloss finish.

2 Every six months or so, the application of a good quality wax polish will help to preserve the body finish and keep damp at bay.

3 If the vehicle is a year or two old, or you have just purchased a used model, it is worthwhile hosing and scrubbing under the wings to remove all deposits of mud. When the undersurface is clean and dry, inspect for damaged underseal or rust and make good as necessary. For a really good job it is worthwhile giving the complete underwing surfaces a fresh thick coat of underseal all over.

4 The treatment of the underbody, fuel tank and sills can be carried

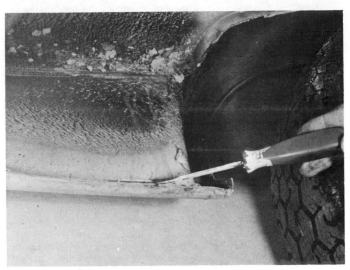

2.5A Clearing a sill drain

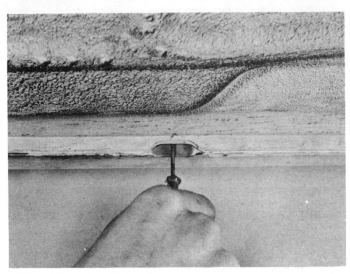

2.5B Clearing a door drain

out in a similar way, but wire brushing will probably be cleaner and more effective than attempting to wash off the undcrneath with water. If underscaling the complete underbody is too much like hard work, consider spraying with one of the wax-based coatings which are available.

5   Remember, rust often appears having worked its way outwards from a box section, a door interior or a double-skinned section. Keep the drain holes in sills and doors clear (photos), and spray out the sections also with anti-rust fluid or wax-based compound. Drill one or two holes if necessary to gain access for the spray gun. Fit sealing grommets on completion.

6   Always touch up chips in the paintwork immediately they are noticed. Even if the finishing paint is not available, a dab of anti-rust primer will prevent matters getting worse until the job can be done properly (see Section 4).

7   Finally, keep all catches, locks and controls regularly lubricated. The door hinges on these models are self-lubricating and do not require oiling.

3   Vehicle interior – maintenance

1   Regularly brush or vacuum clean the carpets and the luggage area.

2   The facia and instrument panel can be wiped free from dust using a damp cloth.

3   To clean fabric upholstery, careful vacuum cleaning should be sufficient, but if it becomes stained, use a proprietary cleaner strictly in accordance with the manufacturer's instructions and leave the windows open afterwards for it to dry.

4   To clean plastic upholstery, a sponge with detergent or certain types of hand cleaner are effective in removing ingrained dirt. Rub dry with a dry cloth after rinsing off.

5   The interior or exterior surfaces of the window glass are best cleaned with water and a leather, although drying with a crumpled newspaper is very effective. To remove greasy deposits from the glass, use a little ammonia in the water.

6   To prevent the glass from becoming scratched over a period of time, periodically wind the windows fully down and wipe along the contact edges of the inner and outer glass weatherseals. This will remove any accumulations of grit or dirt.

7   Discolouration of the headlining can be removed sometimes by gently wiping with a sponge or cloth soaked in washing up liquid. Rinse off afterwards.

4   Body damage – repair

The photographic sequences on pages 270 and 271 illustrate the operations detailed in the following sub-sections.

Minor damage

Small dents and scuffs are well within the ability of the home mechanic to repair (see below). Distorted or damaged doors, tailgate and bonnet, bumpers and grilles can be replaced with new components or ones in good condition which can often be obtained from a vehicle dismantler.

Refinishing to the vehicle colour will be required on completion as new body panels are supplied in primer.

Major damage

Where damage or corrosion has affected any welded or structural part of the vehicle, repair should be left to your dealer or a body builder having the necessary alignment jigs which are essential for safe and satisfactory repair of this range of Escorts.

Repair of minor scratches in the car's bodywork

If the scratch is very superficial, and does not penetrate to the metal of the bodywork, repair is very simple. Lightly rub the area of the scratch with a paintwork renovator, or a very fine cutting paste, to remove loose paint from the scratch and to clear the surrounding bodywork of wax polish. Rinse the area with clean water.

Apply touch-up paint to the scratch using a fine paint brush; continue to apply thin layers of paint until the surface of the paint in the scratch is level with the surrounding paintwork. Allow the new paint at least two weeks to harden: then blend it into the surrounding paintwork by rubbing with a paintwork renovator or a very fine cutting paste. Finally, apply wax polish.

Where the scratch has penetrated right through to the metal of the bodywork, causing the metal to rust, a different repair technique is required. Remove any loose rust from the bottom of the scratch with a penknife, then apply rust inhibiting paint to prevent the formation of rust in the future. Using a rubber or nylon applicator fill the scratch with bodystopper paste. If required, this paste can be mixed with cellulose thinners to provide a very thin paste which is ideal for filling narrow scratches. Before the stopper-paste in the scratch hardens, wrap a piece of smooth cotton rag around the top of a finger. Dip the finger in cellulose thinners and then quickly sweep it across the surface of the stopper-paste in the scratch; this will ensure that the surface of the stopper-paste is slightly hollowed. The scratch can now be painted over as described earlier in this Section.

Repair of dents in the car's bodywork

When deep denting of the vehicle's bodywork has taken place, the first task is to pull the dent out, until the affected bodywork almost attains its original shape. There is little point in trying to restore the original shape completely, as the metal in the damaged area will have stretched on impact and cannot be reshaped fully to its original contour. It is better to bring the level of the dent up to a point which is about $\frac{1}{8}$ in (3 mm) below the level of the surrounding bodywork. In cases where the dent is very shallow anyway, it is not worth trying to pull it out at all. If the underside of the dent is accessible, it can be hammered out gently from behind, using a mallet with a wooden or plastic head. Whilst doing this, hold a suitable block of wood firmly against the outside of the panel to absorb the impact from the hammer blows and thus prevent a large area of the bodywork from being 'belled-out'.

Should the dent be in a section of the bodywork which has double skin or some other factor making it inaccessible from behind, a different technique is called for. Drill several small holes through the metal inside the area – particularly in the deeper section. Then screw long self-tapping screws into the holes just sufficiently for them to gain a good purchase in the metal. Now the dent can be pulled out by pulling on the protruding heads of the screws with a pair of pliers.

The next stage of the repair is the removal of the paint from the damaged area, and from an inch or so of the surrounding 'sound' bodywork. This is accomplished most easily by using a wire brush or abrasive pad on a power drill, although it can be done just as effectively by hand using sheets of abrasive paper. To complete the preparation for filling, score the surface of the bare metal with a screwdriver or the tang of a file, or alternatively, drill small holes in the affected area. This will provide a really good 'key' for the filler paste.

To complete the repair see the Section on filling and re-spraying.

Repair of rust holes or gashes in the car's bodywork

Remove all paint from the affected area and from an inch or so of the surrounding 'sound' bodywork, using an abrasive pad or a wire brush on a power drill. If these are not available a few sheets of abrasive paper will do the job just as effectively. With the paint removed you will be able to gauge the severity of the corrosion and therefore decide whether to renew the whole panel (if this is possible) or to repair the affected area. New body panels are not as expensive as most people think and it is often quicker and more satisfactory to fit a new panel than to attempt to repair large areas of corrosion.

Remove all fittings from the affected area except those which will act as a guide to the original shape of the damaged bodywork (eg headlamp shells etc). Then, using tin snips or a hacksaw blade, remove all loose metal and any other metal badly affected by corrosion. Hammer the edges of the hole inwards in order to create a slight depression for the filler paste.

Wire brush the affected area to remove the powdery rust from the surface of the remaining metal. Paint the affected area with rust inhibiting paint; if the back of the rusted area is accessible treat this also.

Before filling can take place it will be necessary to block the hole in some way. This can be achieved by the use of zinc gauze or aluminium tape.

Zinc gauze is probably the best material to use for a large hole. Cut a piece to the approximate size and shape of the hole to be filled, then position it in the hole so that its edges are below the level of the surrounding bodywork. It can be retained in position by several blobs of filler paste around its periphery.

Aluminium tape should be used for small or very narrow holes. Pull a piece off the roll and trim it to the approximate size and shape required, then pull off the backing paper (if used) and stick the tape over the hole; it can be overlapped if the thickness of one piece is insufficient. Burnish down the edges of the tape with the handle of a screwdriver or similar, to ensure that the tape is securely attached to the metal underneath.

Bodywork repairs – filling and re-spraying

Before using this Section, see the Sections on dent, deep scratch, rust holes and gash repairs.

Many types of bodyfiller are available, but generally speaking those proprietary kits which contain a tin of filler paste and a tube of resin hardener are best for this type of repair. A wide, flexible plastic or nylon applicator will be found invaluable for imparting a smooth and well contoured finish to the surface of the filler.

Mix up a little filler on a clean piece of card or board – measure the hardener carefully (follow the maker's instructions on the pack) otherwise the filler will set too rapidly or too slowly.

Using the applicator apply the filler paste to the prepared area; draw the applicator across the surface of the filler to achieve the correct contour and to level the filler surface. As soon as a contour that approximates the correct one is achieved, stop working the paste – if you carry on too long the paste will become sticky and begin to 'pick up' on the applicator. Continue to add thin layers of filler paste at twenty-minute intervals until the level of the filler is just proud of the surrounding bodywork.

Once the filler has hardened, excess can be removed using a metal plane or file. From then on, progressively finer grades of sandpaper should be used, starting with a 40 grade production paper and finishing with 400 grade wet-and-dry paper. Always wrap the abrasive paper around a flat rubber, cork, or wooden block – otherwise the surface of the filler will not be completely flat. During the smoothing of the filler surface the wet-and-dry paper should be periodically rinsed in water. This will ensure that a very smooth finish is imparted to the filler at the final stage.

At this stage the 'repair area' should be surrounded by a ring of bare metal, which in turn should be encircled by the finely 'feathered' edge of the good paintwork. Rinse the repair area with clean water, until all of the dust produced by the rubbing-down operation has gone.

Spray the whole repair area with a light coat of primer – this will show up any imperfections in the surface of the filler. Repair these imperfections with fresh filler paste or bodystopper, and once more smooth the surface with abrasive paper. If bodystopper is used, it can be mixed with cellulose thinners to form a really thin paste which is ideal for filling small holes. Repeat this spray and repair procedure until you are satisfied that the surface of the filler, and the feathered edge of the paintwork are perfect. Clean the repair area with clean water and allow to dry fully.

The repair area is now ready for final spraying. Paint spraying must be carried out in a warm, dry, windless and dust free atmosphere. This condition can be created artificially if you have access to a large indoor working area, but if you are forced to work in the open, you will have to pick your day very carefully. If you are working indoors, dousing the floor in the work area with water will help to settle the dust which would otherwise be in the atmosphere. If the repair area is confined to one body panel, mask off the surrounding panels; this will help to minimise the effects of a slight mis-match in paint colours. Bodywork fittings (eg chrome strips, door handles etc) will also need to be masked off. Use genuine masking tape and several thicknesses of newspaper for the masking operations.

Before commencing to spray, agitate the aerosol can thoroughly, then spray a test area (an old tin, or similar) until the technique is mastered. Cover the repair area with a thick coat of primer; the thickness should be built up using several thin layers of paint rather than one thick one. Using 400 grade wet-and-dry paper, rub down the surface of the primer until it is really smooth. While doing this, the work area should be thoroughly doused with water, and the wet-and-dry paper periodically rinsed in water. Allow to dry before spraying on more paint.

Spray on the top coat, again building up the thickness by using several thin layers of paint. Start spraying in the centre of the repair area and then, using a circular motion, work outwards until the whole repair area and about 2 inches of the surrounding original paintwork is covered. Remove all masking material 10 to 15 minutes after spraying on the final coat of paint.

Allow the new paint at least two weeks to harden, then, using a paintwork renovator or a very fine cutting paste, blend the edges of the paint into the existing paintwork. Finally, apply wax polish.

5　Bonnet – removal and refitting

1　Open the bonnet and support it on its stay.
2　Disconnect the screen washer pipe on the underside of the bonnet lid (photo).
3　Mark round the hinge plates on the underside of the bonnet lid as an aid to refitting.
4　With an assistant supporting one side of the bonnet lid, unbolt the hinges and lift the lid from the vehicle.
5　Refit by reversing the removal operations. If a new bonnet is being installed, position it so that an equal gap is provided at each side when it is being closed.
6　The bonnet should close smoothly and positively without ex-

cessive pressure. If it does not, carry out the following adjustment.

7   Screw in the bump stops which are located on the front upper cross rail (photo). Close the bonnet and then readjust the bump stops until the bonnet is flush with the wing upper surfaces.

8   Adjust the striker centrally in relation to the latch. Release it by unscrewing its pressed steel locknut (photo).

9   Screw the striker in or out until the bonnet fully closes under its own weight when allowed to drop from a point 300 mm (11.8 in) above its released position.

6 Bonnet release cable – removal and refitting

1   Working inside the vehicle, extract the three screws and remove the steering column shroud. Open the bonnet. If the cable is broken, the release latch must be operated using a suitably shaped bar through the grille aperture.

2   Extract the single screw and remove the cable bracket from the steering column.

3   Working within the engine compartment, pull the cable grommet from the bonnet latch bracket and then disengage the cable end fitting from the latch.

4   Unclip the cable from the side of the engine compartment.

5   Withdraw the cable through the engine compartment rear bulkhead into the vehicle interior.

6   Refitting is a reversal of removal.

7 Bonnet lock – removal and refitting

1   Extract the three securing screws from the lock and lower it until the cable can be disconnected.

2   Withdraw the lock from below the top rail.

3   Refit by reversing the removal operations.

8 Radiator grille – removal and refitting

1   The grille is held in position by four spring clips (photo).

2   Once these clips are released, the grille can be removed from the body panel.

3   Refit by reattaching the spring clips.

9 Body adhesive emblems and mouldings – removal and refitting

1   The radiator grille emblem, the front wing motif, the tailgate emblems and the body side mouldings are all of the self-adhesive type.

2   To remove these devices, it is recommended that a length of nylon cord is used to separate them from their mounting surfaces.

3   New emblems have adhesive already applied and a protective backing. Before sticking them into position, clean off all the old adhesive from the mounting surface of the vehicle.

10 Overriders (bumpers) – removal and refitting

1   The overrider is held to the bumper by a clamp screw. Find this screw on the underside of the bumper and release it, the overrider can then be lifted off.

2   On versions with the headlamp washer option, disconnect the fluid hose as the overrider is withdrawn.

3   Refitting is the reverse of the removal procedure.

11 Bumper moulding and bumper sections (passenger vehicles) – removal and refitting

Moulding

1   Where so equipped, remove the overriders.

2   Release the moulding from the bumper by compressing the jaws of the retaining clips inside the bumper.

3   Slide the moulding from the end retainers, noting that the front bumper moulding is in two parts.

4   To refit, push the moulding into position and fully engage the clips.

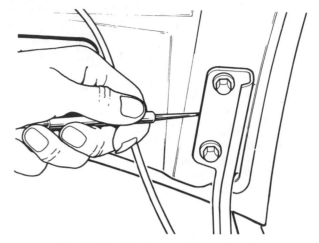

Fig. 12.1 Marking bonnet hinges (Sec 5)

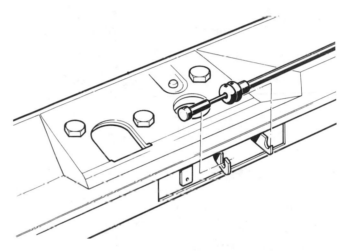

Fig. 12.2 Bonnet release cable at latch end (Sec 6)

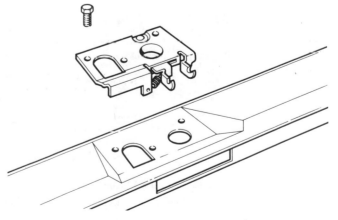

Fig. 12.3 Bonnet lock components (Sec 7)

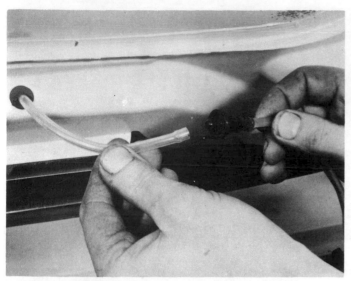

5.2 Disconnecting the windscreen washer fluid pipe

5.8 Bonnet bump stop

5.9 Bonnet striker and safety catch

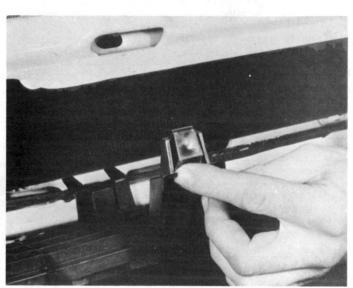

8.1 Radiator grille clip

Fig. 12.4 Removing radiator grille emblem (Sec 9)

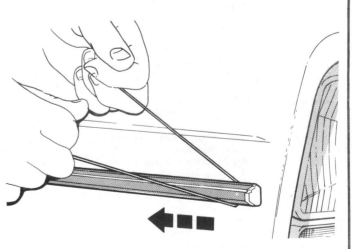

Fig. 12.5 Removing body side moulding (Sec 9)

Fig. 12.6 Removing tailgate badge (Sec 9)

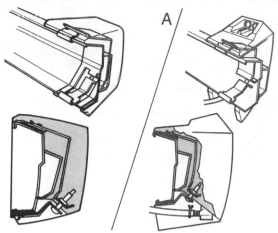

Fig. 12.7 Overrider details (Sec 10)

A   Without headlamp washer   B   With headlamp washer

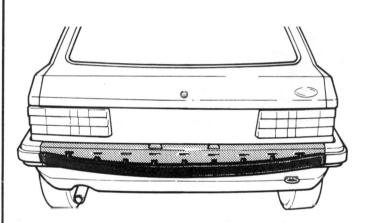

Fig. 12.8 Bumper moulding (Sec 11)

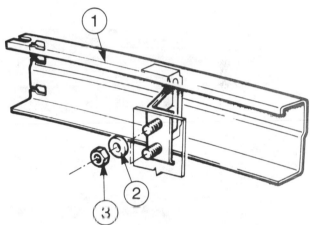

Fig. 12.9 Front bumper attachment (Sec 11)

1   *Bumper bar*   3   *Fixing nut*
2   *Washer*

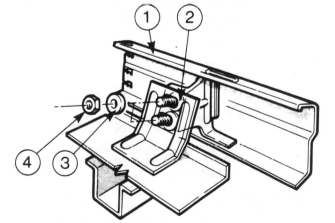

Fig. 12.10 Rear bumper attachment (Sec 11)

1   *Bumper bar*   3   *Washer*
2   *Mounting bracket*   4   *Fixing nut*

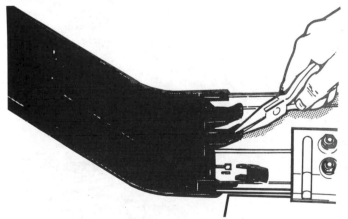

Fig. 12.11 Removing rear quarter bumper retaining tangs (Sec 11)

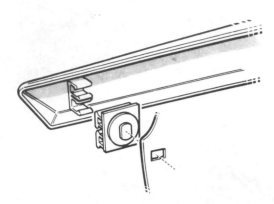

Fig. 12.12 Rear quarter bumper clip (Sec 11)

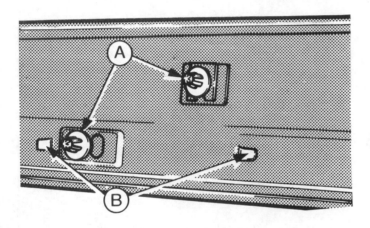

Fig. 12.13 Door trim panel capping (Ghia) (Sec 13)

A   Panel fixing clip   B   Moulding tang

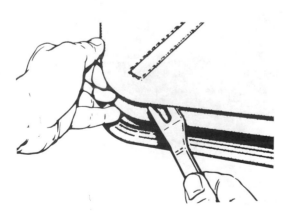

Fig. 12.14 Tool for releasing trim panel clips (Sec 13)

Sections

5   To remove the bumper complete, open the bonnet or tailgate according to whether the front or rear bumper is being removed and unscrew the bumper securing nuts from each end of the bumper.
6   Withdraw the bumper from the vehicle. With the rear bumper, the number plate wiring plugs will have to be disconnected.
7   Release the locking tangs using pliers as shown (Fig. 12.11) and pull or tap the quarter section free using a piece of soft wood to prevent damage. If required the quarter section end retaining clips can be removed from the body by twisting through 90° and pulling free.
8   Reassembly and refitting are reversals of removal and dismantling.

12   Bumpers (Van) – removal and refitting

Removal and refitting of the front bumper is as described in the preceding Section. To remove either rear quarter bumper, prise out the number plate lamp, disconnect the bulbholder, and extract the two Torx screws.

13   Door trim panel – removal and refitting

1   On Ghia versions only, remove the panel capping by carefully prising out the retaining clips using a forked tool similar to the one shown (Fig. 12.14). This can easily be made from a piece of scrap metal.
2   Remove the door window regulator handle. Do this by prising out the plastic insert from the handle and extracting the screw which will now be exposed (photos).
3   On vehicles fitted with electrically-operated front windows, pull out the switches and remove the door pocket finisher.
4   Remove the door pull/armrest. This is held by two screws (photo). On Base models with a door pull only, the end caps will have to be prised up to reveal the screws.
5   Push the door lock remote control handle bezel towards the rear of the vehicle to release it from its retaining lugs (photo).
6   Again using the forked tool, pass it round the edge of the panel betweeen the panel and the door and release each of the panel clips in turn. Lift the panel from the door (photo).
7   The door tidy is attached directly to the trim panel without any anchor screws being used; for this reason the tidy should not be used as a means of closing the door.
8   Refitting the panel is a reversal of removal.

14   Front door window regulator and glass – removal and refitting

1   Remove the door trim panel (see Section 13).
2   Carefully peel the waterproof sheet from the door (photo).
3   Prise off the inner and outer glass weatherstrips.
4   Unscrew and remove the window regulator securing screws (photo).
5   Disengage the window channel from the regulator slides and lower the regulator to the bottom of the door.
6   Remove the window glass by tilting it at the rear and withdrawing it from the outside of the frame. If the glass is so tight that it cannot be tilted, remove the fixing screw from the front channel extension and pull the channel down to release the top clip.
7   The regulator can be removed through the door lower aperture (photo).
8   Refitting is a reversal of removal. Make sure that the waterproof sheet is in good condition, otherwise renew it using plastic sheeting and double-sided self-adhesive tape.

15   Rear door window regulator and glass – removal and refitting

1   Remove the door trim panel as described in Section 13.
2   Prise out the glass inner and outer weatherstrips.
3   Carefully remove the waterproof sheet from the door.
4   Take out the glass dividing channel by extracting the single screw from the door frame and the second screw from the door inner panel. Temporarily refit the window regulator handle and fully lower the window glass. Tilt the dividing channel away from the quarter window glass and then withdraw the channel from the inside of the door frame.
5   Take out the glass and its flexible channel.

13.2A Window winder handle insert

13.2B Extracting window winder handle screw

13.4 Extracting armrest screw

13.5 Removing remote control handle bezel

13.6 Door trim panel removed

14.2 Door waterproof sheet

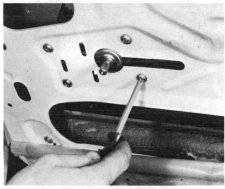
14.4 Removing regulator mounting screw

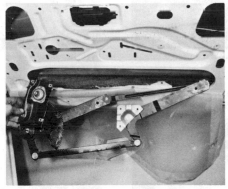
14.7 Withdrawing window regulator

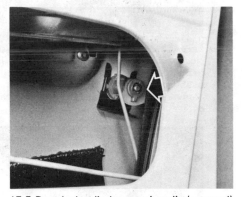
17.5 Door lock cylinder securing clip (arrowed)

6   Remove the regulator securing screws, disengage the window glass channel from the regulator slides and lower the regulator to the bottom of the door.

7   Remove the glass by pulling it upwards and tilting it towards the vehicle interior.

8   Refitting is a reversal of removal.

16 Fixed rear quarter window glass – removal and refitting

1   The glass is removed complete with weatherstrip by pushing it out from inside the vehicle.

2   The lip of the weatherstrip must be released from the top and sides of the window aperture using a suitable tool before exerting pressure to remove the assembly.

3   Refit using a cord as described in Section 24.

17 Door lock and cylinder – removal and refitting

1   Remove the door trim panel as described in Section 13.

2   Pull away the waterproof sheet as necessary to gain access to the lock.

3   Disconnect the control rods from the lock.

4   Remove the lock by extracting the three securing screws and lowering the lock sufficiently to permit the cylinder lock rod to clear the lock housing. Turn the latch around the door frame and withdraw the assembly through the rear cut-out in the door.

5   To remove the lock cylinder, pull out the retaining clip and seal and withdraw the cylinder (photo).

6   The remote control handle can be removed once its connecting rod has been disconnected and the single securing screw extracted.

7   Refitting is a reversal of removal.

This sequence of photographs deals with the repair of the dent and paintwork damage shown in this photo. The procedure will be similar for the repair of a hole. It should be noted that the procedures given here are simplified – more explicit instructions will be found in the text

In the case of a dent the first job – after removing surrounding trim – is to hammer out the dent where access is possible. This will minimise filling. Here, the large dent having been hammered out, the damaged area is being made slightly concave

Now all paint must be removed from the damaged area, by rubbing with coarse abrasive paper. Alternatively, a wire brush or abrasive pad can be used in a power drill. Where the repair area meets good paintwork, the edge of the paintwork should be 'feathered', using a finer grade of abrasive paper

In the case of a hole caused by rusting, all damaged sheet-metal should be cut away before proceeding to this stage. Here, the damaged area is being treated with rust remover and inhibitor before being filled

Mix the body filler according to its manufacturer's instructions. In the case of corrosion damage, it will be necessary to block off any large holes before filling – this can be done with aluminium or plastic mesh, or aluminium tape. Make sure the area is absolutely clean before ...

... applying the filler. Filler should be applied with a flexible applicator, as shown, for best results; the wooden spatula being used for confined areas. Apply thin layers of filler at 20-minute intervals, until the surface of the filler is slightly proud of the surrounding bodywork

Initial shaping can be done with a Surform plane or Dreadnought file. Then, using progressively finer grades of wet-and-dry paper, wrapped around a sanding block, and copious amounts of clean water, rub down the filler until really smooth and flat. Again, feather the edges of adjoining paintwork

The whole repair area can now be sprayed or brush-painted with primer. If spraying, ensure adjoining areas are protected from over-spray. Note that at least one inch of the surrounding sound paintwork should be coated with primer. Primer has a 'thick' consistency, so will find small imperfections

Again, using plenty of water, rub down the primer with a fine grade wet-and-dry paper (400 grade is probably best) until it is really smooth and well blended into the surrounding paintwork. Any remaining imperfections can now be filled by carefully applied knifing stopper paste

When the stopper has hardened, rub down the repair area again before applying the final coat of primer. Before rubbing down this last coat of primer, ensure the repair area is blemish-free – use more stopper if necessary. To ensure that the surface of the primer is really smooth use some finishing compound

The top coat can now be applied. When working out of doors, pick a dry, warm and wind-free day. Ensure surrounding areas are protected from over-spray. Agitate the aerosol thoroughly, then spray the centre of the repair area, working outwards with a circular motion. Apply the paint as several thin coats

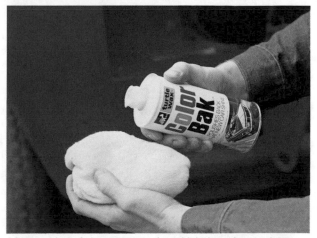

After a period of about two weeks, which the paint needs to harden fully, the surface of the repaired area can be 'cut' with a mild cutting compound prior to wax polishing. When carrying out bodywork repairs, remember that the quality of the finished job is proportional to the time and effort expended

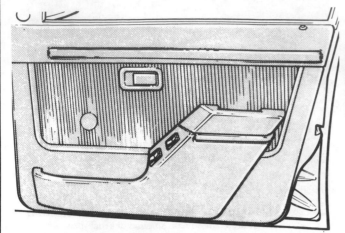

Fig. 12.15 Door trim panel (vehicles with electrically-operated windows) (Sec 13)

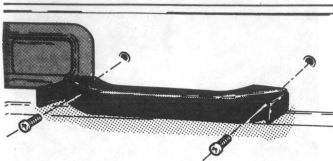

Fig. 12.16 Door pull handle (Base models) (Sec 13)

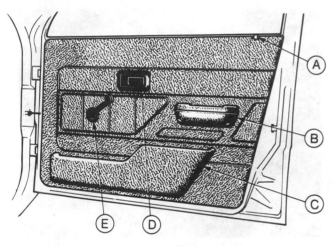

Fig. 12.17 Door trim panel (Sec 13)

A   Lock plunger   D   Bezel
B   Armrest   E   Window regulator handle
C   Door pocket

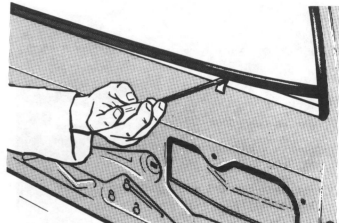

Fig. 12.18 Removing glass weatherstrip (Sec 14)

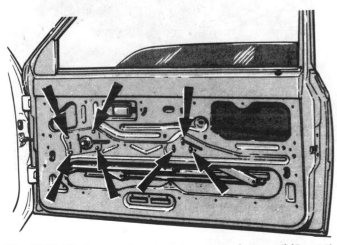

Fig. 12.19 Window regulator securing screws (arrowed) (Sec 14)

Fig. 12.20 Removing front door window glass (Sec 14)

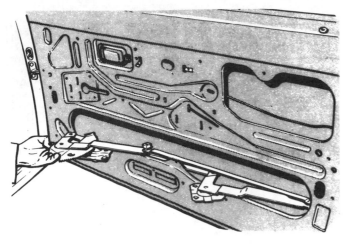

Fig. 12.21 Withdrawing door window regulator (Sec 14)

Fig. 12.22 Removing door quarter glass (Sec 15)

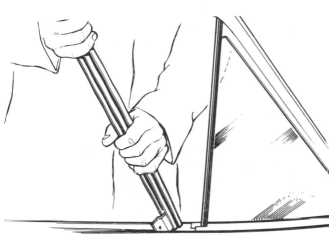

Fig. 12.23 Door window dividing channel (Sec 15)

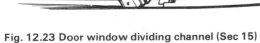

Fig. 12.24 Rear door window regulator screws (arrowed) (Sec 15)

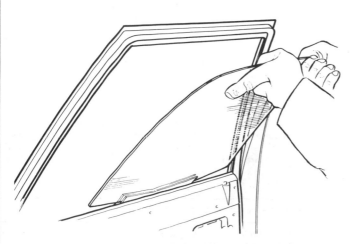

Fig. 12.25 Removing rear door window glass (Sec 15)

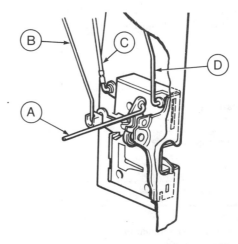

Fig. 12.26 Door lock components (Sec 17)

A   Connecting rod to interior handle
B   Connecting rod to exterior handle
C   Connecting rod to lock cylinder
D   Connecting rod to sill plunger

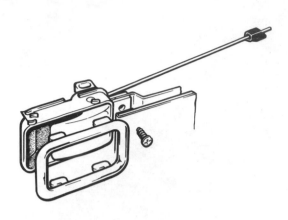

Fig. 12.27 Door lock remote control handle (Sec 17)

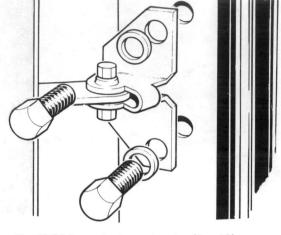

Fig. 12.28 Door check arm bracket (Sec 19)

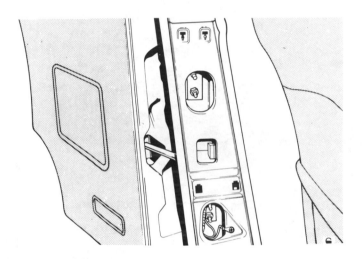

Fig. 12.29 Rear door hinge bolts (Sec 19)

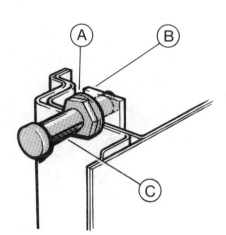

Fig. 12.30 Door striker components (Sec 19)

A   Body pillar   C   Striker pin
B   Reinforcement plate

18 Electrically-operated front windows and central locking system – general

Components of these optional systems are described in Chapter 11.

19 Doors – removal and refitting

Front door

1   Open the door fully and support its lower edge on a jack or blocks, covered with a pad of rag.
2   Unscrew the two bolts which hold the check arm bracket to the body and disconnect the arm.
3   Remove the scuff plate from the sill at the bottom of the door aperture (photo).
4   Unclip the lower cowl side trim panel (photo).
5   Remove the heater duct.
6   Unbolt the door lower hinge from the body pillar (photo).
7   Unbolt the upper hinge from the body pillar, then lift the door from the vehicle.

Rear door

8   The operations are similar to those described for removal of the front door, except that the centre pillar trim panels must be removed for access to the hinge bolts.

All doors

9   When refitting the doors, do not fully tighten the hinge bolts until the alignment of the door within the body aperture has been checked.
10   The door striker can be adjusted to provide smooth positive closure by unscrewing it a turn or two from its captive retaining nut and sliding it as necessary.

20 Tailgate – removal and refitting

1   Open the tailgate fully and disconnect the leads from the heated rear window and the wiper (where fitted).
2   From the top edge of the tailgate aperture, remove the weather-strip and then peel back the headlining.
3   With an assistant supporting the tailgate, unbolt and remove the struts. The strut balljoint is released by prising out the small plastic peg (photo).

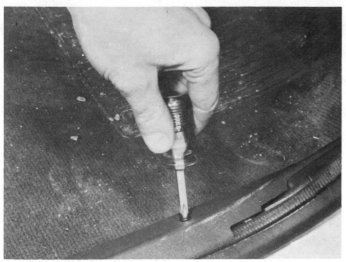

19.3 Extracting sill scuff plate screw

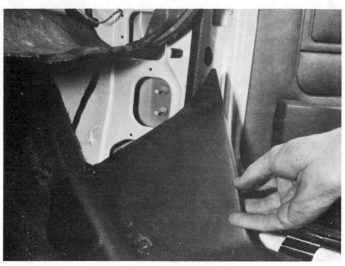

19.4 Removing cowl side trim panel

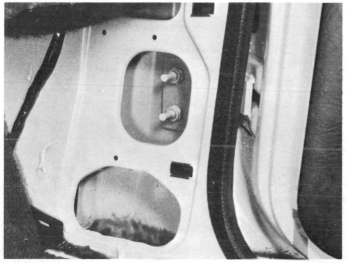

19.6 Door lower hinge

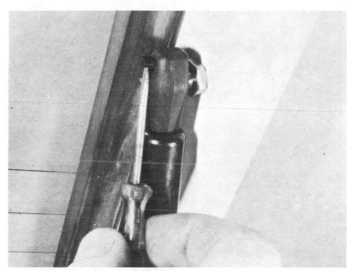

20.3 Releasing tailgate strut balljoint

4   Unscrew the hinge screws, remove them with the washers and lift the tailgate from the vehicle.

5   The tailgate lock and (if fitted) the wiper motor are accessible for removal once the trim panel has been released from its securing clips, which should be turned through 90° to release them.

6   The tailgate lock cylinder is retained by a spring clip. The two tailgate stops are secured with pop rivets which will have to be drilled out if the stops must be removed.

7   Refitting is a reversal of removal, but do not fully tighten the hinge screws until the tailgate has been adjusted to give an equal gap all round.

21 Spoilers (XR3) – removal and refitting

Front
1   The front spoiler is secured by one screw.
2   Once this is extracted, the spoiler can be disengaged from its eight positioning pegs.

Rear
3   Remove the rear wiper arm and blades.
4   From the lower section of the spoiler, extract the three cover pieces and the three securing screws.

5   Open the tailgate and detach the trim panel from its interior surface.

6   Unbolt and remove the rear wiper motor.

7   Unscrew and remove the four spoiler securing nuts and lift the spoiler away. In addition to the nuts, double-sided adhesive tape is used to retain the spoiler. New tape should be obtained for use when refitting, which is a reversal of removal.

22 Wheel arch deflector (XR3) – removal and refitting

1   Prise off the covers to expose the two screws which hold the deflector to the body side panel.

2   Drill out the three pop rivets which hold the deflector to the wheel arch flange and remove the deflector.

3   Refit by reversing the removal operations and secure with new pop rivets.

23 Rear doors (Van) – removal and refitting

1   Begin by opening the door to its full extent and supporting it on a jack or blocks, with a pad of cloth used to prevent scratching.

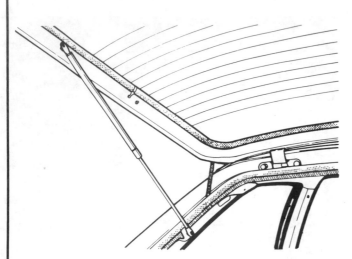

Fig. 12.31 Tailgate strut (Sec 20)

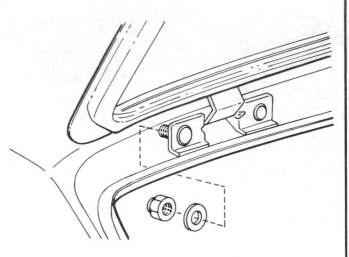

Fig. 12.32 Tailgate hinge detail (Sec 20)

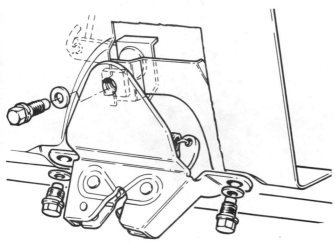

Fig. 12.33 Tailgate lock details (Sec 20)

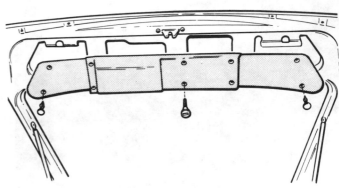

Fig. 12.34 Tailgate trim panel (Sec 20)

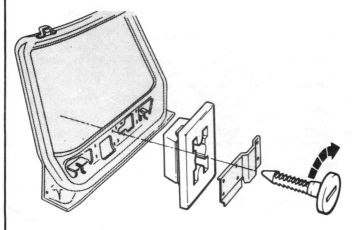

Fig. 12.35 Tailgate trim panel turn buttons (Sec 20)

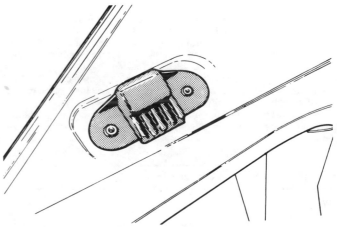

Fig. 12.36 Tailgate stop (Sec 20)

2   Disconnect the check strap from its lower edge.
3   Unbolt the hinges from the door and remove the door from the vehicle.
4   Before the bolts are fully tightened when refitting, adjust the position of the door within its frame to give an even gap all round and even contact with the edge of the second door.

24 Windscreen glass – removal and refitting

The average DIY mechanic is advised to leave windscreen removal and refitting to an expert. For the owner who insists on doing it himself, the following paragraphs are given.
1   All models are fitted with a laminated glass screen and in consequence even if cracked, it will probably be removed as one piece.
2   Cover the bonnet in front of the windscreen with an old blanket to protect against scratching.
3   Remove the wiper arms and blades (see Chapter 11).
4   Working inside the vehicle, push the lip of the screen weatherseal under the top and the sides of the body aperture flange.
5   With an assistant standing outside the car to restrain the screen, push the glass complete with weatherseal out of the bodyframe.
6   Where fitted, extract the bright moulding from the groove in the weatherstrip and then pull the weatherstrip off the glass.
7   Unless the weatherstrip is in good condition, it should be renewed.
8   Although sealant is not normally used with these screens, check that the glass groove in the weatherstrip is free from sealant or glass chippings.
9   Commence refitting by fitting the weatherstrip to the glass. Locate a length of nylon or terylene cord in the body flange groove of the weatherstrip so that the ends of the cord emerge at the bottom centre and cross over by a length of about 150 mm (6.0 in).
10 Offer the screen to the body and engage the lower lip of the weatherstrip on its flange. With an assistant applying gentle, even pressure on the glass from the outside, pull the ends of the cord simultaneously at right-angles to the glass. This will pull the lip of the weatherstrip over the body flange. Continue until the cord is released from the centre top and the screen is fully fitted.
11 If a bright moulding was removed, refit it now. This can be one of the most difficult jobs to do without a special tool. The moulding should be pressed into its groove just after the groove lips have been prised open to receive it. Take care not to cut the weatherstrip if improvising with a made-up tool.

25 Tailgate glass – removal and refitting

1   The operations are very similar to those described for windscreen renewal in the preceding Section.
2   Disconnect the leads from the heated rear window and the wiper motor (where fitted).
3   The tailgate glass is of toughened type, not laminated, so if it has shattered, remove all granular glass with a small vacuum cleaner.

26 Interior trim panels – removal and refitting

Rear quarter trim panel
1   Unbolt the seat belt from its floor mounting.
2   Pass the belt buckle slide through the panel aperture.
3   Pull the seat cushion and backrest forward.
4   Extract the single screw from the quarter panel and then using a suitable forked tool, lever out the clips and remove the panel.
5   The clips and ashtray are detachable after the panel has been withdrawn.

Cowl side trim panel
6   Extract the two screws from the scuff plate.
7   Remove the two clips and detach the panel by pulling it from its two locating pegs.

Windscreen pillar trim panel
8   The windscreen will have to be removed as described in Section 24.
9   Pull off the door aperture weatherstrip.

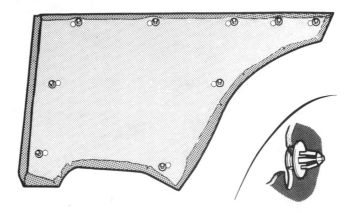

Fig. 12.37 Rear quarter trim panel (Sec 26)

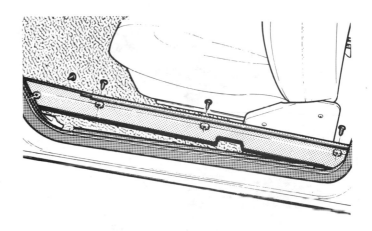

Fig. 12.38 Scuff plate and fixing screws (Sec 26)

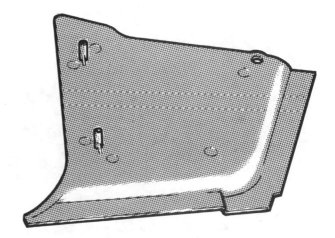

Fig. 12.39 Cowl side trim panel (Sec 26)

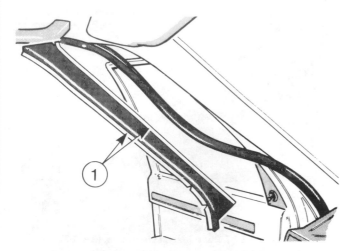

Fig. 12.40 Windscreen pillar trim panel (1) (Sec 26)

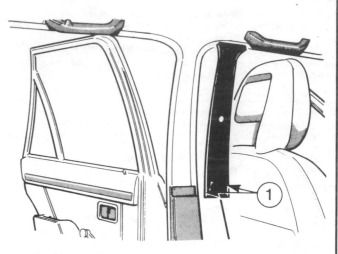

Fig. 12.41 Centre pillar upper trim panel (1) (Sec 26)

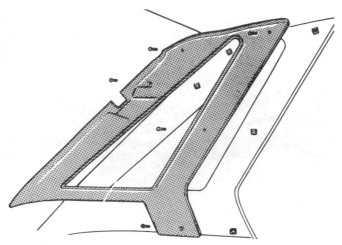

Fig. 12.42 Rear pillar trim panel and screws (Sec 26)

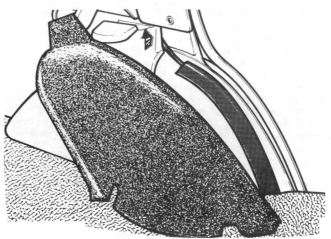

Fig. 12.43 Rear wheel housing cover (Sec 26)

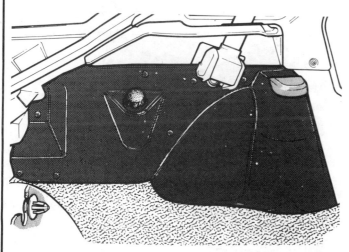

Fig. 12.44 Load space trim panel (Sec 26)

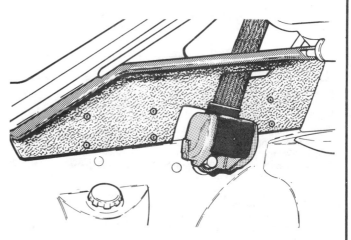

Fig. 12.45 Rear parcel shelf bracket (Sec 27)

10 Peel back the edges of the trim panel and remove it.

Centre pillar trim panels
11 Remove the two seat belt anchorages from the pillar.
12 Pull off the weatherstrips from the door apertures.
13 Remove the upper trim panel from the pillar.
14 On three-door models, the rear quarter window will first have to be removed before the pillar trim panel can be withdrawn.
15 The lower trim panel can be removed from the pillar after the four screws have been extracted.

Rear pillar trim panel
16 Remove the rear seat belt upper anchorage.
17 Fold down the rear seat back.
18 Extract the five securing screws and remove the trim panel.

Tailgate trim panel
19 This comprises a flat panel secured with push-in type clips. If a rear wiper is fitted, this will have a moulded cover over the wiper motor secured by quarter-turn fasteners.
20 To remove the moulded cover, turn the heads of the fasteners through 90° to release them.

Rear wheelhouse covers
21 These are fitted to certain Base and 1100 cc models and are of moulded type. On Ghia versions the covers are cloth covered while on 5-door versions, the covers have an upper finisher held by two screws.

Load space trim panel
22 These take the form of moulded panels on GL, XR3 and Ghia models and flat panels on Base and L versions. The panels are held in position by external clips.

Door trim panels
23 Refer to section 13 of this Chapter.

27 Rear parcel shelf – removal and refitting

1 Open the tailgate fully and disengage the parcel shelf lifting strap loops from the tailgate retaining knobs.
2 Lift out the parcel shelf pivot pins from their notches in the support brackets and withdraw the shelf.
3 Pull each strap loop through its hole in the rear edge of the shelf by disengaging the upper and lower retaining collars.
4 The shelf brackets are secured with pop rivets which must be drilled out if the brackets are to be removed.
5 Refitting is a reversal of removal.

28 Glove compartment – removal and refitting

1 Open the glovebox lid and extract the screws which hold the glovebox to the crash pad.
2 Remove the latch (two screws).
3 Remove the single screw inside the top of the glove compartment which holds it to the moulded bracket. Withdraw the glove compartment.
4 Refitting is a reversal of removal.

29 Passenger grab handles – removal and refitting

1 These handles are secured to the roof by screws concealed by small cover plates.
2 To expose the screws, prise out the cover plates. Remove the screws and handle.
3 Refit by reversing the removal operations.

30 Facia – removal and refitting

1 Disconnect the battery.
2 Refer to Chapter 9 and remove the steering wheel and the column shroud.

3 Remove the steering column switches and detach the electrical wiring harness.
4 Remove the underdash cover panels.
5 Unbolt the steering column mountings and carefully lower the assembly to rest on the front seat.
6 Remove the screw and detach the bonnet release lever.
7 Refer to Chapter 11 and remove the instrument cluster.
8 Detach the heater controls, switches and wiring multi-plugs.
9 Remove the ashtray and cigar lighter mounting panel.
10 Remove the radio and its mounting bracket (Chapter 11).
11 Disconnect the wire from the loudspeaker and remove the speaker (four screws).
12 Remove the glovebox (Section 28).
13 Remove the instrument warning module (Chapter 11).
14 Detach the vent ducts and demister hoses from the heater.
15 Extract the three securing screws and remove the facia panel complete with crash pad.
16 The crash padding can be detached by removing the glove compartment mounting bracket and lock bracket, withdrawing the side and centre face level vents and extracting all the securing clips.
17 Refitting is a reversal of removal.

31 Headlining – removal and refitting

1 Renewal of the headlining is a major operation and will first require the removal of the windscreen, the fixed quarter windows and their weatherstrips.
2 Once this has been done, pull the weatherstrip from the top edges of the door and tailgate apertures.
3 Refer to Chapter 11 and remove the interior lamp.
4 Refer to Section 32 and remove the sun visors.
5 Refer to Section 29 and remove the passenger grab handles.
6 Release the upper edges of the pillar trim panels (Section 26).
7 Where so equipped, remove the sun roof panel slide covers and weatherstrip.
8 Prise off the headlining retaining clips from the door, tailgate and quarter window aperture flanges.
9 Remove the headlining rear support wire retainer and pull the headlining from the roof.
10 Before fitting the new headlining, check that the support wire anti-rattle pads are firmly stuck to the roof.
11 Clean off old adhesive from the door and quarter window apertures amd around the interior lamp and apply fresh adhesive.
12 Fit the headlining by offering it up to the roof, centralising it and fitting the rear support wire retainer.
13 Pull the front edge of the headlining into the windscreen aperture and secure with two clips to the body flange.
14 Pull the rear edge into the tailgate opening and secure in a similar way.
15 Trim and fold the headlining as necessary at the body pillars.
16 Pull the headlining into the door and quarter window apertures and secure with two clips at each location. Check that the headlining appears taut.
17 Trim off any surplus material.
18 Where the vehicle is equipped with a sun roof, carefully cut round the headlining at the sun roof aperture, cut V notches at the corners and then apply adhesive to the flanges and stick the lining down.
19 Refit the passenger grab handles, the sun visors and the interior lamp.
20 Refit the door aperture weatherstrip, the windscreen and the rear quarter windows.

32 Sun visors – removal and refitting

These are secured to the roof by means of a pivot rod held in position by two screws. Removal and refitting are self-explanatory.

33 Interior mirror – removal and refitting

1 The interior mirror is bonded to the windscreen glass. If it must be removed, grip the mirror firmly and push it forward to break the adhesive bond.

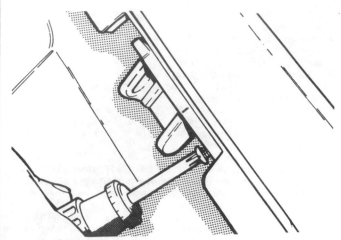

Fig. 12.46 Removing glove compartment latch screw (Sec 28)

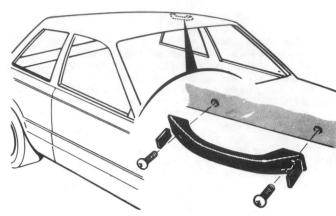

Fig. 12.47 Passenger grab handle details (Sec 29)

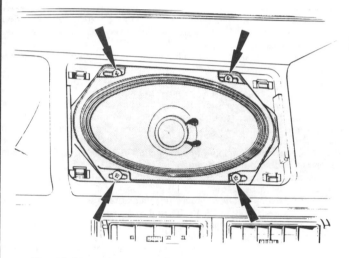

Fig. 12.48 Loudspeaker fixing screws (arrowed) (Sec 30)

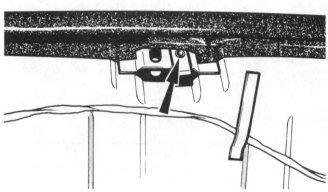

Fig. 12.49 Facia panel centre screw (arrowed) (Sec 30)

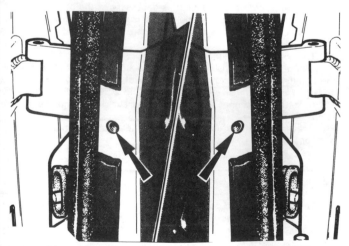

Fig. 12.50 Facia panel end screws (arrowed) (Sec 30)

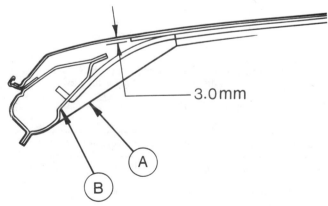

3.0mm

Fig. 12.51 Sectional view of headlining and support wire (Sec 31)

A   Headlining   B   Cant rail

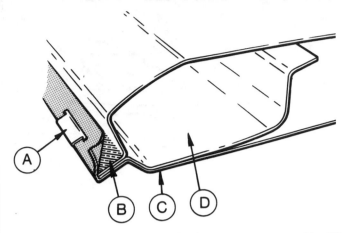

Fig. 12.52 Headlining attachment at windscreen aperture (Sec 31)

A   Clip   C   Lining
B   Adhesive   D   Header rail

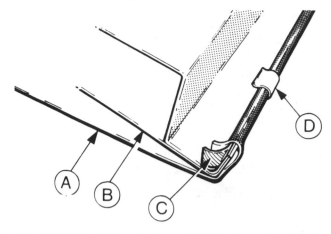

Fig. 12.53 Headlining attachment at tailgate aperture (Sec 31)

A   Lining   C   Adhesive
B   Window frame   D   Clip

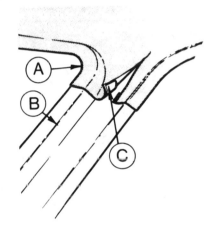

Fig. 12.54 Headlining attachment at windscreen pillar (Sec 31)

A   Headlining   C   Turned-under edge
B   Pillar

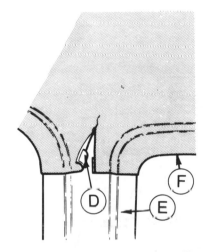

Fig. 12.55 Headlining attachment at centre pillar (Sec 31)

D   Turned-under edge   F   Headlining
E   Pillar

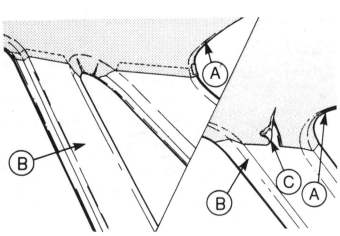

Fig. 12.56 Headlining attachment at rear pillar (Sec 31)

A   Headlining   C   Turned-under edge
B   Pillar

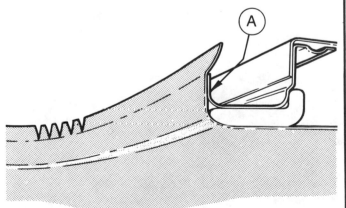

Fig. 12.57 Headlining attachment at sun roof aperture (Sec 31)

A   Flange

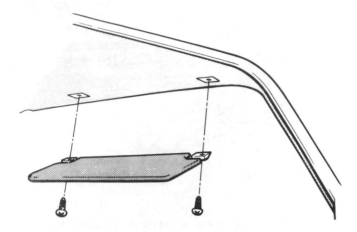

Fig. 12.58 Sun visor attachment (Sec 32)

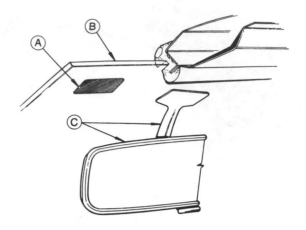

Fig. 12.59 Interior mirror mounting (Sec 33)

A   Adhesive black patch   C   Mirror and mounting stem
B   Windscreen glass

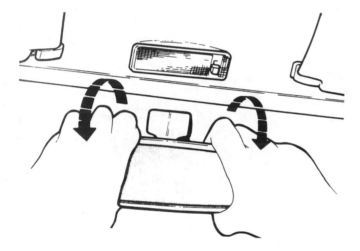

Fig. 12.60 Releasing interior mirror from adhesive base (Sec 33)

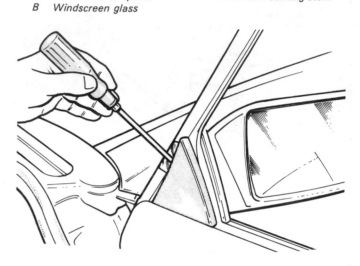

Fig. 12.61 Removing exterior mirror trim panel (Sec 34)

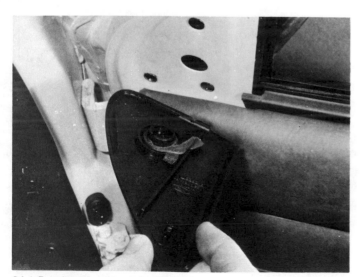

34.1 Exterior mirror mounting cover plate

2   When refitting the mirror, the following preliminary work must first be carried out.
3   Remove existing adhesive from the windscreen glass using a suitable solvent. Allow the solvent to evaporate. The location of the mirror base is marked on the glass with a black patch, so that there should not be any chance of an error when fitting.
4   If the original mirror is being refitted, clean away all the old adhesive from the mirror mounting base, and apply a new adhesive patch to it.
5   If a new windscreen is being installed, peel off the protective layer from the black patch, which is pre-coated with adhesive.
6   Peel off the protective layer from the mirror adhesive patch and locate the mirror precisely onto the black patch on the screen. Hold it in position for at least two minutes.
7   For best results, the fitting of a bonded type mirror should be carried out in an ambient temperature of 70°C (158°F). The careful use of a blower heater on both the glass and mirror should achieve this temperature level.

34 Exterior mirror – removal and refitting

Without remote control

1   Using a screwdriver, prise off the triangular trim panel from inside the mirror mounting position (photo).

2   Unscrew and remove the three mirror fixing screws and withdraw the mirror.

With remote control
3   Unscrew and remove the mirror actuator bezel nut from the triangular trim panel. A special wrench will be needed to release the nut but a C-spanner may serve as a suitable substitute.

All mirrors
4   Refitting both types of mirror is a reversal of removal.

---

35 Centre console – removal and refitting

1   Unclip and pull off the console end cover.
2   Remove the gear lever knob.
3   Pull the flexible gaiter up the control lever and remove it.
4   Extract the four securing screws and remove the console.
5   Refitting is a reversal of removal.

---

36 Front seat and slide – removal and refitting

1   Slide the seat as far forward as it will go.
2   Unscrew and remove the bolts which retain the rear of the seat slides to the floor pan.
3   Slide the seat as far to the rear as it will go and remove the bolts which secure the front ends of the slides to the floor.
4   Remove the seat from the vehicle interior.
5   If the seat slides must be detached from the seat, invert the seat and remove the two bolts from each side. Detach the cross-rod and clips.
6   Refitting is a reversal of removal. Tighten the front bolts before the rear ones to ensure that the seat is located evenly on the floor pan.

---

37 Rear seat – removal and refitting

Cushion
1   Unscrew and remove the Torx (socket-headed) screws from the seat cushion hinges which are located on each side.
2   Lift the cushion from the floor and remove it from the vehicle.

Backrest
3   Fold the seat cushion forward and then fold the seat back down to expose the hinges.
4   Extract the screws which hold the backrest to the hinges.
5   Remove the backrest from the vehicle.

Both parts
6   Refitting is a reversal of removal.

---

38 Sun roof – adjustment

1   The sun roof panel can be adjusted within its aperture and for flush fitting with the roof panel in the following way.
2   To correct the panel-to-aperture gap, bend the weatherstrip flange as necessary.
3   To adjust the panel height at its front edge, release the corner screws, raise or lower the panel as necessary and then tighten the screws.
4   To adjust the panel height at its rear edge, release the two screws at each side on the link assemblies and push the links up or down within the limits of the elongated screw holes. Retighten the screws when alignment is correct.

---

39 Sunroof panel – removal and refitting

1   To remove this type of glass panel, pull the sun blind into the open position and have the sliding roof closed.
2   Wind the sliding roof handle in an anti-clockwise direction for one complete turn.

Fig. 12.62 Centre console end cover (Sec 35)

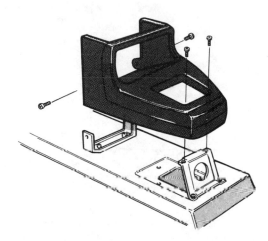

Fig. 12.63 Centre console securing screws (Sec 35)

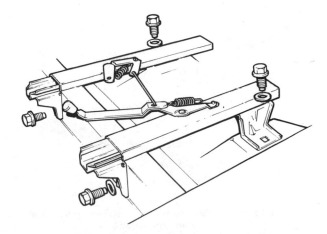

Fig. 12.64 Front seat mounting bolts (Sec 36)

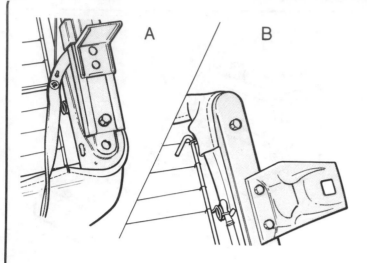

Fig. 12.65 Front seat slide bolts (Sec 36)

A   Front bolt   B   Rear bolt

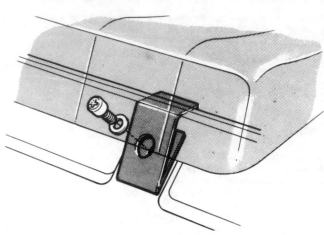

Fig. 12.66 Rear seat cushion screw (Sec 37)

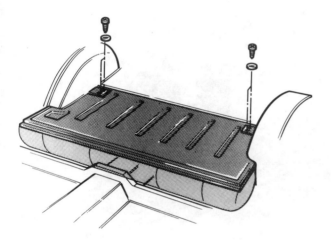

Fig. 12.67 Rear seat backrest screws (Sec 37)

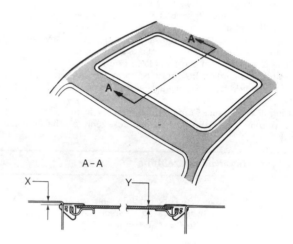

Fig. 12.68 Sun roof panel alignment diagram (Sec 38)

X   Flush to within 1.0 mm below roof line
Y   Flush to within 1.0 mm above roof line

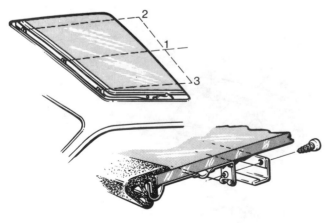

Fig. 12.69 Sunroof glass-to-frame screws. Numbers indicate insertion order (Sec 39)

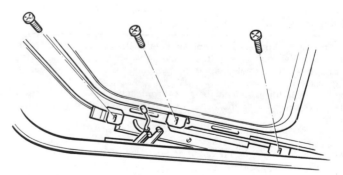

Fig. 12.70 Sunroof glass-to-gear screws (Sec 39)

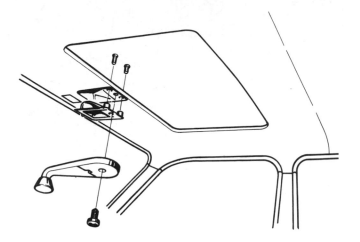

Fig. 12.71 Sliding roof handle and cup (Sec 40)

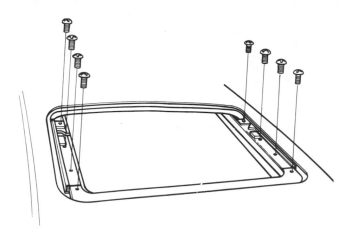

Fig. 12.72 Sliding roof gear-to-roof screws (Sec 40)

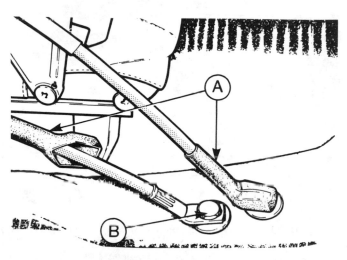

Fig. 12.73 Front seat belt stalk (3-door) (Sec 41)

A   Cover   B   Anchor bolt

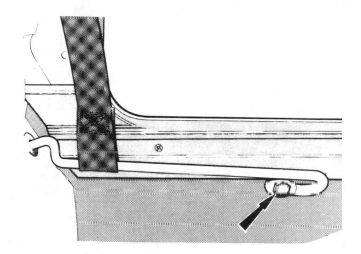

Fig. 12.74 Anchor rail bolt (arrowed) (3-door) (Sec 41)

3   Remove the three screws and clips which connect the lower frame and glass.
4   Turn the handle to close the sliding roof and remove the three screws from each side which hold the glass to the sliding gear.
5   Remove the glass panel by lifting it from the outside of the vehicle.
6   To refit the panel, have the roof closed, locate the glass and secure with the three screws on each side. Once the screws are secure give the handle one complete turn in a clockwise direction.
7   Set the glass to align with the roof panel and locate the lower frame to glass brackets. Insert the clips through the brackets.
8   Insert the retaining screws in the sequence shown in Fig. 12.69.

40 Sun roof sliding gear – removal and refitting

1   Remove the glass panel as described in the preceding Section.
2   Turn the sliding roof regulator handle clockwise to the fully closed position. Extract the three screws and remove the regulator handle and the handle cup.
3   Extract the four screws from each side which hold the sliding gear to the roof. Lift up the front of the gear and withdraw it from the front of the sliding roof aperture.
4   Refitting is a reversal of removal.
5   Adjust if necessary as described in Section 38.

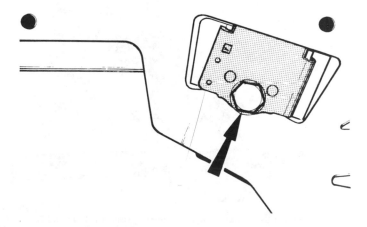

Fig. 12.75 Inertia reel bolt (arrowed) (3-door) (Sec 41)

Fig. 12.76 Pillar anchor bolt (arrowed) (5-door) (Sec 41)

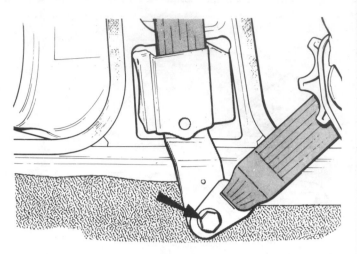

Fig. 12.77 Reel/plate anchor bolt (arrowed) (5-door) Sec 41

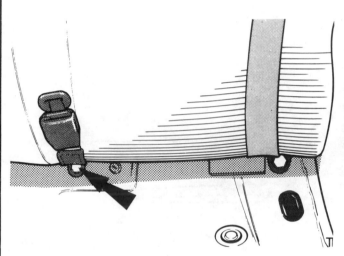

Fig. 12.78 Belt floor anchorage (arrowed) (rear seat – car) (Sec 41)

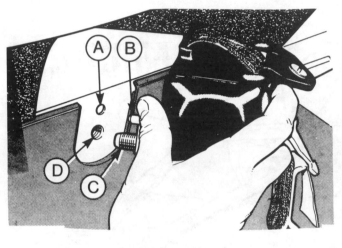

Fig. 12.79 Reel/spacer mounting (rear seat – car) (Sec 41)

A   Spacer pin hole   C   Anchor bolt
B   Spacer alignment pin   D   Tapped hole

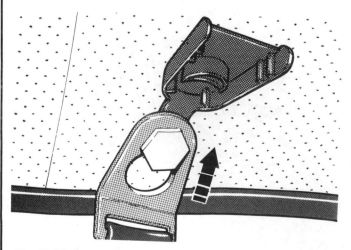

Fig. 12.80 Support strap attachment (arrowed) (Estate) (Sec 41)

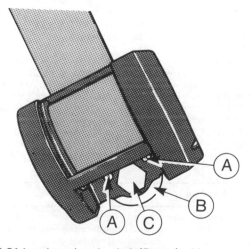

Fig. 12.81 Inertia reel anchor bolt (Estate) with cover removed (Sec 41)

A   Screws   C   Anchor bolt
B   Washer

41 Seat belts – maintenance, removal and refitting

Maintenance

1 Periodically check the belts for fraying or other damage. If evident, renew the belt.

2 If the belts become dirty, wipe then with a damp cloth using a little liquid detergent only.

3 Check the tightness of the anchor bolts and if they are ever disconnected, make quite sure that the original sequence of fitting of washers, bushes and anchor plate is retained.

4 Never modify the belt or alter its attachment point to the body.

Front belt (3-door)

5 Slide the belt stalk cover upwards to expose the anchor bolt.

6 Unbolt the stalk.

7 Unbolt the lower anchor rail, pull the end of the rail away from the panel and slide the belt from it.

8 Prise the moulded cap from the centre pillar anchorage and remove the bolt.

9 Prise the belt guide runner from the rear quarter trim panel and slide the runner from the belt.

10 Remove the rear quarter trim panel (Section 26).

11 Unbolt the reel/belt assembly from the inner rear quarter body panel.

Front belt (5-door)

12 Refer to paragraph 5 and remove the stalk.

13 Refer to paragraph 8 and remove the anchor bolt.

14 Unbolt the inertia reel and the anchor plate from the centre pillar. Remove the pillar lower trim panel (Section 26).

Rear belt (car)

15 Raise the rear seat cushion and remove the anchor bolt from the floor pan.

16 Unclip the elasticated strap from the lower belt buckle.

17 Unbolt the inertia reel anchor plate from the floor.

18 Unbolt the belt from the body pillar upper section.

19 Prise out the belt guide runner from the rear package tray support panel and slide the runner from the belt.

20 Raise the inertia reel cover, unscrew the reel mounting bolt and withdraw reel and spacer.

Rear belt (Estate)

21 Repeat the operations described in paragraphs 15 to 17.

22 Raise the moulded cap from the support strap mounting, slide the mounting plate to one side until the large hole passes over the bolt head and the strap can be removed.

23 Unscrew the cap and bolt.

24 Raise the cover on the inertia reel to expose the bolt and unbolt the reel.

All belts

25 Refitting of all belts is a reversal of removal. Ensure that spacers, plates and washers are in correct sequence and tighten all bolts to the specified torque wrench settings.

Chapter 13 Supplement:
Revisions and information on later models

Contents

1 Introduction

Since its introduction in September 1980, the front wheel drive Escort has had a number of modifications made to it. Although the engines fitted have remained basically the same, the VV carburettor has undergone certain modifications and the emission control system on both British and overseas models has been revised.

The XR3i model was introduced in October 1982 and the details concerning the fuel injection system applicable to this model are also given in this Chapter.

Another significant modification made to the Escort was the introduction of the five-speed manual gearbox, originally fitted on the 1.6 model but later being available as an optional fitting on the 1.3 litre variant.

In 1983 the new Ford automatic (ATX) transmission became available as an optional fitting on the 1.6 models and this is covered also.

The Escort Cabriolet was introduced in late 1983. Based on the 1.3 and 1.6 models in the range, the Cabriolet is the first open top car made by Ford for some twenty years. Whilst mechanically the same as other models, the Cabriolet body shell panels differ considerably from the Saloon/Estate variants in order to strengthen the structure. As well as increased body strength, a roll-over hoop is fitted and this has the dual purpose of strengthening the body and giving protection to the occupants.

This supplementary Chapter is used to its best advantage if studied before the main Chapters of the Manual. This will ensure that any relevant information can be collected and accommodated into the procedures given in Chapters 1 to 12.

2 Specifications

Engine (CVH)
Oil capacity
CVH engines except 1600i:
   Without filter change .... 3.25 litres (5.7 Imp pints)
   With filter change .... 3.50 litres (6.2 Imp pints)
1600i:
   Without filter change .... 3.25 litres (5.7 Imp pints)
   With filter change .... 3.60 litres (6.3 Imp pints)
Note: *above capacities for engines with white or green handle dipstick only*

Torque wrench setting

	Nm	lbf ft
Rocker studs (with nylon insert)	20	15

Cooling system
Capacity
1600i .... 7.8 litres (13.7 Imp pints)

Fuel and exhaust systems
VV carburettor (from model year 1984)
Choke type:
   1.1 ohv and 1.3 CVH .... Manual
   1.6 CVH (manual and automatic transmission variants) ..... Automatic

Idle speed
Automatic transmission models .... 800 to 900 rpm

Weber 2V carburettor (from model year 1984)
Main jet 115/125

Fuel tank capacity
Van .... 50 litres (11.0 gallons)
All other models from May 1983 and XR3i .... 48 litres (10.5 gallons)

Fuel injection system

Type	Bosch K-Jetronic
Idle speed (engine cooling fan on)	750 to 850 rpm
CO mixture	1.0 to 1.5%

Torque wrench settings (fuel injection system)

	Nm	lbf ft
Fuel distributor to sensor plate screws	32 to 38	23.6 to 28
Main system pressure regulator	20 to 25	14.7 to 18
Sensor plate to air cleaner unit screws	8.5 to 10.5	6.3 to 7.7
Air cleaner unit retaining screws	4.5 to 5.0	3.3 to 3.7
Warm-up regulator securing bolts	3.5 to 5.0	2.6 to 3.7
Start valve securing bolts	3.5 to 5.0	2.6 to 3.7
Auxiliary air device securing bolts	3.5 to 5.0	2.6 to 3.7
Distributor intake/return banjo bolts	16 to 20	13.3 to 14.7
Distributor injection pipes banjo bolts	5.0 to 8.0	3.7 to 5.9
Distributor start valve feed pipe banjo bolt	5.0 to 8.0	3.7 to 5.9
Distributor warm-up regulator feed banjo bolt	5.0 to 8.0	3.7 to 5.9
Distributor warm-up regulator return banjo bolt	5.0 to 8.0	3.7 to 5.9
Warm-up regulator inlet banjo bolt (M10)	11.0 to 15.0	8.1 to 11.1
Warm-up regulator outlet banjo bolt (M8)	5.0 to 8.0	3.7 to 5.9
Fuel pump, filter and accumulator banjo bolts	16 to 20	11.8 to 14.7

Ignition system

Lucas distributor drive dog shaft endplay .... 0.08 to 0.42 mm (0.003 to 0.016 in)

Spark plugs

Type:	
1.3	Motorcraft AGP 22C or AGPR 22C
1.6 (Weber carburettor)	Motorcraft Super AGP 12C, Super AGPR 12C or Super AGPR 22C
1600i	Motorcraft AGPR 12C
Electrode gap (1600i)	0.75 mm (0.030 in)

Distributor

Advance characteristics* at 2000 engine rpm, no load:	Mechanical	Vacuum	Total
1.3 (83SF-12100-BA)	2.4° to 8.4°	9.0° to 17.0°	11.4° to 25.4°
1.6 (Van)	0.8° to 6.5°	14.0° to 22.0°	14.8° to 28.5°
1.6 (81SF-12100-BAA)	6.0° to 12.0°	9.0° to 17.0°	15.0° to 29.0°
1.6 (81SF-12100-ALA)	6.0° to 12.0°	14.0° to 22.0°	20.0° to 34.0°
1.6 (81SF-12100-ANA)	0.8° to 6.5°	8.0° to 14.0°	8.8° to 20.5°
1.6 (83SF-12100-FA)	0.4° to 6.4°	12.0° to 20.0°	12.4° to 26.4°
1.6 (81SF-12100-BBA)	6.0° to 12.0°	9.0° to 17.0°	15.0° to 29.0°
1.6 (fuel injection)	8.0° to 14.0°	9.0 to 17.0°	17.0 to 31.0°

Crankshaft degrees; initial advance not included

Transmission (manual four-speed)

Ratios

1.1 litre ohv with 3 + E transmission:

1st	3.58:1
2nd	2.04:1
3rd	1.30:1
4th (E)	0.88:1
Reverse	3.77:1
Final drive	3.58:1

Transmission (manual five-speed)

Transmission type .... 5 forward speeds and 1 reverse, synchromesh on all forward gears

Gear ratios

	1.1 litre and 1.3 litre	1.6 litre
1st	3.58 : 1	3.15 : 1
2nd	2.05 : 1	1.91 : 1
3rd	1.35 : 1	1.28 : 1
4th	0.95 : 1	0.95 : 1
5th	0.76 : 1	0.76 : 1
Reverse	3.62 : 1	3.62 : 1

Final drive ratio – XR3i .... 4.29 : 1

Grease specification (assembly only – see text)

Gears, contact and thrust faces	Molybdenum Disulphide paste to Ford spesc SMIC-4505-A
Synchroniser cones and mainshaft assemblies	Collodial Molybdenum Disulphide in oil to Ford spec SMIC-4504-A

5th gear on input shaft .... Ford grease type ESEA-MIC-1014-A
Selector shaft locking assembly sealer .... Anaerobic retaining and sealing compound to Ford spec S-M4G-4645-AA or AB

Lubrication
Lubricant capacity .... 3.1 litres (5.5 pints)
Lubricant type .... SAE 80 light EP gear oil

Torque wrench settings

	Nm	lbf ft
5th gear housing to gearbox	13	10
5th gear selector pin clamp bolt	15	11
5th gear selector plate to housing	31	23
5th gear housing cover	10	7
Gearbox front mounting to gearbox	45	33
Gearbox mounting bolts	58	43
Selector interlock cap nuts	30	22

Automatic transmission
Transmission type ...... Ford ATX (automatic transaxle), three forward gears, one reverse

Converter ratio ...... 2.35 : 1

Gearbox ratios
1st .... 2.79 : 1
2nd .... 1.61 : 1
3rd .... 1.00 : 1
Reverse .... 1.97 : 1

Axle ratio ...... 3.31 : 1

Oil cooler type ...... Twin tube in coolant radiator

Oil (fluid) capacity
(transmission, converter and oil cooler) ...... 7.9 litres (14 Imp pints)

Torque wrench settings

	Nm	lbf ft
Shift shaft nut	54	39
Starter inhibitor switch	11	8
Oil lines to transmission	33	24
Oil lines to cooler	20	14
Transmission to engine bolts	40	29
Torque converter to driveplate	37	27
Driveplate to crankshaft	84	62
Converter housing cover plate	9	6
Transmission mounting to body (front and rear)	58	43
Shift cable bracket	43	32
Downshift linkage to engine bracket	23	17
Downshift linkage control lever (to damper)	6	4
Damper locknut	6	4
Downshift/throttle valve shaft lever nut	14	10
Selector mechanism to floor	9	6
Selector lever to lever guide nut	22	16

Driveshafts
Driveshaft identification marks – later models
1.1 models from February 1982 .... Orange
1.3 and 1.6 models from February 1982 .... White

Braking system
Brake pedal travel – all models
Nominal at 220 N (50 lbf):
    Disc/drum – LHD boosted .... 53 mm (2.08 in)
    RHD boosted and RHD/LHD unboosted .... 56 mm (2.20 in)

Pedal free height ...... 203 ± 10 mm (7.99 ± 0.04 in)

Rear brake drum diameter – fuel injection models .... 203.2 mm (8 in)

Rear brake wheel cylinder diameter
Saloon and Estate from February 1983 and XR3i .... 17.78 mm (0.710 in)

Steering
Front wheel alignment from 1981

	Castor	Camber
Saloons:		
1.1 Base and L:		
Standard	2° 11′	1° 26′
Heavy duty	2° 10′	1° 55′
1.1 GL and Ghia:		
Standard	2° 09′	1° 11′
Heavy duty	2° 06′	1° 38′
1.3 and 1.6 Base and L:		
Standard	2° 33′	1° 47′
Heavy duty	2° 10′	1° 57′
1.3 and 1.6 GL:		
Standard	2° 31′	1° 30′
Heavy duty	2° 09′	1° 42′
1.6 XR3:		
Standard	2° 39′	1° 22′
Estate (all models):		
Standard	2° 38′	1° 53′
Heavy duty	2° 16′	1° 53′
Van (35 and 55):		
Standard	1° 24′	1° 17′
Heavy duty	1° 24′	1° 17′
Maximum permissible variation – left to right-hand side	1° 0′	1° 15′

Front wheel alignment (from May 1983)

Toe setting tolerance permissible when checking .... 0.5 mm (0.02 in) toe-in to 5.5 mm (0.22 in) toe-out
Adjust to .... 2.5 mm (0.10 in) toe-out ± 1.0 mm (0.04 in)

Castor and camber angles (nominal)

	Castor	Camber
1.1 Saloon, Base and L (3-door):		
Standard	2° 15′	0° 13′
Heavy duty	2° 14′	0° 30′
1.1, 1.3 Saloon (5-door) ATX:		
Standard	2° 24′	0° 10′
Heavy duty	2° 19′	0° 25′
1.6 Saloon (3-door):		
Standard	2° 20′	0° 06′
Heavy duty	2° 14′	0° 30′
1.6 Saloon (5-door):		
Standard	2° 22′	0° 30′
Heavy duty	2° 19′	0° 25′
1.6 ATX Saloon (3-door):		
Standard	2° 19′	1° 14′
Heavy duty	2° 14′	0° 30′
1.6 XR3i:		
Standard	2° 47°	–0° 51′
1.1 and 1.3 Estate:		
Standard	2° 39′	0° 29′
Heavy duty	2° 18′	0° 29′
1.6 Estate:		
Standard	2° 40′	0° 33′
Heavy duty	2° 18′	0° 33′
Van:		
35	1° 39′	–0° 17′
55	1° 19′	–0° 17′
Maximum permissible side to side variation:		
Castor angle	1° 0′	
Camber angle	1° 15′	
Permissible tolerance range:		
Castor angle	± 1° 0′	
Camber angle	± 1° 0′	

Torque wrench settings

	Nm	lbf ft
Steering rack plug	5	4
Tie-rod to rack	80	59

Suspension
Roadwheels and tyres

Wheel size:
   Pressed steel .... 13 x 5.50, 14 x 6.00
Tyres:
   Passenger vehicles .... 185/60 HR 13

Tyre pressure (cold) in bar (lbf/in²) front/rear:
Saloon and Estate:

Tyre size	Up to 3 occupants (or equivalent)	Fully laden
145 SR 12	1.8 (26)/1.8 (26)	2.0 (28)/2.3 (33)
155 SR 13	1.6 (23)/2.0 (28)	2.0 (28)/2.3 (33)
155 SR 13 (auto)	1.8 (26)/2.0 (28)	2.0 (28)/2.3 (33)
175/70 SR/HR 13	1.8 (26)/1.8 (26)	2.0 (28)/2.3 (33)
185/60 HR 13/14	1.8 (26)/1.8 (26)	2.0 (28)/2.3 (33)
Van:		
155 SR 13	1.8 (26)/1.8 (26)	1.8 (26)/2.6 (37)
165 RR 13	1.8 (26)/1.8 (26)	1.8 (26)/3.0 (43)

Rear suspension camber (passenger vehicles)

Ride height	Camber
XR3i:	
308 to 325 mm	−1° 31'
325 to 349 mm	−1° 5'
349 to 372 mm	−0° 30'
373 to 396 mm	0° 30'
All other models:	
349 to 372 mm	−1° 5'
373 to 396 mm	−0° 30'
397 to 420 mm	−0° 14'
421 to 438 mm	0° 52'
439 to 450 mm	1° 22'

Electrical system
Torque wrench setting

	Nm	lbf ft
Alternator mounting and adjustment bolts	20 to 25	15 to 18

---

3 Routine maintenance

Jack point positions – 1600i models

When servicing or repairing the 1600i models it should be noted that the central jacking position at the rear suggested for other models should not be used. This is due to the location of the fuel pump on this model which is mounted at this point. The jacking and safety stand support locations for the 1600i are shown in Fig. 13.3.

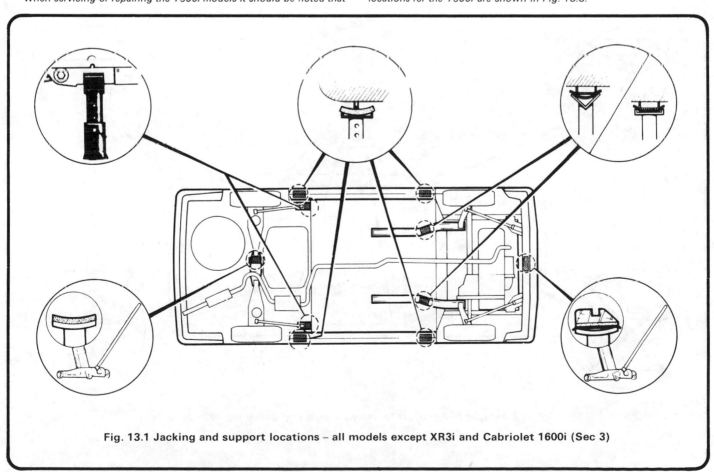

Fig. 13.1 Jacking and support locations – all models except XR3i and Cabriolet 1600i (Sec 3)

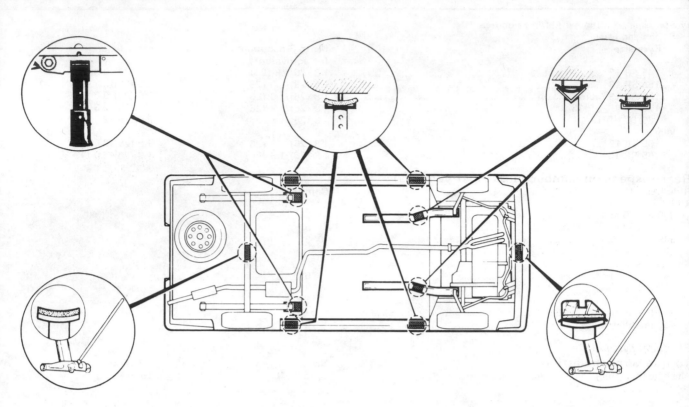

Fig. 13.2 Jacking and support locations – Van (Sec 3)

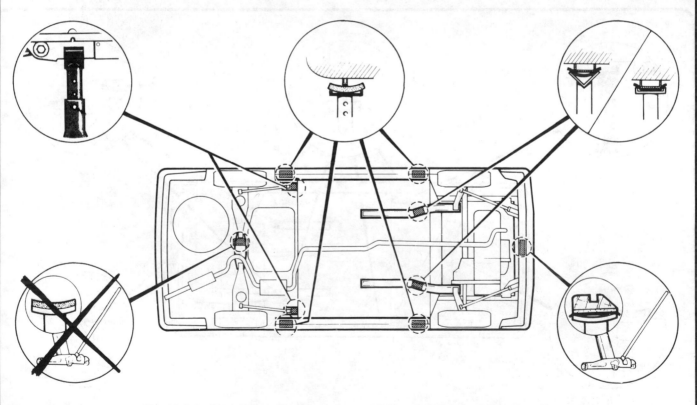

Fig. 13.3 Jacking and support locations – XR3i and Cabriolet 1600i (Sec 3)

In addition to those items mentioned in the Routine Maintenance Section at the start of this Manual, the following additional items should also be incorporated when attending to the service procedures given:

Monthly

Check the automatic transmission fluid level as given in this Chapter.

On fuel injection models check for signs of leaks or any signs of deterioration in the system hoses and pipes.

Every 20 000 km (12 000 miles)

On fuel injection models renew the air filter.

Every 40 000 km (24 000 miles)

On fuel injection models renew the fuel filter.

Every 80 000 km (48 000 miles)

Renew the timing belt on CVH engines.

4 Engine

Engine oil level – CVH engine

1 From mid 1982 the quantity of engine oil was reduced and in consequence the dipstick markings were changed.

2 For identification purposes during an engine oil change, the reduced level dipstick will have a green or white handle. In this instance refer to the Specifications in this Chapter for the amount of oil to be used, whilst for CVH engines, with dipsticks not having these colours, refer to Chapter 1.

Engine mountings

3 To eliminate the tendency of vibration when driving away from rest at certain engine speeds (about 1700 rpm), some Escorts have had a 2 mm (0.08 in) thick washer added to the engine mounting assembly to increase the mounting clearance. Reference to the accompanying figures will show the location of the washers.

4 If new rubber insulators are to be fitted it should be noted that the latter insulators are colour coded to ensure correct fitting. The rear insulator is identified by having a green paint mark on it whilst the front insulator has a black paint mark. The insulators on ohv engines also have an orange line marking.

5 If the fitting of new insulators does not give the minimum allowable clearance (X) then the previously mentioned washer must be fitted (see Figs. 13.4 and 13.5).

6 From August 1983 a revised right-hand side upper engine mounting is fitted to CVH engines. If the mounting squeaks, the lower bump stop surfaces should be smeared with petroleum jelly (Fig. 13.6).

Valve rocker studs and nuts – CVH engine

7 On later models the rocker studs differ from those fitted previously in that they have a nylon insert in the threaded section. The later type stud can be fitted in place of an earlier type, but it should be noted that its torque wrench setting is increased. This also applies to the rocker nuts, see Specifications in this Chapter.

Timing belt renewal – CVH engine

8 Although not specified by Ford it is recommended that the timing belt is renewed at 48 000 miles (80 000 km) since failure of the belt teeth would result in extensive damage to the pistons and valves.

9 On later models the timing belt cover is in two sections, each with its own rubber gasket. The lower section incorporates a mark to indicate TDC. Removal of the lower section is only possible after removing the crankshaft pulley. On reassembly it must be remembered to refit this section before refitting the pulley.

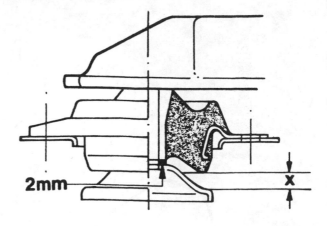

Fig. 13.4 Front left-hand engine mounting showing location for 2 mm thick washer to give minimum clearance of 3 mm required at X (Sec 4)

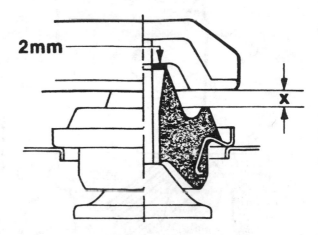

Fig. 13.5 Rear left-hand engine mounting showing location for 2 mm thick washer to give minimum clearance of 3 mm required at X (Sec 4)

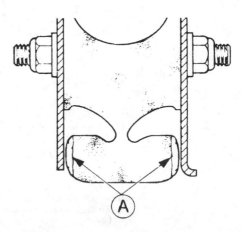

Fig. 13.6 Surfaces (A) to be smeared with petroleum jelly on upper right-hand side CVH engine mounting (Sec 4)

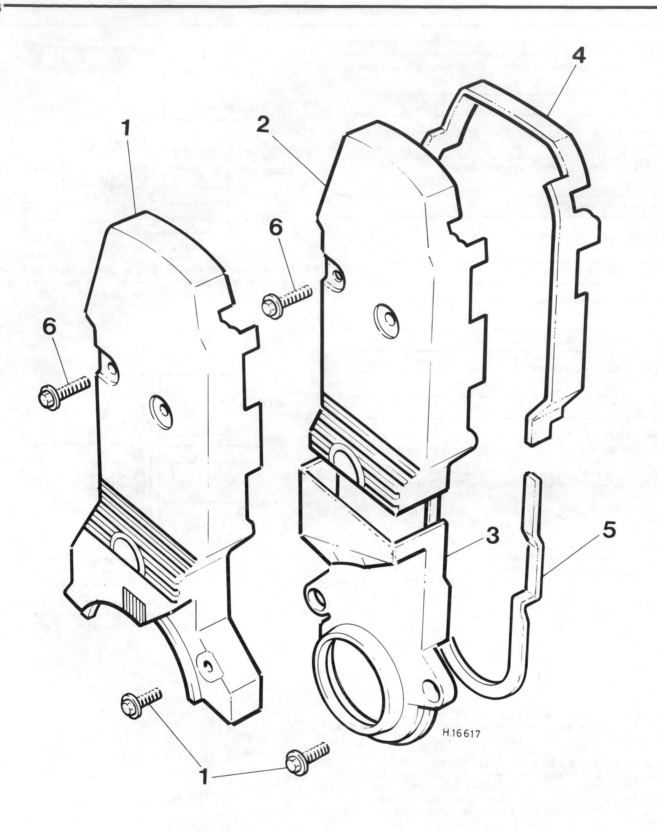

H.16617

Fig. 13.7 Timing belt covers for the CVH engine (Sec 4)

1   Early type   4   Upper gasket   6   Upper bolts
2   Upper section of later type   5   Lower gasket   7   Lower bolts
3   Lower section of later type

10 When fitting a **new** timing belt the initial tension should be greater than that given in Chapter 1, and the procedure given in the following paragraphs should be adopted after completing paragraphs 1 to 11 in Section 25 of Chapter 1. Note that a timing belt may be regarded as used after being run for half an hour.

11 Loosen off the tensioner retaining bolts by half a turn each to allow the tensioner to snap into position against the timing belt.

12 With the crankshaft locked in position at TDC, fit a 41 mm socket and torque wrench onto the camshaft sprocket bolt and apply an anticlockwise torque in accordance with the settings below depending on engine type:

| 1.1 and 1.3 litre engines | 60 to 65 Nm (44 to 48 lbf ft) |
| 1.6 litre engine | 45 to 50 Nm (33 to 36 lbf ft) |

Whilst applying the above torque setting to the camshaft, simultaneously tighten the tensioner retaining bolts, right-hand then left-hand bolt, to their specified torque wrench setting.

13 The remainder of the refitting procedure is as given in Section 25 (Chapter 1).

Engine and manual transmission (carburettor models) – removal and refitting

14 When removing the engine and manual transmission on later models the following differences apply, depending on the variant in question, to those details given for removal and refitting in Chapter 1.

15 Some later models are fitted with a carburettor having a manually operated choke, in which case it will be necessary to disconnect the choke cable from the operating lever at the choke unit. Refer to Section 6 in this Chapter for details of disconnection, refitting and adjustment.

16 On five-speed gearbox models select reverse gear to make gearchange rod reconnection easier.

17 Refitting of the five-speed gearbox is similar to that for the four-speed type, but note that there is no tension spring fitted. When the stabiliser rod is connected proceed as follows to refit and adjust the selector shift rod mechanism.

18 Insert a suitable drift or rod through the selector shaft drilling, then engage reverse gear by rotating the selector shaft clockwise from the neutral position to the point where it reaches the stop and press it fully in.

19 Check that the contacting faces of the shift rod clamp and selector shaft are grease free and loosely attach the two.

20 To adjust the linkage move the gear lever to the reverse gear position being careful not to detach the shift rod from the selector shaft, then push the lever down and move it fore or aft to align the locking holes.

21 Insert a suitable 4 mm diameter bolt (or Ford tool No 16-032) through the housing to hold the gearlever in position.

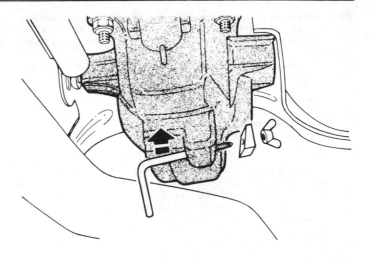

Fig. 13.8 Ford special tool 16-032 securing gearlever in position (Sec 4)

22 Using a suitable pin or rod inserted into the hole in the end of the projecting shaft, turn the shaft clockwise to its stop and hold secure in this position with a strong rubber band (Fig. 1.67 shows this). Now tighten the clamp pinch-bolt.

23 Remove the temporary locking pin from the projecting shaft and pressing down on the gearlever (to relieve the spring pressure) withdraw the bolt or Ford special tool from the housing.

Engine and manual transmission (fuel injection models) – removal and refitting

24 On fuel injection models the engine and transmission removal and refitting details are the same as those given for carburettor models, but information concerning the carburettor and its associated components must be ignored and the following items removed or disconnected instead.

25 Select reverse gear to make gearchange rod reconnection easier when refitting.

26 Disconnect and remove the air hose between the throttle valve unit and the fuel distributor unit (see Fig. 13.9).

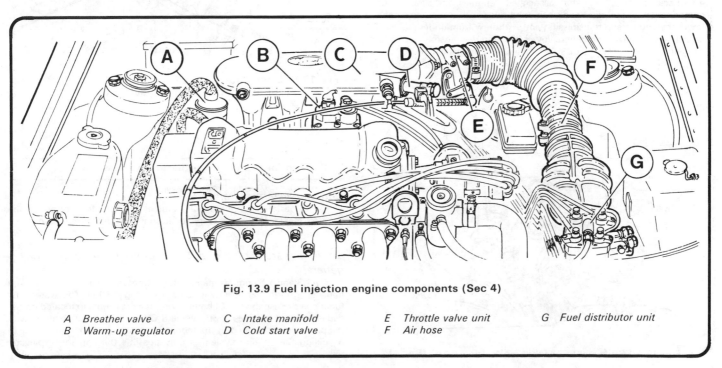

Fig. 13.9 Fuel injection engine components (Sec 4)

A	Breather valve	C	Intake manifold	E	Throttle valve unit	G	Fuel distributor unit
B	Warm-up regulator	D	Cold start valve	F	Air hose

27 In addition to disconnecting the cooling system hoses mentioned in Chapter 1 also disconnect the oil cooler three-way hose at its Y-shaped connector. This is located to the right of centre between the engine and bulkhead.

28 Disconnect the respective wiring connections from the cold start valve, the thermo-time switch, the warm-up regulator, and auxiliary air valve and the earth lead from the throttle valve stop. Label or make a note of the various leads to ensure correct reconnection during assembly.

29 Disconnect the two fuel lines at the warm-up regulator, the single fuel line at the cold start valve and the four fuel lines at the fuel distributor unit. As they are disconnected plug them to prevent the ingress of dirt.

30 Disconnect the vacuum hose from the fuel cut-off valve.

31 Pull free the breather hose from the engine ventilation valve.

32 Disconnect the throttle cable from the throttle valve unit in a similar manner to that described for detachment from a carburettor.

33 All other engine and transmission removal procedures are as given for the carburettor engine models in Chapter 1.

34 When refitting the engine and transmission take care not to allow any dirt to enter the fuel lines as they are attached. Ensure that all fuel and wiring connections are correctly made.

35 When the engine is restarted, check for any signs of leakage around the fuel system hoses and connections. Once the engine is warmed up, check and if necessary adjust its idle speed and mixture settings as described in Section 6 of this Chapter.

Engine and automatic transmission – removal and refitting

36 Refer to Section 8B in this Chapter and proceed as described in paragraphs 43 to 46 inclusive.

37 Jack up and support the front end of the vehicle, raising it sufficiently to allow the engine and transmission to be removed from underneath the vehicle.

38 Connect a suitable hoist to the engine, preferably using a spreader bar and connecting the lift hooks at the points indicated in Fig. 1.35. Engine lift lugs are provided.

39 Raise the hoist to take the weight of the engine and transmission off their mountings.

40 Unscrew and detach the speedometer cable from the transmission.

41 Unscrew and remove the two shift cable bracket securing bolts from the transmission.

42 Disconnect the starter motor leads and the reversing light lead from the actuating switch on the transmission.

43 Proceed as described in Section 8B, paragraphs 55 to 60 inclusive.

44 Unbolt the engine mounting from the side-member and from the wing apron panel. Position a protective board over the rear face of the radiator.

45 Check that all of the associated engine and transmission components are detached and positioned out of the way, then carefully lower the engine and transmission and withdraw from under the car. To ease the withdrawal operation, lower the engine/transmission onto a crawler board or a sheet of substantial plywood placed on rollers or lengths of pipe.

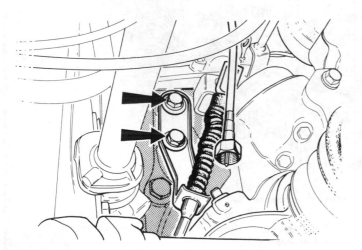

Fig. 13.10 Shift cable bracket bolts (arrowed) (Sec 4)

Separation

46 To separate the engine from the transmission, unbolt and remove the starter motor.

47 Unbolt and remove the driveplate cover, then reaching through the driveplate aperture, unscrew and remove the four nuts securing the driveplate to the torque converter. Turn the crankshaft to allow access to each nut in turn and remove the nuts in a progressive manner, one turn at a time.

48 With the engine and transmission supported, unscrew and remove the engine to transmission flange bolts at the top and bottom, then carefully separate the two units. As they are separated, retain the torque converter against the transmission to prevent it catching on the driveplate bolt. The torque converter is only loosely attached so keep it in position in the transmission housing.

49 Reassembly and refitting of the engine and automatic transmission is a reversal of the removal procedure. Refer to Section 42 in Chapter 1 for further details, but ignore those references concerning the manual transmission.

50 Reconnect the downshift linkage and selector lever as described in Section 8B, paragraphs 26 to 29 inclusive in this Chapter.

Crankcase ventilation system (XR3i and Cabriolet injection models)

51 On these models the crankcase ventilation system consists of hoses from the rocker cover and crankcase directing the blow-by fumes to the intake manifold via a filter.

52 The system has been changed on two occasions and the latest arrangement is shown in Fig. 13.11. In the event of stalling or poor idling on early models the system can be updated by obtaining the new components.

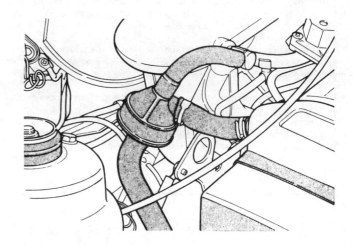

Fig. 13.11 Latest crankcase ventilation system for XR3i and Cabriolet injection models (Sec 4)

---

5   Cooling, heating and ventilation systems

Cooling system – draining

1 On some later models a drain plug is fitted to the bottom of the radiator, making it unnecessary to disconnect the bottom hose when draining the system.

Cooling system (1.3 and 1.6 engines from April 1983) – general

2 On 1.3 and 1.6 engines manufactured from April 1983 the thermostat housing is no longer fitted with a cap (see Fig. 13.12). The system still functions as described in Chapter 2 with the pressure cap located on the degas tank. 1.1 engines (both ohv and CVH) continue unchanged with the pressure cap located in the thermostat housing.

3 Filling the cooling system is only possible through the expansion tank.

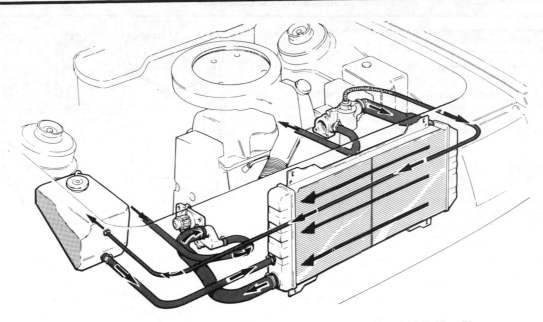

Fig. 13.12 Cooling system (1.3 and 1.6 engines from April 1983) (Sec 5)

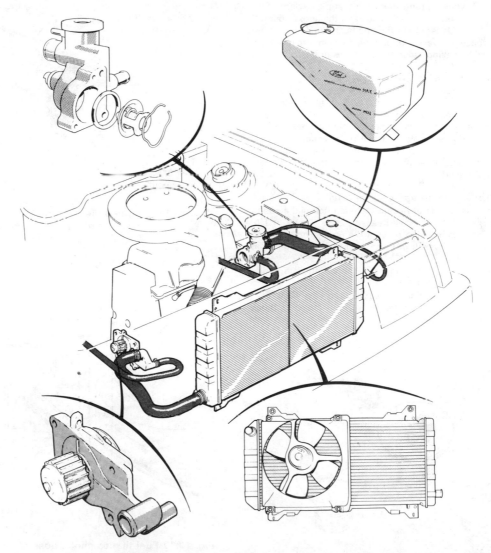

Fig. 13.13 Cooling system (1.1 CVH engine) (Sec 5)

6 Fuel and exhaust systems

Part A: Carburettor systems

Ford VV carburettor

1 On later models the external covers of the VV carburettors are secured by Torx type screws and to avoid damaging them during removal and refitting a T20 Torx screwdriver should be used. This type of screwdriver should be available from a good proprietary tool supplier or Ford accessory shop.

Ford VV carburettor – venturi valve diaphragm

2 An improved venturi valve diaphragm is fitted from early 1985 – being blue in colour as against the previous black version. The new diaphragm is designed to last longer. The version fitted to the carburettor can easily be identified by determining the colour of the diaphragm edge visible between the cover and carburettor body.

3 To remove the diaphragm withdraw the cover (4 Torx screws) followed by the return spring, then extract the circlip and detach the diaphragm from the lever. Refit in reverse order leaving the cover screws loose and ensuring that the vacuum hole is aligned in the cover, diaphragm and carburettor body. Hold the air valve fully open when tightening the screws. Check and adjust the idle speed and mixture on completion.

Ford VV carburettor – automatic choke

4 Whenever the fuel or choke hoses to this carburettor are detached for any reason it is essential when refitting to ensure that a clearance of 11 mm (0.4 in) or more exists between the fuel line and the choke hoses. If the clearance between them is less than this the heat transference from the choke hoses may cause fuel vaporization which will in turn give poor engine idling and possibly stalling when the engine is hot.

Ford VV carburettor – air bled choke system

5 A later type VV carburettor is fitted to all CVH engine models from January of 1982, which has an air bled choke system fitted. Although the servicing adjustments remain unchanged, should it be necessary to renew any of the carburettor components (particularly the choke unit) it is advisable to take the carburettor along to the parts dealer for correct identification of type. This applies to earlier models also, in case they have been updated at some time and will ensure that the correct replacement parts are obtained.

Ford VV carburettor – needle valve assembly

6 On later models a revised type of needle valve is fitted and a spring clip is added to the assembly, the position of which is shown in Fig. 13.19. This modification was made to prevent the engine from stalling shortly after it was started, as a result of the shortage of fuel in the float chamber.

7 The new type needle valve and spring clip can be fitted to earlier models.

8 Remove the old needle valve as described in Section 13 of Chapter 3, but do not under any circumstances loosen off the metering block screws for access to the needle valve.

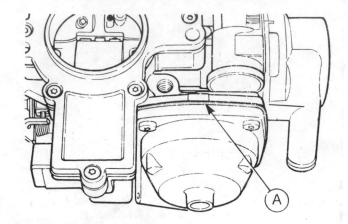

Fig. 13.15 VV carburettor venturi valve diaphragm colour identification (A) (Sec 6)

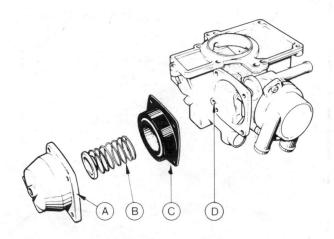

Fig. 13.16 Exploded view of the VV carburettor venturi valve diaphragm (Sec 6)

A Cover   C Diaphragm
B Return spring   D Vacuum hole

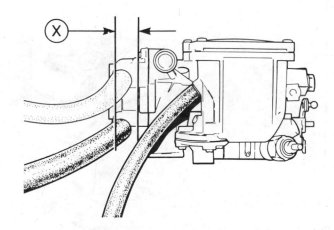

Fig. 13.17 Fuel line to choke hose clearance X must be as specified on the Ford VV carburettor (Sec 6)

X = 11 mm (0.4 in)

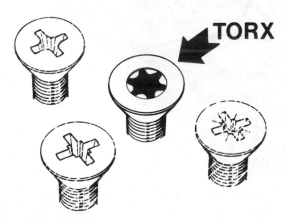

TORX

Fig. 13.14 Torx head screw (Sec 6)

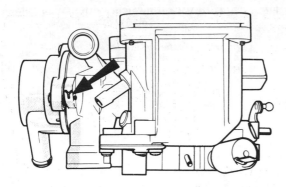

Fig. 13.18 Ford VV carburettor with air bled choke system has code mark at point indicated (Sec 6)

Y code letter   1.1 and 1.3 engines
P code letter   1.6 engine

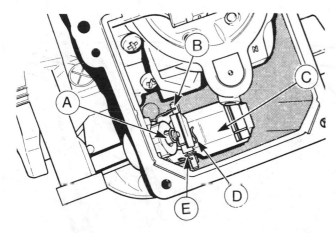

**Fig. 13.19 Ford VV carburettor revised needle valve assembly
(Sec 6)**

A	Needle valve	D	Spring clip
B	Float pin	E	Spacing washer
C	Float		

9   Fit the new needle valve into position and engage the spring clip into the groove of the valve. When refitting the float, check that the spacing washer is located between the float lever brackets and the float, with the pivot pin engaged in the float arm detents. Operate the float and check for freedom of movement before reassembling the remaining components.

Carburettor adjustment – automatic transmission models

10   Whenever carburettor adjustments are to be made on models fitted with ATX transmission, the damper rod of the downshift linkage must be preloaded as follows.
11   Rotate the damper unit so that the damper rod comes into contact with the downshift linkage lever, then scribe or paint an index mark on the damper body and turn it a further four full turns to preload the damper rod.
12   If it is found that four full turns are not possible refer to Section 8B and adjust the downshift linkage, as described in paragraphs 33 and 34.

Ford VV carburettor manual choke unit – removal and refitting

Some later models are fitted with the Ford VV carburettor which has a manual choke unit fitted. This choke unit is actuated manually by a cable, but incorporates a choke pull-down system as with the automatic

type so that the choke is controlled both manually and automatically. Remove the choke unit as follows:
13   Detach the battery earth lead.
14   Remove the air cleaner unit.
15   Unscrew the pinch-bolt and detach the choke cable from the operating lever.
16   Unscrew and remove the three Torx screws which secure the choke lever/housing cover in position. Withdraw the choke lever housing and disconnect the outer cable from its support bracket.
17   Unscrew and remove the three retaining screws from within the choke unit and withdraw the unit from the carburettor.
18   If necessary the choke lever/housing cover and the choke unit must be renewed as a matching pair since they are calibrated during manufacture.
19   Refit in the reverse order of removal using a new choke unit to carburettor gasket. Set the choke linkage at its mid-travel position when reassembling the housing and engage the spring loaded arm over the linkage lever.
20   When assembled, check that the choke lever operation is satisfactory before attaching the cable.
21   When the cable is attached ensure that it allows the choke lever full movement through its arc of travel so that the choke can be fully applied when the cable is pulled on and fully released when the cable is pushed in for the choke off position.
22   On completion check the idle speed and fuel mixture settings, as given in Section 9 of Chapter 3.

Ford VV carburettor accelerator pump diaphragm – renewal

23   Remove the carburettor, as described in Chapter 3.
24   Invert the carburettor then remove the three screws and discard the cover (a modified cover is supplied, together with the new diaphragm).
25   Remove the spring and discard the diaphragm and gasket if fitted.
26   Obtain the new diaphragm kit then, from the following table, determine the correct spacer to fit under the diaphragm:

1.1 engine	Red
1.3 engine	Black
1.6 engine	Blue

27   Locate the spacer in the carburettor body recess, then place the diaphragm over it with the gasket side outwards and the vacuum holes aligned.
28   Fit the spacer, spring and the new cover and tighten the screws evenly.
29   Refit the carburettor.

Fuel pump – CVH engine

30   If the fuel pump has been removed for any reason, or if an oil leak exists between the mating flanges of the pump and the cylinder head, the fitting clearance should be checked as follows.
31   With the pump removed, extract the operating pushrod from the cylinder head and clean the flange faces of the cylinder head and pump.
32   Fit the pump into position without the pushrod or gasket and tighten the retaining nuts down to a torque wrench setting of 2 to 4 Nm (1.4 to 3 lbf ft). Using a feeler gauge check the clearance between the pump and cylinder head flange faces. If the clearance is 0.25 mm (0.010 in) or more then the pump must be renewed.
33   Remove the pump, insert the pushrod, locate a new gasket onto the mating flange and refit the fuel pump. When tightening the fuel pump retaining nuts, tighten them in four stages on alternate sides (whilst simultaneously pressing the pump against the gasket) to the specified torque wrench setting given in Chapter 3.

Speed control system

34   This system is an optional fitting to manual transmission models only. The main components of the system are as follows:-

(a)   Hand control switch: this provides driver control over the system.
(b)   Speed sensor unit: this device passes the road speed information to the electronic control unit.
(c)   Electronic control unit: this gives the actuator assembly throttle position information in accordance with the information received from the hand control switch and the speed sensor.
(d)   Actuator assembly: this device converts the electrical signals received from the control unit to mechanically control the throttle.

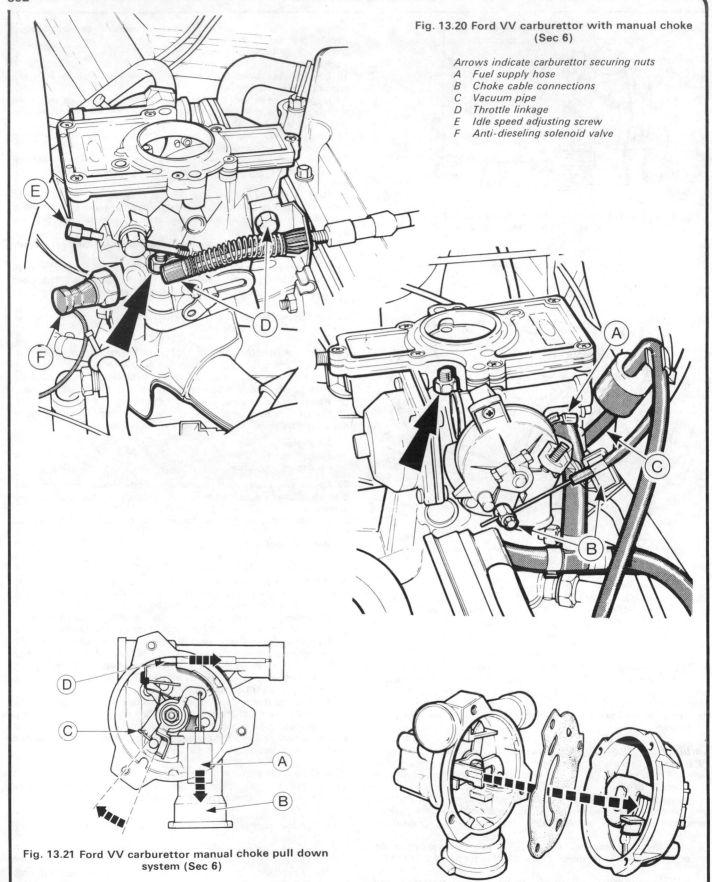

Fig. 13.20 Ford VV carburettor with manual choke (Sec 6)

Arrows indicate carburettor securing nuts
A   *Fuel supply hose*
B   *Choke cable connections*
C   *Vacuum pipe*
D   *Throttle linkage*
E   *Idle speed adjusting screw*
F   *Anti-dieseling solenoid valve*

Fig. 13.21 Ford VV carburettor manual choke pull down system (Sec 6)

A   *Pull-down piston movement*
B   *High vacuum*
C   *Choke lever fully anti-clockwise*
D   *Needle valve closing*

Fig. 13.22 Ford VV carburettor showing choke lever to choke unit engagement (Sec 6)

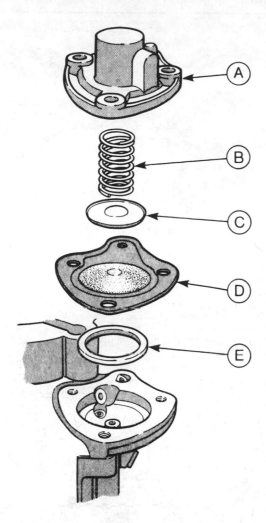

Fig. 13.23 Modified accelerator pump diaphragm
components on the VV carburettor (Sec 6)

A Cover D Diaphragm
B Spring E Coloured spacer
C Spacer

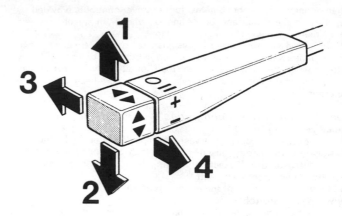

Fig. 13.24 Speed control switch positions and functions
(Sec 6)

Position 1
Set current speed — Move lever briefly and release
Accelerate — Move lever and hold in position
Set accelerated speed — Release lever
Position 2
Set current speed — Move lever briefly and release
Decelerate — Move lever and hold in position
Set decelerated speed — Release lever
Position 3
Cancel speed control — Move lever briefly and release

Note Speed control is also cancelled by actuating brake or clutch
pedal

Position 4*
Resume to last set speed — Move lever briefly and release
(eg, after brake or clutch
actuation)

* Memory function (position 4) must only be used if you are sure of
the previously set speed. The memory function of the system stores
the vehicle speed last set until the ignition is switched off

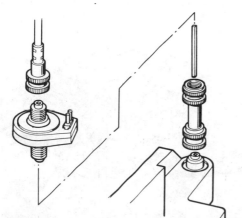

Fig. 13.25 Speed sensor unit location (Sec 6)

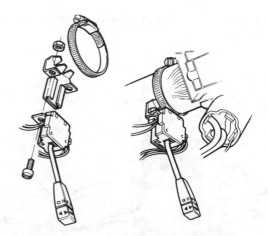

Fig. 13.26 Hand control switch and securing clip (Sec 6)

35 In addition to the above items, further driver control is provided by switches on the clutch and brake pedals, whereby a signal conveyed from either switch will turn off the system.

36 The speed control system is designed for use under normal open road or motorway driving conditions and should not be used in heavy traffic, on winding roads or where the road conditions are slippery. Never engage the speed control system when the driving wheels are clear of the ground.

Speed control system components – removal and refitting

Speed sensor unit

37 This device is located between the speedometer cable and the transmission. To remove, unscrew and detach the speedometer cable from the sensor unit. Detach the wiring from the sensor unit then unscrew the unit from the adaptor.

38 Refitting is a reversal of the removal procedure.

Hand control switch

39 Disconnect the battery earth lead then detach and remove the steering column upper and lower shrouds, as described in Chapter 9 (Section 7). Loosen the control switch clip, detach the wiring connector from the control switch and the switch from the column.

40 Refitting is the reverse of the removal procedure, but centralise the switch in relation to the aperture in the column shroud before fully tightening the securing clip.

Electronic control unit

41 Disconnect the battery earth lead. Unclip and detach the underdash panel on the driver's side for access to the control unit. Disconnect the wiring at the connector, then unscrew and remove the unit retaining nuts and screws and withdraw it.

42 Refit in reverse order of removal.

Actuator assembly

43 This unit is attached to a mounting bracket which is located just forward of the expansion tank.

44 Remove the three mounting nuts, bolts and washers and detach the actuator from the mounting bracket. Withdraw the actuator snout as shown then disconnect the inner cable. Disconnect the electrical wire at the connector and remove the actuator.

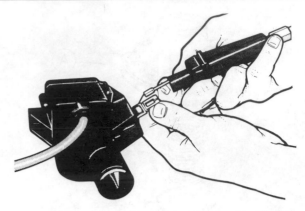

Fig. 13.29 Disconnecting the actuator cable (Sec 6)

45 Refitting is a reversal of the removal procedure, but if locating a new cable into the actuator snout, thread the adjuster in by approximately 13 mm (0.5 in).

Accelerator cable

46 Although the accelerator cable can be removed and refitted in a similar manner to that described in Chapter 3 it should be noted that its attachment at the carburettor differs slightly as shown in the accompanying illustrations.

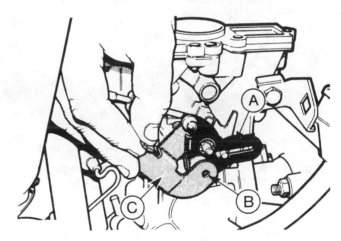

Fig. 13.30 Ford VV carburettor with speed control system accelerator assembly (Sec 6)

A   Original throttle lever   C   Accelerator connection
B   Securing bolt hole

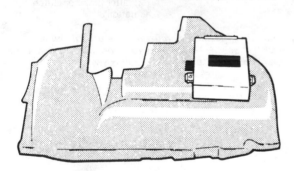

Fig. 3.27 Electronic control unit mounting (Sec 6)

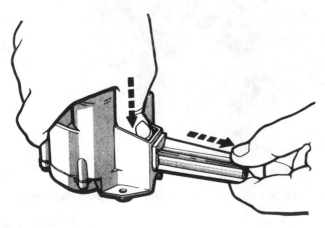

Fig. 13.28 Actuator snout removal (Sec 6)

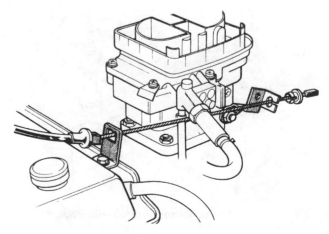

Fig. 13.31 2V carburettor with speed control system has this accelerator connection (Sec 6)

Brake and clutch pedal switches

47 These switches are attached to a bracket which is secured to the main pedal support bracket. Each switch is secured by means of an adjuster nut and locknut. A spade terminal wiring connector fits into the rear of each switch.

48 Whenever the switches have been removed it is essential, when refitting either, to adjust them for position so that when the pedal concerned is in the rest position the switch is depressed by half of its operating travel. Secure in this position by tightening the locknut.

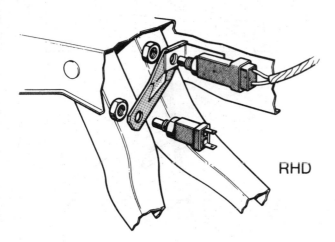

RHD

Fig. 13.32 Clutch pedal switch (right-hand drive) (Sec 6)

Part B: Fuel injection system

General description and principle of operation

The fuel injection system fitted is of the continuous injection type and supplies a precisely controlled quantity of atomized fuel to each cylinder under all operating conditions.

This system, when compared with conventional carburettor arrangements, achieves a more accurate control of the air/flow mixture resulting in reduced emission levels and improved performance.

The main components of the fuel injection system fall into two groups:

Group A

Fuel tank
Fuel pump
Fuel accumulator
Fuel filter
Warm-up regulator
Throttle plate (valve)
Injector valve
Fuel distributor and mixture control
Auxiliary air device
Air box (plenum chamber)
Starter valve

Group B

Thermo-time switch
Safety module and fuse
Speed sensor module
Fuel shut-off valve
Wiring

The fuel tank is similar to the one for carburettor type vehicles except that before removing it, the pipes to the fuel pump and accumulator and the pipe from the pressure regulator must be disconnected and plugged.

The fuel pump is of electrically operated, roller cell type. A pressure relief valve is incorporated in the pump to prevent excessive pressure build up in the event of a restriction in the pipelines.

The fuel accumulator has two functions, (i) to dampen the pulsation of the fuel flow, generated by the pump and (ii) to maintain

fuel pressure after the engine has been switched off. This prevents a vapour lock developing with consequent hot starting problems.

The fuel filter incorporates two paper filter elements to ensure that the fuel reaching the injection system components is completely free from dirt.

The fuel distribution/mixture control assembly. The fuel distributor controls the quantity of fuel being delivered to the engine, ensuring that each cylinder receives the same amount. The mixture control assembly incorporates an air sensor plate and control plunger. The air sensor plate is located in the main air stream before the air cleaner and the throttle butterfly. During idling, the airflow lifts the sensor plate which in turn raises a control plunger which allows fuel to flow past the plunger and out of the metering slits to the injector valves. Increases in engine speed cause increased airflow which raises the control plunger and so admits more fuel. It is important to note that each injection supply pipe connection in the distributor head has a screw adjacent to it. These four screws are not for adjustment and must not be removed or have their settings altered.

The throttle valve assembly is mounted in the main air intake between the mixture control assembly and the air box. The throttle valve plate is controlled by a cable connected to the accelerator pedal. During manufacture the throttle plate is adjusted so that it is fractionally open to avoid the possibility of it jamming shut, and it must not be repositioned. Idle speed adjustment is provided for by means of a screw which, according to its setting, restricts the airflow through the air bypass channel in the throttle housing.

The injector valves are located in the intake manifold and are designed to open at a fuel pressure of 3.5 bar (50.7 lbf/in²).

The air box is mounted on the top of the engine and functions as an auxiliary intake manifold directing air from the sensor plate to each individual cylinder.

The warm-up regulator is located on the intake manifold and incorporates two coil springs, a bi-metal strip and a control pressure valve. The regulator controls the fuel supplied to the control circuit which provides pressure variations to the fuel distributor control plunger. When the coil springs are pushing against the control pressure valve there is a high control pressure and this gives a weak mixture. The coil spring pressure application is controlled by the bi-metal strip which in turn is activated in accordance with engine temperature and an electrical heat coil.

The auxiliary air device is located on the intake manifold. It consists of a pivoted plate, bi-metal strip and heater coil. The purpose of this device is to supply an increased volume of fuel/air mixture during cold idling rather similar to the fast idle system on carburettor layouts.

The fuel start valve system consists of an electrical injector and a thermo-time switch. Its purpose is to spray fuel into the air box to assist cold starting, the thermo-time switch regulating the amount of fuel injected.

The safety module is located under the facia panel on the driver's side and is coloured purple. Its purpose is to shut off the power supply to the fuel pump should the engine stall for any reason or the vehicle be involved in an accident. The module is basically a sensor which senses the ignition low tension circuit pulses. When the pulses stop the module is deactivated and power to the fuel pump is cut.

The shut-off valve system is an economy device whereby air is drawn from within the air cleaner unit, through the shut-off valve and directed into the ducting chamber above the air sensor plate and causing a depression. This then causes the sensor plate to drop which in turn shuts off the fuel supply. The shut-off valve will only operate under the following circumstances:

(a) *Only when the engine coolant temperature is at or above 35°C (95°F)*

(b) *Only when the throttle is closed and with the engine speed decelerating from speeds above 1600 rpm*

The coolant temperature must be above that specified to ensure that the valve does not shut off the fuel supply during the initial engine warm up period.

When the throttle is released to the closed position, it contacts an electrical switch which will only operate once the specified coolant temperature is reached. This switch will activate the shut-off valve when the throttle is fully released and the engine speed is over 1600 rpm, but once the engine speed drops below 1400 rpm the switch and valve are deactivated. The engine speed is sensed by a speed sensing module which is coloured black and located beneath the facia panel on the driver's side.

Fig. 13.33 Fuel injection system principal components and locations (Sec 6)

A Warm-up regulator
B Speed sensing module and fuel pump
   safety module

C Fuel accumulator
D Electric fuel pump
E Throttle housing

F Start valve
G Mixture control unit
H Fuel filter

Note: *Auxiliary air device is hidden below the start valve (to the right of the warm-up regulator). The fuel shut-off valve is in the air cleaner top cover*

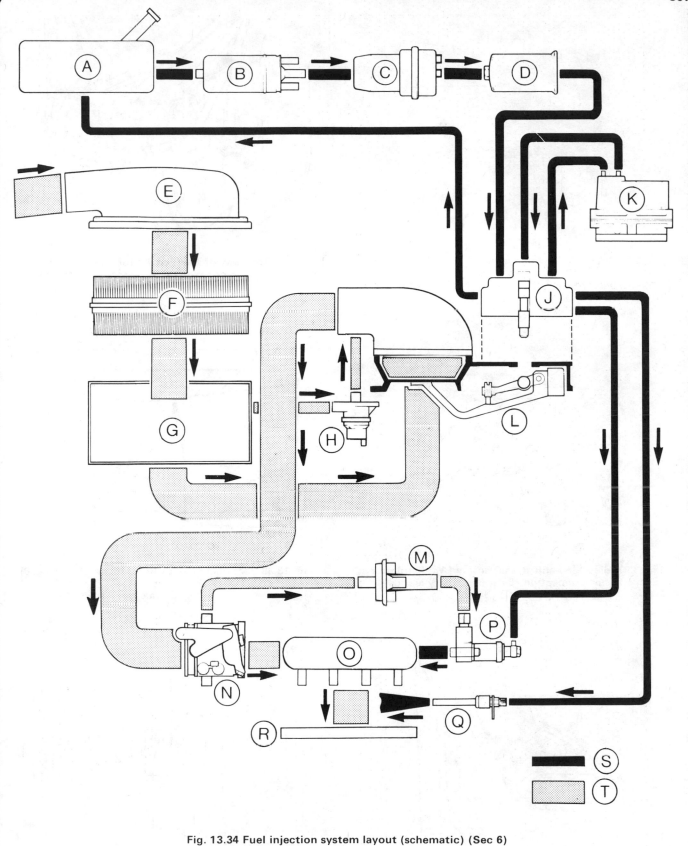

Fig. 13.34 Fuel injection system layout (schematic) (Sec 6)

A	Fuel tank	F	Air filter
B	Pump	G	Cleaner body
C	Accumulator	H	Shut-off valve
D	Filter	J	Fuel distributor
E	Air intake	K	Warm-up regulator

L	Sensor plate	Q	Injectors
M	Auxiliary air device	R	Intake manifold
N	Throttle housing	S	Fuel flow
O	Plenum chamber	T	Air flow
P	Start valve		

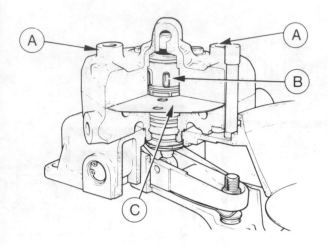

Fig. 13.35 Cutaway view of fuel distributor unit (Sec 6)

A   Fuel outlet connections   C   Steel diaphragm
B   Control plunger and barrel

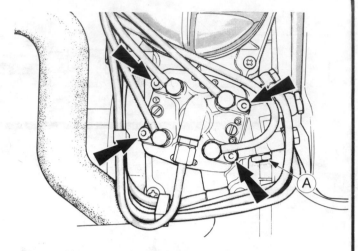

Fig. 13.36 Top view of fuel distributor head and regulator screw (A). Do not remove or tamper with the four screws arrowed (Sec 6)

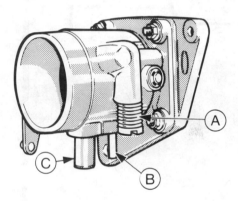

Fig. 13.37 Idle speed adjustment screw (A), distributor vacuum pipe connection (B) and auxiliary air hose connection (C) (Sec 6)

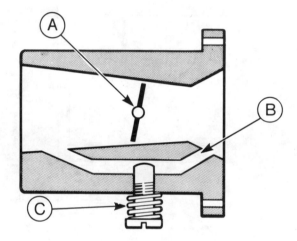

Fig. 13.38 Sectional view of the throttle plate (Sec 6)

A   Throttle plate   C   Idle speed adjustment screw
B   Bypass air channel

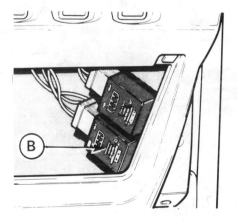

Fig. 13.39 Speed sensing module and fuel pump safety module (B) (Sec 6)

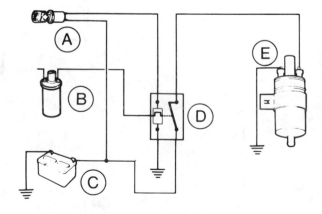

Fig. 13.40 The safety control circuit (Sec 6)

A   Ignition key   D   Safety module
B   Coil   E   Fuel pump
C   Battery

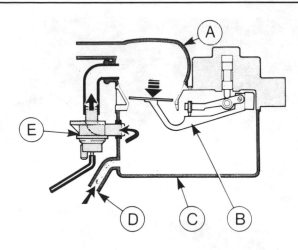

Fig. 13.41 Shut-off valve system components (Sec 6)

A	Air ducting
B	Sensor plate
C	Air cleaner body
D	Air intake
E	Shut-off valve (open)

6B.9A Loosen off the air ducting band ...

6B.9B ... and separate the ducting from the sensor plate

Maintenance, adjustments and precautions – general

1 Due to the complexity of the fuel injection system, any work should be limited to the operations described in this Chapter. Other adjustments and system checks are beyond the scope of most readers and should be left to your Ford dealer.

2 The mixture setting is preset during production of the car and should not normally require adjustment. If new components of the system have been fitted however, the mixture can be adjusted by referring to paragraphs 17 to 29 in this Section.

3 The only adjustment which may be needed is to vary the engine idle speed by means of the screw mounted in the throttle housing. Use the screw to set the engine speed to that specified when the engine is at the normal operating temperature.

4 Routine servicing of the fuel injection system consists of checking the system components for condition and security, and renewing the air cleaner element and fuel filter at the specified intervals (see Routine Maintenance).

5 In the event of a malfunction in the system, reference should be made to the Fault Diagnosis at the end of Part B in this Section. But first make a basic check of the system hoses, connections, fuses and relays for any obvious and immediately visible defects.

6 If any part of the system has to be disconnected or removed for any reason, particular care must be taken to ensure that no dirt is allowed to enter the system.

7 The system is normally pressurised, irrespective of engine temperature, and care must therefore be taken when disconnecting fuel lines, the ignition must be off and the battery disconnected.

Air cleaner element – removal and refitting

8 Disconnect the battery earth lead.

9 Unscrew and loosen off the air ducting to sensor plate unit securing band, then separate the two (photos).

10 Carefully pull free the shut-off valve hose from the air ducting connector. The hose is a press fit.

11 Unscrew and remove the six air sensor plate to cleaner top cover retaining screws, but leave the plate unit in position for the moment.

12 Prise free and release the air cleaner cover retaining clips and detach the hose from the cover at the front (photo).

13 Carefully lift the sensor plate clear, together with its gasket, and pivot it back out of the way. Withdraw the shut-off valve from the rear end of the cleaner case cover then lift out the cover and remove the element from the casing (photos).

14 If the air cleaner casing is to be removed you will need to detach the fuel filter from the side of the cleaner casing (leave the fuel lines attached to the filter) and the air intake hose from the front end of the case. Unscrew and remove the casing retaining nuts from the inner wing panel and lift out the casing.

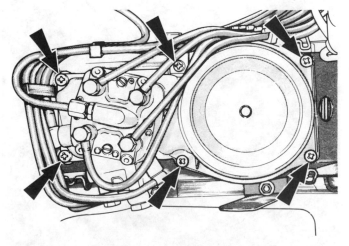

Fig. 13.42 Air sensor plate to air cleaner retaining screws (arrowed) (Sec 6)

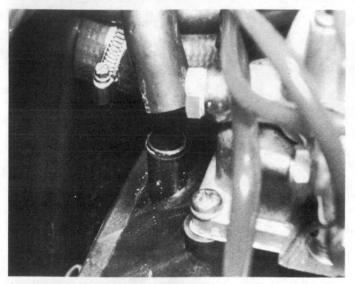

6B.12 Detach the hose from the air cleaner cover

6B.13C ... and, with cover removed, lift out the element

6B.13A Lift off the sensor plate unit ...

6B.15 Locate the sensor plate gasket before fitting

15 Refitting is the reversal of the removal procedure. Wipe the casing clean before inserting the new element. When fitting the sensor plate unit into position on the top cover check that the gasket is in good condition and aligned correctly (photo).
16 Check that all connections are secure on completion.

Idle speed and fuel mixture – adjustment

17 The idle speed and fuel mixture adjustments will normally only be required after the installation of new components to the fuel injection system.
18 The idle mixture screw is located at the rear of the throttle housing and access is severely limited unless the front section of the heater air intake scoop is removed, as described in Section 17 of Chapter 2.
19 The idle is best checked and if necessary adjusted using an externally attached tachometer; connected in accordance with the manufacturer's instructions.
20 Run the engine to warm it up to its normal operating temperature before making any checks and adjustments.
21 With the engine warmed up, run the engine at 3000 rpm and hold it at this speed for 30 seconds, then allow the engine to idle and check the tachometer reading. If idle speed adjustment is necessary, turn the adjuster screw to set the speed at that specified.

6B.13B ... detach the shut-off valve ...

22 To check the mixture adjustment an exhaust gas analyser is needed and should be connected according to manufacturer's instructions. A 3 mm Allen key will also be required to make any adjustments.

23 Before checking the mixture adjustment the idle speed must be correct.

24 Break off the tamperproof cap from the mixture control screw on top of the fuel distributor.

25 Stabilise the exhaust gases, as described in paragraph 21.

26 Insert a 3 mm Allen key into the head of the mixture screw and turn the screw until the correct CO reading is obtained. Readjust the idle speed screw.

27 If the mixture adjustment cannot be finalised within 30 seconds from the moment of stabilising the exhaust gases, repeat the operations described in paragraph 5 before continuing the adjustment procedure.

28 On completion fit a new tamperproof plug and disconnect the tachometer and CO meter.

29 Do not, under any circumstances, touch the screws adjacent to each injector pipe on the fuel distributor head.

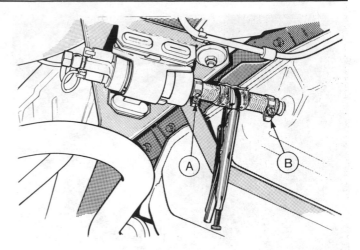

Fig. 13.44 Clamp the fuel inlet hose between the pump (A) and tank (B) connections (Sec 6)

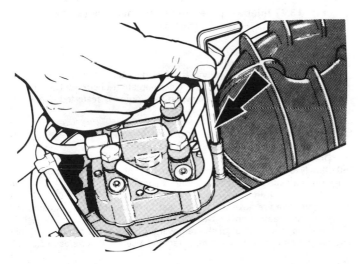

Fig. 13.43 Mixture setting adjustment using 3 mm Allen key (Sec 6)

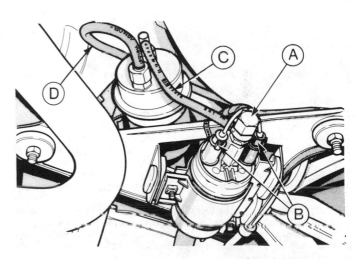

Fig. 13.45 Fuel pump and accumulator connections (Sec 6)

A Outlet union
B Wiring connections
C Inlet pipe to accumulator

D Outlet pipe from accumulator

Fuel pump – removal and refitting

30 The fuel pump is bolted to the underside of the car just to the rear of the fuel tank and to the right of the fuel accumulator. For access raise and support the car at the rear.

31 Disconnect the battery earth lead.

32 To relieve the system pressure, slowly loosen off the fuel feed pipe at the warm-up regulator and absorb fuel leakage in a cloth.

33 Clamp the fuel inlet hose midway between the tank and the pump using a brake hose clamp, grips or similar. If the fuel level in the tank is low, you may prefer to drain the fuel from the tank into a suitable container once the inlet hose is disconnected.

34 Disconnect the fuel inlet and outlet pipes from the pump catching fuel spillage in a suitable container. Once disconnected do not allow dirt to enter the pipes, temporarily plug or seal them if necessary.

35 Note the electrical connections to the pump and disconnect them.

36 Loosen off the pump bracket retaining bolt and then withdraw the pump unit with rubber protective sleeve.

37 Refitting of the fuel pump is a reversal of the removal procedure. Renew the feed pipe from the tank if it was damaged or defective when disconnected and/or clamped.

38 Check that the rubber protector sleeve is correctly positioned round the pump before tightening the clamp bolt.

39 On completion, retighten the warm-up regulator fuel inlet connector, reconnect the battery earth lead, restart the engine and check for any signs of leaks from the pump and warm-up regulator hoses.

Fuel accumulator – removal and refitting

40 The fuel accumulator is mounted adjacent to the fuel pump above the rear left-hand suspension arm.

41 Disconnect the battery.

42 Place the rear of the car over an inspection pit or raise it on ramps or axle-stands.

43 Relieve the system pressure by slowly loosening off the fuel feed pipe at the warm-up regulator. Absorb fuel leakage in a cloth.

44 Disconnect the fuel pipes from the fuel accumulator and catch the small quantity of fuel which will be released.

45 Remove the clamp screw and remove the accumulator.

46 Refitting is a reversal of removal. Check for leaks on completion (with engine restarted).

Fuel filter – removal and refitting

47 Disconnect the battery earth lead.

48 To relieve the system pressure, slowly loosen off the fuel feed pipe at the warm up regulator and absorb the fuel leakage in a cloth.

49 Position a suitable container beneath the filter pipe connections and disconnect the fuel inlet and outlet pipes from the filter (photo).

50 Loosen off the filter clamp bracket screw and withdraw the filter from the bracket.

51 Refit in the reverse order of removal. On completion restart the engine and check the filter hoses and warm-up regulator feed pipe connections for any signs of leaks.

6B.49 Fuel filter

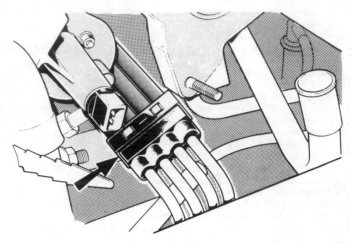

Fig. 13.47 Injector pipes and hoses harness (arrowed)
(Sec 6)

Fuel injectors and injector delivery pipes – removal and refitting

52 Disconnect the battery earth lead.
53 Detach the four supply pipes from the injectors.
54 Unscrew and remove the respective injector retaining bracket bolts then withdraw the injectors and their O-ring seals.
55 The injector fuel delivery pipes can be removed by unscrewing and removing the four banjo bolts at the distributor head. Note the respective pipe connections as they are detached and remove the pipes, complete with the plastic hoses and the injector harness. Do not separate the pipes or hoses from the injector harness.
56 Before reassembling the fuel delivery pipes or the injectors clean all pipe connections thoroughly and use new O-ring seals on the injectors. Use new seal washers on the banjo connections fitting two washers (one at each side) per union. Do not overtighten the banjo bolts, or the washers may fracture.

57 Refitting of the injectors and the fuel delivery pipes is otherwise a reversal of the removal procedure. On completion check that the pipes and hoses are not distorted and when the engine is restarted check for any signs of leaks.

Fuel start valve – removal and refitting

58 Disconnect the battery earth lead connections.
59 Detach the electrical lead connector from the plug.
60 Slowly unscrew and remove the fuel supply pipe banjo bolt. Take care on removal as the system will be under pressure. Soak up fuel spillage with a cloth.
61 Unscrew and remove the two socket-head mounting bolts using an Allen key and remove the valve.
62 Refitting is a reversal of the removal procedure. Do not overtighten the banjo bolt or the washers may fracture. Use a new one each side of the union.
63 On completion restart the engine and check for signs of fuel leakage.

Auxiliary air device – removal and refitting

64 Disconnect the battery earth lead.
65 Detach the electric plug and the two air hoses from the device.

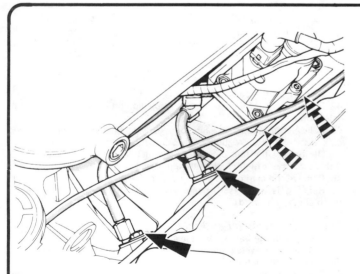

Fig. 13.46 Injector retaining bolts (arrowed) (Sec 6)

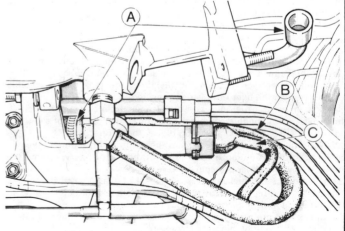

Fig. 13.48 Auxiliary air device connectors (Sec 6)

A   Throttle housing hose   C   Electric plug
B   Start valve hose

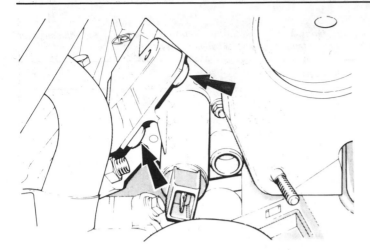

Fig. 13.49 Auxiliary air device retaining bolts (arrowed) (Sec 6)

66 Unscrew and remove the two socket-head mounting bolts using an Allen key and lift the unit away.
67 Refitting is the reversal of the removal procedure.

Warm-up regulator – removal and refitting

68 Disconnect the battery earth lead.
69 Detach the electric pump from the regulator.
70 Unscrew and remove the fuel inlet and outlet pipe banjo bolts, taking care to unscrew the first one slowly to relieve any pressure in the system. Soak up any fuel spillage with a cloth.
71 Unscrew and remove the two socket-head bolts which secure the regulator unit in position then withdraw the unit.
72 Refitting is a reversal of the removal procedure. Use a locking compound on the threads of the unit securing bolts. When reconnecting the fuel lines use new banjo bolt washers (one each side of the union) and take care not to overtighten the bolts.
73 On completion check fuel pipe connections for any sign of leakage with the engine running.

Fuel distributor – removal and refitting

74 Disconnect the battery earth lead.
75 Slowly unscrew and disconnect the warm-up regulator feed pipe connection at the distributor, catching any fuel spillage in a cloth.
76 Disconnect the injector feed pipes from the distributor also the fuel

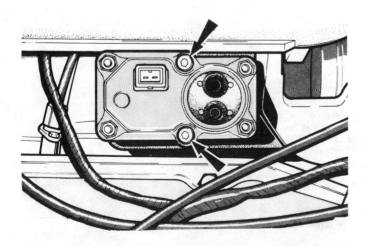

Fig. 13.50 Warm-up regulator showing Torx retaining screws (arrowed) (Sec 6)

inlet and return pipes. Note sealing washers which must be renewed on reconnection of the pipes. Take care not to let dirt enter the pipes on their connection points.
77 Unscrew and remove the three retaining screws from the top face and remove the distributor and O-ring.

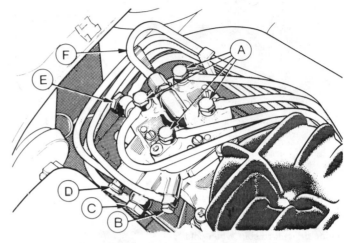

Fig. 13.51 Fuel distributor pipe connections (Sec 6)

A To injectors	D From regulator
B To start valve	E Fuel inlet
C Fuel return	F To warm-up regulator

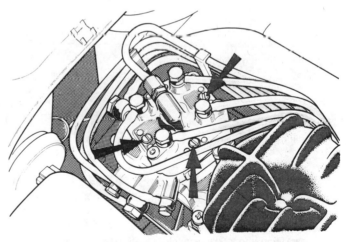

Fig. 13.52 Fuel distributor retaining screws (arrowed) (Sec 6)

78 Refitting is a reversal of the removal process. Ensure that the air sensor plate and distributor mating faces are clean before reassembling together with a new O-ring seal.
79 When reconnecting the pipes to their distributor connection points fit a new oil seal washer each side of the unions. Do not overtighten the union bolts.
80 On completion check for any signs of leaks and have the system pressure checked by your dealer.
81 Adjust the idle speed and mixture, as described elsewhere in this Section.

Fault diagnosis – fuel injection system

Note: *High fuel consumption and poor performance are not necessarily due to fuel faults. Make sure that the ignition system is properly adjusted, that the brakes are not binding and that the engine is in good mechanical condition before tampering with the injection system.*

Symptom	Reason(s)
Engine will not start when cold	Fuel pump faulty Auxiliary air device not opening Start valve not operating Start valve leak Sensor plate rest position incorrect Sensor plate and/or control plunger sticking Vacuum system leak Fuel system leak Thermo-time switch remains open
Engine will not start when hot	Faulty fuel pump Warm control pressure low Sensor plate rest position incorrect Sensor plate and/or control plunger sticky Vacuum system leak Fuel system leak Leaky injector valve(s) or low opening pressure Incorrect mixture adjustment
Engine difficult to start when cold	Cold control pressure incorrect Auxiliary air device not opening Faulty start valve Sensor plate rest position faulty Sensor plate and/or control plunger sticking Fuel system leak Thermo-time switch not closing
Engine difficult to start when hot	Warm control pressure too high or too low Auxiliary air device faulty Sensor plate/control plunger faulty Fuel or vacuum leak in system Leaky injector (valve(s) or low opening pressure Incorrect mixture adjustment
Rough idling (during warm-up period)	Incorrect 'cold' control pressure Auxiliary air device not closing (or opening) Start valve leak Fuel or vacuum leak in system Leaky injector valve(s) or low opening pressure
Rough idling (engine warm)	Warm control pressure incorrect Auxiliary air device not closing Start valve leaking Sensor plate and/or control plunger sticky Fuel or vacuum leak in system Injector(s) or low opening pressure Incorrect mixture adjustment
Engine backfiring into intake manifold	Warm control pressure high Vacuum system leak
Engine backfiring into exhaust manifold	Warm control pressure high Start valve leak Fuel system leak Incorrect mixture adjustment
Engine misfires (on road)	Fuel system leak
Engine 'runs on'	Sensor plate and/or control plunger sticky Injector valve(s) leaking or low opening pressure
Excessive petrol consumption	Fuel system leak Mixture adjustment incorrect Low warm control pressure

CO level at idle high	Low warm control pressure Mixture adjustment incorrect Fuel system leak Sensor plate and/or control plunger sticky Start valve leak
CO level at idle low	High warm control pressure Mixture adjustment incorrect Start valve leak Vacuum system leak
Idle speed adjustment difficult (too high)	Auxiliary air device not closing

Part C: Emission control system

Emission control system (UK models) – description and component renewal

An emission control system is fitted in order to reduce the level of noxious gases that would otherwise be emitted from the vehicle exhaust. The system fitted can vary according to model, but whatever system is used it should be realised that for optimum reduction of exhaust gas CO level, the good tune of the engine (fuel and ignition) and the efficiency of the temperature controlled air cleaner are essential requirements.

To improve driveability during warm-up conditions and to keep exhaust emission levels to a minimum, a vacuum-operated, temperature-sensitive emission control system is fitted to all CVH engines covered by this manual. The system is designed to ensure that the rate of distributor vacuum advance is compatible with the change in fuel/air mixture flow under all throttle conditions, thus resulting in more complete combustion and reduced exhaust emissions.

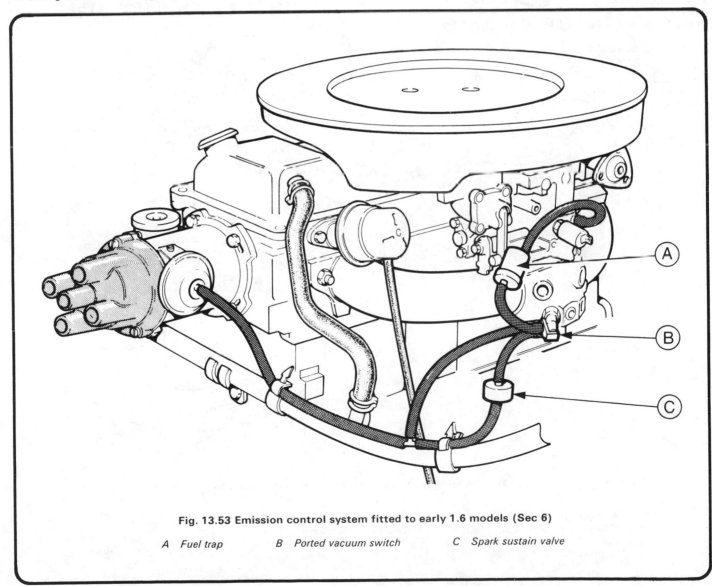

Fig. 13.53 Emission control system fitted to early 1.6 models (Sec 6)

A Fuel trap   *B Ported vacuum switch*   *C Spark sustain valve*

Under part throttle cruising conditions, distributor vacuum advance is required to allow time for the fuel/air mixture in the cylinders to burn. When returning to a part throttle opening after accelerating or decelerating, the distributor vacuum increases before the fuel/air mixture has stabilised. On 1.1 and 1.3 engines this can lead to short periods of incomplete combustion and increased exhaust emission. To reduce this condition a spark delay valve is incorporated in the vacuum line between the carburettor and distributor to reduce the rate at which the distributor advances. Under certain conditions, particularly during the period of engine warm-up, some models may suffer from a lack of throttle response. To overcome this problem a spark sustain valve may be fitted in the vacuum line either individually or in conjunction with the spark delay valve. This valve is used to maintain distributor vacuum under transient throttle conditions, thus stabilising the combustion process.

The operation of the valves is controlled by a ported vacuum switch (PVS) which has the vacuum lines connected to it. The PVS operates in a similar manner to that of the thermostat in the cooling system. A wax filled sensor is attached to a plunger which operates a valve. The PVS is actuated by the engine cooling water and is sensitive to changes in engine operating temperature. When the engine is cold the sensor moved the plunger to open the upper and middle ports of the PVS. Therefore vacuum applied to the middle port is directed to the distributor via the upper port. As the engine warms up and coolant temperature increases, the wax expands and the plunger closes the upper port and opens the lower port. Vacuum applied to the centre port is now directed to the distributor via the lower port. In this way the spark sustain or delay valves can be activated or bypassed according to engine operation temperature. The vacuum applied to the middle port of the PVS is taken from a connection on the carburettor through a fuel trap. The fuel trap prevents fuel or fuel vapour from being drawn into the distributor vacuum unit.

Testing of the various components of the system is not within the scope of the home mechanic due to the need for a vacuum pump and gauge, but if a fault has been diagnosed by a garage having the necessary equipment, the renewal of a defective component can be carried out in the following way.

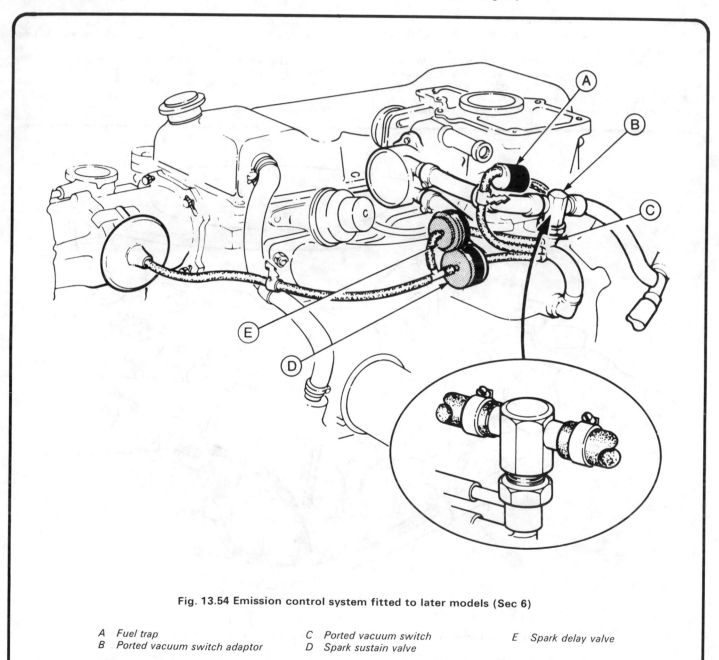

Fig. 13.54 Emission control system fitted to later models (Sec 6)

A   Fuel trap   C   Ported vacuum switch   E   Spark delay valve
B   Ported vacuum switch adaptor   D   Spark sustain valve

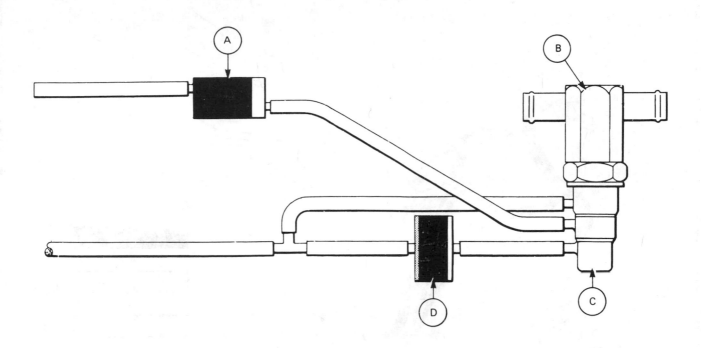

Fig. 13.55 Emission control system with alternative vacuum hose connections to the sustain valve (Sec 6)

A   Fuel trap   C   Ported vacuum switch   D   Spark sustain valve
B   Ported vacuum switch adaptor

Spark delay/sustain valve – removal and refitting

1   Disconnect the vacuum lines at the valve and remove the valve from the engine.

2   When refitting a spark delay valve it must be positioned with the black side (marked CARB) towards the carburettor and the coloured side (marked DIST) towards the distributor. When refitting a spark sustain valve the side marked VAC must be towards the carburettor and the side marked DIST towards the distributor.

Ported vacuum switch – removal and refitting

3   Remove the filler cap from the expansion tank to the reduce pressure in the cooling system. If the engine is hot, remove the cap slowly using a rag to prevent scalding.

4   Disconnect the vacuum lines, and on later models the water hoses, then unscrew the valve from the intake manifold or adaptor.

5   When refitting the valve note that the vacuum line from the carburettor is connected to the middle outlet on the PVS, the vacuum line from the spark delay valve (where fitted) is connected to the outlet nearest to the threaded end of the PVS, and the vacuum line from the spark sustain valve is connected to the outlet furthest from the threaded end of the PVS.

6   Reconnect the water hoses and if necessary top up the cooling system.

Fuel trap – removal and refitting

7   Disconnect the vacuum lines and remove the fuel trap from the engine.

8   When refitting, make sure that the fuel trap is positioned with the black side (marked CARB) towards the carburettor and the white side (marked DIST) towards the PVS.

Carburettor speed control system – description and component renewal

The carburettor speed control system is an integral part of the emission control system on some UK models as well as for some overseas market models.

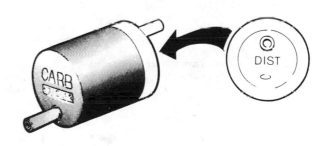

Fig. 13.56 Fuel trap is marked for direction of fitting (Sec 6)

The system's function is to improve the air and fuel mixture when the engine is cold in low ambient conditions. It achieves this by increasing the air volume into the intake manifold in order to weaken the mixture ratio which has been enriched by choke operation.

The carburettor speed control valve is fitted to a vacuum hose which is located between the air cleaner unit and the intake manifold on UK models.

Testing of the system components should be entrusted to a Ford garage. The renewal of a defective system component is given elsewhere in this Section.

Emission control system (Sweden and Switzerland)

Later 1.6 litre manual transmission models destined for these markets are equipped with the carburettor speed control system previously described and are integrated into the emission control system.

The emission control system on later 1.6 models fitted with the automatic transmission has also been changed and the later system layout is shown in Fig. 13.59.

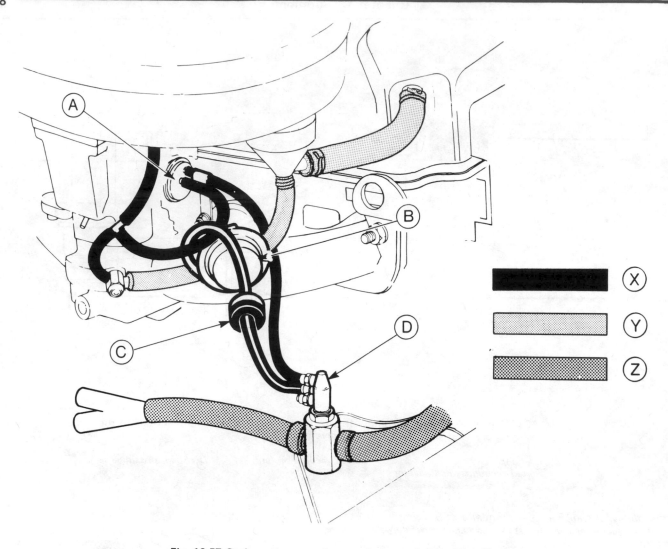

Fig. 13.57 Carburettor speed control system layout (Sec 6)

A Temperature vacuum switch   C Spark delay valve   X Vacuum hoses
B Carburettor speed control valve   D 3-port vacuum switch (PVS) and   Y Air supply hoses
                                         adaptor   Z Coolant hoses

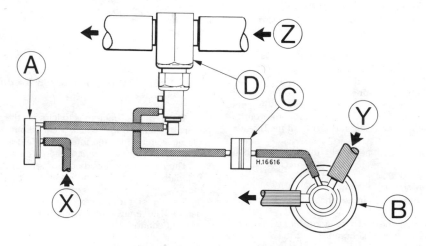

Fig. 13.58 Carburettor speed control system operation (Sec 6)

A Temperature vacuum switch   D PVS and adaptor   Y Air (from air cleaner)
B Carburettor speed control valve   X Manifold vacuum   Z Engine coolant
C Spark delay valve

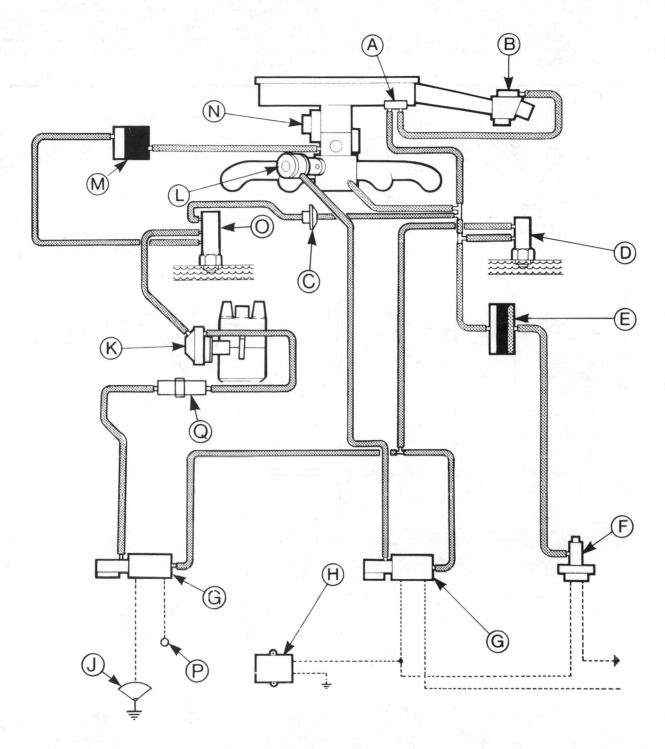

Fig. 13.59 Emission control system layout – Sweden and Switzerland models with automatic transmission and automatic choke (Sec 6)

A	Air cleaner heat sensor	E	Vacuum sustain valve	J	Inhibitor switch	N	Carburettor
B	Vacuum motor	F	Microswitch (vacuum		(transmission)	O	3-port PVS
C	Vacuum check valve		operated)	K	Distributor (dual diaphragm)	P	Ignition switch
D	2-port PVS (distributor	G	Two-way solenoid	L	EGR valve	Q	Vacuum restrictor
	retard and EGR)	H	Speed sensor	M	Fuel trap		

Part D: Exhaust system

Exhaust system (1.1 engine)

As from model year 1984 the exhaust system fitted to 1.1 litre engines is of twin downpipe type, similar to the system fitted to the 1.3 and 1.6 litre engines as shown in Fig. 3.60, Chapter 3.

7 Ignition system

Lucas distributor – overhaul

1 In addition to the information given in Section 16 of Chapter 4 concerning the distributor overhaul procedures, the following additional points should be noted.

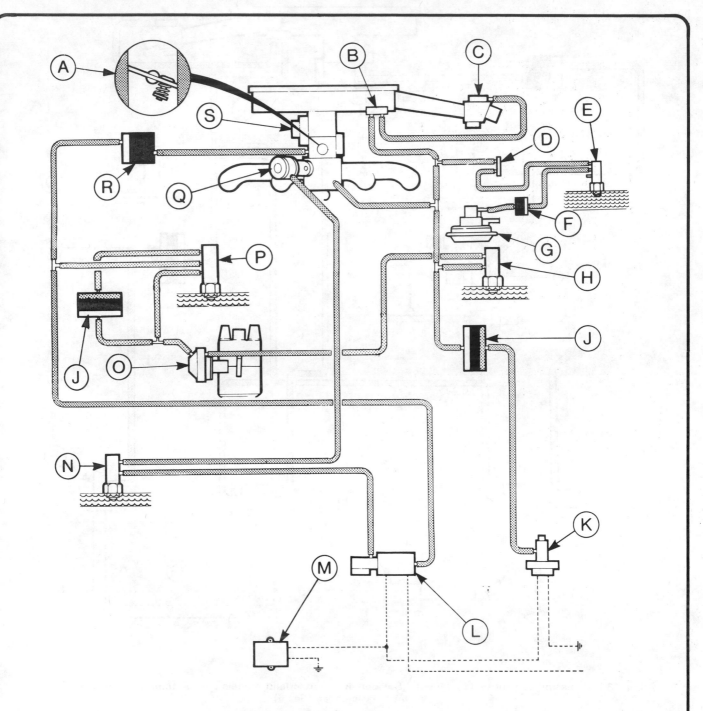

Fig. 13.60 Emission control system for Sweden and Switzerland 1.6 litre models with manual transmission and VV carburettor with automatic choke (Sec 6)

A	Decel (in venturi)	G	Carburettor speed control
B	Heat sensor (in air cleaner)		valve
C	Vacuum motor	H	2-port PVS (distributor
D	Temperature vacuum switch		retard cut-out)
E	3-port PVS	J	Vacuum sustain valve
F	Vacuum delay valve		

K	Vacuum microswitch
L	2-way solenoid
M	Speed sensor
N	2-port PVS (EGR cold
	cut-out)

O	Dual diaphragm distributor
P	3-port PVS
Q	EGR valve
R	Fuel trap
S	Carburettor

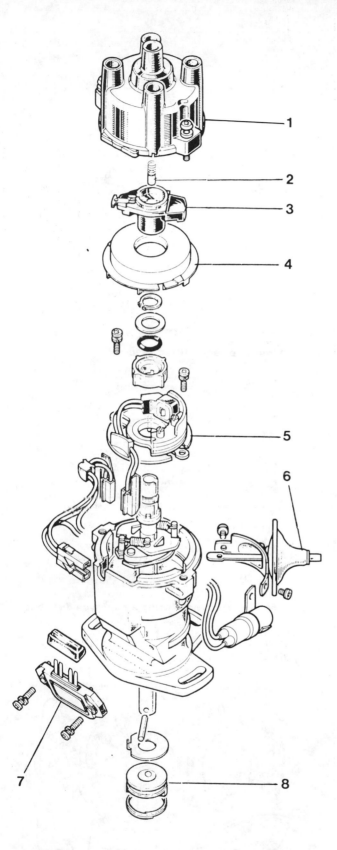

Fig. 13.61 Lucas 57 DM distributor components (Sec 7)

1 Cover	5 Pick-up and baseplate unit
2 HT brush and spring	6 Vacuum unit
3 Rotor arm	7 Amplifier module
4 Flash shield	8 Drive dog

2   If the distributor drive coupling is to be renewed, first remove the coil spring from the coupling. Avoid distorting or damaging the spring since this can be used on the new coupling.

3   Use a suitable pin punch and drive out the coupling retaining pin whilst supporting the distributor. Discard the pin on removal and withdraw the coupling.

4   If a new coupling is to be fitted the replacement must be of the correct type (Bosch or Lucas). The two types are not interchangeable.

5   Do not remove the distributor shaft. Leave the shims and washers in position.

6   The coupling repair set contains three couplings. Select the coupling which when engaged in the camshaft slot has the least clearance. The couplings are code numbered so choose the highest numbered coupling that will fit.

7   Refit the coupling in the reverse order to removal, using the new retaining pin supplied. When fitted check that the coupling can rotate freely and has minimal endfloat. Refit the coil spring.

Ignition coil – XR3i models

8   From June 1983 on, the Escort XR3i model is only fitted with the Bosch ignition coil due to the Femsa and Polmot manufactured coils being longer overall and not providing the minimum clearance of 20 mm (0.78 in) required between the coil and the transmission housing. Without this clearance it is possible for the engine/transmission to foul the coil when they are at their maximum 'rock' position.

Distributor – XR3i model

9   The distributor of the XR3i model is basically the same as that fitted to the XR3 model but its rotor arm differs in having a centrifugal HT cut-out mechanism. The cut-out is designed to actuate at an engine speed of 6500 rpm.

Distributor – all later models with electronic ignition

10   From early 1985 new type Bosch and Lucas distributors were progressively introduced. At the time of writing the only information on these distributors is given in the following sub-sections.

Distributor – replacement with later type

11   Obtain a new set of HT leads suitable for the new distributor, also the LT wire assembly 84AG-12045-BA.

12   Remove the old distributor (Chapter 4).

13   Fit the new distributor with the vacuum unit uppermost and the bolts located centrally in the flange slots. Note that the new distributor uses only the two opposite mounting bolts, the third mounting hole not being used.

14   Tighten the mounting bolts then fit the new set of HT leads.

15   Fit the LT wire plug to the distributor module, and the wires at the other end as shown in Fig. 13.64. The green wires go to the coil negative terminal, the black wires to the coil positive terminal, and the brown wire to earth.

16   Finally check and adjust the ignition timing, as described in Chapter 4, Section 14.

Distributor vacuum unit (later Lucas type) – removal and refitting

17   Remove the distributor (Chapter 4).

18   Remove the cap and rotor arm.

19   Extract the screws and withdraw the ignition amplifier module.

20   Extract the three screws and separate the two halves of the distributor.

21   Prise the plastic ring from the upper half then pull out the module connector.

22   Lift out the trigger coil.

23   Extract the circlip from the lower half and remove the upper shim, stator, and lower shim.

24   Remove the screw and withdraw the vacuum unit.

25   Refitting is a reversal of removal, but make sure that the vacuum unit arm is correctly located in the stator. Check that the distributor shaft rotates freely on completion.

HT leads

26   On some distributor types the HT lead positions may differ from those shown in Chapter 4, Fig. 4.26 for CVH engines. The positions may be one terminal anti-clockwise from that shown (ie No 1 to No 3 position, No 3 to No 4 position etc). However No 1 terminal will still be identified by a dimple in the new position.

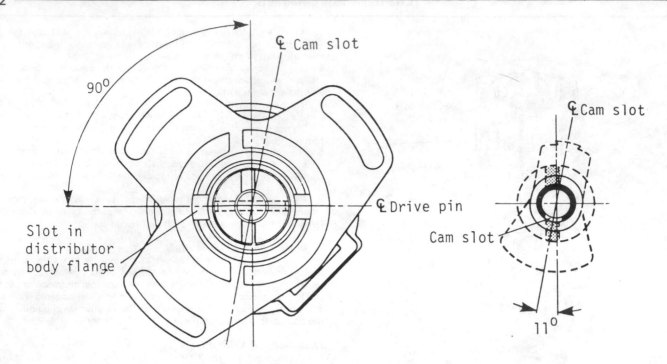

Fig. 13.62 Lucas 57 DM distributor drive dog position when correctly fitted (Sec 7)

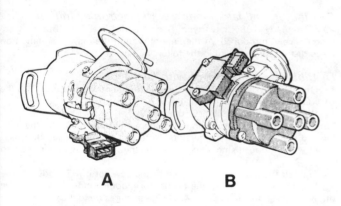

Fig. 13.63 New distributors introduced in early 1985
(Sec 7)

A Bosch   B Lucas

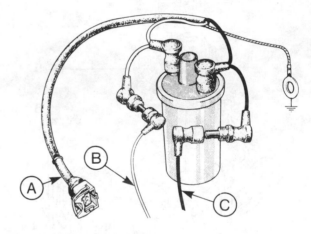

Fig. 13.64 LT wires when fitting a new type distributor
(Sec 7)

A LT wire assembly   C Black wire
B Green wire

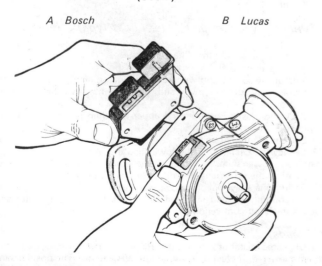

Fig. 13.65 Removing the ignition amplifier module
(Sec 7)

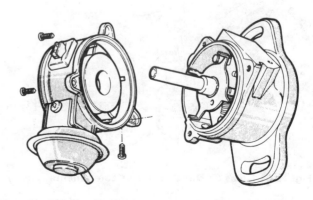

Fig. 13.66 Separating the distributor halves (Sec 7)

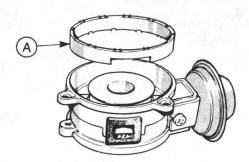

Fig. 13.67 Removing the upper half plastic ring (A) (Sec 7)

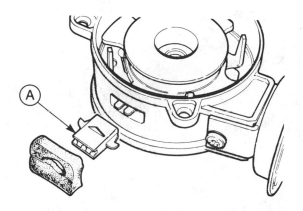

Fig. 13.68 Removing the module connector (A) (Sec 7)

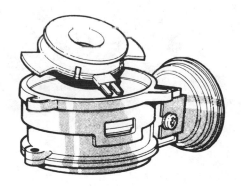

Fig. 13.69 Removing the trigger coil (Sec 7)

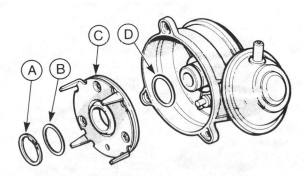

Fig. 13.70 Lower half stator components (Sec 7)

A   Circlip
B   Shim (upper)
C   Stator
D   Shim (lower)

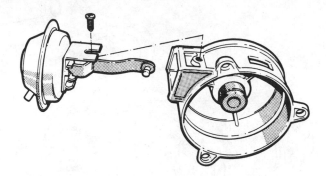

Fig. 13.71 Removing the vacuum unit (Sec 7)

8   Transmission

Part A: Manual transmission

Gearshift stabiliser bar bush – renewal

1   If the stabiliser bush is in poor condition, it can cause engine and transmission noises to be transmitted to the vehicle interior. To renew the bush raise and support the vehicle on safety stands.

2   Disconnect the stabiliser bar at the transmission end then press out the bush using a suitable bolt, nut and two washers, used together with a pair of suitable diameter sockets as shown (Fig. 13.72). During bush removal and refitting do not pull down excessively on the stabiliser bar. Use sockets of different diameters so that one is the same as that of the bush housing and one the same diameter as the fitted bush.

3   Having withdrawn the old bush, insert the new one drawing it into position using the sockets, bolt, washers and nut. Position the voids in the bush as shown in the inset in Fig. 13.72 and take care during fitting not to damage or distort the bush.

4   Disconnect the stabiliser bar to the transmission and tighten the retaining bolt to the specified torque wrench setting.

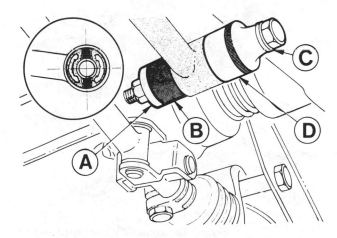

Fig. 13.72 Gearshift stabiliser bush fitting method. Note the void positions in bush (inset) (Sec 8)

A   Washer
B   Bush
C   Washer
D   Socket

Five-speed manual transmission – general

From February 1982 a five-speed manual transmission is fitted as standard equipment on all 1.6 litre Escort models, and is available as an option on 1.3 litre versions and certain 1.1 litre export models.

The transmission is basically the same as the four-speed version, with

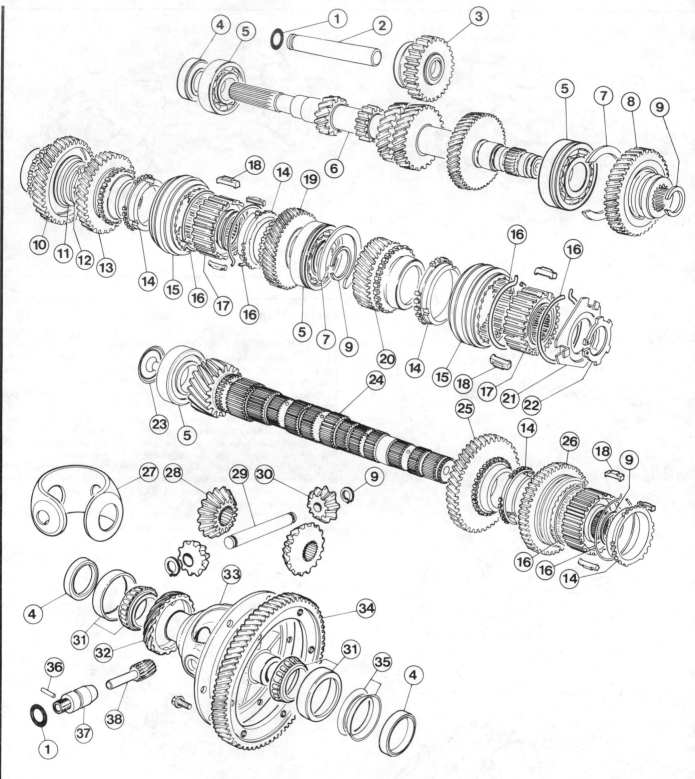

Fig. 13.73 Exploded view of the five-speed transmission internal components (Sec 8)

1 O-ring	11 Supporting ring	21 Retaining plate	30 Differential pinion
2 Reverse idler gear shaft	12 Thrust half washers	22 Circlip	31 Taper roller bearing
3 Reverse idler gear	13 3rd gear (driven)	23 Oil slinger	32 Speedometer drive worm
4 Radial oil seal	14 Synchronising ring	24 Mainshaft	33 Differential housing
5 Bearing	15 Selector ring	25 1st gear (driven)	34 Final drive gear
6 Input shaft	16 Retaining spring	26 Selector ring with reverse	35 Spring washers (2)
7 Snap-ring	17 Synchroniser hub	gear	36 Locking pin
8 5th gear	18 Blocker bar	27 Thrust cage	37 Speedometer drive pinion
9 Circlip	19 4th gear (driven)	28 Axleshaft pinion	bearing
10 2nd gear (driven)	20 5th gear (driven)	29 Differential shaft	38 Speedometer drive pinion

the exception of a modified selector mechanism, and an additional gear and synchro-hub contained in a housing attached to the side of the main transmission casing.

The repair and overhaul procedures for the five-speed transmission are the same as described in Chapter 6 for the four-speed unit, except for the differences described in the following sub-sections.

Five-speed manual transmission – removal and refitting

5   The procedure for removal is basically the same as for the four-speed unit described in Chapter 6, Section 5, except for the minor differences listed below.

   (a) *Before removal of the transmission, engage reverse gear to ensure correct engagement of the selector mechanism when refitting*

   (b) *Note that there is no tension spring fitted to the gearchange rod*

   (c) *To facilitate removal of the transmission from under the car, detach the left-hand front anti-roll bar mounting from the crossmember*

6   The refitting procedure is also as described in Chapter 6. However, the procedure for adjustment of the selector mechanism has been revised for the five-speed transmission and is as follows.

7   Using a drift inserted into the drilling in the selector shaft, turn the shaft as far as it will go in a clockwise direction and push it right in. This will ensure reverse gear is engaged.

8   Refit the gearchange rod to the selector shaft, but do not tighten the pinch-bolt at this stage.

9   Taking care not to disengage the gearchange rod from the selector shaft, place the gear lever in the reverse position.

10   Push down on the gear lever and move it back and forth very slightly until the holes in the selector housing and gearchange rod are aligned. Insert a 3.5 mm (0.14 in) diameter pin or rod through the aligned holes to lock the mechanism.

11   Now turn the gearbox selector shaft clockwise to take up any free play, then tighten the gearchange rod pinch-bolt.

12   Finally remove the alignment pin or rod from the hole in the selector housing.

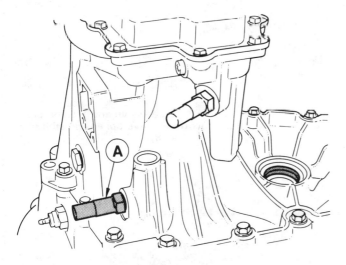

Fig. 13.74 Selector shaft locking mechanism – five-speed transmission (Sec 8)

A   4th and reverse gear cap nut

Five-speed manual transmission – dismantling (general)

13   As stated previously, the five-speed transmission is virtually identical to the four-speed unit, with the exception of an additional gear and synchro-hub and a modified selector mechanism. The overhaul procedures described in Chapter 6 are therefore applicable to the five-speed unit with the exception of the following sub-sections. Note, however, that if any new components are to be fitted to the mainshaft they must be lubricated with the special grease, as shown in the Specifications, during assembly.

Five-speed manual transmission – removal of major assemblies

14   With the gearbox removed from the vehicle, clean away external dirt and grease using paraffin and a stiff brush, or a water soluble grease solvent. Take care not to allow water to enter the transmission.

15   Drain off any residual oil in the transmission through a driveshaft opening.

16   Unscrew the lockbolt which holds the clutch release fork to the shaft and remove the shaft, followed by the fork and release bearing.

17   If not removed for draining, unscrew the selector shaft cap nut, spring and interlock pin. Now remove the additional 5th gear selector shaft cap nut, spring and interlock pin.

18   Unbolt and remove the transmission housing cover.

19   Unscrew the clamp-bolt and lift the 5th gear selector pin assembly off the shift rod.

20   Using circlip pliers, extract the 5th gear retaining snap-ring, then lift off the 5th gear complete with synchro assembly and selector fork from the mainshaft.

21   Extract the circlip securing 5th driving gear to the input shaft. Using a two-legged puller, draw the gear off the input shaft. *Do not re-use the old circlip when reassembling; a new one must be obtained.*

22   Unscrew the nine socket-headed bolts securing the 5th gear casing to the main casing and carefully lift it off.

23   Remove the snap-rings from the main and input shaft bearings.

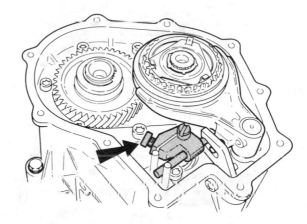

Fig. 13.75 5th gear selector pin clamp bolt (arrowed) – five-speed transmission (Sec 8)

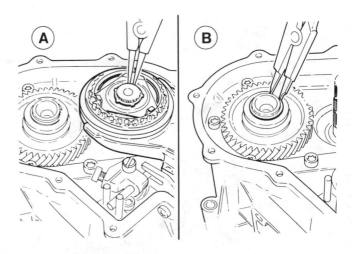

Fig. 13.76 5th gear retaining snap-ring (A) and input shaft circlip (B) locations – five-speed transmission (Sec 8)

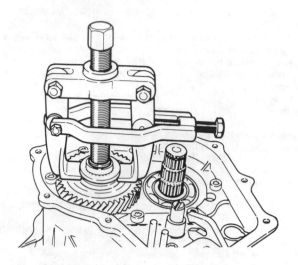

Fig. 13.77 Removal of 5th gear from input shaft with puller – five-speed transmission (Sec 8)

24 Unscrew and remove the connecting bolts and gearbox mounting bolts, then lift the smaller housing from the transmission casing. If it is stuck, tap it off carefully with a plastic-headed mallet.

25 Extract the swarf-collecting magnet and clean it. Take care not to drop the magnet or it will shatter.

26 Release the circlips from the selector shaft guide sleeve and 1st/2nd selector fork. Carefully withdraw the guide sleeve.

27 Lift out the complete mainshaft assembly, together with the input shaft, selector forks and reverse gear as a complete unit from the transmission housing.

28 Remove the selector shaft and the shift locking plate.

29 Finally lift the differential assembly from the housing.

30 The transmission is now dismantled into its major assemblies, which can be further dismantled if necessary as described in Chapter 6, but note the following differences when overhauling the mainshaft.

(a) If overhauling the fifth gear synchroniser unit, note that the blocker bars are secured by means of a retaining plate. When assembling the unit proceed as described for the other synchro units, but ensure that the retaining spring located between the hub and retaining plate is pressing against the blocker bars

(b) When reassembling the mainshaft, fit the 1st/2nd synchro so that the reverse gear teeth on the unit are positioned towards 1st gear, with the selector groove facing 2nd gear

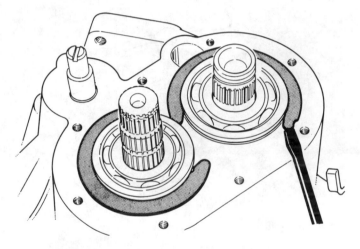

Fig. 13.78 Bearing snap-ring removal – five-speed transmission (Sec 8)

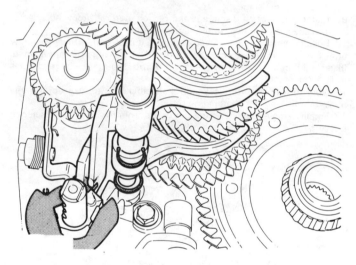

Fig. 13.80 Selector shaft guide sleeve and 1st/2nd gear selector fork circlip locations – five-speed transmission (Sec 8)

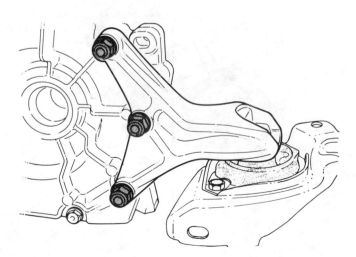

Fig. 13.79 Gearbox mounting retaining bolt locations – five-speed transmission (Sec 8)

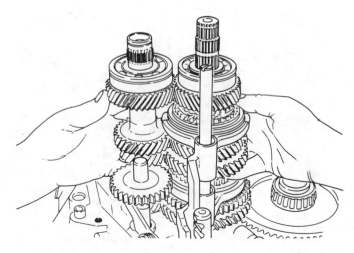

Fig. 13.81 Removal of mainshaft and input shaft as complete assembly – five-speed transmission (Sec 8)

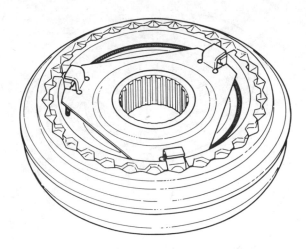

Fig. 13.82 5th gear synchroniser unit showing spring location between hub and retaining plate – five-speed transmission (Sec 8)

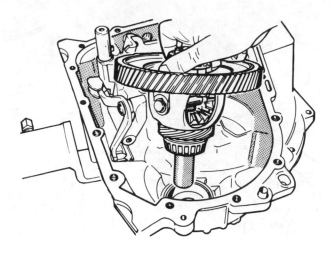

Fig. 13.84 Refitting the differential assembly – five-speed transmission (Sec 8)

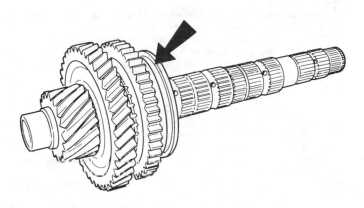

Fig. 13.83 Selector groove (arrowed) to face 2nd gear – five-speed transmission (Sec 8)

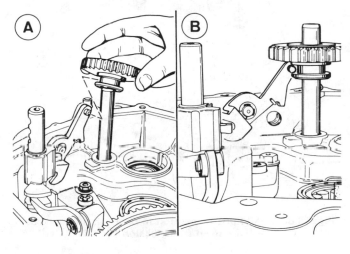

Fig. 13.85 Correct positioning of reverse gear on reverse shaft (A) and engagement of selector lever with groove in gear (B) – five-speed transmission (Sec 8)

Five-speed manual transmission – reassembly

31 With the larger housing section on the bench, lubricate the differential bearings with gear oil and insert the differential assembly into the housing.

32 Slide the reverse idler gear onto its shaft, at the same time engaging the selector lever in the groove of the gear which should be pointing downwards.

33 Refit the selector shaft and shift locking plate.

34 Refit the mainshaft and input shaft as an assembly complete with selector forks. Guide the selector forks past the shift locking plate, noting that the plate must be turned clockwise to bear against the dowel.

35 Install the selector shaft guide sleeve and secure the 1st/2nd selector fork on the guide sleeve using new circlips.

36 Refit the swarf-collecting magnet to its location in the housing.

37 Locate a new gasket on the housing flange and place the small housing section in position. Refit and tighten the retaining bolts to the specified torque. Refit the gearbox mounting bracket.

38 Fit the snap-rings to the ends of the main and input shafts. Cut-outs are provided in the casing so that the bearings can be levered upwards to expose the snap-ring groove. Snap-rings are available in three thicknesses, and the thickest possible ring should be used which will fit into the groove. If any difficulty is experienced in levering up the bearing on the input shaft, push the end of the shaft from within the bellhousing.

39 Tap the snap-rings to rotate them so that they will locate correctly in the cut-outs in the 5th gear housing gasket, which should now be placed in position.

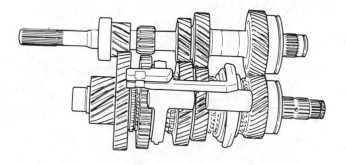

Fig. 13.86 Correct positioning of mainshaft and input shaft assemblies prior to refitting – five-speed transmission (Sec 8)

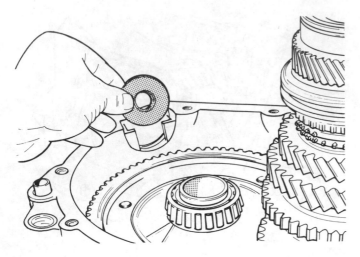

Fig. 13.87 Location of swarf-collecting magnet in casing –
five-speed transmission (Sec 8)

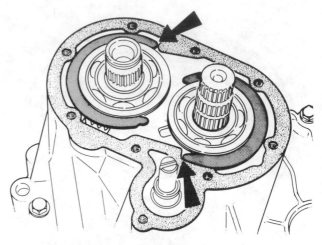

Fig. 13.90 Snap-ring correctly aligned to locate with
cut-outs in gasket (arrowed) – five-speed transmission
(Sec 8)

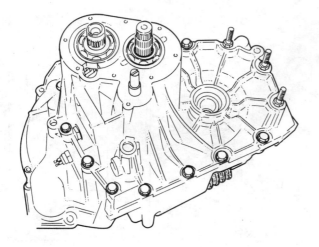

Fig. 13.88 Small housing section in position on main casing
– five-speed transmission (Sec 8)

40 Fit the 5th gear housing and tighten the retaining bolts to the specified torque.

41 Coat the splines of 5th gear and the input shaft wth the special grease (see Specifications). Before fitting 5th gear, check that the marks on the input shaft centering bore and the gear web are the same colour.

42 Heat 5th gear to approximately 80°C (176°F), and then drift it into place on the input shaft. Fit a new circlip to the input shaft using a tube of suitable diameter as a drift.

43 Fit 5th gear, complete with synchro assembly and selector fork into the mainshaft and secure with the snap-ring.

44 Coat the threads of the 5th gear selector shaft locking mechanism cap nut with sealer (see Specifications). Fit the interlock pin, spring and cap nut, then tighten the nut to the specified torque.

45 Insert the 1st/4th and reverse gear interlock pin, spring and cap nut, the threads of which must be coated with sealer (see Specifications). Tighten the cap nut to the specified torque wrench setting.

46 Refit the 5th gear selector pin assembly to the shift rod, but do not tighten the clamp bolt at this stage.

47 Engage 5th gear with the selector shaft by turning the shaft clockwise as far as it will go from the neutral position, and then pulling it fully out.

48 Slide the selector ring and selector fork onto 5th gear.

49 Rotate the shift rod clockwise as far as the stop using a screwdriver and retain it in this position. Coat the clamp bolt threads with a locking compound then fit and tighten it to the specified torque wrench setting.

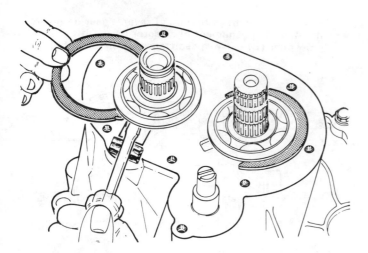

Fig. 13.89 Fitting the snap-rings to the main and input shaft
bearing – five-speed transmission (Sec 8)

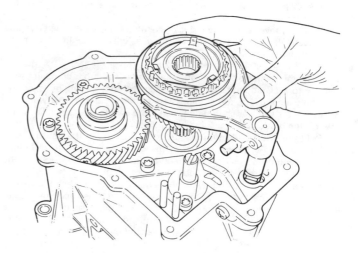

Fig. 13.91 Refitting 5th gear synchro assembly and selector
fork – five-speed transmission (Sec 8)

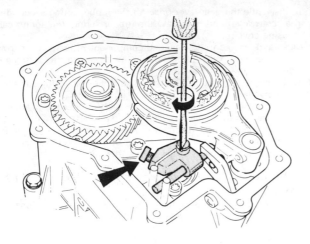

Fig. 13.92 Turning the shift rod clockwise with a screwdriver prior to tightening selector pin clamp bolt (arrowed) – five-speed transmission (Sec 8)

50 Place a new gasket in position and refit the housing cover, tighten the retaining bolts to the specified torque.
51 At this stage check the operation of the selector mechanism by engaging all the gears with the selector shaft.
52 Refit the clutch release shaft, lever and bearing into the bellhousing.
53 The transmission is now ready for installation in the vehicle.
54 Wait until it is installed before filling with oil.

Gearchange mechanism (five-speed transmission) – removal, overhaul and refitting
55 Proceed as described in paragraphs 1, 2 and 3 of Section 4 in Chapter 6, but engage reverse gear instead of 4th.
56 Disconnect the exhaust pipe from its rubber mounting straps at the rear.
57 Proceed as given in paragraphs 5, 6 and 7 of Section 4 (Chapter 6).
58 To dismantle, unscrew and remove the three guide element spring retaining screws, one from each side of the selector housing, and one underneath (which also holds a lock pin). Extract the three springs and the lock pin.
59 Unscrew and remove the four selector housing to stabiliser/ mounting frame and gear lever housing cover bolts. Lift the gearlever and cover away.
60 Unclip the upper guide shell and lift the shift rod out of the selector housing.

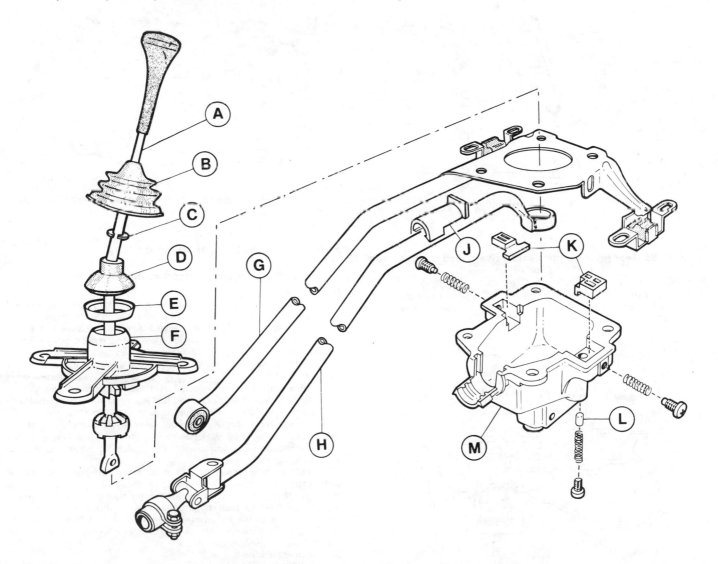

Fig. 13.93 Five-speed transmission external selector mechanism (Sec 8)

A	Gear lever	D	Rubber spring
B	Gaiter	E	Spring carrier
C	Circlip	F	Housing cover

G	Stabiliser	K	Guide elements
H	Shift rod	L	Locking pin
J	Guide shell	M	Selector housing

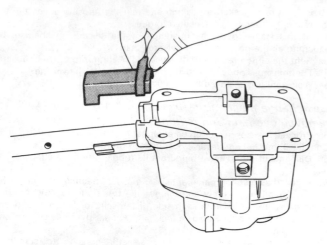

Fig. 13.94 Guide shell removal – five-speed transmission (Sec 8)

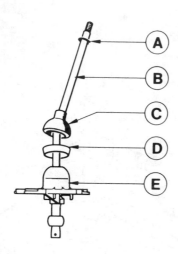

Fig. 13.95 Gear lever components – five-speed transmission (Sec 8)

A   Circlip
B   Gear lever
C   Rubber spring
D   Spring carrier
E   Housing cover

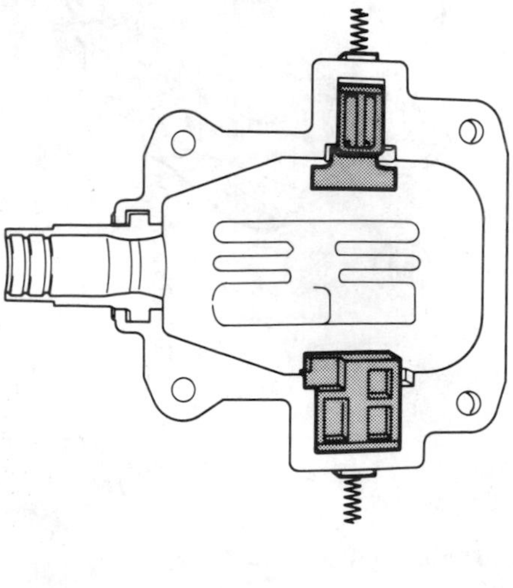

Fig. 13.96 Locate the guides and springs – five-speed transmission (Sec 8)

61 To dismantle the gear lever prise off the rubber spring securing ring using a screwdriver and withdraw the rubber spring, the spring carrier and housing cover.

62 Clean and inspect the dismantled components. Renew any showing signs of excessive wear. Reassemble by reversing the dismantling procedure but note the following points.

63 Make sure that the cut-out at the edge of the plastic cover is aligned with the curve in the gearchange lever.

64 Position the guide shells as shown and check that the gear lever is located in the ring of the shift rod as it is assembled.

65 Refit the gearchange mechanism to the vehicle as described in paragraphs 14 to 19 in Section 4 (Chapter 6) and adjust as described for the five-speed transmission earlier in this Chapter.

Gearchange rod tension tension spring (four-speed transmission)

66 On later models the gearchange rod tension spring is located as shown in Fig. 13.97.

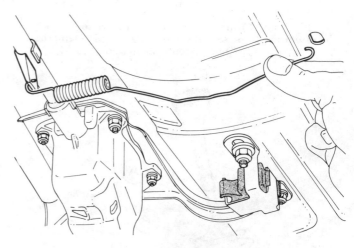

Fig. 13.97 Gearchange rod tension spring on later models (Sec 8)

Part B: Automatic transmission

Automatic transmission – description and safety precautions

The Ford ATX (automatic transaxle) transmission has three forward and one reverse gear. It is mounted transversally, in line with the engine and incorporates an integral final drive assembly. The drive to the axle shafts is transmitted by an axle driving gear from the gearbox through an intermediate gear to the drive (differential drive) gear.

The ATX transmission is a split torque type whereby engine torque is transmitted to the gearbox by mechanical or hydraulic means in accordance with the gear selected and the road speed. This system provides for improved efficiency and fuel economy when compared with the C3 type automatic transmission fitted to other Ford models.

The mechanical torque transference is by a planetary gear set attached to the torque converter unit and a damper assembly reduces the engine to transmission vibrations when operating under 'mechanical drive' conditions.

Owing to the complexity of the automatic transmission unit, if performance is not up to standard, or overhaul is necessary, it is imperative that this be left to the local main agents who will have the special equipment for fault diagnosis and rectification.

The content of the following sub-sections is therefore confined to supplying general information and any service information and instruction that can be used by the owner.

Safety precautions

The following safety precautions must be noted and adhered to where an automatic transmission is fitted:

(a) *Whenever the vehicle is being parked or is being serviced or repaired, ensure that the handbrake is fully applied and the selector lever is in P position*

(b) Never exceed an engine speed of 4500 rpm when stationary

(c) If the vehicle is to be towed at any time the selector lever must
be set in the N position. The maximum towing distance should
not exceed 20 km (12 miles) and the towing speed must be
kept down to a maximum speed of 30 to 40 kph (18 to 25 mph)

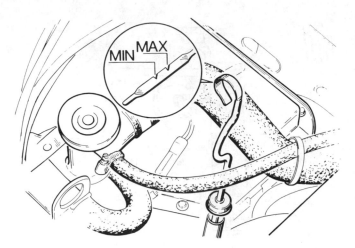

Fig. 13.99 Automatic transmission dipstick location and
fluid level markings (insert) (Sec 8)

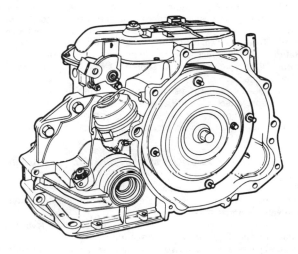

Fig. 13.98 Ford automatic transmission (ATX) unit (Sec 8)

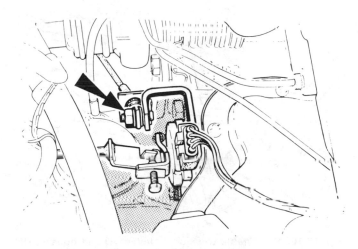

Fig. 13.100 Shift cable nut (arrowed) – automatic
transmission (Sec 8)

Automatic transmission – fluid level checking

1   The automatic ransmission fluid level should be checked every
10 000 km (6000 miles) and a lever dipstick is provided for this purpose.

2   Before making the level check the transmission fluid must be at its
normal operating temperature. Therefore this check is best made directly
after a journey in the car or failing this, run the vehicle on the road for a
distance of approximately five miles (8 km) to warm it up.

3   Park the car on level ground, then fully apply the handbrake.

4   With the engine running at its normal idle speed, apply the footbrake
and simultaneously move the selector lever through the full range of
positions three times then move it back to the P position. Allow the
engine to run at idle for a further period of one minute.

5   With the engine still idling, extract the transmission fluid level
dipstick and wipe it dry, with a clean non-fluffy cloth. Fully reinsert the
dipstick and then extract it again and check the fluid level mark, which
must be between the MAX and MIN markings.

6   If topping-up is necessary, use only the specified type and pour it
through the dipstick tube, but take care not to overfill. The level must not
exceed the MAX mark.

7   If the fluid level was below the minimum mark when checked or is in
constant need of topping-up, check around the transmission unit and
the oil cooler for any signs of excessive oil leaks, and if present then they
must be rectified without delay.

8   If the colour of the fluid is dark brown or black this denotes the sign
of a worn brake band or transmission clutches in which case have your
Ford dealer check the transmission, at the earliest opportunity.

Automatic transmission gear selector – removal, overhaul and refitting

9   Move the selector lever to its D position.

10 Raise and support the bonnet, then loosen off the shift cable nut.

11 Unscrew and remove the gear selector level knob, then carefully
prise up and remove the selector gate cover from the console.

12 Remove the console unit which is secured in position by two screws
at the rear and screws on each side at the front.

13 Remove the selector gate and stop plate which are secured by two
screws, one on each corner at the front.

14 Disconnect the shift cable from the selector lever and housing by
removing the securing clips.

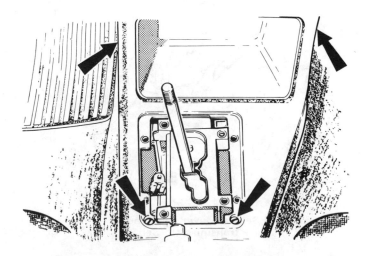

13.101 Console retaining screw positions (arrowed) –
automatic transmission (Sec 8)

Fig. 13.102 Selector gate and stop plate retaining screws (arrowed) – automatic transmission (Sec 8)

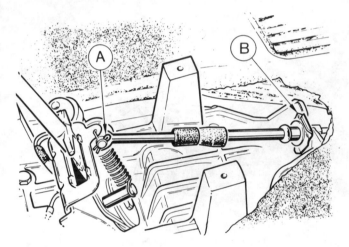

Fig. 13.103 Shift cable to selector lever (A) and housing (B) – automatic transmission (Sec 8)

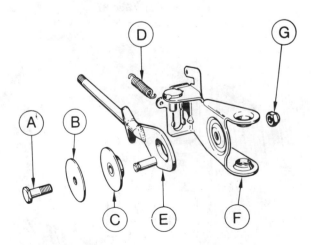

Fig. 13.104 Selector lever components – automatic transmission (Sec 8)

A   Pin   E   Lever
B   Steel washer   F   Lever guide
C   Plastic spacer   G   Nut
D   Spring

15 Disconnect the escutcheon light holder from the lever housing, then unscrew and remove the four housing retaining screws. Lift the housing clear.

16 To dismantle the selector unit, unscrew the lever pivot pin retaining nut and remove the lever assembly from its housing, together with the bushes.

17 The lever can be removed from the guide by unhooking the spring, unscrewing the retaining pin nut and withdrawing the pin, washers and lever.

18 Reassembly of the selector unit is a reversal of the removal procedure. Tighten the selector lever nut to the specified torque wrench setting. The pivot pin nut must be tightened to provide a lever movement of 0.5 to 2.5 Nm (0.3 to 1.8 lbf ft).

19 Refitting of the gear selector unit is a reversal of the removal procedure. Tighten the retaining screws of the lever housing to the specified torque.

20 On completion adjust the shift cable by moving the selector lever to the D position, check that the shift shaft lever is still in the preset D position, then retighten the cable nut. To prevent the threaded pin rotating as the nut is tightened press the cable slot onto the thread.

Automatic transmission downshift linkage – removal and refitting

21 Raise and support the bonnet.

22 Disconnect the downshift linkage from the transmission downshift/throttle valve shaft.

23 Disconnect the throttle linkage from the linkage pivot lever beneath the intake manifold by removing the securing clip.

24 Unscrew and remove the two nuts which secure the downshift cable mounting bracket (on the right-hand side of the engine). Withdraw the linkage and bracket.

25 Disconnect the throttle linkage from the downshift linkage pivot lever by extracting the clip, then remove the clamp bolt and nut to separate the downshift linkage from the control lever. Remove the downshift linkage.

26 To refit, insert the linkage into the bracket and tighten the clamping bolt nut. Check that lever movement is possible.

27 Reattach the throttle linkage to the pivot lever, then refit the downshift linkage and bracket. Slide the linkage onto the downshift/throttle shaft of the transmission, fitting the stepped washer between the lever and linkage on the valve shaft. The bracket securing screws should be tightened to the specified torque setting.

28 Secure the throttle linkage to the downshift linkage pivot lever by refitting the retaining clip. Refit and tighten the downshift/throttle valve shaft nut. Adjust the downshift linkage as follows.

Automatic transmission downshift linkage – adjustment

The downshift linkage adjustment method is dependent on whether the adjustment is made during a routine check or if the linkage has been removed and refitted. For adjustment during a routine check proceed as described in paragraphs 29 to 31. Whilst adjustment after refitting is given in paragraphs 32 to 34.

Before making a routine adjustment check, the transmission must be at its normal operating temperature, its fluid level correct and the carburettor and ignition adjustments as specified.

29 Loosen off the adjuster screw on the throttle valve shaft lever to give a clearance of 2 to 3 mm (0.078 to 0.118 in) between the stop end face and the adjuster screw (Fig. 13.106). Use a feeler gauge to set this clearance.

30 Check that the handbrake is fully applied, start the engine and check that the idle speed is correct, then retighten the adjuster screw to reduce the stop end face to adjuster screw clearance to 0.1 mm (0.004 in).

31 Loosen the control level clamp bolt nut then rotate the downshift linkage control lever to press in the damper rod 5 mm (0.2 in) and retighten the clamp bolt nut (Fig. 13.107).

32 For adjustment after refitting the linkage or damper unit follow the procedure in paragraphs 29 to 31. Refer to Fig. 13.107 and release the locknut (A). Screw in the damper to leave a gap of 2 mm (0.079 in) at B.

33 Loosen the control lever clamp bolt (F) and move the lever (E) to make contact with the damper rod. Tighten the clamp bolt.

34 Scribe or paint an index mark on the damper body then turn it four full turns to give a damper to bracket clearance of 7 mm (0.27 in), including the previously set clearance of 2 mm (0.08 in), and the damper rod is pressed in 5 mm (0.2 in). Tighten the locknut.

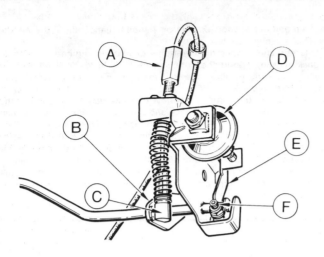

**Fig. 13.105 Damper and downshift linkage assembly –
automatic transmission (Sec 8)**

A   Throttle cable   D   Damper
B   Downshift linkage   E   Control lever
C   Clip   F   Clamp bolt and nut

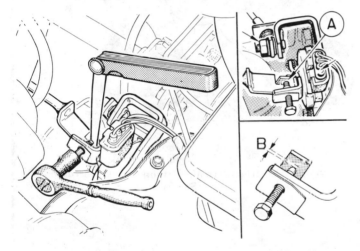

Fig. 13.106 Downshift linkage adjustment (Sec 8)

A   Adjuster screw   B   Final clearance

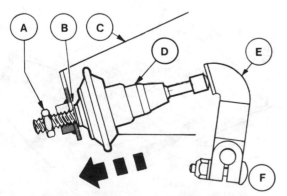

Fig. 13.107 Damper unit adjustment (Sec 8)

A   Locknut   D   Damper
B   Damper to bracket clearance E   Downshift linkage control
   of 2 mm (0.08 in)   lever
C   Damper bracket   F   Control lever clamp bolt

Starter inhibitor switch – removal, refitting and adjustment

35 Disconnect the multi-plug connector from the switch.
36 Remove the retaining nut and disconnect the linkage from the throttle valve shaft on the transmission.
37 To remove the downshift linkage from the transmission, unscrew and remove the two securing screws to the location bracket on the right-hand side of the engine and pull the linkage free.
38 Remove the downshift/throttle valve shaft lever, together with the stepped washer and disconnect the return spring. Unscrew the two retaining screws and remove the starter inhibitor switch.
39 The switch must be renewed if it is known to be defective.
40 On refitting the starter inhibitor switch do not fully tighten the securing screws until it is adjusted for position. To do this first move the selector lever to the D position, then using a 2.3 mm (0.090 in) diameter drill shank as shown (Fig. 13.109), locate it into the hole in the switch body.
41 Move the switch whilst pushing on the drill so that the switch case aligns with the inner location hole in the switch and with the drill fully inserted so that the switch is immobilised, fully tighten the retaining screws to the specified torque.
42 With the switch in position, refitting of the downshift/throttle valve shaft lever and linkage is a reversal of the removal procedure, but readjust the downshift linkage as given previously.

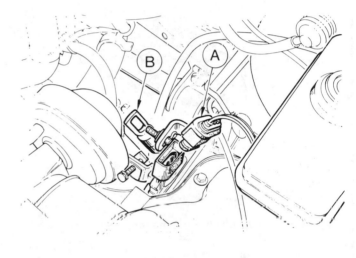

**Fig. 13.108 Starter inhibitor switch multi-plug (A) and shift
cable (B) connections (Sec 8)**

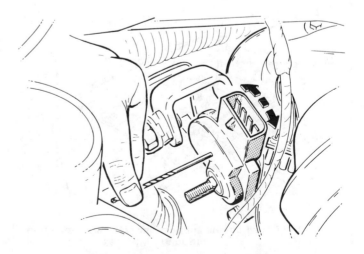

Fig. 13.109 Starter inhibitor switch adjustment (Sec 8)

Automatic transmission – removal and refitting

Any suspected faults must be referred to the main agent before unit removal, as with this type of transmission the fault must be confirmed, using specialist equipment, before it has been removed from the car.

43 Disconnect the battery negative lead.

44 Mark the relative positions of the bonnet hinges to the bonnet, outlining them with a pencil or felt tip pen. Unbolt the hinges from the bonnet and disconnect the bonding strap, then with the aid of an assistant lift the bonnet clear of the vehicle.

45 Disconnect the starter inhibitor switch lead multi-plug connector, then with the selector lever in the D position, unscrew the shift cable to lever retaining nut on the shift shaft.

46 Loosen off the downshift linkage adjuster screw and disconnect the linkage from the downshift/throttle valve shaft which is secured by a single nut. To allow the disconnection of the downshift linkage from the shaft (and eventual refitting) you will also have to remove the downshift

linkage mounting support bracket on the right-hand side of the engine bay. This is secured by two bolts.

47 Unscrew and remove the two upper gearbox to engine flange bolts.

48 Jack up and support the front end of the vehicle. You will need to raise it sufficiently to allow the transmission unit to be removed from underneath the vehicle.

49 The weight of the engine must now be supported. Either support the engine under the sump using a jack and block of wood or attach a hoist to the engine lifting lugs. A third method is to make up a bar with end pieces spaced to engage in the water channel each side of the bonnet lid aperture. Using an adjustable hook and chain suspended from the bar and attached to the engine lifting lugs, the weight of the engine can be taken off the mountings. With this method take care not to damage the wing panels with the support bar. If the drain channels are rusty do not use this method.

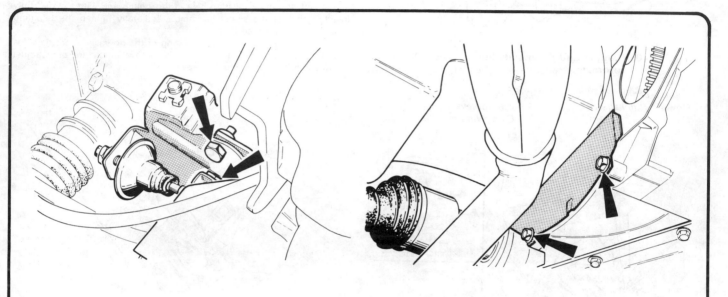

Fig. 13.110 Downshift linkage mounting support bracket (Sec 8)

Fig. 13.112 Driveplate and retaining bolts (arrowed) (Sec 8)

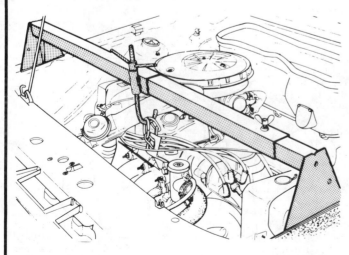

Fig. 13.111 Ford engine support bar (21-060) in position (Sec 8)

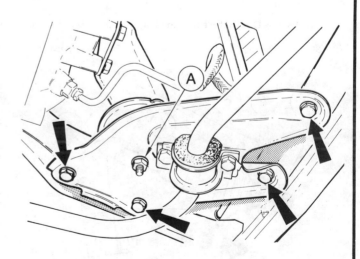

Fig. 13.113 Transmission front mounting attachment bolts (arrowed) and nut (A) (Sec 8)

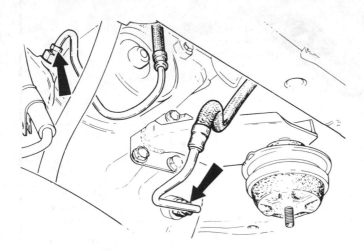

Fig. 13.114 Oil cooler to transmission hose connections (arrowed) (Sec 8)

50 Unscrew and detach the speedometer drive cable from the transmission.

51 Unscrew and remove the two shift cable bracket securing bolts from the transmission.

52 Detach the starter motor leads and then unbolt and remove the starter motor which is secured by three bolts.

53 Disconnect the reversing light lead from the switch.

54 Unscrew and remove the driveplate cover securing bolts and detach the cover.

55 At the outboard end of the right-hand track control (suspension) arm, disengage the arm from the hub (spindle) carrier by unscrewing and removing the pinch-bolt and nut. The pinch-bolt is a Torx type and to prevent it turning when unscrewing the nut retain it with a suitable Allen key.

56 Disconnect the right and left-hand driveshafts from the transmission as given in Section 2 of Chapter 7.

57 The front transmission mounting must now be detached by removing the insulator nut and four mounting to body securing bolts. The stabiliser bar can remain attached to the mounting.

58 Unscrew and disconnect the oil cooler hoses from the transmission allowing for oil leakage. Plug the lines whilst detached to prevent the ingress of dirt.

59 Remove the three retaining bolts and withdraw the front transmission mounting bracket.

60 Remove the transmission rear mounting complete from the body and transmission by unscrewing the five retaining bolts (and two nuts).

61 Working through the driveplate cover aperture, unscrew and remove the four nuts securing the driveplate to the torque converter. For this to be accomplished it will be necessary to turn the crankshaft for access to each nut in turn. Remove the nuts in a progressive manner, one turn at a time.

62 Position a jack and piece of wood under the transmission oil pan and raise to support. Now unscrew and remove the transmission flange bolts at the front.

63 Check that all of the transmission attachments are disconnected then carefully lower the transmission. As it is being lowered press the torque converter against the transmission to prevent it catching on the driveplate bolt. Remember that the torque converter is only loosely attached so keep it in position in the transmission housing during and after removal of the transmission.

64 Refitting is a reversal of the removal procedure. Tighten the respective retaining nuts and bolts to their specified torque wrench settings.

65 When refitting the driveshafts to the differential unit on each side, be sure to use snap-rings.

66 When reconnecting the driveshaft linkage refit and adjust it as follows. First slide the linkage onto the downshift/throttle valve shaft and locate, but do not fully tighten the securing nut at this stage.

67 Refit the downshift linkage mounting (on the right-hand side of the engine compartment) and tighten its securing bolts. Now tighten the downshift linkage on the side of the transmission housing.

68 With the selector lever (inside the car) and the lever on the shift shaft still in the D position, attach the shift cable to the shift shaft lever.

69 Reconnect the starter inhibitor switch multi-plug.

70 When the battery earth lead is reconnected and the transmission oil at the level specified, adjust the downshift linkage as given elsewhere in this Section.

9 Driveshafts

Modifications

Owing to the inclusion of the five-speed transmission to later Escort models, the engine and transaxle assembly have been located 17 mm (0.67 in) further to the right-hand side in the engine compartment (on four and five-speed models). This modification necessitated the fitting to these models of driveshafts having different lengths from those fitted to the earlier models with the four-speed gearbox (pre February 1982).

In addition, on 1.3 litre model Saloons and Estates a redesigned outboard constant velocity joint and stub axle shaft unit have been fitted. As the later joint is smaller in diameter the bellows retaining clamp is smaller to suit. This latter constant velocity joint and stub axle shaft assembly is directly interchangeable with the earlier type on 1.3 models, but must not be used on the Van and 1.6 litre variants.

It should be noted that since the engine and transmission mounting positions have been changed as described above, the pre February 1982 engine and transmission units cannot be fitted to models produced from this date.

10 Braking system

Modified handbrake cables

All Escort models produced after January 1982 are fitted with revised handbrake cables and a modified adjuster. The revised cables can be identified by the coarser wound outer cable and threaded adjusting sleeve incorporating finger grips. On early models the secondary cable is in two sections, each of which may be renewed separately, however, on later models the cable is continuous.

Handbrake cables – removal and refitting

1 The procedure for removal and refitting of the primary cable remains unchanged, and is as described in Chapter 8, Section 17.

2 The procedure for the secondary cable is also as described in Chapter 8 except that it is no longer necessary to unlock the adjuster nut from its sleeve by prising their shoulders apart. On the modified cable, unscrew the locknut then slacken the adjusting sleeve until the cable can be withdrawn from the abutment bracket.

Handbrake (from January 1982) – adjustment

3 The procedure is as given in Chapter 8, Section 16 except that the total plunger movement should be between 0.5 and 2.0 mm (0.020 and 0.079 in), and the adjuster has a normal locknut. The footbrake should be applied prior to adjusting the handbrake to ensure the rear brakes are adjusted by the automatic mechanism. To set the locknut, tighten it 2 clicks by hand followed by a further 1 or 2 clicks using a wrench.

Rear wheel cylinder

4 All Escort Saloon and Estate models produced from February 1983 are fitted with reduced diameter rear brake wheel cylinders, the diameter now being 17.78 mm (0.710 in) in diameter. The Escort XR3i has had this small wheel cylinder fitted since its introduction in October of 1982.

5 The servicing instructions for the later 'small' type wheel cylinder are the same as those given for the earlier types in Chapter 8, but it is important that when ordering spare parts or a replacement wheel cylinder you identify which cylinder type you have. Cylinders of different sizes must not be fitted on opposing axles. The respective cylinder types can be identified by the letter mark stamped into the body of the cylinder unit on its rear face next to the brake line connection aperture.

Automatic adjustment strut

6 A modified automatic adjustment strut is not being fitted to later Escorts (all variants). The new and earlier type struts are identified by a difference in profile.

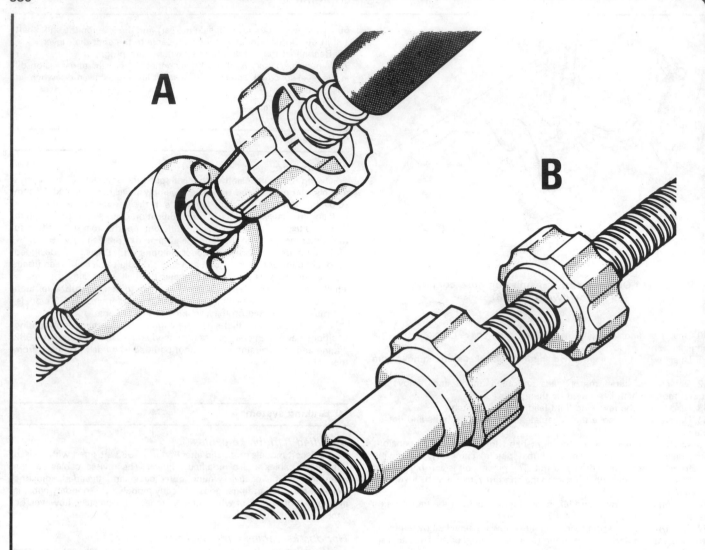

Fig. 13.115 Early type (A) and modified type (B) handbrake cables (Sec 10)

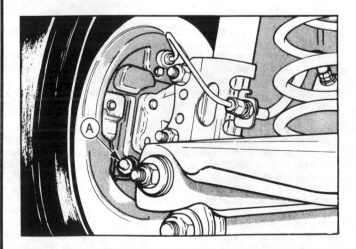

Fig. 13.116 Handbrake adjustment plunger (A) (Sec 10)

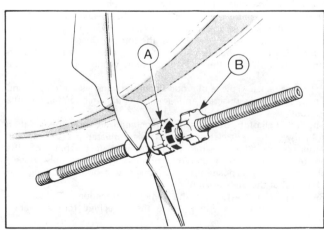

Fig. 13.117 Modified handbrake cable adjusting sleeve
(A) and locknut (B) (Sec 10)

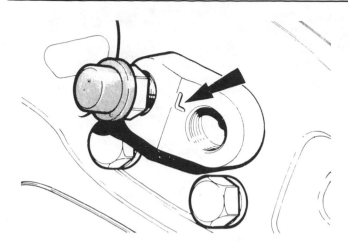

Fig. 13.118 Rear wheel cylinder type identification mark (Sec 10)

T – 22.2 mm diameter cylinder   H = 17.78 mm diameter cylinder
L = 19.05 mm diameter cylinder

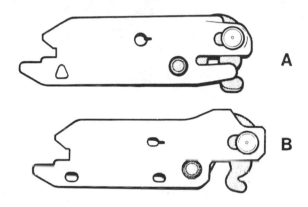

Fig. 13.119 Rear brake automatic adjustment strut types (Sec 10)

A   Late type strut   B   Early type strut

check through the brake system and its components for signs of defects or excessive wear. Also check the wheel bearing free play and renew as necessary, then repeat the above procedure.

14 To check the pedal free height measure the distance between the top face of the pedal and the floorpan metal panel at the point shown in Figure 13.121 and compare it with the figure given in the Specifications. If the pedal free height is not as given, check that the brake pedal, its bushes and linkages are not excessively worn or that the floorpan is not distorted.

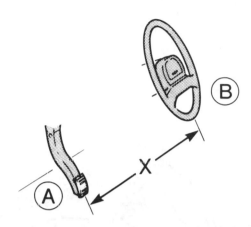

Fig. 13.120 Brake pedal free height (released) check (Sec 10)

A   Brake pedal   X   Free height distance
B   Steering wheel

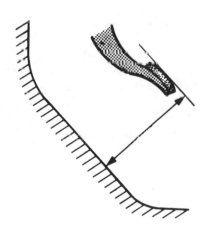

Fig. 13.121 Brake pedal to floorpan height check (released) (Sec 10)

Footbrake pedal travel check

7 If the footbrake pedal travel is thought to be excessive it can be checked in the following manner. It is also advisable to check the pedal travel after the brake hydraulic system has been bled for any reason.

8 On models fitted with a servo unit the check must be made with the engine switched off and the servo vacuum used up by fully depressing the pedal a minimum of eight times.

9 On all models check that the hydraulic fluid level in the master cylinder reservoir is topped up to its maximum mark and fully release the handbrake.

10 Apply a reasonable pressure to the footbrake pedal to ensure that the rear brakes are fully adjusted then release the pedal.

11 Measure the distance between the free height (released) position of the brake pedal to the underside of the steering wheel rim at its lowest point. Now depress the pedal fully (as much as the travel will allow) and check the pedal to steering wheel distance as already described. Calculate the difference between the two readings and check the figure recorded with the nominal pedal travel given in the Specifications at the start of this Chapter.

12 If the pedal travel is excessive then the brake system should be bled, as described in Chapter 8.

13 If, after bleeding the hydraulic system, the travel is still excessive

Rear brake linings

15 In consequence of the introduction of the modified strut described in paragraph 6 the upper shoe return spring differs from the original arrangement (Fig. 13.122). To release the leading shoe from the strut it is now necessary to move the automatic adjuster to the maximum position (Fig. 13.123).

Brake drum and hub (fuel injection models)

16 On fuel injection models the brake drums are detachable from the hubs as for Van versions. The wheel bearing adjustment is the same as that described in Chapter 8.

17 Although it may be possible to remove the brake shoes with the hub *in situ* it is recommended that the hub is removed first.

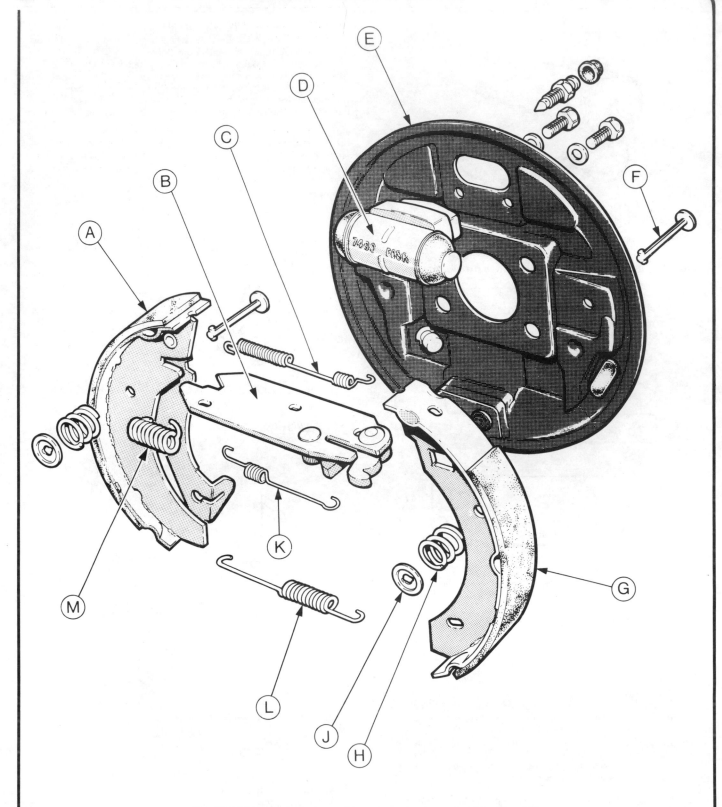

Fig. 13.122 Exploded view of later rear brake assembly (Sec 10)

A	Trailing shoe	D	Wheel cylinder	G	Leading shoe	K	Ratchet pawl spring
B	Adjuster strut	E	Backplate	H	Spring	L	Return spring
C	Spring	F	Hold-down post	J	Dished washer	M	Return spring

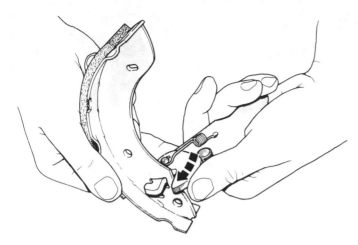

Fig. 13.123 Removing the leading shoe from the strut on later models (Sec 10)

11 Steering

Steering gear (rack and pinion) modifications and overhaul

The steering gear unit fitted to all Escort variants from May 1983 is of a type similar to that developed for the Sierra model. Whilst the removal and refitting of this later unit can be achieved as described for the earlier type, the overhaul procedures differ and you will need the use of Ford special service tool 13-009-A to complete the overhaul. To overhaul the unit proceed as follows.

1 Clean the exterior of the steering gear with paraffin and wipe dry.

2 Mount the steering gear in a vice then remove and discard the clips and slide the rubber bellows off the tie-rods.

3 Move the rack fully to the left and grip the rack in a soft jawed vice.

4 If the original tie-rods are fitted, use a pipe wrench to unscrew the balljoint from the rack and remove the tie-rod. If service replacement tie-rods are fitted use a spanner on the machined flats.

5 Remove the right-hand tie-rod in the same way. Each tie-rod must be refitted to the same end of the rack so keep them in order of fitting.

6 Unscrew and remove the slipper plug and remove the spring and slipper. Unscrew the slipper plug using the hexagonal end of service tool 13-009-A.

7 Now engage the segmented end of the service tool into the slots in the head of the pinion retaining nut and unscrew it. Remove the nut and the seal. Withdraw the pinion and bearing using a twisting action.

8 The rack can now be withdrawn from the steering gear housing.

9 Clean all the components in paraffin and wipe dry. Examine them for wear and damage and renew them as necessary. If necessary the rack support bush in the housing can be renewed.

10 Lightly coat the rack with the specified semi-fluid grease and insert it into the housing.

11 Centralise the steering rack within the tube then coat the pinion and bearing with grease and locate it in the housing, meshing it with the rack. When in position the pinion flat must be at 90° relative to the slipper plug on the pinion end side of the tube.

12 Before fitting the pinion nut, smear its threads with sealant and tighten it to the specified torque wrench setting using the special service tool (13-009-A). Lock the nut by peening the housing in four places.

13 With the rack still centralised, refit the slipper spring and plug. The plug threads should be smeared with a suitable sealant before fitting (Locktite 542 or similar). Tighten the plug using the special service tool to the specified torque wrench setting, then loosen it off 60° to 70°.

14 Using a piece of string and a spring balance check that the turning torque of the pinion is between 0.3 and 1.3 Nm (0.22 and 1.0 lbf ft). To do this accurately turn the pinion anti-clockwise half a turn from its central position and measure the torque while turning the pinion clockwise through one complete turn.

15 If necessary tighten or loosen the slipper plug until the torque is correct. Then lock by peening the housing in one of the slots.

16 Refit the tie-rod inner balljoint units to the steering rack, reversing the method used for removal. If reusing the original tie-rod units they must be fitted to their original sides and tightened so that their original staking marks align with the steering rack grooves. When tightening ensure that the rack (not the tube) is secured in a soft jawed vice. If new tie-rods are being fitted they must be tightened to the specified torque wrench setting using an open-ended torque wrench adaptor then staked to the steering rack groove.

Steering tie-rods and steering gear bellows

17 As from May 1983, non-repairable steering tie-rods/inner balljoint units were fitted to all models. In addition the rack bellows are secured by a single clip fitted at the rack housing end and the tie-rod end engaged in a groove in the tie-rod. However, it is recommended that clips are fitted to hold the bellows in the tie-rod groove, as in certain circumstances the bellows may slide from the groove causing oil to escape and dirt and water to enter. As from late 1984 clips are again fitted by Ford.

18 Whenever new bellows are to be fitted, check that they are the correct type to suit the diameter of the tie-rods which will be 11.8 mm (.46 in) or 13.3 mm (0.52 in).

19 After renewal of the bellows and/or overhauling the steering gear unit on models produced from May 1983 it should be noted that the steering gear lubricant has been increased to 120 cc. This should be added to the tube, whilst 70 cc of semi-fluid grease should be inserted into the housing end of the gear. If, however, only a partial loss of steering gear lubricant was experienced when renewing the bellows then top up accordingly with the required amount of lubricant.

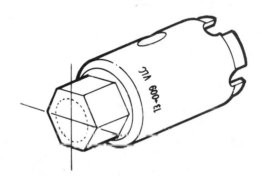

Fig. 13.124 Ford special steering gear service tool 13-009-A required on later models (Sec 11)

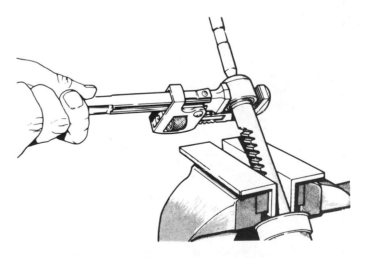

Fig. 13.125 Unscrewing tie rods from steering rack (Sec 11)

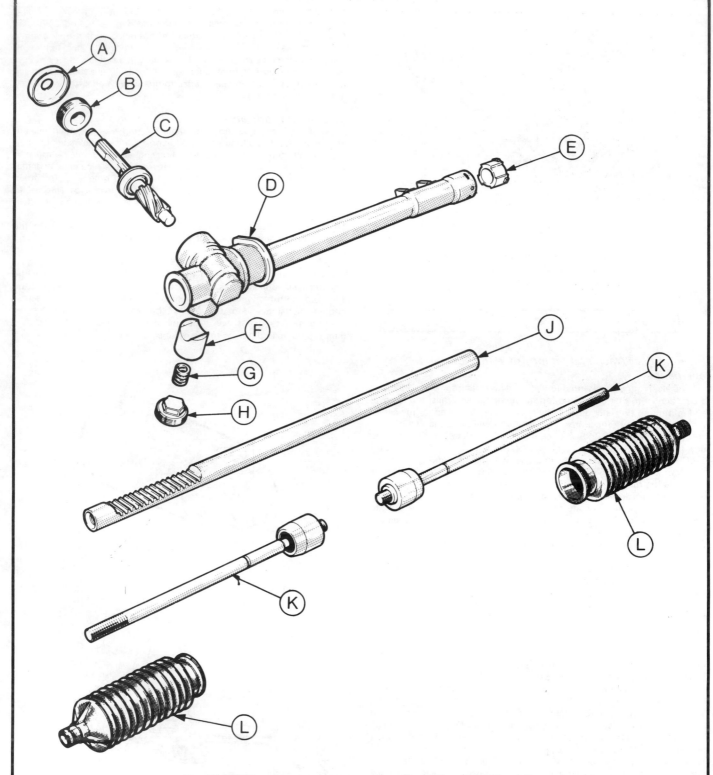

Fig. 13.126 Steering gear components – from May 1983 (Sec 11)

A	Dust cap	E	Rack support bush	J	Rack
B	Pinion cover	F	Rack slipper	K	Tie-rods
C	Pinion	G	Spring	L	Bellows
D	Rack housing	H	Slipper plug		

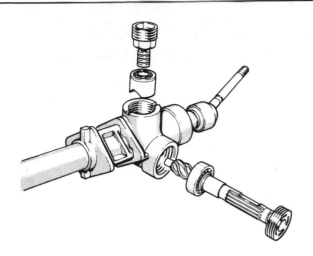

Fig. 13.127 Steering pinion and slipper assembly (Sec 11)

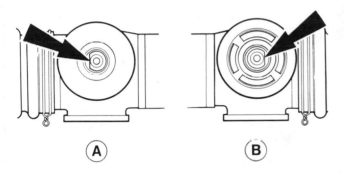

Fig. 13.128 Pinion alignment to be as shown according to type (Sec 11)

A   Left-hand drive   B   Right-hand drive

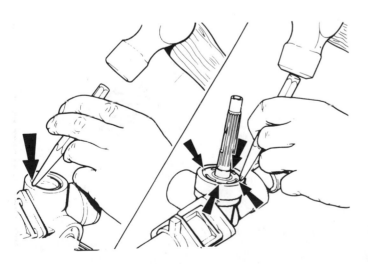

Fig. 13.129 Peen to lock set positions of the pinion cover and the slipper plug (Sec 11)

12 Suspension

Front tie-bar
1   All 1.1 litre models produced from May 1983 are fitted with an anti-roll bar, as used on the 1.3 and 1.6 litre models, in place of the tie-bar.

Front suspension strut
2   All models produced from May 1983 are fitted with front suspension struts which have a redesigned top mounting and the mounting location on each side has been moved inwards.
3   The hub (spindle) carrier has also been revised in design and steering (suspension) arms are 7.3 mm (0.287 in) longer.
4   These modifications have resulted in a change of front wheel alignment data, as given in the Specifications at the beginning of this Chapter.
5   The late type suspension struts, hub carrier and steering arms are not interchangeable with the earlier types.

Front suspension strut – removal and refitting
6   The removal and refitting details for the suspension strut on models produced from May 1983 are basically the same as those given for the earlier type in Chapter 10, but the following differences apply:

(a)   Prior to dismantling the suspension strut from the hub carrier, the brake hose and grommet must be detached from the suspension unit support
(b)   When disconnecting the strut top mounting, detach the top nut cap, then unscrew the nut and remove it and the cup washer

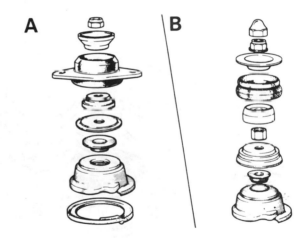

Fig. 13.130 Front suspension strut top mounting on early (A) and late (B) models (Sec 12)

Front hub bearings
7   All Escort fwd models are fitted with non-adjustable front hub bearings, the bearing play being set when the hub nut is tightened to its specified setting during initial assembly or overhaul.
8   A small amount of endfloat may be detected when checking for play, even after fitting new bearings, but when the wheel is spun there should be no sign of roughness, binding or vibration caused by the bearings.
9   When lubricating the wheel bearings, use a grease to the Ford Specification SAM - 1C - 9111A as used during production.

Anti-roll bar bushes and rear tie-bar bushes
10   The above mentioned component bushes have been revised to improve the ride quality on all models produced from August 1983. When renewing the bushes at the front or rear they must be renewed as a set since the early and late type bushes must not be mixed on the same axle. The removal and refitting procedures are otherwise the same as those described in Chapter 10.

Rear axle and suspension modifications

11 All models (except Van) produced from May 1983 had minor improvements made to the rear suspension system, which include dropping down the lower arm inner pivot location and raising the tie-bar to chassis locating point.

12 These modifications have reduced the nominal toe-in per wheel to 1 mm (0.04 in).

13 Late type lower suspension arms and tie-bars are not interchangeable with the earlier types, although longer tie-bars can be fitted to earlier models, but only in pairs and the rear wheel toe settings will need adjustment during fitting, so this is therefore a task best entrusted to a Ford dealer.

14 It should be noted that whenever the tie-bars are removed for any reason, the spacers, washers and bushes must be reassembled in the same order of fitting as when removed. The washers are fitted during production to give the correct rear wheel toe setting adjustment, an equal number of washers being fitted on each side.

Rear shock absorbers (passenger vehicles) – removal and refitting

15 The rear shock absorbers are identical on each side of the car and this means that the brake hose/pipe mounting bracket on the right-hand side is located further behind the coil spring than on the left-hand side. If difficulty is experienced reaching the bracket nut with a normal spanner, a cranked spanner may be used or alternatively the coil spring can be removed.

Oversteer at high speed – rectification

16 If oversteer at high speed is experienced, such as when changing lanes on a motorway, the front anti-roll bar to suspension arm flexible

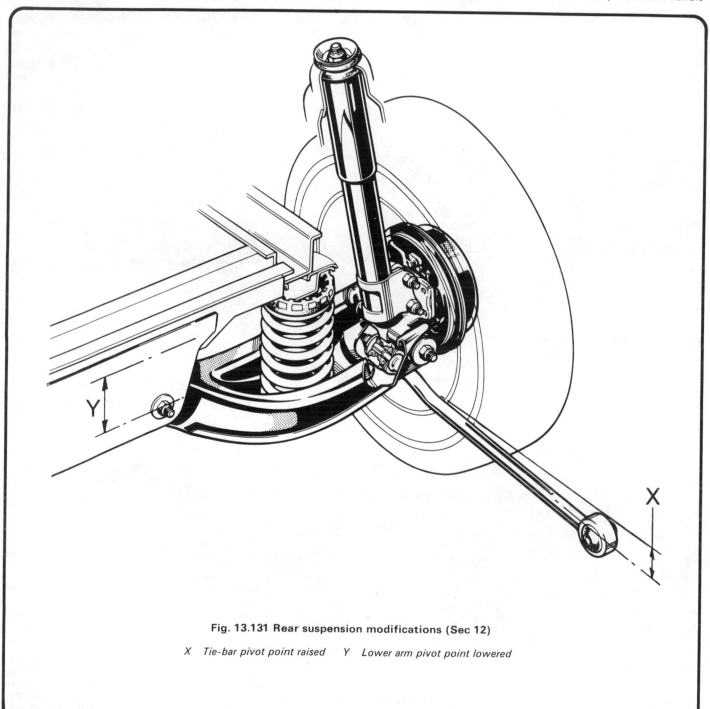

Fig. 13.131 Rear suspension modifications (Sec 12)

X   Tie-bar pivot point raised   Y   Lower arm pivot point lowered

bushes and rear tie-rod to suspension arm flexible bushes should be renewed and the wheel alignment adjusted to the following specifications.

Front wheel toe-out   – 4.0 ± 1.0 mm (0.158 ± 0.040 in)
Rear wheel toe-in   – Minimum of 3.0 mm (0.118 in), maximum of 3.87 mm (0.152 in)

17 Adjustment of the rear wheel alignment is made by changing the number of washers against the front flexible bushes (refer to Fig. 10.23 and 10.24, Chapter 10). There must always be an equal amount of washers on each side of the car and a minimum of one washer.

Wheels and tyres – general care and maintenance

Wheels and tyres should give no real problems in use provided that a close eye is kept on them with regard to excessive wear or damage. To this end, the following points should be noted.

Ensure that tyre pressures are checked regularly and maintained correctly. Checking should be carried out with the tyres cold and not immediately after the vehicle has been in use. If the pressures are checked with the tyres hot, an apparently high reading will be obtained owing to heat expansion. Under no circumstances should an attempt be made to reduce the pressures to the quoted cold reading in this instance, or effective underinflation will result.

Underinflation will cause overheating of the tyre owing to excessive flexing of the casing, and the tread will not sit correctly on the road surface. This will cause a consequent loss of adhesion and excessive wear, not to mention the danger of sudden tyre failure due to heat build-up.

Overinflation will cause rapid wear of the centre part of the tyre tread coupled with reduced adhesion, harsher ride, and the danger of shock damage occurring in the tyre casing.

Regularly check the tyres for damage in the form of cuts or bulges, especially in the sidewalls. Remove any nails or stones embedded in the tread before they penetrate the tyre to cause deflation. If removal of a nail *does* reveal that the tyre has been punctured, refit the nail so that its point of penetration is marked. Then immediately change the wheel and have the tyre repaired by a tyre dealer. Do *not* drive on a tyre in such a condition. In many cases a puncture can be simply repaired by the use of an inner tube of the correct size and type. If in any doubt as to the possible consequences of any damage found, consult your local tyre dealer for advice.

Periodically remove the wheels and clean any dirt or mud from the inside and outside surfaces. Examine the wheel rims for signs of rusting, corrosion or other damage. Light alloy wheels are easily damaged by 'kerbing' whilst parking, and similarly steel wheels may become dented or buckled. Renewal of the wheel is very often the only course of remedial action possible

The balance of each wheel and tyre assembly should be maintained to avoid excessive wear, not only to the tyres but also to the steering and suspension components. Wheel imbalance is normally signified by vibration through the vehicle's bodyshell, although in many cases it is particularly noticeable through the steering wheel. Conversely, it should be noted that wear or damage in suspension or steering components may cause excessive tyre wear. Out-of-round or out-of-true tyres, damaged wheels and wheel bearing wear/maladjustment also fall into this category. Balancing will not usually cure vibration caused by such wear.

Wheel balancing may be carried out with the wheel either on or off the vehicle. If balanced on the vehicle, ensure that the wheel-to-hub relationship is marked in some way prior to subsequent wheel removal so that it may be refitted in its original position.

General tyre wear is influenced to a large degree by driving style – harsh braking and acceleration or fast cornering will all produce more rapid tyre wear. Interchanging of tyres may result in more even wear, but this should only be carried out where there is no mix of tyre types on the vehicle. However, it is worth bearing in mind that if this is completely effective, the added expense of replacing a complete set of tyres simultaneously is incurred, which may prove financially restrictive for many owners.

Front tyres may wear unevenly as a result of wheel misalignment. The front wheels should always be correctly aligned according to the settings specified by the vehicle manufacturer.

Legal restrictions apply to the mixing of tyre types on a vehicle. Basically this means that a vehicle must not have tyres of differing construction on the same axle. Although it is not recommended to mix tyre types between front axle and rear axle, the only legally permissible

combination is crossply at the front and radial at the rear. When mixing radial ply tyres, textile braced radials must always go on the front axle, with steel braced radials at the rear. An obvious disadvantage of such mixing is the necessity to carry two spare tyres to avoid contravening the law in the event of a puncture.

In the UK, the Motor Vehicles Construction and Use Regulations apply to many aspects of tyre fitting and usage. It is suggested that a copy of these regulations is obtained from your local police if in doubt as to the current legal requirements with regard to tyre condition, minimum tread depth, etc.

13 Electrical system

Maintenance-free battery

From 1982 Ford models have progressively been fitted with a maintenance-free battery during production. The maintenance-free battery is of sealed for life cell design and does not require routine topping-up with distilled water. The only maintenance requirement with this battery type is to inspect the battery lead terminals for security and any sign of corrosion. Being of sealed cell design it is not possible to check the electrolyte in each cell by using a hydrometer to assess the state of charge. With the maintenance-free battery the procedure is as follows.

Maintenance-free battery – testing

1 To check the condition of a maintenance-free battery you will need a voltmeter.
2 If the battery has been under charge within the previous six hours (and that includes normal engine running), switch on the headlamps for 30 seconds to stabilise the battery voltage.
3 Switch off the headlamps and check that all other electrical components of the vehicle are off, then allow an interval of about five minutes to pass, before making the test, to stabilize battery voltage. Check that the battery terminals are clean whilst waiting.
4 Connect up the voltmeter to the battery and check the reading. If the reading is less than 12.2 volts the battery is deeply discharged, whilst a reading between 12.2 and 12.5 volts indicates that it is partially discharged
5 If the battery is found to be in need of recharging the procedure differs from normal and the method used is dependent on the state of discharge. In either case, remove the battery from the vehicle before recharging.

Maintenance-free battery – charging

6 As mentioned above the method used to recharge a maintenance-free battery is dependent on whether it is partially discharged or deeply discharged.
7 If the battery is partially discharged, it can be recharged to a usable condition of 12.5 volts within about three hours if connected to a 'Constant Voltage' type battery charger. The charger voltage must be set to operate between 13.9 and 14.9 volts and the charger current must not exceed 2.5 amps. It should be noted that full charging by this method could take two to three days and in this instance charging is best entrusted to your Ford dealer or automotive electrician.
8 If the battery is fully discharged it will need to be charged in a similar manner to that described for a partially discharged battery in which case it will take several days. In this instance full supervision is required during charging and it must therefore be entrusted to a Ford dealer or automotive electrician.

Alternator mounting

9 To prevent undue strain and possible breakage of the alternator mounting lugs, it is important to ensure the mounting bolts and washer are correctly fitted, as shown in Fig. 13.132. The adjustment strap bolt should be tightened first, followed by the front then rear bolts. The current torque wrench setting is given in the Specifications.

Rear lamp and bulbs (Cabriolet)

10 The rear lamp clusters fitted to the Cabriolet are identical to those on the Estate version, however access to the rear of the lamps is gained from inside the boot compartment by pulling open the trim access flap.

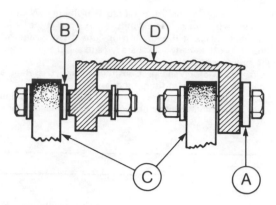

Fig. 13.132 Correct fitting of alternator mounting components (Sec 13)

A   Large washer
B   Small washer (pre 1985
    CVH engines only)

C   Bracket
D   Alternator

Radio – removal and refitting

21 On later models the Ford radio removal and refitting details differ from that described in Chapter 11, the procedure being as follows:

22 Disconnect the battery earth lead.

23 Pull free and remove the radio control knobs, together with the plastic tone control lever and the tuning knob spacer.

24 Unscrew and remove the two cover trim panel retaining nuts and washers. Withdraw the trim panel.

25 Using two lengths of wire rod with their ends bent over, reach into the aperture on each side of the radio front face and release the retaining tangs by pulling them inwards enabling the radio to be released and partially withdrawn.

26 Detach the aerial lead, the power input lead, the aerial feed, speaker lead plug and earth lead from the radio and fully remove it. The radio can then have its plastic support bracket and location plate removed from the rear and the front bracket detached.

27 Refitting is the reversal of the removal procedure. When the various lead connections are made, push the radio into position to the point where the retaining tangs are heard to snap into position.

28 When locating the trim panel its top edge is marked on its inside face.

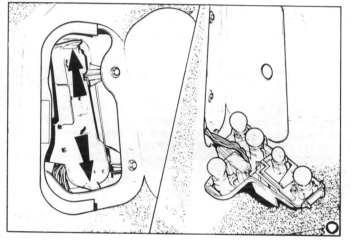

Fig. 13.133 Removing the rear lamp bulbholder on the Cabriolet (Sec 13)

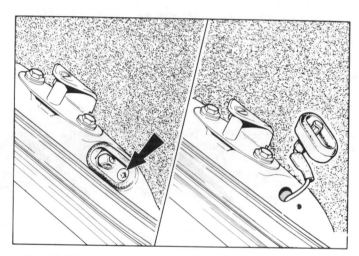

Fig. 13.134 Removing the load space lamp switch on the Cabriolet (Sec 13)

Retaining screw arrowed

Load space lamp switch (Cabriolet) – removal and refitting

11 Open the boot lid then remove the cross-head screw, lift out the switch, and disconnect the wiring. Tape the wire to the rear panel to prevent it dropping in the hole.

12 Refitting is a reversal of removal.

Load space lamp bulb (Cabriolet) – renewal

13 Open the boot lid and prise out the lamp with a thin screwdriver.

14 Depress and twist the bulb to remove it from the bulbholder.

15 Refitting is a reversal of removal.

Headlamps – alignment

16 To assist when making a hedlamp alignment check/adjustment as described in Chapter 11, Section 25 the accompanying diagram shows the provisional headlamp beam alignment.

17 When set correctly, the centre of a dipped beam light should be below the headlamp level, as shown.

Auxiliary warning system

18 The fuel low level warning lamp is now activated when the quantity of fuel in the tank falls below 5.0 to 8.0 litres (1.1 to 1.8 gallons).

19 The brake pad wear indicator is now activated when the friction material is worn down to 1.5 mm (0.059 in) thick.

20 On some models the low coolant level switch is retained with a screw type cap, as shown in Fig. 13.137.

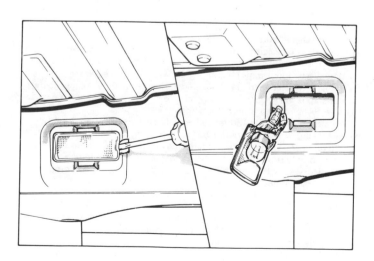

Fig. 13.135 Load space lamp bulb removal on the Cabriolet (Sec 13)

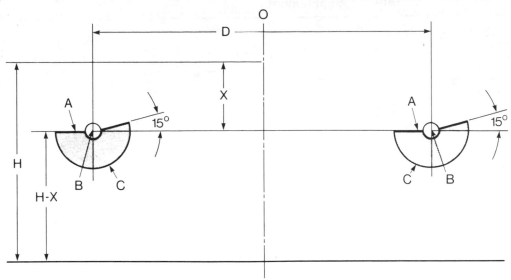

Fig. 13.136 Basic headlamp alignment diagram for use in conjunction with details given in Section 25 of Chapter 11. Transpose 15° beam inclination from right to left for right-hand models (Sec 13)

A   Light/dark boundary
B   Dipped beam centre
C   Dipped beam pattern
D   Distance between lamp centres 1004 mm (39.50 in)
H   Headlamp height of individual vehicle
0   Centre line of vehicle
X   130 mm (5.10 in) saloon, estate and van; 110 mm (4.30 in) XR3 and HD

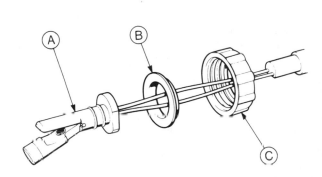

Fig. 13.137 Low coolant level switch (A), spacer (B) and cap (C) (Sec 13)

Fig. 13.138 Remove the radio trim panel securing nuts (arrowed) (Sec 13)

Fig. 13.139 Release the radio unit retaining tangs (arrowed) (Sec 13)

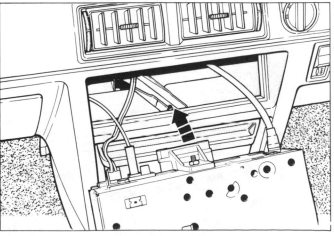

Fig. 13.140 Radio refitting. Align plastic support bracket and slide (Sec 13)

Radio/cassette player – removal and refitting

On later models this unit is removed as follows:

29 Disconnect the battery earth lead.

30 To release the radio cassette unit from its cavity you will need to fabricate two lengths of suitable wire rod bent into a U-shape with the ends spaced to fit into the two slots on each side of the facia. Insert the two rods into the slots at each end and pull them slightly outwards to release the retaining clips and pull the radio/cassette unit from its location aperture. Pull the unit out keeping it square.

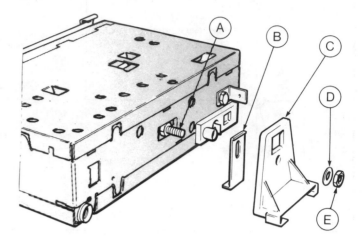

Fig. 13.144 Radio/cassette rear support bracket assembly
(Sec 13)

A   Securing stud   D   Washer
B   Locating plate   E   Securing nut
C   Bracket

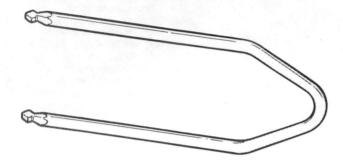

Fig. 13.141 Radio/cassette removal tool (Sec 13)

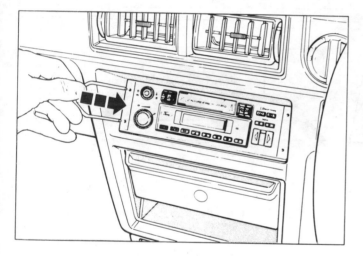

Fig. 13.142 Insert removal tool into holes in front face
(Sec 13)

31 Disconnect the aerial lead, aerial feed lead, the speaker plugs, the power supply lead, the light and memory lead (if fitted) and the earth wire then fully remove the unit.

32 Disengage the release wires by carefully pushing back the securing clips with a small screwdriver.

33 The plastic support bracket and location plate can be removed from the rear of the unit.

34 Refit in the reverse order of removal. When the various leads are reconnected locate the unit into its aperture and push it in until the retaining clips are heard to snap shut.

Loudspeakers (rear parcel shelf mounting) – removal and refitting

35 Prise the speaker cover free by inserting a screwdriver blade into the slots in the side face of the cover. Unscrew and remove the four speaker retaining screws, pull the speaker away from the shelf and disconnect the wires.

36 Refit in the reverse order to removal.

Fig. 13.143 Radio/cassette unit withdrawal method using
special tools (Sec 13)

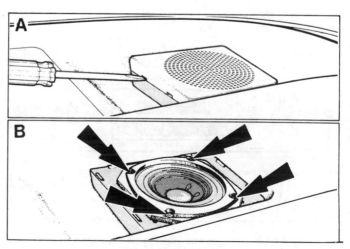

Fig. 13.145 Rear parcel shelf mounted speaker unit removal
(Sec 13)

A   Prise free the cover   B   Remove securing screws (arrowed)

Loudspeakers (rear parcel tray mounted) – removal and refitting

37 Unscrew the collar and pull the wiring plug from the loudspeaker.
38 Remove the rear parcel tray then unscrew the four retaining screws and remove the speaker.
39 Refit in the reverse order to removal.

Aerial mast (power-operated type) – removal and refitting

40 Switch on the radio so that the aerial fully extends then switch it off and disconnect the battery when its length is reduced to 400 mm (16.0 in).
41 Unscrew the upper retaining nut then pull the bottom part of the aerial from the body. Clean the plastic drive cable.
42 Unscrew the knob from the top of the aerial, lower the top section, then unscrew the mast (Fig. 13.146).
43 Refitting is a reversal of removal.

Speaker balance control – removal and refitting

44 Prise the bezel from the control with a screwdriver.
45 Pull the cassette stowage unit from the facia, then turn the clip unit anti-clockwise, release the control and disconnect the wiring.
46 Refit in reverse order.

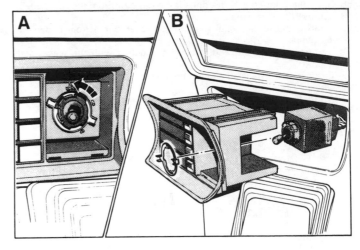

Fig. 13.148 Speaker balance control removal (Sec 13)

A Turn the clip   B Remove the cassette storage unit

Loudspeaker (cowl panel mounted – Cabriolet) – removal and refitting

47 Extract the screws as necessary from the scuff plate.
48 Extract the end screw from the facia panel.
49 Prise the door weatherseal from the cowl panel.
50 Remove the cowl panel and, if required, unclip the speaker grille.
51 Extract the four speaker mounting screws and withdraw the speaker until the leads can be disconnented.
52 Refitting is a reversal of removal.

Loudspeaker (rear quarter panel – Cabriolet) – removal and refitting

53 Fully open the roof and lock it.
54 Pull off the roof release lever knob and remove the window winder.
55 Pull back the rear quarter trim panel then remove the three screws and withdraw the trim panel with the speaker.
56 Disconnect the wiring then extract the screws and detach the speaker and grille from the panel. Note the location of the rubber washers.
57 Refitting is a reversal of removal, but position the speaker so that the terminals face forwards.

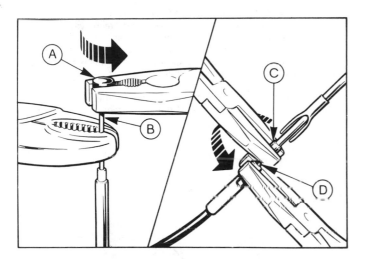

Fig. 13.146 Removing the aerial mast (Sec 13)

A Knob   C Locknut
B Top section   D Thread

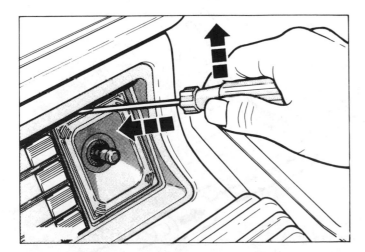

Fig. 13.147 Prising out the speaker balance control bezel (Sec 13)

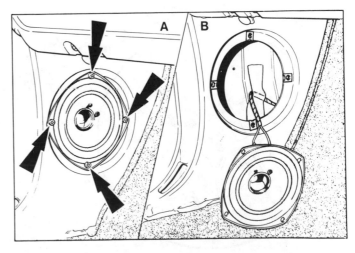

Fig. 13.149 Remove the screws (A) and withdraw the speaker (B) – Cabriolet (Sec 13)

Aerial (Cabriolet) – removal and refitting

58 Open the boot lid and disconnect the gas strut from the side panel.
59 Remove the trim panel.
60 Remove the lower aerial mounting bracket screw from under the quarter panel.
61 Unscrew the top nut and remove it, together with the spacer and washer.
62 Unscrew the aerial lead and, on the power-operated type, disconnect the wiring.
63 Withdraw the aerial from inside the luggage compartment.
64 Refitting is a reversal of removal.

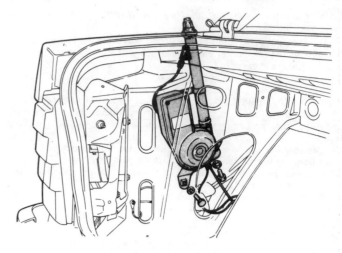

Fig. 13.151 Power-operated aerial on the Cabriolet (Sec 13)

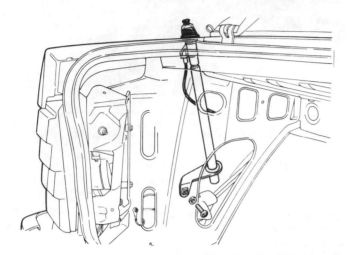

Fig. 13.150 Manually operated aerial on the Cabriolet (Sec 13)

Twin jet windscreen washer system

Later models are fitted with a twin jet windscreen washer system instead of the single jet type used on earlier models.

The jets are now located as shown in Fig. 13.152, one each side on the bonnet inner panel. The washer supply hose is connected to a central T-piece connector which directs the fluid to each jet.

The twin jets can be adjusted in the same manner as the earlier single type. They should be set so that the fluid jets hit the windscreen about 250 mm (9.8 in) from the top edge of the windscreen.

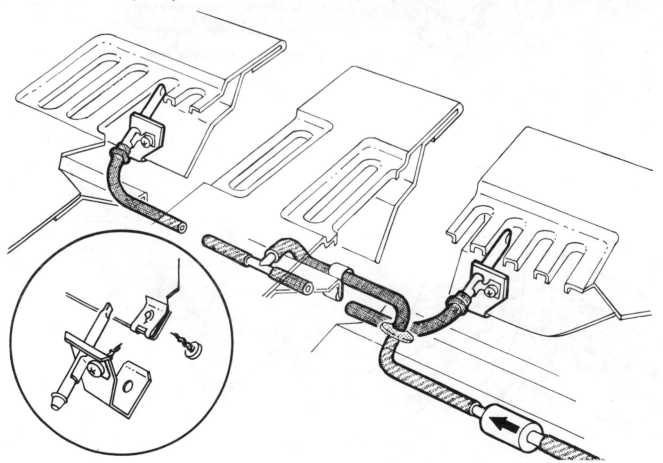

Fig. 13.152 Twin jet windscreen washer system showing jet locations (Sec 13)

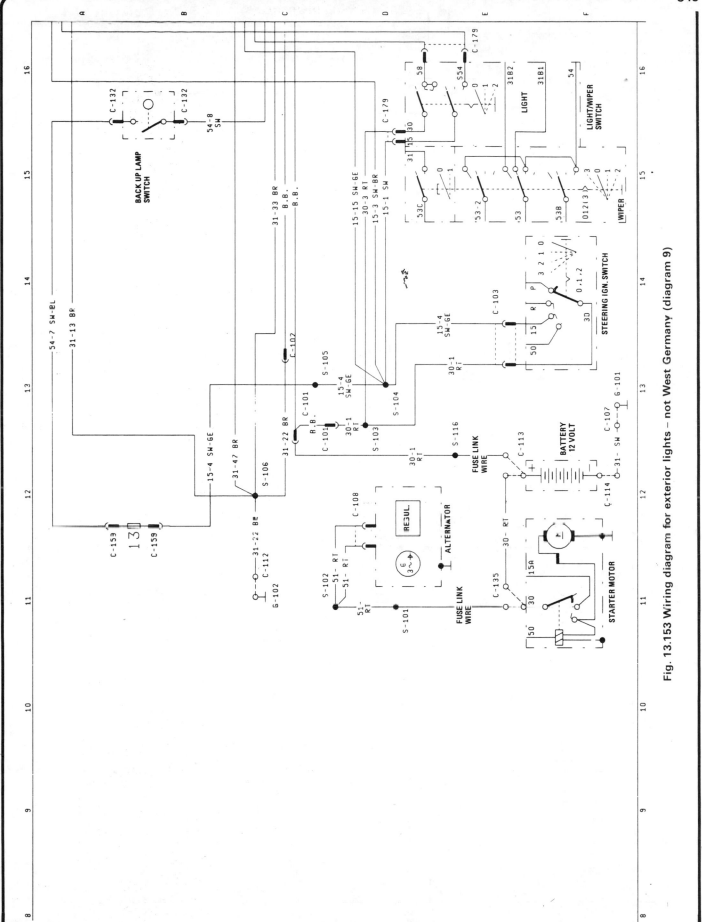

Fig. 13.153 Wiring diagram for exterior lights – not West Germany (diagram 9)

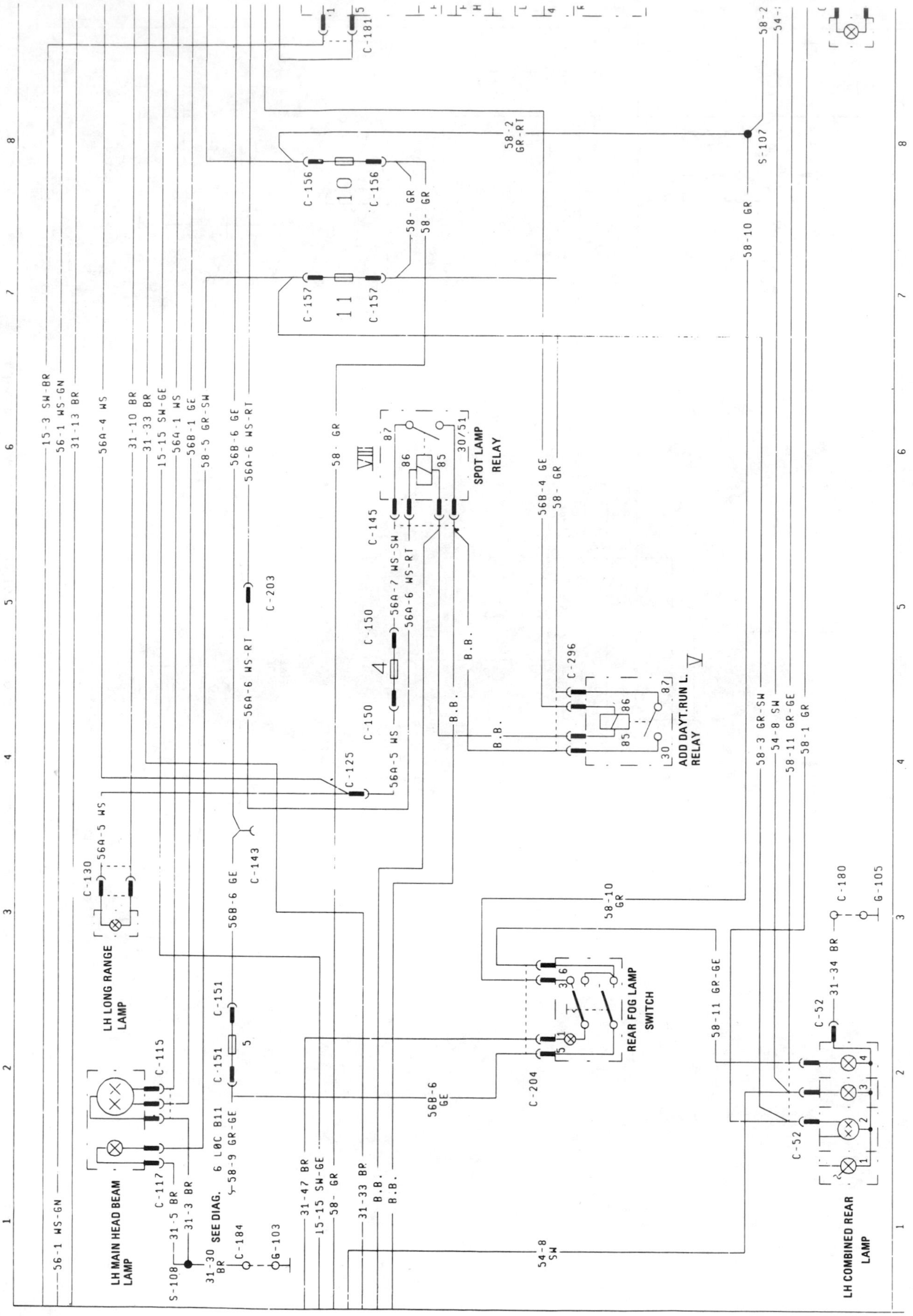

Fig. 13.154 Wiring diagram for exterior lights – not West Germany (diagram 10)

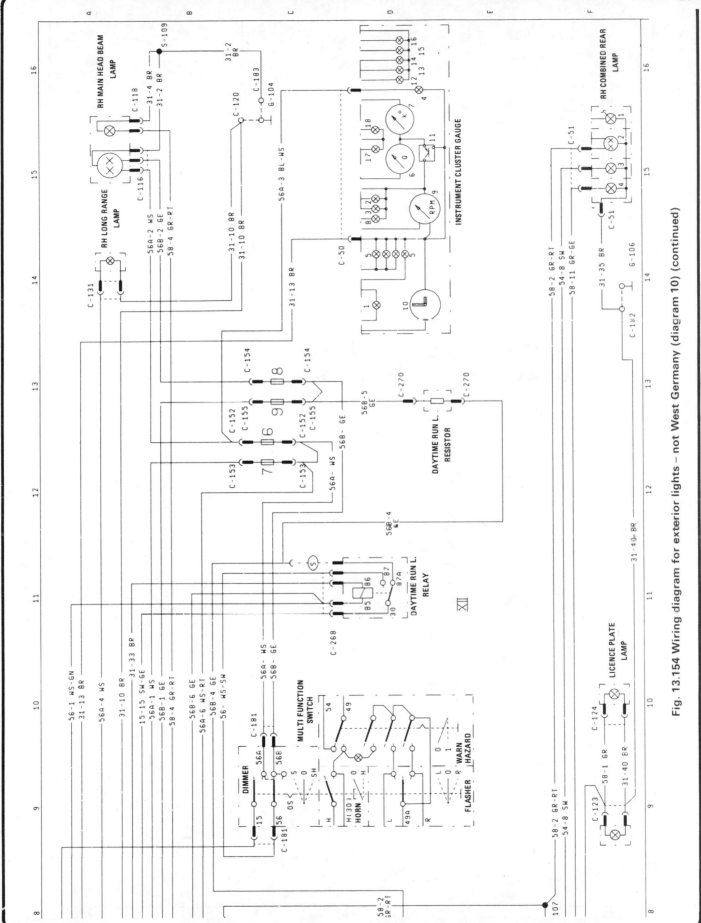

Fig. 13.154 Wiring diagram for exterior lights – not West Germany (diagram 10) (continued)

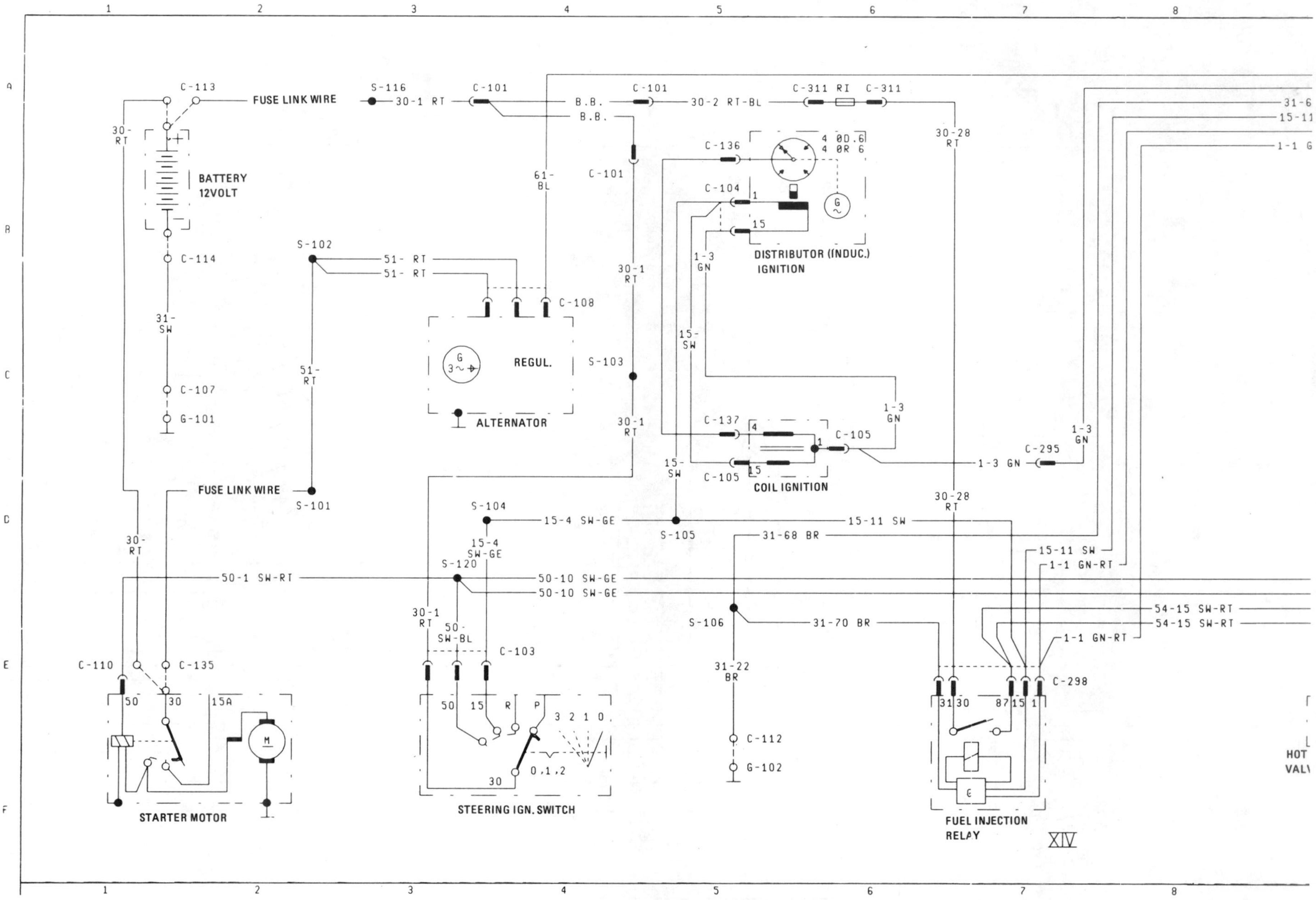

Fig. 13.155 Wiring diagram for fuel injection (diagram 11)

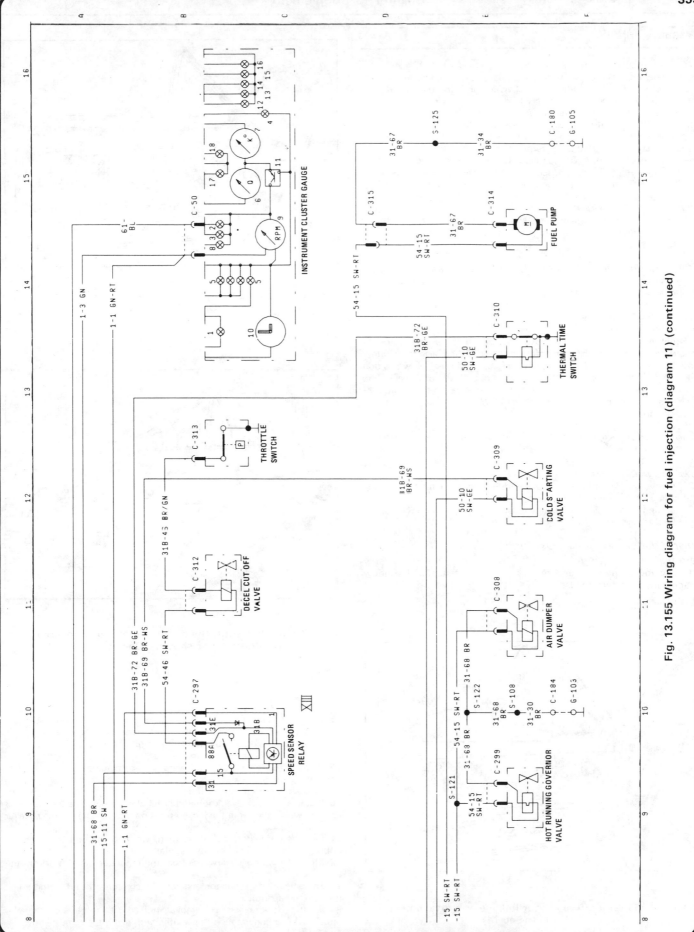

Fig. 13.155 Wiring diagram for fuel injection (diagram 11) (continued)

14 Bodywork

Door window regulator

1   On later models the door window regulator is retained by seven rivets instead of screws as on earlier models. When removing the regulator on later models it is therefore necessary to drill out the rivets.

2   Since the screw fixing regulator is no longer being manufactured, replacing the regulator on early models with the later type regulator necessitates drilling out the retaining holes to 7 mm (0.276 in). Special J-nuts must then be fitted to the regulator positioned in line with each of the seven securing holes. The regulator can then be attached to the door shell using seven M6 x 10 mm screws. Do not use any other screw type.

3   On later models the regulator is reattached using new rivets.

Plastic bumper and sections

4   The plastic bumper end sections should be renewed if removed from the metal centre section as they are distorted during the removal operation.

Door window glass (Cabriolet) – removal and refitting

5   Remove the door trim panel and peel off the waterproof sheet.

6   Remove the door weatherstrip and rubber end block.

7   Lower the window and, working through the aperture, disconnect the linkage arms from the bottom rail.

8   Lift the glass upwards from the door.

9   Refitting is a reversal of removal, but adjust the window stop as follows. Loosen the adjustment bolt (Fig. 13.157) then raise the window until the top edge of the glass touches the top guide seal. Now position the stop on the regulator mechanism and tighten the bolt. Check that, with the door shut and the window fully raised, the top front corner of the glass is under the lip of the weatherstrip. Make any final adjustments as necessary.

Door window regulator (Cabriolet) – removal and refitting

10   Remove the door trim panel and peel off the waterproof sheet.

11   Lower the window and, working through the aperture rail. Fully lower the window glass into the door.

12   Remove the seven screws and withdraw the regulator through the aperture.

13   Refitting is a reversal of removal, but adjust the window stop as described in paragraph 9.

Rear quarter window glass and regulator (Cabriolet) – removal and refitting

14   Fully lower the roof and remove the weatherstrip and window channel from the centre pillar.

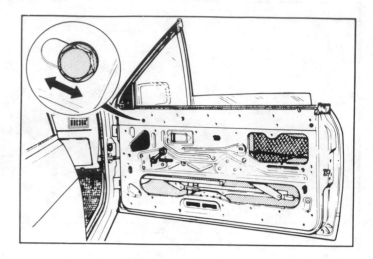

Fig. 13.157 Window regulator stop adjustment bolt location – Cabriolet (Sec 14)

Fig. 13.158 When shut, the window glass must locate under the weatherstrip as shown – Cabriolet (Sec 14)

15   Extract the clip and pull back the trim to expose the upper seat belt anchorage. Unscrew the bolt and place the seat belt to one side.

16   Lower the window and remove the regulator handle.

17   Fold the rear seat cushion forwards.

18   Remove the inner and outer window weatherstrips and the quarter panel rubber end block.

19   Remove the front quarter trim panel.

20   Remove the roof lever knob and bezel, then remove the trim panel (3 screws) with the lever in the locked position and disconnect the speaker wires.

21   Peel off the waterproof sheet then, working through the aperture, unbolt the window rail from the regulator.

22   Move the window rearwards from the regulator then lift it from the car.

23   To remove the regulator, extract the six screws and withdraw it through the aperture.

24   Refitting is a reversal of removal, but adjust the glass so that the upper and rear edges touch the weatherstrip using the screws shown in Fig. 13.159.

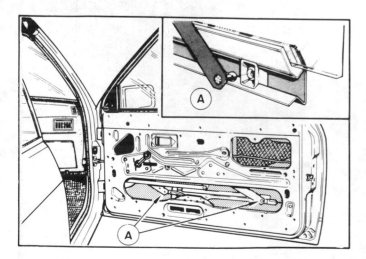

Fig. 13.156 Window regulator linkage arm attachment – Cabriolet (Sec 14)

Rear window glass (Cabriolet) – removal and refitting

25 Disconnect the heated rear window wiring and pull the wiring from the weatherstrip.

26 Have an assistant support the window frame from outside then push out the glass from the inside.

27 Remove the weatherstrip from the glass and clean away all traces of sealant.

28 Refit in reverse order to removal using the method described in Chapter 12, Section 24, and finally apply suitable sealant beneath the outer lip of the weatherstrip.

Folding roof (Cabriolet) – removal and refitting

29 Remove the rear side, wheel arch and roof stowage compartment trim panels.

30 Disconnect the heated rear window wiring and pull it from the weatherstrip.

31 Release the roof front locking catches.

32 Unscrew the nuts and remove the rear window frame guides.

33 Remove the screws shown in Fig. 13.161 from each side.

34 Unscrew the nuts at both tensioning cable blocks.

35 Pull the roof and cable from the rail and release the cable.

36 With the roof frame upright, unbolt the strap retaining brackets.

37 Remove the headlining wire screw and unhook the wire.

38 Disconnect the gas struts.

39 Lower the front of the roof then unscrew the three mounting bolts on each side.

40 Lift the complete folding roof from the car.

41 Refitting is a reversal of removal, but do not tighten the mounting bolts or tensioning block nuts until the front of the roof is locked and the rear beading is in the rail. It may be necessary to use a tamping tool to ensure the tensioning cable is fully inserted in the rail. A little sealant should be applied at the points where the cable passes through the covering.

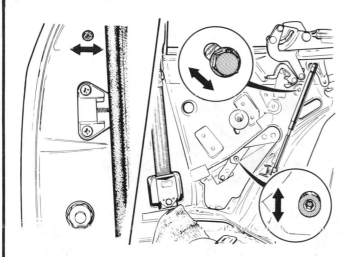

Fig. 13.159 Rear quarter window adjustments – Cabriolet (Sec 14)

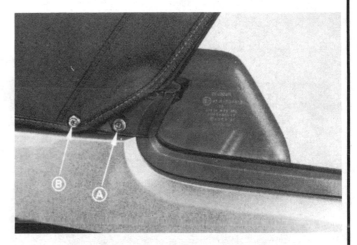

Fig. 13.161 Protection cover screw (A) and tensioning screw (B) – Cabriolet (Sec 14)

Fig. 13.160 Rear window frame guide nuts (arrowed) – Cabriolet (Sec 14)

Fig. 13.162 Cable tensioning block nut (arrowed) – Cabriolet (Sec 14)

Fig. 13.163 Removing the tensioning cable (Sec 14)

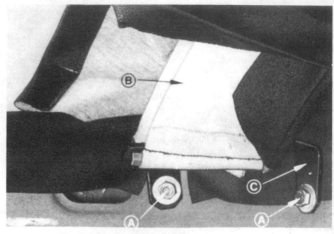

Fig. 13.164 Rear strap mounting – Cabriolet (Sec 14)

A Bracket bolts   C Bracket
B Strap

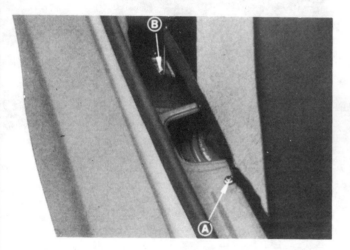

Fig. 13.165 Headlining wire screw (A) and wire (B) –
Cabriolet (Sec 14)

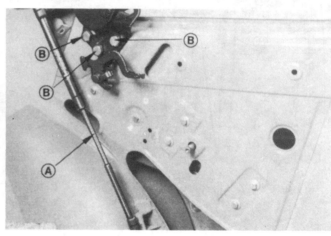

Fig. 13.166 Gas strut (A) and roof mounting bolts (B) –
Cabriolet (Sec 14)

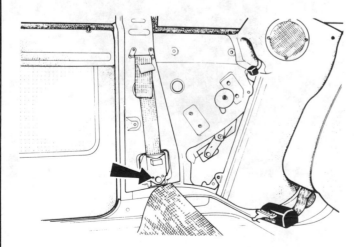

Fig. 13.167 Front seat belt inertia reel unit and bolt
(arrowed) – Cabriolet (Sec 14)

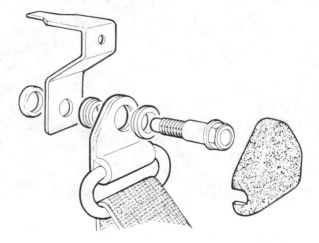

Fig. 13.168 Front seat belt upper anchor components
(Sec 14)

42 With the roof ready to be locked, its front edge should be between 2.0 and 4.0 mm (0.079 and 0.158 in) from the header rail, the upper edge nut protruding, and the lower edge not more than 1.0 mm (0.039 in) below the rail. If necessary, the locking hooks can be adjusted to provide even pressure on each side after releasing the collars. Tighten the collars on completion.

Front seat belts (Cabriolet) – removal and refitting

43 Unbolt the centre stalk.
44 Remove the clip and pull back the trim to expose the upper anchor. Unscrew the anchor bolt.
45 Unbolt and pull out the lower mounting rail. Slide the belt from the rail.
46 Remove the rear quarter trim panel then pull the belt through the slot in the panel and through the pillar guide.
47 Unbolt the inertia reel unit.
48 Refitting is a reversal of removal.

Rear seat belts (Cabriolet) – removal and refitting

49 Raise the rear seat cushion.
50 Release the buckles from the elasticated straps.
51 Unbolt the seat belts from their floor mountings.
52 Refitting is a reversal of removal.

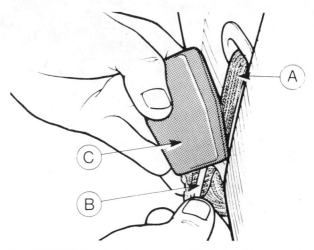

Fig. 13.169 Releasing the rear seat belt buckle from the elasticated strap (Sec 14)

A Elasticated strap
B Clamping piece
C Buckle

General repair procedures

Whenever servicing, repair or overhaul work is carried out on the car or its components, it is necessary to observe the following procedures and instructions. This will assist in carrying out the operation efficiently and to a professional standard of workmanship.

Joint mating faces and gaskets

Where a gasket is used between the mating faces of two components, ensure that it is renewed on reassembly, and fit it dry unless otherwise stated in the repair procedure. Make sure that the mating faces are clean and dry with all traces of old gasket removed. When cleaning a joint face, use a tool which is not likely to score or damage the face, and remove any burrs or nicks with an oilstone or fine file.

Make sure that tapped holes are cleaned with a pipe cleaner, and keep them free of jointing compound if this is being used unless specifically instructed otherwise.

Ensure that all orifices, channels or pipes are clear and blow through them, preferably using compressed air.

Oil seals

Whenever an oil seal is removed from its working location, either individually or as part of an assembly, it should be renewed.

The very fine sealing lip of the seal is easily damaged and will not seal if the surface it contacts is not completely clean and free from scratches, nicks or grooves. If the original sealing surface of the component cannot be restored, the component should be renewed.

Protect the lips of the seal from any surface which may damage them in the course of fitting. Use tape or a conical sleeve where possible. Lubricate the seal lips with oil before fitting and, on dual lipped seals, fill the space between the lips with grease.

Unless otherwise stated, oil seals must be fitted with their sealing lips toward the lubricant to be sealed.

Use a tubular drift or block of wood of the appropriate size to install the seal and, if the seal housing is shouldered, drive the seal down to the shoulder. If the seal housing is unshouldered, the seal should be fitted with its face flush with the housing top face.

Screw threads and fastenings

Always ensure that a blind tapped hole is completely free from oil, grease, water or other fluid before installing the bolt or stud. Failure to do this could cause the housing to crack due to the hydraulic action of the bolt or stud as it is screwed in.

When tightening a castellated nut to accept a split pin, tighten the nut to the specified torque, where applicable, and then tighten further to the next split pin hole. Never slacken the nut to align a split pin hole unless stated in the repair procedure.

When checking or retightening a nut or bolt to a specified torque setting, slacken the nut or bolt by a quarter of a turn, and then retighten to the specified setting.

Locknuts, locktabs and washers

Any fastening which will rotate against a component or housing in the course of tightening should always have a washer between it and the relevant component or housing.

Spring or split washers should always be renewed when they are used to lock a critical component such as a big-end bearing retaining nut or bolt.

Locktabs which are folded over to retain a nut or bolt should always be renewed.

Self-locking nuts can be reused in non-critical areas, providing resistance can be felt when the locking portion passes over the bolt or stud thread.

Split pins must always be replaced with new ones of the correct size for the hole.

Special tools

Some repair procedures in this manual entail the use of special tools such as a press, two or three-legged pullers, spring compressors etc. Wherever possible, suitable readily available alternatives to the manufacturer's special tools are described, and are shown in use. In some instances, where no alternative is possible, it has been necessary to resort to the use of a manufacturer's tool and this has been done for reasons of safety as well as the efficient completion of the repair operation. Unless you are highly skilled and have a thorough understanding of the procedure described, never attempt to bypass the use of any special tool when the procedure described specifies its use. Not only is there a very great risk of personal injury, but expensive damage could be caused to the components involved.

Conversion factors

Length (distance)
Inches (in)	X	25.4	= Millimetres (mm)	X	0.0394	= Inches (in)
Feet (ft)	X	0.305	= Metres (m)	X	3.281	= Feet (ft)
Miles	X	1.609	= Kilometres (km)	X	0.621	= Miles

Length (distance)						
Inches (in)	X 25.4	= Millimetres (mm)	X 0.0394	= Inches (in)
Feet (ft)	X 0.305	= Metres (m)	X 3.281	= Feet (ft)
Miles	X 1.609	= Kilometres (km)	X 0.621	= Miles

Volume (capacity)
Cubic inches (cu in; in^3)	X 16.387 = Cubic centimetres (cc; cm^3)	X 0.061 = Cubic inches (cu in; in^3)
Imperial pints (Imp pt)	X 0.568 = Litres (l)	X 1.76 = Imperial pints (Imp pt)
Imperial quarts (Imp qt)	X 1.137 = Litres (l)	X 0.88 = Imperial quarts (Imp qt)
Imperial quarts (Imp qt)	X 1.201 = US quarts (US qt)	X 0.833 = Imperial quarts (Imp qt)
US quarts (US qt)	X 0.946 = Litres (l)	X 1.057 = US quarts (US qt)
Imperial gallons (Imp gal)	X 4.546 = Litres (l)	X 0.22 = Imperial gallons (Imp gal)
Imperial gallons (Imp gal)	X 1.201 = US gallons (US gal)	X 0.833 = Imperial gallons (Imp gal)
US gallons (US gal)	X 3.785 = Litres (l)	X 0.264 = US gallons (US gal)

Mass (weight)
Ounces (oz)	X 28.35 = Grams (g)	X 0.035 = Ounces (oz)
Pounds (lb)	X 0.454 = Kilograms (kg)	X 2.205 = Pounds (lb)

Force
Ounces-force (ozf; oz)	X 0.278 = Newtons (N)	X 3.6 = Ounces-force (ozf; oz)
Pounds-force (lbf; lb)	X 4.448 = Newtons (N)	X 0.225 = Pounds-force (lbf; lb)
Newtons (N)	X 0.1 = Kilograms-force (kgf; kg)	X 9.81 = Newtons (N)

Pressure
Pounds-force per square inch (psi; lbf/in^2; lb/in^2)	X 0.070 = Kilograms-force per square centimetre (kgf/cm^2; kg/cm^2)	X 14.223 = Pounds-force per square inch (psi; lbf/in^2; lb/in^2)
Pounds-force per square inch (psi; lbf/in^2; lb/in^2)	X 0.068 = Atmospheres (atm)	X 14.696 = Pounds-force per square inch (psi; lbf/in^2; lb/in^2)
Pounds-force per square inch (psi; lbf/in^2; lb/in^2)	X 0.069 = Bars	X 14.5 = Pounds-force per square inch (psi; lbf/in^2; lb/in^2)
Pounds-force per square inch (psi; lbf/in^2; lb/in^2)	X 6.895 = Kilopascals (kPa)	X 0.145 = Pounds-force per square inch (psi; lbf/in^2; lb/in^2)
Kilopascals (kPa)	X 0.01 = Kilograms-force per square centimetre (kgf/cm^2; kg/cm^2)	X 98.1 = Kilopascals (kPa)

Torque (moment of force)
Pounds-force inches (lbf in; lb in)	X 1.152 = Kilograms-force centimetre (kgf cm; kg cm)	X 0.868 = Pounds-force inches (lbf in; lb in)
Pounds-force inches (lbf in; lb in)	X 0.113 = Newton metres (Nm)	X 8.85 = Pounds-force inches (lbf in; lb in)
Pounds-force inches (lbf in; lb in)	X 0.083 = Pounds-force feet (lbf ft; lb ft)	X 12 = Pounds-force inches (lbf in; lb in)
Pounds-force feet (lbf ft; lb ft)	X 0.138 = Kilograms-force metres (kgf m; kg m)	X 7.233 = Pounds-force feet (lbf ft; lb ft)
Pounds-force feet (lbf ft; lb ft)	X 1.356 = Newton metres (Nm)	X 0.738 = Pounds-force feet (lbf ft; lb ft)
Newton metres (Nm)	X 0.102 = Kilograms-force metres (kgf m; kg m)	X 9.804 = Newton metres (Nm)

Power
Horsepower (hp)	X 745.7 = Watts (W)	X 0.0013 = Horsepower (hp)

Velocity (speed)
Miles per hour (miles/hr; mph)	X 1.609 = Kilometres per hour (km/hr; kph)	X 0.621 = Miles per hour (miles/hr; mph)

Fuel consumption*
Miles per gallon, Imperial (mpg)	X 0.354 = Kilometres per litre (km/l)	X 2.825 = Miles per gallon, Imperial (mpg)
Miles per gallon, US (mpg)	X 0.425 = Kilometres per litre (km/l)	X 2.352 = Miles per gallon, US (mpg)

Temperature
Degrees Fahrenheit = ($^{\circ}$C x 1.8) + 32

Degrees Celsius (Degrees Centigrade; $^{\circ}$C) = ($^{\circ}$F - 32) x 0.56

*It is common practice to convert from miles per gallon (mpg) to litres/100 kilometres (l/100km), where mpg (Imperial) x l/100 km = 282 and mpg (US) x l/100 km = 235

Index

Printed by
J H Haynes & Co Ltd
Sparkford Nr Yeovil
Somerset BA22 7JJ England